THE
PGA

THE
PGA

The Official History of the
Professional Golfers'
Association of America

HERB GRAFFIS

THOMAS Y. CROWELL COMPANY
Established 1834   New York

Designed by Abigail Moseley

Manufactured in the United States of America

Library of Congress Cataloging in Publication Data

Graffis, Herbert Butler, 1893-
    The PGA: The official history of the Professional Golfers' Association of America.
    1. Golf—History. 2. Professional Golfers' Association of America—History. 3. Golf—United States—History. I. Title.
GV963.G67   796.352'0973   75-9967
ISBN 0-690-00919-4

1 2 3 4 5 6 7 8 9 10

ACKNOWLEDGMENTS

I'D like to express my great thanks and appreciation to:

Harold Sargent, Charles Evans, Jr., Jack Mackie, Jr., Tom Walsh, Joe Novak, Harry L. Moffitt, Lou Strong, Frank T. Sprogell, John Inglis, Wally Mund, George Hall, W. W. Wotherspoon, Max Elbin, Leo Fraser, William Clarke, Tom Crane, Bud Harvey and his staff of *The Professional Golfer*, Lloyd F. Lambert, Tom Boyle, Ed Newkirk, Mark Cox, Ed Carter, Marshall Dann, Otto Probst, Lillian Harlow, Leo McNamara, Mike and Grace Brady, MacGregor Hunter, Harry Pressler, Joe Murdock, Robert Kuntz, Irene Strong Harrison, Frank Faulkner, Fred Corcoran, George Aulbach, Joe Graffis, Ed Worthington, Angus J. Ray, Chet Posson, Emil Beck, Joe C. Dey, Clifford Roberts, Bob Jolly, Leonard Strong, Fred Brand, Jr., Ted Payseur, Ernie Sabayrac, Harry Chapman, Johnny Vasco, Marty Cromb, James M. Anderson, Charles Mayo, and Robert Rickey.

Also Fred Newnham, Eddie Duino, Pat Markovich, Tom LoPresti, Toney Penna, Frank Mitchell, Joseph D. Schwendeman, John Ross, Irvin R. Schloss, Gary Wiren, Dudley Green, Hubert Smith, Willie Low, George Vitense, Jack Clark, John Reuter, Jr., John Gaucas, Bob Lavacek, Brien Boggess, Gary Loustalot, Allan Mitchell, Jackie L. Maness, Marilyn O'Pace, Dick Forester, Connie Madsen, Tom Pace, James Gaquin, Charles S. McBride, Kathy Andorfer, Louise Twohig, Ted Smits, Jerry Rideout, Bruce Herd, George M. Smith, Don Dunkelberger, and Joseph P. Zeilic.

For photographs: Except where otherwise credited, the following abbreviations indicate the sources of the photographs, for which I make grateful acknowledgment:

AG: Nevin Gibson's Archives of Golf.

GH: Golf House, courtesy of the United States Golf Association.

PGA: Professional Golfers' Association of America.

CONTENTS

THE
PGA

FOREWORD

AS a sports reporter and amateur historian I often wondered why re-
nowned professional historians never noted the significant relationship between particular national sports and the histories of the nations
themselves.

Plato theorized that the athlete should be a superior citizen of the
Republic. Not that his hope has been realized to any marked degree,
despite the questionable liberality of today's athletic scholarships, but
the association of sports and history was heeded by some very practical ancient politicians—the Roman rulers who promptly gave the natives bread and circuses whenever they got restless.

And much closer in location and time, I remember the sponsorship
of sandlot and semipro baseball teams and prairie football teams by
politicians and businessmen in and around Chicago when I was a
youth there. Later I saw that the association between these foresighted
backers of ballclubs and the vigorous and influential young players
had considerable effect on the political and business history of Chicago,
Cook County, and the State of Illinois. But I have never seen that development mentioned in the many histories of Chicago that I have
read.

Because of lively though not especially proficient participation in
high school and prairie sports, I got my first newspaper job in Chicago.
One noon I was refreshing myself at the free-lunch counter when an
elderly gentleman edged to the bar close to me and the bonus cuisine,
which was a staple of many a newspaperman's diet in those days. He
greeted me kindly. "I've seen you around the shop. What's your name?
What do you do?"

I told him and added proudly, "I'm in sports."

He laughed. "Oh, in the Toy Department. Have fun. Here's how."
Then he tilted his chin and gulped his drink.

I must say I was hurt by his slighting reference to what I regarded as enlistment in a holy order. When I returned to the disorderly establishment in which the newspaper art flourished, I asked the sports editor about my new friend.

"He's been around. He's a fine newspaperman, but he won't be here long." The editor shook his head. "He's a real scholarly drunk."

Pigeonholing sports as the Toy Department of life troubled me but also helped me to take a calm and contented view of my job as a sportswriter. From the most amusing comic relief on the field or in the arena to the dismal economics of scalpers' prices, traffic jams, and room shortages of a World Series is no stretch at all. And if money talked back then, it speaks even more loudly today. Now, the mercenary element has taken over in professional sports and much of collegiate football; still the pleasure of the sport is retained because it is traditional even though there's hard money in it.

When I began writing about golf, as well as other sports and business, about fifty years ago, I soon became aware of the unique and powerful influence of a comparatively new game that was to become big business. It's startling to realize that fifty years after an American golf club hired the first professional, there are more Americans playing golf than the total of our fellow citizens of all ages playing baseball, football, tennis, and basketball, or perhaps any other indoor or outdoor game you could name.

What accounted for the vast growth of golf in the United States? Certainly not publicity of the sort that baseball, football, horse racing, and boxing received in the newspapers. The achievements of such outstanding amateurs as Francis Ouimet, Chick Evans, and Bobby Jones had a glamour and prestige that inspired youngsters and aroused the admiration of influential adult males, but these three young golfers were not celebrities to be classed with Jim Thorpe, Red Grange, Ty Cobb, Babe Ruth, or other stars of their years of glory.

My brother Joe's foresight and a kindly Providence got me into the onrushing tide of golf. Joe had been with *Golfer's Magazine,* now long extinct, then had gone to France in 1915 as an ambulance driver, then had flown with the French and the pioneer American pilots. After some golf publishing work on his return, he got the idea of *Golfdom, the Golf Business Magazine,* which we began in 1927. Until we sold that periodical and *Golfing,* a player magazine, which we started at the suggestion of several leading club- and golf-ball makers, we had the privilege of being close to developments in amateur and professional golf as a game and a business.

Joe and I treasure awards given us for our service to golf and golfers. They have been received with gratitude and embarrassment; we feel that there are many more deserving than we are. But the greatest reward for working in golf has been in knowing the hundreds of men and women who made golf a tremendous national asset. As I watched the business of golf grow to an American capital investment of nearly

$4 billion, I was constantly impressed by golf's professionals who not only served their own sport and business uniquely well but also, in my opinion, influenced American economic and social history more than men in sports anywhere ever had done before. By his efforts, the American golf professional lifted the standard and the social acceptability of the professionals in every other sport.

There is evidence that golf was played in the United States as early as 1779 and in possibly fifty places where immigrant Scots dug holes in fields to play their favorite game. Only after the early pros got busy did golf take root in this country. The early Scottish pros quickly saw that to make a living they had to make golf popular. But then the Scots long have been successful at making a living under tough conditions.

Time after time I ran across stories of golf clubs being formed and courses laid out and built on the edges of select communities or where the best families had summer places not far from the sweltering towns and cities. Dad soon learned he could wear his old clothes and have fun playing golf Saturdays, Sundays, and holidays. He also had a few drinks and gambled a little with the boys and came back to work Monday feeling much better than when he had spent the weekends overeating and sleeping it off in the hammock.

Then Mom and the girls began playing weekdays just as the Four Hundred did at Newport and Tuxedo and Southampton. Soon the local and neighboring farm kids were picking up some quarters caddying, and that was so easy nobody who'd ever had to mow a lawn or toil on a farm could call it work.

Before long more and more of the best families began going to Mac or Jock or Sandy or Alex—or whatever the pro was called—and taking a few lessons and buying clubs and balls and bags, and even dressing sort of fancy and playing with business friends in the big cities. As a consequence the pioneer pros soon had so many customers that better roads had to be built to the golf courses. That wasn't difficult. Usually the country club members carried plenty of weight around city hall and the county headquarters and with the governor.

Next, the farms around the golf clubs began to be sold, first for summer homes, then as suburban real estate, and the country club folks began driving out to the course in their horseless carriages. Then came the Model T's, followed quickly by sports models such as the Stutz Bearcat, which people bought after seeing photographs of them parked in front of a golf clubhouse that was truly an American baronial hall worthy of the Great Gatsby and combining the most impressive features of Buckingham Palace and the Taj Mahal.

By now, the influence of the golf professionals had spread to the tailors and the fabric makers. The cinema moguls, reported by *Variety* as "N.Y.-to-Hollywood," wore smartly tailored knickers on the *Chief*. Then an ex-caddie from Boston, who was a leader in the textile industry, got the idea of summer-weight clothing. By adroitly promoting the

fabric with the golfing set, he transformed the summer-clothing business for men and women until sportswear (which golf wear came to
be known as) was the uniform of the day. Every time you spot a man
wearing a jacket and trousers of different materials today, you are seeing the influence of golf on American fashion.

It was also the American golf professionals who first broke through
the social barrier dividing the nice people and those who were paid for
playing games. Folklore has it that the wall fell in 1914 at the Midlothian Country Club in suburban Chicago, when golf professionals
shared locker-room accommodations and all other clubhouse amenities
with the members. This marked the first time this had happened at a
National Open Championship in either the United States or Great
Britain. The fitting winner on that historic occasion was the personable Walter Hagen, once a caddie for Herge Eastman, Eastman Kodak's
top man, at Rochester, New York.

Hagen certainly was the first golf professional to live like a merry
millionaire, and nobody in pro golf has come near to equaling his record at having fun with money, but he was hardly the first to be a guest
at the homes of prominent club members. Many of the early American
professionals and their wives were churchgoers. Though the wives had
to represent the family at Sunday morning services, the husband normally attended on Sunday evenings and at Wednesday evening prayer
meetings. Social acceptance became certain when the communities
found they'd acquired solid, respectable citizens in the golf pros.

I had had business-journalism experience in the telephone, gas, oil,
retail-store, and management fields before I began reporting about golf
pros and their work, and it was fascinating to see how men ostensibly
untrained in business built the huge golf operation in the United
States, an achievement with worldwide ramifications. There isn't another business story in the world like that of American pro golf, and
it's all the more amazing because not only were most pros untrained as
well as temperamentally unsuited to conduct a short-season business
that required considerable capital, but they also did not have the faintest idea they were involved in a sport that required their having to
finance their club members' purchases.

Some professionals at the first-class clubs were fortunate enough to
get valuable advice from members who were golf enthusiasts and nationally known businessmen. I used to wonder how Jack Mackie, an
early president and for years treasurer of the PGA (more than any
other pro, he brought the PGA from its cradle through bewildered infancy to sturdy, brawling youth), who was pro at Inwood, Long Island,
guessed right so many times. He depended on businessmen who were
not often able to break 100 on a golf course, but who were champions
walking to the bank. So did John Inglis, the pioneer American professional who headed the Metropolitan PGA for many years and was professional at Fairview where members used to bring basket picnics on

Sundays, and whose grandsons and granddaughters saw memberships sell for $15,000.

The first really first-class pro shop I ever saw was that of one of the Ciuci boys at Fresh Meadow, another famous club. Good pro shops, once a novelty, are vital to the golf business. As the game increased in popularity, so did its profitable sidelines.

The PGA itself made one of the early efforts at industrial Social Security. It started out like a cross between a family reunion and an acknowledgment of responsibility absolutely unparalleled in sports. The PGA was an American phenomenon. In different areas the association was formed primarily as individual social, educational, disciplinary, or benevolent groups. These all came together in 1916 as an organization of responsible businessmen with an undefined social objective new to the American sports picture.

When I began golf reporting, I felt that many PGA officials were winners of popularity contests but hardly qualified to cope with the growing pains of a national federation of regional organizations that had only simple, limited functions. The main job of the PGA section was to arrange and operate monthly tournaments during the season. At these gatherings, the pros discussed matters of collective interest, such as the ability of pros and their assistants to ensure enthusiastic member approval, the maintenance of standards of personal professional conduct, and the development of mutually helpful relationships with regional amateur associations and the USGA.

PGA headquarters did a slack job of coordinating sectional activities. For the first thirty years of the national organization, the PGA championship and the Ryder Cup matches got more attention from the PGA than did the association's teaching and business-training programs. As the PGA continued to share in the explosive growth of golf, it became plain that the association's hundreds of national and sectional officers were handicapped. They did not know the lessons the PGA had learned in its long growing experience. All PGA members were losing because the association had not achieved the authoritative golfing status to which it was entitled by virtue of its service record and its trials, errors, and triumphs.

Often, in reporting PGA business stories, I realized that the PGA was wasting time, money, and words, and delaying progress by going over the same ground year after year and settling very little. In a way, the PGA was trying to run the business destinies of thousands of its members by using the same irrational methods that private golf clubs often employ. One set of officers experiments expensively and disastrously until it learns the answers, usually leaving enduring mistakes in the process. Then another administration is elected and continues with the same flawed, uninformed policies until still other new officers take over to demonstrate how little has really been learned from costly past errors.

I also noticed that pro job security was strongest at the pleasanter and more efficiently operated country clubs. There was the normal turnover of elected officers at these clubs, but their able and discreet professional seemed to supply the bond of sound policy and practice that ran through the years. His experience, judgment, and diplomacy made all the difference.

The pro knew the golf business—and that's a mighty peculiar business. The grounds superintendent was an expert gardener. The house manager was a fine restaurant and bar man, with the warmth and charm of a premier hotelman back when hotels were living places instead of institutions.

But the club professional was, and is, somebody different. He is a golf businessman, and the golf business is very special. The successful professional knows how to take care of people. He has the gift of sensing the right approach to situations that make a golf club seem like an extension of your home and the professional like one of the family.

The temperamental qualifications of a first-class professional are not textbook subjects. Nevertheless, I think these qualities shine out in the history of how golf professionals have managed their own occupational organization.

Not that there haven't been problems. When the playing stars of preceding generations were enjoying the profits of the PGA's work in building the tournament circuit, as well as the ancillary revenues it brought to the publicized professionals, it appeared that the misunderstandings and mistakes that later resulted in the split of the PGA into the service-pro and show-pro divisions had already been met and solved. These included such controversial matters as the players' traveling personal caddies and the mandatory participation of higher-ranked players in the "designated" or preferential tournaments on the circuit, which had been confronted and satisfactorily resolved by the PGA years earlier. But as you will read, the pro golfers don't learn from history.

I have said repeatedly that a history of the PGA should be written as a matter of pride and as an educational record. Eventually, when he was PGA president, I got the same treatment from Leo Fraser that is given a club member who complains about the food, service, drinks, and prices at his club. Naturally, he is immediately made chairman of the house committee—and that cures him the hard way.

After Fraser and his companion PGA officials had me cornered, I tried to pass the assignment to a genuine pro in writing history, because I believe in competent professional service in all specialized fields. So I asked Paul Angle, then secretary and director of the Chicago Historical Society, and now chairman of its Educational Advisory Committee, what professional historian I should get to do the job about the PGA and the immense and unique effect professional golf has had on the nation's development since about 1895. Since Angle writes history like a reporter who was there when it happened, I hoped he would write the history of the PGA.

"Do it yourself," he told me bluntly. "You've been in and around the subject longer and closer than any other writer."

So I was stuck.

How many letters I wrote, how many personal interviews I conducted, how many telephone calls I made, and how many books, magazines, and PGA national and sectional reports I used in digging and checking material, only the good Lord knows. A serious defect in vision slowed down the job and almost stopped it. Luckily, and with a great deal of cheerful and competent help, I learned how to beat that trouble.

To begin with, the split of the PGA into its original function as a sports public service and an auxiliary show business was the dividing stage in the organization's history. Since the formation of the Tournament Players' Division of the PGA, developments indicate that there may be a reunion before long. Since it has not had to contend with the Tournament Players' Division's problems, the PGA has been able to make decided progress in business-management and golf-instruction requirements because of revolutionary changes in the overall policy and operations of golf clubs and public golf enterprises.

The Tournament Players' Division finds itself more than ever becoming subsidiary to the television networks—charitable organizations that have been using touring pros as they would games of keno or bingo, but for a bigger take because more free workers sell the cards and run the show. In the first six years after the TPD split from the PGA, no appreciable improvements were made in the operation of the Tournament Players' Division. Meantime, the financial position of the home professionals was improving, while the tournament purses showed the first yearly losses since the end of World War II.

In researching this picture of professional golf in the United States, I have interviewed many pro employers at private and public courses, at amateur associations of men and women golfers, and among senior amateur association members. I found the seniors especially helpful in determining the course of pro golf history as the veteran amateurs viewed the home pros and the tourists.

When I got tired and discouraged, and the difficulty of getting to some facts seemed insurmountable, I always was refreshed by the enthusiasm of Lewis Gillenson, golfing president of Thomas Y. Crowell Company.

So here, for better or worse, is the history of the PGA and professional golf in the United States. And I dedicate it with warmth and affection and pride to the hundreds and hundreds of professional golfers I've known during the years they have been contributing to a happier and healthier country.

Herb Graffis

1

How It All Began Way Back When

HUNTING, fishing, and boating became sports long after they became vital to the business of living in the United States. Golf is a sport that grew into a huge business because it contributed greatly to the happiness and health of living in this land.

The phenomenal growth of American golf made the business of the game the third-largest American sports business in fewer than seventy years from the time the first golf clubs, balls, and bags were imported. Golf in the United States continues to grow as the industrial and commercial strains and the tensions of life in the concrete jungle become more severe, and renewed association with the good green grass, the fresh air, the trees, and the water—even the sand—becomes highly important to sanity and survival.

For 1973, a National Golf Foundation survey estimated the capital investment in the 12,000 golf courses of the United States at $3.5 billion. Replacement value of the eighteen- and nine-hole private and public courses of all types would bring the investment close to $4 billion. Approximately 1,175,000 acres are used for golf facilities by the 13,550,000 golfers. Of these golfers, about 2,550,000 played fewer than 15 rounds a year. The rest of them played 15 to over 250 rounds annually. Close to half of the golf courses in the United States are nine holes, and the foundation, in compiling its estimate of 260 million rounds a year, figures nine-hole play at half a round. It costs about $500 million a year to maintain American golf courses.

According to the Sporting Goods Manufacturers Association Census Report for 1973, the sale of American-made golf equipment at factory prices indicates golfers spent more than $360 million for golf balls, bags, and clubs that year. It is estimated that for years now, golfers have spent half as much for equipment as have those who play all other sports—baseball, softball, football, hockey, basketball, etc.

The 1970 survey of the U.S. Department of the Interior showed that 33,-158,000 fishermen spent $470 million for fishing equipment, and 14,336,000 hunters and marksmen spent $566 million for equipment. The Boating Industry Association estimates for 1973 show, for watercraft in use: 5,350,000 outboard motorboats, 780,000 sailboats, and 2,420,000 rowboats, canoes, and miscellaneous craft.

More than 21 million hunting licenses and 28 million fishing licenses are issued annually in the United States, but hunting and fishing equipment rarely is used as often as golf equipment. Though the life of a fine gun is long, the life of tackle used by the multitudes is short enough to make this sports line a gigantic market.

Fishing equipment has been in commerce probably almost since the invention of barter. Guns became an item of commerce in Europe in the thirteenth century. For almost three centuries more, guns were used only for war and food. The bow and arrow were losing the killing market to the gun, but not all that quickly in Scotland where bowmakers were kept busy with their new sideline of golf clubs.

But how did it all get started? How was it that golf's professionals turned a simple shepherd's game into a tremendous worldwide business? Where did the game originate? Who devised the game itself and why?

The Columbia Encyclopedia defines golf as a "game of hitting a small hard ball with specially made clubs over an outdoor course called a links." Super-

ficial as it is, the description is essentially accurate, even though it makes the game seem deceptively easy. The encyclopedia goes on to say that the origin of the game is unknown, but it takes no effort of the imagination to speculate on how it all began.

While no cave drawings have been found showing early man swinging a golf club, surely there was a primate who discovered that a stick could be used as an extension of his arm. And if in his few moments of leisure, in what must have been a constantly hostile world, he learned that he could use this stick or club to knock a small stone through the air in what can be seen as a primitive kind of baseball, he could just as easily have knocked this same stone along the ground in an equally primitive kind of croquet or golf. Eventually, perhaps, some kind of gimmick was attached to the end of his specialized club or stick, producing a useful tool, weapon, or toy that could be used to propel the stone he swung at toward a designated "hole."

In passing, it might be added that many a modern golfer has hit a shot with a beautiful, expensive club, then ruefully admitted that it might easily have been bettered by a caveman using a limb wrenched from a small tree. And even today, some golfing specialists unconsciously invoke the game's origin when they are permitted to play a particular course with the prospect of a five-figure payment for four days' activity on the links. When they don't fancy the course at which they are playing as guests, they are apt to sneer, "A monkey could play here just as well as a man." Then their fellow professionals, as well as the other gentlemen sportsmen who pay in labor, cash, time, and convenience to present the rich show, are apt to look at each other, nod, and say something like, "It's quite possible, but the monkey would be the one with the better manners."

In any case, while the game's origin remains unknown, golf is most clearly and closely identified with Scotland, where, in 1457, it was legally outlawed as being against the national interest. King James II was on the throne, and the Scottish Parliament felt that the nation's defense was being weakened because golf was interfering with crucial archery training. Scotland was a beleaguered nation with a severe shortage of good wood for puncturing invaders; not only was the court alarmed at the inadequacy of first-grade bows and arrows in the royal military arsenal, it also believed that the king's archers were perhaps getting too enthusiastic about the new hobby, golf. This would surely mark neither the first nor last time that golf would be damned as a source of civic distraction, fraternal disunity, neglect of duty—or call it what you will—and yet the game's popularity quickly increased as can be seen.

Some sixty or more years later, Catherine of Aragon, first wife of Henry VIII (and luckier than most, since she escaped the block) wrote to Cardinal Wolsey that "all his [the king's] subjects be very glad, Master Almoner, I thank God, to be busy with golf, for they take it for pastime." Along with royal recognition of the game, this is perhaps the first historical reference to golf as a national pastime. Catherine's reference to "all his subjects" implies that English women as well as men were playing the game, which indicates that, along with golf itself, golf widows were perhaps first prevalent in Scotland.

Some historians mention versions of golf in both ancient Italy and Holland, but these seem to have been variations of field hockey and shinny and not the true golf of Scotland, where the land itself proved highly compatible with the sport. Somehow the coastline of Scotland, with its sand dunes, its gorse, heather, and other tangled vegetation that kept the land from blowing into the sea, and the tough grass that only sheep and rabbits considered worth nibbling, provided the Scots with ready-made golf courses on ground that was unfit for any other practical use. The sheep themselves may have played a role in the emergence of golf. They are boring company for the most part and need little supervision in the absence of predators, so it was only natural to turn the job of tending the flocks to the smart collies who followed their masters along these primordial fairways. Thus the dogs baby-sat the sheep while the shepherds improved their game.

If the shepherds enjoyed swinging at the ball, their friends, followers, and assorted hangers-on were bound to take a whack at it. The word no doubt spread, and in the long summer twilights of Scotland, fishermen, sailors, carpenters, masons, and blacksmiths enthusiastically sampled the game and became devotees. After all, there was little for an adult male to do in a Scottish village in the evening. Besides, whisky cost money, and the country was so poor that its population could barely manage the necessities. So, apparently, golf was the answer. And it must have been popular if, as we've seen, Parliament had to ban the sport so that healthy males would concentrate on military preparedness and the proper use of the bow and arrow.

Boys, always eager to imitate their elders, quickly took up the game and were also used to carry the primitive equipment and to spot balls in the gorse-and-heather rough. Even centuries ago, the meager revenue of caddying recruited youngsters. The label "caddie" was a Scottish application of the French word *cadet,* meaning an acolyte in the military service. As a pastime that probably diverted the rugged Scots from killing enemy clansmen and the English, golf remained a simple pastoral sport bringing together congenial drinkers, gamblers, farmers, workmen, and toughs who didn't relish sitting around indoors after the hard day's labor. Even back then, the game was pure fun.

But along with the fun came the usual problems as a sport is developed and refined and gathers its experts and those who profit by providing the equipment. Business competition was keen in the early dawn of golf, but apparently too much money was going out of Scotland to Holland to pay for golf balls. It seems the king was against that. A royal prohibition of the usual angry sort was issued by the Scots' ruler. Naturally, then, the balls were bootlegged into Scotland, and the Scots seem to have taken a livelier interest in the pastime played on the grazing grounds and dunes of the seashores.

While records are vague on the construction of the balls, the indications are that the Dutch sold the Scots golf balls of wood, bone, and leather shells into which were stuffed various materials. Feathers seem to have been the most satisfactory stuffing for golf balls. With restrictions on the importation of Dutch golf balls, a few deft Scots were able to master the craft of golf-ball making so well that the kingdom's outward flow of money for golf balls was halted. Then, as invariably happens when a profitable manufacturing business is established, market development occurred. And with that, special privileges and monopolistic practices followed. Political larceny was as common then as it is today.

James IV of Scotland (1473–1513), who lost his life with 10,000 other Scots, including most of the aristocracy, at Flodden while fighting the English, was noted in the Lord High Treasurer's report for the years 1502 and 1503 as paying pioneer professionals for his golf clubs and balls. Balls were apparently in short supply and difficult to manufacture. James VI of Scotland (1566–1625), who was also James I of England (1603–25), granted a twenty-one-year golf-ball monopoly to one James Melvill, beginning on August 5, 1618. The king's men put this into the record as evidence of money spent at home and a good reason for not going to Holland for golf balls. But let it be noted that the references to golf-ball imports from Holland are viewed as fiction by some cold-eyed historians.

Let it also be noted that Melvill wasn't a manufacturer. He had made arrangements with the William Berwick company, which made the balls, and thus assured of his supply, received the royal monopoly. King James didn't miss a chance when it came to tying executive privilege to golf. During his reign William Mayne of Edinburgh was appointed royal clubmaker "during all the dayes of his lyif-tyme." And some people still believe that golf professional merchandising is a recent development!

Both balls and clubs were crude by today's standards, but they were all handmade, relatively expensive, and hard to come by. The balls were goose-feather-stuffed and covered with stitched leather; the clubs were sturdy thin shafts improvised from the limbs of native hardwood trees. They were carved, whittled, and smoothed down to size by hand with axes, chisels, and planes. As more Scotsmen played the game, there was more demand for the "right" specialized equipment, and the primitive experts and manufacturers of golf equipment were only too eager to oblige. It has been estimated that balls were nearly as costly as clubs in 1672, with balls worth today's equivalent of $1.75, and a golf club worth about $2.50. But it was still a time when a golfer could devise his own equipment if he had the skills—and there were no dues or initiation or greens fees.

One can imagine that there were few lost balls in those early golf games. Players had to find them because there were so few around. As for the clubs themselves, probably the heads were so flimsy, with so many breaking off on repeated impact, that some clever player suggested that they be made out of metal for durability. A local blacksmith, perhaps a devotee of the game himself, was no doubt talked into pounding out an iron head for the club, and thus evolved the first irons.

Golf-club making in Scotland in those far-off days wasn't a specialist's job as ballmaking appears to have been. There were enough Scottish carpenters, blacksmiths, sailors, and fishermen to blend their various skills into the design and manufacture of implements for lofting or rolling a ball around the rugged and variegated golf links. This was fortunate because grazing sheep, rabbit warrens, roadways, sandy pits, and mounds covered with rough grasses, weeds, gorse, and other scrubby shrubs provided golf-playing problems that had to be solved in part by ingeniously designed clubs. The golfing Scot from 1500 on had to play the ball as it lay. That was the only rule. There were no "winter rules"; there was no improving the lie or lifting the ball and dropping it into an easy situation two club lengths from a television tower.

The abundance of pebbles and stones in the sandy links usually called for a sweeping flat swing and a wooden club with a long, narrow face. Considering the destructive conditions under which these early wooden clubs were used, it is remarkable that any of them survived as museum pieces. The iron heads were forged and set on the shafts so that these clubs required precision for cutting into the soil under the ball and lofting it out of a close lie in the sand, dirt, or tangled rough.

The early club designer also had to devise iron heads that would not excessively damage the golf balls. From the stage when almost every golfer improvised his own clubs, production of clubs increased until there was a good market for the specialist in clubmaking, or the blacksmith, carpenter, or cabinetmaker who made clubs as a sideline.

Each club was suited to the individual, with the result being a wide and significant range of useful features. Back then, nobody used a club because it was reputed to be a copy of one used by a great player. The early Scottish golfer believed that when he had a shot to make, there was no golfer greater than himself for the job.

Wooden clubs designed to suit many conditions of play were made by carpenters and joiners headed by Hugh Philp, who was clubmaker to the Royal and Ancient Golf Club of St. Andrews, appointed in 1819. He was considered the best of the clubmakers. A kinsman, McEwen, worked with, then succeeded Philp. Their wooden putters are now regarded by collectors, as they were by players in the mid-1800's, as classics of the clubmakers' art.

Other noted clubmakers whose wooden clubs are prized museum pieces are Jackson, Patrick, Davidson, Ballentine, Munro, Sandison, Cockburn, Poke, Beetson, Sharp, Dunn, and Forgan. The Forgans later got into iron-club production with success, although the Forgan iron heads were not given highest favor by the pioneer American pros, mainly Stewart and Nicoll, who imported iron heads. Collecting old golf clubs has long been a hobby. In the early 1800's an ardent British collector already had more than two hundred old clubs. The Golf Collectors' Society periodical, issued by Joseph S. Muroch of Lafayette Hill, Pennsylvania, frequently describes old clubs and balls that have been discovered or have changed ownership. The condition of some of these relics is amazingly good. There's a group of such collectors that conducts an annual tournament in California and plays with the old clubs. They call themselves the Hickory Hackers. Hickory-shafted woods and irons fifty to sixty years old are fairly common. Occasionally an old gutta-percha ball, or "gutty," is played.

Perhaps golf truly became an official game when the Royal and Ancient Golf Club of St. Andrews, Scotland, was founded in 1754. The club naturally became the international shrine of the sport, and the basic rules it set for the game came to be accepted and adopted all over the world as golf developed. As one reads the minutes of meetings held at the earliest Scottish golf clubs, it is apparent that the members played hard, drank hard, and had a roaring, rollicking good time playing their favorite game. This is only as it should be.

They paid off their bets and club penalties in liquid form, generally with claret (which we call Bordeaux), and then available for what would be 15 cents a bottle today. The minutes of St. Andrews mention fines of two bottles of claret for absent members and caddie fees that had a top limit of about a dime in U.S. money. Any member who paid more was also fined two bottles of claret. This seems to be in the honorable tradition of Scotland, but then would any grateful caddie tattle on his benefactor?

The Royal Burgess Golfing Society of Edinburgh is believed to have started in 1735, thus antedating St. Andrews by nineteen years if this is true, but there is little official record of club proceedings until July 1, 1774. At that time it was the opinion of the members that "a boy should be made choice of and engaged to call on each member every Saturday morning, and take the names of those who propose dining on that day, and that he shall serve as waiter in time of dinner, and also serve as caddie for carrying his clubs."

For a century or so, there are no references in the society's minutes to a club professional as such. But there are many earnest citations regarding thirst. Bets were recorded in whisky. On July 30, 1816, "a quantity of rum" was received from a member in the Caribs, but the society's funds were not enough to pay the required duty of about $300. The members were assessed and paid up cheerfully.

The first of the regular series of minutes of the Honorable Edinburgh Company of Golfers began in 1755. In addition to formally regulating a few prize competitions and the eating and drinking routine of the company over the years, the appointment of the Reverend Dr. John Dun as chaplain was announced on March 15, 1764. For the glory of God, as well as for the good souls of the Edinburgh Company, Dr. Dun, who also served as chaplain to the Earl of Galloway, seems to have been pleased to accept the honor. It took a few years for the reverend to get in his good works and curtail the betting to one guinea a round, along with the customary forfeits of wine, no doubt to ensure that the kirk was not shortchanged at the Sunday collection.

The minutes of the Edinburgh Burgess Golfing Society record pleasant hoistings of champagne at the expense of a member soon to be married. The Musselburgh Golf Club limited the wagering on "club day" to sixpence (about 15 cents) a hole. It also restricted charges on members' liquor bills to "port wine and sherry, rum, brandy, gin and small beer." This was in 1788, when Scotch whisky was presumably served in lieu of water, and golfers could be a rough, roistering lot.

A story of the period tells of a stalwart laird who became involved in a high-proof brawl with other Highland noblemen in an Edinburgh hotel to which a golfers' fiesta had transferred after a lusty day on the links. Unfortunately a waiter aroused the vigorous displeasure of his lordly clients, and the laird was the leader in flinging him out of the nearest window. The party went on merrily, and soon the golfers needed refills and clamored for a waiter. Finally the landlord opened the door carefully and told the merrymakers, "You'll just have to be patient. You killed the other waiter we sent up here." The laird shrugged at the news. "Too bad," he said. "Put him on the bill and send us a fresh waiter!"

When you look over the minutes of the meetings of the foremost Scottish golf clubs of the 1700's, a story about a new member of the Augusta National Golf Club, where the Masters is held, comes to mind. He was having dinner of a winter evening and asked his waiter, "Where are the golfers? I didn't see many while we were playing this afternoon."

"They'll be here," the waiter assured him. "Right now, this is mainly a drinking club."

And that's an ancient and honorable practice, too.

Employee relations figure in the minutes of the Bruntsfield Links Golf Club for January 22, 1822. It seems that Mrs. Gilchrist and her daughter Mary, who ran the club, "were not disposed to remain unless at reduced rent." The consensus was that, in the interest of the club, Mrs. Gilchrist and Mary—particularly Mary—should remain on the job "so the comfort and pleasure of the Members might, as hitherto, be secured." After recording that Mary was voted a higher raise than her mother, the minutes concluded with the entry: "Mary the Maid of the Inn for Me." Nowhere in the history of professional golf is there testimony indicating such unanimous satisfaction at what a club paid an employee.

The entry of August 29, 1801, in the minutes of the Bruntsfield club states that: "There being fourteen members present, Mr. Maugham, agreeable to last minute, was admitted. The members as usual cracked their jokes over a glass, and enjoyed the evening harmoniously with a song."

But note a few of the items in the minutes of these old club meetings. You'll see that the boys back in the early 1800's encouraged junior golf by giving balls to scholars in the local schools. And as early as 1810 there were ladies' days with prizes of pocketbooks and Indian scarves, the latter no doubt contributed by club members with some sailor kin. Astonishing, too, are the references to the long, useful service of unpaid club officials. John Whyte-Melville served St. Andrews in an official capacity for "upwards of sixty years" and was chairman of the Committee of Management for over thirty years. Stuart Grace was honorary secretary of St. Andrews for forty-four years before he retired.

The club's Committee of Management served a vital function. It helped revive a dying golf establishment to the extent that, in 1893, the minutes record that "The Club has of late years developed enormously, so that 'Royal and Ancient' may now be fairly called without dispute the 'National' Golf Club of Scotland." It might be added that the Committee of Management seems to be an idea that American golf clubs might find effective to adopt. (More about St. Andrews's largesse to one of its esteemed longtime golf pros a little farther along.)

The present clubhouse of the Royal and Ancient Golf Club of St. Andrews was opened in May, 1854, with the Royal and Ancient Club and the Union Club sharing the building before merging in 1877. In contrast to the United States when high society took up golf and the country club itself became the hub of the community and a focal point for all the families who had achieved success, in Scotland golf clubhouses were considered a luxury having little to do with the simple pastoral nature of the game. The expense involved in building a spacious, comfortable clubhouse was contrary to thrifty Scottish principles except when such a structure could be used as a convivial meeting place and a center for easy, enthusiastic drinking deemed so essential to combat the rigors of the Caledonian climate and the chill and storm of playing conditions.

Veteran members of the Royal and Ancient links were prone to criticize the food served at the clubhouse, hark-ing back longingly to the superior meals and service provided when the club met at Adamson's Inn, the Cross Keys, Mrs. Peerie's, Glass's Inn (which in the 1770's was the granddaddy of all clubhouses), the Black Bull Inn, the Bunch of Grapes, and other cozy hostelries where the waiters or waitresses were discreet. The annals of the R & A record the merry and championship drinking that was done and the substantial wagers made in currency, whisky, wine, and even mutton.

Just like today, members voiced complaints about the price and quality of the whisky served at the club, about the keeper of the links, and about a certain ballmaker who was sacked and eventually replaced by David Herd and Alexander Pirie, the heads of families later to become prominent as providing the early professionals who laid the foundations of American golf.

Along with entries on meetings, course achievements, and affairs, and the assorted mischief of wayward members, the R & A annals also include references to the club's dances, festive events never held in the clubhouse itself. There doesn't seem to have been much change in the tone of the meetings or in human frailties over the years. One member was fined a bottle of claret "for reflecting on the Secretary," evidence that the practice of damning club officials was common Royal and Ancient procedure, just as it is today. In 1840 Robert Hay, an R & A member, was fined half a guinea (about $2.50) for tearing up a scorecard in competition. Even then, clubs were faced with the problem of devising a trustworthy handicap system and policing their members so they wouldn't hustle each other.

Just as at the other golf clubs existing at the time, members of the R & A appear to have been aware of the perils of polluted water. It was used cautiously as a chaser, if at all, and bathing and toilet facilities at the big clubhouse were distinctively primitive compared to what that master architect, Stanford White, provided at the Shinnecock Hills clubhouse, the first U.S. luxury "country club" and certainly an extravagant par for all American private golf clubs.

One thing can be said for sure about golf way back when: As entered in the minutes of the old club, the record usually focuses on everyone having fun and lots of it. That's the way professional golfers developed and the way the great and glorious game itself was nourished and sustained—and prospered.

No one seems to have determined for certain when the term "professional" was first applied to the commercial golfer, but references to it can be found dating back to about 1859. The label was neither initially nor generally used in the United States. *Harper's Golf Guide* of 1901 usually referred to professionals as "greenkeepers," which was an accurate description of the primary duty of men later known as "pro-greenkeepers" or "greenkeeper-pros." Prior to the export of commercial golf from Scotland to England, France, Canada, and the United States, the chief officers of such clubs as St. Andrews, Musselburgh, and Bruntsfield, where the facts of golf life were usually matters of record, had their own officially appointed ballmakers, clubmakers, and uniformed caddies. Their duties were limited, and the professional, in the modern sense of the golfing term, was a development of the late 1880's when his responsibilities involved keeping the course in good playing condition, supplying and repairing equipment, tutoring the amateur aspirants in putting and other aspects of the game, and supervising starting and score collecting during competitions.

It is revealing to learn that the one thing that truly identified the pioneer professional was that he always played for money. He seemed to be in the position of constantly having to prove his privileged status by beating all the local hotshots at their own game for cash on the line. He was a gentleman who excelled for cash and glory.

Gambling also made golf a spectator sport, but no record exists of how many were in the gallery when the Duke of York and an Edinburgh amateur, John Patersone, were winners of the first international golf match. For nearly three centuries a little house in Edinburgh has been evidence that betting on golf was a pleasant way for a talented Scottish lad to rise quickly above limited local note as a "poor shoemaker" to celebrity status with a coat of arms to which was affixed a dexter hand grasping a golf club and the motto "Far and Sure." The motto indicates that John Patersone was a long hitter with a deadly accurate game.

It is likely that his neighbors suggested to the shoemaker that his poverty might be eased if he'd spend more time at his trade and less on the Leith links. It was at Leith, though, that Patersone's far-and-sure game caught the attention of the then Duke of York, later to become King James II. In 1681 and 1682 the duke was in Edinburgh representing his brother the king at the Scottish Parliament.

The duke wasn't the only one at court with golf occupying his spare time. There were two English noblemen who fancied their golf, and the Duke of York hustled them as the earliest recorded employment of a practice that has become tremendously popular in the game. The Englishmen wagered "a very considerable sum" against the duke and a partner of his choice, and he wisely chose Patersone. When he and his companion won, the Duke of York gave Patersone all the stakes. From this liberality the shoemaker built his home. Thus was a beautiful example set by a royal golf hustler—something that later golf-betting men have emulated with like generosity.

However, while comments can be found in the records of old Scottish golf clubs indicating that substantial sums were wagered on golf matches, there are also suggestions that the spectators may have been more attracted by the extent of the bets than by the skill displayed by the contestants. It was distinctly not all *pour le sport*. (The same charges were to be leveled more than 250 years later concerning the notorious Calcutta pools at various Opens, the Masters, the Bing Crosby pro-amateur, and other tournaments where the money involved was in the hundreds of thousands. The USGA was shocked, and the IRS all eyes and ears.)

A story printed in a September, 1859, issue of the *Dundee Advertiser* shortly after his death called Allan Robertson "the greatest golf-player that ever lived, of whom alone in the annals of the pastime, it can be said he never was beaten."

His grandfather, Peter Robertson, who died in 1803, was a ballmaker, and Allan's father followed the same trade. In the course of time, Allan, who was born at St. Andrews September 11, 1815, the year of Waterloo, took up the awl and feathers himself and learned how to make golf balls.

The *Dundee Advertiser* said: "Allan would rise betimes, and with shirt sleeves rolled up for better muscular

play, start along for practice across the deserted Links still wet with dew. Allan had improved in his day on the old theories of golf, and to him are owing many of the improved methods and styles of the present game. . . .

"The life of a professional golfer [note this early reference to a pro], like Allan's, is so composeed of continuous matches and a certain recurring sameness of incident that we have found it impossible to trace in anything like a consecutive story the incidents of Allan's life. . . .

"Suddenly a golfer appears at the clubhouse door; he looks about for somebody who is evidently lacking. 'Where's Allan?'—the cry is repeated by telegraphic caddies right up to the champion's little garden. A minute elapses and down comes the champion in hot haste to the clubhouse. . . . But now the match is arranged. Allan has evidently got to nurse an elementary golfer. It is a foursome; Allan and his *protégé* against two rather good hands. Remark how pleasant the little man is; no miss of his partner causes a shade to his habitual good nature, and, ten to one, when the match comes in from their round the new player swears by Allan and gives his adhesion to golf for once and all."

Another golfer in Allan's Army in the 1850's! So, what else is new?

The old minutes book also records that the Royal and Ancient Golf Club of St. Andrews, ever mindful of its golfing greats, voted an annuity to Allan Robertson's widow after his untimely death. It's interesting that this was ages before any American club gave the widow of its longtime pro anything more than a farewell paycheck and flowers on the casket. Nor did the PGA go farther than handing her one of

Tom Morris. GH

those group insurance "bye-bye" checks for which the late lamented had paid himself.

One of the clearest early uses of the term "professional" occurs in the minutes book of the R & A for May 4, 1864: "Major Boothy moved, That Tom Morris of Prestwick, formerly of St. Andrews, be brought here as a professional Golfer, at a salary of Fifty pounds a year, on the understanding that he shall have entire charge of the Golf Course under the Green Committee."

James Balfour in 1887 wrote: "The Links are far more carefully kept than they used to be. Tom Morris superintends this with great assiduity, and he has two men under him who are constantly employed in keeping the bunkers at the proper size, in filling up rabbits scrapes and other holes, and in returfing places which have given away. The putting greens also, instead of being left in their natural state as formerly, are now carefully rolled with a heavy roller—mowed with a machine —and watered in dry weather from a well that has been sunk near each of them."

On January 1, 1895, "Tom Morris left the Club House with his barrow, his spade and his shovel and for the next forty-four years was to become an outstanding figure in St. Andrews golf, beloved and honored by all who knew him, until that tragic day in May 1908 when the venerable gentleman, then in his eighty-seventh year, had a fall in the New Club, from the effects of which he never recovered."

As a professional, old Tom won the second British Open in 1861, when there were only eight contestants, and also the Opens of 1862, 1864, and 1867. His son Tom, Jr., won that same championship in 1868, 1869, and 1870. When young Morris's three consecutive victories made the Championship Belt his property, the British Open was held in abeyance for a year. Young Tom won again when it was resumed in 1872, then died shortly after his victory.

Yes, money undoubtedly made the matches in the dawn of golf just as it made the tournament circuit in the United States many, many years later. While there was plenty of it in these one-on-one matches, the British Open winner was awarded only a Championship Belt, and then, beginning in 1872, the present Open Cup, which was donated by four clubs. And old Tom, a true pioneer professional who taught his son and many others, was a good man to bet on as a match player. If he also took care of an eighteen-hole course with the help of only two men, then he surely wasted little time in idleness.

We should also add that all that fussing about getting science into the golf swing and into club design seems to have started with young Tom Morris. He made the discovery of the golfer's steady head as the hub of the swing. (You can still hear it today in the commands to "Keep your head still!" "Don't look up!" and so on.) From that point the arc of the swing developed so that, theoretically at least, the bottom of the swing brought the leading edge of the club exactly under the ball. From that epochal finding, all the discussion, pseudoscience, and confusion regarding stance, posture, approach, swing, balance, timing—and the good St. Andrew alone knows what other refinements—began.

The last of the famed Scottish golfers to star in the big-money matches was Willie Park, Jr., a member of a famed golfing family. He was the architect of many golf courses in the United States and several in Canada. That activity

Willie Park, Sr. Photo from Nevin Gibson, *A Pictorial History of Golf*

curtailed his money-match programs and brought on a breakdown from overwork that caused his death in 1921.

Willie was born to golfing glory. His family had lived in Musselburgh for four hundred years. Musselburgh was a fishing port about five miles east of Edinburgh, near the mouth of the Esk. The shore, like that of St. Andrews, was by nature good for golf and not much else.

The first professional at Musselburgh was Willie Park, Sr., and the job gave him plenty of time for working on his own game. He was the first golfer to be famed and feared for his putting. His son upheld his father's reputation. Through the years come the story of Willie, Jr.'s, practicing putting for eight hours for days on end, and attaining such proficiency that he was accurate from six yards in and on the greens of those days. His deadly weapon was a putting cleek, an iron that had a trifle more loft than today's usual putter. In-

stead of rolling the ball over the bumpy greens, the club combined a chip and roll that seems to have shot the hearts out of Park's opponents.

The senior Park won the British Open Championship in 1860, the first year it was played, then again in 1863, 1866, and 1875. Young Willie won that championship in 1887 and 1888. The skill ran in the family. After working at sea for several years, Mungo Park, a brother of Willie, Sr., came ashore to win the 1874 British Open at the old home course, Musselburgh.

For twenty years Park, Sr., had a standing challenge published in *Bell's Life* of London, offering to play "any man in the world" for £100 a side. There is no record of his victories and defeats. Willie Park, Sr., and Tom Morris, Sr., often played against each other; their big-money matches were held in 1856, 1858, 1871, and 1882. The last match was at Musselburgh and ended when the gallery became unruly. Park was 2 up with six to play. Robert Chambers, a prominent Edinburgh publisher, was the referee. He halted the match when the spectators began interfering with the balls. Then Chambers and Tom, Sr., went into a public house near the links. After waiting for old Tom to return, Park sent word that if Morris didn't resume play, he would play the remaining holes and claim the match. So the long competition of the historic figures finished on a sour note.

Willie, Jr., is named in the *Golfer's Handbook* as winner of many money matches for "private stakes." He took time off from golf architectural work in Europe and the United States to defeat J. H. Taylor in a £200 stake match in 1907 at Musselburgh. Taylor had won the British Open in 1894, 1895, and 1900, and was to win it again in 1909 and 1913. In 1898 Park, Jr., fin-

ished a stroke behind Harry Vardon, winner of that year's British Open. Park then challenged Vardon to a home-and-home match at Musselburgh and Ganton. The match was eventually played in 1899 at North Berwick and is reported to have been "watched by the greatest golf crowd up to that time or for many years afterward." Figures of the estimated size of this gallery, if ever guessed, have eluded researchers. But that is no great loss to golf history as guesses of gallery size invariably are excessively optimistic.

When Park lost to Vardon, 11 and 10 in the thirty-six-hole match, he claimed he had stayed away from playing too long because of business. He thus became the first big-name golfer to present a now common explanation for defeat. The Park-Vardon match actually was more of a turning point in golf history than is realized. By his own recorded testimony, Park had a magic putting touch, while Vardon, in the printed reports of his ghostwriter, was uncertain, worried, and inconsistent and even missed a lot of two-footers when he was the greatest golfer of his time.

It is part of the lore of golf that Harry Vardon was so accurate that in the afternoon he would hit a ball into the divots he'd left in the morning round. Upon hearing that legend, a thoughtful locker-room lush once asked, "If the guy was that good, how come he hit them into the divots?" The grillroom bartender remained discreetly silent.

The matches of the old Scots were the preliminaries of the modern programs in which the head-to-head contest on the last few holes of the regulation route of a big-money championship of stroke or match play has proved to be the most exciting aspect of today's golf television show.

Those early contests were the tournament circuit of their times. The working golfers and the amateurs competed for their own stakes and sometimes for a share of the winnings of their backers. The amateurs were in two classes. One group consisted of men with higher incomes and social position; the others were the artisans who made their living the hard way. Again, looking ahead in our story, when golf began growing in the 1880's and the American golf boom came, many of the Scottish artisans became professionals. Then, professional and amateur team matches and individual contests, almost always at match play, were popular.

Notwithstanding their reputation for thrift to an extreme, the Scots are a generous and gambling people. They want odds that will make a wager fair, and that desire accounted for the introduction of the handicap system into golf. The early preference for match play over stroke play seems to have come about primarily because matches were man-to-man contests and scoring by holes was easier than with a pencil and card in the play of any one man against the field.

Harry Vardon. GH, courtesy of United States Golf Association

2

Golf Reaches the United States

IN all the centuries-old history of golf, back to the early 1500's in Scotland, the game was just a game among the homeland and transplanted Scots until it became firmly rooted in the United States. Then, much like tennis with its early boost by high society and the right people, there began a phenomenal growth of golf, a growth of such worldwide ramifications that it effected a multitude of social changes and accounted for wealth far beyond the estimates of the imagination.

And perhaps it cannot be said too often that through his personality and artistry in presenting his game, the American golf professional changed the face of American society in general. His influence in this regard has never been fully appreciated, nor has he ever been recognized for his major role in the economic development of the United States. It is no exaggeration to add that

no other sport ever had the great good fortune to have the kind of stalwart and dedicated pioneers that American golf had.

These pioneers were a very special breed. They came to an alien country to work at a trade that had originated as the pastime of shepherds who had been saved by golf from becoming as bored as their sheep. They arrived when their pastoral game had become the fad of a parvenu society of pretenders to a royalty that never really existed outside its own exalted attitudes and behavior. And in less than twenty years these proud Scottish golfers had solidly set the foundation of a sport that was to replace baseball as *the* American National Game, that became an economic factor accounting for billions of dollars in investment and annual expenses, and that proved a sociological lifesaver in getting stodgy, over-

24

weight Americans off their seats and backs out into fresh air, grass, sunshine, and the pleasant, carefree simplicity of country-club life where, in time, it cost members only $5,000 to join and $1,500 in annual dues.

But golf had been around many years before it really caught on as a national game. While there were a few golf courses around New York and Boston, Foxboro, Pennsylvania, Oakhurst, near White Sulphur Springs, West Virginia, and Burlington, Iowa, early in the 1890's, the Carolinas saw golf played so long ago that the records have all but vanished. John Campbell, curator of the Golf Museum of the James River Country Club at Newport News, Virginia, discovered a reference to a golf club being formed in Charleston, South Carolina, in 1786. This was in a copy of the *South Carolina and Georgia Almanac* for 1793 and lists a Dr. Purcell as president, Edward Penman as vice-president, and James Gardiner as treasurer and secretary. Other references to the club's meetings in 1791 and 1794 were also found.

Charles Evans, Sr., father of Chick, the famed amateur champion, was a noted librarian whose bibliographical research has been the source of considerable writing on early American golfing history. In the *Georgia Gazette*, dated September 22, 1796, he came on a request that members of the Savannah Golf Club attend an anniversary meeting on October 1. This plainly indicates that there must have been a golf club in that seaport in 1795. He also found other notices of meetings of the Charleston and Savannah clubs, but nothing about competitions. According to golf historians, the courses were probably on the order of pasture par-3's.

Even in those pristine days the members made it a habit to gather for good times. Chick Evans has a copy of an invitation to the Savannah Golf Club Ball for December 20, 1811. It's interesting to note that the managers of the ball—George Woodruff, Robert Mackay, John Craig, and James Dickson—all bore good Caledonian names. Charleston was also the birthplace of the St. Andrews Society, the oldest benevolent and social organization of any Americans who had been born overseas. And while the Carolinas and Georgia were certainly rich colonies and no doubt closely associated in vast coastal- and transatlantic-shipping enterprises, there isn't the slightest indication that golf was any bond between them. The Carolinas' later importance in the rapid growth of American golf centered on Pinehurst, and we'll come to that farther along.

Yellowed newspaper clippings, old magazines, and letters also attest to golf's being played in the United States before 1890—generally by Scottish immigrants and their friends—in New York, Massachusetts, Connecticut, Pennsylvania, Virginia, West Virginia, Ohio, Illinois, Iowa, Nebraska, Kentucky, Florida, Georgia, North Dakota, California, Colorado, and Texas. This was a primitive golf played on the lawns of country homes, town greens and parks, pastures on the edge of town, and even ranch meadowlands. Alex Findlay, for example, brought along some golf balls and clubs when he came over from Scotland to be a cowhand in Nebraska. Now and then he demonstrated his native game to curious Americans, really scoring as a missionary when he organized a club in Omaha. Later he worked for Wright and Ditson in Boston and for John

Wanamaker's golf department, and in 1935 he managed the exhibition tour of Joyce Wethered, the smooth-swinging British woman champion in the United States.

Edward Blackwell, another prominent Scottish golfer, came to California in 1886 with his two brothers with the intention of turning some family-owned property into a vineyard. For six years he didn't have a club in his hand because there were no courses in the area. Then he returned briefly to Scot-

land, won the major autumn competition at St. Andrews, and went back to California for another five years without golf. He finally returned to his homeland to resume his golfing career, and in 1904 finished second to Walter J. Travis in the British Amateur Championship. Apparently in those years long layoffs did not harm the game of dedicated players.

Willie Dunn was the Scotsman who gave golf a great boost in the United States, with a notable assist from high

Alex Findlay. Wide World Photos

society. The tycoons were widely traveled individuals with plenty of time
and money on their hands and a great
interest in new fads, games, and sports
that they could take over as their own.
Golf became a very "in" thing for these
favored few, and it may be that, indirectly at least, France is partly responsible for golf's popularity over here. In
any case Dunn was building a course in
Biarritz when he fired the shot heard
round the golfing world. Biarritz was
a popular French resort with an international flavor, and a number of prominent Americans were present when
Dunn whacked the ball at a 125-yard
hole, later to become famous as the
Chasm Hole, then smacked a few more
shots across the ravine close to the temporary flag.

Willie Dunn. Photo from Nevin Gibson, *A
Pictorial History of Golf*

"This game beats rifle shooting,"
William K. Vanderbilt told his Yankee
companions. "It will go in our country." And then, to back up his words,
in March, 1891, he, Edward S. Mead,
and Duncan S. Cryder brought Willie
Dunn over to the United States to build
the country's first professionally designed golf course near the Shinnecock
Indian reservation at Southampton,
Long Island, where many wealthy New
Yorkers had summer homes.

Too bad Willie never found the time
to write his memoirs. He took a gam-
ble on employment in the United
States, since he first believed that
France would be the ideal country in
which to promote golf because it provided a mild climate, medicinal waters
at its resorts, and an urgent need for a
sport that would divert royalty and the
haut monde from its usual round of
enervating amusements. Eminent phy-
sicians of those days, just like their
contemporary counterparts in the
United States, may have been limited
in treating illnesses, but they did real-

ize that their rich patients had a better
chance of survival walking in the sun
and fresh air, engaging in a fascinating
if hardly strenuous pastime, than they
would have remaining indoors eating
and drinking to excess and pursuing
their fancy ladies.

Golf was healthy, elite, and fun, and
the importation of Willie Dunn by
William K. Vanderbilt, a leading big
spender, came at just the right time for
American big business and society.
Shinnecock Hills was a landmark for
the game. Dunn built the original
course with 150 Indians from the reservation as his working crew. The only
equipment they had was picks, shovels,
and a few horse-drawn road scrapers.
The fairways were natural grass on
sandy, rolling land. The rough was
rugged, with blackberry bushes that
tore tweed pants and shredded stockings; the hard turf, boulders, and rocky
gullies ruined many clubs. The hick-
ory-shafting business was brisk for
Dunn and the other clubmaking professionals he brought over from his

Shinnecock Hills Golf Course. GH

homeland to Shinnecock Hills and the other new clubs that were springing up in the East.

Willie Dunn should also be credited with having the first pro shop in the United States. According to H. B. Martin, newspaper golf writer and author of *Fifty Years of American Golf,* Dunn had brought over from Scotland a good supply of clubs, balls, and bags, which he sold to members. He also gave lessons and trained Indians from the Shinnecock reservation as caddies. One of them, John Shippen, of Indian and black parentage, became an instructing and playing pro in the New York metropolitan district and did well in early USGA Open championships.

There is no record of the number of Scots who migrated to golf work in the United States at the bidding of the trailblazing Dunn, but according to early American pros it must have been between twelve and twenty. Besides being a golf-course builder and topflight player, Willie was also an employment and travel agent, always good for a loan

for passage when a lad he thought would be good for a job barely had enough to pay his way to the port of embarkation. The Scottish founding fathers of pro golf in the United States disproved the legend that their countrymen are tighter than a warped door. The contrary was generally true—they were inclined to be too generous because they had little experience in handling money.

It was found that the original Shinnecock Hills course, consisting of twelve holes of fairways and greens, could be maintained adequately without undue expense. And this was just as well because, for some reason, the rich who came by yachts and private railroad cars to their summer homes were not of a mind to throw away money on golf-course building and maintenance or on the services of professionals as course architects, construction foremen, or instructors. Still, although moderate even by the American wage scale of those days, the pay was better than the professional could get in Scotland, England, or in France where the few resort courses were popular.

When Shinnecock Hills was being organized as a club, its first seventy members paid $100 a share for stock. It is significant to note that as soon as these reigning males began to play, they decided that "the links have become congested," and an additional nine holes were built exclusively for the use of women members. This was also a time when the original course at The Country Club in Brookline, Massachusetts, was built for $50, when sheep did the mowing, and when the rental fee for the one set of loan clubs the club owned was 25 cents an hour.

From this it is obvious that golf in the United States at the time offered social prestige at bargain prices. It was also just as plain that only the super-thrifty Scots could afford to take a chance on it as a business career. As a sport for amateurs other than the Scottish immigrants it would appear that American golf in the 1890's was not destined to survive. As a society fad and as "pasture pool" to give the sedentary businessman a mild workout, or as a gambling game that helped a sport to walk off a severe hangover, golf was considered to be gently effective if hardly habit-forming.

Consider that Horace Hutchison, the famed British amateur golf champion, once gave a demonstration of the game at the Meadowbrook Club, Hempstead, Long Island, while a guest of member Robert Purdy. Meadowbrook was primarily a hunt club at the time, and the horsey set remained coolly unimpressed. They clearly preferred the aristocratic cry of "Yoicks!" to the vulgar "Fore!"

To get back to Shinnecock Hills, if the usual thrifty policy prevailed at this rich man's club, the clubhouse broke sharply away from the simple, practical European model. Stanford White, the noted architect, was hired to design it, and set an enviable standard for opulence. It didn't take other wealthy new golfers long, once they saw the glory of Shinnecock Hills, to get the feeling that, while the simple clubhouse might be adequate for the needs of ordinary golfers, it did not reflect the social prestige of the first families of the area. So, whether or not Papa really felt the expense was warranted, the grand and glorious white-elephant-to-be clubhouse had to come into its own.

It was all too easy to find architects who thought they could build a better clubhouse than Stanford White. Soon there were pseudobaronial castles, towering edifices on the style of exclusive summer resort hotels, imitation Mount Vernons, and big barnlike structures spread over an area large enough for a railroad station. Most of them cost far too much money and were hard to maintain. They were way out in the country where there was insufficient fire protection available, and as a result a lot of them burned to the ground. However, with the insurance money, the club promptly repeated its mistakes and put up another monstrosity at still higher prices.

Those pretentious clubhouses usually incorporated three costly errors so far as golf was concerned. They were not designed for efficient operation; they didn't have employees' quarters of the sort to attract and hold the kind and number of help needed; nor did they have a professional's shop located for convenient service to members and for the merchandising, manufacturing, and management functions of the professional. Until the steel shaft displaced hickory in about 1930, the making and repair of clubs was a major duty of the professional and his assistants. One of the advantages of belonging to a club was the opportunity to say proudly, "Yes, it is a beautiful club. I had Mac make it up for me."

Perhaps this healthy vanity had much to do with golf's becoming *the* society game. People were climbing. But that meant they were elevating themselves. It can be said that the rise in social standing and selectivity accounted for much of the basic growth of American golf.

It should be added that White's association with the rich sportsmen of his time also extended to designing deluxe log cabins for them near one of the finest and most exclusive fishing spots in North America. They still house avid fishermen on the bluffs above the Restigouche River on the Quebec–New Brunswick border. These same men, who were attracted by the great salmon fishing, also paid for the palatial White clubhouses at Shinnecock Hills, Newport, Rhode Island, and Jekyll Island, Georgia. Much like their titled British counterparts, White and his wealthy golfing friends had a hunting place on the lovely Jekyll Island, and for added amusement, it was only natural that they send Willie Dunn down there to have him build the first of the Southern resort courses exclusively for their use.

Willie Dunn had expected to return to Scotland quickly after laying out the Shinnecock Hills course, but then he built another one at Jekyll Island and stayed on to build even more courses. The few pioneer pros generally took days off to lay out courses in metropolitan suburbs or on cheap land at the edges of the smaller cities. The jobs generally involved a fee of $25 for a nine-hole course. The "architect" took eighteen sticks and stuck nine of them at places where the greens were to be and nine more where the tees were to be located. Then the farmer, who was to do the construction and maintain the course, was given an idea of what it was all about. What happened then was up to local spirit, the basic appeal of golf itself, and the skills of the imported talent who usually came shortly before the ground for the course was cleared, and who usually had to complete the building job himself.

He was called the professional or greenkeeper. His job was everything about the new club. He got it ready for play; he showed the men, women, and children how to play; he provided the clubs and balls and bags they needed; and repaired the hickory-shafted clubs that so often broke on the rocky terrain of those early courses. He taught a farmboy how to take care of the greens, then the fairways and tees. He had a workbench and a little store with a stock of golf goods in a corner of the small clubhouse, where there were lunches and occasionally a dinner for members, who were already being talked about as "the country-club people."

This young Scot got the club lively with competitions that had the men discovering they could enjoy golf as much in the daylight as they did their poker games in the evenings. For the first time the high school and college girls and their mothers had a game with competitions just as exciting as the programs at Newport and Tuxedo and Southampton.

Recruiting and training caddies was a bright and busy part of the job for Jock or Mac or Sandy or whatever the young man with the burr in his talk still echoing Scotland was named. The kids could use those easy quarters earned by caddying. Those were days when spare change meant a lot to many families.

The canny young Scot had been a caddie himself. He gave the youngsters elementary instruction and had them doing jobs around the shop. They sandpapered the iron heads, gave a polish of the pro's own mixture to the hickory shafts and the wooden club heads, wrapped the string binding that broke loose from the grips or where the wooden heads and shafts were joined, and learned how to put new leather grips onto clubs. The members gave the caddies their old clubs that were decidedly secondhand, and the pro showed the kids how to get them into prime playing condition for themselves. The caddies also had a few holes for pitching and putting in back of the clubhouse where the pro could keep an eye on them.

There was discipline among those kids with Scotty in charge of them. He was from a hard-nosed no-nonsense school himself. In the homeland respect for parents and obedience were closely associated with self-preservation and the development of the young. And in the early 1900's quite a few of the British youths who became professionals at new golf clubs in the United States had been serving Her Majesty the Queen in the army, navy, or merchant marine. From this experience the young pros got the notion that boys should behave themselves—or else. The basic training they passed along was of immense value to the young Americans who got their prep schooling as caddies.

It was the young Scottish pros in the United States who first thought of a Monday caddie tournament when nobody else was playing the course. They had wanted to hold such competitions back home, but there the youngsters had been forced to grab their golf during the very few times when their active elders weren't playing. Here the pros were heads of young families and only too glad to let their boys play golf on a notoriously slow day for members.

A practically-good-as-new club or a sure-enough-brand-new golf ball the pro gave to the caddie winner was somehow squeezed out of a meager income, but such prizes really inspired youngsters. The Mike Bradys, Tom McNamaras, Johnny Inglises, Jack Burkes, Johnny McDermotts, Chester Hortons, and the hundreds of other American boys who graduated as caddies went on to become noted players and instructors in their own right. And the glorious achievements of former caddies such as Francis Ouimet and Chick Evans reminded the kids that they, too, had the clubs of champions in their worn old golf bags, or as Napoleon, a pretty fair pro in his own line, put it: "Every French soldier carries in his knapsack a marshal's baton."

One sure sign of a game's having arrived in the United States is the appearance of a how-to book about it. The first such golf book on the American scene appears to have been *Golf in America—A Practical Manual*, written by James P. Lee and published by Dodd, Mead and Company on May 25, 1895. It was certainly the first of the thousands of golf-instruction books that were to follow in the next eighty years and that are still continuing to flood the stores. This volume is part of a collection of rare golf books bequeathed to the PGA by Judge Earle Tilley of Chicago and is kept in a locked case at PGA headquarters.

Another indication of a game's popularity as it filters down from the upper brackets to the man in the street is its acceptance by the college crowd. The

Charles Blair MacDonald. GH

early American professionals naturally had a strong influence in promoting the game among the undergraduates, who at this period, it must be admitted, were something of an elite group. The first national intercollegiate tournament was played in 1897. The Big Three seem to have dominated the game, as they did with football, with Yale winning the first team championship, and L. B. Bayard, Jr., of Princeton emerging as the first individual intercollegiate champion. By 1900 a few Eastern universities had what were called golf courses of their own or had arranged for student playing privileges at nearby courses. The professionals at these courses showed a keen interest in the college players and developed hundreds of them into national amateur championship status.

But the game was still far from being a national pastime and was more noted for its society trappings and snob appeal. It was the plaything of the likes of such Chicago millionaires as Potter Palmer, as can be seen in the observations of popular humorist Finley Peter Dunne's creation, Mr. Dooley. In 1896 Dunne's mythical Chicago bartender had this to say about golf: "Out-iv-dure golf is played be the following rules. 'If ye bring yer wife f'r to see the game, an' she has her name in the paper, that counts ye wan. So the first thing to do is to find the rayporter, an' tell him ye're there. . . .

"Whin ye get to th' tea grounds, ye step out and have yer hat ironed by th' caddie. Then yer man that ye're going up against comes up, an' he asks ye, 'Do you know Potther Pammer?' Well, if ye don't know Potther Pammer, it's all up with ye; ye lose two points. But ye come right back at him with an upper cut: 'Do ye live on Lake Shore Dhrive?' If he doesn't, ye have him in the nine hole. Ye needn't play him any more. But if ye do play with him, he has to spot three balls. If he's a good man an' shifty on his feet, he'll counter be askin' you where you spent th' summer. Now ye can't tell him that you spent th' summer with wan hook on th' free lunch an' another on th' ticker tape. . . .' "

This quotation is taken from Charles Blair Macdonald's book, *Scotland's Gift —Golf,* and he calls Dunne, the columnist and then editor of a Chicago newspaper that went bankrupt, and later an official of a New York City bank, a "friend to whom I'm devoted." He also recalls Dunne's story of a time when he, Marshall Field, and Robert Todd Lincoln, the late President's son, were playing at the Chicago Golf Club. The humorist and Field argued about which one of them could knock a ball across a pond hole. The first Field, not a man inclined to give long odds, complained that he had lost his drive. Then Dunne, not one to be awed by millionaires, said, "Marshall, why don't you put a dollar on the ball? You can make a dollar go farther than any other man in America." That was probably the first tee gag in the history of golf in this country, at least of printed record.

Many of the rich amateurs who were the first to become members of American golf clubs were men who knew how to squeeze a nickel. Robert Todd Lincoln had a large income as a Chicago corporation lawyer, spent his summers at his Manchester, Vermont, home playing golf, and during the cold winter months ventured from Chicago to Augusta, Georgia, to play the game. A former caddie at Augusta, who later became a Pullman porter on the *Twentieth-Century Limited,* liked to tell the story of a black caddie who grumbled when the Great Emancipator's son

tipped him only a dime after a round. "Northern gentlemen usually give me a quarter," he said.

Lincoln glared. "Didn't my father do enough for you people?"

"I don't know. I never caddied for your father."

Macdonald was the moving spirit of the Chicago Golf Club, one of the founders of the USGA, and with Laurence Curtis of The Country Club of Brookline, Massachusetts, headed the first Rules of Golf Committee of the USGA. He was born in Canada, moved to Chicago, and then was sent to St. Andrews, Scotland, to school. He returned to Chicago in 1874 and got the Chicago Golf Club started in 1893. Macdonald designed it, and it was the first eighteen-hole course in the United States. Macdonald, an excellent golfer who was runner-up in the two amateur championships held in 1894, moved to New York in 1907 and began building the National Golf Club course adjoining Shinnecock Hills. He was able to get his wealthy friends to back him, adapted many famous holes of British courses into his design, and produced a golfing masterpiece of its day.

The controversial Macdonald and the majority of those who might be called golf's official first family in the United States were not the kinds of individuals destined to play pied piper leading the American multitudes to the game. Valid testimony identifies them as a snobbish, domineering lot, cuddling up to the rich and socially important and keeping others at a well-chilled distance. Macdonald, Findlay Douglas (another Scot who became wealthy, a USGA National Amateur Champion and a USGA president), and Walter J. Travis (the Australian-born amateur who in 1904 became the first of U.S. registry to win the British Amateur and who won the USGA Amateur title three times) were said by old-timers in American golf to be the three coldest mortals short of the polar regions. They were the type who had to be boss or else. And their attitude probably heightened the need to organize golf under strict controls in the United States.

Macdonald's book is an entertaining, informative view of the infancy and youth of golf in the United States as seen by a fervent and dictatorial evangelist who had to run the show at all costs. It is an interesting reflection, after all these years, of the temperamental assets and liabilities with which the early American professionals had to contend. Macdonald never refers to business or to his source of income in his engaging chronicle, and his carefree attitude toward money indicates how he must have regarded the working classes, including the professionals and golf writers, as well.

In his book Macdonald said, "As we all know, there is nothing the sporting reporters love more than a row. It makes copy. For twenty years they have kept it up—thank heaven to no purpose." What he was referring to was the "Western refractory contingent," which resented Eastern domination of the USGA. This was a situation that the Easterners (including Macdonald as an official Western representative of the USGA from 1894 to 1899) said "didn't exist." It was a delicate matter for Macdonald because his son-in-law, H. J. Whigham, was an Oxford graduate and an American newspaper reporter, and Macdonald didn't seem to be able to decide which side of his son-in-law was to be trusted. But when Whigham won the 1896 and 1897 USGA Amateur championships, all was in order.

To make a point, we have to digress a little, as we find ourselves increasingly inclined to do in these necessarily rambling opening chapters, but it was clear that the press did not consider golf to be news when the game first began to be played in the United States. If it got any mention at all, golf was jokingly tied to its wealthy and aristocratic devotees on the society pages. However, if the editors ignored the sport, or as was far more likely, were ignorant of it, then the sportswriters should have given it at least part of the attention that they did to baseball, boxing, and the other manly pursuits. But these competent clerks in the Toy Departments of newspapers had their own pet playthings and just did not see what was happening to and with golf in the United States.

Golf is probably the one American game that hit the sports section headlines without a deliberate professional push. Pleasant company, a few free meals, and booze with congenial drinkers who had class reconciled the golf writers to covering a sport that was usually played way out in the boondocks. Along with the difficulties involved in reaching the tournament, the reporter had to trudge all over the county to see what was happening to a hundred or more competitors instead of eighteen-or-so baseball players or a football team or a couple of boxers having at each other while the same reporter watched from the press box with a Western Union or Postal Telegraph operator alongside.

Once in a while a sports editor was chewed out by a managing editor who had received the word from the front office that a big advertiser's wife, who had won a championship in C Flight at her club, had not got her name in type. When the same lady attended a charity tea she made headlines in the society news, while here, in golf, something that meant real class, she was completely overlooked. And don't think that didn't show the power of the game. One of the most brilliant and able sports editors in this country was fired from his job because he didn't appreciate the power of golf—women's golf in particular.

This was also a time, when golf was growing up, that the professional, along with all his other duties, had the additional task of telephoning scores to newspaper sports departments.

Macdonald's irritated remarks about golf reporters loving to create rows where none existed showed how far the press had progressed in taking the game seriously. Along with his other peeves it is amusing to read at this late date Macdonald's vehement comments on professionalism in *his* sport. In a 1901 issue of his magazine *Outing,* Casper Whitney indicted Walter J. Travis and A. G. Lockwood as professionals for receiving hotel board and railroad transportation "during a Florida golfing campaign." Macdonald joined in the censure. "We all knew that President Robertson [of the USGA] had not been imbued with the ancient and honorable traditions of the game in his youth any more than Travis had been," he wrote in his book, "but we thought that after their spending three months together in Scotland and England during the summer they would have absorbed some reverence for these same ancient and honorable traditions. We were doomed to disappointment. As Rider Haggard said: 'Golf, like Art, is a Goddess whom we woo in early youth if we would win her.' "

Travis became editor and publisher of *The American Golfer* in 1909. He also became active as a golf architect and for a while was associated with Macdonald, who had asked him and Jim Whigham to collaborate in the design of "The National Golf Course of America." But Travis had sinned, and Macdonald wrote, "Eventually I dropped Travis."

Just as in the old country, there were some gigantic hangovers during golf's infancy over here. Pioneer Scottish-American professionals were reputed to have amazing thirsts, but available testimony indicates that the amateurs of the early American golfing years could match them glass-for-bottle-for-case along the way. Charles Macdonald records the evening, after the first day's play at St. Andrews in Yonkers, N.Y., when Stanford White (who was shot and killed in 1906 by Harry K. Thaw because of trouble over Thaw's beautiful showgirl wife, Evelyn Nesbit Thaw) gave him a dinner party that lasted until 5:00 A.M. Macdonald had led the first day with an 89, but he felt the party had finished him. En route to his room at the Waldorf, Macdonald ruefully told White he didn't think he'd be able to show up at the first tee that day. As is the custom with every host who isn't as stoned as his guest, White said simply, "Leave it to me."

When he got up, feeling terrible, Macdonald found a few pills labeled "strychnine pellets" and a note on their use from White. They worked. After Macdonald and Willie Lawrence, his opponent in the morning round, had breakfasted, they took the train for Yonkers, where Macdonald defeated Lawrence 2 and 1.

"I was fading fast away," Macdonald recalled. "Stanford White came out to luncheon with me. Again he insisted upon pulling me together. He had evidently read Horace Hutchinson's article in the *Badminton Library* book on

golf: 'If you ever see a man who has tied with another for a medal, toying in the luncheon interval with a biscuit and lemon and soda, you may go out and bet your modest half-crown against that man with a light heart. But if you see him doctoring himself with a beefsteak and a bottle of beer, or, better still, a pint of champagne, you may go forth and back that man with as stout a heart as though you had yourself partaken of his luncheon.'

"Stanford insisted on a bottle of champagne and a steak. I do not wish the reader to think that Stoddard would not have beaten me anyways. That I do not know. I played wretched golf all that afternoon."

L. P. Stoddard of St. Andrews won on the last hole. Some considered that tournament the first national amateur championship of the U.S. Macdonald didn't and criticized the affair so much that formation of the USGA was spurred. So it might be said that the USGA is the result of a tremendous hangover.

Macdonald also underscores the liquid nature of early American golf in his story of a match between ten men from the Chicago Golf Club who traveled by private railroad car to Cleveland to play ten Country Club of Cleveland amateurs, among whom was Coburn Haskell, who later invented the cored, rubber-thread-wound golf ball that helped transform the game. On their arrival at 7:00 A.M. the visitors and hosts drank a hearty breakfast at the Union Club, then went to the country club to play a preliminary nine holes before imbibing luncheon. Macdonald coyly comments that "The luncheon was of a character not calculated to improve a person's golf."

In case their guests were stricken by fresh-air poisoning, at the fifth hole the hospitable Clevelanders had "a table set out with attractive libations, presided over by an excellent Negro waiter." The two competitors ahead of Macdonald and his opponent, T. S. Beckwith, refreshed themselves, then staggered off after balls struck across a creek, and Macdonald later learned that the two golfers preceding had had their caddies hit the tee shots.

This sort of thing fitted neatly into the ever-growing legend about the traditionally gargantuan thirsts of Scottish and English golf professionals. But just like today's expert shotmakers, the fact remains that while some may have drunk heavily, others drank only moderately, and still others were teetotalers. Though they were chilly, superior, and little tin gods of the sport in their prime, there are still veterans in American golf who knew Macdonald, Travis, Douglas, and other pioneer hammerheads who will say that when the old boys got near the end they really became affable. Maybe they heard the angel voices calling. But it must not be forgotten that all the way, according to their lights, they did what they thought was best for golf.

Whether they were democratic businessmen such as Robert Lockhart and John Reid, who started the Apple Tree Gang at Yonkers, or society-oriented individuals such as Charles Blair Macdonald, the early Scottish amateurs had relatively little influence in establishing golf as a popular game in the United States. The groundwork was laid by and the impetus came from such early American professional golf families as the Auchterlonies, Gourlays, Hutchisons, and Forgans. It was David R. Forgan who wrote that poetic tribute to the game that began: "Golf—it is a science—the study of a lifetime in which you may exhaust yourself but never

Walter J. Travis. GH

your subject." And at the time, not un-
mindful of the business it did with
golfers, the American Banknote Company reprinted the Forgan paean on a
fancy throwaway and distributed it
widely to banks and premier accounts.
This public-relations effort is an accurate indication of golf's status among
the wealthy in the United States in the
dawning 1900's.

While Forgan's observations were
more emotional than practical, it became plainer as the years went on that
golf was not so much a science as an art.
But the game itself, as with so many
new sports that demand special equipment and special places in which to
play them, was also a business—and, as
it proved, big business. At any rate, it
was the Scottish professionals, who
came over to nurse the transplanted
game through the weaknesses of its infancy, who were actually responsible
for making golf popular here with, as
noted, an initial boost from high society in the persons of the Astors, the
Goulds, the Vanderbilts, the Havemey-
ers, the Chatfield-Taylors, the Biddles,
the Stillmans, the Morgans, the Bel-
monts, the Goelets, the Winthrops, the
Oelrichs, the Potter Palmers, and the
others. This all came about in a heady
atmosphere when the rich were getting
fantastically richer—and there were increasingly more of them and, of course,
the poor—and ambitious middle-class
males and females were clawing their
way up the social ladder and eager to
play follow-the-leader on the nearest
links.

3

The Game Spreads and Spreads and Spreads

THE first American Open Championship was won by Willie Dunn, who defeated Willie Campbell 2 up in eighteen holes. There were only four in the field at the St. Andrews Club in Yonkers in 1894 in this competition, which preceded the official USGA Open by a year, and this was considered a fairly good showing, considering the informal nature of the affair.

The first USGA Open Championship was played at the Newport Country Club's nine-hole course on October 4, 1895, with eighteen holes played in the morning and eighteen in the afternoon. There were ten professionals in the field and one amateur, A. W. Smith of Toronto, and the Open tournament followed on the heels of the newly formed USGA's Amateur Championship, which had been played at the same Newport course on October 1 to 3.

To clarify matters, the Open was almost an afterthought of the United States Golf Association, which had been organized to eliminate the confusion surrounding the two amateur championships in 1894. One had been held at the Newport Country Club and been won by W. G. Lawrence, a member, and the other was played at St. Andrews. The latter was also won by a member, L. B. Stoddard, and Charles Blair Macdonald, the outspoken Chicago Golf Club founder, was runner-up in both events.

Horace Rawlins, the Newport club's nineteen-year-old assistant professional, who had come over from England in January, won the 1895 USGA Open with a 173. Willie Dunn was second at 175; Smith, the amateur, finished in a tie for third at 176 with James Foulis, professional at the Chicago Golf Club; and the home professional, W. F. Davis, was fourth. Prize money was split five ways. Rawlins got the first prize of $150 and a $50 medal, Dunn got $100 for second place, and the other prizes were $50, $25, and $10. In the next year's championship, young Rawlins was registered as professional at the Sadaquada Golf Club, Utica, New York, and by mutual agreement the Open Championship Cup went to the winner's club until the next Open was played.

Considering the size of the purses, it's quite likely that club professionals expected their members to help pay expenses to the one-day affair. James Foulis's trip from Chicago to Newport was the longest of any competitor, and it can be assumed that a frugal Scot would hardly make such a jaunt on his own.

Charles Blair Macdonald was also one of the five men who signed the agreement founding the USGA at the Calumet Club in New York City on December 22, 1894. He signed as captain of the Chicago Golf Club, and the other signers were John Reid, president of the St. Andrews Golf Club; T. H. Barber, president of the Shinnecock Hills Golf Club; F. Murray Forbes, chairman of The Country Club; and Theodore A. Havemeyer of the Newport Golf Club. Havemeyer, the Sugar King, was so rich, famous, and important that he didn't need any club title, and naturally he became the first president of the USGA. He had a combination of sideburns and moustache that was impressive back in the 1890's when a lot of big men ran to facial bush, and would be even today, when beards and moustaches are again in fashion.

He seems to have been a gentleman of great courtesy, charm, and generosity, as was Henry O. Tallmadge of the St. Andrews Club, who was host at the organizational dinner. Somehow these two successfully accomplished a delicate diplomatic task in bringing together clubs and members who were just as patrician, wealthy, and aloof as the founding body of the Amateur Golf Association of the United States, as the USGA was first called. The name was soon changed to the United States Golf Association, when it was suggested that the new national group should assume control of professional golf, too, and hence the "Amateur" limitation had best be avoided. The objective seemed to be total and absolute control of all phases of golf.

Neither in print, nor in memory, nor in legend is there any indication that the amateur founding fathers of American golf viewed the pioneer professionals in any kindlier light than that which was shining on the working stiffs of the 1890's, which were not so gay for the average man and woman either here or in Great Britain. The situation was perfectly agreeable to the early American professional golfers. They had all they wanted of the members' company during working hours anyway. Some of the first American golfers were financially substantial Scottish-born businessmen who as university students in England never became clubby with the "working" golfers (the nucleus of the American pros) or with the clubmakers or caddies. Even on the golf course every man was created equal, but clearly some were more equal than others.

Golf follows the seasons, and when the winter winds blew and the rich had to leave their courses in Newport, Brookline, Yonkers, Long Island, and Chicago, they were delighted to play their favorite game in a more salubrious climate. Some went to Georgia and Florida to swing a club and lie in the sun—and others went to Pinehurst, North Carolina. We've recorded historical mention of golf in the Carolinas after the Revolutionary War, but its

Pinehurst Golf Course. Pinehurst Photography Studio

later importance was marked by Pinehurst where James W. Tufts of Boston, a soda-fountain manufacturer in the mid-1890's, bought a lot of land in the sandhills of North Carolina to build residences for ailing Northerners who couldn't stand New England winters.

In 1896 Leonard Tufts, son of James W., and Dr. George Carver laid out a nine-hole course. Dr. Carver was hopeful that the pine-flavored air of the area would help cure tuberculosis and that golf would help build Pinehurst's reputation. Then in 1900 Donald Ross came to Pinehurst as professional and started building courses. Ross was one of those gracious, beloved characters out of Scotland via New England with the kind of winning personality that meant a few hundred million dollars

to American professional golfers, and maybe a few billion to golf in general.

Pinehurst soon grew out of being merely an overnight stop between North-and-South winter transit. The North and South Amateur began there in 1901, and the first North and South Open was held in 1903. The home professional, Donald Ross, was the winner, and Jack Jolly, a grounded sailor from St. Andrews, was second. The Women's North and South tournament started in 1903.

The North and South Open was a tremendous factor in the development of American professional golf. Employment was aided when officials of clubs met nomadic professionals at Pinehurst, and golf architecture, instruction, and finesse in playing technique were worked out by experts at "Maniac

Hill," the Pinehurst practice area where, perhaps more than on any other ground, American technical golf education was cradled.

It was wonderfully happy publicity for Pinehurst, Inc. The professionals were roomed and boarded by the management at clergymen's rates, and that was a Pinehurst, Inc., expense. The prize money, not fat by today's standards, was good in the old days and a frost-free bonus when pros moved South for the winter with their stomachs so pleasantly packed by the Pinehurst American plan they could have hibernated in Florida for the next five months.

To round out the history of Pinehurst as a cradle of golf and a mecca of the game, it should be added that the Tufts family ultimately sold out their interest to the Diamondhead Corporation, which paid $9.3 million for 9,000 acres and built a sumptuous sports and recreational complex on the property with the emphasis remaining on golf. The place is ringed with condominiums, artificial lakes, tennis courts, and golf courses, and Horace Sutton, writing in the *Saturday Review/World* for November 30, 1974, says it offers "one of the most complete resort centers in the hemisphere."

And he adds: "But golf remains the center attraction (even the rentable villas bear names of such famous courses as Pebble Beach, Thunderbird, and Broadmoor), and under the new owners Pinehurst assured its preeminent position in the sport by building the World Golf Hall of Fame, a $2 million extravaganza with splashing fountains, moats, and floodlights. In marble magnificence it lies somewhere between Versailles and the Taj Mahal. President Ford came down to inaugurate it last September [1974] and stayed long enough to play nine holes and to give a speech in the ballroom of the hotel.

"In the lobby of the Hall of Fame, one is faced with an enormous statue of Bobby Jones, larger than Lenin in a Soviet pavilion at a world's fair. The cases are stuffed with golf mementoes of the famous, charts and plaques displaying the history of the game, costumes of the early players . . . , and a collection of scoring pencils from famous golf clubs. A prized acquisition is a rut iron especially designed to extract a ball that had come to rest in a rut left by a wagon. A quotation on the glories of golf has been etched on a large stone tablet to be hung prominently in this Valhalla. 'When it's lighted up, it will look just like the Lincoln Memorial,' the curator assured me. And I believe him."

The Florida courses offered ideal winter employment for Northern and Central States' professionals who would otherwise be lucky to get jobs making golf clubs or to have saved up enough from summer work to cure homesickness with a trip back to bonnie Scotland. The Florida East Coast Railroad had resort hotel courses at St. Augustine, Ormond Beach, Palm Beach, Miami, and Nassau as early as the winter of 1898–99, and called Alexander H. Findlay its "golfer-in-chief." Florida's West Coast Railroad had John Duncan Dunn as golfer-in-chief of its courses. Dunn, one of a family of noted professionals from Musselburgh, Scotland, was stationed in New York in the summer, and from January 1 to April 1 at the Tampa Bay Hotel. James Foulis, 1896 National Open Champion, worked under Dunn at Tampa, and Dunn also supervised Laurie Auchterlonie, winner of the 1902 National Open, at the Belleview course in Bellair, Willie Marshall at Kissimmee,

J. M. Watson at Winter Park, and J. S. Pearson at Ocala.

The larger Florida resort courses had Bermuda greens, and these, together with grassy fairways of a sort, gave the Southeastern playgrounds an advantage over Southern California and other Southwestern courses where the climate was also inviting but the links were scrawny pastures, more adobe than grass. The Flagler and Plant railroad and hotel systems made profitable use of professional golfers' services. Years later, Steve Hannegan, the public-relations hustler who worked for Carl G. Fisher in ballyhooing Miami Beach from sandy strand to steel and concrete, mortgages, and opulence, always felt that newspaper photographs of gorgeous young ladies in tight bathing suits had done far more for the cause than golf. But the dynamic, high-pressure Steve was talking about golf long after its pioneer professionals had blazed the big-money trail into the tip of the promised land where Ponce de León had thought to find eternal youth.

For years golf was suspect in the United States as "a sissy game, cow pasture pool and old men's shinny," an effete game for the effete, but the statistics of the early years had already long disproved this tired theory. According to *Western Golf,* one of the first American golf magazines, in 1899 the United States Golf Association had 133 "allied" member clubs and 21 "associates." The magazine also estimated a capital of somewhere between $200 million and $500 million being "shut up in golfing lands" in 1899, and added that there were more than 200 golf courses in states neighboring Illinois. And according to authorities more than $1.5 million was to be spent in the East for the construction of golf clubhouses. An-

other indication that golf was destined for a long and prosperous future in the United States appeared in the February, 1900, issue of *Golf Magazine.* The editor wrote: "From the amounts furnished me which various clubs spend on caddies each year I am able to state that golfers in the United States laid out the surprising sum of $1,250,-000 in caddie fees last year. The Chicago Golf Club alone paid out $3,-319.32 for caddie service."

The reference to 32 cents in the accounting from the wealthy Chicago Golf Club suggests that the caddie fee total was based on some precise data. Such fees varied at the time from 25 cents for nine holes to 50 cents for eighteen, plus a dime tip from the big spenders. It was considered easy money for the kids—indeed there had been nothing like it available before—and there was resentment when they went on strike for higher wages. One caddie strike took place at a course in Sellwood, Oregon, where the boys had been getting 15 cents for nine holes and 25 cents for eighteen. There were also reports that Long Island caddies had become "haughty" and "intend to form a trust," and, the news item added, it seemed that club members "propose to retaliate for remonstrances."

The point was that these youngsters were ruining the game by being difficult; they should be grateful for the golden opportunity golf had presented to them. Interestingly enough, when the Western Golf Association was formed in 1899, it had caddies in mind. One of its objectives was to "Settle all questions that may arise as to payment of caddies and the highly desirable disciplining of them." Later on, this same association changed its attitude, and with its Chick Evans caddie scholarships, originated a plan that brought these bag-toting, ball-spotting boys millions in educational grants.

An advertisement in an 1899 issue of *Golf* showed two caddies in the foreground, and a background of three golfers and a caddie on the green, with this inspiring message from a pioneer manufacturer tying his product directly into the new craze:

> If a caddie meet a caddie
> Comin' through the green,
> If a caddie ask a caddie
> Why his clubs are clean,
> It's ten to one he'll answer, "Oh!
> I rub them with
> Sapolio."

From the early American golf magazines it would appear that the professionals were unified in one way: They unanimously rejected numerous invitations and encouragements that the amateurs extended them to get formally organized. In the first issue of *Western Golf,* May 1, 1899, the lead article told of the formation of the Western Golf Association, into which had been merged the Associated Golf Clubs of Chicago, which had been organized in April, 1899. Among the aims of the new association was to: "Adopt a general policy in regard to the engagement of professionals, their pay, the perquisites to be allowed, etc. One feature of this branch of the association's work will be the arranging of matches among the many professionals now in this part of the country. Such events will be of the highest interest and incalculable value to amateur spectators. Next to personal instruction from a high class professional, it is beneficial to watch him at his work. The men are anxious enough to play for a purse, large or small, and it rests with the association to extend to them the proper encouragement."

How eager professionals were "to play for a purse, large or small," may be questioned as one reads in the July, 1899, issue of *Golf* that "The story about a strike of the professionals for higher prize money on the eve of the Open Championship was without a grain of truth." Golf was suffering from growing pains, and if there were rumors of strikes, then surely the professionals had similar grievances that had to be glossed over somehow.

The Open of 1899 was played at the Baltimore Country Club on September 14 and 15, with eighty-one entries playing for a total purse of $650, with $150 first money. In 1899 eight professionals were in the money, instead of six as in the previous four National Opens. Willie Smith of the Carnoustie family, who'd recently arrived to become one of the professionals at Midlothian in suburban Chicago, was the winner at Baltimore with 315, a comfortable margin of eleven strokes over George Low of Dyker Meadow.

James Foulis of the Chicago Golf Club had won the second National Open at Shinnecock Hills, and in 1898 Fred Herd of Washington Park, Chicago, had won the fourth National Open with 328, seven strokes ahead of Alex Smith, also of Washington Park. The championship was played at the Myopia Hunt Club, Hamilton, Massachusetts, in mid-June. The contestants needed a goodly amount of traveling money to get a chance at a $150 first prize, and club members chipped in to defray expenses for their pros. The Chicago area boasted that its professional colony was the equal of that of any other city in the country, and "if no amateur champions are developed here in the next year or two, it will not be for lack of teaching talent."

Western Golf said that, including teachers and clubmakers, Washington

Park had five professionals in 1899. They were listed as James Herd, Frederick Herd, and William Yeoman and Alex Smith of Carnoustie, with the fifth professional unnamed.

Who paid those five, how much they received for lessons, how much for clubs, balls, and bags, and what amount for what other services (direction of the course, maintenance, and so on), is not known. But Washington Park had a professional staff of all-around proficiency and size that no other club could then afford. Two of the staff were National Open champions and three (the Herds and Yeoman) were internationally famous as clubmakers. Their artistry and sound Scottish business management led them into the successful establishment of small factories and the enlistment of other skilled clubmakers, so that the three became happily and solidly set among the "well-to-do," as the class between the "average" and the "rich" used to be called.

As a sidelight it is revealing to see that some things never change. In the early years of golf in the United States, the courses were outside the cities and in the deep country, or what is now the suburbs. And it didn't take any longer to get from downtown to the far-out suburbs at the turn of the century than it does in, say, 1975. When the United States Golf Association's fifth Amateur Championship was played at the Onwentsia Club, Lake Forest, Illinois, in 1899, the Northwestern Railroad advertised that the trip between the Chicago station and Lake Forest took only an hour. More than seventy years later Northwestern's time for the same railroad journey of approximately forty miles is still about an hour.

While there were some rich home professionals at the private clubs, the majority were probably lucky to break

even on the job or perhaps show a slim profit for their labors. In the early years, the sales of candy, sandwiches, and soft drinks to caddies were vital to the net income of professionals or of caddie masters, when golf had grown enough to need caddie masters. So winning tournaments was as important for survival as it was for prestige.

Yet the USGA Open prize money in its first year, 1895, was only $335, with the winner getting $150. The other four prizes for a field of ten pros and an amateur were $100, $50, $25, and $10. Nor did purses increase significantly for some time. As a consequence a pro made more money being backed by his own members in a stakes match arranged against the professional of a neighboring club. The members bet on their own respective pros, there were many side bets, and the winner could acquire a nice bundle. And for some years, when a considerable percentage of the Open purse came from the pros' entry fees, United States and British pros complained bitterly at having to play for their own money.

Traveling professionals got fare and living expenses, if little more, if they were fortunate enough to win one of the first three places in the early Western and Southern tournaments. In January, 1900, the Oakland, California, Golf Club held an open tournament that was won by Horace Rawlins, winner of the first USGA National Open. After him were Alex Smith, D. Stephenson, James Melville, and Willie Anderson. Obviously the Scots were engaged in winning the West for golf.

Starting the 1900 circuit in Florida, George Low won from a field that included Willie Smith, the 1899 National Open Champion, Horace Rawlins, and others, at Magnolia Springs. Another tournament was held to mark the opening of the Tampa Bay Hotel course designed by Tom Dunn. This was won by Willie Smith, with 150 against 157 for Horace Rawlins.

Driving contests were a feature of these early tournaments. Really blazing one out there always appealed to Americans, and some of the pioneer players whacked the "gutty" ball 230 to 260 yards, carry and roll over hard, lumpy fairways. It can be. assumed that the winners picked up some cash and side bets for their herculean efforts with ball and club.

With golf becoming thoroughly at home in the United States and an increasingly important fact of economic life, its growing pains continued on through such controversial matters as strikes by caddies and professionals to the inevitable one of the fine line dividing the exemplary simon-pure play-for-fun amateur and the gross commercial play-for-pay professional. The story concerned Charles S. Cox of the Fairfield County Golf Club who had applied to the USGA for reinstatement as an amateur. As manager of a department of certain branches of sport at A. G. Spalding and Brothers, including "golf, tennis, polo and cricket and other minor games" doing roughly about $1 million worth of business a year in 1898, Cox, who was also editor of Spalding's annual *Golf Guide,* had found it obligatory to "go over invoices and accounts with certain of our professional customers . . . who are not businessmen themselves and it frequently is necessary to explain to them personally about discounts, credits and other matters connected with their business."

And for that association with pro golf, the USGA, in an exhibition of stuffiness reminiscent of Avery Brundage and his Olympic Games pro-

nouncements in the years to come, officially declared Cox *not* an amateur. He was a good player and resigned his membership when his club insisted that he play in team matches regardless of the USGA ruling. The USGA finally reinstated Cox but continued this sort of smug arbitrariness by later excommunicating Francis Ouimet and John Dawson as tainted amateurs. Both, of course, were reinstated. Ouimet became the first American captain of the Royal and Ancient and winner of numerous amateur championships. Dawson also won amateur championships, and more than anyone else, was the developer, with golf, of the immensely valuable Southern California desert resort area.

It was second nature for the early American golf professionals to give women their first planned, persistent encouragement in sport. The tutoring of women pupils of all ages by pioneer golf pros began the growth of feminine participation in sports that continues to this day.

Prior to golf, the only sport considered ladylike and suited to the gentler sex was tennis. It started in England in 1873 and bounced to Bermuda, an oasis where British immigrants were yearning to take up a new outdoor game. And it was a vacationing guest, Miss Mary Ewing Outerbridge, whose parents belonged to New York's Staten Island Cricket and Baseball Club, who brought the game back home with her. Her brothers started playing, and, along with other early male tennis players fascinated by the game, proceeded to organize it. They started the United States Lawn Tennis Association, which held its first national championship matches in 1881 at Newport, Rhode Island, where fashionable pastimes always enjoyed the blessing of high society. The first women's national tennis matches also got under way at Newport in 1887.

A young lady from Pau, a French resort where golf had been played in the late 1880's, came to visit the Arthur Hunnewell family at Wellesley, Massachusetts, in 1892. She brought her clubs and a few balls with her, and since there was no course available, she promptly improvised one on the Hunnewell estate and the adjoining property of Hunnewell's brother-in-law, R. G. Shaw, and a nephew, Hollis Hunnewell. The seven-hole course had flowerpots as holes and proved to be a popular diversion. Laurence Curtis, a Hunnewell friend, began playing on the pasture course. He and Hunnewell and a neighbor named Robert Bacon liked the game and persuaded The Country Club of nearby Brookline to authorize construction of a course at a cost not to exceed $50. A six-hole course was built at The Country Club and opened in April, 1893.

So the young lady from Pau was instrumental in getting golf started in New England. There is no record of her name, another indication of the attention paid to women in sports until comparatively recently.

The British Open was established in 1860, the British Amateur in 1885, and the Ladies Championship of Great Britain was first played at St. Annes in 1893. But not until the fifth Ladies Championship was it played on a Scottish course, Gullane.

Despite the legends you may have read or the drawings you may have seen of Mary, Queen of Scots, playing golf in the fields beside Seaton a few days after the murder of her husband Darnley, on February 10, 1567, the Scots were not enthusiastic about women playing golf. While Darnley does not seem to have been the perfect husband for the beautiful Mary, and although folks said she wasn't one to fight off a bonnie laddie, the kind of a girl who would play golf in Scotland in February was hardly the ideal wife, mother, or fireside companion. Understandably, centuries passed before the Scots endorsed golf for women.

In the *Golf* volume of the *Badminton Library of Sports and Pastimes,* edited by Horace G. Hutchinson, winner of the second and third British Amateur championships, Lord Wellwood was quoted in 1890 as saying: "The ladies are advancing in all pursuits with such strides, or leaps and bounds, whichever expression may be thought to be the more respectful, it will, no doubt, not be long before a claim of women's absolute equality in golf be made. . . . Golf is not more unfeminine than tennis and other sports in which ladies nowadays engage freely."

But his Lordship had his doubts as he pondered: "It will be convenient to consider this delicate question under three heads: (1) the abstract right of women to play golf at all; (2) their right to play the 'long round' with or without male companions; and (3) their right to accompany matches as spectators.

"On the first question our conscience is clear. We have always advocated a liberal extension of the right of golfing to women. Not many years ago their position was most degraded. Bound to accompany their lords and masters to golfing resorts for the summer months, they had to submit to their fathers and brothers playing golf all day and talking golfing shop the whole of the evening, while they themselves were hooted off the links with cries of 'Fore' if they ventured to appear there."

After commenting that ladies' links have been provided at most of the larger clubs, Lord Wellwood recommends that: "Ladies links should be laid out on the model, though on a smaller scale, of the 'long round'; containing some short putting holes, some longer holes, admitting of a drive or two of 70 or 80 yards, and a few suitable hazards.

"We venture to suggest 70 or 80 yards as the average limit of a drive advisedly; not because we doubt a lady's power to make a longer drive, but because that cannot well be done without raising the club about the shoulder. Now, we do not presume to dictate, but we must observe that the postures and the gestures requisite for a full swing are not particularly graceful when the player is clad in female dress."

Lord Wellwood cavalierly observes that if ladies choose to play when male golfers are feeding and resting, no one can object, but: "At other times—must we say it—they are in the way; just because gallantry forbids to treat them exactly as men. The tender mercies of the golfer are cruel. He cannot afford to be merciful; because if he forbears to drive into the party in front he is promptly driven into from behind. It is hard to follow a party of ladies with a powerful driver behind you if you are troubled with a spark of chivalry or kindness."

In those prudish male-chauvinist days in Scotland, it must have been hell for a gentleman "troubled with a spark of chivalry or kindness" to play eighteen holes "being driven into from behind" by the ladies, even though his flanks were protected by Scotch tweed as substantial as that armoring tanks in World War I or as thick as that worn by overdressed early American golfers until they died of heat prostration.

If attitudes were rigid in his homeland, the pioneer American professional quickly perceived the changes in women's golf in his adopted country. It didn't take him long. The first USGA Women's Amateur Championship was held at the Meadow Brook Club, Hempstead, Long Island, on November 9, 1895. With an exclusive women's course designed by Willie Dunn, and a Taj Mahal of clubhouses designed by the fashionable Stanford White, it would seem that a Shinnecock Hills Country Club member had to emerge a winner in the field of thirteen women who played nine holes in the morning and nine in the afternoon. And so it proved, as Mrs. Charles S. Brown took the honors with a 69, 63—132. The women contestants had to play from the men's tees, and the USGA red-facedly admitted that the championship "was arranged on short notice."

The next year the USGA Women's Amateur Championship was at match play. It was held at the Morris County Golf Club, Morristown, New Jersey, in October and had twenty-nine entrants contesting for eight places. Miss Beatrix Hoyt, sixteen, again of Shinnecock Hills, was medalist and winner. She was the youngest contestant, and that was the first of her three consecutive championships.

With the early pros serving as mother's helpers and baby-sitters, women's golf had developed to such an extent in 1901 that the Women's Western Golf Association had a good field for its initial championship. Miss Bessie Anthony won the first three of those Women's Western championships, which are the oldest consecutive women's championships in the world. They were played through two world wars by contestants who took time off from military nurs-

Mrs. Charles S. Brown. GH

Bessie Anthony. GH

ing, factory work, auxiliary service, war-bond selling, and those Sister-Susie-sewing-shirts-for-soldier jobs to play championships at courses close to town. All this blooming of women's golf started in the United States and actually rebounded into Britain.

The early professional soon noted that his adult male members, whether very rich or merely well-to-do, were definitely of the working classes and did not get to the golf club except on weekends. During the week, business came before pleasure, and as a consequence the professional hadn't the opportunity to make as much money as he felt entitled to in this land of plenty and of the free. So, since Papa had to stay at the office while the mothers and daughters of these better families had time and money and interest in golf, the professional wisely took the women to his heart as daughters—and certainly as grateful customers.

Photographs taken in 1892 show women in long flowing skirts playing golf with the Shinnecock Hills clubhouse in the background. One shows a woman in a white skirt kneeling on a green and studying her putt, while another woman is putting and two others watch, shading themselves with parasols. (The World Golf Hall of Fame in Pinehurst has among its displays costumes worn by early players, showing that women golfers of the period "wore two petticoats under a wasp-waisted skirt bound at the bottom with leather, a red jacket with brass buttons, and a straw skimmer . . .") It's all nice and proper, but these photographs are a landmark because they symbolize the emergence of women in sports on an international scale. In 1900 there would be women's tennis singles at the Olympic Games in Paris; in 1908 women would participate in figure skating; and in the 1912 Olympics at Stockholm they would have their own swimming and diving events. (Golf made its only Olympic appearance when the games were held in St. Louis, and the event was won by George S. Lyon of Canada over a rather pick-up field. Like tennis, golf seemed unsuited for Olympic competition and was dropped.) The point can be made that with the help of the early golf professionals American women set world records in the development of sports.

In 1900 it was estimated that there were about 982 golf courses in the United States. *Harper's Golf Guide* listed 715 of them as nine-hole courses, 90 as eighteen-hole courses, and 66 as six-hole courses. The number of holes in the remaining 111 was not given, and perhaps they were rather primitive. But the fact that approximately two-thirds of the courses were nine-hole layouts indicates that there was a considerable sampling of golf by Americans and that this called for the expert attention of professional golfers if the game was to become more than just a passing fad. By the time of the St. Louis Fair in 1904, the number of golf courses had reached close to 2,000, according to available records, and women were serving as club officials as well as playing the game.

This was especially true of Connecticut, where the old directories show that Miss Evelyn Goodsill of Bridgeport was secretary and treasurer of the Woodmont Golf Club when General Joseph R. Hawley was president. Miss J. A. Deming was chairman of the House Committee at the Litchfield Country Club, Miss Partridge and Miss Foote were on the governing committee of seven at the Nokomis Gold Club in Mystic, and Mrs. J. B. Lathrop was president of the Cochegan Golf Club at

Mickey Wright, one of the greatest all-time woman golfers. AG

Montville. Golf clubs at Waterbury, Watertown, Stonington, Wallingford, and Westport also had women officials, according to the old records.

A number of other clubs in the country had women presidents at the time, but the most fittingly named was the King's Daughters Golf Club in Evanston, Illinois, which was headed by Mrs. S. S. Davis, with Miss Frances Poole as secretary and treasurer. The club had a 2,785-yard nine-hole course and was a block from the Chicago and Northwestern Railroad tracks.

Along with the sale of clubs and balls, lessons to women were major factors in the pioneer professional's income. His lessons to men also accounted for a good part of his instruction revenue up to about 1914, but typically, the independent American male didn't see why he should pay for golf lessons any more than he should pay to be taught baseball or football. After a few elementary golf lessons, he thought he knew it all. Ask the club professional and he'll tell you that's the way it still is. The strange part of it is that golf is essentially such a simple game that the professional's task is that of "unteaching" most of his pupils who have been playing six months or so.

Just as in the old days, golf's most effective teachers operate on the basis that golf instruction is an art. The early teachers were brutally candid among themselves and sometimes remarked that the first five years a fellow had a pro job he should have paid his pupils for taking lessons.

A 1930 inquiry indicated that more than 60 percent of golf lessons were given by professionals to women. The percentage is about the same now. There were no "surveys" on golf in the early 1900's, but surviving veterans estimate that more than half the lessons were given to women. Men received instruction in what were called playing lessons. The professional would play around with his pupil for nine holes, then turn him loose.

The lesson and practice tee didn't come into golf education until the course construction of the early 1920's. It originated at "Maniac Hill," at Pinehurst, as previously mentioned, where professionals gathered for the North and South Open under the sponsorship of the Tufts family and their professional, Donald Ross. This was the first university of professional golf. Professionals first gathered there to hit balls for exercise rather than for self-examination. At that time they didn't practice before rounds, believing that if you didn't know how to play when you got to the first tee of a championship, it was too late for you to learn. At Maniac Hill they began to discuss and experiment with technique collectively.

Every angle had to be played to get the American public educated to watching golf. The old reliable society theme that had figured in golf's successful introduction to the United States also served to put pro tournament golf into the entertainment and publicity picture. The upper-crust note was sounded very effectively at Palm Beach and from there spread along Florida's east coast. The association was adroitly promoted by Ray McCarthy, a sportswriter for the *New York Herald Tribune,* who made his golf-promotion debut in 1922 by signing Jim Barnes and Jock Hutchison for exhibition matches. Barnes was an able golfer but so colorless that he was soon replaced by the more dynamic Gene Sarazen. Then, in 1924, McCarthy brought Hutchison and Sarazen to Miami for an exhibition and ar-

Marilynn Smith, who became a pro in 1949. AG

Jock Hutchison in the 1940s. Photo from Nevin Gibson, *A Pictorial History of Golf*

ranged a match between this team and Leo Diegel and Mike Brady, who got $50 each to play.

Mayor Everett Sewell of Miami was impressed by the size of the gallery and promptly hired McCarthy to promote golf in the area. McCarthy got room and board at the Royal Palm Hotel and came up with the idea of the Miami International 4-Ball. He brought over Arthur Havers, British Open Champion, and Jim Ockenden, another English player, to play in the event, which was won by Horton Smith and Bill Melhorn, who faced Brady and Hutchison in the finals. The Miami 4-Ball lasted for twenty-five years, and McCarthy later promoted the Championship of Champions (amateur) at the Breakers in Palm Beach. The flossiest of all the earlier invitational tournaments that sprang from McCarthy's Palm Beach gatherings was the Seminole Pro-Amateur event, which ran from 1937 through 1959.

McCarthy continued to play the Palm Beach society theme melodiously when he promoted his annual Artists and Writers Golf Tournament. It brought many magazine and book writers, illustrators, editors, and cartoonists down from New York. For a week or so they were pleasantly wined and dined by the local peerage as news and photographs of sunny Florida appeared to advantage in the Eastern newspapers.

In the old days the pros paid no tournament entry fees at the resorts. The Open championships at Florida hotels were financed by the guests who paid $5 to $250 each, and exhibitions were often run in the same manner. Jacksonville fell in line for golf spectacles when the municipality offered $5,000 for an Open tournament. No gallery fees were charged so that the local residents would not feel the tax-payers' money was being tossed loosely to the knickered gypsies. It was ama-teur interest in both Florida and Cali-fornia that gave the pro-tournament circuit a foundation. In 1932 Florida paid $25,000 for six winter tourna-ments, while California paid $21,500 for four. In 1934 and 1935, the dates for tournaments conflicted in these two states, and that began a costly decline for the journeymen professionals.

An interesting experiment began in Florida during the 1923–24 winter sea-son; this was the "golf league," which, unfortunately, proved unprofitable. Walter Hagen and Joe Kirkwood played for the Pasadena real-estate de-velopment; Temple Terrace at Tampa had Jim Barnes and Freddie McLeod; and Hollywood had Sarazen and Diegel. The Winter Haven team consisted of Cyril Walker and Eddie Loos. Bobby Cruikshank and Johnny Farrell made up another Tampa duo; Orlando's men were George Low and Tommy Kerri-gan; and Tommy Armour and Bill Melhorn represented Miami. The teams never did play out their schedule as ad-vanced because it was learned that cad-dies did not make for a remunerative gallery.

Perhaps the public would have re-sponded more favorably if some celeb-rities had joined the pros during their play. Actors and famous personalities had a great deal to do with populariz-ing the game and making pro golf glamorous entertainment. This was evi-dent as early as the first World Series of Golf played in 1921 at the Sound View Golf Club, Great Neck, Long Island, where Jim Barnes, that year's American Open Champion, beat Jock Hutchison, the current British Open titleholder. The Barnes-Hutchison match started a series that had Hagen playing Sara-zen, then Hagen against Walker, and in 1928, Hagen against Farrell.

Among the theatrical notables of the day playing at the Sound View and Lakeville clubs were Ernest Truex, Ring Lardner, Gene Buck, John Golden, Ed Wynn, Frank Crummit, Arthur Hopkins, H. B. Warner, Henry E. Dixie, Oscar Shaw, Alan Dale, De Wolfe Hopper, Raymond Hitchcock, Frank Craven, Tom Meighan, Donald Brian, and T. A. (Tad) Dorgan. Dor-gan wasn't an actor but an amusing sports cartoonist who kept actor's hours. There also was Grantland Rice, who even took a crack at writing a comedy about golf, but it didn't last much longer than a fast backswing.

It's perhaps not so surprising that show-business people heightened the game's public appeal and also made its professional aspects a sporting phase of show business. Bing Crosby and Bob Hope came along later to put golf pros into the big-money bracket. Crosby es-tablished the celebrity pro-amateur tournament in his characteristically casual way, and Hope got a pro-amateur going for a hospital. Both made golf the sport that made the greatest finan-cial contribution to a multitude of worthy causes. The Crosby-Hope team also accounted for other actors and ac-tresses following them as sponsors of benefit tournaments that didn't cost them a cent for the immense publicity they generated for a good cause, profes-sionals, golf as a fun game, and last but hardly least, themselves.

4

Regional PGA's, Clubs and Balls, and the British PGA

PEOPLE with common goals learned very early that strength and efficiency come from banding together, and that accounts for the amazing number of solid voluntary organizations in the villages, towns, and cities of the United States. The amateur's recognition that groups had to become firmly organized to get things done stands in solid contrast to the attitude of professionals in many fields. This was certainly true of golf, where the professionals, if they only knew it, had clearly the most to gain by organizing, but continued their foolishly and recklessly independent ways even long after their British brethren had seen the light. If the American amateurs were snobbish and aloof in their own refined manner, so were the professionals, who considered the game their own.

The idea of the professional golfers of the United States becoming organized was hardly a new one. The PGA of America was first proposed by Arthur R. Pottlow, editor and publisher of the magazine *Golf*, as far back as 1897. For a mere golf writer, Pottlow must have had a high rating among the early amateurs, as his magazine was the official organ of such groups as the United States Golf Association, the Western Golf Association, the Southern Golf Association, the Intercollegiate Golf Association, the Metropolitan Golf Association of New York (which was founded in 1897), and the Central New York Golf League.

But apparently he was a nothing-weight with the few American professionals of that time, who were mostly an assortment of competent gentlemen of excellent character, plus perhaps a few uncouth, unsavory, and unshaved Scots gladly relinquished by their homeland and harbored in backwoods clubs where green golfers didn't know what a golf professional was supposed to be like. At any rate, Pottlow got nowhere with his warnings that properly qualified professionals should join to protect and advance their own interests and to develop the game. While the PGA was formed twenty years after his urging, there had been collectives of professionals in Massachusetts and Illinois and other areas in the interval, and the Eastern Professional Golfers' Association was organized in 1906, with George Low, then professional at Baltusrol, as president, and Charles Kirschner, one of Spalding's golf salesmen, secretary-treasurer.

Harry Bowler was president of a professionals' organization that began in the Boston area in 1914, and Robert White, who was named the first president of the PGA of America in 1917, headed the Chicago-based professionals who decided to organize back in those days. His background will be covered in detail in the next chapter, but it will suffice here to say that he was a sort of scoutmaster to American golf's trailblazers. The professionals around Chicago regarded him as a man of sound judgment and foresight, and club officials depended on him for advice at a time when they weren't in the habit of consulting professionals about their golf problems. White represented the early professional as an understanding businessman in what was a curious and precarious new business.

The professionals in the Chicago area had a schedule of monthly tournaments from April through September at one or another of the pleasant courses in the district. It was their custom to gather informally at Spalding's store on Wabash Avenue, and when they decided to organize on a formal basis, White was the natural choice for president. They paid $2 a year dues to their association. The entry fee at each tournament was $5, which was generally a prize-money contribution, with amateur friends at the host clubs generally adding to the purses.

There were a number of superior professionals in the Chicago area when White headed the Illinois organization. They included Fred Herd, Willie Smith (who went to Mexico as pro for a couple of years), Jim Foulis, Harry Turpie, Laurie Auchterlonie, Freddie McLeod, Bob Simpson, Fred Mackenzie, Alex Taylor, Willie Marshall, John (Skokie) Watson, Dave Foulis, Dave McIntosh, Arnie Tollifson, John and Otto Hackbarth, Alex Gourlay, Dave Bell, Alex Baxter, Willie Lorimer, Frank Bartsch, Chester Horton, Stewart Gardner, Walter Fovargue, Jimmy Donaldson, George Simpson, Dave Livie, Jack Croke, Tom Vardon, and others whose names are lost in the faraway mists of legend. The native caddies were growing up to compete with their tutors.

The territory of the Eastern Professional Golfers' Association consisted of the New York metropolitan area, parts of Connecticut, Pennsylvania, and most of New Jersey. The boundaries were apparently set up as a matter of convenience; they were arranged so that the members could easily commute to and from the monthly summer tournaments. Dues were $5 a year, and on Mondays, their usual shopping days, many of the professionals had lunch at the Umbrella, a saloon across from the Spalding offices on Nassau Street, New York City. Here organization was attended to on a purely informal basis.

One particular pub, a saloon-restaurant, and later on, a restaurant doubling as a speakeasy, was the professional's club away from his home club on idle Mondays. The place had to be near the branch offices of Spalding, MacGregor, Wilson, Burke, St. Mungo, Horton, and the other major suppliers of golf equipment, and most importantly, had to have a genial and astute credit manager as owner. Some customers needed credit because their clubs were inordinately slow in paying their professionals the fees collected from members. They were rated "Careless," "Good but slow," "Will pay if catching a long shot," "Will pay when he sobers up," "A lush, will be out of his job, too," with the majority classified as "Wish I was as good pay." That was the highest tribute in the speakeasy days when terms on the stuff were "Now—or else." But there were few consistently alcoholic nuisances in these growing-up days of professional golf.

The Eastern Professional Golfers' Association held its first Championship at the Forest Hill Field Club in New Jersey on October 23 and 24, 1906, eleven years before the PGA of America inaugurated its competition. Alex Smith of the Nassau Country Club, Glen Cove, New York, who had triumphed in the National Open at Onwentsia in suburban Chicago by a comfortable margin of seven strokes over his brother Willie, was the winner with two 73's. He got $125 and a gold medal. Alex Campbell, who was second with 149, got $85. Third and fourth money of $120 was divided between David Hunter and George Thomson at 152. The best a home-bred pro could do in this first American PGA Championship was fifth place, for which Orin Terry of California got $40. Right behind him was another home-bred, Mike Brady, who tied with George Pearson at 155 and split $50. The seven following contestants divided $30. Terry and Jock Hutchison won a four-ball event with 69, and Willie Norton and George Turnbull had a 70.

There was a significant play of personalities in that first official professional association championship. George Turnbull, who was then stationed at Sadaquada in Whitesboro, New York, later became professional at the Columbia Golf and Country Club, then went on to the Midlothian Country Club, outside Chicago. Here legend has it that Walter Hagen, then a brash, personable professional who supposedly didn't know any better, promptly made himself at home in the members' locker room, thereby setting an example that forever elevated professionals from their lowly status in this country, and particularly around British clubhouses, which, it must be said, seldom had facilities comparing in comfort and attractiveness with even small-town American golf club quarters.

When questioned about the precedent-shattering treatment of young Hagen and the older professionals during the 1914 National Open, where Hagen burst into fame, veteran Midlothian members declared that there was nothing unusual about their courtesy. They'd simply asked their professional what should be done and followed the advice of the estimable George Turnbull.

The durable Chick Evans, who finished second to Hagen at Midlothian in 1914, has said: "Midlothian had a lot of famous professionals, and they were congenial men. You couldn't find in all golf any finer gentlemen than Fred McLeod and George Turnbull. And Willie, the quiet Smith, was a modest fellow who knew how to help golfers enjoy themselves. So, with all due credit to the wonderful Walter, I'd have to say that maybe Midlothian's own professionals, such as George Turnbull, set the stage for what's been called the social revolution in American golf."

References can be found in old golf

magazines and newspapers to the hosts at the initial Professional Golfers' Association tournament being pleased and surprised at receiving thank-you notes from their pro guests. This marked a nice, old-fashioned exercise in good manners that long ago was so instrumental in raising purses to $300,-000. Plainly those pioneers were great masters of sound, simple public relations. Now, regrettably, tournament sponsors rarely hear from the enriched contestants who have enjoyed their hospitality. It has all become a coldly cash-and-carry business.

The British professionals were also slow in getting together. Perhaps the self-contained nature of the intense golfer, combined with the independent temperament of the Scottish professional, was responsible for the due deliberation in organizing the British PGA, which was formed in 1901. The first British Open was played in 1860, well over a century after professional golf had become an established, if not profitable, fact of life in Scotland. As we've seen, at this primary stage golf was merely a sideline to such occupations as fishing, carpentry, masonry, painting, thatching cottage roofs, sailing before the mast, or soldiering in some godforsaken spot thousands of miles from home. The original golf professional jobs were those of the ball-maker, when golf balls were made of leather stuffed with feathers, and the clubmaker, when clubmaking began to emerge as an art and a science. They antedated the professional golfer, who generally played for cash on the line and side bets, and the much-later teacher, who instructed amateurs in "playing lessons."

Since the formation of both the British and American PGA's was spurred by manufacturers of golf balls, it's per-tinent to continue with the development of balls, clubs, and other accessories of the game as golf became an ever more popular sport and growing business in the United States. Chapter 1 described the early stages, the first clubs, the golf ball monopoly sanctioned by the king in the seventeenth century, and on up to the Robertson ball's being favored by tournament players in the 1840's. The feather-stuffed ball was serviceable enough at the time, but it was no bargain in human values as can be seen in *The Curious History of the Golf Ball,* a bright, informative book by John Stuart Martin, a remarkable one-armed golfer and all-around sportsman who played an important role in the founding of *Time, Fortune,* and *Life* magazines. It's very good reading for the golf enthusiast, professional or amateur, who wants to know about the game's implements.

Martin says that the best ballmakers of the 1840's and 1850's could stuff and stitch no more than four or five "featheries" in the course of a long, nonunion day. Oddly enough, just as today when occupational hazards are finally being recognized among workers who use asbestos, uranium, mercury, and other life-endangering substances on their jobs, making those early golf balls had its own built-in risks. The persistent pressure against the chest involved in the stuffing and stitching process, plus the inhaling of feather particles, cut short the lives of the ballmakers.

Allan Robertson's staff, which included Auld Tom Morris, produced 2,425 balls in 1844. That's only a few more than 200 dozen, and figuring the modern rate of around $3,000 for the same amount, nobody would get rich then or now. But Allan had another important first going for him. Because

Hand-nicking and hand-painting guttie balls—Robert Forgan Golf Shop, 1900. GH

he was *the* topflight golfer of his time, and consistently won big matches on which great wads of money were bet, he established the practice of having the ball played by champions proclaimed as the ideal ball for every other golfer—good, medium, fair, duffer, and whiffer. The golf business has always been like that.

Nor was there much money in the gutta-percha balls that came along next and were promoted by the Gourlays. Just how the new ball evolved is not entirely clear, but some people believe that it was the result of an experiment by some Scot with the backing of W. T. Henley's Telegraph Works Company, makers of rubber-insulated cables for long-distance underwater service. On the other hand, according to a letter in

the *St. Andrews Citizen,* the molded gutta-percha ball began when a local boy, who was serving Her Majesty the Queen in India's sunny clime, shipped home an Indian idol carefully packed in a protective rubbery substance conveniently available there. Someone then discovered, apparently, that the packing material from India bounced and was easily molded into a ball when heated. Thus was introduced the gutta-percha ball that was played from the late 1860's until the American inventor Haskell produced a ball of rubber thread wound around a core and with a treated rubber cover. In 1901, when Alex (Sandy) Herd won the British Open with the new wound ball, the gutta-percha ball became obsolete.

In any case many golfers promptly

hailed the "gutty" ball as the best around by far—"white as snow, hard as lead, and elastic as whalebone"—and far superior to the leather-covered, feather-filled Robertson. While the public is always captivated by something new on the market, the gutty ball was cheaper than its feathery predecessor. It went like lightning, too, and far, but it tended to duck, soar, hook, or slice in an unpredictable manner, despite the dexterity of the old experts. From the data available it can be concluded that they had marvelous club control and handled the treacherous gutty skillfully. The pioneer American golfers were pretty good at this sort of sleight of hand themselves. Freddie McLeod and Chick Evans, both of whom won national championships, used only seven clubs for their feats. They played all the shots with six clubs and their putters—and don't think they used that putter just for rolling balls into holes on the greens! But perhaps the greatest advantage of the gutty ball was that it could be remolded if knocked out of shape. It was good business for the professionals, as they only had to heat the cut, misshapen balls, remold and paint them, and they were good as new.

Just as the British professionals loathed the American Haskell rubber-cored ball when it arrived on the scene, Allan Robertson hated the new gutty ball as a player, and most of all, because he rightly feared that it would ruin his business as well as that of the other makers of feather-stuffed balls. However, old Tom Morris liked the ball, and this caused a falling out with Robertson. But the gutta-percha golf ball did account for the entry of a large manufacturing company into the golf business. Some employees of a Scottish maker of rubber-insulated wire (the Telegraph Works Company referred to above) used samples of the insulating material to fashion themselves good golf balls. When this came to the attention of a factory executive, also a golfer, he decided that this might be a profitable sideline for his company. So it seemed for a while, but this did mark the first time a big, going concern had ventured into the golf business.

McLeod and Evans played the hard-rubber ball, which when the newness wore off and the outside was scarred, behaved well. When it was discovered that marking the cover kept the ball more accurate in flight, the next step was to hand-hammer markings on the ball. This was done until about 1880 when the balls were put into molds. When something is radically changed in any system, sooner or later the remaining components have to be altered. The wooden clubs, with their thick heads and slender necks adapted for the feather-stuffed ball, soon broke when playing the rubber balls. The new ball obviously demanded a new club; a new design was made, and the club business soared. So with the introduction of a cheaper ball and a remodeled club, golf's popularity further increased in the 1880's, and what Allan Robertson and others had seen as a threat to their business only proved to make it better. It enlarged the market by making golf a sport more people could afford to play.

The golf market was further revolutionized when Walter Travis won the 1901 U.S. Amateur Championship playing the $1.25 top-grade, rubber-cored, thread-wound ball, and as mentioned, Sandy Herd used it to beat Harry Vardon by a stroke in the 1901 British Open. Circumstantial evidence indicates that Herd used an American-made ball sent to him by his brother Fred, a professional in the Chicago area who had won the fourth U.S. Open in 1898. This was a time when excellent wood and iron clubs for the new ball sold at $2.50 each, and in passing, it might be said that, considering inflation and the many other factors reducing the purchasing capacity of the dollar, it's surprising how comparatively small the dollar increase has been in the cost of golf equipment since the game became firmly established in the United States.

The sale of equipment at the pro shops in golf clubs played a unique role here. The shops supplied golfers at the convenient point of use with authoritatively selected merchandise and personalized fitting. What perhaps isn't remembered nor is highly regarded about this immensely valuable service is that it used the professionals' character as a credit rating and practically as a medium of exchange. Pro merchandising was necessary because the professional himself received only a courtesy salary that was barely enough to support the man and his family on a tight budget. Whatever he could make over and above that minimum was his incentive. To a considerable degree that is still the policy at many American golf clubs, whose increased prestige and superior operating standards derive from the aspiration, dedication, and ability of their professionals.

Before digging further into the development of clubs and balls, something should be said about how players, professionals as well as amateurs, carried their extra balls and clubs as they played their rounds. With all the studious attention they've given to golf equipment, both making it and selling it, the professionals of the old school confess that they never had much to do with the design and construction of golf bags. They were much more con-

cerned about caddies, most of them having been caddies themselves. At any rate, golf bags did not come into use until early in 1880. Prior to that, the six or seven clubs the contestants or players used were carried loose under the right arm of each man's or woman's caddie. This can be noted in some of the early golfing photographs, and it must have been an awkward business, especially when the caddie had to look for lost balls or otherwise be of assistance to the player.

Members of the Golf Collectors' Society have been consulted about when golf bags were first used, but they can only say that they made their appearance in 1895 when the game was a novel pastime in the United States. The golf tee itself probably came along sometime after World War I. Before that, there were handy boxes of sand at every tee, the golfer or his caddie made a little mound of it, perched the ball, and the golfer was teed up and ready for his drive.

The golf bag grew in size and weight until the 1930's when they were as big as elephant legs, swollen with twenty to twenty-three clubs and so heavy that child-welfare authorities were alarmed that the caddies' burdens might account for many American youngsters having curvature of the spine. Along with changing times, costs, and the difficulty of finding kids to caddie, the sheer heft of these gargantuan bags may have had something to do with the emergence of the two-wheeled caddie cart, and later the golf cart.

Materials used for making golf bags also changed. The early ones were probably made out of some kind of cloth, with canvas being the sturdiest. In one significant instance, the Wilson Packing Company in Chicago had an excess of leather, and in seeking an outlet, bought the Western Sporting Goods Company, which soon became a big factor in the marketing of leather golf bags and also in other aspects of the golf business. Today, of course, leather golf bags sell at a premium, and most of them are made of plastic and artificial materials resembling leather.

The cornerstone of the American golf industry was probably laid in 1892 when a foresighted young man named Julian Curtiss returned from Scotland to bewilder his associates in the A. G. Spalding & Brothers Company with his purchase of a $500 assortment of golf clubs. Three years later, in 1895, Spalding was in the golf business. According to stories, Curtiss, a member of the Yale crew in 1878 and 1879, was sent over to Scotland to buy leather for footballs. Golf intrigued him. While enjoying congenial company and sampling some good Scotch whisky, he somehow found himself signing for a big order of golf equipment. Back in New York, after he got through explaining what had happened as nearly as he could remember, he moved his unwanted goods to his home in Greenwich, Connecticut. With the equipment at hand, and the money to do the job, he soon got his brother, Edwin B. Curtiss, and a next-door neighbor to put in a five-hole course on his property. Then he invited his friends to play with the stock of balls and clubs Spalding had been stuck with because of his "bad guess."

It was just about this time that the golf craze peaked, and high society created a demand for golf equipment. So Spalding immediately recalled the clubs and profited from Julian Curtiss's "mistake." And perhaps on his example, the Greenwich Country Club was formed not long afterward. In any case there were golf clubs advertised in

Spalding's 1896 catalogue, the early golf magazines, and the succeeding Spalding catalogues.

By 1900, enterprising professionals were advertising their benchmade clubs in the national golf magazines. Their specialties were mainly variations of the standard wood models. A few of these professionals employed other pros in the winter to build up stock for the coming season, but Spalding employed most of these otherwise unemployed Scots during the winters up to about 1908. The company's employees had a golf course alongside the factory in Chicopee Falls, Massachusetts. It was the first industrial golf course in the world.

Prices encouraged early buyers of golf clubs. In 1897, Spalding woods of persimmon, dogwood, or "compressed hickory" were $2, and for $1.50 the golfer could get an "iron niblick to jerk the ball out of the steep face of a bunker or extract it from the rough stone or the deep tracks of cart wheels." In 1899, a Diamond-back cleek was $1.50.

A golfer in the 1890's and early 1900's accepted conditions as he or she found them, and nobody ever dreamed that the USGA would someday have its Green Section study the standardization of fine-grain bunker sand. The shifting sands and the stony or hard clay ground on which many of the first American courses were built were totally unlike Scotland's golfing terrain of rolling fields, open pastures, and windswept dunes. Clubs got rough wear on the shallow-rooted grass of American courses, so new clubs had to be developed for the way the Yankees played the game. They didn't play as much as the Scots did, for one thing, and they needed special clubs for their shots. New to the game, the American amateurs simply hadn't acquired dexterity in the manipulation of the few clubs the Scots had mastered.

As a consequence, American golfers had available a driver, brassie, cleek, driving mashie, midiron, light iron, niblick, mashie iron, mashie putting cleek, and putter, lofter, and lofting mashie.

From the very start of golf, there was a compulsion to improve the tools of the game. Most golfers seem to have had the feeling that they might do better with clubs that were better for them, and that instinctive conviction of the golfer has accounted for immense and continuous improvement in the hitting implements of the game.

The search for improved materials for golf clubs has been unending. Happily the supply of American hickory for shafts and persimmon for wood heads became abundantly available in the early 1900's when the game of golf blossomed into a business boom.

The Scots-forged Nicoll, Forgan, and Stewart iron heads, in material, design, and individual craftsmanship, continued to be in highest favor with American golfers after American forgings became available. They were generally made by Scots who played good golf themselves. Their forgings didn't need as much filing and grinding as American forgings did before an acceptably finished club was produced. But wood club heads of American material were being turned out in the rough for export to the United States until the end of the 1800's.

American shoe-last manufacturers, especially Crawford, McGregor and Canby, and the Burke Company, seeking an operation to fill in the seasonal slump in their shoe-last business, found that their machinery also could turn out nearly finished wood club heads

using persimmon from sources not far away. They had a ready market in supplying most of the pro clubmakers. In 1897, Spalding and Crawford, McGregor and Canby started making a complete line of golf clubs, followed by the Burke Golf Company in 1904. The Vulcan Golf Company, also originally a shoe-last manufacturer, also got into the golf club business late in the 1920's, but didn't stay long.

The Scottish wood heads were copied almost exactly for the first American-made heads, and the Jack White type of driver head stayed in high popularity for years. There was considerable variety in the design of the American brassies, as the harder, gravelly nature of most of the early American courses called for a wood club with a brass sole to do a versatile job.

After some experience with American golfers and American playing conditions, professionals who had been good clubmakers in Scotland, and pioneer Americans, Johnny Inglis among them, began fashioning their own models of woods. They advertised them in the golf magazines and supplied thousands of golfers scattered around the country before golf club distribution was extensive.

South of Chicago, a number of able clubmakers got together to make clubs in the winter. They were headed by Robert White, professional at Ravisloe, who later became the first president of the PGA. The group advertised as the Professional Golfers' Association ten years or so before the PGA was organized. These professionals were better clubmakers than they were industrial executives. They made excellent products and sold the factory output for delivery in early spring. But payment for most of the clubs didn't come in until well after the eventual purchasers had bought them; although there was high praise for the clubs, lack of capital and a sharp rise and fall in production ended this early pro collective business effort.

And somehow, the more the scholars probed into the mechanics of the stroke, the more obvious it became that the artistry of the individual determined the difference between mastery and mediocrity in performance. Variations in the application of the essentials of golfing methods are innumerable. Tommy Armour noted, "All there is to putting is keeping the head dead steady and the face of the putter moving squarely across the line to the hole, and there are at least a thousand different ways of doing these two things." There certainly have been thousands of variations in the design and construction of the clubs intended for the simple job of rolling the ball into the hole.

The putting cleek, a short-shafted iron club with very little loft, was the primitive club for the specialized function of striking the ball with minimum deviation in direction over the uneven early greens. After a few hundred years, putter designers were thinking about getting away from the vertical face of the putter. An indication of the efforts of ingenious clubmakers to devise an effective connection of player with club is seen in the variety of putter grips, some of which are illegal, as shown in the USGA Rules of Golf. Other evidence of the search for a grip that promoted satisfactory joining of the hands and the club is in the club grip material and in some golf gloves.

The earlier clubs usually had grips of calfskin or sheepskin. In 1906, Spalding offered rubber grips. The novelty was popular for a short time, but the grips got hard and slippery and could not be restored to their original secure and sensitive feel. Experiments with rubber grips continued, but about forty years passed before a satisfactory rubber composition grip became extensively used.

Bench clubmaking showed that importance was attached to the diameter of the grip in correctly fitting clubs to the individual. The thickness and character of the leather, the kind of listing beneath the leather, and of course, the weight and length of the grip material to have the club in good balance, afforded the clubmaker opportunities for demonstrating his skill in filling the club user's individual requirements. Often, players had the butt end of their grips wrapped with a few inches of gauze tape to give a left-hand grip that was more pleasing.

Beech, apple, oak, and other woods native to Britain were materials used for wood club heads until, by experimenting with all possible timber, persimmon was found to have the qualities that were best suited to manufacture and use as club heads. Widely varying climatic conditions of golf club use was a factor that helped account for the general adoption of hickory for shafts and persimmon for heads. These woods, seasoned and treated with oil and varnish, retained factory condition remarkably well.

In 1901, golf gave to the world of pro sports an idea that was to make millions for conspicuously talented professionals. Spalding introduced the Vardon woods and irons. Prior to the use of the famed British champion's name, clubs bore the names of men who were proficient clubmakers rather than the names of the golfers who used them.

The Vardon Flyer ball was short-lived because the Haskell type of con-

Alex Smith. GH

struction soon came onto the market. But the Vardon clubs really began to shine in the market. Vardon himself was not much of a clubmaker, according to George Sargent, a PGA of America founder who had been assistant to Vardon in England. Vardon was a big man. He had been a gardener before he got into golf, and his hands were strong and not especially large. He had artistic hands. There are bronze casts of his hands holding a golf club grip; one set is in the clubhouse of the Long Meadow Golf Club, Lowell, Massachusetts, a club home of numerous Spalding executives. Sargent said that Vardon had the sharpest eye and most sensitive feel of a golf club of anyone he ever knew.

All the deals that reward professional athletes for the use of their names to advertise anything from golf balls to shoes, socks, clubs, balls, chairs, cars, lawn mowers, airlines, resorts, and you-name-it, date back to Harry Vardon. He was the first professional to endorse the tools of his trade. From the golf clubs bearing the Vardon name, the star-player endorsement as a sales theme came down through the years to hundreds and hundreds of beneficiaries in professional golf, baseball, tennis, football, basketball, boxing, skiing, and any commercial sport under the sun.

Not only was Julian Curtiss instrumental in getting the golf industry started in America, he was also the first to introduce the sports star system in money with Vardon. Yet, has Julian Curtiss been named for a place in a sports hall of fame in the United States? This blindness of golf's historians, causing so obvious an omission of the one man who laid the foundation for the beginning of American golf history, has amused and bewildered the cynical realists.

Every man and woman who has collected money for the use of his or her name on sporting goods owes a bow to the memory of Julian Curtiss, who in golf, and with Harry Vardon, made the pro athlete's name a selling point. As golf grew in popularity, misuse of the names of athletes on cheap equipment became a common commercial exploitation of the buyers that must haunt the merry and estimable Julian Curtiss in the hereafter.

There were some early Spalding woods bearing the name of an amateur, Walter Travis, before USGA amateur status rules prohibited such advertising. Travis won the USGA Amateur Championships in 1900, 1901, and 1903, and the British Amateur in 1901. He wasn't much of a distance driver, but he stayed on the fairways and had a short game that cut the hearts out of his opponents. He had three kinds of Spalding drivers: the pull, the slice, and the regular. The slice head was for golfers who chronically hooked, and the pull head, which was toed in, was for players who habitually sliced. The clubs sold well. Pro-shop clubmakers who knew the games of their customers made woods to adjust in the way the Travis models corrected customary faults. Scottish clubmakers hadn't thought much about getting the ball into the air as the winds of the seashore courses required that shots be low rather than up into the windy zones.

Iron clubmaking didn't advance much until the Haskell type of ball construction came with a more durable cover than the feather-stuffed leather ball or the molded gutta-percha ball, which could also be cut easily and severely by iron clubs. With pro bench-

made clubs still taking most of the small market from the American manufacturers in the period from 1895 to 1903, and the ball market uncertain in the switch from the solid rubber ball to the new Haskell type, Julian Curtiss, who had put Spalding into the golf business, financed a tour of the United States by Harry Vardon to promote the sale of the Vardon Flyer, for which the Spalding company had exclusive distribution rights in this country. The Vardon Flyer was a solid gutty ball, Bramble-marked, and made for the great golfer in England. But when he won the 1900 USGA Open at the Chicago Golf Club, he was playing a Vardon Flyer manufactured at the Spalding plant in Chicopee Falls. Vardon had a fat percentage arrangement with Spalding, one that might have made him the first of professional golf's millionaires *if*. . . .

The big *if* was the new Haskell ball and the new Kempshall ball, another innovation, with liquid centers. The Vardon Flyer, the gutty ball that Spalding first imported in 1898, then manufactured on its own, was expected to dominate the American market after Vardon won the 1900 Open with it. Although the victory was hailed in the limited golf journalism of the period, it couldn't hold back the Haskell ball. And yet the Haskell seems to have had slow, reluctant acceptance among American players.

Willie Anderson won the 1901 National Open at Myopia after tying with Alex Smith at 331, the highest score in the U.S. Open, then beating Smith 85 to 89 in the play-off. There is no printed evidence to show that either Anderson or Smith played the new ball, and the scores do not point to any progress in the ball. It's probable that the American invention figured in a championship victory abroad sooner than it did in the United States. Although Spalding had added golf to its 1895 sports line and continued to develop and improve golf equipment, it suffered the first of the bumps, inevitable to the pioneer, when Vardon's American tour, supplemented by J. H. Taylor in its later stages, didn't pan out as a product booster.

The Goodrich Rubber Company at Akron, Ohio, had a leading part in the invention and development of the Haskell wound ball. Coburn Haskell of Cleveland was in the Goodrich plant at the suggestion of his friend Bertram Work, a Goodrich official, when he spotted some thin strips of rubber lying on the floor by a machine and got the idea they could be wound into a golf ball. Coburn patented his hunch and got Work interested to the extent that the Goodrich official got bright young men in the plant working on ball-winding machines, devising cores, and making a rubber casing that would keep the wound ball fairly well protected.

The first wound balls were produced in 1898 but were not quickly accepted by professional or amateur golfers. They were called Bounding Billys, and although they played longer than the gutta-percha balls, they were too lively to be satisfactory for approach shots to the hard greens of that time.

The Kempshall ball was promoted by a St. Andrews professional, Jack Jolly, who quit his club job at Forest Hill, Bloomfield, New Jersey, to go into the golf ball business and immediately got caught in the middle of a battle of the giants, with Spalding and Goodrich on one side, and on the other, Haskell Construction and Kempshall, originally a celluloid collar maker who had

come up with a novel golf ball idea himself and a connection with the St. Mungo Golf Company of Glasgow. Jolly had charm, intelligence, and energy. As United States sales chief for the St. Mungo people he not only got the kinks eliminated from his new ball, which was called the Colonel, but kept traveling until he had solidly established his product. In time he knew every member of the Professional Golfers' Association and the PGA Seniors. George Braid was his Midwestern representative. He had a bad arm—one of the handicaps that had to be surmounted by Ed Furgol when he won the National Open in 1954—and was an amazingly good golfer. He and Jolly did extremely well as two little guys against big business.

Few people really understood the commercial realities of the situation because golf wasn't regarded as much of a business at the time, even though the market was growing and expanding at an enormous rate and many firms and individuals were battling for their share of the pie. While imported golf equipment continued to have the snob appeal of Rolls-Royces and Jaguars today, and there was no doubt that much of it was of better quality than that made in the United States at the time, more and more manufacturers were finding the American market promising and lucrative. However, Spalding continued to dominate golf sales in the early days of the game. There was a main branch in New York, another store in Chicago where the Scots Herbert and Douglas Tweedie were in charge, while in Boston Wright and Ditson, another Spalding satellite, was headed by John Morrill, of whom Francis Ouimet wrote: "A kindlier and more lovable character never lived." And as we shall see, it was to counteract the Spalding lead that Tom McNamara of the Wanamaker pro golf department got young Rodman Wanamaker, son of the founder, interested in launching the PGA.

At this period golf clubs were being made by Crawford, McGregor and Canby and also the Burke Golf Company. But these manufacturers, like a number of others, were not particularly concerned with pro employment as a marketing aid. It wasn't until the Goldsmith sporting goods interests acquired Crawford, McGregor and Canby that the accent was placed on the business of professional golfers. Deftly capitalizing on the Scottish element in advertising and sales, the new owners put an "a" into the name of one of the original founders and made the golf line "MacGregor." Clarence Rickey was hired to push the professional end, and in a few years he had MacGregor climbing fast as a major contender with Spalding and Wilson, another recent entry, for the pros' business. After his father died in a car crash, young Robert Rickey came into the MacGregor executive family and worked successfully on the company's pro interests.

George Worthington, another Yale (and Andover) graduate, got into the golf ball business via the bicycle tire business. Knowing Coburn Haskell, he built a golf ball factory in Elyria, Ohio, and with the merchandising of a Scot named Jim Brydon, Worthington became one of the big makers of golf balls and developed the private-brand ball business as advertising.

Spalding remained well ahead of the field because it had been quick to set up retailing connections with the professionals, then continued as practically the only employment agency for professionals during the first decade of American golf. Hence, when the Has-

kell type of ball came in, and Julian Curtiss decided to take it over, Spalding had its distribution all arranged.

The first Haskell-type balls were made only by Goodrich; then Spalding began ball manufacture and for many years got uncovered balls from Goodrich. Then, about 1903, the Staughton Rubber Company began making golf ball covers of balata. Balata was tougher than rubber, took cover marking well, and was white. It was a considerable improvement over rubber as golf ball cover material, although at times there was difficulty in bonding the balata cover and the inner ball so they stayed tightly together.

Spalding bought the Staughton company and moved its ball-covering equipment to its plants at Chicopee Falls as the company progressed rapidly with its ball business. The Spalding Wizard was the leader among the early wound balls. Then came their Glory Dimple and Baby Dimple balls with their recessed round markings. Soon square-mesh recessed markings became popular, and the search for other golf ball treatment for endurance, distance, and accuracy in flight has never ceased.

Golf balls were black and floated prior to the Spalding Baby Dimple of 1910, which was painted white and was smaller and heavier than the 1907 Dimple and their Bramble-marked ball, which had also floated. The Bramble marking had been discontinued because it scuffed and was worn down too quickly. Covers were a problem with all ballmakers. They were easily cut, and the paint came off or turned yellow even in pro-shop showcases. The difficulty lay in getting covers to adhere to the inner-construction winding. The vulcanized cover, which Spalding introduced in 1921, was an advance; then a team of inventors developed a process that came into general use as the most durable and cohesive of covers.

Getting a wound ball core that stayed round during manufacture, storage, and use presented another difficult problem that the makers tried to solve with every kind of spherical core from a steel ball bearing to honey as a liquid center. In 1921 Spalding began winding their top-quality balls on dry cores that had been kept round by being frozen in dry ice.

All this time Wilson-Western Sporting Goods Company had been vying with Spalding for the professionals' business. The sideline company had been formed when Thomas E. Wilson and his associates in the meat business saw a profitable market for leather in making baseball gloves and golf bags and golf club grips. Lawrence B. Icely, a supersalesman of sports equipment, was brought in to head the Wilson sports branch, then Western Sporting Goods Company was taken over with Dave Levinson as its president. The Icely-Levinson combination would provide tough competition for most firms, but Spalding had a big edge on the ball business, and that, along with its close working relationship with professionals, helped the firm to hold onto its major share of the rapidly growing market.

United States Rubber and Dunlop soon began to enter the golf ball business in a big way, with Dunlop also adding clubs, and with Vincent Richards, once the Boy Wonder of tennis, as head of its sports department. Eddie Conlin, a prominent tennis official, took over U.S. Rubber's golf ball division, and following Spalding's successful tie-in with Great Britain's famed Harry Vardon, moved on into ball promotion with Walter Hagen, a rising American pro, in the show window. Conlin made a deal when The Haig

wanted to become a golf-business magnate, and both profited. Of course, Walter Hagen was one of the most extraordinary figures and wheeler-dealers in the history of American professional golf and will rate the space he deserves further along.

Herbert Lagerblade, another former professional, was in charge of the golf department of the Horton Manufacturing Company, which had just introduced the steel golf club shaft as a companion to its Bristol steel fishing rods. Lagerblade managed to get the Western Golf Association to legalize the steel shaft and saw to it that Horton made good clubs, although they didn't sell particularly well in the pro shops.

The Burke Golf Company was more of a comfortable family business, with W. C. Sherwood, a pioneer professional, as production boss and director of sales policy. Burke made excellent clubs but never was going to battle anyone for first place in sales. All during this period Spalding stayed at the head of the pack because of its affiliation with professionals at the most active clubs. These men assembled at the Spalding plant once a year to discuss the new lines, and the company got expert advice from knowledgeable professionals who were usually graduates of bench clubmaking, good players, and observant teachers.

Meanwhile Icely did his best to build up a star system of tournament players for Wilson. The selling value of professional endorsements, long a Spalding strongpoint, was the envy of its competitors. With payments that would be sneered at by players today, plus bonuses for winning the National Open, the Western Open, or the PGA Championship, the pros were eager to sign. It must be admitted that the "staff" players of various companies weren't always true to their contracts. It was then that a bright little ex-caddie, Eddie Darrell, built up a checking system by attending the major tournaments and reporting who was playing what brand of balls and clubs, who was wearing whose shoes, and so on.

But as golf continued to grow in popularity, the influence of professionals as merchants weakened the value of the star system. A competent professional had a sound knowledge of the game and the needs of his student; he also had expertise in the technique of clubmaking and the feel and looks of a perfectly made club. With these outstanding advantages he could easily direct the choice of buyers who wanted the best for themselves.

Besides, many of the store clubs bearing the names of professionals were cheaply made by poking a steel shaft into a head and pushing a composition grip onto the other end. As a result, the name on the product had about as much selling power as that of an athlete on a chewing-gum card. Naturally there were a few conspicuous exceptions where the professional insisted on the highest quality of the equipment bearing his name, regardless of what arrangement his hungry manager wanted to make in the United States or other countries. History has long proved that excesses are bound to follow any new and exciting development, and golf was no exception. But all this stumbling and fumbling in the early days of golf merchandising pointed to the simple truth that the professionals had to get together in order to best serve and profit from the market they had created.

All the same, it took them some time to become educated as golf merchants. Even as late as the 1930's, when Eddie

Conlin published a primer on pro-shop management called *Pros, Players and Profits,* many pros were still unaware that they were part of a business that was becoming a giant in the sports industry. In fact, not until a number of years after the organization of the PGA of America was professional golf as a merchandising service considered a career that might make a fellow one of the helpful and prosperous small businessmen of his community.

Consider the case of "Uncle Ed" Tufts, who ran a sporting goods business (mostly guns, ammunition, and fishing tackle) in Southern California. He was a prime mover of the Los Angeles Country Club and kept rigid control of the marketing of golf equipment in the area. As a consequence the club did not give its professional the equipment sales concession. Who can say whether Ed Tufts's desire to keep the early Southern California professionals from making a living by golf goods merchandising was helpful to golfers? For years some clubs in and around Los Angeles refused to allow their professionals to operate an expert personal business. Very few still continue such a policy. At any rate, who pays for that deviation from the usual nationwide practice of allowing pro earnings commensurate with ability, effort, and proper attention to the needs of customers depends perhaps more on bookkeeping than on traditional policy.

And it must be said that bookkeeping at golf clubs has had its entertaining, if not informative aspects, with the clubs themselves all too frequently having no more idea of the real financial score than did the early professionals. Nor did they get straightened out until the IRS got into action, and for better or worse, for right or wrong, for foolishness or sense, told them how to keep

J. H. Taylor. GH

score. A few specialized accounting firms also helped the clubs with their books.

As we look back on the development of the Professional Golfers' Association, it is clearly apparent that economics and inherent Scottish thrift accounted for golf's becoming the gigantic business it is. Naturally the early professionals made mistakes. They weren't trained as businessmen, but neither was Abraham Lincoln. He went broke, too, as a general storekeeper on his way onward and upward, but what historians don't mention is that Lincoln probably served his community in a very valuable way by going broke, just as many of the early professionals nursed American golf into healthy condition with credit ratings that were minus nothing, but hopeful. So anyone looking back, way back, can see the PGA being born as golf business.

We seem to have gotten a little ahead of our story, but all these factors had a great deal to do with the birth of the PGA. While it would be expected that the New World would know better and hence take the first steps to organize for the good of the game and its players, it's perhaps significant that the golf professionals first organized in the Old World. After all, wasn't it their game to begin with?

The new golf ball, the American Haskell in particular, seems to have been responsible for the formation of the British Professional Golfers' Association. The idea was suggested by Frank Johnson, a golf salesman, who was probably as concerned with promoting his interests as he was those of his clients. Major J. Bywaters, secretary of the British PGA, summarizes the beginning of the organization that provided a pattern for the PGA of America:

"A meeting of golf club professionals was held on Friday, 12th of July, 1901, in Paternoster Square, London, when it was unanimously voted that a group be formed under the title of The London and County Professional Golfers' Association, to include professionals and assistants from Berkshire, Hertford, Essex, Surrey, Middlesex and Kent, and all other counties surrounding the Capital of London.

"At the first annual general meeting of the new association in September of the same year, it was announced that Mr. A. J. Balfour, who was British prime minister from 1902 to 1905, had accepted the presidency of the Association and Mr. J. H. Taylor was elected chairman.

"At a subsequent meeting, in December 1901, it was unanimously agreed that the Association should be re-named the Professional Golfers' Association. At this time there were 59 professionals and 11 assistants, making a total of 70 members as the organization attained practical working condition. The treasury then had the equivalent of $235.

"Prior to the formation of the PGA there was a Midland Professional Golfers' Club, which was formed in 1897. There also was a Northern Counties Association. Both these were amalgamated with the PGA in April, 1902, as the Midland and Northern sections. Other sections were formed and the British PGA has eight sections and approximately 2,000 members."

Major Bywaters has a letter written by J. H. Taylor, five-time British Open winner, telling of the early days of the British PGA, and surprisingly, noting an American influence, the new Haskell ball, as impelling the professionals to get together.

Taylor knew numerous American professionals who were British-born. He won his first Open in 1894 and his last in 1913. He was nearly ninety-three when he died in April, 1963, and he corresponded frequently with pioneer American PGA officials. His handwriting was a work of art, his English classic, his advice sound, and his devotion to golf exemplary.

"It is but just to say," Taylor wrote, "that the formation of the London and County PGA in July, 1901, from which sprung the present association, was the idea of a Mr. Frank Johnson, an astute businessman, a supplier of golf requisites, who, presumably, thought that such an organization would further his interests.

"As its name implied, the membership was confined to professional golfers on the outskirts of London when the game was making an enlivened appeal. Rumour of a newly invented, revolutionarily constructed ball in America, the 'Haskell,' was reaching this country. It was perhaps a natural urge in the circumstances that James Braid, John Rowe, Rowland Jones, myself and a few others arrived at the conclusion that an association designed and founded on the principles of self-help and protection of mutual interests would be of benefit to all professional golfers.

"With this compelling motive as an incentive there was required little persuasion for the few to get together and formulate plans for a more ambitious, comprehensive scheme. With the ready concurrence of Mr. Johnson, the London and County was consigned to oblivion and the Professional Golfers' Association was born with James Braid as captain and myself as chairman of a small committee.

"At first membership was confined to professionals located in the south of

Harold Hilton. GH

England. It is in no spirit of boasting to say that the newly arrived Association's influence was immediate and hailed as being praiseworthy. It was so recognized by all whose minds were progressive and free from inconsequential fears.

"Professionals in other parts of the country clamoured for admission. The demand became so insistent, especially from the Midlands, that it was decided that it would be best served if they formed a section of their own with a separate Committee to supervise and control the administration of their own particular district. This was done smoothly, without ostentation or conflicting passions of any kind, and the Midland members have proved themselves steadfast, loyal and devoted.

"In due course, and from pressure of events, a Northern section was formed along the same lines, followed by Scottish and Irish sections whose faithfulness to the ideals of the Association deserve a similar tribute.

"With the steady, uninterrupted growth of the Association in numbers and in prestige, Amateur Golfers were not negligent in their approval of the high standard of conduct that is demanded and the code of honour that PGA membership involves; conduct that is strictly and impartially enforced. It is pleasing to note that penalties for violation of the code seldom are put into operation.

"Membership of the PGA is its own safeguard," Taylor concluded. "Growth of the association since its early days has been continuous. I make the proud claim as one of the PGA founders that it has raised the standard of professional golfers to a degree that is more than enviable, comparable to any other section of society, and what is of nobler significance, its members have enhanced the glories of the game that they are proud to serve."

The British professionals' concern about adjusting to the loss of the gutta-percha ball remolding and repainting business and the prospect of having to buy, sell, and play the new American cored balls was justified. In 1902, the year after the British PGA began, Alex (Sandy) Herd won the British Open at Hoylake with a 307. He was the only one in a field of 112 playing the new ball. The last time the British Open had been played at Hoylake, in 1897, the great amateur and brilliant golf writer Harold Hilton had won with 314, ahead of James Braid, Sandy Herd, Harry Vardon, and J. H. Taylor. Hilton had also won in 1892 and was the last amateur to win the British Open until Bob Jones came along in 1926.

So some part of Herd's triumph in the 1902 Open must have been due to the ball. There weren't seven strokes' difference between the players, and the Hoylake course was the same. This was long before golf courses were significantly altered for genuine championship play; it was also long before competent players supposedly capable of playing any competitive course anywhere were crybabies. If the contestants didn't like a course chosen as the test of a true champion, then they could stay away, for they surely wouldn't be missed. In the unanimous opinion of the early golfers, these bellyachers just didn't have the qualifications of a champion.

There is an indication in the Taylor letter that some professionals feared their organizing would be regarded by amateurs as establishing a union at a time when neither Britain nor golf was cordial toward unions. Perhaps an "association" is not quite a union.

The admission of assistants into the

new British PGA was an interesting feature. The PGA of America accepted that idea cautiously after a few years and has ever since debated how to determine the true rating of a golf professional. The player can make his own judgment easily on the basis of the scorecard alone, but there's so much more to the home professional's job that it's difficult to evaluate the men needed for the work of highest value and responsibility in commercial golf.

For the benefit of readers interested in learning more about the operations of the British PGA, we print the following information from the *Golfer's Handbook:*

"The Professional Golfers' Assn. was founded in 1901 to promote interest in the game of golf; to protect and advance the mutual and trade interests of its members, and to hold meetings and tournaments periodically for the encouragement of the younger members, to institute a Benevolent fund for the relief of deserving members, to act as an agency for assisting any Professional Golfers or Club-maker to obtain employment, and to effect any other objects of a like nature as may be determined from time to time by the Association.

"No candidate shall be eligible for election as a Professional until a period of five years has been served as Professional to a *bona fide* Golf Club, but such period may include any time served as an assistant to a Professional attached to a Club or Course.

"Women may apply for election to the Ladies Section of the Association.

"No candidate shall be eligible for full membership until a period of three years has been served as an assistant to a Professional attached to a Golf Club or Course.

"Suitable qualified amateurs may apply for election to the Association as Tournament Playing Members; so too may Professionals and Assistants awaiting election become registered for tournament play. No Tournament Playing Member shall be permitted to take prize money until a period of six months has elapsed from the date of his registration.

"The objects of the Benevolent Fund are to relieve deserving members of the Association in distress through poverty by:

"(1) Grants, temporary or permanent;

"(2) Assisting, in cases of sickness, accident, death and internments;

"(3) Providing, should Funds ultimately permit, small annuities to the aged and incapacitated,

"(4) And allowances to widows and orphans."

5

The Professional Golfers'
Association of America Is Finally Born

AS recorded in the previous chapter, the golf professionals in and around New York, Boston, Philadelphia, Baltimore, Washington, Chicago, and St. Louis, who had been casually and informally organized about eight years prior to the creation of the Professional Golfers' Association of America, were principally concerned with conducting tournaments during the warm, playable months. Otherwise, temperamental differences and lack of time and office facilities had limited the effectiveness of these regional PGA pioneers. But they were vastly successful in promoting golf; they formed congenial associations with officials and members of clubs where the tournaments were held and also with the amateur addicts of the game, who took part in the first friendly pro-amateur matches that eventually changed the attitude of Americans toward those who played for pay.

The camaraderie of the course and a few drinks after the round helped the amateurs understand the problems and aspirations of the professional golfer. Many of the pioneer pros, foreign-born and natives, were men of sound education, fine character, and admirable family background. They fitted well into the American social pattern, and in the early stages of American professional golf they naturally felt responsible for a number of their golfingly adept but rough colleagues who either had to be schooled into occupational and social acceptability or risk being thrown out of pro golf. The professionals were advancing securely but slowly, and as proud mortals didn't want their progress endangered. Their high standard of personal and business conduct was not reached in other professional sports of the period for the simple reason that so many of those pros were not policed by the rigid standards professional golf-

ers applied to themselves and their colleagues. These men thought of their
home pro jobs as more than an opportunity for mercenary connections; they
felt a real sense of responsibility toward the sport and the many amateurs
who participated in it.

There was no difference between the
home professionals and the playing
professionals in job status in 1916 when
Tom McNamara, a pleasant and competent salesman for John Wanamaker's
pro golf department, assembled the nucleus of the Professional Golfers' Association of America.

McNamara had been a caddie
around Boston, then a professional at
the Fall River and Wollaston clubs. He
was second in the National Opens of
1909, 1912, and 1915. When he finished
two strokes back of John McDermott's
294 at the Country Club of Buffalo,
golf history was made because those
were the first four rounds played at par
in the National Open. The United
States Golf Association had only established "par" in 1911. But work as a
club professional held little interest for
McNamara, so he got a job with the
Wanamaker golf department handling
professional business in the New York
metropolitan area and in New England. His wide acquaintance among
professionals, his playing ability, and
the high regard in which he was held
by the British-born and home-bred professionals brought him constantly in
contact with those who thought that
professionals in the United States
needed a nationwide organization similar to the British PGA.

Just like Frank Johnson, the golf
salesman who played such a key role in
the organization of the British PGA,
McNamara was motivated by sound
business and personal reasons in leading the movement for an American
counterpart. There was stiff competition between Wanamaker and Spalding in those days, and as it turned out,
the promotion of the PGA by Wanamaker, at the instigation of McNamara,
helped to cut down Spalding's lead.

At any rate, McNamara mentioned
the professionals' hopes during an office conference, and Rodman Wanamaker, son of the boss, quickly saw the
merchandising and customer relations
possibilities. He suggested that McNamara invite prominent professionals in
the area to get together at lunch on
Monday, January 16, 1916, to discuss
their proposed association. The place
was the Taplow Club in the Hotel
Martinique on Broadway near the
Wanamaker store in New York. Since
this was the first time any competitor
had been able to get the jump on the
Spalding company's near monopoly of
major developments in professional
golf, Wanamaker was delighted to
make the best of all lunch and dinner
announcements: "Waiter, give me the
bill."

In addition to leading professionals
who had been talking about an American PGA, McNamara and Wanamaker
invited several well-known amateurs.
Among these were Francis Ouimet,
John G. Anderson, A. W. Tillinghast,
Joseph Appel, W. W. Harris, P. C. Pulver, and Jason Rogers. Pulver was one
of the first New York newspaper golf
writers, having started in 1895 on the
Daily Advertiser. Ouimet, the 1913
National Open Champion and first of
the home-bred winners, later became a
golf salesman and got into amateur-
status trouble with the USGA, but
when he went into the stock-selling
business, his amateur golf virginity was
officially restored with such complete

Tom McNamara (right) was runner-up to Jerry Travers in the 1915 U.S. National Open at Baltusrol Golf Club in New Jersey. Courtesy of Leo E. McNamara

Francis Ouimet, GH

success that he was either a player or nonplaying captain on every USGA Walker Cup team from 1922 until 1949. He was even elected captain of the Royal and Ancient Golf Club of St. Andrews for 1951–52, the first non-British golfer to be so honored.

John G. Anderson, for several years a Wanamaker golf salesman, was the winner of numerous championships in the metropolitan New York area. Tillinghast was a well-known Philadelphia player and writer who later became a golf architect. As a consultant sent around by the PGA, he was instrumental in curtailing excessive bunkering. W. W. Harris was a New York writer, Joseph Appel was the Wanamaker advertising director, and Jason Rogers was prominent as a New York lawyer and club official.

Tom McNamara made up a list of those attending the lunch after the affair, and there is some question as to its accuracy. Those McNamara recorded were William Gourlay, Robert White, W. G. Green, Alex Pirie, Jack Pirie, Gordon Smith, Carl H. Anderson, T. B. Whitehead, C. W. Singleton, Jack Williams, John D. Dunn, J. Crabbe, E. Calligan, Jack Hagan, Frank Belwood, Tom Skipper, Joseph Mitchell, David Stevens, John Hobens, Herbert Strong, Walter C. Hagen, Bert Battell, James Hepburn, Frank Noble, Tom McNamara, W. G. Fotheringham, P. J. Gaudin, F. N. Noble, James J. Crossan, Willie Collins, Walter Stoddard, Harry Vinall, Gilbert Nicholls, Jack Mackie, and Dan Mackie.

Rodman Wanamaker gave the discussion some substance when he offered to provide the new organization with cash prizes and a trophy similar to the News of the World Award given to the winner of the PGA Championship of Great Britain. The Wanamaker trophy remains as the PGA of America Championship award.

In the expectation of holding the first American PGA Championship that summer, the meeting got down to the business of organizing formally. James Hepburn was chosen as chairman of the organizing committee, whose members were James Maiden, Robert White, Gilbert Nicholls, John Mackie, John Hobens, and Herbert Strong. All were British-born.

It was hardly the best of times for a professional golfers' association to be organized. World War I was going badly for the British. Tens of thousands of young Englishmen were being slaughtered on the battlefields of Europe, and among the appalling casualties were many of the kingdom's most promising golfers, including some younger professionals who hadn't applied for American citizenship and had gone back to Britain to enlist. Virtually all British-born American professionals had war casualties in their families overseas. World War I losses to British golf accounted to a large degree for the accuracy of Johnny McDermott's opinion, after he'd won the 1911 U.S. National Open, that it would be a long time before a British golfer won the U.S. Open.

Ted Ray, a British elder of the world golf congregation, won at Toledo's Inverness in 1920, and Jim Barnes, then a naturalized U.S. citizen, at the Columbia Country Club in Washington, D.C., in 1921. Cyril Walker, also a naturalized citizen, won at Oakland Hills near Detroit in 1924. Willie Macfarlane, who'd taken out his American citizenship papers, beat the budding Boy Wonder, Bob Jones, at Worcester in 1925. Another naturalized Scot, the war-battered Tommy Armour, won the U.S. Open in 1927. After World War

Rodman Wanamaker. PGA

II the first foreigner to win the U.S. Open was the South African Gary Player in 1965.

War also prevented the development of younger American professionals. The infant PGA had its first championship in 1916 with Jim Barnes winning, then skipped 1917 and 1918 because of the war. Barnes won the second PGA Championship in 1919. It wasn't until 1921 that a home-bred player, Walter Hagen, won the PGA title. The naturalized Armour won in 1930, and Australian-born Jim Ferrier won in 1947.

The organizing committee met on January 24, 1916, with the purpose of outlining a constitution but accomplished nothing. It then decided to get a copy of the constitution of the PGA of Great Britain, and Jason Rogers offered to adapt it to the requirements of American professionals. It should be added that several amateurs who had been helpful to professional golf in the metropolitan area also attended these early meetings.

On February 7 a committee was appointed to prepare the constitution and bylaws, and on February 24 that assignment was reported completed by the committee of John Hobens, John Mackie, Herbert Strong, and two amateurs, the lawyers Jason Rogers and C. C. Ennever. Early records of the PGA followed the custom of referring to amateurs as "Mr.," and the prefix was continued in USGA scoring until 1930.

With organization formally effected, the PGA's thirty-five charter members were Carl H. Anderson, Bert Battell, J. Crabbe, J. Crossan, Willie Collins, John D. Dunn, Frank Belwood, W. G. Fotheringham, William Gourlay, W. G. Green, E. Galligan, P. G. Gaudin, Jack Hagan, John Hobens, Walter Hagen, James Hepburn, Joseph Mitchell, Tom McNamara, Jack Mackie, Dan Mackie, Frank Noble, F. N. Noble, Gilbert Nicholls, Alex Pirie, Jack Pirie, Gordon Smith, C. W. Singleton, Tom Skipper, David Stevens, Herbert Strong, Walter Stoddard, Robert White, T. B. Whitehead, Jack Williams, and Harry Vinall.

At the meeting of the organizing committee, April 10, 1916, at the Hotel Martinique in New York City, ninety-two applicants for membership were voted on. Of these, seventy-eight were elected to Class A membership. Assistants, generally called apprentices and lacking experience for master pro jobs, were Class B members. Salesmen and unemployed pros were put in other classes.

George Fotheringham was chairman of the organizational meetings and of the first PGA annual meeting, which was held June 26 and 27, 1916, at the Hotel Raddison in Minneapolis. Her-

bert Strong was secretary of those meetings. The twenty-second National Open Championship of the USGA was played at the Minikahda Club of Minneapolis June 27, 28, 29, and 30. Of the eighty-one starters in that competition, thirty-nine were members of the seven PGA sections that had been organized.

The 1916 Open was an inauspicious occasion for the newly formed PGA, since an amateur won for the third time in four years. Chick Evans triumphed with a 286, breaking par in all four rounds and establishing a record that stood for twenty years. He also avenged his loss to Walter Hagen by one stroke in 1914, when Hagen's 290 gave him his first National Open title at Midlothian. Jock Hutchison was two strokes higher than Evans at 288; Jim Barnes was third at 290; Wilfrid Reid, Gilbert Nicholls, and George Sargent tied at 293 for fourth; and Walter Hagen was fifth with a 295. Three months later Evans also won the 1916 National Amateur. But it should be noted that the pain to the professionals' ego was eased by the increase in prize money to $1,200.

About the only thing the PGA could agree on when it began was its name— the Professional Golfers' Association of America. This was an improvement over the USGA, which had first called itself the Amateur Golf Association, then dropped that name because the organization first proposed to involve both professional and amateur golfers in the United States. The next choice, the Amateur Golf Association of America, was discarded because of possible objections from Canadians who might quite rightly object that they had had golf clubs in North America before there were any in the United States.

The difficulty in finding men who knew the pros and amateurs in the various areas, who were qualified by education, experience, and temperament to develop the infant organization, and who also had the time to do the job properly, delayed the selection of officers for the new association. Nevertheless, an Executive Committee of twenty-four members covering seven sections was established to operate the PGA, with each section entitled to the same representative proportion on the committee as its individual membership had to the total PGA membership.

Each section was required to elect officers as vice-presidents on the Executive Committee, while the Executive Committee itself was empowered to appoint the president, vice-president, and secretary-treasurer of the association.

The original sections and their Executive Committee members were as follows:

Metropolitan: president, Robert White; vice-presidents, James Maiden, James Hepburn, Herbert Strong, John Hobens, Gilbert Nicholls, John Mackie, William Robertson, Tom Kerrigan.

Middle States: George Fotheringham, Stewart Gardner, John Croke, W. G. Fogargue, William Marshall, David McIntosh.

New England: M. J. Brady, C. J. McGrath, George Gordon.

Southeastern: J. R. Thompson, Wilfrid Reid, William C. Byrne.

Central: William V. Hoare.

Northwestern: George Sargent.

Pacific: Charles G. Adams.

In its first year the association had vice-presidents James Maiden representing the Metropolitan section, George Fotheringham for the Middle States, Michael J. Brady for New England, and J. R. Thompson for the Southeastern, George Sargent for the Northwestern, W. V. Hoare for the Central, and Charles G. Adams for the Pacific sections.

The Central section was large geographically, taking in the courses south of Missouri and from Tennessee to California, and Willie Hoare, a product of England's Westward Ho course, was in Memphis when the PGA was organized. The Northwestern section was also roomy, reaching from Wisconsin to Washington. George Sargent, its representative, was pro at Interlachen in Minneapolis and was the third president of the PGA from 1921 to 1926.

In appointing Robert White, then professional at Wykagyl, as its first president, the newborn Professional Golfers' Association of America got a man who was particularly qualified both by experience and character to bring his fellow workers together. White had been a schoolteacher in Scotland and came over to the United States in 1894. His first job was at Myopia, then he went as professional to the Cincinnati Golf Club, the Louisville Golf Club, and then on to the Ravisloe Country Club in suburban Chicago. This was one of the best-paying jobs in the area.

White, who was also in charge of course maintenance, had been laying out golf courses almost since his arrival in this country and became the first turf expert among the pro-greenkeepers of his time. Like Willie Dunn, he got $25 to lay out a nine-hole links. It was a morning's job, and he'd put in nine sticks for tee locations and nine more for where the greens would be. He might also suggest a few bunker locations, and a neighboring farmer, who had been brought into the planning by the club's organizers, was instructed about mowing and digging out the bunkers and given a few tips about fertilizing and smoothing greens. Next

White informed the founders where they could buy a greens mower and a fairway mower, and furnished the names and addresses of New York and Chicago seed dealers who could supply the German mixed bent and other seed suitable for greens. After that, course maintenance was up to the farmer at his convenience, the pro-greenkeeper hired by the infant club, and the kindly Lord Almighty.

White's reputation as a course builder naturally put him in a position to recommend professionals for employment. He was a good judge of men and admirably impartial—meaning that he would endorse any clean, competent immigrant Scottish golfer even if the kid didn't come from St. Andrews, White's hometown. It's quite possible that either by blood, marriage, or occupational sponsorship White was related to about a third of the PGA's approximately one hundred charter members.

White was hardly one of the playing stars of his period. The first time his name appears in the USGA record book is for the 1897 Open at the Chicago Golf Club. In the field of thirty-five playing thirty-six holes, and led by Joe Lloyd of Essex, he finished twenty-seventh with an 89–97, twenty-four strokes behind the winner. He is also in the USGA book for the sixth National Open, played at the Chicago Golf Club in October, 1900. He was still pro at Cincinnati and finished fortieth in a field of sixty with a 378 against the 313 of Harry Vardon, the winner. Being a mere sixty-five strokes back did not discourage White. He probably enjoyed the championship as much as Vardon. Open championships were then as much gatherings of the clans as they were competitive events.

Vardon, as described previously, was playing because Spalding had brought him across the ocean on tour to promote the Vardon Flyer, a gutty ball that was doomed because the cored, rubber-thread Haskell ball was coming in and the molded ball was out. (Recently, with the use of synthetic materials, the molded ball, domestic and foreign, is returning to favor.) In any case Vardon's hopes of riches from royalties on American ball sales never materialized. He died near London, moderately well-to-do, in 1937. White survived him by many years, coming to his end at Myrtle Beach, South Carolina, where he was part owner of a golf course and had extensive property holdings. He'd seen how golf courses developed property values, and related his golf course architecture and investments wisely; so the first PGA president went to his Maker from a beautiful home, leaving a substantial estate.

During the years from 1902, when he went to Ravisloe, through 1914, when he left to go to Wykagyl at New Rochelle to design and build the course and stay on as professional, White was noted as the leading businessman of golf. He continued to play fairly well, considering his other golfing interests. The last time he appeared as a contestant was in the National Open of 1906 at the Onwentsia Club at Lake Forest. Alex Smith won with a 295, and White, then at Ravisloe, was thirty-nine strokes higher, tying for forty-second in a field of sixty-six.

White was also a fine clubmaker and one of the founders of the Professional Golf Company, a clubmaking firm in suburban Chicago. In addition to instruction, clubmaking, caddie training, and outside jobs designing courses, White is primarily distinguished for applying the first scientific approach to golf course maintenance to his club.

Bob White. Wide World Photos

Ravisloe, like many other courses in the Chicago area and elsewhere in the United States, was built on land unsuited to farming because of poor soil and drainage. If the site of Ravisloe had been good farmland that close to Chicago, it would never have been selected as a leisure-time playground for the city and suburban rich. But White was dissatisfied with the condition of the course and determined to do something about it.

He had heard about the winter classes in elementary agriculture (then known as the "Farmers' Schools") held at the University of Wisconsin and decided to attend them. White attended these three- and four-day sessions over a period of eleven years and was the only student specializing in golf club grass and turf. The knowledge he acquired enabled him to pass on enough valuable basic training to improve course maintenance throughout the Midwest. With the Chicago stockyards close at hand, his use of cow, sheep, and poultry manure grew excellent turf on ground that had long been lacking in fertility and was almost as unfavorable for golf as it had been for farming. As a result of the Farmers' Schools, short courses on golf grounds maintenance were later introduced at many state agricultural colleges. They were given nationwide impetus by the classes organized by Professor L. S. Dickinson and his associates at the Massachusetts State Agricultural College at Amherst.

White's contribution to the game takes on major importance because, as we have seen, the duties of the pioneer professional were so varied. In appraising their services to their clubs, considerable attention has to be given to their ability to get and keep their golf courses in attractive playing condition long before the period of piped water-

ing, adequate drainage, and fertilizing and weed-control programs. It cannot be emphasized too strongly that in the early days the professional was *all* the business of golf at his respective course. Like Robert White, he had to be versatile and competent, an enthusiastic evangelist, or the new club wouldn't survive. Some clubs in lively small towns and suburbs just couldn't keep going because they lacked professional guidance. The new young professionals were resourceful, personable, and determined individuals. They had to be to make a living in a strange land, and one of the major purposes of the PGA was to show them how to do it.

John B. Mackie, who was named president in 1920 and then served as treasurer for twelve years, was a sturdy, canny Scot who showed traditional genius in stretching the meager funds of the PGA and in increasing its revenue. He was also a cool hand in helping to settle arguments with an apt quotation. Unquestionably, there has been no other group of professional sportsmen as literate as professional golfers and as much addicted to poetry. In its first twenty years of existence it could be said that the PGA was run more by the authority of quotations from Robert Burns than by citing *Robert's Rules of Order.*

In one session Tom Boyd, a professional of Gaelic stock and a man who had never taken the vow of silence, got into a heated controversy with Mackie, the Scottish-born treasurer of the organization. It reached the point where Boyd advanced menacingly toward Mackie, with both of them in a fist-swinging mood. Just then a member grabbed Boyd by the coattail and spoke briefly to him. Whatever it was he said, Boyd calmed down quickly.

"Mr. Treasurer, I apologize," he

said. "Jack, I'm told I was misinformed. I'm sorry."

"These things happen to all of us," Mackie replied with a smile. "Forget it and remember what Burns said: 'An honest whore is the noblest work of God.' "

Although Boyd was soothed, he sat down wondering why the Scots always had to quote Bobbie Burns. When he learned that Mackie had used a common misquotation, he laughed and threatened to quote an Irish poet to Mackie. Considering the PGA's growing pains, its chronic shortage of money, plus what is now called "deficiency in communication," the early annual meetings were distinguished by good, wholesome turmoil. Along with honest differences of opinion, national origin often played its part in forcing the PGA members of the 1920's and 1930's to choose up sides. The Scotch, English, Irish, Italian, and home-breds of mixed ancestral backgrounds sometimes mixed with more vigor than harmony. However, no issue ever arose that could not ultimately be agreed on and laughed away. And in the heat of the argument nobody considered face was lost if a plain statement of fact settled the matter.

Herbert Strong's clear handwritten figures and concise observations record on now-yellowed paper the birth pangs of the PGA. He continued to serve as secretary of the organization through 1919, then declared he'd had enough. The offices of secretary and treasurer were separated in 1920.

Herbert Strong's brother, Leonard J., was also valuable and prominent in the golf business. For many years he was superintendent in charge of the courses of the Saucon Valley Club in Bethlehem, Pennsylvania, for which the Bethlehem Steel Company president

wanted to have the best-maintained links in the world. He provided the money, and Leonard Strong the talent and management.

Establishing a durable precedent that has been faithfully and energetically observed to this day, after its formal organization the PGA promptly got into an argument about something many of the members thought had already been settled. At the second session of the first annual meeting, Secretary Strong read the offer by Rodman Wanamaker to donate $2,500 and a trophy for a PGA Championship that was to be played along the lines of the News of the World tournament that determined the British PGA Championship.

Although Wanamaker's offer had been informally accepted six months earlier and had accounted for the organization of the PGA, now it was moved that the proposal not be accepted. The acceptance motion was withdrawn after considerable discussion, but arguments never wilt and die easily in PGA meetings, so eventually the Wanamaker offer was accepted. Then, the minutes show, the offer was "tabled."

It is amusing and amazing to read PGA Executive and Tournament Committee and annual meeting minutes over the years and note how often formal agreement on an issue one year didn't mean anything the next. This holds true for the split that eventually resulted in spinning off the tournament players into a separate division. It was a civil war that was unnecessary because the points of disagreement had been smoothed out to the mutual satisfaction of all concerned, moved, seconded, put into print, and greeted with sighs of relief and hosannas at least three times at Tournament and Executive Committee meetings, as well as annual meetings.

But the PGA from the beginning was a with-malice-toward-none-and-charity-toward-all outfit and as quickly forgot what members had agreed upon as what they'd fought about. So it is pleasantly indicative of the spirit of the organization that at its first annual meeting it was moved and seconded that a subscription be taken up for J. J. McDermott, the first home-bred National Open winner in 1911. McDermott was mentally ill and permanently confined to an institution; he died almost fifty-five years after the PGA first attempted to ease the financial burden his sisters had borne for so long.

It quickly became plain that keeping the PGA records would require more time than a professional golfer would be able to give as a sideline, so employment of an assistant secretary at $1,200 a year was authorized. In a few months Mrs. Irene Blakeman was hired for this job, and she stayed with the association as a valuable employee until shortly after 1948, when the offices were moved to Dunedin, Florida. She then retired.

The first meeting of the Executive Committee was held July 14, 1916, at the Garden City (New York) Golf Club, during the Metropolitan Open. The National, Western, and Metropolitan Opens then were the major professional competitions of the golf year in the United States, and the PGA hoped to get its championship into that class.

The Executive Committee, with Robert White president, officially moved to accept Rodman Wanamaker's offer of $2,500 for the tournament, a cup, a gold medal to the winner, a silver medal to the runner-up, and bronze medals to the winners of the qualifying rounds. Then, on October 9, 1916, the

Executive Committee met at the Siwanoy Country Club and discussed sending a letter describing the PGA to the secretaries of all golf clubs. The organization was beginning to get a little publicity and needed more, and the proposed letter was to be mailed after the approval of the PGA sections.

However, if such a letter was ever written and mailed, no copy of it exists. Most probably, this notice outlining the purposes and services of the PGA and its potential help to golf clubs and their members was lost in the dark, quiet store of unfinished business. Nationally and sectionally, the PGA was always able to get publicity about tournaments, but when it came down to promoting organizational benefits for its own members, other golfers, and golf clubs, it never seemed to manage a sound and lively operational program. Yet among all professional sports groups it was unique in the value, scope, and intimacy of its services to the employers of professional golfers.

Another letter to clubs that was discussed at early Executive Committee meetings asked for cooperation in the PGA Benevolent Plan. Pros received comparatively low pay during a short season and even with revenue from clubmaking were seldom in a position to manage accident and sickness expenses.

The initial vice-presidents, George Fotheringham of the Middle States section and James Maiden of the Metropolitan section, were active in early Executive Committee meetings, which were usually held in the New York metropolitan area. They and other founding fathers of the national PGA soon received the warm backing of men who were prominent in amateur organizations. These distinguished and enthusiastic amateurs saw the immense potential value of an informed, organized, and aspiring nationwide association of golf businessmen in extending the game and helping golf club officials and all other amateur players. Professionals of the regional associations had shown such admirable spirit in promoting the good of golf, and in assuming responsibility for the members of their groups, that the USGA, the Western, and other amateur bodies had asked for the professionals' advice in the arrangements for open championships.

A number of the pioneer PGA officials were diplomats with winning ways and finesse. They deserve much of the credit for breaking down the age-old barriers of caste that had kept sports mercenaries from entering the sacredly segregated temples of those who engaged in sport for fun only. The invitation of honorary officials was a custom of British golf organizations, and invariably royalty accepted. So it was fitting that G. Herbert Windeler, who'd been president of the USGA in 1903 and 1904, was named the association's first honorary president at a PGA Executive Committee meeting on November 27, 1916.

Windeler was one of the convivial individuals who begat The Country Club of Brookline and the USGA. He was on familiar speaking terms with the Cabots, the Lodges, and God; he was of Plymouth Rock stability financially; and he was the hero of an epic match between the St. Andrews team of the New York City environs and The Country Club. It seems The Country Club's cause was lost, and when the valiant Windeler and his St. Andrews opponent met in the last match, both seem to have been well lubricated. But the eminent Windeler stood up under the strain, just as a proper Bostonian

should, and nosed out his adversary 12 up, according to an item picked up by the diligent H. B. Martin and printed in his immensely interesting *Fifty Years of American Golf*. Windeler was the sort of understanding soul the budding PGA needed.

R. S. Worthington, Julian W. Curtiss, and Jason Rogers were also honorary vice-presidents with Windeler. R. S. Worthington was one of three ardent golfing sons of C. C. Worthington, a prominent engineer, industrialist, and early member of the St. Andrews Golf Club. Worthington Senior owned some land at the Delaware Water Gap that was the largest individually owned tract of land east of the Mississippi. On it he built Buckwood Inn, a resort hotel, and close by, in 1911, A. W. Tillinghast designed and built the Shawnee Country Club course where the Shawnee Open was started in 1912. C. C. Worthington, who designed one of the earliest golf course tractors, which were to replace horse-drawn mowers, also designed gang mowers for fairways and greens. Worthington's son Edward ran the golf course equipment business, and Edward's brother, R. S. (Reginald), operated the Buckwood Inn and conducted the Shawnee Open so successfully and entertainingly that he was in high favor with professional golfers. In time, the Worthington property was bought by Fred Waring of Waring's Pennsylvanians musical enterprises.

Julian W. Curtiss was president of Spalding. We've already read how he became commercially entangled with some thirsty companions on a trip to Scotland and came home with unwanted stores of golf clubs, balls, and bags, and still came out ahead. The beloved and vigorous Uncle Julian got the Spalding salesmen and stores pushing golf as a game of the British upper classes that could be played in any pasture, was a good gambling game, and was easier on the legs than shinny.

Jason Rogers, an attorney who had Wanamaker's among his clients, was the honorary vice-president who kept the young PGA out of trouble with the law. He believed that the incorporation of the Eastern PGA was adequate for the PGA of America, which practically became the Eastern association's successor. The PGA became incorporated only in the 1920's when Albert Gates was commissioner, and there were legal problems that couldn't be avoided. Among them was the PGA's effort to get preferential prices from manufacturers for its members. This was suspected as a violation of antitrust legislation, but after finding it difficult to decide who could be sued, the government apparently lost interest.

P. R. Hollander and John G. Anderson were also made honorary members of the PGA at the meeting when the honorary president and vice-presidents were named. A month before, a young priest, the Reverend J. B. Kelly, had been made the first honorary member of the PGA and the unofficial chaplain of the then predominantly Scottish-American organization. Father Kelly continued to be chaplain of the National and Metropolitan sections of the PGA for many years. No other chaplain has been appointed by the national body.

On December 15, 1921, Sylvanus P. Jermain of Toledo was made an honorary vice-president, and on November 20, 1922, he was appointed honorary president of the association. Jermain was a kindly, quiet man, not known to many golfers away from his own bailiwick, where he was president of the local golf association. As a member of the USGA's subcommittee on public links and municipal golf courses, Jermain, with James Standish of Detroit, a member of the USGA Executive Committee, prevailed upon the USGA to establish the Public Links Championship, which was first played in 1922 at the Ottawa Park course in Toledo.

The PGA later curtailed awarding honorary offices, and the practice was established of naming retiring presidents as honorary vice-presidents, then honorary presidents until they were replaced by the officers next in line. Since 1930 honorary vice-presidents have included Robert T. Jones, Jr., Walter C. Hagen, and Dwight D. Eisenhower.

Plainly, in its first ten years of existence the PGA had enough growing pains without the public relations frill of honorary officials or advisory committees of prominent businessmen and theatrical notables. From April 10, 1916, until the June 5, 1916, meeting, sixty-one Class A members were elected, bringing the membership in the main class to 139. Right from the start, there was a cordial and cooperating relationship between the PGA and the USGA, which was having its own problems, as golf seemed about to become the national game of the United States.

The USGA's amateur status rule was of concern to the PGA as well as to the amateur ruling body. A few years before World War I, and for fifteen years or so afterward, proficient and personable amateurs were taking numerous professional jobs. They had pleasant personalities, played impressive golf, and were hired on this basis by club officials. These amateurs generally expected to make a good living having fun as glamorous front men for their clubs; they had no conception of the essential hard-work part of the pro job. So when one after the other began to be fired for incompetence, many decided to abandon the golf business as a career.

The USGA welcomed the PGA by extending the privilege of selecting the host club for the 1917 Open Championship to the new group. At the meeting of the PGA Executive Committee on November 27, 1916, the Whitemarsh Country Club at Philadelphia got one vote, Brae Burn Country Club in suburban Boston got two votes, and the Shawnee Country Club at Shawnee-on-Delaware got three votes. War prevented the 1917 and 1918 Open Championships, but a fund-raising tournament was held for the Red Cross at Whitemarsh on June 20 to 22, 1917. Jock Hutchison won with 292, and Tom McNamara was second with 299.

The practice of charging spectators to see golf competitions was established in the United States at the Red Cross exhibitions during World War I. All spectators were required to contribute something to the Red Cross and were given tags to wear as evidence of their payments. The best of the men and women amateur talent and the professionals participated. Among the most active pro fund-raisers as clubs staged Red Cross events were Jock Hutchison, Jim Barnes, Mike Brady, Gil Nicholls, Tom McNamara, George Sargent, Wilfrid Reid, Walter Hagen, Bob Macdonald, Otto Hackbarth, Fred McLeod, Alex Campbell, Tom Kerrigan, Dave Livie, Jack Croke, and Jack Jolly.

Foremost among the amateurs in the campaign was Chick Evans, the 1916 National Open and National Amateur Champion. He had enlisted in the Army to become a flyer but soon was told by his realistic superiors that he would be more useful as a highly effective fiscal aide to the Red Cross than he'd be flying in the wild blue yonder. With Chick in the amateur contingent

of golf's Red Cross campaigners were Max Marston, Bob Gardner, Francis Ouimet, Frank Blossom, Oswald Kirby, Ned Sawyer, Nelson Whitney, Woody Platt, John Anderson, Jesse Guilford, and two boy stars from Atlanta, Bob Jones and Perry Adair.

In those World War I Red Cross golf matches, women played before fairly large galleries, and their games amazed the male spectators. The more proficient women amateurs were Alexa Stirling, Dorothy Campbell Hurd, Elaine Rosenthal, Mrs. Caleb F. Fox, Marion Hollins, Edith Cummings, and Glenna Collett.

Of course nobody imagined it then, but for a far more important reason than the admission fee, the American Red Cross golf matches were significant as the start of the tournament circuit in the United States that loosed the worldwide flow of money to the boys who play golf for cash.

The actual work of putting on those Red Cross matches was done by women. They were the lassies who knitted bales of sweaters and socks for the AEF. They were the ones who put up the advertising signs in the stores, who sold the tickets, who collected the tickets, who made and sold the sandwiches at the Red Cross exhibitions. Their successors were the wives of the Junior Chamber of Commerce members. They gave the tournament circuit the first view of well-coordinated, energetic, attractive, unpaid service ever seen in the operation of professional or amateur sports events.

At a meeting of the PGA Executive Committee on November 4, 1918, at the Martinique Hotel in New York, Robert White was reelected president of the organization. Jack Mackie was elected first vice-president, George Sargent, second vice-president, and Herbert Strong, secretary-treasurer, while Wilfrid Reid, Jack Hobens, and James Maiden were elected to the Executive Committee. The new administration must have done well, as a mail vote taken on a midyear proposal to raise the annual PGA dues to $25 had a comfortable majority of "Yes" ballots. The Middle States section, which had grown around the pro group in the Chicago area that had been actively functioning even before the national association was formed, had expanded to the point of hiring Joe Davis as its secretary. And the PGA Executive Committee authorized paying Davis $300 a year out of its national treasury.

Joseph Garibaldi Davis, who had a great affection for the game and its players, was golf editor of the *Chicago Tribune* from 1896 to about 1928. An Englishman who also covered cricket matches and the illicit cockfights often staged in the rural areas around Chicago, Davis was a kind, knowledgeable man, widely acquainted with the amateur and professional golfers of his day. He usually had a cigar stub jammed under his unkempt moustache. It was so seldom lit that once, when Davis was in the pressroom of a golf tournament in the 1920's, a colleague exclaimed in alarm, "Joe, your chew is on fire!"

Pioneer golf writers like Joe Davis were very helpful to the professionals, one reason being that the stiff-necked amateur officials viewed lowly reporters and golf pros in the same dim social light. So the golf writers took every opportunity to stress that the errors made by the USGA in tournament planning and management all stemmed from a failure to consult the experienced men whose business was golf. The jabs obviously registered after the National Open was renewed on June 9 to 11,

1919, at Brae Burn, where Walter Hagen defeated Mike Brady in a play-off, 77 to 78, after the two had tied for first at 291. Then, at the request of Howard Whitney of the USGA Executive Committee, who became USGA president in 1921, the PGA Executive Committee meeting of October 19, 1919, instructed Joe Davis, secretary of the Midwest section, to seek a host club for the 1920 USGA Open. The tournament went to the Inverness Club of Toledo, Ohio.

Just for the record it should be added here that at the 1919 Executive Committee meeting, in addition to receiving the pleasant news that the USGA considered it a grown-up outfit, the PGA received its first request to go coeducational when a Gertrude Harrison applied for membership. Unfortunately, Miss or Mrs. Gertrude Harrison remains a maid of the mists of golf history. Considerable inquiry has failed to identify her, although a few veteran pros dimly recall that the lady in question was in the golf department of a store.

The 1920 Open was played on August 12 and 13, after two days of qualifying rounds for the record entry of 265. A gale disturbed play on the last day of the championship, and Harry Vardon, then fifty years old, was blown out of a five-stroke lead, scoring the last seven holes in even 5's. Ted Ray, another Briton, won by a stroke at 295, and at forty-three he was the oldest player yet to win the Open. Vardon, Jack Burke, Leo Diegel, and Jock Hutchison all tied for second with 296. In that big field an unknown eighteen-year-old amateur named Robert Tyre Jones, Jr., made his Open debut. He finished eighth. Gene Sarazen, Tommy Armour, and Johnny Farrell, all of whom were eventually to win the event, also were first-time Open contestants at Inverness.

Neither the PGA nor the USGA records reveal the extent to which the PGA counsel was heeded in conducting the 1920 Open, but at least the PGA had been recognized as a tournament authority. An important precedent was also set at the annual meeting at the Secor Hotel in Toledo just before the 1920 Open, when the generous American practice of exemptions was established. It was decided that the first thirty-one PGA members to finish in the National Open Championship were automatically qualified for the PGA Championship, a tournament that was gaining in prestige. The PGA was played for the first time at a Middle States course in 1920; the site was the Flossmoor Country Club in suburban Chicago where Jock Hutchison won this third of the PGA's title contests by defeating Douglas Edgar 1 up.

George Sargent was elected president of the PGA at the December 15, 1920, meeting at which James Harnett, a circulation man for *Golf Illustrated,* was voted expenses to raise funds for a professional team match between the United States and Great Britain. Harnett had conceived the idea as a circulation promotion stunt, but potential readers hadn't warmed to the idea and the PGA advance was welcome. The rivalry eventually developed into the esteemed and prestigious Ryder Cup matches, but John Mackie, the outgoing PGA president at the time, saw the proposal in the nature of a vendetta between the home-breds and the imports who wanted a free trip back home. In an effort to eliminate freeloaders, Mackie offered and had passed a motion limiting the foreign-born players on the American tour to golf

professionals who had been in the United States five years and had declared their intention of becoming citizens.

The first U.S. team in international professional golf competition met the British at Gleneagles on June 6, 1921, and was beaten 6 to 3 with three matches halved. The American team consisted of Jock Hutchison, Walter Hagen, Emmett French, Fred McLeod, Tom Kerrigan, Wilfrid Reid, George McLean, Dave Hackney, Charles Hoffner, and Bill Mehlhorn. They faced Willie Dunn, George Duncan, Abe Mitchell, Ted Ray, J. H. Taylor, Harry Vardon, James Braid, Arthur Havers, J. Ockende, J. G. Sherlock, and Josh Taylor.

The only Americans to win in the singles were Emmett French, who beat Ted Ray, 2 and 1; Wilfrid Reid, who defeated Arthur Havers, 2 and 1; and Fred McLeod, who won over J. H. Taylor. The best the Americans could do in the foursomes was to halve the matches of Hutchison and Hagen against Willie Dunn and Mitchell, and Hackney and McLeod against Braid and Taylor. Two of the remaining matches easily went to the British, but Charlie Hoffner and Bill Mehlhorn lost by only one hole.

This was the same year a bevy of Americans went across for the British Open at St. Andrews. Jock Hutchison won easily in a thirty-six-hole play-off with the British amateur Roger Wethered. Wethered had penalized himself into a tie after he'd stepped on his ball at the fourteenth hole in the third round; he was backing up, after looking over the line to the hole, when the accident happened.

Jim Harnett persisted in his efforts to get enough in circulation bonus money

First U.S. Ryder Cup team, 1927. GH

to continue sending a pro team from the United States to Britain in later years, but didn't sell enough papers. However, he did keep pounding, and the PGA of America paid partial expenses for another ten-man team in 1926. They faced the British on June 4 and 5 on the Wentworth course, and the Yankee pros absorbed the worst licking ever in international competition. The British obliterated them 13 to 1, with one match halved.

Bill Mehlhorn won a match from Archie Compston by one hole; Emmett French and E. R. Whitcombe halved a match. The five foursome matches all went to the British by convincing margins. Abe Mitchell and George Duncan overwhelmed Jim Barnes and Walter Hagen, 9 and 8! In 1922 Hagen had won the British Open, Barnes had won it in 1925, and the amateur from Dixie, Bob Jones, had won it in 1926. So, depending on which side you viewed them from, the 1926 international pro matches were either electrifying or shocking.

The matches proved such an international success that the British and American PGA's decided to make the competition official. As the proposal was under discussion, Samuel Ryder, a British seed merchant whose company had British and American courses as patrons, was prevailed upon to offer a trophy. The presentation of what came to be known as the Ryder Cup settled the matter, and the initial contest was set for Worcester, Massachusetts, June 3 and 4, 1927. The National Open that year was played at Oakmont, near Pittsburgh, June 14 to 16, so the British Ryder Cup team, captained by Ted Ray, would have plenty of time to prepare for the Open.

With Walter Hagen as captain the Americans easily won the first official Ryder Cup competition. Nine matches went to the Yankees, two to the British, and one was halved. Thus began the series of matches every other year (except during World War II), with the United States and Great Britain alternating as hosts.

The story of the Ryder Cup matches —the different ways the teams are selected, the varying pattern of play designed to keep both sides happy and the competition equitable and interesting, plus the international niceties practiced by the respective international hosts— would make a long volume in itself. But certainly it was the PGA of America that took the lead in developing this transatlantic golfing event that proved so invaluable to American professionals. The overseas publicity immediately increased the value of their services.

Today, when modern American professionals get revenue from the use of their names in British and other foreign markets, they are harvesting from a market the PGA primed with the Ryder Cup competition at a time when it had little money for show business or even more urgent affairs. Just as with becoming organized, the pros again lagged behind the amateurs in United States–Great Britain matches. The first competition between the amateur teams was played at Hoylake, May 21, 1921 (the Americans won nine matches and the British three), sixteen days before the first international pro matches at Gleneagles. The USGA and the Royal and Ancient lost little time in making these competitions official.

The first Walker Cup matches were played at the National Links, Long Island, on August 29, 1922, almost five years before the British and American PGA's established the official Ryder Cup matches.

During this period golf was considered one and the same game for professionals and amateurs, for players and spectators alike. No alterations or changes were made on courses where the National Open championships were to be held. They were not made *deliberately* more difficult for these special events, with the occasional exception of the rough being allowed to grow. The theory was that a golfer skilled enough to win the Open ought to be able to stay out of the rough, which might be almost knee-high unless it had been cropped to enable club members to find their balls more easily.

Naturally the club hosting the Open wanted its course in the best possible condition for the event. With this aim in mind, there were some unfortunate experiments in the area of scientific turf management, particularly the chemical greens treatment at the Columbia Club in Chevy Chase, Maryland, in 1921. When the Open was played there in July, the greens were almost bare of grass. Jim Barnes won that tournament with a nine-over-par 289; Walter Hagen and Fred McLeod, the home professional, tied for second at a record nine strokes behind the winner.

Just as there have always been differences between the amateur and professional factions of the same sport, whatever it may be, so the PGA was in conflict with the USGA over the rules of golf almost from the time the professional organization began. To the average club member this controversy about rules seemed nonsensical. To him there had to be one golf law for all, even though the club member wasn't sure what the law was and often observed it only at his convenience. Brought up in rules of orthodoxy, the early imported pros used to snort and say: "Golf is a different game here and in Scotland. Back there they hit the ball around the course, and over here they carry it around." Tommy Armour put the case another way at the conclusion of a first-tee, odds-making filibuster with his playmates at Boca Raton. "What are we going to play?" he asked. "Golf or that game you make up as you go along?"

As the tournament players grew in numbers, prominence, and affluence, they began to protest that the Rules of Golf were too tough for professionals (that is, those who play golf for a living). And they often resented having to play on poor courses early in the morning only two or three hours after paying patrons all over the country had waited to play on public courses. So here was a threat of golf becoming two different games—the easy job for a lot of money on the tournament circuit, or the game that tested skill, character, and versatility that the ordinary golfer had been —and was—playing. The argument quickly turned acrimonious, with many of the USGA's five-hundred-and-some committeemen and officials complaining to the golf writers that "if these tournament stars think the rules are tough, why don't they go to work as we've done and see what really tough rules are?"

It was a more delicate situation than the tournament players realized, and a distinct embarrassment to pro tournament golf. The menacing impasse that existed is clearly indicated in the words of Hord W. Hardin, retiring president of the USGA, in his farewell address:

"I cannot recall a single instance in my thirteen years of committee service which was aimed at making the game harder." The strong, skilled professional heroes were whining for Daddy to make the game easier, while the men who had made the stars rich were finding the going more uncomfortable, more exacting, and more expensive. Their attitude was such that public regard for tournament golf was suffering, and realists on the PGA Tournament Committee didn't want their crybaby colleagues making up their own rules for whatever they wanted to call what used to be known as golf.

It was at this point that Lou Strong, then president of the PGA, dampened the rules controversy that was threatening permanent discord between the PGA and the USGA. An adroit politician, he played along with Joe Dey, then executive director of the USGA and an authority on the Rules of Golf. Dey knew the game and he knew how to put his ideas across in meetings of either pros or amateurs. He was respected and admired, and ultimately, like so many other problems in PGA history, the rules dispute worked out for the good of all. In the process Joe Dey was vividly identified as a man who was for golfers—not the pros or the amateurs—and for the good of the game for all concerned. And much later on, when the playing pros needed a front man to bail them out of the disrepute into which they had fallen with their policy of using golf only to take money from chumps, Dey proved to be their main and only hope.

Not that the playing professionals were ever quite so stupid and mercenary as they appeared to be. They had been enticed into the publicly untenable position of only being interested in squeezing more and more cash out of the game at whatever cost. The playing pros, at least the gullible and normally greedy innocents among them, had become captives of the coldest and most calculating exploiters who ever tried to make a sport over into an entirely commercial racket. The exploitation of pro golfers to make a buck for their managers, many of whom had only contempt for "the good of the game," certainly reached new depths, but the movement was never powerful enough to undermine the Rules of Golf.

Warren Orlick, who became president of the PGA, was the first professional to be invited to serve on the USGA Rules of Golf Committee. Orlick had been a sound educator and proponent of rules among pros and amateurs. He began with the simple point that you can't go wrong giving the ball a break, and explained the reason for and the equity back of each rule so convincingly and masterfully that his hearers couldn't help but be convinced. Watching him in action, USGA officials decided: "This man is for golf and for us." The complaints of tournament players—some involving valid questions of fair play and the inevitable element of luck, and others the bellyaching of mortals with more of a muscular temperament than an intellectual one—have been soundly appraised by Orlick. His sole objective was always the good of the game.

PGA officials soon discovered that arranging championships took more time and red tape than did their own business affairs as club professionals. Territorial problems nagged the PGA during the golf boom of the early 1920's. Each section wanted to remain cohesive and independent, including running its own sectional championships without any outside interference. This de-

sire was cordially approved by the national body, which already had about all the detail work it could handle. As it was, the PGA had enough jurisdictional problems with manufacturers, golf clubs, and the USGA. The jobs of national officials were more complex than they had imagined. They involved as yet unexplored grounds for the promotion of professional golf and called for time away for the clubs that employed them. This meant not only a loss of income but larger out-of-pocket expenses than the thrifty officials had envisioned.

Truthfully, the duties, responsibilities, and sacrifices of PGA officials have never been especially remunerative, nor have the jobs warranted the political effort necessary to gain election. Politics developed late in PGA official life, and for no rational reason except that mortals are that way. All the same, the PGA has been fortunate to find men willing to accept national and sectional office under the circumstances.

The PGA took a major step when George Sargent, a scholarly English pro, was president during the 1921–26 period. Then professional at Scioto, Columbus, Ohio, and a former U.S. and Canadian Open Champion, Sargent was an unusually good organizer but soon discovered that the president of the PGA was forced to carry too much of a load. The job simply demanded more administrative attention than the association had available. How best to solve the problem had been brought out in studies made for the PGA by two business management firms. One of the recommendations was that the PGA should have a business manager.

This was at a time when professional baseball had been making unfavorable headlines. As a result of the ugly Black Sox gambling scandal, the public had lost confidence in what had been the beloved national pastime, and something had to be done quickly to restore it. So in 1921 baseball executives hired the colorful and exemplary Judge Kenesaw Mountain Landis as the game's clean-up man and shining symbol of purity. He was given the title of commissioner and a seven-year contract at $50,000 a year. Perhaps baseball's belated effort to discipline itself provided a good lesson for golf, which was growing apace all across the United States. While professional golf did not need to employ an upright and celebrated citizen to display its probity, it could certainly use a strong head man at the administrative wheel—and some efficient showmanship in its relations with other associations as well as the great golfing public.

The subject of hiring a business manager for the game was first on the agenda at the PGA's annual meeting at the Wardman Hotel, Washington, D.C., on July 22, 1921. Then there began a search for a distinguished amateur executive to take the job of commissioner at $20,000 a year, a generous salary for an organization of slightly more than 1,200 Class A members. The PGA had started with dues of $10, upped them to $25, and now another increase would be necessary to pay for the doctor and director needed to keep the association growing and prosperous.

In time, the job of PGA commissioner was offered to a number of prominent amateur officials, among them William C. Fownes, Jr., a fine amateur player, a successful businessman, and one of the builders of the famous Oakmont course in suburban Pittsburgh. When he was asked by Alex Pirie to accept the position, Fownes politely and firmly declined with what might be considered a prophetic comment: "I'm afraid the man you'll get to take the job isn't the man for it."

Albert R. Gates, a wealthy Chicago corporation lawyer and four-time president of the Western Golf Association, was finally selected for the post in 1930. He was a courtly, affable man, one of those admirable old-fashioned sportsmen much like the pros he became associated with, and the salary he received was not an important factor. His guiding principle was "What good will it do golf?" and if that essential question was satisfactorily answered, he was prepared to get down to business. And that's generally the way it was in the good old days before exploiters greedy for the fast buck swarmed all over the game.

It must be remembered that when the search for a commissioner began in 1921, there was no expectation that tournament affairs would ever become a substantial element in PGA business. The only tournament and road-show campaigner specializing in play was Walter Hagen, who was earning good money on his exhibition circuit. People had to pay for tickets to watch the great man in action, and this same tag idea used by Hagen and in the Red Cross exhibition matches was picked up by the PGA at its December 15, 1921, meeting when it voted to ask clubs holding PGA championships to permit tagging the gallery for the PGA Benevolent Fund. The USGA, because it was interested in helping the professionals improve their financial status, particularly in regard to increasing prize money, soon took notice, and the next year, charged admission for the Open held at the Skokie Golf Club near Chicago. This was the first time this had been done, and it quickly became established procedure at all major championships. And after conferring with

PGA officials, the USGA decided to make the Open a three-day tournament, with the low sixty-four and ties playing thirty-six holes the third day. The USGA also adopted a PGA suggestion, made in 1922, that the Open was to be played in June every year instead of being scheduled for later months. The USGA procedure on qualifying rounds, starting times, pairing, and entry fees was also discussed with the professional group. But PGA requests to have all entry fees become prize money and to appoint PGA representatives to the USGA Rules of Golf Committee were turned down, although Willie Kidd, Jack Mackie, and George Sargent were appointed by the PGA as consultants on the rules and, as such, unofficially received by the USGA. And in 1924 the PGA requested that the USGA establish sectional qualifying and helped work out the basic pattern for this convenience in obtaining a representative national field.

For its part, the PGA sent a letter to all its members urging that they do everything possible to ensure that their clubs were USGA members. There was a tacit understanding between the two groups that the USGA was the organization of the amateur players and the PGA the trade group of golf. From shortly after the formation of the PGA until the mid-1930's, the pro associa-tion was regarded by the USGA as a weathervane reflecting the moods and needs of the average golfer, fee course players as well as private club members. Older professionals and young men or veterans in the best pro jobs considered this consultant status an honor and a responsibility, and it worked out well for all concerned.

Then the PGA began to get so deeply involved in tournament circuit affairs that the USGA, district amateur organizations, and the general golfing public had the impression that the PGA was preoccupied with furthering the interests of a small segment of the nation's golfers—the playing specialists who were in golf just to make money—and were indifferent to the amateurs except as cash customers. The changed image of the PGA in the eyes of millions of golfers was doubly unfortunate; it put the professionals in the same crass, greedy category as other commercial athletes—always taking instead of giving—and stirred up a great deal of personal resentment. And since right from the beginning of golf in the United States, players had depended on their home pros to heighten their enjoyment of their favorite game, this new, callously mercenary attitude represented a dramatic, and even rather shocking, reversal of values.

6

A Review of the PGA's Early Years

THIS apparent change in attitude and direction on the part of the PGA came at a bad time for the USGA, which was experiencing difficulty in getting highly desirable clubs to host the National Open, despite its undeniable status as the country's premier golf tournament. This further ruffled feelings between the amateur and professional organizations. And there were other prickly issues. While such minor matters as recognizing PGA member badges as admission tickets at USGA championships were settled quickly, prize money in the Open continued to be a major source of argument.

It may surprise some professionals to be reminded that, as they should have learned years ago, some USGA officials had made strenuous efforts to raise Open purses. However, this move had been questioned by other officials, who pointed out that the USGA, which had

never been noted for overpaying its own employees and had Green Section agronomists who were doing more for golf than any ten players, had been operating close to or in the red for years. So it was high time to worry more about household expenditures, since memberships were bringing in more money than the Open itself. Besides, whenever the USGA did manage to put aside money for stormy weather, the Internal Revenue Service came through with prompt reminders of its non-profit-organization status.

In the 1920's the older professionals had proved effective recruiters by assuring club officials that unless a club belonged to the USGA it lacked the golfing and social rating it aspired to and merited. The amateur organization's money cramps were the result of a sluggish increase in membership and its commendable effort, as the governing body of America's fastest-growing sport, to back every aspect of the game. The USGA had started its Green Section in February, 1921. Probably no other correlated activity of a sports group has had so vast an effect on the beautification of the United States as the Green Section of the USGA. Its spurring of turf-grass research and development has been of immeasurable value not only to golf courses but also to home, park, factory, and cemetery lawns, to roadsides and airfields. The Green Section definitely was a strong push behind the "Beautify America" campaign for at least forty years after its inception.

A great deal of fantasy persists regarding the fringe benefits of a National Open victory, even though the title is about the only one of golf's annual triumphs that is sure to be remembered. The Masters comes second. In recent years the PGA Championship has outranked the Bing Crosby tournament, which has enjoyed a decided advantage because of being the first winter golfing TV event of much color and consequence. The amount of prize money in most tournaments is remembered for a few days, and the name of the sponsor of the commercial event for even less time. But such mercenary factors rarely concern the winners, who have the checks and are girding themselves for new onslaughts on tax-exempt tournaments and the inevitable hassles with managers, lawyers, and tax experts.

Testimonial revenue also tends to be exaggerated and uncertain except for the big names among pro golf's established favorites. Sports celebrities' advertising testimonials are customarily used to advertise low-cost items that have a wide margin of profit and have to depend on some glamorous gimmick to attract buyers. The professional athletes' testimonial market was once rather productive, but the athletes didn't sell, and the demand for their endorsements has declined, with the significant exception of the game's current hotshots.

During the first decade of the association's existence, the PGA had strengthened the game and enriched its members by calling attention to expert instruction, pro department service in conveniently supplying merchandise to golfers, and other supplemental services of the pro department. The association's educational program began with inquiries and discussions about the methods of the young American stars, McDermott, Hagen, McNamara, Brady, -Evans, Ouimet, Travers, and whiz kids such as Sarazen and Jones. The graduate caddies had learned by imitation and improvisation. Trial and error and competition with other caddies was their schooling. Bob Jones was the first brilliant product of pro tuition, and he took the game far beyond his teachers in becoming the finest of all American golfing stylists.

The usual ghosted books and articles of instruction followed the generalized British pattern and certainly didn't produce any improvement in instruction. All the while, teaching and golf course maintenance as a pro duty were accented by PGA officials in the association's early years. But increased demands for professionals' services soon forced pros at most of the larger clubs to neglect the greenkeeping part of the customary pro-greenkeeper post, a dual responsibility necessitated by lack of money to pay two fair salaries, as well as the rarity of an experienced course maintenance manager.

George Sargent (1961). PGA

Teaching was a primary duty of the pro on the job; consequently, teaching pros how to teach was primary in the PGA schooling plan. George Sargent, the association's third president and a former U.S. and Canadian Open Champion, was an intense student and analyst of the golf stroke. He'd been an assistant to Harry Vardon before leaving England. While Vardon wasn't an especially competent clubmaker nor the best of teachers back in those days when all lessons were playing lessons, he was undoubtedly the most effective player of his period. Naturally Sargent and many others tried to discover what made Vardon tick. In his swing, Vardon's left arm was bent until it straightened in the hitting area. His hand action was magical in the way he could finesse the club face at contact. Action photographs of the Vardon hands made by George Beldam, a gifted golf photographer, student, and ghostwriter of the early 1900's, remain works of art and are still appreciated by authorities on golf technique.

Vardon had a genius for knowing where to hit shots and putting the ball where it should be. He was unsurpassed at reading courses. Tommy Armour, who paid for lessons from Vardon, observed that he was the supreme master of golf tactics in placing shots so that the next ones were easy.

When asked to suggest a replacement, when the pro post at East Lake in Atlanta became vacant, it seemed only natural that Bob Jones should name the scholarly George Sargent. Sargent, George Jacobus, Joe Novak, and Horton Smith, all of whom were PGA presidents, were extraordinarily successful teachers. They stressed the teaching responsibilities of the professional, and with many willing and competent fellow members greatly improved golf instruction, even though this was not always reflected in the scoring average of the nation's club members.

In recent years there have been indications that the older pros were looking at the golf instruction problem backward. They should have been creating an understanding of tuition as a partnership, with the pupil responsible for learning. The lesson, most experienced professionals agreed, was about 25 percent teaching and 75 percent learning. Hence the basic job of the pro was to teach the pupil how to help himself. But the golf professional rarely had a physically adept pupil who could be kept on an orderly plan of instruction and be disciplined and supervised as are beginners and novices in other sports. A drastic change was needed in the policy of golf instruction, and Bob Jones sensed this when he wrote in the introduction to his book *Golf Is My Game* (Doubleday and Company, 1960):

"I have never tried to teach golf, always being on the receiving end of such exchange, but I have spent many years in trying to learn something about the game.

"At times I had thought that I had learned pretty well, but I always found more to learn."

Jones, who in 1930 retired undefeated as the only Grand Slam winner (the National Open, the National Amateur, the British Open, and the British Amateur championships) the game has known, had plenty of time for reviewing golf instruction.

The fundamentals were difficult to put across on a uniform PGA instruction basis. For many years at the PGA annual meeting and educational sessions, the foremost players of the period tried to explain how they thought they made their strokes. There were confused explanations and unsuccessful interpretations, but only rarely were the stars able to describe how they happened to *learn* unusually good golf.

The primary principles of golf pedagogy that PGA founders hoped to give to PGA members never were simply acquired despite all the association's educational efforts. Somehow, the Big Idea was missed. Maybe there was an explanation in the remark of Dr. Robert Dyer, an excellent golfer and an instructor and lecturer at the University of Illinois Medical School and at PGA meetings, who said, "The fellows can't be made to go at the job the right way. They stage public 'clinics' without realizing a clinic should exhibit treatment of the ailing. They exhibit performances by the healthiest of expert golfers."

Slowly, but very slowly, the idea was getting across that *the pupil,* not the PGA member, was the headliner of the golf instruction act. The accent had been too much on the teacher. Even in collegiate golf instruction, where all the emphasis of physical education was supposed to be applied, it continued to be the same routine. There were infrequent breakthroughs, such as when Lester Bolstad, a competent playing and instructing pro golfer on the Physical Education staff of the University of Minnesota, showed his students a few simple exercises in golf technique and let the youngsters work out the rest of the routine for themselves. Bolstad had a practice area with out-of-bounds over a fence at the right. Many balls went over until he got the students holding their clubs mainly with the last three fingers of their left hands. Then they started hitting balls farther, straight or hooked—or both.

Tommy Armour was not only a fine

golfer but claimed he had taken more lessons than he had given. Armour was talked about as a lazy teacher who would take a drink under an umbrella while the pupil was hitting shots in the sun. But the plot was exposed after the pupil had hit the customary twenty balls, then sat down with Tommy to explain how and why the shots had been hit. The pupil was made the star of the act. Armour was the stage director who got the money for teaching the pupil how to learn, and he died leaving a substantial estate based on his success as a golf instructor.

It took many years for the PGA to learn that the big lesson of teaching golf was to teach the pupil to learn. The veterans used to say they should have paid their pupils for lessons, and that laughing remark shows how accurately the pioneer professionals understood the situation. They had a big job of instruction to do, and they paid a lot of attention to showing caddies the elements of the game. The earliest American professionals had so much work in instruction they couldn't take care of the customers with playing lessons, so the instruction-and-practice tee was established. Nobody is sure of the who, when, and where of the first practice tee, but the best guess is that it happened at a course Donald Ross designed prior to 1910. Before that, lessons were given at the side of a fairway near the clubhouse.

Instruction proficiency was the primary reason, often the only reason, for a professional's employment up to the mid-1920's. He could usually hold his job if his game was good enough for him to defeat all but a few of the members and if he was a "nice guy." The pro could hire a competent clubmaker as an assistant, and recruiting, training, and supervising caddies was also

part of his job at the average club. At the larger clubs a caddie master worked under the professional. The pro shop was beginning to pay off as a retail golf store, but the critical part of the pro job was teaching, and members increasingly sought good teaching pros. Consequently, professionals were carefully studying the teaching methods of their colleagues.

Not until 1933, when George Jacobus became president of the PGA, was much planned formal attention given to teaching pros how to teach. Jacobus, who had a considerable reputation in this line, said he had given as many as 1,500 lessons in a year. A number of professionals declared they gave 1,000 lessons or more a year. Considering that the golf "year" at most clubs was twenty-eight weeks and that most club professionals were not at their clubs on Mondays (when clubs usually were closed except for caddie play) and that they rarely gave lessons on Sundays, the pro who claimed to be giving 1,000 lessons a year must have averaged more than eight lessons a day. Perhaps some did follow such a grueling schedule. At any rate, lessons usually lasted a half hour, and the price almost until the 1950's ranged from $2.50, if an assistant taught, to $4 or $5 at a first-class club for a lesson from a professional who was a first-class instructor. There were exceptional cases of higher fees.

The playing lesson, the original Scottish type of instruction, practically vanished from the American picture in the early 1930's. Professionals didn't have the time for this sort of individual lesson on the course. They did play with various members as often as convenient, and instead of spreading their booking widely among members, some were inclined to play with select groups whose bets made the time and occasion profitable. Beating the pro for hard cash was heady stuff—and comparatively rare.

A version of the playing lesson program became popular about 1940. In it the professional played three to six holes with different foursomes one day a week and in this way got to know many of his members and their respective games. The idea became a feature of ladies' day at many clubs.

It was in the late 1920's that the group lesson began to boom, particularly in lessons for women and juniors, and by 1930 nearly a hundred professionals were teaching winter indoor classes at night programs in high schools, YMCA's, YWCA's, and also at factories for employee recreation. This was in the first decade of the PGA, when an avalanche of golf instruction books was ghosted for such famous players as Jock Hutchison, Walter Hagen, Gene Sarazen, Jim Barnes, and others, and syndicated newspaper golf instruction articles filled the sport pages. Chick Evans and Bob Jones wrote their own newspaper features, while Chester Horton and Alex Morrison had their pro teaching pieces running in many newspapers.

With the increased popularity of the game, golf magazines also proliferated. Those aimed at the sporting and playing aspects of the game came first, then the merchandising and trade publications. Condé Nast, publisher of *Vogue* and *Vanity Fair,* added *American Golfer* to his magazines for the wealthy, the sophisticated, the socially arrived, and the climbers. It was a time when movie magnates and other millionaires had their own private golf courses built. Grantland Rice and Innis Brown edited the *American Golfer.* One of the editors of the slick, handsome *Golf Illustrated* was the genial and gifted

Max H. Behr, an Eastern intercollegiate star golfer who became an able course architect and later died in a plane crash en route to the 1929 National Amateur at Pebble Beach. While accenting the swank, *Golf Illustrated,* as we have seen, played a major role in developing the Ryder Cup matches.

Golf remained very much a status symbol of the quality folk during the Roaring Twenties. Among other flowerings of golf in that flamboyant period of F. Scott Fitzgerald novels, flappers, the Charleston, bathtub gin, and the speakeasy was the Women's National Golf Club on Long Island. This was a pretentious and hopeful venture with the accent on the Social Register. Ernest Jones, whose simple method of swinging a club was the result of his losing a leg as a British soldier, was the National's professional, and his relaxed swing was quite effective for women golfers, who were not often able to get much power into their strokes. The Women's National was the first club exclusively for women in the United States since the King's Daughters Golf Club was organized at Evanston in 1899, and both were short-lived. The 1929 market crash ended the Women's National's dreams of glory.

The majority of professionals quickly observed that the security of their club jobs often depended on the influence of women members. The men had a disturbing habit of becoming involved in club politics, with the poor pro caught in the crossfire. And not infrequently, younger and more inexperienced club members decided that a glamorous, sharpshooting young professional, recently out of the amateur ranks, should replace an older professional who cared for the interests of all members and the club in general in a competent, reliable, but unexciting way.

The children's classes conducted by the earlier PGA members usually were most successful when the women's committee at the club helped the professional organize them. This established a pleasant family relationship between the professional and his members, and it was one reason why many veteran professionals stayed in their jobs from twenty-five to more than forty years.

Sometimes women members, whose husbands didn't understand them and who got carelessly inflamed on Prohibition gin, were among the occupational hazards faced by some of the more immature and susceptible professionals. Liquor was abundant at many golf clubs and accounted for out-of-bounds trysts with women members and club waitresses. The affairs usually ended quickly, with the pro being divorced from his job, often in midseason, and leaving behind him a mourning group of orphaned creditors.

The PGA had a ten-year start on other national business organizations in golf. The National Association of Greenkeepers (later to be called golf course superintendents) was formed in 1927 and held its first annual meeting in Chicago. The Club Managers' Association of America was formed the same year. It also held its first national meeting in Chicago.

In February, 1927, *Golfdom, the Business Journal of Golf,* forecast that golf was growing from a pastime into a gigantic business that would account for billions of dollars of increase in property values, sales of sporting goods, and enormous spending by the golfers in addition to the essentials of the sport. *Golfdom* became a powerful force in the economic progress of professionals, golf course superintendents, and managers, while also serving officials of private and public courses and owners of fee courses. The magazine participated intimately and effectively in the planning, operating, and publicizing of the growing PGA. It had the same close and constructive relationship with the superintendents' association when the expert in charge of the basic and costly golf courses was emerging from the elementary and limited agricultural duties of the pioneer "greenkeeper" to recognition as the executive responsible for the outdoor part of the golf investment on which every other aspect of the game depended.

Golfdom conducted an educational campaign that brought club managers out of the old steward and maitre d'hotel jobs they had commonly held, under the earlier plan at American golf clubs, into executive responsibility for all phases of clubhouse operation. The serious deficits of restaurant, bar, and other services in clubhouses that were not architecturally designed for efficient business operations could only be balanced by heavy assessments at many first-class golf clubs. At *Golfdom*'s urging, managers were eventually allowed to manage. Once the club's figures on all departments were kept in the clubhouse, the manager finally was able to appraise the financial situation quickly and clearly, and then to make his report to club officials, as well as to his associates in the course maintenance and professional departments. This group lesson in elementary accounting wasn't well received by the department heads involved, but it was the beginning of genuine business management of golf clubs, and it saved and improved many jobs.

Joe Graffis, who with his brother Herb (the author of this book) founded *Golfdom,* was experienced in the golf publishing business. He'd been advertising manager of the *Golfer's Maga-*

zine in Chicago before going to France in 1916 for military service with the French and later in U.S. naval aviation. Craft W. Higgins, secretary of the Western Golf Association, was editor of the magazine. Harry B. McMeal and Hiram D. Fargo, publishers of other magazines in Chicago and avid golfers, were publishers of the *Golfer's Magazine*. After World War I Joe Graffis returned to the *Golfer's Magazine;* then, with his brother Herb, who had had newspaper sports and business magazine experience, Joseph G. Davis, veteran golf writer of the *Chicago Tribune,* and Irving Vaughan, another *Tribune* sportswriter, he established the *Chicago Golfer,* a district golf magazine, which they sold in 1926.

As the business nature of golf expanded and became vividly noticeable on financial statements, the PGA became more clearly money-minded. That was the beginning of the never-ending discussion with the USGA about increasing the Open prize money so that, to a great extent, the pros wouldn't be playing for the money of their own entry fees. At this point the PGA lacked clout. While it grew slowly but solidly in public regard and membership because of the esteem in which its older members were held by golfers, the PGA's small income from dues limited its powers as a business organization until after World War II. In the late 1920's it was estimated that the PGA had members at about only half the courses in the United States, and many of these were nine-hole links that couldn't afford professionals.

Internally the PGA operated simply and smoothly during its first ten years. The paperwork was handled by Mrs. Blakeman in the office at New York and again when the headquarters were moved to Chicago. In New York, Jack Mackie came into the office Mondays on his days away from his club job at Inwood and checked up on the work. Alex Pirie did the same thing in Chicago during the three years he was president, but after Albert Gates was engaged as executive director in 1930, the visits of Pirie from his club, Old Elm at Fort Sheridan, became more in the nature of pleasant formalities. Mackie, who continued in PGA office until late in 1939, was a frequent Chicago office visitor and concerned that the operation should not waste money. After Gates left his job in 1934, Secretaries R. W. Treacy and Tom Walsh spent their Mondays and many winter weekdays working in the PGA office at Chicago.

Communication between the Executive Committee and the many other committees, which frequently needed prodding and help from headquarters, and liaison between the central command and the autonomous geographical components, required a competent, active man with enough initiative and personality really to represent the elected officers, who were expected by their clubs to stay on the pro jobs for which they were paid.

Eventually, several sections hired men and women as secretaries, who became, in effect, business managers of those sections. After some years of considering the need, the PGA hired Don Fischesser as liaison man between headquarters and the various sections. When he resigned, Don Smith took over the job. Fischesser had been an Indiana PGA official, and Smith had been an officer of the Pacific Northwest section.

The association was intent on becoming national as quickly as feasible. The Executive Committee voted on July 23, 1927, to hold a PGA national "convention" in the Midwest section in the fall, with the expenses of one delegate from each section to be paid by headquarters.

Reports of Midwest section meetings were as brief and to the point as the meetings were. Unfortunately, this material was lost to history, as Joe Davis, the secretary, had a filing system on and in his desk that fellow workers usually called the Billy Goat's Nest. When the *Chicago Tribune* moved from its location at Madison and Dearborn streets to its present building, the priceless Davis collection of golf history in picture and ink was destroyed. Colonel Robert R. McCormick, *Chicago Tribune* publisher, had ordered that all desk material be filed in an orderly manner for handling by movers. Joe was not the orderly type.

Hence, records of the Midwest, later to be known as the Illinois, section were lost. Records of almost all other early sections, scanty as those records were, also vanished for one reason or another. But the sectional PGA secretary couldn't be blamed. He usually had more reading, writing, and recording about his own operations than could be handled. It wasn't until the late 1950's that pro-shop design allowed for office space for most professionals. An indication of the frightening growth of pro paperwork came from William Wotherspoon, professional at the famed Southern Hills club in Tulsa. Wotherspoon said that when he was professional at a fee course in Kansas City, he and his wife could handle their monthly accounts with twelve checks. At Southern Hills, as that fine club grew, Bill Wotherspoon was signing well over a hundred checks a month and had a heavy volume of tax records, employment records, and other accounting to do for the city, county, state, and federal governments.

During efforts to get on a business-like basis, records were discovered among the papers of veteran members. Among them were the papers incorporating the New England Professional Golfers' Association, which antedated the PGA of America and was allowed to expire. By 1921 it was found that the sections were getting too large for necessary membership contacts. Yet it took years before New Jersey spun off from the Metropolitan section, and Texas, California, and Ohio, each later to be divided into northern and southern sections of these states, were separated from their parent sections.

During the PGA's first half century there were extensive complaints that too much of the association's revenue (mainly in dues) was being spent on tournament development for a comparatively small group of playing specialists. Then, when television revenue began mounting and purses became larger, the tournament players complained that the PGA was not spending enough on tournament circuit promotion.

Unfortunately, the PGA has always had a problem explaining its financial operations to its members. About as much as anything else, the PGA-TPD split resulted from the players' belief that PGA administrative costs were too high and that tournament television revenue was making the PGA rich. Expenses were allocated by the PGA according to sound accounting practice, but that didn't make any difference because balance-sheet figures usually are as baffling to athletes as to the average man. When the Tournament Players Division was formed and expenses greatly increased thereby, the PGA members on the tournament circuit continued to be in a deep fog about operation finances.

When the PGA was young, its original Class A annual dues of $25 were adequate for the few operating expenses of the headquarters office and the relief fund. Entry fees of the PGA Championship took care of a large part of the prize money. The relief fund was for emergencies, and the minutes of early meetings contain frequent references to the possible needs of Johnny McDermott, 1911 and 1912 U.S. Open Champion, who, as noted earlier, suffered a mental breakdown shortly after his championship competitions. Even to this day fringe benefits that apply to workers in many other lines do not apply to professional golfers or to golf course superintendents and managers at private or semiprivate golf clubs.

The emergencies of the PGA relief fund were backstopped by the Benevolent Fund, which continues to aid indigent PGA members whose need extends over many months or years. The Executive Committee always has been reticent about disclosing the names of pros on relief or recipients of the Benevolent Fund, mentioning these unfortunates by name only to keep clear in the bookkeeping.

As the PGA grew, so did its sources of revenue. The first extra income the PGA got was for the use of the PGA insignia on golf balls and clubs. For several years in the late 1920's and early 1930's, some ballmakers had their own names on one pole of a top-grade golf ball and the PGA insignia on the other pole. Usually the royalties were divided between the professional selling the balls and the PGA. There were also royalty deals for the PGA insignia on the clubs of a few manufacturers, but the club deal never got very far in the earlier period, especially in the hickory-shaft days when skilled bench clubmakers were available and professionals wanted their own names on clubs. Only rather recently has the PGA name on clubs, balls, and other merchandise been a substantial factor in the upper strata of the market because of advanced design and strong advertising and merchandising. Moreover, the PGA Championship rarely showed a profit until the 1960's, nor, until recent years, did the Ryder Cup matches do much better than break even.

The bewilderment of members with PGA accounting began when the tournament circuit income and expenses, the PGA National Golf Club at Dunedin, Florida, the educational and insurance programs, the tax laws, and stiff legal fees compounded the confusion. The PGA-TPD civil war rapidly enriched lawyers with $350,000 and other legal bills incurred in unexpected situations such as sporting goods dealers' suits to end the "pro only" assurance of top-quality golf merchandise, the cancellation and settlement of Robert Creasey's contract as executive director, and the settlement with John MacArthur when the offices were moved from Palm Beach Gardens and the PGA National Golf Club name was taken from golf facilities on the MacArthur property. There were also heavy expenses when the PGA was involved in a tax dispute about the PGA manner of billing members' insurance with annual dues.

These abnormal expenses could not be readily explained in the annual treasurer's report, and most members weren't interested. The ramifications of PGA accounting made it impossible for the association to show its financial picture as clearly as the USGA, the Western Golf Association, and the superintendents' associations.

In recent years PGA treasurers' reports have been printed in the *Professional Golfer* to help members understand that they are in big business. In getting to significant features of the 1972 statement, Treasurer Henry Poe pointed out that the PGA Championship at Oakland Hills produced a record net of $388,500, an increase of $269,300 over the previous year. The general fund total revenue was up only $12,800 over fiscal 1971, for a total of $569,800. The increase was mainly because of a net gain of 167 members and Approved Tournament Players.

The restricted funds earmarked for specific uses had a 1972 revenue of $1,470,468. This money was income of the PGA Corporation, which was organized for profit and to protect the PGA against having what tax authorities might regard as too much in undistributed assets. The restricted funds were mainly for educational and apprentice departments but also included the construction, liability, and benevolent and relief funds.

The National Golf Day income was another item of revenue to be distributed annually for caddie scholarships, golf-turf research and scholarships, amputee golf tournaments, and golf therapy and welfare programs at veterans' hospitals. Eventually the PGA Credit Union called for attention, and the prospect of PGA participation in a pension plan loomed.

The responsibilities and management of PGA funds ultimately became a full-time job for an experienced treasurer keenly alert to policy matters and the protection of capital against unwarranted spending. To a large extent the details were handled by Thomas A. Boyle when he became controller of the PGA in the 1960's. While Boyle gradually simplified the association's record of income and outgo, it still re-

mained too involved to be readily understood by most members. The construction-fund item proved a particularly confusing bookkeeping entry. Members believed they were being assessed to build a golf club that would be the front yard of their retirement homes. That had been the Dunedin dream and the hope at Palm Beach Gardens, but there never was enough money to provide utopian courses for retired pros. Even the modest amount required for maintenance of the Dunedin course and its small, weatherworn clubhouse was a strain on PGA funds and was regarded as an unnecessary expenditure by Western PGA members with little interest in a PGA course in Florida. Nor did the Palm Beach Gardens project for a pro winter resort turn out to be a dreamland.

Not many PGA members had bought residential property at Dunedin or Palm Beach Gardens, but those who did saw their investments increase in value, so they didn't suffer. Those others who contributed to the construction fund continued to hope. The membership generally felt lucky at having refused to authorize borrowing $2 million to build a clubhouse and offices alongside the MacArthur courses. Nevertheless, the PGA name is a definite asset in promotion of a winter resort; invitations for the association to become financially involved in real-estate developments continue to this day.

According to Robert Creasey, the lean and worried days of the PGA ended in the late 1950's when dues, television and other revenue from the cosponsored circuit tournaments, the PGA Championship, and equipment royalties began mounting until the association actually had more money than it knew how to handle.

Although the founders of the PGA

realized that they and their companions were building a huge sports business, they sensed that golf professionals would harvest only a minor share of the crop that they were planting. They had no conception of the enormous peripheral profits such as real estate that would develop from the professionals' success in enlarging American golf; their main concern was simply the playing equipment business.

Much of the PGA's effort in the early years was devoted to getting a larger share of the manufacturers' profits for association members and the PGA's expansion of services. Those early hopes of manufacturers' substantially financing PGA marketing operations were unrealistic, since the profits of the club- and ballmakers were rather small and the rapidly growing but specialized market was keenly competitive. Professionals were serving the needs of the free-spending playing members of the active clubs, and the cheaper club and ball volume was split up between sporting goods stores and other retailers, whose experienced buyers traded prices down until none of the manufacturers of clubs and balls had any hope of getting rich quick. One of the first cases the PGA officials handled involved a manufacturer who was selling American-made golf balls to a large wholesale house at prices considerably below the pro price.

Then, in 1919, the PGA considered establishing cooperative buying along the lines the British PGA had adopted. Nothing came of the idea nationally, although much later there was pro coop buying around Kansas City and in Indiana. For years the British PGA's successful operation of cooperative buying was cited as an indication the Americans might do better. However, the British market, smaller geographically and financially, with quicker shipping, lower shipping costs, and prompt payment of bills, proved better suited for coop marketing than the U.S. market.

From about 1910 to nearly 1930, ball sales accounted for approximately half the pro-shop revenue. Then for about twenty-five years the pro-shop percentage from golf balls stayed at around 33 percent. More balls were sold because many more people were playing golf. But sales volume failed to increase proportionately because of tougher covers on balls, lower cutting of rough, and the absence of concealing broad-leafed weeds.

As golfing apparel sales increased at pro shops, naturally the percentage of revenue from ball sales went down until ball sales dollar volume was slightly under 25 percent at some rapid-turnover pro shops.

Up to the mid-1920's woolen golf stockings and sweaters imported from our Scottish friends were the only apparel sold in most pro shops, although some select ones did sell knickers, either imported or made by local tailors. The wives of several Scottish-born professionals made hosiery for sale to members. These same swift and expert knitters had turned out large amounts of knit goods to be sent to the troops during World War I. They were women who couldn't stand being idle, and with their husbands as pros modeling the hosiery and sweaters, the market made itself.

The wives of the professionals also played a crucial role in World War II, when most golf clubs barely managed to keep going, using reduced staffs. With new balls and clubs either at a premium or unavailable, they all but converted the pro shops into apparel stores and took over while their husbands were away on war jobs or in military service. While these practical women carried on as a matter of survival, they were also perhaps unknowingly promoting a new and highly profitable sideline of the golf business. For by the time normal peacetime operations resumed, it was discovered that a ready apparel market existed at golf clubs on a foundation that was worth millions.

The pro-shop development in apparel merchandising seems to have occurred while quality competition was sleeping. The pro shops at the private clubs were stores of convenience, offering unquestioned credit, easy parking, and enough styles, sizes, and colors to satisfy the country club set's impulse to buy. The downtown quality stores in the larger cities were often inconveniently located for the woman country club member, while the suburban branches of the big department stores and the smart specialty shops were slow in accurately sensing the tastes of the country club women who were fashion leaders in sports.

When they were getting vigorously into the apparel business in the late 1950's, the pros learned that the cheap stuff was not for them because there were always stores that could get the cheap stuff cheaper. It was the same with golf clothing and shoes as it was with golf clubs and balls. In the case of golf apparel, the women members were instinctively better judges of value than the pros. Because so many women members bought for their husbands and sons, the pros' market in male apparel was also kept on a high-quality plane.

While women members, pros' wives, and a few exceptionally talented saleswomen in pro shops may have "made" the apparel market for professionals,

earlier and more clearly, the professionals themselves had established the market for balls and clubs. From 1900 on, the only things other retail outlets could sell, in any appreciable amount, were the golf balls and club brands for which professionals had developed consumer acceptance. This pro market power continues and is the reason that the courts have consistently ruled against pros in the "pro only" suits.

As has been discussed, ball-marketing power was one of the reasons for the PGA's being formed at a time when pro business leaders had a vague idea that they could play one manufacturer off against another if they had the kind of unity that would give them some muscle. Wanamaker, the major importer, and Spalding, the chief domestic producer, were contending for pro favor and volume, with Spalding pulling ahead because of an improving product and closer nationwide contact with the professionals. The promotion efforts included bonuses of balls, which amounted to a discount, and also some moderate salaries paid for "advisory," "consulting," or other vague services that naturally resulted in lowering prices to professionals. As a consequence, Wanamakers' hope of capturing a major part of the pro golf ball market never materialized, in spite of its cradling of the PGA and the gift of the championship trophy and prize money.

What loosely were called "promotional deals to secure pro-shop push in golf ball retailing" became a costly trade practice that government trade policemen questioned so sharply that the manufacturers agreed among themselves to greatly reduce giving free balls to club professionals and to curtail the number of pros getting cash payments. But the practice had grown so extensive that it took many years to get it cut to a rational business basis. It even persisted to a minor degree into the 1960's, when the payments were called "subsidization" and the PGA considered a resolution barring from national office any professional who was "subsidized" by a manufacturer. The resolution was defeated.

By that time the services for which the professionals were paid had to be definite and worth the money. Accounting and legal departments of the companies were taking hard looks at expenses, and executives were struggling to earn dividends for stockholders. The days of buying pro business and of salesmen leaving clubs "on consignment" in pro shops were over. There had never been enough profit to justify the extravagant competition for pro business, but many PGA founding members were misled by the apparent largesse of the ball-and-club giveaways as inducements or rewards for pro patronage. These professionals were convinced that if the golf manufacturing business could afford that careless expense, the margin of profit must be large. Some association officials claimed that the money involved in "free goods" promotion deals could be much better used in developing the PGA, but that was an unpopular view. The majority of pros wanted to continue to get as many "free" balls as possible directly from the manufacturers.

The Prohibition era brought on further personality problems that the PGA tried hard to control. One of these difficulties was drinking at championships. There were probably fewer cases of conspicuous imbibing at the National Open, the PGA, and major championships than there were at the usual business conventions during the 1920's, but baseless charges about the pro golfer's thirst persisted. Actually, those who played well enough to be contenders were temperate men. The PGA felt that it was responsible for those who got roaring drunk and disorderly as well as for those who behaved themselves, but this was a problem with swarms of hospitable salesmen. In 1923 the Executive Committee requested that manufacturers discontinue serving intoxicants at championships. There was also a brief period when activities in the manufacturers' "hospitality rooms" at PGA annual national and sectional meetings became overly enthusiastic, but that wasteful nuisance was tactfully corrected by PGA officials and manufacturers.

Considering the peculiar problems of market development, consumer education, merchandising methods, credit, and financing, the PGA and the manufacturers got along amazingly well while making golf a huge business and a national pastime. Even the difficulties of transition from hickory to steel shafts were not unduly troublesome, although the shift meant unemployment for professionals and a change in financing and manufacturing schedules for clubmakers.

With the Western Golf Association first legalizing the steel shaft, then the USGA and the R & A making it unanimous in November, 1929, there was little demand for large inventories of hickory shafts being seasoned or ready for heads and grips. Still, it should be remembered that Bob Jones won his Grand Slam with hickory-shafted clubs. When you think of the variations in temperature and humidity at St. Andrews, Hoylake, Interlachen, and Merion when Jones won his 1930 championships, you have to marvel at the expert selection of hickory, the workmanship, and the finishing treatment those shafts got. They went through the four competitions and now, looking as trim and true as ever, are displayed (with two exceptions) at the Augusta National Golf Club.

Billy Burke, who had been testing steel shafts for the American Fork and Hoe Company, won the 1931 National Open at Inverness. A week prior, in the Ryder Cup matches at Scioto, Burke had won his single match and his foursome, with Wiffy Cox as his partner, playing the same steel-shafted clubs. The visiting British pros were impressed by what they called Burke's "pipes," and the better-playing professionals accepted the steel-shafted woods without much hesitation, but said that the steel shafts didn't give iron clubs the correct feeling for precision shots.

They'd been accustomed to going through many raw shafts and working long and delicately on the finishing process before getting the completely satisfactory "wood" for the club. It was not uncommon for a good clubmaker to go through fifty or more shafts in his stock before choosing one for a club to be used by a discriminating, favorite player. Club sets, regardless of how many clubs were included prior to the fourteen-club limitation, were matched by feel of the club head and flexibility of the shaft as well as overall weight. Swing-weight determination came with the steel shaft, since those shafts were uniform in weight.

The breaking of hickory shafts, plus the eternal hope of increased distance, made most golfers eager to try the highly touted steel-shafted clubs even before they had reached the retail counters. The price of the new clubs promised to be little more than for good hickory ones, and while there had been some breakage of the earlier metal

shafts, that didn't last long. Materials and tempering quickly corrected these flaws. But all the same, despite their advance public acceptance on the basis of the usual extraordinary claims of manufacturers, the change from wood to steel shafts struck the older professionals as just as dramatic, revolutionary, worrisome, and even regrettable as the shift from the horse to the automobile had seemed to lovers of the breed around the turn of the century. To purists of the game, golf was never quite the same again.

At the 1929 PGA annual meeting, there was worried discussion about hickory shafts being doomed; the manufacturers were pushing steel, almost completely stopping the purchase of hickory for shafts. (Although a satisfactory steel shaft wasn't available then, progress was so rapid in the factories that the 1932 club lines for pro shops and stores were all steel-shafted.) The annual meetings in 1931 and 1932 were marked by bitter reflections on the hickory-to-steel shift, exchanges of experiences in installment selling, and the problem of what to do with unsold hickory-shafted PGA clubs.

The cost of replacing hickory-shafted clubs with a complete new outfit of steel-shafted ones was considerable, as golf costs were regarded in those days. Hickory-shafted clubs had been bought one, two, or three at a time. Installment payments did induce buying in some cases, but these were the Depression years, club members found it burdensome to spread payments over a few months, and the pro rarely dared push for quicker action. Nor could hickory-shafted clubs be used as a down payment for steel; the trade-in arrangement was six or seven years in the future and became a costly nuisance to the professional, who had to make two sales instead of one in disposing of the used clubs.

Some stores disposed of their stocks by selling them at a cut rate, but the bulk of the hickory-shafted clubs, new and used, were given away by the professionals to thousands of caddies and youngsters in every state. This was perhaps one of the most successful recruiting campaigns a sport ever experienced. With these gifts a new and eager army was brought into the game; boys swarmed onto the public courses. In a couple of years, no doubt, most of the wooden clubs had been broken by the kids, who then were golfers happily ever after.

The 1929 crash and the Great Depression that followed had its effect on the pros just as it did on other working people. Some clubs went out of business, others went into a form of bankruptcy that allowed years for recovery, and the new courses that had been planned stayed on the drawing boards. Some pros lost their jobs; those who stayed on had to accept lower pay, and there were no other openings. The economic slump probably hit the golf course equipment manufacturers and dealers most severely. Oddly enough, golf balls continued to sell at about the normal annual rate, with the buying average in the 1928–34 period approximately a dozen new balls per player per year. But these figures were probably distorted by the recent surge in the golf ball repairing and repainting business, which has continued to be a tremendous one to this day. The business has paid professionals and clubs substantially for the privilege of reclaiming balls from water holes.

The Depression inertia, the continuing drop in sales, the changeover to the metal shaft, and the slow, determined effort of the PGA to make its membership an educated power in the golf business all had their effect in forcing the manufacturers to work together more closely than ever before to stabilize and improve the industry. Once again the government intervened, and even the PGA was warned by its attorneys that it risked being accused of violating federal laws if it persisted in its alleged concerted and monopolistic efforts. Then, in 1932, when George Jacobus became PGA president, he appointed a Manufacturers' Relations Committee, consisting of himself, Tom Boyd, John Mackie, who had been PGA president in 1920, and John Inglis, a charter member of the PGA and president of the Metropolitan section for many years.

From their experiences with the PGA brand on clubs and balls, the members of the committee were quite satisfied that their problems with the manufacturers were balanced by the manufacturers' problems with the pros. Taking this into consideration, as well as the reaction of the ball-and-club dealers toward the manufacturers' use of the PGA label, it appeared that trade improvement was progressing. For a couple of years the situation seemed promising, then progress was halted when lawyers for both sides warned of possible collusion, illegal agreements, and violations of federal statutes. This ended the hopes of the pros of saving money for golfers, improving playing equipment, and making its manufacture and distribution more profitable for maker and seller.

However, the club- and ballmakers and the pros continued their efforts, and gradually the committee effectively handled a number of routine matters on a mutually satisfactory basis. What was called the "Fourteen Points Agreement" was made by the PGA and the manufacturers in a Manufacturers' Relation Committee meeting that preceded the annual PGA assembly of officials and delegates. *Nobody signed anything* regarding the agreement, which covered billing, repairs, return of merchandise firmly ordered, contracts with home and playing professionals, who was entitled to buy PGA items for resale, who was qualified to be called a professional golfer, the status of golf ranges as retailers for PGA merchandise, and as always when the PGA and the manufacturers talked, their mutual prickly subject of pro credit.

7

A Review of the PGA's Later Years

THE reference just above to golf ranges as possible retailers for PGA merchandise brings up one of the most phenomenal, prolific, and remunerative offshoots of the game. Beginning in the late 1920's, the golf range business grew rapidly and attracted prominent instructors who were either dissatisfied with club pro jobs or didn't like the tournament strain and monotony. Some of these teaching stars, such as Bob Macdonald of Chicago, drew many pupils who were members of private clubs but found the range and the Macdonald instruction more convenient and effective. At many ranges in metropolitan areas the professionals made more money than they'd made at private clubs. The tutoring fees were good and were coming in, weather permitting, as long in the day as the pro wanted to work. From 7:00 P.M. until midnight was the gold-mine time for the floodlighted ranges. Forenoon and

early afternoon business was almost altogether confined to women, and many ranges were patronized by young mothers who had babies sleeping in carriers of one sort or another back of the tees. Some businessmen would start to work early and spend a half hour at a golf range en route as exercise.

Marshall Field III, grandson of the Chicago merchant who founded a huge fortune, was a golf range regular. He must have been a member of six to a dozen private golf clubs around the nation, but this business-burdened financier and publisher would invariably stop at a range in a prairie of northwest Chicago and hit a couple of baskets of balls. He was Mr. Anonymous sandwiched between a couple of fellows also en route home after wearying, worried days in an office or factory.

Field's handicap was around 16. He didn't seem to have a burning desire to be any better and thoroughly enjoyed golf, and others enjoyed golf with him. He considered the golf range his great discovery as the convenient place where a businessman could cure his cares of the day. He said a golf practice range was a perfect place for thinking without interruption. He liked the atmosphere of the golf practice tee as a school in which, according to his observation, after confusion and complication the correct way was discovered to be the simplest way.

There are successful veteran golf teachers who maintain that for many people the golf range with a competent professional available was the practical way of learning sound golf. The pupil with expert inspection and intermittent supervision could work out the correct method of hitting a golf ball.

Bob Macdonald, who had been professional at fine private clubs before going into teaching at ranges, said that twenty minutes or more of lesson time for most pupils was wasted. To prove his case, he would take the doubter to where a hopeful was swinging away and comment, "Not bad. You might be a golfer if you would hold the club with the fist of your left hand and the fingers of your right. Try a couple." The fellow would, and Macdonald might make simple adjustments. "Now, work on that and nothing else until you've hit these balls."

When he noticed that the customer had a half dozen balls left, Macdonald would return, observe the results of the advice, and make more useful comments. In the majority of cases the golfer showed indications of improvement. Many rented an extra basket of balls.

The golf range was anything from a mowed few acres with a small, box-like building for rental ball and club storage, an office for the pro, and a shelter, to expensive, beautiful establishments with canopies over the tees, automatic ball-teeing devices, restaurants, excellent lighting for night play, and balls of better than fair quality. A few ranges had a deck of tees above those at ground level. Several had warming areas where the golfer could have cold-weather practice in comfort.

The range had to be on a well-traveled thoroughfare to get enough patronage to justify a pro's interest. In many of these installations the net income of the range not only paid taxes on the property but enabled the professional to buy the property. Clem Wittek, a pioneer in supplying ranges with balls, clubs, and operating equipment, and now one of the largest in that department of golf business, estimates that at least fifty professionals are worth from $150,000 up to the millionaire bracket because of increases in the price of property they bought for golf range use.

The golf range became almost an essential at American military locations at home and overseas. It is an American professionals' idea that has spread throughout the golfing world. Inquiry among veteran professionals has not determined who established the first golf range. Whoever the innovator was, he'd be amazed to see how his idea has reached a magnificent summit in a multidecked range in the center of Tokyo. It's really a golf range country club. It is crowded day and night and has been a factor in accelerating the astonishing growth of golf in Japan.

The golf range proved to be another of professional golf's great contributions to the American economy. It helped golf, golfers, and people in the real-estate business. Soon the range was followed by a par-3 course, which at first was called a pitch-and-putt course.

Most of the earlier layouts adjoined ranges, and a few of them were lighted for night play. They didn't get the wild welcome of the miniature course craze, nor did they expire so quickly. Hundreds of them continued operating to the degree their profits paid the taxes on expensive property.

Out of the par-3's came the short course that had a few par-4 holes. These usually were facilities of residential developments on property that otherwise would have been so ordinary and unattractive that it wouldn't have justified the prices asked. With the lush, well-groomed short course as a home's front yard, the home took on value in excess of the building and maintenance costs of the golf course.

For high-rise apartments to border on a short course was an especially valuable feature. Far too many people who retired to big condominiums in Florida and the Southwest had no outlets and needed the green grass and sunshine and fresh-air treatment available in a two-hour round on the demanding little course. The courses often were called "executive," using the name an early builder had applied in the 1960's, or identified by their par, which usually was 60.

We've already touched briefly in an earlier chapter on the beginning of intercollegiate golf and the strong influence of professionals on the college players. From 1897 on, the National Intercollegiate Championship was a regular event and the 1920 Intercollegiate marked the first time the tournament was held west of the Mississippi. In 1922, National Intercollegiate officials joined forces with the USGA in supervising intercollegiate golf, but the association was not a binding one and the Intercollegiate became a stepchild tournament. Then, in 1938, the college

coaches, many of whom were PGA members, took over sponsorship of the Intercollegiate Championship because they felt their players were more important in the golf picture than the cold, distant USGA appeared to realize.

The USGA was worried about the Intercollegiate Championship's threat to the USGA National Amateur competition as the premier amateur contest of the year. Besides, big money prizes and television coverage of the pro contests had reduced the amateur events to matters of practically no consequence to the golfing public. First the Western Golf Association, then the USGA went on a crossbreed of stroke and match play for championships, and the Intercollegiate became a generation-gap stroke-play campus "Open" of interest mainly to the contestants and their coaches and the scouts from golf equipment manufacturers eager to supply free golf equipment, plus money, to tournament winners whose triumphs often didn't carry enough endorsement power to sell the average amateur golfer a package of wooden tees.

The formation of the ICAA (Intercollegiate Athletic Association) Golf Coaches' Committee in 1939 tremendously stimulated collegiate golf, and the championship at the Wakonda course in Des Moines, Iowa, seemed to revitalize the tournament, as well as remind the students back home that collegiate golf was important. Not many of the students intended to be playing football or basketball during their business careers, but they did plan to play golf the rest of their lives.

With the approval of a new intercollegiate golf organization reaching nationwide—from the veteran Ben Thompson of Yale to Eddie Twiggs of Stanford—the Golf Coaches' Committee of the NCAA (National Collegiate Ath-

Lawson Little, Jr. PGA

letic Association) was quick in becoming one of the strong groups in golf and was closely, but informally, associated with the PGA. Besides Thompson and Twiggs, those who formed the collegiate Golf Coaches' Committee were Bourne of Princeton, Ericson of the University of North Carolina, Smith of Minnesota, Hagan of the University of Pittsburgh, and others whose names now rest in contented anonymity but whose achievements in fitting golf into the pursuit of happiness and extending a college sport beyond the interest of muscular students might someday justify a thesis by a scholar exploring a neglected part of American sports history.

Lawson Little, Jr., of Stanford, was the first collegiate golfer to be a top champion. Arnold Palmer of Wake Forest and Jack Nicklaus of Ohio State came much later. Little's victories in the U.S. and British Amateur cham-

pionships of 1934 and 1935 and his triumph in the 1940 USGA National Open after a tie with the durable Sarazen had golfers wondering whether collegiate training would soon be the route to the heights. Yet Little, who played on Eddie Twiggs's team at Stanford, hadn't distinguished himself in collegiate golf, and Bob Jones, who had been an excellent scholar at two universities, hadn't participated in collegiate golf competition.

As in so many other facets of golf, the PGA helped college golf from the start and nursed it until it became highly important to the game. But it must be said that the PGA had much more to do with prompting collegiate golf than it ever did with the development of the Ladies' PGA. The women got their outfit going after vainly seeking PGA help.

Before hailing the LPGA, toward which the lordly PGA so long expressed a typical male chauvinist attitude, we should also pay tribute to the women's associations that have helped make golf an immense game and business in the United States. The Women's Western Golf Association, the Women's Trans-National Golf Association (formerly the Trans-Mississippi), the Women's Committee of the USGA (which is practically an autonomous group that the USGA wisely lets attend to its own business), possibly nearly seventy states and smaller groups of women golfers, the Swing Clubs, and the American Women's Voluntary Service, who bring the big heart of golf to hospitalized veterans and their families, are, beyond any doubt, the most valuable and least publicized groups in golf. There wouldn't be the tournament circuit there is today if there hadn't been the free work of women golfers selling tickets, scoring, driving service cars, and doing the multitude of other chores that ensure the success of these events. And women continue to earn praise from professionals for putting over the junior programs at many clubs. These programs managed by mothers have meant more to clubhouse and pool revenue than most club officials possibly realize.

The Ladies' PGA had trouble getting organized, but when the determined and businesslike Patty Berg took command, the association really began to move. It took a lot of promotion, lovely manners, and pleasant sportsmanship before the LPGA became a flourishing business operation. There were many personable young women among its members. There always had been. Just like tennis, golf came to the United States as a society sport, and there were as many delightful women among those who wielded clubs as those who swung rackets. Even the girls that Paul Gallico rather unfairly labeled Muscle Molls in the 1920's and 1930's showed social graces on golf courses. And it now seems terribly old-fashioned to recall how these competitive young women were stigmatized for daring to take up an exclusively male sport instead of hiding in the kitchen as nice girls were supposed to.

These pioneer pros had just as much poise as today's women professionals. They deliberately chose the name "Ladies' PGA," and they are responsible for making the organization as successful as it has become. And the LPGA scored in the best way when an international cosmetic company began sponsoring its tournaments. Long gone, if it ever truly existed, is the saddle-skin look of yesterday, and the women pros are doing very well indeed on their own tournament circuit, as teachers, and as golf executives in their own right. As in

every other field in these enlightened days, it's a whole new ball game for women. And it's about time!

"Is it good for golf?" That was the first test of any problem involving the game or business that confronted the PGA, and it helped make the association strong and detoured it around many puzzles and perils. "Is it good for golf?" was what every man and boy in the profession was taught to answer in his heart and had become a tradition when George Jacobus, the first American-born PGA president, was elected in 1933.

But it was this very question that was to lead to a civil war within the PGA that split the association into the home professionals, the sections of home professionals, and the Tournament Players' Division. Probably some separation of the PGA was inevitable because of the different interests and responsibilities of the home professionals and the playing professionals. The home pro's responsibility was to see that amateurs got the most out of the game; the playing professional was interested in good purses and playing conditions on the tour. The home professionals at their club or fee course jobs were in golf business. The tournament professionals were in show business, which had been popularized by the effective public education work done by the home pros.

These hemispheres of golf's world were widely split as the money in show business golf got larger and attracted a new type of exploiter who was more concerned with what was good for himself than for what was good for golf. But you couldn't really blame the managers who had the playing pros on a tight string. It was the same way in other pro sports with managers, lawyers, and tax tricksters working all angles. In a $60,000 prize money year, a

Patty Berg. GH

tournament journeyman was able to net about $15,000 after a lot of road-work, acres of ulcers, and absence from contented family life. The boys learned that the road to headlines was paved with headaches.

Yet the promise of a fortune for playing golf, instead of having to pay for playing the game, had youngsters striving for golf scholarships at colleges and universities that were becoming the same sort of favored farm system that football, basketball, and to a lesser extent, baseball had established in the halls of higher learning. The golf scholarships often made laughable the USGA rule calling for forfeiture of amateur status by one "taking any action for the purpose of becoming a professional golfer."

The gold rush of amateurs into tournament golf made it necessary for the PGA to establish a screening procedure. Candidates had to qualify by playing in a circuit candidate tournament before a player's card was issued. There was schooling in tournament conduct, the Rules of Golf, and public relations at these qualifying sessions. The procedure continued after the Tournament Players' Division split and took charge of eligibility for most of the events on the circuit. The National Open, the PGA, and the Masters, of course, were major events in which the TPD did not determine eligibility.

Young men were required to show proof of financial responsibility before getting a player's card. The PGA had gone through the embarrassing period of early tournament players leaving unpaid bills when the jumps were long and the purses low as the tournament circuit was being built. In a few cases, after the playing card and financial responsibility system was established, there were questions about the repu-

Barbara Romack became a professional in 1958. AG

Betsy Rawls was elected to the Golf Hall of Fame in 1960 after a season of ten victories. AG

tations of the young men's sponsors, but never has a candidate failed to conduct himself in an honest, businesslike manner.

Some youths got stage fright in the qualifying rounds and failed the first time only to succeed in later trials. Those who were confident of their ability to play successfully against a sharp pro competition got another chance in the so-called minitournaments that became popular in the early 1970's. These events had entry fees of $5,000 and up and were usually at resort courses. The fee paid the living expenses for the player and sometimes for a player's wife during the weeks the competitions were being played, while the promoters deducted expenses and usually a good profit. The purses were substantial. The players were playing for their own money, or that of their sponsors. The problem of purses largely derived from entry fees was something the PGA had corrected long before the Tournament Players' Division was formed.

Certainly, by 1928 the pattern of PGA policies and procedure had been well formed. By instinct, habit, and deliberation the organization shared with the amateur governing body (the USGA) an unselfish, complete dedication to the good of golf. The PGA had also succeeded in achieving one of the objectives set forth in its constitution: "to elevate the standards of the professional golfers' vocation." As a result of natural selection and discipline, in 1928 the PGA had acquired a membership that in desirable character was unsurpassed by personalities in any other sport and equaled by few pro sports rosters. The game always came first, the professional second in PGA motivation, and the pro was reminded that his reputation and his prosperity depended on how well he served the amateur players. This service often was free. Few professionals in other sports have contributed the free work in promotion of the game that golf professionals have. In the building days of the game and business of golf in the United States, the playing experts were as generous as the home professionals in promotion activities.

This intelligent liberality was to come to almost a complete halt when tournament purses got large and tournament players' managers went into a state of shock when their clients gave away anything on which they, the lawyers, and the tax evasion counselors did not collect a commission. The situation became so greedily controlled that it embarrassed even the golf writers, who knew that admirable young men were becoming so notoriously mercenary they'd take $5,000 or $10,000 for playing in charity matches with famous actors (who played free and drew galleries), yet allowed the Tournament Players' Division to be the lowest contributor of all PGA sections on National Golf Day, the PGA's one nationwide fund-raising operation.

National Golf Day is a PGA operation unique in sports. PGA member professionals and the players at their clubs contribute a minimum of $1 each in an annual net score competition against the champions of the National Open, the PGA, the Women's Open, and the LPGA. Beneficiaries are golf therapy programs at veterans' hospitals, blind golfers, indigent professionals, golf turf research, and amateur organizations that annually provide approximately a thousand scholarships for caddies.

Although getting more of their circuit prize money as the top cut from charity benefit events with purses over $7 million, the tournament players in

Sandra Haynie ranks No. 2 in all-time earnings, with over $387,389 in career winnings. AG

recent years contributed only about $400 in cash to the PGA's own charity and welfare public service fund. Obviously the humiliating showing was not caused by individual stinginess but by inexplicably bad management.

The PGA continues to insist on "conduct becoming a gentleman" as essential to membership. There have been few instances in which contempt of the PGA code of noblesse oblige has warranted official notice. Flagrantly bad manners usually are controlled and corrected by the chill of fellow competitors, host officials and members, and sportswriters in cases of tournament players, or by unemployment if a club player is at fault. While the tournament player must have some charm as well as a creditable playing record to qualify himself for testimonial money, the home professional must be subjected to closer character appraisal each day than any other sports professional.

The surreptitious meetings of the tournament rebels in planning the break from the PGA were juvenile plots rather than meetings of minds qualified to run a multimillion-dollar entertainment business. They were much like children eager to blame domineering parents for everything that happened to them. In every tournament there are few galleries of any size following individual golfers. As a mortal groping for an alibi, the tournament golfer accompanied only by his caddie and his next of kin (if convenient) would have to blame somebody far, far away. Hence, the PGA in its vague, all-embracing way, was identified as the cause of the gallery quarantine.

However, golf writers were misled when they thought the revolt of tournament players in the PGA wouldn't amount to much because the popular

big stars didn't seem especially concerned with the internecine quarrel. In doing one of the greatest favors to tournament golf, Bing Crosby unwittingly sharpened the pin of tournament players who didn't draw enough customers to pay caddie fees. When Crosby started his "clambake" at Rancho Santa Fe in 1934, he did three things that were to make tournament golf big business. He introduced the celebrity pro-am tournament as a preliminary instead of the tired and dull shot-making demonstration called a "clinic." He got a lot of colorful hams as an added attraction, and as expected, they brought into the paid-admission category fans who have the idea that golf is fun. And by giving the proceeds to charity on a good, sound tax-exempt basis and tipping other show business people off on how to get under the tent for publicity and stooging for millions in charity, Crosby really established tournament golf.

There has been a great deal of talk about what accounted for the swift and tremendous rise of tournament golf. President Dwight D. Eisenhower, TV, prize money, and Arnold Palmer have been named as the causes. But a review of the Crosby classic shows that the genial and generous Bing, more than any other one man, made tournament golf big business.

For this he got no credit from the professionals. To the contrary, some of the minor mercenaries wanted the pro-amateur feature of the Crosby tournament eliminated in order to make more room for professionals and to curb the disturbing influence of an amateur partner who was taking too many bogeys and thus reducing the team's prize money. The amateurs paid $1,500 each to get into the play, and that money went to charity. More than three thousand applicants for amateur entry were turned down each year. Very, very few people in show business other than Bing Crosby could or would take the risk of being called hard names by the disappointed entrants.

Without the pro-am competition the Crosby affair would be just another tournament; without the star-sprinkled field of amateurs the tournament wouldn't draw much of a gallery to the Monterey peninsula, which is noted for its uncertain weather early in the year. The Monterey charities would slump seriously. An ordinary tournament, no more distinctive than any of the games of a routine major league baseball season, would go into the gap in the golf calendar. In that precarious balance the Crosby tournament continued because of the patience of an illustrious benefactor of tournament golf.

Controversies about tournament dates and differences of opinion about the extent to which sponsors were to be allowed to direct their tournaments were frequent long before the Crosby show had led the parade to fortunes for the touring professionals. The differences usually were inevitable; somebody was sure to have his feelings, if not his pocketbook, hurt.

Notwithstanding the cordial public relations individual professionals had with their club members and the general golfing public, the PGA was collectively handicapped by misunderstandings in developing the tournament circuit. The healing of time repaired much of the damage done to the PGA by pressures to force the development of the tournament schedule. The problem was an immensely complex one.

Few American amateur sportsmen realize that professional baseball, football, hockey, and basketball are sponsored and operated by experienced businessmen who own clubs and parks and who control the commissioners of those sports. On the other hand, from the beginning the PGA has been an organization of individuals without commercial experience other than in golf clubs, usually only in the shops they operate as a service to golfers. When the contrast between the PGA and other professional sports authorities is considered, the remarkably sound record of professional golfers is bound to be recognized.

There was foresight in the PGA plan, and all through PGA history there has been no lack of men of good judgment, high character, and energy to serve as sectional and national officers. A commissioner functioning as in other professional sports was not needed in professional golf because the officers and Executive Committee made policy. The sections, through their delegates at annual meetings, provided the directives that were adequate even to cover the crisis of the family fight that produced the Tournament Players' Division. Numerous PGA members and some officials were all for dropping the tournament pros from membership and forming a new tournament circuit, although it might mean lawsuits to enforce contracts signed between sponsors and the PGA.

By a margin of one vote the Executive Committee approved a compromise. Dollarwise, the decision soon was validated when the PGA-backed Sunol tournament held practically in competition with the Los Angeles Open, which presented a field of leading players, was a failure. The Sunol event cost the PGA almost $100,000. That amount probably was a bargain, considering the beating the PGA and the TPD took in lawyers' bills and the

Tom Crane (left) on PGA Executive Committee with Joe Novak and Horton Smith. PGA, photo by Kuehn

prospect of enough litigation to explain why the United States has one lawyer to about every 550 citizens.

The PGA got its first commissioner in Albert Gates because PGA officials' duties were taking time that association officers thought they owed their clubs and because the central management and legal problems of the pro association's growing pains required an experienced executive. The PGA also needed an outstanding "front man" who could acquaint officials of amateur golf organizations and manufacturers with the conscientious efforts the PGA was making to serve golf.

Gates got PGA headquarters operating as a corporation office and awakened amateurs to what the PGA was doing to help all golf. Gates deeply believed in the potential of the PGA as a tremendous force for the develop-

ment of golf, but he was ahead of the PGA. It couldn't afford him, and after salary cuts he separated from the PGA with respect and a sigh of relief. He didn't need the PGA money. He was like the pro and amateur officials of those days: He wanted to do something for golf.

Thomas Crane came in as executive secretary after Tom Walsh became PGA president in 1940. Tom was lawyer, nursemaid, business manager, and third-man-in-the-ring for the PGA when it was growing up. Crane, a battered young ex-Marine, proved to be the right man to run the store for the PGA. He'd been one of those hopeful Chicago lawyers specializing in small cases for businessmen. For the time and the place, Tom Crane was the Million-Dollar Boy for the PGA, taking it through the perils of government and

lesser suits that always confront a growing business. Crane had the soft answer that turneth away wrath, which
was often needed in cases that might be
gently described as "differences of opinion" in the PGA.

As the PGA's affairs grew more complicated, the organization became a
customer of one of the big Washington, D.C., law firms. The lawyers
weren't spectacularly successful for the
PGA. They three-putted the cases with
PGA landlord John MacArthur, the
pro-only merchandising suits, and the
contract settlement with Executive Director Robert Creasey, who succeeded
Crane.

Although they couldn't "win 'em
all," what the PGA did win out of the
big wholesale lawyers in Washington
was an assistant to Crane, Lloyd Lambert. He was farmed out by the Washington law company to its client and
became very valuable to the pros in
handling a multitude of routine legal
matters, getting the office work on a
smooth system, arranging meetings, and
discreetly editing minutes of meetings
so salient information was recorded
and nobody was in print as having
spoken out of turn. Lambert eased the
load on the overburdened Tom Crane
and seemed to be able quickly to supply the information officers wanted.

When Crane retired and was succeeded by Robert Creasey as executive
secretary, Lambert became Creasey's assistant and was named acting executive
director after Creasey's contract was
canceled and he was paid off for time
remaining on the employment agreement. Creasey, a Washington lawyer,
had been an Assistant Secretary of Labor under President Harry S. Truman.
He was a member of the Burning Tree
Club when its professional, Max Elbin,
was PGA president and Tom Crane

was retiring because of poor health.
Creasey enjoyed playing golf and
thought the PGA post would be paradise with two golf courses outside the
office. He soon learned different.

If Creasey had been Super Lawyer,
he could not have avoided being judged
wrong when he was right and right
when he was wrong by those of his employers who were divided into the Max
Elbin and Leo Fraser political camps.
Elbin as president believed that the
PGA should continue as an entity and
that differences between the home and
journeymen professionals could be settled within the house. Fraser was secretary when the internal conflict was
hottest, and succeeded Elbin as president. Fraser was for a compromise with
the dissatisfied tournament players,
turning them loose to operate the part
of pro business that did not have the
traditional PGA responsibility of service to the amateur golfers. Elbin and
his supporters insisted that the tournament players, if they were to be identified as Professional Golfers' Association members, either share the obligations and expenses or get out.

Elbin and Fraser were admirable,
able professionals, dedicated to the
PGA. Both of them were personable
men whose charm and dedication mag-
netized vigorous partisans. But secret
meetings of tournament players had
created suspicion and mistrust new to
the PGA, and this unhealthy atmosphere spread in the organization's official quarters. It took years to dissipate
this miasma and restore to the PGA
the wholesome condition of frank and
vigorous differences of opinion that had
helped build it.

But the PGA civil war wasn't about
golf. It was about money, and money
only. Golf had no more to do with the
split than if the argument had been

between two groups of horseshoe pitch-
ers—those who were going to country
fairs and pitching for fabulous $100
prizes and those who stayed home and
competed informally with other local
talent after supper and on Sunday af-
ternoons.

The split of the journeyman performers from the home pros probably
marked the end of the sentimental era
in American golf; the last time a sort
of sweetheart attachment to the game
was to figure in its commercial development. With the TPD golf was cash and
carry.

So, into a head-on political confrontation walked Bob Creasey, thinking
that he was to be like a tournament
player, getting paid for what he'd been
paying to do. As the man in the middle
he couldn't possibly come out happy
and healthy. However, by accident he
did a great service to the PGA: He was
there to be blamed for everything.
Creasey treated too many of the tournament stars as lucky caddies, and
many PGA members seemed to be prejudiced against him because he was
making more per annum than they
were. So when the TPD split happened,
it was his fault. Just why, nobody could
explain, except that he was blunt about
saying tournament players had been
brought into the big money on a pass
by PGA members, and he got into a
jam when the PGA and John MacArthur bumped nose-to-nose on the office
lease. There were also tax technicalities in which Creasey was censured for
guessing wrong, although he appeared
to have worked toward an acceptable
retirement program for club pros.

The pattern of organization followed
by the Tournament Players' Division
had been worked out in the main by
the PGA and had proved successful
with the golfing public, the press, and

television. Either the personalities of
dissident pros or the change in the atmosphere of golf from a game to a cold
business accounted for the difficulty of
adjustment.

At any rate, the idea of the PGA
executive director, the Tournament
Committee chairman, and the Tournament Bureau manager, which had
lighted the way of tournament golfers
from rags to riches, with Hagen as
drum major, was no longer acceptable.

The family fight that followed tar-
nished the image of the tournament
players more than could have been
imagined when the feuding started.
The most active brawlers seemed to be
players with little public appeal. These
comparatively anonymous parties were
actually pleasant and earnest fellows
who were surprised at getting more
money than they would have been paid
in pursuits away from print and public
view. The situation was confusing to
them; under the circumstances sound
judgment that would consider public
opinion was not to be expected.

It seemed to be the opinion of the
sports public—golfers and nongolfers—
that golf pros who complained about
getting $10,000 to $20,000 for four af-
ternoons that did not involve risk from
tackles, pitched balls, flaming automobiles, left hooks, or even mining coal
for that matter, were crybabies.

The more intelligent and successful
tournament players rightly feared that
the way the journeymen were handling
their case, which had some merit,
would alienate the public that had
given pro golfers high rank among professional athletes. They were right—
and they included Arnold Palmer and
Jack Nicklaus, two young men who had
their names on "pro-only" lines of clubs
that were showing promise of becoming
as profitable and popular as pro-only

lines bearing the names of Walter Hagen, Tommy Armour, and Ben Hogan.

The battling club pros ended those hopes. The sales of the two good new lines dropped abruptly. Palmer and Nicklaus, who had discreetly avoided leading troops in the professionals' civil war, were injured commercially as innocent bystanders.

Only for a few days was there much public interest in the pro quarrel. Bob Jones made the news when he counseled that the journeyman pros sensibly and swiftly settle their differences with the club professionals, as golf was primarily a participants' game and the professionals should be unified for the best interests of the amateur players who supported all the professionals. Another time there was amateur comment on the dispute was when members of the Burning Tree Club in Washington supported their professional, PGA president Max Elbin, lauding his service to golf and censuring the avaricious tournament professionals whose behavior they felt was contrary to the needs of golf and golfers.

Generally the attitude of private club golfers was that the journeymen were a favored class whose conduct was not up to the expected standard. Now many excellent clubs were reluctant to be host to Open championships, and the PGA split intensified an antipro feeling in that sector.

Most golfers were unconcerned about the journeyman pros' rebellion. The golfing public had little idea what the fight was about; neither did most of the pros. There'd been so much print about pro golfer millionaires that the ordinary golfer thought of the controversy as merely some millionaires wanting more money for easy work.

Only the baseball players in their short and senseless strike were able to get the sports public a bit more than casually interested in the issues involved. The baseball fans were entirely reconciled to a strike, but their cynical reaction—"Let 'em go on strike and stay out! Baseball is dying anyway"—forced baseball players and club owners to get together swiftly while they still had a business.

The PGA family split was undoubtedly the most serious slump in social status—whatever that is—that ever happened in sports. In this democracy and abroad, the tournament golf pros slumped from being guests at the first table with their bibs up, to the strata of professional wrestlers, who, although they are hardworking laborers, you probably wouldn't want your sister to marry. The change was severe, socially and economically. The rebels had blundered into public disrepute as just another greedy group. They were pleasant fellows, if not Phi Beta Kappas, but you can't have everything.

Obviously they needed to be restored to public acceptance, and quickly. Leo Fraser, who had been blamed for encouraging the split, came up with the right answer. He suggested Joseph C. Dey, Jr., as the commissioner of the Tournament Players' Division. Dey, formerly a sportswriter in New Orleans and Philadelphia and for years the executive director of the USGA, was the perfect front man for the best-run sports operation in the world—amateur or professional. USGA Executive Committee members traditionally have had extensive and successful business experience. Their association duties demanded considerable sacrifice of time and money, and they are not men with an urge to enjoy publicity. They needed someone to take charge of the USGA office work and fill in for association officials at a great many meet-

Joseph C. Dey, Jr. PGA

ings with other golf groups, when USGA official contact was mutually valuable.

Dey soon demonstrated his aptitude so well that some officials thought their new young man needed to be reminded he was outranked in the table of organization. A sharp little suggestion was all he needed. He became unquestionably discreet and valuable in effectively transmitting USGA policies; he also became an authority on the Rules of Golf. In addition to relieving the USGA officials of roadwork, Dey graduated to participation in USGA delegations consulting with the Royal and Ancient on the growing common problems resulting from golf's development as a closely joined, worldwide game. The moot subject of uniform golf ball specifications was one of these puzzling areas.

In his work as the USGA's Man in

the Window, Joe Dey had frequent contacts with the PGA nationally and sectionally. He came out of potentially dangerous situations smiling, unscratched, and usually with new friends.

When the PGA family quarrel was raging, the USGA, as might be expected, maintained an attitude of neutrality and studied indifference to the bad manners in the servants' quarters. Dey, as was becoming to a USGA employee, looked the other way. He had learned to conduct himself so carefully in delicate situations, his newspaper friends said, that he could walk across Niagara Falls on a rubber band.

Dey's $50,000 salary was a bargain for the journeyman pro golfers who needed a name to restore them to public favor. The golf pros were impeccably honest in their play. What they didn't realize was that their split with the parent body had been engineered without the slightest consideration for public relations, nor had their secret meetings given sportswriters the opportunity to present the position of the tournament specialists to the public. The players themselves were unaware that only about a dozen of the field in a tournament circuit event are known to the public that's paying to see the show.

Except for the Dey name and establishment of the TPD offices in New York, there wasn't really much of a change in the program of tournament management. The policies of tournament circuit development that the PGA had worked out by trial and error over the years had the TPD all set for going out into the big, rich world on its own. Player directors were elected by TPD members. There were four of them and three directors chosen from PGA officers. Three "Independent Directors representing the public interest" were named, indicating the journeymen had learned to mind their commercial manners in the presence of the people who pay. A Young Players' Advisory Council was also selected from the anonymous hopefuls to consult with the Tournament Policy Board. This was to avoid another revolution in case Big Names wanted to stay too long and eat too high at the first table.

Besides tournament players and PGA officials, the Tournament Policy Board included three businessmen of such sublime solvency and prominence that the journeymen—even the touring millionaires—would take off their caps and be silent in the presence of the triumvirate. They were perfect blockers in case Dey wanted to carry the ball. They were John D. Murchison of Dallas, J. Paul Austin of Atlanta, and George H. Love of Pittsburgh. Love had some acquaintance with professional golf, having brought into being the Laurel Golf Club near Ligonier, Pennsylvania, where the 1965 PGA Championship was played and where there had been a fervent desire to establish a summer championship something on the order of the Masters.

The TPD side of the divorce retained custody of Samuel E. Gates as counsel. An affable and adroit lawyer, Gates did all right by the journeymen, who were apparently setting up a tournament schedule and knocking down their own standing with the public.

When the agreement to split was made, the PGA turned over to the TPA a tremendous asset in the person of PGA tournament director Jack Tuthill. A former FBI agent, Tuthill was a quiet, competent, almost anonymous man in tournament golf and unquestionably the most competent man in arranging for a tournament and conducting it, including handling the emergencies that without his smart, strong management might explode from the sports section onto the front page. With Tuthill and his field staff and an emphatically able publicity staff at headquarters, the job of Commissioner Dey was immensely simplified.

When the TPD insisted on having its office in New York, the PGA continued to keep its headquarters in Florida, where it had first located, in Dunedin, as the caboose to a real-estate deal for a golf course to be used a couple of months in the winter. It continued to play the other man's game when John MacArthur brought it over to his Palm Beach Gardens development, then evicted it. By that time the PGA had forgotten why it was in Florida.

However, the PGA tournament program had taken a forward look. By the time television income became important, tournament golf had been fixed as a target of general sports interest. Later its TV rating advanced far beyond the point where only the National Open Championship and the Masters got attention.

Golf, although slow and spread over much ground, was well suited to television because of the intermittent excitement inherent in all phases of the game. Booming drives, long fairway irons, amazing recovery shots from bunkers, and well-executed approaches brightened the lens picture. And, of course, a putt that meant thousands of dollars on the last green gave TV programs more thrills than a track meet.

Television has also been charged with driving thousands of players away from the game because of the slow play, especially on the greens, of the tournament experts. While imitation of these tedious parties has not accounted for any noticeable improvement in putting, it has slowed golf play by about an hour per round since 1960. Though important in popularizing the game, television has never created a colorful reputation for a player or established a distinguished championship. Those achievements have been the work of the golf writers.

In its formative decade the PGA never envisioned anything like television as a promotion aid, but it always worked closely with the gifted reporters and writers who had a passion for the game. The PGA tournament circuit certainly was made by early golf writers about as much as by the professionals themselves and the PGA. Hal Sharkey, the *Newark News* reporter who made a pioneering trip to Southern California with the wandering pros and filed copy to Eastern newspapers, wrote the genesis of the tournament circuit. Then Bob Harlow became PGA Tournament Bureau manager and provided pro golf with the liveliest reporting talent in the field. Harlow was to American golf writers, including Bob Jones's "Boswell," O. B. Keeler, and the fluent and versatile Grantland Rice, what Bernard Darwin was to the British golf writers. Harlow discovered and encouraged "color" in tournament golfers; he made and abetted personalities.

Times change. The PGA's publicity men and their successors with the TPD continue to exercise their efforts and genius in writing up new heroes, but for some reason the PGA has never told the unique story of its home professionals as the leading businessmen in professional sports. Occasionally local stories would get into print on what a professional was doing as a businessman, instructor, or women's sports fashion sponsor or business educator. There would be golf business news in the press on these matters, but the PGA never realized what might be done nationally in acquainting the public with the accomplishments of its members in a gigantic sports business. As the leading business organization of golf, the PGA could not identify itself as a business authority.

Volumes of press releases that never were printed were sent to newspapers and magazines on winter competitions at the PGA courses. As national sports information this material was no more newsworthy than the winners of the ball sweepstakes at the pros' clubs. Little, if any, information was sent to newspapers on the nationwide PGA program of making thousands of pros and their assistants better businessmen and more useful to golf.

The annual PGA Merchandise Show has a strong effect on golf goods sales and on golf fashions for women and men, but only the golf business magazines publicize this event. The PGA seems officially unaware that there are business and women's pages as well as sports pages in newspapers. In the planning of national PGA publicity nothing has been made of the fact that golf professionals' business operations are worth approximately forty times the prize money of all PGA national and sectional tournaments. There are probably twenty-five times more PGA members intensely engaged in the business of golf than in competitive playing.

Because of individual contacts with newspaper, television, and radio people, the sections usually get far more coverage about the business of the professional than the PGA gets nationally. Likewise, the sectional merchandise shows get good publicity and draw crowds that make the displays effective preseason advertising for the pros.

In many ways the development of the

sections has been the biggest part of PGA growth after it got its foundation established. A number of the sections hired full-time men or women who functioned as business managers, regardless of the official titles held. It has often been suggested that the achievements of PGA headquarters would be more clearly identified if the man in charge were known as the PGA business manager. But the rapid and informative way in which the PGA national headquarters staff handles its work and its contacts with the press, the golfing public, and the manufacturers has always drawn praise.

In any case, it can honestly be stated that, in building on the framework of its crucial first ten years of existence, the policies of the PGA have generally proved to be sound and wise. Perhaps only in the split of the Tournament Players' Division and in its inability to publicize itself as a major sports business organization has the PGA failed to confirm its basic premise. And probably even the relationship the TPD retained with the PGA showed that the original plan was correct and that the separation was primarily the result of the times in putting tournament players in the vicinity of more money than they could comfortably handle. Already tournament players are forecasting that

their division will be back in the PGA as one of the sections. Show business isn't always a land of sunshine and roses even for the professionals who hit it rich.

The story of the PGA's progress since its shaky and uncertain beginning way back in 1916 has really been a remarkably successful one, considering the complexities of the gigantic growth in the business of golf and the fact that the PGA is operated as a sideline by conscientious men trained as athletes rather than as businessmen.

From the minutes of annual meetings, from bales of committee reports, magazines, and other printed material, and from countless individuals who were intimately connected with PGA history, the progress of the organization, and its problems and conflicts, will follow year by year until the time of the PGA and Tournament Players' Division split. There will also be some intervening chapters dealing with some of the memorable personalities and extraordinary sidelights that are so much a part of the wonderful world of golf. It should also be noted that in tracing the course of the PGA through the years a certain amount of repetition and duplication of material is almost unavoidable. But then, what's a mulligan or two among friends?

8

PGA Growing Pains Continue, Gates and the Steel Shaft Come In – and So Does the Depression

[1928, 1929, 1930]

THE story of the PGA is formally told in minutes of the annual meetings. The controversies that got into the record during the early years usually concerned territorial boundaries, applications for membership or reinstatement, and the development of a successful tournament circuit.

When certain rugged characters were denied PGA membership because of unbecoming conduct, they invariably had defenders who declared that the party in question had valid reasons for either his excessive thirst, chronic insolvency, unlucky love affairs, or congenital inefficiency. These discussions probably took up more time than was warranted, but they did a lot to establish a respectable standard of gentlemanly conduct for professional golfers. Bad manners that brought professional golfers into disrepute were not condoned whether the boor was a club professional or a journeyman. No fines

were necessary. The social "freeze" plus uncomfortable pairings and starting times soon had ill-mannered fellows behaving themselves.

Minutes of the PGA annual meetings were discreetly edited from the earlier days to 1936 by secretaries Herbert Strong, Alex Pirie, Ernest Anderson, Joe Mitchell, Jack Pirie, and R. W. Treacy. Then Tom Crane became executive director and so carefully edited the minutes that, without distorting the debates, he elevated the plane of parliamentary discussion enough to ease the way for Robert T. Creasey as executive director and Lloyd F. Lambert as the secretary who followed Crane in PGA management jobs. Even during the civil war between the club professionals and the touring pros many years later, the debates in print read no more dramatically than differences of opinion at a Parent-Teacher Association meeting.

Prior to 1928, minutes of the PGA annual meetings were kept in journals neatly and concisely recorded by secretaries who weren't excessively fond of writing. When court stenographers began recording the proceedings in 1928, more oratory got into type, but the substance was no more than might be expected from a lively collection of individualists who were not easily classified.

After the first four British-born PGA presidents, there was a great deal of political maneuvering, with sections vying to elect favorite sons and put home-bred professionals in command. The transition was inevitable, and in 1931 Charles W. Hall of the Country Club of Birmingham, Alabama, was elected president, although he had never been in the national official family before. He was a personable fellow, big, friendly, a good player, and so competent as a businessman that he became a bank director. Hall was reelected, and his two terms were critical but peaceful in preventing PGA members of Scottish, Irish, and Italian descent and the ethnically unaffiliated from trying to run the show. (This rancorous background never got on paper except in bills for room service in hotels where the PGA annual meetings were held.)

From the few handwritten pages covering the first annual meeting, the PGA yearly meeting minutes and committee reports grew until they filled eight hundred mimeographed pages in the 1960's. The minutes of the Executive Committee accounted for another bale of typewritten matter nobody read completely. And as one damages his sight and tests his endurance pawing through these reports, it's interesting to note how many times the club professionals' and tournament players' differences apparently were settled with mu-

tual satisfaction. But the word never seemed to get around. Players at some tournament would get together, and when they heard what their representatives had decided at the PGA annual meeting, the fight would be on again.

The proceedings of the PGA annual meetings and the Executive Committee meetings became too much to be digested. Two business management organizations tried to solve the problem but apparently only managed to get the PGA office work simplified on a sound business basis. The minutes of earlier annual meetings were boiled down by R. W. Treacy when he was PGA secretary in 1933 and the three years following.

In 1928, the twelfth annual meeting of the PGA was held at the Hotel Hollenden, Cleveland. It was the last of the three terms of Alex Pirie as president and the last administration of the PGA to be dominated by foreign-born members. W. H. Way and J. A. Patterson were vice-presidents, and Joseph R. Mitchell was secretary. Jack Mackie, who'd been the association's second president in 1920 and had been elected treasurer in 1923, was also elected to that post in 1928, and continued through 1939, when George Jacobus completed his sixth term as the PGA's sixth president.

Whether or not Mackie was an office-holder, all PGA expenses had to pass his examination in the early years. At the 1928 annual meeting the twenty-seven delegates from twenty-four sections felt rich when Mackie reported that the PGA had a balance of $6,609. Of the $4,000 "war fund" raised in 1928, only $50 was paid out, for a purpose not mentioned. During the year the Benevolent Fund had paid out $50 a month to a widow with three children. She was not identified, and this was O.K. with the comrades of her late husband so long as Jack Mackie was handling the cash. There were critics who said that to get money from the Benevolent or Relief funds of the PGA a pro had to be so long dead the payment wouldn't do anybody any good. But the evidence is to the contrary; Mackie was tough but compassionate, and when cash was urgently needed, he paid out what the PGA could afford, often supplementing payments from his own pocket.

Before the PGA got into the group insurance plans common with most organizations now, collections for afflicted members and indigent families were common. The Scots, reputedly a parsimonious people, proved to be generous. Most recipients at that stage of the PGA's history naturally were of Scottish origin, and there was sharp comment about this. Mackie, the man under fire, replied with a concise summary of those who had charitably kicked in and those who had not, concluding with, "An empty barrel makes the most noise." End of debate.

The Benevolent Fund money came mainly from royalties paid for use of the PGA name on club heads (generally iron heads) because many professionals wanted their own names on wood clubs that they could finish into works of art. Imported iron heads were being replaced by American manufacturers' machine-forged production. For the calendar year 1927, PGA club and ball revenue from manufacturers was $81,948. Of that amount the greater part came from royalties on 23,092 dozen balls. The PGA name was stamped on one pole, the manufacturer's name on the other.

The recently legalized steel shaft was authorized for PGA clubs made by Spalding, MacGregor, Wilson,

Wright and Ditson, Burke, and Wanamaker. The matched sets of woods and irons that came in with steel shafts were slow starters, according to reports at the annual meeting. And members felt that the steel-shafted clubs had increased the competition of chain stores and other retailers getting into the market the professionals had established.

There was talk about starting a PGA nationwide cooperative buying operation on the order of that of the British PGA. It was noted that the Mid-West Golfers Supply Company, a buying organization formed by forty professionals around Kansas City, was doing fairly well in a limited area but running into difficulties with warehousing and distribution, although the backing of the members had prevented credit problems.

Winston, Strawn, and Shaw, a Chicago law firm headed by a former president of the USGA, incorporated the PGA, and with its annual proceedings being printed for the first time, the PGA began to get organized as a business. In this regard, officials and delegates at the 1928 annual meeting argued about whether the association's financial statement should be printed and sent to members and the press or just sent to the sections.

Considering the unquestioned integrity of PGA officials, plus the bonding formality of common business practice, it is puzzling that PGA annual financial statements were regarded almost as state secrets until William Wotherspoon was elected PGA treasurer in 1928. A native of Monifieth, Scotland, he came over to a pro job in Kansas City, then became pro of the newly formed Southern Hills Country Club of Tulsa. Wotherspoon promptly began educating PGA members in the fi-

William Wotherspoon. PGA

nances of their organization. By having pie charts showing income and expenses printed in *The Professional Golfer,* sent to all members, and otherwise freely circulated, Wotherspoon's report answered the usual questions: "What's the PGA doing for me?" "How do we stand?" "Why should we pay higher dues?"

Wotherspoon also stressed that if professionals could understand the annual financial statements of their own clubs, they'd be better qualified to improve club operations. In theory his point was valid. In practice, though, until two nationwide firms began specializing in club accounting and helped the Club Managers' Association's campaign to get club accounting standardized, country club financial statements were murky—concealing honest indifference, incompetence, and carelessness about keeping up with changing conditions. This all added up to poor man-

agement of clubs whose members had to be good businessmen to be able to afford membership.

But the Wotherspoon innovation continued until the PGA presented its annual financial statement as freely as the USGA, the Western Golf Association, and other amateur golf associations. However, Wotherspoon's belief that free circulation of PGA financial figures would prove educational to all professionals was unfounded.

Nobody got down to the simple business basis of examining the figures, so the argument continued to separation forty years later. This seems incredible in a business where the players have the responsibility of knowing the figures and keeping their own scores, but failure to refer to available figures exploded the PGA civil war. Then, after peace had been restored and the divisions had become compatible, the Tournament Players' Division of the PGA got coy about its own financial statement.

At the 1928 meeting there was evidence that the association's decade of campaigning for tournament golf was beginning to register. Willie Hunter, Southern California delegate, and PGA vice-president J. A. Patterson presented bids for the PGA Championship of $12,000 from the Los Angeles area (provided an acceptable championship course could be obtained) and $10,400 from the Santa Barbara Chamber of Commerce. Previously, if there had been just one offer for the PGA Championship, it was quickly and gratefully accepted. This time the Hillcrest Country Club at Los Angeles got the 1929 PGA Championship, the first to be held on the Pacific Coast. It was played December 2 to 7, and Leo Diegel won, defeating P. O. Hart, Herman Barron, Gene Sarazen, Walter Hagen,

Leo Diegel. AG

and Johnny Farrell, all by comfortable margins.

This same year an argument that has never ended popped into print for the first time; it concerned the touchy business of exemptions from qualifying for PGA championships. British-born members were against them. Willie Kidd, longtime professional at Interlachen in Minneapolis, said, "The game of golf is not what I did yesterday—it's what I do today." Laurie Ayton, who left the pro job at the Evanston Golf Club to return to Scotland, remarked, "I'm also a member of the British PGA and have played in their championships and have seen former champions who didn't qualify but made no complaint. In golf you have to take your chances. Ease the qualifying and you'll see the day when men who are not worthy to be champions win on exemptions."

It was also suggested that the USGA have sectional qualifying rounds for the National Open and increase National Open prize money so that professionals would be playing for substantially more than the total of their Open entry fee. The PGA was able to get both suggestions adopted and patterns established for the decided benefit of tournament players.

It was about this time that PGA national officials were finding that the work of the rapidly growing organization took more time and money than they could afford in justice to their families and their jobs. Hence the talk about hiring a business manager or commissioner along the lines of Judge Kenesaw Mountain Landis, who had

been hired by organized baseball to revive and discipline the game. Landis
was tough and smart and weathered
well with the gentle, trusting souls of
the American sports-loving public, so
naturally PGA officials hoped for someone of his integrity to whom they could
pass their holy trust. But they had no
clear idea of how the proposed commissioner was to be paid. Since the PGA
now had 1,897 members, it was suggested that dues be increased to $10 a
year. This was done despite a delegate's
plea that one of his section's members
had complained that he was working
hard to make $2,000 a year.

"It would cost us probably $25,000
a year to hire a man of the Landis
type," President Pirie told the 1928 assembly, "and you couldn't put that
kind of a man in the dump of an office
we have in New York."

"Sandy" Pirie was a man who belonged to the spirit rather than the
realities of a commercial sport. He and
men like him were kindly, industrious,
and far from their birthplace in a troublesome and fast-moving land they had
enriched by their goodness. Pirie's
"Now, gentlemen" aborted many a
PGA brawl that promised to bust heads
and furniture. He was professional at
Old Elm, a for-men-only, ultraexclusive
club in northern suburban Chicago,
and he thought of his members as his
family. They admired the faithful,
competent Pirie, but when he retired
it was not any appreciable aid from his
club that helped pay the bills of his
long illness. Regardless of their affluence, in those days club members just
didn't know any better. It was far different from today when gentlemen
sportsmen provide retirement benefits
for people who have served them long
and well. To its credit, the PGA quietly
took care of some of the costly medical

expenses of the fine man who had done
so much for the organization.

While the PGA pension plan was
still a long way off Jack Mackie summarized the progress and the future of
the association as follows: "In 1920 we
had 400 members. This year we have
about 1,900. It took Moses forty years
to bring the children of Israel out of
the desert into the promised land. You
will have to look ahead ten years before
you get 2,000 golfers paying $50 a year
dues."

Then Hagen was announced as captain of the Ryder Cup team of 1929 to
play (and be defeated by the British) at
Moortown, Leeds. A couple of places
were left open on the team to be filled
by players who showed well before the
sailing date. Not recorded in the first
printed proceedings of a PGA annual
meeting was the customary formality
of Fred Brand leading the lads in sing-
ing "Auld Lang Syne" at the conclusion of the yearly gatherings.

In 1929 the PGA faced the problem
of building Southern membership.
There were approximately 5,000 golf
courses in the United States then, with
about 2,000 of them nine-hole courses.
A 1928 survey had indicated that the
average eighteen-hole club pro shop
had sales of less than $12,000 a year,
while the nine-hole clubs averaged annual sales of about $2,500. No decided
improvement was evident in 1929, but
obviously the pro's salary, his lesson income, and his club-cleaning and storage net had made his job worth keeping. In contrast, assistants' salaries were
not much more than a good, steadily
employed caddie could make.

Considering the number of clubs in
the United States, the PGA had a
pretty good representation with 2,022
members of all classes, the great majority being Class A. Of the entire

membership, according to the report of Treasurer Jack Mackie, only 581 hadn't paid dues for 1929.

The 1929 annual meeting was held in Atlanta, the hometown of the idolized Bobby Jones, the youth the pros most desired to beat on the field of honor. A genial local professional, Howard Beckett, was head of the host committee, and he saw to it that his visiting colleagues were educated in the qualities of Georgia corn, which the temperate Scots of the conclave pronounced a palatable and wholesome refreshment after a hard day's work.

President Pirie urged the delegates to be realistic about the changing economic picture, which would certainly not be limited to the effect of the switch from the hickory to the steel shaft. He proudly commented on the golf playing equipment market, built and dominated by professionals, which he reported might amount to $40 million in 1929 retail prices. (This was a minor figure compared with sales that pros would have in future years. Before this book was put into type, pro-shop sales for a year had already reached $250 million. One professional, whose club has two courses, is doing $400,000 a year in pro-shop sales and is providing convenience and a variety of quality merchandise priced under the usual specialty shop markup.)

There was noisy debate at the 1929 meeting on whether the pro was better off having the shop as a full concession and being entirely on his own as a merchant, as well as an instructor, caddie master, and manager of golf operations, or by having the club guarantee him a satisfactory annual income along with taking care of the salaries, inventory, financing, and risk. The question still continues, with the decision generally in favor of the pro's being on his own

and making out of the job whatever he can. Usually that catch-as-catch-can system also worked out better for the club as well as for the professional, although it meant that the pro had to use his own money for the club's service.

At the smaller, more exclusive clubs, such as Old Elm north of Chicago where Pirie was pro, the concession basis would be painful. There was no chance of the pro's coming out in the black because shop sales were minimal. Alex Pirie had about a hundred members, all of whom belonged to one of several other golf clubs; hence, the sensible thing in his position was to deduct shop sales profits from a substantial guarantee and pay himself the rest.

Parallel situations continue. In recent years, when PGA convention delegates and Tournament Committee members agreed to prohibit PGA tournament circuit play at golf establishments where the pro did not have shop concessions, comparatively few courses were affected. They were the resort payplay courses. Exclusive private clubs where professionals were on a satisfactory income basis made it plain the last thing they wanted was a tournament, so being denied one was not cruel and unusual punishment. To that their professionals agreed.

Since the 1929 PGA annual meeting was held shortly after the stock-market crash, the delegates naturally worried about what was going to happen to golf's big spenders. The pro market had been quick to respond to Wall Street's easy money. Club members who were riding high in the market bought new sets of clubs for themselves, their families, and as gifts to others rather new to golf. Because the steel shaft was a novelty, it became a popular gift item in spending the tape profits.

But luckily, not everybody was playing the market. There were so many new players that 1930 was a good year in golf sales. Only in 1931 and 1932 did the bottom drop out of golf sales, and in 1933 a number of new clubs that were planned as deluxe community playgrounds went broke while some vanished forever.

Older pros weren't caught by the market crash. The elder Scots had never believed that money came as easily as they'd been told it came via Wall Street. Luckily for the younger pros, few of them had had enough spare cash to bet themselves into deep-red debt playing the market. But until the dust from the market crash settled, the PGA delegates faced an urgent employment problem. They discussed whether to become unionized as with Actors Equity or even the plumbers, some of whose union members then, as now, were earning far more per hour than a master professional who was a PGA Class A member.

Cooperative buying was again considered. Professionals were said to be retailing 70 percent of the golf goods sold in the United States and having problems making profits. The Midwest section cooperative venture started the previous year had narrowed down to nine professionals participating. Free golf balls were being given away as advertising come-ons. Losing a considerable volume of benchmade, hickory-shafted clubs and having them replaced in shop inventory by factory-made clubs had members wanting four or five brands of clubs stocked. That meant tying up too much of the pro's "good credit" money without improving his position as an authority who could expertly fit clubs to each individual's needs.

There were twenty-five delegates representing the following sections: Carolina, Central New York, Illinois, Indiana, Kentucky, Metropolitan, Michigan, Mid-Atlantic, Midwest, Minnesota, New England, Nebraska, Northeastern New York, Northern California, Ohio, Oklahoma, Pacific Northwest, Pacific Southwest, Philadelphia, Southeastern, Texas, Tri-State, Western New York, and Wisconsin. The Kentucky section, which had only nine members, boasted that all of them were paid up. Sections were allowed two delegates if each paid the expenses of one man to the annual meeting. One delegate's expenses came out of the national treasury. Convention expenses were on an austerity basis.

At the 1929 meeting official note was taken for the first time of the idea that blossomed into the PGA's big annual Merchandise Show, which eventually began at the PGA National Golf Club at Dunedin and expanded at the PGA headquarters at Palm Beach Gardens. There were also merchandise exhibits at annual meetings of several sections, and efforts made at Las Vegas and Los Angeles to extend the success of the PGA's big show early in the year at Palm Beach Gardens. At the Atlanta gathering, small as it was, enough salesmen were present to suggest to the foresighted that the pro salesmen's shopping should be organized and coordinated with marked savings of time and money.

The PGA had so much urgent work to do and so little money to work with that it was proposed to raise the annual dues from $10 to $50. Discussion was stormy. There was much to be said against increasing dues, but the majority was determined to move ahead. After considering a budget for progress, delegates voted the increase.

If—a big *if*—the PGA could finance

its pressing needs, a committee on raising dues (Willie Kidd, chairman) planned spending as follows: business administrator, $10,000; district organizers (three at $3,500), $10,500; clerical help (four at $1,800), $7,200; office rent and light, $4,000; stationery and printing, $2,000; telephone and telegrams, $1,500; travel expenses, $10,000; and miscellaneous, $3,500.

The careful dreamers even broke down "miscellaneous" to medals, $300; auditor, $250; tournament expenses, $400; Executive Committee expenses, $2,000; and "other." Tournament expenses were figured on the basis of: Ryder Cup, $2,500; PGA Championship, $5,500; and Benevolent Fund, $6,000.

Against these expenses of $62,500, the budgeted revenue was $62,350 for 1,247 Class A members at dues of $50 each.

That budget, as with other plans of mice and men, gang aft agley. Sections threatened to withdraw if the dues were boosted. A lot of Cokes, tea, and "Gawgia" corn couldn't oil through the dues raise. Some delegates said many of their members were talking about quitting even at $10 per year. Joe Devaney of the Michigan section reported that members of that section had threatened to resign if dues were raised and was told, "O.K., the rest of us will form a new section of professionals who want to go first class."

The 1929 Ryder Cup matches, the first Ryder Cup matches abroad, and the 1929 PGA Championship at Hillcrest Country Club, Los Angeles, put the association in show business, although that development wasn't realized at the time. The British–United States professional match, after being played unofficially at Gleneagles in 1921 and Wentworth in 1926, was adopted by the PGA of Britain and the United States and officially began when the American team defeated the British at Worcester, Massachusetts, in June, 1927, for the trophy presented by a British seed merchant.

In the 1929 matches at Moortown, Leeds, the American team, again headed by Hagen, took a beating, losing six matches, winning four, and halving two. But it was a gala loss, and the pain was eased by Hagen, Farrell, and Diegel finishing one-two-three in the British Open at Muirfield. Hagen at 292 was six strokes ahead of Farrell.

There were fund-raising exhibitions at Woodland (near Boston), Chester, Pennsylvania, Pinehurst, and Wilshire (at Los Angeles). Jones, Glenna Collett, Johnny Farrell, Gene Sarazen, Helen Hicks, Hagen, Farrell, Leo Diegel, Willie Hunter, George Von Elm, Horton Smith, and others played matches as though the Redcoats were firing at the bridge at Lexington. They all raised more than $6,000, and U.S. golf manufacturers kicked in $2,650. Henderson and Company, a seed company that was putting grass on American golf courses, PGA sections, and amateur associations and clubs kicked in around $2,000, so the first U.S. Ryder Cup team to play overseas didn't have to swim to the first tee or back home.

But what has been bypassed in charting the progress of golf in American social and economic history is the game's association with the movies. Hillcrest as the host of the 1929 PGA Championship was inevitable. Hillcrest was smarter than the rest of the clubs that sniffed at the PGA Championship as exceedingly small potatoes.

Hollywood's trend setters sensed that golf was the coming thing. As culture wended its way westward on the Santa Fe *Chief*, cinema moguls lolled and pontificated in golf knickers and sports jackets of costly wool and admirable buttonhole work, with a herd of blonds and yes-men. Their knowledge of ancient and honorable pastimes was not comprehensive, but they knew with certainty that golf had the status-symbol glamour of polo, tennis, and other rich men's games. It was royalty's cup of tea, too, judging from the photographs of Walter Hagen on the fairways with the Prince of Wales.

Hollywood created the picture of the country club set, and the Hollywood hierarchy and its highly paid hirelings lived it up in the sunny playground they had devised. It was a far cry from the bleak Scottish shores where the clubhouse was a dark little pub, and the new school of American professionals was an important part of the tinseled package. At least that's what many of the youngsters in the Hollywood wonderland believed. A caddie yesterday, a Hagen playing with the wealthy and beautiful tomorrow. And all that big money for having fun!

The older pros didn't live a moment in that dreamland. Not after the crash when some of their fellows seemed to have trouble paying $10 a year for PGA dues. It was a rough world, too, for the dreaming lads when they couldn't meet the payment on their shiny new cars, when manufacturers wouldn't ship balls or clubs until they got "something on account," and when big spenders who cut the young pros in on $100 Nassau winnings dropped out of the club, broke. Yet a hundred young professionals were after each job that opened.

The year of the big bust was a year of planning by the deans of the PGA. Tough times were nothing strange to them; they had to have hope to keep in the pro golf business, and there was hope that the PGA by nursing encouraging tournaments could provide opportunities that would develop more Walter Hagens. President Pirie appointed a Tournament Committee consisting of Tommy Armour, Al Espinosa, and J. A. Patterson. Mrs. Armour and Mrs. Espinosa began writing letters to tournament sponsors, present and potential; they produced a coordinated schedule in the Southwest and West for the winter, and with their tactful and compelling paperwork pioneered what the PGA Tournament Bureau was to do later.

Purses in 1929 were nearly $150,000. The Junior Chamber of Commerce of Los Angeles became the sponsor of the Los Angeles Open and worked so energetically and successfully at the job that other Junior Chambers of Commerce got into golf tournament promotion. Jaycees conducted Open tournaments at St. Paul, Minnesota, Phoenix, Arizona, and Greensboro, North Carolina, that became fixtures. They also staged PGA championships at Buffalo and Milwaukee and sponsored other Open tournaments that contributed to the growth of the PGA circuit. In fact the Jaycees played an important part in making tournament golf a going business. The Junior Chamber of Commerce's way of organizing, financing, and managing a tournament, with the immense amount of free work done by the young community leaders and their wives, established the pattern of tournament business operation generally used today.

In 1929, Hal Sharkey agreed to manage the tournament circuit, such as it was, with his salary and expenses to be paid out of 10 percent of the purse winnings of the players. This arrangement was revised because too many players didn't pay. Then the PGA proposed that the sponsors deduct 10 percent as the Sharkey management fee, but the sponsors refused. They preferred to pay the advertised prize money in full.

Sharkey was covering winter events for the *Newark News* and with his salary, plus his revenue from supplying Jersey Club event scores to New York newspapers in the summer, the easygoing and industrious Sharkey wasn't fussy about pay. That was fine with the pioneer tournament circuit players; they weren't fussy about paying.

With the PGA Championship of 1929 at Hillcrest, the Los Angeles Open, and other Southern California, Texas, and Arizona events away from the snow, and some action handy in Mexico, the players who could afford the fare switched from Florida to the Southwest. As a bonus Sharkey arranged for a tournament in Honolulu with "appearance money" provided for the "leading" players.

You can readily imagine that Sharkey's choice of "leading" players raised hackles in the ranks. But as J. A. Patterson commented in reviewing the PGA's tournament promotion with Sharkey in 1929, "God help the man who has to go through all the grief that man has in his job."

Sharkey wound up in the red for his first year's labor as Big Daddy of the tournament circuit. Few if any of today's harvesters of a multimillion-dollar annual purse have ever heard of Hal Sharkey, the plump young reporter who started many a caddie on the road to riches, but even with all his imagination and his sales talk about golf's being America's new national sport, Sharkey never dreamed about making much money out of what he did for golf. Nobody in PGA work ever did think about money for their toils for golf and golfers. These men were in

love with golf. Jack Mackie, formally to be paid $600 a year as PGA secretary, turned the money over to the Benevolent Fund, of which he was a trustee.

After annual dues had been lifted from $10 to $50 at the 1929 annual meeting, the PGA went into 1930 as though professional golf were knee-deep in dollars. Nobody seemed to worry that the dues increase might reduce the membership. This hopeful attitude was justified by the picture presented at the 1930 annual meeting, which was held at the Palmer House in Chicago, November 17 to 19.

Alex Pirie was again president. His cousin Jack was secretary; vice-presidents were Willie Ogg, W. H. (Bert) Way, Charlie Hall, and John R. Inglis. J. B. Mackie remained as treasurer and perennial watchdog of the cash box.

Charles Hall, a newcomer to the official family, was a native of Leeds, England, who got his first U.S. job as assistant to Bob Simpson at Blue Mound in Milwaukee, then went to the Nashville Country Club as pro, and eventually to the Country Club of Birmingham. John R. Inglis, a home-bred who was professional at the Fairview Country Club, Elmsford, New York, was the educator of many fine young professionals, and for years president of the Metropolitan section of the PGA.

The main attraction at the annual meeting was Albert Gates, a corporation lawyer of Chicago, who had been Western Golf Association president in 1907, 1908, 1921, and 1922. He had been hired by the PGA Executive Committee early in 1930 as the association's business administrator and legal adviser at a salary of $80,000 for five years, and took office May 1.

Gates was a handsome man in his lively sixties who loved golf and wanted to do something for the game. He had more money than he ever would need. After screening a dozen applicants and being politely turned down by five or six more prominent amateurs, the association's officers and Executive Committee decided Gates was their man. The decision was not unanimous. The New York Metropolitan and New England sections wanted an Eastern man, and the Pacific Coast sections didn't much care for the commissioner arrangement.

Alex Pirie prevailed upon Gates to take the post, which proved to call for more work and responsibility than Gates had contemplated. Jack Mackie approved the choice of Gates, although he knew this meant moving PGA headquarters from New York to Chicago. Along with leaving the old homestead —that drab and disordered little office on Fifth Avenue—it meant separation from P. C. Pulver, who'd been in a secretarial, publicity, and editorial capacity with the PGA almost since the organization and its magazine *The Professional Golfer* were started. Pulver began golf reporting in 1895 with the *New York Daily Advertiser,* then went to the *Evening Sun,* where he wrote a golf column for twenty-five years. He was a good golfer and valuable to the PGA. He lived in New Jersey with his wife and an invalid son, and in presenting a case for a good separation arrangement with Pulver, Pirie referred to professionals who had been with clubs ten to twenty years, then were let go on short notice without a nickel. He hoped the PGA wouldn't follow the same poor example.

Mrs. Irene Blakeman, who was on the job six long days a week in New York and was the PGA office force, went along to Chicago when the associ-ation moved into the First National Bank Building there. Without Mrs. Blakeman's knowledge of the PGA's problems and personalities, Administrator Gates would have had far more headaches than he got—and he got more than enough.

As one expression of the Gates plan to show the PGA how to operate as a business, the 1930 meeting saw a financial statement from April 1, 1930, through October 31, 1930, plus another sttaement on the Tournament Bureau Fund from July 1, 1930, through October 31, 1930. The increased dues were coming in well, and there had been no drop-off in membership. The Tournament Bureau confusion was being diminished.

The cash score:

	April 1 Balance	Receipts	Disbursements	Balance
General Fund	$ 4,735	$58,492	$44,206	$19,020
Benevolent Fund	15,777	3,707	6,425	12,999
Tournament Bureau		5,713	1,825	3,888
War Fund	4,267	85		4,352
Ryder Cup	260			260

Dues receipts for the period were $42,881.

The PGA Championship was also looking a little better as a potential moneymaker. The 1930 Championship had been played at Fresh Meadow Country Club, Great Neck, New York, with Armour defeating Sarazen 1 up in a thrilling combination of psychological warfare and golfing skill.

Fresh Meadow's club members each paid $10 for tickets and briskly promoted other sales. The PGA got $5,000 in gate receipts. Entry fees were $2,185. The PGA got $750 as its share of the program revenue, and the tournament program, which made its initial appearance at the National Open of 1928 at Chicago's suburban Olympia Fields, was an adaptation of an advertising idea effectively used when labor unions were running balls, picnics, or other fiestas. Advertisers were assured by the space salesmen that "the boys" would show appreciation of the printed complimentary greetings, accompanied by a goodwill offering in cash.

The polite revision of the friendly fund-raising was conducted by Joe and Herb Graffis and Jack Fulton, Jr., with Olympia Fields and the three young men splitting the net. It compared favorably with admission revenue at that championship, which had an extra day's sale when Johnny Farrell defeated Bob Jones in the play-off.

At the Open the next year, the program-advertising selling was repeated, with proceeds being divided between the club and the publishers. The program was so profitable that the USGA cut itself in as a partner and in succeeding years took a fat amount as its share, with the host clubs getting more. The program publishers at the championships and at lesser tournaments where the union-dance program-advertising gimmick was employed did very well for themselves. From the $750 start at Fresh Meadow, the PGA Championship program grew until, in one year, it brought over $100,000 into the association.

That initial report of the PGA under Gates's direction showed the net cost of the championship was only $2,500. There was another bright spot in the championship that year when the Rodman Wanamaker trophy came out of hiding. Nobody knew where or how it had been lost (which was typical), but it was discovered when somebody snooped into a big box at the Walter Hagen Golf Company ware-

house in Detroit. Hagen had won his fifth and last PGA Championship in 1927; he'd also won it the three previous years.

The Tournament Bureau tangles were being straightened out, but Hal Sharkey had "had it." He had collected some money from players who were willing to pay for his help and some more from tournament sponsors who needed his promotional and management aid. He turned over $5,435, minus $435 for work he'd done for PGA headquarters. With that $5,000 from Sharkey, plus $690 the St. Paul Open had paid the Tournament Bureau for the services of the bureau's newly acquired Bob Harlow, the Tournament Bureau was off and running.

It wasn't a smooth start by any means. After a little more than five months, Gates told the convention, "You see before you a man with more gray hairs than I hope any of you will ever have, and I venture to say that half of them are there because of the Tournament Bureau. It has been that department of your work that has caused me more grief than any other feature."

There was sharp controversy about the tournament players getting far more out of the PGA than the home pros. The outspoken J. T. Shea, a New England delegate, remarked, "We all are paying five times last year's dues to increase money for fellows who always are crying and won't pay to help themselves in their own department of golf." His sentiments were echoed by other delegates. This was at a time when few pros were playing specialists; most had to depend principally on club jobs, and getting away from their clubs to play in tournaments was a problem.

This points up the fact that the PGA at that date, and even earlier, was already a family divided. At the 1930 meeting, George Sargent had suggested that "the PGA name be changed to Golf Instructors' and Players' Association of America. There are two distinct kinds of men in our organization: the instructor class who develop the players who make the game and business and which is the major class of our membership; then there is the group of high-class players who are the advertising fellows. They get the most publicity. The instructors should have more recognition."

History, always a pleasant exercise in second-guessing, makes remarks such as Sargent's tragically prescient—and to be disregarded at the PGA's peril. He was about forty years ahead of his time in contemplating a division that ultimately cost enough money in lawyers' fees alone to run all PGA activities for many years, and which also apparently did little to advance the business interests of the playing specialists or the home pros. Sargent was even further ahead in his suggestion that the instructor and home professional be accorded due recognition. Despite the home professional's being the key figure in the biggest commercial sports development in the United States, forty years after George Sargent's advice the PGA had yet to organize a department to make known the nature and extent of his status as a business authority. In the interim George's son Harold had become the twelfth president of the PGA and one of the most successful professionals in the world in serving his members by pro-shop merchandising.

But in 1930 the big-business dream was far ahead of pro imagination. That year Jones completed his Grand Slam, playing hickory-shafted clubs. What the steel shaft was going to do to pro-shop sales, nobody dared to guess, but

what Jones was doing to golf, millions and millions knew. Even in retrospect, Jones continues to rank with veteran sportswriters as well as with golfers as the Number One ideal sports idol. He was the Frank and Dick Merriwell of the All-American Boy sagas when athletes played for fun and glory. In victory and defeat, in public and private life, Jones conducted himself like a true champion.

In 1930, at twenty-eight, Jones was through with competitive golf, and his retirement figured in numerous discussions at the PGA annual meeting. There was talk about combining the National Open and PGA championships. The PGA was on a match-play basis because the British PGA Championship had been that way for years, while the National Open at stroke play had been making money ever since 1922, when admission was first charged.

"What makes the Open a money-maker?" asked Willie Ogg, a vice-president.

Treasurer Jack Mackie answered: "Bobby Jones!"

The stroke play versus match play argument continued annually, with the USGA's National Open far ahead of the PGA as a profitable show until 1958, when Dow Finsterwald won it with 276 at the Llanerch Country Club in suburban Philadelphia.

As Tournament Bureau manager of the PGA, Bob Harlow was to prove the founder of professional golf as it is today. He was the son of a New England minister, a graduate of the University of Pennsylvania, and his parents hoped he would become an evangelist. He did —for professional golf, and that was one of the luckiest breaks pro golf all over the world ever got.

Harlow had been in newspaper work in Pennsylvania, Massachusetts, and

Bob Harlow. AG, courtesy of Mrs. Robert E. Harlow

New York. He quit his job with the Associated Press in New York to concentrate on business management of Walter Hagen when Hagen wanted to get more exhibition dates and H. B. ("Dickie") Martin, a veteran New York newspaperman who had represented Hagen for years, didn't want to risk a steady income on The Haig. "Business management" of Hagen by Harlow was a loose and poetic use of the term.

Bob Harlow thought that every player owed the game first consideration, and by insisting on that policy put professional tournament golf and golfers beyond the reach of grasping promoters and their eternal query: "What's in it for me?" His start was stormy, his in-between years were rocky, and his finish as Tournament Bureau manager came after a political brawl. But his plans for professional tourna-

ment golf were brilliantly imaginative and his attachment to the game a never-ending love affair.

When Harlow came to the PGA job on May 1, 1930, he was accused of being a "dictator," insisting on "this and that" from tournament sponsors. The stories were spread by sportswriters who had not troubled to learn the facts. Later on, even the quiet, slim youngster Horton Smith was tagged a "dictator" by a Los Angeles writer and a PGA official for repeating what Harlow demanded from tournament sponsors as PGA services.

The Harlow plan was that the bureau provide a tournament organization pattern; publicity service in print and promotion talks by players and Harlow; scoreboard personnel; instructions to scorekeepers; marshals; locker room and meals; general instructions; course condition; tee and cup placement; and transportation and housing cooperation. There was no marked change in the procedure, but Harlow convinced sponsors that the service eased work and got results. Not every sponsor paid, but enough of them did to provide help for the PGA in financing the growth of the tournament circuit.

What kept sponsors from going all the way with the Harlow payment plan for PGA services was the bureau's inability to guarantee an attractive field of good players. "Appearance" money guarantees didn't solve the problem. When $100 was made nearly a standard fee for better players, some of them wanted $200. Bob Harlow reported that among cities interested in holding PGA tournaments were Omaha, Denver, Colorado Springs, Seattle, Vancouver, Spokane, Tacoma, Phoenix, and "several in Texas." He also said he hadn't been paid a cent by the PGA for about six months' work.

Gates incorporated the PGA in 1930 as a "not for profit" organization. Use of the PGA mark on clubs and balls had only recently been trademarked, and *The Professional Golfer* was copyrighted as the name of the association's magazine. Gates was getting the house in order.

The American Sports Publishing Company, which had been publishing *The Professional Golfer,* was paid $3,468 due it when the magazine was moved to Chicago. Circulation was increased from 1,300 to 4,000, with club officials being placed on a complimentary list. The advertising rate was $150 a page, and the magazine was losing money. The PGA asked Joe and Herb Graffis, publishers of *Golfdom,* to publish *The Professional Golfer,* but they declined. They believed it would be unwise for the PGA to risk compromising its independence by making any outside publishing alliances.

Willie Ogg urged stronger bonds between section headquarters and the national headquarters and pointed out that shortly after the PGA had been formed, a New England Professional Golfers' Organization had broken away on its own and incorporated. However, when hot heads cooled, the house divided was brought together in less than a year.

Although the slow-motion form pictures of Hagen, Vardon, and Joyce Wethered that George Sargent made (mainly in England) cost the PGA $5,227 in a lean year, there was no griping about the start of the PGA educational program. In watching the films, each PGA member thought he saw something new for instructing his pupils or got confirmation of his own ideas. But George Sargent himself wasn't sure what the pictures showed. Jones had the straight left arm that was

to be a style mark of the new school. Vardon and Hagen didn't, yet all of them came into the ball on normal strokes from the inside out. Golf films were a risky business. Warner Brothers had signed Jones for a series of features that pros at the 1930 meeting were sure would bring Bob at least $1 million. They didn't. The moviegoing public was interested in Jones as a winning Prince Charming in the glamorous Lindbergh mold, not as a game technician.

The PGA counted noses after its first year of higher dues and found, at annual-meeting time, that out of a total of 1,100 members, 760 Class A members had fully paid, 222 Class B members had fully paid, and 118 Class B members had partially paid. A group life insurance arrangement was made, covering each paid-up member for $1,000 in case of death. Delegates also wanted fire and theft insurance on their pro shops, but it was years before PGA members were able to get such protection at reasonable terms.

The 1930 meeting also tried to organize a PGA employment bureau, but the idea has never materialized on a national basis, although PGA sections have developed a custom of employers making inquiries. The problem wasn't so much that of identifying a qualified professional as it was of determining how good the job was. Delegates to the convention reported that pros in their sections hadn't been paid for months by their clubs. In some cases the pros were on a salary basis; in others they were on concession income with the club collecting members' accounts.

The controversy over salary versus concessions as the basis of pro income was very much alive in 1930, as many professionals were still in charge of courses and paid a substantial part of their income for that work. The argument continued for years.

Charles Lorms, a Columbus, Ohio, professional, got the annual meeting on a sensible business track when, after one of the innumerable tournament discussions, he said, "We are wasting our time talking about matters that actually concern only about ten professionals. My members read that the PGA is in a quarrel about tournaments at Los Angeles, Agua Caliente, Catalina, Pasadena, and Glendale and wonder how I happened to get into such a mess concerning professionals who'd never done a thing for them. I think we should help everyone in professional golf, but I wonder if we're not spending too much time and money on some of our members who get more money easier than money comes on a club job."

Jack Forrester, a New Jersey delegate and a Scot who had been one of the better playing pros, asked, "If these players are so important, why do manufacturers put the players' names on the cheapest trash that can be sold to people who don't know any better? If these players haven't any respect for themselves, why should we worry about building them up so they can steal from people in the name of professional golf?"

Loud applause greeted his pertinent comment, but nothing has been done over the years in this regard. Which brings to mind an incident that happened much, much later on when Jack Nicklaus was reminded of the questionable business management involved in selling a champion's name. Nicklaus's name was carried on a cheap ball, which, of course, he didn't play. In this instance, after one of his mighty shots at the 1970 Masters, Nicklaus lost his ball in a wooded area. He and his caddie were busy searching for it when a sacrilegious galleryite called out, "Quit looking for it, Jack! You can buy three of them for a buck and a quarter!" Proving, as the French put it, *"Plus ça change, plus c'est la même chose."*

A historic development came out of the Chicago meeting when the PGA decided to work with the British PGA on a committee that might carry international relations beyond the Ryder Cup matches. The teaching hopes of the PGA were also evident in a suggestion by Harold Sampson, a Northern California delegate, to have a PGA textbook compiled that professionals and their pupils could use.

The PGA knew the change from benchmade to factory-made clubs was bound to alter drastically the professionals' business as retailers. President Pirie had assigned Herb Graffis, editor of *Golfdom, the Business Magazine of Golf,* to interview manufacturers, golfers, club officials, and sports goods retailers, and report. Graffis suggested that the association appoint a merchandising committee to hold conferences at major trading centers where pros and assistants could listen to experts on purchasing, display, selling, and accounting, and get prepared for a huge market that was certain to develop swiftly and that should be commanded by professionals if they continued to qualify themselves as authorities. He added that the pro shop had the ideal location for selling.

9

Gloom, Doom, the Depression, and the Light at the End of the Fairway

GOLF was finishing the gloomiest year of its American history when the PGA annual meeting was held at the Hotel Statler, Boston, November 16, 17, and 18, 1931.

Country club waiting lists had practically vanished, and the most exclusive clubs were eager for members and had a hard time getting them at any price. One famous old club, whose distinguished senior members were badly hurt by the Depression, made a special low-price offer to recruit younger members, but only a few sons of members signed up. One young man, whose father had been noted in amateur golf for many years, explained his refusal: "Father and the rest of his foursome played together since they ran the Indians off the course. They didn't seem too happy about making us welcome then when the club needed some life, and now I'm not rushing to bail them out. I've got my own troubles."

A number of courses "reorganized"— a polite way of saying: "went bankrupt." Golf course equipment and supply dealers carried past-due accounts of clubs until their own bankers began shutting down on them. Daily-fee and public courses were in better condition, so those who no longer could afford private clubs were not giving up golf entirely.

Probably a hundred professionals, to repeat an informed guess of the time, were of vital importance in keeping their clubs from closing. They acted as managers and greenkeepers, some of them splitting their lesson income with their clubs, and what they could make out of their shops kept these professionals and their families eating in 1931.

Charles W. Hall of the Country Club of Birmingham, had been elected president of the PGA after Alex Pirie had refused to run for another term.

Hall was the last foreign-born president of the PGA of America. His parents had brought him to the United States from Leeds, England, when he was three years old. They settled in Oxford, Mississippi, then moved to Memphis. After he got through high school, Bob Simpson, a family friend who knew the lad was one of the few who'd been playing pretty good golf, took him on as an assistant at Blue Mound in Milwaukee. His first pro job was at the Nashville Country Club; he was there for four years, then went to Birmingham. Hall played in the PGA and National Open championships and won the Southeastern PGA Championship twice. He could drive the ball so far over those unwatered fairways that other pros wouldn't believe it. Hall had numerous authenticated drives of 400 yards or more, and that undoubtedly established his high standing with his brother pros more than did his distinction of being the first American golf professional to become a bank director. Hall was a sound but not spectacular merchant in his pro shop, but he was a very good teacher and a good manager of his club's golf operations.

When Hall became PGA president, in this troubled period, the emphasis was on how to keep pro golf jobs. As usual, the tournament minority made the most noise. Not that the tournament circuit was without its troubles, although Bob Harlow persevered as Tournament Bureau head. Golf tournaments usually provided excellent publicity for cities and towns where they were held, but unemployment problems were so severe throughout the nation that he couldn't find a single Chamber of Commerce willing to sponsor a professional event. These were the brother-can-you-spare-a-dime days, not a time when the sports pages headlined the top money winners of the year on the tournament circuit.

Oddly enough, Harlow got some tournaments during that period of economic ebb at places where about the last thing the ailing community needed was a golf tournament. Unquestionably the farthest reach was in staging a $5,000 tournament at aptly named Hazard, Kentucky, a small coal-mining town where the valley widened out just enough for a nine-hole course. The event had been sponsored by an Ohio company that owned the mines there, and the prize money was more than many of the miners would be paid all their lives working underground. The small gallery watched the tournament just as the wail of hymns came from the small church built on a ledge of the hill, where burial services were being held for some miners killed in an explosion. As the mourners silently followed the coffins along the narrow bridge over the river, the golfers stopped complaining about the poor condition of the greens. Perhaps the pros realized that there were harder ways of making a living than playing in golf tournaments.

Always eager to follow through on his job, during a stop in Texas Harlow began to publish *Golf News,* a four-page weekly of tournament information, propaganda, and player personality pieces. The venture was financed by ads from hotels and restaurants, an occasional golf manufacturer, and business advertising that Harlow's golfing friends contributed.

Delegates at the 1931 meeting were more concerned about the association's championship fixtures, the PGA Championship and the Ryder Cup matches, than with the latest chapter in the troubles of the Tournament Bureau, and how it, like everyone else, needed money. The championship at Wanna-moiset, Providence, was a financial success. The club put up $12,000, prize money was $7,200, and travel mileage for the contestants was $4,321. The program made money, with Bob Jones refereeing the final match September 7, when Tom Creavy defeated Denny Shute, 2 and 1.

Creavy was a dark horse, but he got past rugged competitors in beating Peter O'Hara in the second round after O'Hara had been a surprise victor over Hagen in the first round. Then Creavy beat Cyril Walker and Gene Sarazen before meeting Shute. Sarazen, who played in eighteen of the thirty-five tournaments that year, had been named to represent the tournament players in the PGA official family.

Albert Gates had gone smoothly through another year of getting the house in order, and the efficient, pleasant Mrs. Blakeman was proving to be the "businessman" the PGA needed. Membership was 22 percent ahead of the previous year. There were 937 Class A, B, and C members paid in full, 146 paid in part. Class D members, which included pros employed outside golf during the lean years, had 300 paid in full. The 1,383 members, although showing PGA representation at only about a quarter of U.S. golf clubs, usually were located at the better clubs.

Although 1931 was the worst year American golf clubs ever had financially, the PGA improved its own financial position. Receipts from all sources were $113,777. Disbursements were $78,133. The income included $1,000 from the USGA for the Ryder Cup fund. The PGA balance as of October 31, 1931, was $62,980. President Hall was a careful manager, and Jack Mackie, continuing as treasurer, maintained traditional Scottish frugality.

American boys were now coming into the PGA's royal family—Harold Sampson from San Francisco and Dan Goss from Birmingham were new home-bred vice-presidents.

A new Merchandising Committee was formed with Elmer Biggs, of the Country Club of Peoria, as its head. Its function was to promote concerted development of pro-shop sales, reflecting the consensus of the meeting that "Somebody's making a lot of money out of golf goods, but it sure isn't us. Why?"

"This is a business as well as a game," President Hall said, "but we don't seem to be able to get ourselves regarded as businessmen. However, as I hear of the way professionals are keeping their clubs surviving, it seems we've got a golf lesson to teach American business."

PGA annual meetings had always excluded sportswriters because they might write up the family brawls between the tournament artists and the club pros. Hall thought of opening the meetings so all golfers might learn what the PGA was trying to do for the game. The idea was quickly abandoned because some delegates were so outspoken they didn't want to be quoted.

There was even more worrying about job security at the 1931 meeting. Turnover of club officials was higher than ever, and the incoming officials often wanted to hire new professionals. Pros were quick casualties in club politics. A pro who happened to play golf with one group more than another quickly became a political casualty. It was not a situation to nurture the kind of club loyalty that many of the old pros had and that was keeping some clubs going in the years of calamity.

The PGA was becoming more political itself, with the foreign-born pros diminishing in proportion to the PGA membership as a whole. The ex-caddies of Irish and Italian parentage were jockeying for position, and other American-born pros who didn't know, didn't care, or weren't reminded of their ethnic origins were getting involved in the ridiculous game of choosing up sides. It was a bad show, and the old founding-father Britishers who were passing on, subconsciously aware they'd been a bloc, didn't know what was happening. The most adept politician ever in professional golf was coming in from the Ridgewood, New Jersey, Country Club, where he'd been an assistant to a relative and had fallen heir to the top job when he was seventeen. This master of the divide-and-conquer tactic was George Jacobus, and he did the PGA a lot of good at a time when Hall, a solid businessman, was wondering why in the name of the good Lord anybody would want to be a PGA official.

Money for clubs, pros, and manufacturers concerned Hall as PGA president, and he probably had the broadest business view of any PGA official. Hall worried about the employment situation of PGA members, and there was almost a free-for-all at the annual meeting when it was charged that leading manufacturers, in an effort to have the pros pay back accounts long past due, deliberately pushed them into lucrative jobs so they could collect in cash. The fights resulting from this move never were recorded, just as some controversies in the Continental Congress were glossed over in print.

What did come into the open, though, was that the hard-line Old Boys realized once and for all that too many clubs were sending back to Britain for professionals, when kids who'd been developed as caddies and assistants in the United States could do the job just as well, and that pride in their

protégés was the reason why the U.S. "old pros" had started the international competition that blossomed into the Ryder Cup matches.

George Sargent explained the background of the Ryder Cup matches in a way that winks at the high avowals of international competition: "Too often when American clubs needed professionals they would get lads from the old country, and we had been training very good American boys as pros. So, to show a strong offense as the best defense, we went along with Jim Harnett, who was selling subscriptions for *Golf Illustrated* in a campaign to finance an American team to the British Open in 1921 and quit waiting for them to come over and lick us. That began the Ryder Cup matches, and it also stopped the idea that British golfers were easy superiors of American professionals." And that from a British-born American who had been assistant to Harry Vardon.

There continued to be rumblings about pampering the playing pros. PGA members asked why, if the association could pay from $5,000 to $8,000 a year to keep the playing pros busy, couldn't an equal amount be spent on getting jobs for home pros?

The start of junior programs at many clubs having PGA professionals was also reported. These free class lessons for young people and also for women made clubs active nurseries for golf, thus creating a new market that helped lift the game out of the Depression. George Jacobus, who followed Hall as PGA president in 1933, was especially energetic in the junior class teaching.

The PGA had already come close to a split between the home professionals and the traveling players. Gene Sarazen and Alex Pirie were the two who pleaded for the two camps to play it cool. Pirie said it would be fatal for the tournament professionals to go on their own just when the long educational campaign to develop spectator interest in golf and the fun of the game was beginning to bear fruit.

Pirie recalled that the golf galleries had at one time consisted mostly of other professionals, then picked up spectators whose interest had been aroused by the home professionals who had taught them the fine points of the game. With these new fans, plus the caddies who grew up and became golfers and club members, a hope of the country's pioneer pros was being realized. But Pirie's plea for continued financial support of golf as a potentially great American spectator sport found little response among the home pros.

Reflecting that if the home professionals were taken out of the golf picture there wouldn't be any tournament professionals in a few years, George Sargent asked: "Then why is our business administrator, who is being paid $15,000 a year, spending 75 percent of his time on the tournament players?" A delegate remarked it was a case of the tail wagging the dog, and the comment was so wholesomely and completely insulting that everybody laughed.

Then a delegate told about his caddie training, which had been remarkably successful in reducing the theft of balls from his practice range. He said the kids then seemed to teach the members not to steal range balls, and ball losses were reduced to the point where practice range operation became financially possible.

The sale of golf balls through slot machines in pro shops was also discussed. The one-armed bandits had increased ball sales immensely, but there was one very bad thing about them. They were controlled by hoodlums—or whatever name you choose to call the community's lawless element. As a matter of malodorous fact, quite a few of the country clubs, including some of the socially uppity ones, were getting by on revenue brought in by slot machines, few of which were privately owned.

The underworld was in charge everywhere and of course couldn't operate without a payoff of one sort or another to local police. A political ruckus erupted at a big Metropolitan district club when some officers and directors were accused of getting a share of the slot-machine take. One professional—and a good businessman-professional he was—was murdered because of his big-money ambitions. He wanted a "piece" of the machines *and* the bootlegging to club locker rooms. Other professionals in his area had also been invited to share in nefarious but profitable operations during this period of severe fiscal depression for country clubs and their professionals, but they had declined, murmuring that their colleague was not long for this world. They were right. He was the only pro golf victim of the mob during Prohibition.

Gene Sarazen closed the 1931 annual meeting on a strong note. When he was asked what could be done to stop tournament pros from endorsing shoddy golf goods, Sarazen admitted he didn't know, adding that some of his colleagues were so hungry they'd fight with guns to take breakfast away from a sparrow.

Sarazen was, and continued to be, one of the foremost realists of pro tournament golf and far more of a builder of that department of the game than has ever been acknowledged. He quit a good club job to become a journeyman

Gene Sarazen. PGA

pro, entirely on his own. Hagen, ten years older, was the circus darling and never handicapped by bookkeeping, while Sarazen had been brought up on a cash-and-carry basis. He got into the dreamland of the stock market and the real-estate boom but came back to earth quickly when his investments soured. Always resourceful, Sarazen was not one to nurse crybabies. Like Ben Hogan later on, he refused to coddle grown men who couldn't win a good living with their clubs.

At the Los Angeles Open, where only 150 of the 200-and-some contestants were PGA members, Sarazen coldly asked: "Why carry along anybody who won't pay his way?" Ben Hogan, a genuinely heroic and rugged competitor who came along years after Sarazen, said the same thing to other tournament competitors, hardly endearing himself to the crew who played the circuit because they thought it was less "work" than work. And, like Sarazen, Hogan couldn't have cared less. They were both individualists with color and guts.

The 1932 annual meeting at Peoria was the PGA's Valley Forge. The convention was scheduled for only two days, November 21 and 22, because the PGA couldn't afford to meet any longer, and was held at the Pere Marquette Hotel because the owner was a friend of Elmer Biggs, pro at the Peoria Country Club, who gave the members rock-bottom rates. And the site was chosen because the travel expenses of the thirty-four delegates and officials were the lowest of almost any place the nationwide organization could find shelter.

Hundreds of pros were out of golf work, not only because clubs were cutting their budgets, but because the switch from hickory to steel shafts put a lot of fine clubmakers out of work. And these men couldn't get employment at golf club factories because the manufacturers all were losing money and laying off help. Indeed, times were so bad that even the club pros and the tournament pros quit arguing; they were just trying to survive. The club professionals generously came through to preserve the Tournament Bureau and organized circuit golf when the tournament phase of golf, other than major championships, seemed about to go on a catch-as-catch-can basis, with the nomads in the Southwest and Southeast barely getting by on winter eating and room money and a few summer tournaments.

PGA revenue was so low that Administrator Gates made history of a sort in announcing that, instead of drawing the $18,000 salary he had contracted to get, he was being paid less than half of that. The reduction was his own suggestion. Salaries of all employees were cut 15 percent, too. It was announced that from November 1, 1931, to November 1, 1932, Class A, B, and C membership paid in full had dropped from 937 to 772. With partially unpaid and Class D members, membership had fallen to 1,228, about 150 fewer than the year before. Practically 20 percent of the dues was being paid out for group insurance, but there was no criticism of that. There were no rich widows of professionals.

One bright spot was the PGA Championship at the Keller public course in St. Paul, where Olin Dutra defeated Frank Walsh, 4 and 3, for the title. After losing money on two St. Paul opens, the Junior Chamber of Commerce had guaranteed $10,000 for the PGA.

To raise money for the American PGA team to go to the 1933 Ryder Cup matches at Southport, England, a home-bred versus foreign-born match was held at the Oak Park, Illinois, Country Club, August 25 and 26, 1932. It lost money. The U.S. team, captained by Horton Smith, defeated the foreign-born team, headed by Tommy Armour. The score: 10 to 8. Smith's team had Walter Hagen, Leo Diegel, Denny Shute, Johnny Farrell, Tom Creavy, Olin Dutra, Ed Dudley, Billy Burke, Al Espinosa, Al Watrous, and Joe Turnesa. Armour had on his side Jock Hutchison, Clarence Hackney, Dave Hackney, Harry Cooper, Harry Hampton, José Jurado, George Smith, Bob Macdonald, Francis Gallett, Laurie Ayton, and Leonard Gallett.

Bob Harlow had lined up the Miami-Biltmore $10,000 Open for the winter, then had his contract terminated on April 1, 1932, simply because the PGA no longer had the money to pay him. In any case, this was an important event for the PGA and for golf itself in the doldrums of 1932. And thereby hangs a tale.

It seems that Henry L. Doherty, head of the Cities Service utilities and owner of the Miami-Biltmore Hotel, got into some kind of a difference of opinion with Uncle Sam about taxes. So, a bright young man named Gerry Hammond, working for the eminent Carl Byoir, a New York publicity genius, got the correct angle, working with Harlow. Warm Springs, Georgia, a health resort visited by the ailing President Franklin D. Roosevelt, needed money, and plenty. Byoir, Hammond, and Harlow thought it might be a nice thing if a profitable golf tournament at Doherty's Miami hotel course would add operating revenue for the Georgia spa. Furthermore, the Miami-Biltmore charitable event might ease the pain Washington was giving the Doherty interests.

It worked out just that way, and the tournament happened to be more than just another ordinary arrangement between politicians and citizens. The Miami-Biltmore event teed off a fund-raising campaign that became the "March of Dimes" and financed the research to defeat polio. It also was the tournament that showed how hundreds of hospital and other welfare operations could benefit from golf tournaments. And it definitely showed how golf tournaments could survive and flourish. Without the hospital-auxiliary organization women doing the vast amount of free work they've done for golf tournaments, the circuit couldn't have grown.

Bob Harlow's background as a minister's son had acquainted him with the possibilities of getting women active in an affair having a charitable, civic, or educational objective. The wives of the St. Paul Junior Chamber of Commerce were the first group of women to demonstrate what could be done in golf tournament promotion and operation. Then came the Miami-Biltmore affair with a hospital tie-in. Mrs. Doherty, an attractive, energetic woman, had been a nurse, and she got the idea of the society woman–Florence Nightingale combination in a practical way. Harlow was let go before the Miami-Biltmore production, but he helped set the pattern that made golf-playing experts wealthy.

Francis J. Powers, a Chicago sportswriter, then took over Tournament Bureau correspondence and publicity as assistant to Administrator Gates. Powers put out press releases on home and tournament professionals that were

well received, but he found the job had more headaches than he was paid for. His contract was terminated after a year, and Harlow was rehired as Tournament Bureau manager at the players' suggestion.

In 1932 the PGA issued its first official press badge, and 125 writers received them, although it took some years for the PGA badges to mean much. They were supposed to admit their wearers to press quarters at tournaments and inside the marshals' ropes that controlled the excited galleries when tournament golf was growing up. The USGA press badges did what they were intended to do at USGA championships, but the PGA championships and earlier tour events had host club officials who issued their own press badges and other credentials. The PGA press badges frequently struck club officials as presumptuous and consequently worthless.

The Pinkerton and Burns detective agencies were now in the golf tournament ticket-collecting and gallery-control business. In their haste they enlisted representatives of all ages, undistinguished by judgment or instructions, gave them badges and firearms, and turned them loose. The result was as might have been expected. The rented gendarmes had no use for the PGA press badge wearers, and the reporters reciprocated. Eventually the policing agencies recruited qualified personnel for this sort of work and trained them well.

The effort to train assistants in the repair of clubs was fairly successful in 1932. James P. Gallagher, an ingenious clubmaker, was hired by the PGA to teach youngsters how to repair and alter clubs so that they wouldn't have to be returned to the manufacturers. Initially, there was a lot of breakage of the steel shafts. Nor did golfers get the same "feel" as with the hickory-shafted clubs. So there was a lot of weight changing and loft alerting in steel-shafted woods, and the lies and lofts of irons were changed. Making the leather grips shorter or longer, thinner or fatter, was a customary job.

Gallagher was paid $40 a week and expenses by the PGA. By the time of the annual meeting he had visited 275 pro shops in seven states. He had a New England tool company make special tools for the club-repair work and a scale that was a prototype of today's swing-weight scale. The earlier steel-shafted clubs were not in accurately matched sets.

The Gallagher workbench, one of the vanishing ateliers of the gifted artisans of golf, is now a relic in the USGA Museum at Far Hills, New Jersey. It needs only a whisky bottle partially filled with shellac or varnish to typify the benches in pro shops when most of the better players bought their clubs custom-made.

Hickory shaft royalty paid to the PGA between November 1, 1931, and the same date the following year was $95.11, and contracts with Spalding, MacGregor, and Vulcan Golf for clubs bearing the PGA trademark were not renewed.

Again the need for publicity in behalf of the home pro was brought up, and this was to be provided in the newspaper and radio material submitted by Powers. The effort was not a success. For almost forty years the club pro, or the "working pro," as he called himself in deliberate contrast to his fortunate brother, the "playing pro," had received little recognition. Eventually sectional and national awards were made to the Golf Professional of the Year, and a national

award was made by the PGA to the Professional Golfer of the Year in recognition of playing achievements. This is the Robert E. Harlow Award, named in honor of the man who did so much to establish the touring professionals in headlines and high finance.

The one faintly cheerful note in the overall situation was that golf was in better shape than baseball, collegiate football, or boxing, where attendance in 1932 was about half that in 1931.

Although the leading golf goods manufacturers had abandoned contributing to the Tournament Bureau fund, there was a carry-over of tournament promotion that had Lakeland, St. Petersburg, and the Bellaire-Biltmore Hotel, all in Florida, offering $1,000 or $1,500 for two-day tournaments. San Antonio, which had been kept on the circuit in 1931 by a $1,250 loan from the Manufacturers' Fund, via the PGA, refused to stage a tournament in 1932. The 1931 tournament repaid the loan and turned over a small profit to the city's Unemployed Committee. New Orleans and other cities indicated interest in having tournaments in 1933 if the PGA would pay "incidental expenses." The PGA couldn't.

At the 1932 annual meeting, the tournament circuit, in addition to the National Open and PGA championships, was announced as: the National Capital City Open, $2,500; Mid-South Senior PGA at Pinehurst, $2,300; Miami-Biltmore, $10,000; San Francisco Match-Play Open, $2,500 plus gate; Pasadena Open, $4,000; Los Angeles Open, $5,000 plus gate; Santa Monica Pro-Am, $2,000; Agua Caliente Open, $7,500; and Phoenix Open, $2,500.

And that was the program that kept the tournament circuit alive. It took blood, sweat, and tears of pleading and

promising by Harlow and Gates to arrange that survival schedule, with prize
money much less than caddies get in a
few circuit events now.

In its search for urgently needed increased revenue, one large club in the
Chicago district leased its pro department to a leading retailer of men's apparel. The pro shop blossomed with
attractively displayed equipment, accessories, and apparel. But the shop
didn't blossom with profit. This arrangement between the Medinah Country Club and the Henry C. Lytton (the
Hub) store was the first strong, coordinated effort to stock, display, and
energetically merchandise sportswear at
a pro shop. It didn't make money and
after a very few years was discontinued.

In 1932, a firm of accountants examined the books (such as they were)
of several professionals in the metropolitan New York, New England, and
Chicago areas and found that the pro
costs of doing business were deadly.
This discovery was made at a time when
club officials and members thought that
with no rent, no light bills, no advertising, and low wages the pro should be
getting rich. But with a six- or seven-
month season, an active market of
about 225 members, male and female,
at a typical good club, burglary and
fire insurance high, club cleaning boys'
and assistants' pay also high for the
times, and sales, teaching, and club-
storage income low, most pros were
lucky to get through the year in the
black. State sales and federal taxes
jolted pros into an adjustment of
charges in line with costs and compelled them to study their business income and outgo carefully.

At the 1932 meeting, it was reported
that 59 members—good men—were unable to get jobs in golf. One delegate
commented that PGA annual dues

were more than some members made
out of their jobs at nine-hole courses.
Before that year's meeting was concluded, a collection was made for the
Peoria Community Fund. Each delegate was asked by President Hall to donate something for "those less fortunate than ourselves."

Hall had done very well in keeping
the PGA and its tournament organization afloat in the rough seas of the Depression and refused another term.
Hall had learned that being president
of the PGA was an exacting task, a responsibility more than an honor, and
an expense to the man and his club.
And it was a job that must be handled
capably and conscientiously, beyond
the call of duty, for the good of golf.

The Hall administration had the satisfaction of bringing tournament golf
through one of the most dangerous periods any commercial sport had experienced. Amateur play in those lean
years was at a good figure, although
ball and club buying slumped severely.
Those Americans who played golf
learned that the golf course was a place
to escape troubles and get refreshed for
the next round of the battle.

For the first time the PGA was told
it should have a course of its own. Bob
Barnett, professional at Chevy Chase
in Washington, told the delegates,
"There are real-estate men in New
York and Chicago who would give the
PGA land, a golf course, and a clubhouse for a club of its own and make a
large profit out of what a PGA club
would do in increasing the value of surrounding property."

There had been considerable political wheeling and dealing prior to and
at the 1932 meeting. George Jacobus,
an energetic and ambitious young professional who had been head of the
New Jersey section for some years, felt

that the day of the Old Guard was over and that he was the fellow to take over. With Hall declining to run, it seemed there might be a battle in electing his successor, but Willie Ogg, one of the PGA's founders, cautioned delegates about divisive quarreling in the association when it was having enough troubles and moved that George Jacobus's nomination be made unanimous. Another home-bred, R. W. ("Doc") Treacy, was elected secretary, and John B. Mackie stayed on as treasurer.

A strange thing about the Depression, despite the wailing of the comparatively few fellows who were following Hagen and Sarazen into playing specialization for exhibition and tournament money, was that it did a great deal to make tournament golf a successful enterprise.

Club jobs in which a professional could make a living were impossible to get, and the good jobs were solidly held. So a man who wanted to play golf and couldn't get other employment was reduced to hanging around courses where the resident pro might allow him to give lessons or hustle bets for eating and lodging money, or perhaps play in the few local tournaments or exhibitions.

The roll call of unemployed professionals trying to make ends meet with a knife and fork and golf clubs reached 100 at the Capital City Open, according to those at the 1933 PGA annual convention at the Palmer House, Chicago, November 21 and 22. There were 38 delegates at the first annual meeting with George Jacobus as president and James Wilson, Dan Goss, Harold Sampson, and W. Crimann as vice-presidents. R. W. Treacy was secretary, and Jack Mackie was treasurer. Albert Gates was in his finale as PGA business adminis-

trator, and Charles Hall had the new title, honorary president, which was to become customary with PGA ex-presidents.

An exhibition match at Pinehurst with an all-star cast headed by Johnny Farrell had been played for the PGA Unemployment Relief Fund but hadn't relieved the unemployed very much, according to the report at the Chicago meeting. There'd been better luck with the Ryder Cup team playing a team of amateurs at Metropolis Country Club in suburban New York where $3,000 was raised for the relief of unemployed pros.

Jacobus's first clash was with the tournament players, and he met with them in Tampa on February 10 and also at the Capital City Open on November 11. Other meetings were held during 1933 over the differences with the home pros and within the PGA, and the same story was to be repeated for years. The script never varied. The artists had time on their hands and were punchy from three-putting and "hitting the ball well but not scoring" —occupational troubles of their trade. Then one of them who was not among the leading money winners (even when the leader had a $3,000 year) would say, "If the PGA would get on the job, we'd be doing a lot better, so let's get our own thing going." Next morning and a few aspirins later, an earnest malcontent would ask a comrade, "What was it you were to demand of the PGA or else?" The comrade would reply, "Damned if I know, but they're giving us a raw deal and I'm gonna tell them!"

So the word would get to the PGA officials, whose customary reaction was, "Give them what they want. They've got men on the Tournament Committee, and they're getting more action for their dues than the home pros. If you can figure out what else they want, give it to them. What difference does it make to the rest of the fellows who pay the most dues?" But when it came to a showdown, the complainers had difficulty in specifically stating their wants. Thus it continued. The journeyman pros and the home pros were like a husband and wife so used to quarreling that they forgot what the nagging was about. So, not having the money to afford lawyers, they lived more or less happily forever after—or at least until somebody got rich enough to hire lawyers to find something to fight about.

Johnny Farrell, successful in the dual role of playing and home professional, told the 1933 meeting: "Last winter there was a lot of unfavorable publicity about the playing professionals starting their own organization. I don't think they really felt that way about it. They have to come off their high horse and work out any conflict with other professionals as intelligent businessmen should for the good of their business and the game. I know that some playing professionals are carried away by their egotism. They think they're different from the professionals who work with and for the amateur golfers. The Depression has been a great leveler for boys who were talking loud on the top."

Most differences between the playing specialists and the home professionals serving others, psychologists say, are explained by the egocentric nature of the game. The golfer whose interests are mainly concerned with his own score is compulsively seeking an explanation for his failure to do better. The home professional keeps his job and flourishes by thinking primarily about his customer's game. Hence the lack of understanding at the root of long years of

conflict between the home pros and tournament pros, according to a psychiatrist who is familiar with golf as a proficient amateur and in treating several professional golfers.

In the 1932–33 winter, the playing professionals pressing for a split with the PGA were not the most prominent and successful players, as was the case all the while until the division eventually came. Frustrated players found the PGA a convenient whipping boy. The yearly leaders were seldom involved in the family quarrels except as bystanders who couldn't get out of the way.

Complaints about tournament player misconduct were few and chiefly about bad checks, a not uncommon thing in business in those days. Golf goods manufacturers had forty players under contract and were able to control their men. However, the PGA and the manufacturers didn't agree on the use of prominent players' names on cheap clubs. The Southern California section introduced a resolution asking that a player be disbarred from the PGA Championship if he allowed the use of his name on "inferior clubs, balls, and other golf merchandise causing the public to believe that such merchandise is used by the player." The resolution was unanimously passed—and didn't mean a thing.

Albert Gates was through as business administrator of the PGA as of January 1, 1934, but was to be paid $6,200 as the association's general counsel and for such legal services as might be needed until June 1, 1935. In his farewell address, Gates remarked that November seemed to be open season for ducks and business administrators. He was happy that the contract had been terminated early and amicably because he now would have an opportunity to play golf. He'd played only a few rounds

George Jacobus. PGA, photo from City of Miami News Bureau

a year since going to work for the PGA, which, he noted, was unable to afford his services and had more urgent needs for money.

President Jacobus pointed out that the sections said they didn't know what was going on at PGA headquarters, so there was no chance of coordinating nationwide PGA work. The complaint confirmed the need of organizers who would visit the sections, arrange merchandising, educational, and local tournament programs and recruit new members. But again the answer was: "No money."

The Connecticut section, with 51 members, was spun off from the New England section. The membership had

dropped to 1,009 of all classes from a 1932 high of 1,228. There had been 85 taken off the roster for nonpayment of 1932 dues, and the USGA and Western Golf Association also reported membership losses in 1933.

Nevertheless, the delegates discussed raising membership standards. Three years as an assistant and the ability to score better than 75, plus examination by a screening committee, were among requirements proposed at the meetings, but the three years' apprenticeship requirement was the one accepted by the delegates.

Discussion of teaching, which had been spurred by the PGA motion pictures of Hagen, Vardon, and Joyce Wethered and the Warner Brothers movies of Bob Jones, continued. So great was the interest that delegates at the 1933 meeting remarked that golfers would be better off if the PGA thought more about how to teach and less about how to get more tournament money for about 5 percent of its members. Jacobus proposed a standardized teaching program and appointed several committees to prepare preliminary plans, but the committees could not agree that teaching could be standardized. Golf was too individualized, an art rather than a science or mechanics. There were many more diagnoses of methods than there were suggestions of ways of effectively applying the findings of technique. The conclusions of professionals regarded by their peers as most successful in instruction were that: (1) the better members play, the more they play, and (2) effective instruction is about 25 percent teaching and 75 percent learning.

The exchange of experiences on instruction moved the veteran Fred Brand to say, "If we'd spend as much time thinking about improving the golf of our members as we do working for our own fine players who don't help themselves, the PGA would be a big, wealthy, and respected organization."

Then the delegates heard about the difficulty in getting 95 Milwaukee businessmen to raise $9,000 toward the 1933 PGA Championship at Blue Mound Country Club, August 8 to 11, which lost $2,400. And Bob Harlow, back as Tournament Bureau manager, reported $57,300 in tournament prize money signed for the winter and 1934.

The educational program was expanded when Professor L. S. Dickinson, who'd started the golf course management school at Massachusetts State Agricultural School at Amherst, lectured on course maintenance to PGA members and their officials at Kansas City and Detroit. He charged no fee, only expenses of $246.

Jim Gallagher continued his tour in showing young professionals and assistants how to repair clubs.

That year there was begun what developed into the PGA Advisory Board. They were called honorary members then and included H. Windeler, R. H. Worthington, Julian W. Curtiss, Jason Rogers, the Reverend J. B. Kelly of New York, P. R. Hollender, John G. Anderson, and S. P. Germain.

The economic situation was getting better, but money was still tight. Bob Harlow announced with pride that he'd made economical arrangements for tournaments, as, for example, at the Miami-Biltmore the $1 entry fee for the $10,000 Open to be held December 8, 9, and 10, with the winner to get $2,500. Room rates for players were $5 single and $3 double. At Agua Caliente, with a $7,500 four-day tournament, the entry fee was $5, the caddie fee was $2 a round, and players got 25 percent off room rates. At the Pinehurst, tournament players' rooms were free, and they were on the American plan. The boys liked that.

10

The Incomparable Sir Walter, Some Later Charm Boys, and How the Stars Established Today's Sportswear

FOR a time, especially after high society took over the game, the golf professional was treated like hired help and considered in the same category as a head coachman, gardener, butler, chef, chauffeur, or headwaiter. True, he was an expert and indubitably superior at his trade, but he was paid to do—the shame of it!—what his betters did for fun. And if the home pro at least had some standing by virtue of his connection with an elite club—notwithstanding his insignificant salary—then he stood a few notches higher than his touring brethren, who simply played for purses like so many gamblers.

With a few exceptions like Chick Evans, Francis Ouimet, and later on, Bobby Jones, the prominent amateurs were also high society. While they played with professionals, they did not mingle with them off the course. And when the professionals competed with the amateurs in open competitions held at private clubs, they were not expected to share the same facilities. The locker room was *verboten* to them as—let's face it—a species of rather crude, grubby journeymen in the category of professional boxers or baseball players.

Whether legendary or not, since he was always a legendary character in the world of golf, it's typical that Walter Hagen, who was to become the golf companion of the Prince of Wales and others in the upper echelons, should be credited with crashing the barrier separating the sleek *fun* players from the uncouth *money* players. Just how this came about isn't clear, but The Haig, as he came to be known, somehow maneuvered this historic first at the Midlothian Country Club outside Chicago during the 1914 Open. Whatever Hagen said or did, from then on golf professionals used the same locker room and shared the same clubhouse amenities as the members. Whether words

Walter Hagen. GH

were exchanged or some sort of coercion used, or whether the professionals were simply formally accepted, remains an intriguing mystery, but giving the astonishing, incredible, and indomitable Walter C. Hagen all the credit is no problem at all.

Hagen occupies a unique niche in the Valhalla of professional golf. He deserves the credit for many firsts. Along with being the first to buck clubhouse class consciousness, he was the first American golf professional to win repeatedly in big-time play, to market a successful ball and set of clubs bearing his name, to play golf exhibitions for money, to dress impeccably and set style fashions, and to leave a memorable and enduring mark on professional golf as one of a very special breed. As was said about him in the Foreword of this book, he was also the first "to live like a merry millionaire, and nobody in pro golf has come near equaling his record at having fun with money." The Haig loved the good life on and off the course; he was a true and original playboy. And all the amazing stories about him are no doubt absolutely true.

One of the best concerned the time that he failed to show up on time at the tee during the second round of some tournament somewhere. His fellow pros knew he had probably been out all night partying, and it looked as if it had been too much for Walter. But then, just as the officials were about to disqualify him, a chauffeured limousine drove up, and The Haig, regal and composed in his tuxedo, got out after a lazy wave to a mink-wrapped lovely in the tonneau. He signaled his waiting caddie, carefully selected his driver, and, the story goes, went on to play the round in tuxedo, boiled shirt, and patent-leather shoes. Did he win? Oh, surely! The Haig in his prime was

tough, tenacious, durable, and inde-
structible.

He had caddied for George Eastman
in Rochester, New York, and his first
big win at the age of twenty-two was
the 1914 Open. He won the American
Open again in 1919, and the British
Open in 1922, 1924, 1928, and 1929. He
took the PGA Championship five times
(1921 and 1924–27), won the Australian, Canadian, French, and Belgium
opens, plus innumerable other tournaments and titles, and played on five
Ryder Cup teams. He was an interna-
tionalist before there were internation-
alists and professional golf's greatest
personality and celebrity to match
baseball's Babe Ruth, tennis's Bill Til-
den, and football's Red Grange.

In his own keen way, The Haig revolutionized the classic pattern of winning golf; he realized that whoever was
in the cup in fewer than two putts per
green won the hole, and ultimately, the
tournament. Hagen put it positively.
He went for one-putt greens, regardless
of where he had to come from onto the
green. He had a mashie niblick—now
called a 7-iron—that would flash his
ball out of haylike rough close enough
to the cup so that he had a chance to
roll the putt in. In his time, even on
the greens abroad as well as in this
country, he never thought that a putt
involved anything more than rolling
the ball into the hole. His nerves were
ice because he didn't regard putting as
a personal problem any more than he
would consider shooting ducks out of a
blind early on a frigid morning as anything more than a test of luck and skill
between himself and the duck. Walter
Hagen was a master psychologist.

Hagen always had a carefree attitude
toward bills, but a study of the PGA
annals reveals that he was an original
PGA member with the longest dues-

paying record of them all. He was one
of the thirty-five leading professionals
to attend the founding dinner given by
Rodman Wanamaker in 1916. The
Haig was registered as Walter C. Hagen
of the Country Club of Rochester when
Tom McNamara, a golf pro, salesman
for Wanamaker's and the man who had
the idea of getting the professionals together to discuss forming an association, compiled the luncheon list. Not
until his death did sportswriters learn
that The Haig's middle name was
Christian and not Charles.

Never one to worry about what he
got for any amount of money, Hagen
got plenty for his PGA dues. He also
gave plenty to the PGA and its ambitions to make a place for playing professionals in the golden sunshine. The
earliest drain on the PGA treasury was
for items concerned with the promotion of tournament play, but oddly
enough, only Hagen among the PGA
founders had great years ahead of him.
What eased the strain on the PGA
treasury when the tournament idea
needed promotion was the resourceful-
ness of the old-timers in what was then
called "syndicate golf." When Hagen
was coming into his own, the stars
teamed together to share their winnings. It was a better deal for the tournament sponsors because, when "syndicate" quartets played, the field attracted
a gallery and the stars generally got
their money.

Hagen said he didn't like the "syndicate" idea and finally went on his own
—all or nothing. On his first trip South
in 1913, he and Tommy Kerrigan, then
professional at the Dedham club in
suburban Boston, teamed in the hopes
of grabbing money usually won by such
stars as Mike Brady, Gil Nicholls, Tom
McNamara, Johnny McDermott, Jim
Barnes, and Alex Smith. The Hagen-

Kerrigan combination managed to eat, sleep sheltered, and move on by winning low-down money on the Florida circuit. The next year, after Hagen won the Open, he was through with cutting in other pros on what he won.

He went on a Pacific Northwest tour with Jim Barnes in the winter of 1914–15. Jim had been professional at Tacoma for some years, and they hoped that his play would attract golfers in the area. However, Hagen as the added attraction was the showman Long Jim was not. The Haig raised the curtain for all the rest of the golf circus that hit the road in the years to come. On that tour Hagen and Barnes each kept their winnings. The Haig already needed all he could get, and Barnes, a shrewd Cornishman, was a tight one with a dollar. On that tour Hagen won the first $1,000 prize by taking the Panama Exposition Championship at Ingleside in January, 1915.

Hagen always had a nice, easy, though humanely selfish, way of doing things. Why he ever got involved in the birth of the PGA no one ever knew —and he never did. When the question was put to him, he answered with a laugh, "It's never a bad idea to give all the boys a chance." So it could be said that, even though there were no tournament specialists as such in 1916, the presence of the young, personable, and pleasantly threatening Hagen at the PGA's founding accounted for a balance between the home or service professionals and the playing experts in directing the interests of the PGA at its formation.

The Haig got into the golf ball business through Eddie Conlin when the latter took over U.S. Rubber's golf ball division. The association worked out well for both, and Conlin was always there to back up his star. When Hagen and his manager, Bob Harlow, were homeward bound from European triumphs and needed to be bailed off the gangplank, Harlow would send a telegram: ED PLEASE TOSS A LIFE PRESERVER OR MONEY. So Conlin would send funds to the conquering hero and his companion, and that was it. It's hard to imagine something like that happening today.

Walter was a charm guy, and so was his manager Harlow. Without a doubt in the world Harlow as a publicity man for golfers and for golf was so far ahead of any of the rest of the golf writers, then or now, that there was never a close second. And every knowledgeable golf writer agrees. Subconsciously, Harlow played more angles effectively for Hagen than any manager or public-relations man of a later professional has before or since. But Harlow was a man who loved golf more than he loved money, and promoters like that haven't been around for years, if ever.

By then The Haig had started his pro-only manufacturing company, but incompetent management, inadequate capital, and the unfavorable climate of Longwood, Florida, had proved ruinous to the venture. These were the days before air conditioning, and the air at Longwood, a little north of Orlando, was so heavy with moisture that the hickory shafts that had fitted perfectly into club heads at the factory dried out when shipped to other parts of the country. Hagen had lost $200,000 before he and his partners, ex-baseball players Joe Tinker (of Tinker-to-Evans-to-Chance triple-play fame) and John Ganzel, closed the plant and sold it to L. A. Young of Detroit in 1925.

Hagen had insisted that his company restrict its distribution through professionals' shops, and that continued to be the marketing policy after Young took over. Hagen got $75,000 for his name, and the company took out a $500,000 insurance policy. As was his habit, he expected to be paid money on demand, and L. A. Young was always screaming about the size of the checks he asked for. L. B. Icely then bought out Young, and Glen Morris came from the Wilson Sporting Goods Company as manager. Morris was routinely checking through business correspondence and records involving Hagen when, to his consternation, he found a paper stating that The Haig had given the Burke Golf Company the use of the Hagen name on golf equipment for a payment of $500.

Fearing that it would be an expensive business to correct a typical Hagen lapse of memory, Morris hurried to the Burke plant in Newark, Ohio, and discussed the matter with W. C. Sherwood, a veteran professional who was an executive of the company, then later returned to a professional post at the Memphis Country Club. In recalling the visit, Morris said, "I told him, 'Sherry, I'm trying to unscrew some of those deals The Haig made when room service was slow. Do you know anything about anything Walter signed with Burke?'

"Sherwood grinned. 'Funny thing—ran across it a few days ago. Bob Crandall or somebody else around here told me Walter had signed "W. C. Hagen" some places and "Walter Hagen" on other papers because he found out "W. C." meant the "can" to the English. Now Walter likes the British very much, but not that much, so he's been signing "Walter Hagen" to everything for years.'

" 'Let's see it,' I asked worriedly.

" 'I've got it in here in my desk,' Sherwood said, taking out a paper. 'Like to have it? Walter is your problem now. Take it along.' "

After his uneasy visions of lawyers and expensive legal damages, Morris sighed with relief, and then they began talking about there being no one else in sports quite like the great Walter Hagen. He had originally been with Spalding, beginning in 1915, getting paid for playing with Spalding clubs and balls, then came a friendly split in 1922, with Hagen wanting a new contract for $20,000. With his guarantee and his bonus from Spalding matching his prize money in major tournament victories, up to the time of the North and South Open in the fall of 1921, Hagen received $9,600. His purse for winning the 1922 British Open was £100 (then equivalent to $500), which The Haig promptly gave to his caddie.

Like Sarazen, Hagen also played as the social representative of manufacturers who wanted to make contacts with big buyers or engineers who could use their products. After the pleasant softening process, the salesmen followed up. The procedure was called "bird-dogging," and Sarazen was good at it. Hagen wasn't. He had fun playing business golf, but he was inclined to forget for whom he was working. In some respects he wasn't a good businessman because he just couldn't be bothered.

It is significant to recall that when the PGA first began its search for a golf commissioner back in 1921 there was no expectation that tournament affairs would ever become a substantial element in the association's business. At the time The Haig was the only tournament and road-show campaigner specializing in play. He'd given up his job at Oakland Hills near Detroit to take a crack at the brokerage business, but this was an abortive effort. Walter didn't know the business, didn't want to work, but did love to play golf and loaf day and night with the country club set. And people were more than willing to pay to see him play. Tickets for his exhibitions at $1 weekdays and $2 Saturdays, Sundays, and holidays sold briskly, and Robert Harlow, his manager for thirteen years, had Walter playing at least five days a week from late spring to early fall, when The Haig went to Florida and California to pick up more loose golf money.

As noted earlier, the tag idea Harlow thought up for the Hagen exhibitions was picked up by the PGA in 1921 for its own championships, and admission money was charged for the first time at the National Open Championship at the Skokie Country Club near Chicago in 1922. This soon became standard procedure at all major golfing events. But it wasn't until 1926 at the Royal Latham and St. Anne's, where Jones won his first British Open, that admission money was charged for this event in England. And this would all seem to stem back to still another Hagen first.

What isn't generally realized is that the public did not take readily to golf as a spectator sport during the game's developing years in the United States. Perhaps its early association with society and the rich had something to do with this, as well as the individualized nature of the tricky and specialized game. The fact was that, when Hagen won his first Open Championship in 1914, two hundred was considered a large gallery. Nor was educating golfers to follow other golfers around a course, even when the galleries were so small a spectator could get close enough to see all the strokes and take in all the play, a quick, easy process. Baseball, football, boxing, and even tennis were spectator sports—besides, you could *sit* and

watch them comfortably—but golf was fundamentally a player's sport. Unless you liked hitting a golf ball yourself or hunting, walking over the fields had little sporting appeal for most Americans.

About the only reason for the public to follow professional golfers around a course then was to bet on the outcome of the match. And the well-known amateurs drew more people than the professionals, possibly because of some stigma still attached to playing a society game for money rather than fun and glory. Golfers were interested in seeing Ouimet and Evans, then Jones. But even the magnetic Hagen was second in drawing power to Jones until a gallery mood had been created. Undoubtedly, the largest galleries in golf up to 1935 were those at Merion, the last two days, when Jones was completing his Grand Slam. The galleries at Interlachen, Minneapolis, when Jones was winning the 1930 National Open, weren't especially large, but July 10, 11, and 12 on that course were hotter than somewhere east of Suez, and the nearby cool, shady resorts of the Land of Lakes were much more tempting.

So, in quitting his job with the Associated Press in New York to get exhibition dates for Walter Hagen, Bob Harlow took a long chance. Hagen was a big-town boy in the Era of Wonderful Nonsense, and the country club set of that period hadn't acquired the habit of watching golfers perform. Even a National Open at one's own club was regarded by many members as something less than thrilling. For years it was difficult to get clubs to be host to PGA championships.

At many golf clubs in the smaller cities, Hagen played for between $100 and $160, and Harlow ticketed the spectators who had paid at the club entrance or clubhouse. If he hadn't been able to get a golf enthusiast at the club or, once in a while, the local professional to sponsor the exhibition, then the admission payments guaranteed the Hagen fee. Sometimes there were Sunday appearances for $500 and a few record ones where the great man collected as much as $1,000.

Harlow's work as a publicist and advance man for Hagen gave just the right boost needed to get nationwide acceptance of golf as a spectator amusement. It was only possible with the Hagen personality. Those world championship matches between Hagen and Sarazen, Jones, Farrell, Dutra, Shute, and others nursed golf along as something to be watched while on foot instead of cozily resting on the seat of the pants.

The Haig was more than a celebrated golf champion competing against the local pros and amateurs. He was a very pleasant fellow to have around on the course, in the clubhouse, or about town at homes, hotels, or cafés. Unquestionably, there were times when the Lord didn't brag about Walter Hagen as an example of His best day's work. But nobody could rap Walter for bad manners toward his hosts or guests—and don't think that Walter, a come-ye-all host, didn't have some sterling nuisances as guests.

But when he was touring on the exhibitions that Bob Harlow set up in proselytizing for golf, Walter often found himself playing on cow pastures that even the cows shunned as barren, inhospitable stretches of rock and sod. Did the man who made millions for his successors complain? Did he sniff at the impossible playing conditions? Did he beg off for fear his game might be af-

fected? Not Sir Walter. He'd gaze at the pathetic imitations of golf courses and say with his jauntiest smile, "Sporty little course you've got here."

On one such occasion in Iowa, when the exhibition was over, The Haig again attested to the virtues of the sporty little course and suggested that a slight snort might be in order after his valiant efforts. A budding young lawyer was an official of the club and also an understanding soul. He was in a tight spot as a defender of legal Prohibition in a neighborhood of untrustworthy snitches, but he took the chance one human takes for another.

When Hagen departed, his newfound friend, James Cooney, remained to serve the community. In time, Judge Cooney became, in many legal and financial ways, the head of the Wilson Sporting Goods Company, and despite all the chances and twists of fancy financing, the old lawyer, still a golf nut and not a bad chopper, never forgot Hagen's good manners. So between L. B. Icely and Judge Cooney, Walter Hagen wound up as a Wilson property, eventually getting $110,000 annually as his cut of the Hagen division (and that was a good bargain all around), plus a substantial amount annually for Walter Hagen, Jr., as an inheritance after his delightful father had joined his old playmates Tommy Armour, Mac Smith, et al in proving that the Kingdom Beyond wasn't a nine-o'clock town. If $110,000 a year forty years after a man has won his last major championship isn't a little lesson in the importance of good manners, what is? Sorehead tournament specialists and course carpers, take note.

Always a keen and aggressive competitor, along with living well, The Haig also wanted to look and feel good out there on the course before the eyes of the gallery. While he reigned in the days before golf stars endorsed sports clothes, Hagen paved the way for to-day's champions to pose as models for what the well-dressed man wears on and off the fairway. He had great clothes sense, and this was heightened by his intimacy with high society in the United States, Great Britain, and on the Continent. In his autobiography, which was published in 1956 when he was sixty-four, Hagen made it clear that in his first championship he was deter-mined to appear as the best-groomed contestant in the field. And he was. When he traveled to Great Britain to play, as was his annual custom, he al-ways allowed plenty of time to embel-lish his wardrobe with the choicest suits from Savile Row and Bond Street, the finest examples of the bootmaker's art, and shirts from the famed Izod. And when he teamed with his colleagues he insisted that they appear at their sar-torial best.

In 1933, Hagen was captain of a Ryder Cup team that was bound for Britain in what PGA officials had deemed was impressive enough style to represent the United States. The Haig carefully inspected the outfits his team was going to wear for the matches, sniffed, then told his players to go to two of the most expensive tailors in New York, one for slacks, the other for jackets. He then explained to the tail-ors what was required to display the American professionals to British gal-leries as champion exhibits of Ameri-can haute couture.

"And what do you want to spend, Mr. Hagen?" he was asked.

"Whatever is necessary—think noth-ing of it," Mr. Hagen airily replied, which perfectly expressed his attitude toward tailoring bills.

Naturally, his attitude was not shared by Jack Mackie, then treasurer of the PGA, when the bill came in. Jack's cry of pain could be heard clear to Carnoustie. And much later, the in-cident was recalled with grins by veter-ans as they heard and read of the young and uninformed tournament profes-sionals bitterly complaining that the PGA had never done anything to help the show business boys.

The testimony of durable golf enthu-siasts here and abroad is that Sir Wal-ter Hagen was the strongest gallery at-traction to come down the fairway. In the United States, people who had never seen golf played before, especially young women, came and paid money to see Hagen play. The Haig was the first professional to draw Walter's Wacs or The Haig's Waves, or whatever you want to call a large gallery of sophisti-cated, wealthy women attended, strangely enough, by their ever-loving spouses or boyfriends who were also Hagen fans. This wasn't a T-shirted aggregation, it was the jet set of the day and night. It was the class that reflected the original high-society and high-fi-nance atmosphere that established the game in the United States.

When there was talk about Tex Rickard and his "Hundred Million-aires" putting on the big-purse cham-pionship fights in what Westbrook Pegler called the "Days of Wonderful Nonsense," Joe Williams of the *New York Telegram* wrote that wherever Hagen was, you would also find the Hundred Millionaires—and any of the rest of the millionaires who could get close.

Maybe Williams was prejudiced. When he'd been a young sportswriter coming up, Hagen had spotted him at the Youngstown (Ohio) Country Club, left behind without transportation into town after finishing his tournament story. The Haig, relaxing as usual in the grill room, noticed the lost youngster who was new on the job, and adopted him as a companion and passenger.

Joe Williams became a great artist in his field. Brilliant sportswriters now look at some of the old Williams stuff that caught and held readers and wish they could write like Joe did. But the Williams prose, and that of other sportswriters to whom Hagen was companionable, kind, and considerate, was what built up the tournament golf circus in the United States. Conditions no longer encourage the spontaneous endorsement of the golf-playing specialist. He gets the benefit of a few spectacular strokes on television, then is brought into a pressroom where he gets the same sort of interview given suspects in a police station lineup. The star may have time for a few words with a reporter before his manager hauls him off to talk about endorsement deals. Meantime, the reporter on whose free publicity the tournament expert's commercial value depends is heartily nominating the inconsiderate performer as an ill-mannered heel.

Hagen was the star of stars as far as golf writers were concerned. What Walter didn't do for himself, his manager and publicity representative Bob Harlow did for him. But The Haig always had the time of day for the press and his admirers. Good manners were not unusual among the golfers who made the tournament circuit a multimillion-dollar business. Besides Hagen, there was that gentleman among gentlemen, Bob Jones; then Horton Smith; Craig Wood; Tommy Armour; Denny Shute; Paul Runyan; Harry Cooper; Gene Sarazen, who was a marvelously articulate fellow to be interviewed freely

about anything; Ed Dudley; Lawson Little, who was a pleasant young man and never bashful about sounding off; Sam Snead, who would go for colorful hillbilly lines; and Ben Hogan, who, if you'd stay with him and wait patiently until he'd come up with an answer that had been churning between his ears, would give out with answers that made so much sense he even made the reporter look good.

But it all narrows down to a matter of good manners as the crowning feature of showmanship that was so instinctive with Walter Christian Hagen. The old boys, such as Freddie McLeod, George Sargent, Tom McNamara, Mike Brady, Jock Hutchison, Wilfrid Reid, Bob Macdonald, Charley Mayo, Willie MacFarland, and George Low in the building-up era, players such as the Turnesas, Johnny Farrell, Tom Harmon, Joe Novak, George Aulbach, and others who were also truly gentlemen sportsmen, made tournament golf by their charm.

What gave Arnold Palmer a bigger publicity splash than his tournament performance might warrant were his superior, decent manners, an inheritance from his parents, rather than the opulence of increasing prizes for which he was not in the slightest responsible. Palmer, Gary Player, Bill Casper, Julius Boros, the late Tony Lema (so charming, immaculate, and well-spoken in the Hagen mold, and in the habit of serving champagne all around when he won), Jack Nicklaus, and of late, Johnny Miller, have been the only recent headliners in tournament golf to get anywhere near close to the high emotional ratings of their illustrious predecessors.

While being the beneficiary of the luckiest money line in the sports pages, "Arnie's Army," Palmer was in danger

Arnold Palmer.

markable golf record from being one of the most glamorous champions in golf history cannot be pinned down. Maybe he stili will be. He was not at ease, not warmly direct, and yet he handled himself wonderfully well when he didn't make the cut at Brookline the year after he was National Open Champion. Sometimes he was slightly on the arrogant side in runaway interviews with worried reporters who were not in a drawing-room mood themselves. But as much as they might have disliked Nicklaus at the prices he was getting in terms of what they were being paid, they gave the young man a "pass," charitably figuring he was overwhelmed by it all, and on a higher plane, not wanting to hurt the feelings of his wife.

One time a writer on a Palm Beach newspaper included a reference to "Fat Jack" in a story concerning Nicklaus, who lived in a Palm Beach suburban villa with his wife and kids. Kindly neighbors wrote irate letters asking the managing editor to fire the cad who had had the gall to refer to the spare tires protruding over the belt of the slacks our hero was being paid to advertise. The complainants all felt that the crude references to Jack's girth might hurt his wife's feelings.

The managing editor stood up for his sportswriter, who had probably written many worse things but wrote such a funny column about not being able to ride herd on his help that it perhaps came to "Fat Jack's" attention. In any case, Nicklaus got the message, took off the excess poundage, and started to play a lot better golf. Instead of whining like a low-grader and wanting to see a man canned for an accurate story, Nicklaus exhibited himself as a young man with class. And, incidentally, he began to look a whole lot better on TV and in those clothing ads

of becoming identified as a grasping, all-for-money golfer exploiting his worshipers until somebody got smart and hired "Doc" Griffin, a PGA Tournament Bureau publicity man, to switch the spotlight to Our Arnie, the Boy Next Door, just happening to hit the jackpot. What made it easier for Griffin to divorce his subject from his growing image as an instrument of cold, calculated avarice was the high regard golf writers had for Arnie's appealing wife Winnie.

The same held true for Barbara Nicklaus, Jack's wife, another remarkably pleasing young woman. What has so far prevented Nicklaus with his re-

Jack Nicklaus. PGA

Tommy Bolt. AG

and became known as the "Golden Bear."

Frankly, it is difficult to evaluate the clothing testimonials of a number of the models who parade the fairway runways. There are artistic differences of opinion, of course. Tommy Bolt, a snappy dresser on and off the course, said that he had a caddie who dressed more smartly than Doug Sanders, and Sanders, an outstanding golfer and pleasant personality, has outshone the rainbow with his colorful ensembles and come close to blinding the galleries.

But there are tricks in that trade. The Merry Super-Mex, Lee Trevino, had a pants deal set up for him by his first manager, Bucky Woy, that meant so much money in pants that Trevino could have bought back the Alamo. But when they looked at the advertising photographs, Super-Mex bulged all over. An advertising genius gasped, "Goddlemighty, no. This will put pants out of style!" But the quick-thinking Woy, who was brought up as an assistant in pro shops and learned never to let a dollar get away, easily soothed the advertising man with, "Oh no, don't look at it that way. Just remember, every golfer who sees these pictures is going to think, 'I've got to look better than this,' and that is going to sell you a lot of pants." Woy was right. But he and Super-Mex, for whom he brought in around $400,000, split up after a lawsuit. Probably both sides were lucky as well as happy.

Johnny Farrell was the first of the playing experts to make money as a mannequin. Elmer Ward, the Palm Beach clothing magnate who was a golf enthusiast from his boyhood days around Boston, hired Johnny, and the 1928 National Open Champion was crowned with annual best-dressed awards that were as funny and foolish then as they are now. Johnny was a trim, handsome, personable youth, liked by everybody, and he got money and free clothes on the deal. Who can rap that? Furthermore, as a promotion tournament, Ward put on the Palm Beach Round Robin, which involved a competitive pairing schedule so tricky it had university mathematics professors tangled trying to determine who played whom and who gave a damn. In the process, he gave hot-weather clothes by the rack to contestants, becoming virtually the first clothingmaker to use tournament professionals as show window dummies.

When getting Palm Beach advance or tournament play copy filed from, say, New York or Cincinnati, sports editors became confused by the geographical slant of the Palm Beach promotion. And newspaper advertising departments complained, "Why give the outfit free space—make them lay it on the line like our paying advertisers." But Ward kept at it until he got into an argument with the Tournament Bureau.

Elmer Ward certainly used professional golfers effectively in establishing hot-weather fabrics in men's wear; he showed all other advertisers how to put on a golf tournament and get more free advertising than they could possibly buy. He quit the tournament circuit as one of the biggest winners ever on it, taking along an excellent player, Harold (Jug) McSpaden, who became an executive in the clothing business and an owner of two profitable fee courses.

Yes, The Haig started it all. It got so that, when an American professional on a Ryder Cup team came back home looking so smartly turned out that his stunned friends asked, "What happened?" the new representative of the

Johnny Farrell. PGA

beau monde merely laughed carelessly and said, "No one can make my shirts like Izod."

Then a big, bright merchandiser named Vince Draddy began selling Izod shirts in the United States. He made a deal to sell the long-tailed sports shirts that René Lacoste, the French tennis champion and father of the sunny winner of American women's golf championships, had designed. This shirt, with René's alligator symbol on it, traded up the golf shirt market so the quality sportswear makers had a chance and could afford to pay testimonial fees to the tournament stars, instead of being ruined by the sweatshop producers who turned out cheap stuff on which stores could cut prices far under pro-shop figures.

11

The Pro Picture Brightens –
The Masters Begins; The PGA Promotes
Japanese Golf, Suffers From Politics,
Eliminates 7,427 Traps

[1934, 1935, 1936]

THE eighteenth annual meeting of the PGA was held November 20 and 21, 1934, at the Morrison Hotel, Chicago, with George Jacobus in his second round as president. Jim Wilson, Tom Boyd, Dan Goss, Jack Martin, Johnny Farrell, and Willie Maguire were vice-presidents, R. W. Treacy was secretary, and Jack Mackie again was treasurer. Thirty-three delegates assembled to hear Mackie read his report backward, like a Chinese laundry ticket, and the news was good—a welcome change. Ball royalties were around $37,000, general fund receipts were about $70,000, and disbursements approximately $54,500, leaving a cozy margin over the previous year. Dues had been reduced from $40 to $25 for Class A members, and there had been a membership increase of 255, with 211 of them Class A.

The financial statements of the PGA fluctuated wildly—black or red, with no middle ground. Its books were so complex that an amateur could get lost trying to track a dollar through the forests of the General Fund, the Benevolent and Relief funds, the Ryder Cup Fund, the Championship money, then through the devious Tournament, Royalty, and Educational funds with tax angles. All this bookkeeping was so confusing from the start that only certified public accountants and lawyers knew where the PGA really stood.

Tournament routine was handled quickly, with Harlow giving the startling good news that $100,000 in prize money was signed for the 1934–35 winter tournaments and that the 1935 PGA Championship set for the Twin Hills Country Club, Oklahoma City, promised $7,800 prize money.

When Bob Harlow arranged for the championship at Oklahoma City, he told sportswriters that the club was in the heart of the "zero-rolling country." In other localities, Harlow informed

Johnny Revolta. AG

Augusta National Golf Course. PGA

the journalists, a man with $1,000 might be considered wealthy, but in Oklahoma they rolled a lot of zeros after first the dollar mark, then a comfortable number, and three zeros as a starter. Bob also informed the group they could tell a genuinely rich oil man because he dressed as though he owned a service station with two pumps.

The owner of Twin Hills ran into a string of dry wells in his drilling operations shortly before the championship, and the PGA was worried before it got its guarantee, but all came out well.

Johnny Revolta won the final match and title from Tommy Armour, 5 and 4. Revolta started his championship

campaign by defeating Walter Hagen on the eighteenth hole when Hagen knocked his approach over the green under a car in a parking lot. Revolta won $1,000 with the title and became the leading money winner in 1935, with $9,543. Revolta never was a long hitter but was deadly in chipping, pitching, and playing out of bunkers and was one of the best putters. He also became one of the foremost teachers of the game.

The year 1934 was significant to golf in marking the beginning of the now classic Masters Tournament at the Augusta National Golf Club. Played at a time when spring was greening lushly in the South, in a setting that had been a famed botanical garden for a century and on a course designed to be as uniquely American as the Old Course at St. Andrews was pure Scotland at its best, the Masters had perhaps the most nearly ideal staging yet devised for a golf tournament.

Bob Jones and his companion Clifford Roberts, unquestionably the top quality team in American golf, conceived a golf course that gave spectators advantageous viewing points and tested to the utmost the mental as well as the physical capacities of players of all degrees of ability.

Watching the Masters remains one of the most pleasant and revealing experiences for the individual who pays to see a golf tournament. Despite the frequent uncertainties of a Georgia spring, the Masters is always in the finest conditions of any course on the winter circuit. Besides its superb turf, the cup and tee placement have also been given such careful, exacting study that the Masters has scared away those lacking valid championship credentials.

Facilities at the Masters for spectators, players, and press soon became the best in golf's world. Because of the Jones and Roberts planning, many considered the Masters the premier golf tournament, outranking the U.S. National Open, the PGA, and the British National Open. The Masters was settled in Augusta because the city that charmed General Sherman and had been a favorite fall and spring golfing resort of President Lincoln's son, Robert Todd Lincoln, and his golfing friends was also the home of the lovely young woman Bob Jones married. It had the Augusta Country Club and the Forest Hills and other resort courses, so it looked like the promised land to Jones and Roberts, who main-

tained there could be excellent national championships in the South.

After Dr. Alastair Mackenzie, consulting architect for the Royal and Ancient Golf Club of Andrews, had designed the Augusta National course with mounds and waters in strategic locations and only a few sand traps, revisions were made by course experts Robert Trent Jones and George Cobb. Cobb also designed the nine-hole, par-3 course on which is played the curtain raiser to the Masters. It is rated by competent authorities as the best of all par-3 courses.

The story of the Masters Tournament is relevant to PGA history because the Masters came along at the right time to prove that class outranked money in the public eye where golf tournaments were concerned. The Masters has been top class from the start. There have been no robbery prices at the concessions, no parking in remote spots at fancy prices, and no program advertising waste. Sheets on pairing and starting times and information booklets on contestants are provided free to the public.

So the Masters became world famous as the tournament most intelligently conducted by men whose dream was to share a wonderful show with others who also loved golf. And the dates of the Masters are right. Jones had retired as master of all he surveyed and sat at the top of the mountain as the Perfect Gentleman Sportsman. Roberts, a country boy who'd tamed the wolves of Wall Street and had a passion for anonymity and the quiet, friendly pleasures of golf, turned his genius to Augusta National. Of course, there were problems during its infancy, but Roberts and Jones triumphed by maintaining the high quality that was part of their character.

The Augusta National membership list was and continues to be a high-bracket golf Who's Who. Before Dwight Eisenhower knew whether he was a Republican or a Democrat, his presidential destiny may well have been born at Augusta National with Roberts and Jones as midwives. Both of them were just too old-fashioned honorable to think of Ike in any way other than the best man for the country, and away from work, a perfect golfing companion.

Roberts had the sentimental sense to call the Masters pressroom (the best golf writers have seen) the Bartlett Lounge, as a memorial to Charles Bartlett, longtime secretary of the Golf Writers' Association, who had written reams of copy about the event. It was also Roberts's idea to put a plaque on the bridge leading to the fifteenth hole where Sarazen slipped in an eagle 3 to tie and then win the 1935 Masters.

Roberts and Jones kept the Masters so firmly identified with the highest class that they allowed only television sponsorship of top quality, while other televised golf events went for any that would buy the time. So, in 1934, the beginning of the Masters was more significant than anything the PGA Tournament Bureau could do. In other ways the Masters has been beneficial to the PGA, contributing $5,000 a year for many years to the PGA Educational Fund.

At the 1934 meeting, the delegates listened to the report of a Chicago golf business school innovation that began sectional programs that have benefited pro golfers immensely. Professionals from Illinois, Wisconsin, and northern Indiana met in a two-day session to listen to successful golf teachers and merchandisers of their own group and to outside experts in merchandising,

accounting, and the mental and physical makeup of the golfer. Club officials also spoke on the details and spirit of the professional's value to his club and its members and his relations with other club employees.

The New England section had a similar educational program crowded into one day. It was an appraisal of experiences of professionals who'd weathered the economic storm of the previous few years and done mighty well in helping their clubs. Unfortunately, the club business-professional publicity was touched on only lightly at the New England conference. Out of the two meetings came the educational pattern that later became customary at PGA sectional spring meetings and was instrumental in developing pro-shop annual sales of approximately a quarter-billion dollars.

It's remarkable how little the fundamentals of pro-shop operation have changed in about forty years. Reports of the Midwest school tell of a store-display expert telling professionals that, as a club member, he had noticed pros kept the balls they most wanted to sell in a locked showcase, while the secondhand balls were easy to reach. He also urged showing golf merchandise in light as near as possible to the natural light of playing conditions. This was a problem, considering the dark basement pro shops common to the mid-1930's when clubs and fee courses began to appreciate that attractive pro shops were of valuable service to golfers.

The University of Wisconsin conducted a short course on course maintenance that was especially helpful in the pro educational program, inasmuch as 90 percent of the pros at nine-hole courses were pro-greenkeepers and the Depression had forced pros at larger clubs into dual jobs where they were not qualified to handle course management.

PGA ball sales for the year were 35,-556 dozen—Spalding leading with 19,-870 dozen, followed by U.S. Rubber with 4,961, Acushnet with 4,026, Wilson with 2,910, L. A. Young (Hagen) with 1,772, St. Mungo-Burke with 336, and Worthington with 76.

Some delegates complained about the free balls given by manufacturers to professionals. It was charged that the distribution of free balls was unfair and of no help in maintaining a firm retail price or improving credit ratings. It was also decided that something should be done to get golf into more college physical education programs. Golf professionals at colleges and universities with golf courses had been doing an excellent job of developing young men and women into good golfers and had actually had far more influence on postgraduate life than the highly publicized football coaches, but they rarely got any publicity away from their schools.

The junior programs that professionals had been conducting at their clubs were succeeding with kids and their parents beyond the expectations of many pros. The professionals who put across these programs so skillfully were those who tied women's committees at their clubs into the work. The women organized and supervised the classes and tournaments; the pros did the free teaching.

It was proposed that the PGA establish a national junior championship. Even at that time, professionals in the Carolinas and Georgia had junior tournaments going, with contestants being fed and housed at the homes of young people in the tournament host town while the professionals spent hours and off-days and spare cash and automobile

mileage touring their protégés. There's never quite been anything in sports promotion done to equal the performance of the enthusiastic and unsung pros, especially in the Southeast, who got the junior golf program started and continued to develop it so successfully.

The United States Junior Chamber of Commerce national and international junior championships stemmed from the PGA pros' juvenile programs. The USGA was dubious about the professionals' promoting junior golf. It feared there might be some commercialism staining the young people—for instance, soft-drink companies paying the travel expenses of the young players and their coaches. Nevertheless, the work continued while the USGA sat on its hands and raised its eyebrows in alarm. Then, after the PGA had created lively, nationwide interest in junior golf, the USGA began to stir and started its own junior championships.

Other items at the 1934 meeting included the usual discussion about how to select the next Ryder Cup team and changes in membership classifications and qualifications. There have been so many changes in PGA membership classifications that nobody has tried to keep track of them. It didn't make much difference what the classes were; most of them would be changed the next year anyway. At the 1934 meeting, the Northern California section insisted that a man, to be a Class A PGA member, had to be able to score 75 or better. Other delegates asked, "On what course, what day?" There were entertaining reminiscences. The motion didn't pass.

Success was reported with the use of material from a PGA publicity "clipsheet" containing stories on pro business at clubs as well as the tournament circuit news. Bob Harlow wrote the tournament circuit material, and Herb Graffis wrote the pieces about the job of the pro at a club and pay-play course in coaching players and supplying them with equipment. Graffis had ghosted a story on the home professional for Alex Pirie in *The Saturday Evening Post* that drew considerable favorable comment about home pros, but it was never followed up until the 1934 PGA releases. Then, for some reason nobody remembers, or for no reason at all, the public information campaign on the home pro lapsed for years and years.

The three-day annual meeting was resumed when the PGA met at the Morrison Hotel, Chicago, on November 19, 20, and 21, 1935, and there was plenty of business for the forty-one delegates. George Jacobus was president. Vice-presidents were Jimmy Anderson, Tom Boyd, Dan Goss, Jack Martin, Johnny Farrell, and Willie Maguire. R. W. Treacy continued as secretary, and J. B. Mackie as treasurer.

Politics took over this time, meaning that the true politician's first duty was to get elected at all costs; what happened after that was secondary. Naturally, many professionals who had done well for their clubs, then promptly lost their jobs because of club politics, were alarmed when they saw the campaign for the PGA presidency threatening to take priority over other activities of the association.

George Jacobus liked his job as PGA president and wanted intensely to keep it. He had done well for the PGA in trying to get the association coordinated and in planning to take advantage of an upturn in the golf business curve and the general economic situation. He was a good pro at his club and got his employers, the Ridgewood Country Club, to hold the 1935 Ryder

Cup matches. The contest, which was played September 28 and 29 and easily won by the United States team, also made a little money, and the club members were satisfied, even though the 1935 competition wasn't quite the show that had been put on during the previous matches in this country in June, 1931, at the Scioto Country Club, where the Americans had also won handily. The National Open was at Inverness, Toledo, that year, and a world heavyweight championship fight at Cleveland combined with it to draw sportswriters from many countries. As a result, the Ryder Cup competition received the biggest coverage it has ever had in the United States.

In any case, the Ridgewood members were happy. Their pro was an able and faithful servant to them, which was why they cheerfully had gotten him and the PGA out of a bind by taking on the international professional contest. Jacobus had a pretty and competent secretary who did more to put the PGA on a business basis than even she realized. She wrote a lot of letters for her boss. PGA sectional officers who rarely heard from the president began getting frequent chatty communiqués, and Jacobus also visited many sections personally. He was doing his job, and his political motivation was sincere, but it stirred up the PGA.

At the annual meeting, delegates heard a report on a forgotten PGA service that proved to be of great and timely value to golf clubs in general. The PGA had hired A. W. Tillinghast, a prominent golf architect, for a flat two months, and had assigned him to visit golf courses where PGA members were employed as professionals and to suggest design improvements of the courses. Tillinghast was a good ama-

A. W. Tillinghast. GH

teur player in Philadelphia, an entertaining golf writer, and a capable editor. He got into course design and produced several courses on which national championships have been played. He was gifted at the design of greens with contours and bunkering that made them works of art that are distinguished even now.

It was said that "Tilly" would visualize a green, then sit under a tree and yell directions to a black aide-de-camp and his mule. Then the black man and the mule and a Fresno scoop modeled earth presumably as Michelangelo worked on marble. How and why Tillinghast happened to be engaged as the PGA architectural consultant, nobody explained at the time, since there were good architects who were PGA members.

As it was, professionals had learned from club experience that excessive sand trapping was adding heavy costs and diminishing rather than adding to the charm and testing qualities of a golf course. Tillinghast, and other architects of the golf artist type, believed that golf should primarily be fun for those who paid for the courses. They felt that lack of distance penalized the majority of players enough without cutting in bunkers that contributed nothing to the strategic interest of play.

Tillinghast advocated eliminating a lot of traps, converting some traps near greens from sand pits to grassy hollows, and having the fairway mowers control the wise line of play by letting the rough grow and making it an inexpensively maintained hazard. The advisory service was free. In one day, Tillinghast went over the course and the plans with the club officials, the pro, and the greenkeeper, and outlined changes that took little time or money.

Word of the Tillinghast service got around quickly, and there was such a demand for his advice that his time with the PGA was extended. Then it was terminated after having been the best thing the PGA had done to present the professional to his employers as a helpful authority on golf courses. As a matter of fact, this two-year architectural service was so successful it embarrassed Tillinghast. It had disclosed the widespread need of revision in course architecture and the vital need for competent architectural advice. But with the PGA providing the Tillinghast genius free, why should any club with a PGA pro pay an outside architect to do the job?

From that time on, sports section stories began mentioning courses of the "PGA type," and later of "USGA character," when there actually were no such specifications. However, in about

Japanese Golf Team, 1935. GH

a year the PGA had an impact on golf that altered the trend of golf architecture. Neither before nor since has the PGA been so influential in directing club operations.

With a minimal Tournament Bureau budget the PGA had given international professional golf an impetus that was proudly reported at the 1935 PGA meeting. In addition to the Ryder Cup matches, there'd been American representation in the Lakes tournament in Australia, and Jimmy Thomson had won the Melbourne Centenary tournament with a $5,000 first prize, which was big money for that time.

But the international golf show that drew most spectators consisted of the forty-two matches and five tournaments in which a six-man team of Japanese professionals competed. And Kanekichi Nakamura of the Nipponese team did well enough to play seventy-two holes in the National Open at Oakmont in 1935.

It had taken Harlow more than three years to work up the Japanese team's trip, which was financed mainly by the Japan Golf Association. The first Japanese pro to come over was Tom Myamoto in 1934, and he did fairly well in a few tournaments, including the Western Open, for a man who, as Harlow said, had learned most of his golf out of picture books. Hagen also played exhibition matches with Myamoto that brought in nearly enough to pay off the Japanese sponsors of Myamoto's tour.

During the tour the Japanese team won twenty-five matches and lost thirteen against teams of U.S. professionals and one against an all-amateur team in Chicago, after the Japanese had played a team of Illinois professionals. More than two hundred PGA members played against the Japanese.

The artistic and educational crest of the tour for the Japanese came at Atlanta, where they met Bob Jones, who was his usual gracious self. He made such a lasting impression that, at the international pro championships at Tokyo in 1957, members of that 1935 Japanese team looked up American golf writers to ask about Jones and express their gratitude for his kindness.

Harlow was kind to them, too. He got the PGA to go mad with extravagance by advancing Harlow $500 as a down payment on a used Packard-trailer combination. The rest of the expenses came out of gallery fees. Harlow also arranged welcome parties for the visiting team with Japanese residents along the tour and press parties with "delicatessen"—as near as Harlow could translate "cocktail snacks" into Japanese. Between the Harlow program of feedings and the jerking and bouncing in the trailer towed by Harlow and his secondhand Packard, the Japanese team quickly learned American for "service station" and how to transmit emergency signals from trailer to pilot.

That Japanese pro tour of the United States ignited a golf boom in the Orient. It must have been the cheapest and most successful promotion in sports history. The Japan Golf Association got gift transportation and rations for the team on Japanese steamships to and from the United States. That was the start of the vast golf activity among wealthy Orientals, visiting businessmen, vacationers, and occupa-

tion troops following the war in the South Pacific.

There were sportswriters who served in the armed forces or as correspondents in the South Pacific who'd written about the Harlow rolling golf circus; a few of them even rode with Harlow in the beat-up Packard or in the trailer with the touring pros. A Los Angeles golf writer suspected Pearl Harbor originally was intended only to get even with Harlow for his driving.

Interestingly enough, at the time, neither the golf writers, the PGA, nor golf in general had the slightest idea that the trip of the Japanese, together with the invasion of Australia by Yankee pros, was making the United States, rather than Great Britain, the primary world power in professional golf.

The disturbed situation in pro golf at home, per custom, came before the PGA annual meeting with the outspoken Sarazen as the voice of the Tournament Committee. He warned that pro golf was on the way out because of the failure of professionals to show commercial confidence and class, and he urged a decided increase in tournament entry fees. He said tournament fields were jammed with too many "service station amateurs" who paid a little money for the distinction of playing with professionals and for practice rounds that beat the cost of green fees. He advocated having the host club take the gate fees, and he was seconded by Neil McIntyre, professional at the Highlands Country Club of Indianapolis, where the Veterans of Foreign Wars had paid for the use of the course for a tournament that didn't pay the prize winners. McIntyre remarked that his members believed that pros hacked up too many divots to be welcome guests.

Sarazen was promptly knocked by

other pros, saying, "With your way we'd be playing for our own money," a statement to be repeated later about National Open prize money. Sarazen, never one to give an evasive answer, said, "I'm playing for my own money all the time like every other man trying to build a business."

Among the top playing pros, Sarazen and Hogan are, on the record, the coldest, toughest, most defiant proponents of the policy that tournament golf is a problem whose answers are worked out by clubs, balls, and the scorecard, instead of being a playground of the welfare state. There were some, like Ralph Guldahl and Lawson Little, who never went to the trouble of trying to understand what the Tournament Bureau fuss was all about. To pros of the Hagen and Lloyd Mangrum stripe, the Tournament Bureau fussing was something they heard out with a casual big ear and a laugh, much as one washerwoman would listen to the sounding off of the lippy biddy across the fence. With their keen sense of public opinion, Hagen and Mangrum thought, "Who gives a damn about anyone making money by having the fun of playing golf?"

Armour was much the same way, except that he believed a man should elevate his profession. He got in wrong when he said that certain PGA officials should think, speak, and act like mature businessmen instead of caddies, and was threatened with being excommunicated from the PGA for heresy, but he laughed himself out of that rap and had the PGA president red-faced but smart enough to call off the controversy.

There were numerous cases of pros regaining shop concessions after clubs had tried unsuccessfully to get out of the red by taking over the store and

making the money they believed the pros made. These cases were gleefully related in detail at the meeting. There were also the usual comments about the bad credit of professionals at busy first-class clubs where professionals had good salaries for those times, full shop concessions, reasonable revenue from club storage and cleaning, and a split with the caddie master on soft-drink, candy, and sandwich sales to the caddies.

The apparel field, which is such big golf business today, was just getting started and having its own particular problems. Johnny Farrell told the delegates that at Baltusrol he was stuck with a big stock of knickers and hose when the fashion suddenly switched to slacks. Johnny Manion, an energetic professional at St. Louis, added that knickers must be out of style because at his course he saw so many golfers wearing trousers that he thought truck drivers were taking over the course. This was the ultimate sartorial accident and came about when the Prince of Wales and Walter Hagen, playing without taking time to change to the formal knickered attire, established a fashion that rapidly caught on, first for the roomy-leg trousers of British undergraduates, then for the Hollywood pants with that air of "studied carelessness." The switch to the sports-coat-and-handiest-pants ensemble begun by golfers had an immense effect on fashions.

At the 1935 meeting, the pros had no conception of what seemed to be influencing golf apparel, but there was a good hunch that the PGA was missing the boat in public relations for the club pro. Grange Alves, a Scot transplanted to Ohio, asked his fellow delegates, "Why not let golf writers into the meeting so they can see what we are up against in trying to help our clubs and golf and ourselves? They can do more for us than we can do for them." Alves was never able to get his simple story across, and the PGA is still suffering.

Much later on, during the PGA's civil war, the tournament players were having one of their meetings when a graduate caddie slugged a newspaper photographer in a display of what a press-service writer called "a ten-cent brain and two-dollar knuckles running a big business. To his credit, it must be said that the valiant party did apologize; he thought the meeting was "secret." Things were that silly then in public and press relations.

What Grange Alves had in mind for overall PGA publicity was rational but probably as impossible as getting full and open coverage of a Newspaper Guild meeting or a meeting of professional baseball, football, or basketball clubs, strictly private affairs that are, rightly or wrongly, considered none of the public's damned business.

Unfinished business from the previous year's conclave was still smoldering when the twentieth annual meeting of the PGA, at the Congress Hotel, Chicago, on November 10, 11, and 12, 1936, was called to order. "Order" was not always the right word for the tone of the proceedings at times, but differences were healthy ones between men eager to stand up anywhere and be counted.

There was some shouting when the New Jersey section proposed that President Jacobus be given a five-year contract with power to approve or disapprove committee recommendations. The yowls about that idea became louder when Ed Dudley and Leo Diegel said they'd been told during the Ryder Cup matches at Ridgewood that Ja-

cobus, the Ridgewood professional, was to be the PGA president for years.

Another jumping blaze that wasn't stomped out was the charge that manufacturers were subsidizing PGA officials, thus planning to control the PGA. That was the countercharge of the Jacobus supporters to the Diegel and Dudley report of the Jacobus plan to take over. And of course the home versus touring pros debate was bound to get hotter as the PGA got bigger and stronger.

Frank Sprogell, one of a couple of dozen Philadelphia caddies who became fine players, although not so good as their companion Johnny McDermott, who had been on home pro jobs for years with only short vacations for tournaments, noted: "If the playing pro does interest people in golf, after these people are converted, to whom do they go for counsel and help—who gets them acquainted with how to play golf and makes them welcome? It's the home pro. There's not enough money in that work for the playing pro, and he hasn't got the time."

The playing pro wasn't happy with the PGA because, as Sarazen said, the PGA did not hold its championship in June, July or August so the winner could make $5,000 or $10,000 out of his victory. The Sarazen suggestions didn't accomplish a thing. The 1936 PGA Championship was at Pinehurst in November, the only place and time the PGA could get. Denny Shute beat Jimmy Thomson, 3 and 2, for the title.

Instead of splitting the PGA, the differences actually brought the organization closer together by giving members something specific to argue about for a year. Jacobus and his administration happily announced a recovery note in the sale of 174,389 dozen PGA balls and $133,000 in royalties for the year.

Jimmy Thomson. AG

A delegate remarked that the PGA ball royalties meant that all professionals who sold the balls were subsidized by the licensed manufacturers, so why be concerned about what manufacturer had what pro on his payroll?

Club professionals were learning that sponsoring a tournament was difficult. The event scheduled for Portland was canceled because pros in the Pacific Northwest couldn't raise the prize money. The area came up with the right answer to tournament financing when Robert A. Hudson, a wealthy food broker, club official, and golf enthusiast, became the angel of a PGA Championship in Portland and of the Ryder Cup matches. He picked up enough tabs for American and British Ryder Cup players and officials to relieve them of the worry that they might have to swim the Atlantic.

A pro-shop sales promotion idea that enlisted pros at 350 clubs (and still is a good hunch) was *Pictorial Review* magazine's nationwide women's golf competition, with winners paid in pro-shop merchandise. This was the first time any prominent merchandising element had realized the potential of the woman golfer–pro-shop combination in quality marketing to women.

The government, through the WPA, was building golf courses as part of the public works program of recovery from the Depression. The PGA hoped to get a line on pro jobs from this work but couldn't find a direct answer. The same lack of success in capitalizing on the expansion of the pro job market was experienced when federal guarantees of low-interest loans through the FHA accounted for building hundreds of courses around 1960.

During 1936, the PGA was getting well financially, with $110,065 coming into the general fund. Thirty-five tournaments were played in the United States and Canada, and $148,945 was paid out in prize money. Harlow continued to develop the American golf picture internationally. Gene Sarazen won the Australian Open, and Tony Manero and Johnny Revolta finished third and fourth in the Argentine Open in 1936 after Manero had won the U.S. National Open. Lawson Little won the Canadian Open. Torchy Todo and Chick Chin came from Japan again to play in U.S. tournaments. They did fairly well.

The Tournament Bureau reported that American pros had scored better in their events than the British during their summer tournaments, but nothing was said about the possibility that the British might have played more

difficult courses. Australia sent a team, virtually unannounced, to the United States in the middle of the winter season to play a return match for the Lakes Cup, which the Australians had won at home in 1934. The Tournament Committee and the Southern California PGA arranged a match with a team captained by Paul Runyan. The hastily assembled American team won. The match was to be played every four years but faded after the 1936 event.

The Tournament Committee was reduced from nineteen to three by Executive Committee action. Horton Smith, the chairman, was a careful man with money. He saw a championship performance in "carefulness" when he discovered that the PGA gave Harlow $5 per day as an expense allowance in handling Tournament Bureau business. Smith told the annual meeting he thought $5 a day was "a bit too low." He suggested Harlow might have "access to funds" for entertaining tournament sponsors and the press. The "entertainment" bill Harlow had presented for 1936 was $63.

A. W. Tillinghast told the delegates that during the past fifteen months he had inspected 370 courses and indicated 7,427 unnecessary traps as the PGA course architectural consultant. At a conservative estimate of $25 per year for raking traps, cutting grass on slopes, and replacing sand, those traps cost clubs more than $164,000 a year of money wasted. Most of those bunkers, he said, caught the shots of the 90 percent of club members who couldn't break 90.

Tillinghast described eliminating 92 traps at one club and 41 at another. He proved his contention that the sand wedge made it easy for a playing specialist to get out of green trapping fairly close to the hole and maintained that a grassy hollow as green trapping was in many cases a better test of the expert than sand. Again the PGA was lauded for Tillinghast's work. One club official said the service had saved his club $10,000.

Clubs at Charlevoix, Michigan, and Lake George, New York, had been talking about holding annual championships for PGA members fifty years of age or older, but nothing definite had happened. The pro seniors were too busy in the summer. In 1937, the PGA sponsored its first Senior Championship at Augusta and played the event there again the next year.

There was the usual criticism concerning the names of prominent players appearing on inferior clubs and balls, and the usual suggestion that members allowing their names to be used on the cheap stuff be refused entry in PGA tournaments. A delegate said that since there were laws against misleading advertising, the manufacturers misusing pros' names should be brought into court by the PGA. Nothing happened. A resolution prohibiting PGA members on manufacturers' payrolls from holding association office was passed but was, apparently, promptly forgotten.

Political infighting of long standing brought many polite refusals to run for vice-presidential spots. "Doc" Treacy declined to run for another term as secretary. His club was very active again, and he said that in trying to put across the PGA Championship at Milwaukee, which had lost $4,600 during a Depression year, he'd worked harder free than he would have for money. There was no argument when Walter Hagen and Bob Jones were elected honorary vice-presidents.

The PGA ball came in for more hot debate. A ball with "PGA" on one pole and the manufacturer's name on another, made by several licensed manufacturers, had been available for nine years with rebates per dozen going to the PGA, the member buying the balls, or being split between the two. Some members declared that it was just another private-brand ball and the rebate came out of the cost. Treacy and others took the position that the PGA ball rebate was the sensible way for a member to pay his dues, promote his association, and increase ball sales. He admitted, though, that when a man was told that for paying $25 dues he could get $2,000 back, he would suspect something queer about the deal.

Private-brand balls as give-aways or sold at low prices as advertising were running up into the millions, and pros told of members at their own clubs who were competing with them for ball business. Other PGA members brought up successful reprisal campaigns they'd conducted. The most quickly effective was against a soft-drink manufacturer whose sales at clubs slumped sharply and even had the caddies active in reminding the soft-drink maker to attend to the soda business while the pro would attend to the golf ball business. An automobile-tire maker and a maker of electric lightbulbs also got backfire from PGA pros on private-brand ball deals. In some areas pros had printed circulars telling golfers: "We can't afford to give away tires or lightbulbs with first-quality golf balls. Don't think you're getting first-quality, or something good, free from anybody who gives you free golf balls."

The anti-private-brand-ball campaign was a hot subject with the PGA for several years, then cooled as pros learned that private-brand balls were competing with stores selling cheap balls rather than with top-grade, pro-only balls. More important, PGA ball sales had begun to make a marketing impression. Makers of a shirt, a golf bag "with patented features," and golf shoes had expressed interest in making PGA-branded products.

12

Pioneer Personalities – John Shippen, Dewey Brown, John Inglis, and Caddying as Golf's Prep School

SOME scholars maintain that history is basically the story of individuals and that the details are merely accidents beyond the control of the celebrated subjects, who are far more famous dead than alive. This view may well be sniffed at by intellectuals to whom the sports pages are nursery stuff, but it gets solid confirmation from the lives of intelligent athletes. And it is not too much to say that professional golf probably has sports' highest percentage of that category of muscular mortal.

The professional athlete often has been a kid of a poor family and not any too well schooled except in the essentials of making a living. The earlier professionals, foreign-born or native, were youngsters of families in which responsibility, self-reliance, and industry were cardinal virtues. They went wherever a job or opportunity offered itself, be it fishing out of a Scottish port, working as apprentice to a trades-

man, serving in the army, navy, or merchant marine—or even filling a post overseas, as did Freddie McLeod, National Open Champion in 1908, when word got back to North Berwick, Scotland, that a professional golfer was needed in far-off Rockford, Illinois.

Little Freddie worked in a bakery and delivered mail and still got a chance to play thirty-six holes of golf a day. In Scotland it's light at 3:00 A.M. in the summer, and at 10:00 P.M. they still can see the ball and play. Water fare (steerage), train fare (sitting up all night, of course), and rations en route cost about $75 in the late 1890's and early 1900's. But that was a fortune then in a small Scottish town, and when a lad left for the United States he had his own savings, help from his family, a loan from some kin, plus funds from trailblazers from home who met the young immigrant at New York.

The first-comers among the professionals needed assistants right off, and they were careful about their selections. They imported good stock. The Newport Golf Club professional, W. F. Davis, brought over Horace Rawlins from England in January, 1895, and on October 4 that year the nineteen-year-old Rawlins won the first National Open in the United States. Rawlins's score (45–46–41–41–173) beat the nation's first pro, Willie Dunn, who was still at the Shinnecock Hills course he'd built, by two strokes. Jim Foulis, recently shipped from Scotland to be professional at the Chicago Golf Club, and Rawlins's boss, Davis, tied at 176.

For many years Rawlins was distinguished as the youngest professional to win the U.S. Open, the only pro to win the Open on a course at which the winner was employed, and also the only assistant professional to win the event. The victory helped Rawlins get a pro job of his own in 1896 at the Sadaquada Golf Club at Utica, New York. He kept that a couple of years, then went to Equinox, then continued to work in New England at Waumbek and Spring Haven. He came to Wykagyl in the New York metropolitan district in 1905, then for several years was on a summer resort job at Ekwanok, Manchester, Vermont, before he went back to England for the rest of his days. Rawlins was a good player for his time. He followed his victory in the initial National Open by finishing second, three strokes back of the 152 of James Foulis's 152 in the 1896 Open at Shinnecock Hills.

That year Willie Dunn had gone from Shinnecock Hills to the new Ardsley club as professional, but Shinnecock Hills was well represented professionally by R. B. Wilson, Oscar Bunn, and a caddie who'd been brought along as a clubmaker, player, and teacher by

Dunn. The kid, John Shippen, as mentioned in Chapter 2, was of mixed Shinnecock Indian and black parentage. He was a pleasant, well-mannered man and died in the late 1960's. Toward the end of his life he was on the pro staff of a club in New Jersey. He was on a catch-as-catch-can income basis and managed only a slim living as an old man, but he wasn't the only athlete to die old and broke and entirely forgotten by the cheerleaders when he needed a buck.

Available evidence indicates that Shippen was helped a lot to jobs and on jobs by pioneer British pros and their employers in the United States. Dim and kindly recollections have Shippen as cheerful but not especially competent at shop work or teaching. As with many other assistants, then and since, he was far more eager to devote time to his own game than to concern himself teaching members. He started in golf as a member of the crew building the course at Shinnecock Hills, originally an Indian reservation, and appears to have been a satisfactory greenkeeper, but he always preferred to play.

Shippen did well in his first Open in 1896 at his home course, tying for third at 159 with H. J. Whigham, the socialite son-in-law of the noted Charles Blair Macdonald, winner of the second and third USGA National Amateur Championship. Shippen didn't play in the 1897 Open at Chicago Golf or the 1898 Open at Myopia, probably because the events called for more expense money than he could raise. This was something that kept many contenders out of the early Open championships. A fair percentage of the entrants were always homesick Scots probably more eager to see old friends and kinsmen than hopeful of winning the competition.

John Shippen. GH

At the Baltimore Country Club in the 1899 Open Shippen entered from Aronimink and tied for twenty-fourth with two former Open champions, Horace Rawlins and Fred Herd. Next year, when he got a job as greenkeeper at the Marine and Field Club in Brooklyn, he was doing well enough to make the trip to Chicago Golf where he got in the record as "J. Shippen, Jr." There he tied for twenty-fifth. His name is not in the record of the 1901 Open at Myopia, but in 1902 at Garden City "John H. Shippen," registered from New York, finished tied for fourth at 318. He doesn't appear in the USGA record book again until the 1913 Open, when Ouimet won at Brookline. Then, as "John Shippen, Maidstone," he finished in a tie for forty-first.

After that Shippen does not appear in USGA records of the Open. These records are incomplete as only qualifiers for the full route of Open championship play generally are in print, nor are there any written records or recollections of pioneer PGA members that he ever applied for PGA membership.

The first black man to become a PGA member was Dewey Brown, who'd been a caddie, then assistant in New Jersey and the Philadelphia area, then assistant to the veteran Willie Norton. He was hired by Norton at the famous Buckwood Inn resort course owned by C. C. Worthington at Shawnee on Delaware. The course was host to the Shawnee Open, one of the events of the pretournament-circuit days.

Brown had the reputation among visiting professionals and the resort's other guests of having one of the neatest, most attractive golfer "service stations" in the country. He was a competent clubmaker and an encouraging teacher. He knew all the big-name pros

John Inglis. PGA

in golf's growing-up days, and they thought him a distinguished man. Brown was resourceful. Give him soap, water, paint, a few new boards and nails, and some pretty new cloth for window curtains, and he'd risk electrocution and fire hazards to transform a dark basement corner in a clubhouse into a nice bright little store that reflected a good pro's personality. He was the owner of an inviting little course and resort hotel in upstate New York when he died.

The original native professionals of the United States all began as caddies, literally learning the game from the ground up, and they never seemed to consider golf as a field of social differences. They found they could make money and have fun at golf, and what better spare-time avocation was there? There were a few caddie strikes in the late 1890's by kids who felt they were being ground under the heel of capital-

ism at 25 cents plus a dime tip. But with the 1892 Homestead steel mill strike, the Pullman strike, and Coxey's Army in 1894, such labor unrest was bound to overflow a generation gap. When the folks at home asked the young family man about his contribution toward the tight budget, discussion eventually revealed that caddying was a better-paying job than selling newspapers, intermittent work as an errand or delivery boy, a neighborhood chore performer, or otherwise as one of the hard-core unemployed.

So back to work, if it might be called that, the boys went. Caddie wages increased because of the difficulty in getting boys, especially as the clubs were out in the country where there were few prospects. More players meant more of a demand for caddies and improved training and performance helped raise caddie wages.

American-born pioneer professionals were men of sound character who, by accident alone, became acquainted with an utterly new livelihood that combined sport and industry, social development and travel. Typical of this select group was a keen little man who continued to play golf as an octogenarian. The career of John Inglis is paralleled by a dozen of his kind, and John Inglis, a charter member of the PGA, is truly representative of the genuine builders of American golf.

Inglis began caddying in 1896 at the old nine-hole course of the Apawamis Golf Club in Rye, New York, whose professional was the previously mentioned W. F. Davis. Davis saw promise in the Inglis kid and gave Johnny a couple of clubs in junk condition. When Davis saw how the boy had picked up enough about clubmaking to make his implements effective and presentable, Davis put Inglis to work making and repair-

ing clubs—and discreetly getting ears-
and eyesful of golf teaching between
caddying jobs.

Young Inglis was a precocious organizer and leader of kids as well as quick
to show that he was mastering golf as a
trade. At that time, caddies weren't inclined to think of golf as a career. In
1901 Frank Greatorex, pro at the
Larchmont (New York) Yacht and Golf
Club, hired Inglis as assistant and caddie master, and he was soon named
head professional to succeed Greatorex.

By then Inglis had also picked up
enough about course construction and
maintenance to get himself work in the
winter of 1907–1908 building a nine-
hole course for the Royal Palm Hotel,
on the shore of the Caloosahatchee
River at Fort Meyers, Florida. He stayed
on as professional and showed wealthy
Northerners there was more to the
place than tarpon fishing. Thomas A.
Edison, Harvey Firestone, Henry Ford
and Dr. Franklin Miles were among his
pupils, but Inglis was unable to get
them playing golf. They tried, but the
game was too difficult and took too
much time.

When Inglis went North in April,
1908, he was hired as professional by
the Fairview Country Club, then at
Tuckahoe, New York, and went along
when the club moved, in the autumn,
to its new eighteen-hole course at
nearby Elmsford. That proved to be a
steady job. He was there until he resigned at the end of 1959, after fifty-
one years of service and a record as a
home professional.

In the fall of 1908 Inglis was engaged
as professional for the Hampton Terrace Hotel course at North Augusta,
Georgia, two miles from Augusta, staying there as fall-winter-spring pro until
the hotel burned down in 1915. The
next fall, he went from Fairview to the
Highland Park Hotel course at Aiken,
South Carolina, twenty miles from
North Augusta. He was there until
1939 when that hotel also burned.
(Parenthetically, it's a wonder more of
those big wooden winter and summer
resort golf hotels didn't burn and cre-
mate every human being, cockroach,
and mouse on the premises. They were
firetraps. Electrical wiring was inadequate, fire escapes existed in name only,
and fire protection was unmention-
able.)

When Inglis got in on the winter
resort jobs he was one of the pioneer
home-breds in that extension of the
earning season. His course design, construction, and maintenance abilities
were put to work at Hampton Terrace,
where he built a new nine, and at
Highland Park, where he added nine
holes. While he was at the last-named
club, Inglis continued his unselfish promotion of golf by staging women's open
invitational tournaments and arranged
for Patty Berg, Babe Zaharias, Marion
Miley, and other early women professionals to get welcome income in the
off season.

Inglis was recruiter, teacher, banker,
manager, cheerleader, judge and jury,
publicity man, and employment agent
for hundreds of youngsters who first
came to his attention as caddies and because of his efforts and influence graduated as estimable young men in
schools, business, industry, and professional golf. John Inglis and other
American and British professionals like
him who established American golf
never have been recognized as among
the most effective teachers and molders
of character that this country has had.

These almost forgotten men, the
pioneer pros, applying golf's caddie
factor to the changing social and economic conditions, discovered and ac-

Mildred "Babe" Zaharias. AG

celerated the progress of boys most likely to succeed. This was a revolutionary development. Until caddying came into the fringes of metropolitan territories, the chances of poor kids getting a few dollars ahead while moving up in the world were slow and slim. The professionals sensed the difference between the caddie situation in the old country and in the United States and instinctively put the kids into relationships that produced what later were called "business contacts."

Professionals of the John Inglis stripe helped set the stage for the invaluable caddie scholarships that Chick Evans began when he donated the money he had received for phonograph golf in-

struction records. If he had taken the cash, it would have cost him his amateur standing. But Chick liked being an amateur and wanted to help caddies. Golfers aren't any too quick to learn the caddie story. Possibly they don't care because golf is an egocentric game. But notwithstanding the golfer's selfishness, in contributing more or less cheerfully and voluntarily to the Evans and the twenty-five other caddie scholarship funds, golfers have accounted for a youth-aid project that outshines the fervently publicized Rhodes and Fulbright scholarships.

The old pros, such as Inglis and his contemporaries, kept supervising and encouraging the caddies with promise, and by making sure they got assignments often kept the boys from dropping out of school. This foresight resulted in many more ex-caddies becoming millionaires than have the great tournament stars. At a Palm Springs club, several knowledgeable brokers were once talking about the "millionaire professionals," and after referring to the sources of the wealthy pros' income, laughed and cited the ex-caddies who were hiring the "millionaire professionals."

While today's tendency is to score everything in dollars, Inglis scores high by a more rigid measure. He was elected president of the Metropolitan section of the PGA from 1928 to 1949 inclusive, and during most of those years it was by far the largest chapter of the PGA. Inglis was elected by knowing professionals as the one of their group who always did the best for golf. He was a vice-president of the PGA of America two terms and served on numerous committees. He gave so much more than he got in pro golf that his colleagues didn't want to let him go.

But Inglis was by no means unique. In every section of the country you could find his counterpart among the pioneer professionals. The Boys' Club national movement came long after John Inglis was a young caddie master and professional in Westchester County. Johnny got the idea across in his own nice, easy, deep way. For instance, what Inglis thought and did for youngsters of Italian parentage enriched the United States and golf, and of primary importance, made the boys proud and happy.

Writing in *The New Yorker* in 1937 about the standard of golf improving "incredibly fast," Noel F. Bush surmised that "better tournament golf scoring was partially due to the depres-

sion because it induced thousands of urchins who might otherwise have been playing baseball or annoying their parents, to earn an honest dollar or two by caddying." *The New Yorker* writer went on to say that "If, as American universities are rated by their football teams, golf clubs were rated by the expert golfers produced by their caddie masters, Fairview Country Club at Elmsford, N.Y., would occupy a position analogous to Notre Dame's. . . . The Knute Rockne of Fairview is John Inglis, a fatherly little man who, with no children of his own, took an interest in the more promising boys and let them listen when he was giving members lessons."

Johnny gave his kids every chance to learn and encouraged them. He was the godfather of the Westchester County school of professionals, a group that was to New York's golf what the lads of Carnoustie, St. Andrews, and Monifieth were to Scotland's game.

Inglis impressed upon boys that there was an ordinary way to caddie and a kid could get by doing it like that, but there was also an artist's way of doing the job better so the golfer knew that he had a real expert working for him. That artistic note particularly appealed to youngsters of Latin ancestry, and there were a lot of them around. The Turnesa boys, sons of Johnny's friend, the greenkeeper at Fairview, were especially adept. Phil, Frank, Joe, Mike, and Jim became professionals and good ones. Joe finished second to Bob Jones in the 1926 National Open, and Walter Hagen beat Joe in the final of the 1927 PGA Championship; Jim was defeated by Sam Snead in the finals of the 1942 PGA Championship, and Ben Hogan beat Mike Turnesa to win the 1948 PGA title. The youngest Turnesa son, Wil-

Chick Evans. PGA

lie, stayed amateur and won the USGA Amateur championships in 1938 and 1948 and the British Amateur in 1947.

Many Inglis assistants became professionals at fine clubs. When a boy made good working for Inglis, he was definitely good enough to start on a job of his own. Johnny and the rest of the pioneer professionals who successfully conducted the U.S. pro business prep school taught those kids that they were in golf to work, not to waste time loafing. The kids applied this intensity to developing their own games. Tony Manero, who won the Open in 1936, had been an Inglis assistant who early learned to use his time effectively.

Jack Nicklaus never caddied. He was heir to the fabulously rich domain discovered by caddies who preceded him and by their teachers in golf's school. The earlier golf professionals, because of their selection, training, supervision, and encouragement of caddies, had far more influence on American boys than ever was exercised elsewhere in American sports. By 1910, leaders in American professional golf, such as John Inglis, had unmistakably established the obligation of the professional as an example to the caddies. This influence was an important factor in pro employment. The growing demand for good caddies and the necessity of having youngsters who lived near the courses and who would be readily available brought into caddying many thousands of boys who spread the story of the professionals' merits and defects.

Although only a small percentage of the caddies have gone on to professional golf careers, each of them clearly reflected the characters of their mentors in the profession and did them credit by preserving the traditional amenities. Youngsters who became successful and honored in other fields of endeavor often expressed their gratitude and affection for the men who were their pros when they were caddies. Here was another unique distinction to be added to the glories of the old pros: They were the headmasters of a prep school that had no parallel in American education. Many stories have been handed down about young men being helped along with their careers by the helpful, understanding businessmen they first became acquainted with as caddies, but there have only been discreet references to the numerous instances in which pioneer professionals like John Inglis often risked their jobs by asking surly, demanding members to *please* treat their caddies in a more kindly manner.

By around 1910, the ever-expanding duties of the early professionals called for an American innovation in golf— the caddie master. At the beginning, the pro had to hire and pay him, but the man added something to his income by the sale of candy, sandwiches, and soft drinks to the boys. Soon the caddie master became an important member of the club's official family. First of all, he had to recruit caddies when the supply was running short and the clubs were moving farther away from mass transportation. On Chi-

cago's Northwest Side, at the end of the Milwaukee Avenue streetcar line, caddie masters or their assistants had buses to transport youngsters to clubs and guarantee them work and return transportation.

In time, the crude leantos that served as shelters while caddies awaited assignment gave way to caddie clubhouses with showers, lockers, and dining tables. George S. May, the colorful party who put the tournament golfers into big money, was one of the first to build a miniature clubhouse for caddies. The experiment had an unsatisfactory start. Some of the kids were generally as untidy and careless as club members, and the caddie masters had to use genius and muscle to curb them. In this case, the man was John Shavonec, who for years was invaluable in conducting Chicago District Golf Association tournaments.

Part of American professional golf history that never will be written in detail is that of the pro-caddie relationship. There are thousands of stories about the old pros and the boys they helped. The Western Golf Association, the Massachusetts Golf Association, and other amateur organizations and individuals produced caddie manuals to help in organizing the training of caddies, but there never has been any method to equal the personal attention of the old pros. Nor is there any telling how many caddies have been influenced by the compassionate professionals at the clubs where they worked. In 1955, it was estimated that there were 300,000 caddies intermittently employed. In 1970, with golf carts going strong, there were about 1,200 young men in colleges and universities on caddie scholarships. The spirit of John Inglis and the old pros lives on strongly in American golf.

13

The Game Becomes Big Business, The Year of the Missing Report, and the Players Threaten to Strike

[1937, 1938, 1939]

TWO 1937 developments that proved to be highly profitable to PGA members were given only casual mention when the PGA held its twenty-first annual meeting, November 9, 10, and 11, at the Morrison Hotel, Chicago. One was a great increase in the number of sectional tournaments in which professionals played with various categories of their members; the other was considerable advertising by professionals to their members. In previous years professionals' advertising to their members or to potential customers had been rare, but suddenly it sprouted in letters, circulars, and enclosures in members' bills.

Frank Sprogell, a veteran professional attached to the Meadowbrook Country Club in suburban Detroit and chairman of the PGA Publicity Committee, had the inspired hunch that the best publicity a professional could get was to have his name in the papers together with the name of one or more members. In January, 1937, he started a letter campaign of his own to PGA sectional officials, urging them to get their own members and amateur groups in their sections to arrange pro-president, pro-ladies, pro-seniors, pro-green chairmen, pro-junior, and other events in which the pro would be teamed with amateurs.

Sprogell had observed that many younger pros quickly lost their jobs because they failed to play with enough of the members. They were generally men who scored well and liked to bet but weren't noted for the volume of their pro-shop business. They were eager to play and not happy about staying around the shop and taking care of all the members; they thought they could make more money playing the sharpshooters than in tending to the store where business had been poor for a couple of years anyway. But these

Frank Sprogell. PGA

young pros guessed wrong. The majority of members were club-oriented and soon found another pro who cared about them and the club.

Sprogell also sought to overcome the reluctance of higher-handicap members to play with their club professionals. Men and women who scored 95 or higher were embarrassed to exhibit their poor play in pro company. "We are the ones who should be blushing if our members can't play well," Sprogell warned fellow professionals. "We've got to get as close to our members as professionals were when the game really began to grow in the United States." Other experienced pros took up the Sprogell campaign, and a new tone of pro-amateur partnership soon came into the game.

George Aulbach, who was showing professionals they could make profitable use of advertising to a limited market, was pro at the Dallas Country Club, moving to Texas after winning PGA championships in New England. One of the early collegians to turn pro golfer, he lost on the twentieth green of the first USGA Public Links Championship at the Ottowa Park course in Toledo in 1922. He became one of the faculty of the early PGA business schools at Dunedin, Florida. The Aulbach story presented at the 1937 annual meeting rounded out the professionals' use of advertising that led to today's vast marketing through pro shops.

Much of the advertising by pros and golf goods manufacturers was wasted in repetition and poor circulation. As a result, in 1933, with the support of several leading manufacturers, Joe and Herb Graffis, publishers of *Golfdom, the Business Journal of Golf*, began publishing *Golfing*, a player magazine sent without cost to members of private clubs. The lists were supplied by club officials and professionals with the understanding that they'd be used for no other purpose than *Golfing* circulation. Although increasing postal rates handicapped the program, the venture awakened professionals to what sharply directed advertising could do for them.

With the brisk action in marketing, President Jacobus was able to report a solid improvement in the PGA financial position at the 1937 meeting, although membership had increased by only 12 members, to a total of 1,181. Twenty-eight sections were represented at the meeting, and the high command was the same as the previous year, with Jacobus as president; Tom Walsh, secretary; and Jack Mackie, treasurer. Vice-presidents were Grange Alves, Tom Boyd, Al Collins, Ed Dudley, Ray Hall, Dewey Longworth, Willie Maguire, and R. W. Treacy.

The Western PGA members felt they were not being informed about what was going on in the PGA. There didn't really seem to be much excitement and even less communicating. The one explosion came in the firing of Bob Harlow as Tournament Bureau manager and the hiring of Fred Corcoran to succeed him. Jacobus and Harlow never were in close harmony. Harlow was getting more publicity than Jacobus, and that didn't please the president. The exigencies of tournament promotion and management in those days did not allow formalities of correspondence and chain-of-command decisions, and Harlow had tournament deals closed before Jacobus had a chance to say "Yes" officially. Furthermore, Harlow had given tournament golf a solid foundation and such a bright outlook that it seemed a good time to drop out. The action was resented by tournament players and the majority of otherwise interested PGA members.

Jacobus later became a good promoter of a golf sideshow himself, presenting a baseball players' winter golf tournament in Florida that got a lot of sports section space and was the first of the multitude of winter resort tournaments now enlisting athletes of prominence in other fields as golfers.

Fred Corcoran, an affable and able young man from Boston who had been in charge of amateur tournament pairings and scoring in New England, then moved into taking charge of scoring at Pinehurst and points south in the flowering winter tournament circuit, was a lucky choice to follow Harlow. In imagination, showmanship, publicity sense, genuine love of golf, and the capacity to keep from being driven mad by temperamental pro golfers, Harlow and Corcoran were brothers under the skin in the headache of building tournament golf. The PGA had its own troubles with the PGA Championship, then with the Ryder Cup matches and other tournament circuit problems. Harlow and then Corcoran were the nursemaids who had to change their charges, bring them through the kindergarten of golf, and sit in the back row when their protégés got their diplomas from sports pages, headline writers, and bankers. In the process, Harlow and Corcoran conceived and constructed the immense business of modern international tournament golf.

At the 1937 annual meeting, there was a furious family brawl between the adherents of Harlow on one side and those of Corcoran on the other. The storm almost blew Jacobus out of the presidency. Harlow and Corcoran restored calm by urging their partisans to remember that the tournament part of golf was a sideshow for the PGA, and the pros' most important business was to take care of the amateurs, not to get

Bob Harlow and George Jacobus. GH

mixed up in the tantrums of a few hundred fellows who did nothing else but play golf.

For a while Harlow and Corcoran fought each other everyplace from alleys to cathedrals, but they were open and honorable brawlers and quickly made up. Both liked excellent food and drink and cheery companions late into the night and evangelized for wholesome sport in the fresh air where everybody could count. Harlow didn't handle any testimonial rackets for his clients from Hagen down, and there were only a few, but Corcoran got a fine testimonial contract for his client Sam Snead. Neither Harlow nor Corcoran would ever take any percentage of the purse winnings of their clients.

Harlow and Corcoran prevailed in the dimming days of golf as the foremost of the games gentlemen played, whether as pros or amateurs, for money or for fun. They masterminded far bigger earnings, considering time, risk, intelligence, and social status, than were made by professional athletes in other fields. Changing times shoved them into the shadows of sports history, but Corcoran was able to preserve the whole spirit of golf as entertainment instead of as an instrument for hustling a buck out of the trusting chumps. Still, he had to be eternally vigilant to protect golf from becoming just another racket used by promoters.

The trouble with all the background elements of the game is that, while the pros carefully refrained from mentioning them out loud at PGA meetings, they did talk about them seriously in small groups where discussion of club and fee-course operation was candid and room service bad. In those informal sessions, there was little interest in the Corcoran report that $135,500 prize money had been offered in sixteen tournaments, or that Elmer Ward of Palm Beach summerwear was putting up a bundle for a new event, the Palm Beach Round Robin.

Ward was the first smart merchandiser to promote lightweight apparel. He came into golf tournament promotion at a time when sports editors and their superiors, the newspaper advertising managers and publishers, thought, "If a businessman pushing a product wants sports-page advertising, why doesn't he pay for it?" Between them, Corcoran and Ward devised a round-robin invitational tournament with a system of scoring that confused everybody, and playing a Palm Beach tournament in Cincinnati (where the coats and pants were made) only compounded the confusion but got Palm Beach on the sports pages. After a while Ward learned that by spending money on newspaper advertising he could tie his golf-apparel sales promotion in with the tournament's free publicity. Elmer Ward was the first in the golf business, and among the first in all sports-accessory sales promotion, to demonstrate that the retail outlet had to be identified in print with any sales promotion involving sports on radio or television.

The $12,000 International Match Play tournament at the Belmont Country Club near Boston was an innovation on the tournament circuit for the year, and one that reflected the American interest in developing worldwide competition. Byron Nelson defeated Henry Picard in the final match, but the field didn't quite rate "international" significance. In other activities, the Chicago District Golf Association put up $10,000 for an open tournament at the Medinah Country Club, and the PGA advanced $3,000 for a tournament to be promoted and played at Houston, with Willie Maguire and Jack Burke trying to get Houston businessmen interested. The effort was unsuccessful, and the check was returned to the PGA.

Plans for a summer tour of the Pacific Northwest were also ineffective, because no money was forthcoming. Nor did a previously discussed autumn tournament schedule materialize, because collegiate football would take the sports-section space and the customers the proposed tournaments needed. But the United States won the Ryder Cup matches at Southport and Ainsdale, with the American pros winning seven matches, the British three, and two halved. Hagen was the Americans' nonplaying captain.

A spat arose about a proposal to replace the Vardon trophy given to the professional with the best scoring average in the year's leading tournaments. The new award was suggested by Harry

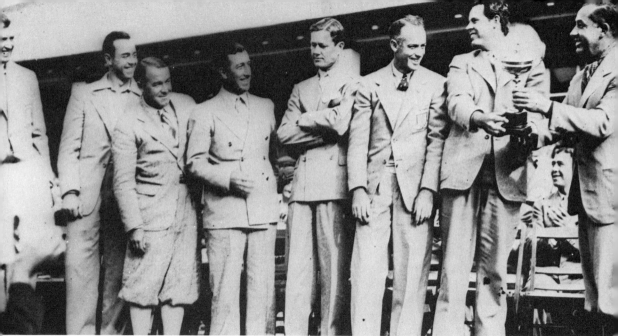

U.S. Ryder Cup team, 1937. GH

Radix, a wealthy Chicago golf enthusiast, club official, and friend of numerous professionals, who in his lifetime had attended more open golf championships in various countries than any other amateur except golf writers and association officials. The Radix offer was declined, but in his will he provided for awards of platinum and diamond cuff links and other jewelry to the Vardon trophy winner, and a trophy memorializing Radix is played for yearly by teams of Illinois professionals versus state amateurs.

Manufacturers informed the PGA that, on their lawyers' advice, the ball contract would not be renewed. This meant a sharp reduction in PGA and individual pro revenue, and it also meant that the golf business was getting big enough for the federal government to keep a watchful eye open.

The continued recovery of golf from the Depression showed the business speeding toward high volume in sports goods sales, but in 1937, as the PGA began to be increasingly plagued by legal matters, it was guided by able and

honest lawyers. Among them were the pioneers Albert Gates and Tom Crane, who was first a lawyer for the PGA, then for many years its executive director.

PGA section officials and a few committee heads continued their work on what was then known as the Golf Promotion Bureau and later as the National Golf Foundation, a golf market development service that had been started in 1936 as promotion by Joe and Herb Graffis, *Golfdom* publishers. Its primary purpose was to get professionals volunteering their services in the free design of golf courses in small towns, in school and college class instruction, and in night-school golf class instruction at high schools, YMCA's, YWCA's, and with factory recreation groups. Golf course superintendents were enlisted to demonstrate how to build good golf courses in rural areas and also how to build practice greens, tees, and fairways at schools and hospitals.

The demand for these services quickly outgrew the capacity of the professionals and superintendents to do the required work. The Graffis brothers, struggling through lean times with a golf business and a golf-player magazine, had critical problems with the payroll, printers, paper, postage, and other essentials, but outstanding golf manufacturers, headed by L. B. Icely of Wilson, Charles Robbins of Spalding, Clarence Rickey of MacGregor, and Edward C. Conlin of the United States Rubber Company, were impressed by the results of their golf market promotion with limited money and personnel.

So when the PGA ball-refund deal was halted by the threat of government action, the manufacturers decided to finance a vigorous effort to develop the golf market. The National Golf Foundation was organized and conducted on a small budget, with Glen Morris as its first executive director. Morris had been Wilson's advertising manager, then was with the L. A. Young Golf Company as its general manager after Wilson bought the Hagen outfit from Young. Morris was followed as head of the foundation by Rex McMorris, Harry Eckhoff, William Pack, and Don Rossi. These men extended the foundation's work with the PGA and other professional and amateur organizations and in schools and other phases of market development. The foundation's field staff and publications have been so effective in building the golf market that it accounts for more than a half of the annual sales of athletic goods. Almost all interests actively engaged in the golf business are National Golf Foundation members, and it is considered to be one of the country's most successful recreation market and service developments.

Professionals were becoming aware of the value of the organized promotion of golf as a game and a business,

and at the 1937 meeting Dewey Longworth offered the Northern California section's proposal for forming a promotion committee. The suggestion got lost in talk, but there was another splurge of politics as the meeting neared the finish, when George Jacobus was reelected president by a landslide. Only a veteran Scot, Alex Cunningham of Illinois, ran against him.

Not many PGA officials and members realized it in 1937 and in 1938, but golf's big show was going on outside the PGA. The association was to learn that its membership wasn't growing as fast as the game was in general. The number of golf courses and players and playing equipment sales were increasing at a rate showing that the PGA needed to adjust to all the phases of big business.

Oddly enough, very little on the 1938 meeting at the Auditorium Hotel, Chicago, is available. The minutes of the meeting and the committee reports have disappeared from the PGA headquarters files, and nobody has any explanation. "Lost" is the only answer; why and how, nobody knows. George R. Jacobus again was president, the enduring Jack Mackie again treasurer, and Tom Walsh, who had been elected secretary in 1937, continued in office.

Walsh recalls that at the conclusion of the meeting the secretary's and treasurer's reports and the usual stacks of committee reports were collected and delivered to the association's office in Chicago. There certainly was a treasurer's report that was carefully checked, and Mackie with characteristic Scottish prudence had himself bonded. But if the proceedings were printed in any form, copies have vanished.

The PGA's magazine carried no story on the meeting, nor was there a word on the gathering in *Golfdom, the*

Business Journal of Golf, which, being nonpolitical and strictly business, usually carried reports of the annual meeting high spots.

Apparently the meeting opened on a note of high confusion. Illinois professionals had been telling golf writers that the PGA's aim was to improve services to players and golf in general, thus improving the pros' public relations and earning power. The controversies of tournament players, sponsors, and the PGA during the previous few years had been of little help to professional golf, certainly not to the club pros who were in closest contact with the golfing public.

The PGA annual meeting coverage by the Associated Press, United Press, and International News Service had been limited to listing newly elected officers and a short paragraph or two about plans for improving instruction. Newspapers in the annual meeting cities rarely had a PGA story big enough for a two-column head in the sports section.

After the Illinois section officials had assembled Chicago sportswriters in the belief that everything that went on at the PGA national meeting would be good for the public to know, an embarrassed officer of the national body announced to the press that they would not be admitted to the meeting. The announcement was received calmly by the reporters. They laughed and told irate local pros not to take the situation with blushes, as it was not uncommon for professional and amateur athletic organizations that are dependent on public understanding and support to have a Ku Klux Klan way of holding meetings.

Although the unofficial effort to get news of the pros' nationwide endeavors for amateur golfers was unsuccessful at the 1938 annual meeting, it was also the last time for many years that anyone in the PGA even tried to sell its story of yearly progress to the golfing public. Nobody seemed to be able to decide whether the PGA annual meeting was entirely an affair of inside legislation and troubles, or whether it involved committee reports of activities of concern and value to all golfers. Tournament professionals had publicity men on the job the year round. Club professionals had friendly golf writers in their sections who intermittently wrote news and feature stories advancing the club professionals' interests. But nationally, publicity for the club pro was scanty and unplanned. Yet, club professionals wondered why their story of earnest, able work for amateurs and clubs wasn't told.

Unfortunately, although the PGA was ardently engaged in a campaign of selling the services of well-qualified professional golfers to the public, it was tardy in hiring well-qualified men in public relations to represent it. Sectional pro groups and club pros individually got excellent newspaper publicity on what they were doing to help golfers, but collectively the PGA didn't score in print as a factor in the golf business.

The contrast between the failure of the PGA to express itself as a business institution in golf and the dynamic growth of the National Golf Foundation as a golf industrial service operation eventually jarred an Executive Committee into the association's long-overdue need of making known its character and strength in the golf business. It wasn't easy to stir this awakening; not until the 1960's was a hopeful, though feeble, attempt made to get national publicity on the business of a PGA annual meeting. Members of the PGA official family were named to hold press conferences after each day's annual meeting session. These men did their best, of course, but it wasn't their field. They had no more idea of what had been done in the meeting that would warrant a national news story favorable to club pros than the reporters knew about telling the pros how not to three-putt.

During the administration of Max Elbin, the PGA hired John Ross, an experienced publicist and former *Golf Magazine* editor, to develop recognition of the PGA as a golf business force. The assignment was vague and ran into conflicts and misunderstandings, so Ross didn't last long. Then Leo Fraser as president made another try to get the PGA identified as golf big business. Naturally, results were slow.

The press-relations error at the 1938 meeting was costly, but at least the PGA itself was in better membership condition than it had ever been before in the relation of Class A members to the number of eighteen-hole courses in the United States. There were 1,739 members. The 1938 PGA Championship at the Shawnee Country Club at Shawnee-on-Delaware also made money. It was played July 10 to 16, and little Paul Runyan beat big, strong Sam Snead, 8 and 7, that year.

In 1934, at the Park Club of Buffalo, "Little Poison" Runyan had gone thirty-eight holes to defeat another big, strong, handsome man, Craig Wood, for the PGA title. Runyan was the world's best with long woods to the green. Wood and Snead were seventy-five yards ahead of him on drives. If the average golfer had been as far behind as Runyan on the par-5 holes, he would have put the ball in his pocket. But then Runyan always hit one of his longest shots and one-putted, and his opponent was lucky to tie.

Some of pro golf's elder scholars believe that, if it hadn't been for Runyan with his putter cutting Snead's heart out at Shawnee, Slamming Sam would have been the greatest winner of all golfers. Snead was a phenomenally long putter, lagging them up to the lip and holing plenty of them, but after Runyan got through with him, Snead seemed to have the feeling that anybody playing him was down in one putt from sixteen feet away and he might miss, so what was the use? At least that was the analysis of pros who had missed enough putts to qualify as experts.

Tournament prize money in 1938 was another record for a year. Although records of prize money are incomplete, indications are that prize money had increased every year since 1926. In 1938, the Argentine Golf Association again financed a trip for two players of its choice to play in the Argentine Open. Paul Runyan, the PGA Champion, and Harold McSpaden were selected. Runyan won the Argentine Open, which Henry Picard had won the previous year.

Ryder Cup planning for 1939 got nowhere in 1938. The British wanted to play over here in late October or early November when collegiate football would be getting the big play in the sports sections. There was difficulty in getting a host for the event, but eventually the Ponte Vedra Club at Jacksonville was secured, and the dates were November 18 and 19, 1939. But by that time, World War II had the British Ryder Cup team in more serious business.

President Jacobus had been building his political fences in 1938, visiting eight sections and rarely touching base at PGA headquarters. He loved the work and the position but was never able to figure out how the office in Chicago could be used as a communications connection among PGA officials, committees, and members.

It was reported that the manufacturers had agreed to contribute substantially toward Tournament Bureau expenses. Most professional tournament contestants were on the payrolls of manufacturers and were provided with equipment as an advertising expense. A small amount was given to the PGA Hole-in-One Club, which awarded a membership card and emblem to those making a hole-in-one when the scorecard of the lucky sharpshooter was endorsed by the PGA professional at his club or fee course. Normal progress had also been made with the PGA teaching program during the year, but no innovation in turning it into a concerted nationwide PGA effort had been achieved.

Jacobus told the annual meeting that he had personally made a deal with Twentieth Century–Fox to make a movie short of several of the stars, including Sam Snead, Harry Cooper, Walter Hagen, Patty Berg, Glenna Collet Vare, and possibly one or two other pros. The picture company was to give the PGA credit, then give films to the PGA for instruction and promotion after theater showings. The pros were to be paid by the picture company.

Somehow the supercolossal deal didn't come off. A few golf shorts were made, but they flopped. Warner Brothers gave the PGA a print of the Bobby Jones picture *How to Break 90,* but PGA members made little use of it.

Jacobus referred to the volume of

paperwork and telephone calls handled by his office in New York. The official headquarters in Chicago continued to be operated by Mrs. Irene Blakeman, who'd come along when the PGA capital was changed from New York to Chicago. She had a few girls with her to care for routine and details of records, and Secretary Tom Walsh came in often to help, but there wasn't too much for him to do. The big stuff had to go "right now" to the president. The Chicago office was a frontier outpost for defense in case the natives got restless. So there's a possibility the missing state papers mentioned earlier were sent to New York, then vanished into limbo.

In his recommendations, Jacobus urged that pros "take immediate action to secure lower prices on golf balls, clubs, and other equipment." This balanced the manufacturers' action in August in supplying funds to operate the PGA Tournament Bureau and other promotion and in requesting that the PGA ask pros to bear down on their slow-pay members.

Jacobus did some pioneering investigating among organizations of small retailers, especially druggists, in the New York area to see how they handled competition. He did not report findings the PGA could apply, but he did see that the PGA had available the advice of highly successful businessmen who were enthusiastic amateur golfers and very much interested in the welfare of pro golfers. Like other successful professionals, Jacobus had profited from the valuable advice of experienced businessmen at his own club who liked him and wished him well. They were certainly qualified to advise him expertly on matters of mutual interest to the club and its professional, and in a casual way the advice of prominent businessmen had also been solicited and sometimes used by PGA officials in their perplexing and unpaid association work.

Jacobus now proposed that an advisory committee be appointed for such a purpose. Eventually it was, and has included men who have been or are officials and directors of huge corporations. However, for many years the Advisory Board was just so many names, with the members being consulted briefly, usually on how the PGA could get out of some annoying or menacing situation that might have been avoided had the Advisory Board been consulted in the first place.

In recent years, with the PGA being operated as a business organization, the Advisory Board has served a useful function. PGA Executive Secretary Lloyd F. Lambert has provided the advisers with summaries of "Actions and Important Matters Considered at PGA Annual and Executive Committee Meetings."

The last of the six terms that George Jacobus served as the first of the PGA native-born presidents was not particularly noteworthy. Jacobus was diligent and ambitious. He spent a lot of time away from his job at the Ridgewood Country Club in working for the PGA. He had a good staff backstopping him at Ridgewood, but he was away from his family a lot and he spent plenty of his own money for the PGA, which wouldn't go for his sort of a travel program. George had been a caddie who was promoted to a pro job at an early age by a relative. Having been on a job and doing acceptably at it since around his sixteenth birthday, he knew all the answers. But his constituents were getting tired of him, and other bright young men were coming along.

He had done very well for the PGA

by shaking it up, and he had a hunch he was going to be shaken out of the high command when the twenty-third annual meeting was held at Chicago in November, 1939. Tom Boyd, a vice-president from New York, who said he'd been the first foreign-born PGA member to propose Jacobus as president, told George to retire gracefully, as the delegates of the twenty-eight sections were beginning to think more about politics than about PGA business. His club's concern about the time it was getting from its professional, the personal expenses of the PGA presidency, and his absences from home also reconciled Jacobus to quitting as PGA president.

As the first American to rise from caddie to president of the PGA, Jacobus felt his distinction keenly, and if he overreacted, who could blame him? He knew from the membership figures and the tournament purses that the PGA was growing, and who was responsible for that but the head pro, even though sectional officials and members thought they had the right answer nearer home? They regarded themselves much nearer to their clubs than to their own PGA. Nevertheless, their realization that they needed a strong and active association was becoming more acute.

It also was becoming increasingly evident that the PGA had a split personality. One-half was the home professional who did best by himself and his members or fee customers by first attending to the interests of those who paid him; the other half was the playing pro who was preoccupied with his own game and had little concern for other golfers or tournament sponsors who provided the prize money.

A division was inevitable. The stronger the PGA home pros made the tournament circuit with financing the

Denny Shute. PGA

tournament players would not or could not provide for themselves, the more certain it was that the tournament players would inherit a big, self-sustaining golf business that would carry itself along.

The crack in the temperamental structure of pro golf appeared early, and it's surprising that it didn't break into a civil war until the opulent 1960's, when income tax deductions overruled any reason that the two divisions of golf should stay together. But it almost happened at the time of the 1939 PGA Championship at the Pomonok Country Club, Flushing, New York, when the PGA was almost blown apart.

Pomonok hadn't been eager for the match, but the fervent golfers in the club overruled the foot-draggers when invited to be tournament hosts. Then, after the closing time for entries had passed, it was discovered that Denny Shute, the 1936 PGA Champion, was not among those enlisted.

Shute, the handsome, quiet son of a fine English pro transplanted to the United States, had won the 1933 British Open at St. Andrews after a play-off with Craig Wood. He was a brilliant shotmaker with a swing as sweet as a Viennese waltz, a golfer who preceded Julius Boros as the lazy, velvety stylist who did what everyone thought was easy to do, but wasn't.

When Shute's entry came in late, the PGA officials ruled him out of the PGA Championship and thought the Post Office Department with its postmark on the envelope had made their decision for keeps. Nor did Denny make much of an effort to explain the delay—something like the spit not sticking to the stamp or the entry getting in with some letters he was going to mail for his wife constituted the Shute case. But that was good enough for his fellow tournament players! They threatened to go on strike unless Shute was allowed to play.

Shute was a sure winner against the Establishment. Several of his defenders played loud practice rounds at the Pomonok bars and in the locker room while golf writers and bartenders kept the score. It was a showdown case of tournament players against PGA officials who were convinced they represented golfers at large. However, the customary "compromise" was in favor of the play-for-pay boys.

Shute beat Ted Luther in the first round, 1 up; knocked out Leo Diegel in the second round, 2 and 1; then lost in the third round to a dark horse from Detroit, Emerick Kocsis, who lost to Byron Nelson. Henry Picard beat Nelson in thirty-seven holes for the title. After Shute lost, people forgot that the man who might have halted the championship had even played in it. Which all goes to show that the pros who threatened to strike might possibly have overestimated their influence on the golfers of the nation. After his retirement from tournament play, Shute became one of the most successful and highly regarded of home professionals and was pro at the Portage Country Club of Akron for many happy years.

The instruction program picked up steam with PGA members talking about uniform teaching. Aspiring golfers sampled it, and at least the publicity got them to the lesson tee. Big-time movie instruction finally made it in *Shooting for Par,* with the producer of films for cowboy Tom Mix getting the swings of Hagen, Cooper, Snead, and Patty Berg before the eyes of hopeful amateurs.

The picture in the cash register was also pleasant—total cash was $144,123,

and the general fund $54,214. As had always been the case, and continues to be, the PGA had funds spread all over acres of bookkeeping paper, and as long as auditors were watching the money and the officials were honest fellows, no time was needed for counting the change. Membership had increased during 1939 by 77, for a total of 1,813, of whom 1,400 were Class A, and tournament purses for the year had been $185,000.

A publicity operation known as PROmotion issued many lessons with the PGA imprint and supplied pros freely with metal ball markers the size of a dime. On one side was stamped: "My handicap is . . . ," with the handicap figure to be inserted by the professional. On the other side was stamped: "My pro's lessons could improve me." The soft metal markers were very popular until some fiend discovered that they worked in the dime slots of golf ball slot machines paying off in fifty-cent balls. Ball-marker promotion was then quickly discontinued.

Many of the most successful educational, public-relations, and public golf school operations of the PGA were started in 1939. The *Chicago Tribune,* in association with the Chicago Park District and the Illinois PGA, started a series of night class lessons at park courses. Charles Bartlett, golf editor of the *Tribune,* got dozens of professionals from private and public courses to do the teaching. Attendance, despite uncertain spring weather, was in the high thousands, although not so large as reported by the volunteer professors at the schools. Spring business schools, exhibitions of playing equipment, and often free instruction clinics and demonstrations were also held by PGA sections at Philadelphia, Chicago, Minneapolis, Detroit, Des Moines, and Newark.

There had been a brisk debate earlier that year about why "personalities" in tournament golf did so much for themselves and so little for the game. The discussion was ruled out of print in the PGA magazine, as was an article by a pro who, with the help of a sportswriter, showed how few golfers would be able to afford their memberships in his club if its customers and clients bought "wholesale." The subjects were too "hot," and would be today.

There was a sunny time of brotherly love and cheerful, nostalgic drinking at the Midlothian Country Club celebrating the twenty-fifth anniversary of Walter Hagen's first National Open victory there on August 19 to 21, 1914. The anniversary match was played August 24 to 27 by an invited field of sixteen. Ed Dudley and Billy Burke got $575 each as the winning team, plus $100 for the most birdies (fifty-one) and the lowest eighteen holes (sixty-two). The team of Hagen and Sarazen finished fourth. Hagen was the only one in the field who'd played at Midlothian a quarter-century before, at the first National Open of any nation at which visiting professionals were as welcome in the locker room as the members.

An interesting switch in the tournament schedule was that of having the Western Open played at Houston in February. That was the first and only time the Western Open was played in the winter, and it was done to nurse along the tournament circuit.

After the mess during the PGA Championship at Pomonok had been forgotten, it was recalled in a nice way. The Tournament Committee, consisting of Ed Dudley, Leo Diegel, Harold McSpaden, Olin Dutra, Jimmy Hines,

Dick Metz, and Ted Luther, formally apologized to the Executive Committee for issuing its "Shute or else" edict that got Denny Shute into the championship. And George Jacobus apologized to the Executive Committee when he overruled them after they'd said the rules of the championship shouldn't be changed to accommodate anybody who couldn't tell time. It was a gleeful orgy of "Pardon me," and the PGA lived happily for some time after.

The boys were understanding of each other, at least temporarily. Ed Dudley remarked, "There are fifteen or twenty of us who play in tournaments and hold club jobs. Guldahl, Snead, Shute, and a couple of other boys I call 'tournament players.'" Vice-president Ray Hall pointed out that being a tournament player was a risky business, as it could easily cost a man $1,500 a year to concentrate on tournaments.

After the tournament wrangling had abated at the annual meeting, the delegates again applied themselves to a discussion of teaching. Harold Sampson of the Northern California section forecast that, "Someday we are going to have teaching short courses as the greenkeepers have." There was talk about the use of motion pictures in the study of golf technique and in teaching. This was to be developed for years by the PGA with Irv Schloss using a great deal of film of stars' methods and analyzing and lecturing on the photographs.

Exhibitions began at the 1939 meeting in which leading players showed how and why they thought they were swinging. This became a popular closing feature of annual meetings. Pros known for their success in instruction rather than for championship performance demonstrated their teaching methods. Ernest Jones showed how he got pupils to swing the club so most details would fall into line. Jack Fox, a New Jersey professional who'd been a British Army drill instructor, exhibited his method of teaching the golf swing "by the numbers" as the manual of arms is taught soldiers. Fox produced many good men and women players with his method, but it was never widely adopted. Then Wally Mund, a Minnesota delegate, proposed that a teaching conference be a feature of the annual meeting, and he got his idea across.

A lecture on the elemental physiology and psychology of the golfer was given by Dr. Robert Dyer of Chicago, and it fascinated the professionals. Dr. Dyer, an excellent golfer, owner of a golf course, and a lecturer at the University of Illinois Medical School, outlined how and why the golfer should, but often didn't, function. Officials and delegates and other professionals requested that the PGA reprint Dr. Dyer's remarks. Nothing happened.

The 1939 meeting, some recall, was historic in that John Budd, a tall young professional who'd started out to be a country preacher, insisted that the meetings be conducted in an orderly way. He declared that professionals should obey *Roberts Rules of Order* in conducting their meetings just as they heeded the Rules of Golf in their play.

Political fevers cooled as the 1939 annual meeting came near its close. The old officers were tired. They'd found that the path of glory didn't lead to PGA office. Some of them were beginning to suspect that the way to get even with someone who had been giving you a bad time was to elect him to PGA office, where he could work his head off and his heart out, get much criticism and little thanks.

Jack Mackie, who'd been a PGA officer longer than anyone else in his time (or after) and whose shrewdness had brought the PGA through the years of fiscal famine, wanted to stay home and read Bobby Burns and have his family about him. The Old Guard were going. For the first time since the PGA was formed, Fred Brand of Pittsburgh wasn't at a meeting, vigorously debating, then leading "Auld Lang Syne" as the meeting closed. So the election returns were as follows: president—Tom Walsh, 45, Ed Dudley, 22; secretary—Captain Charles Clarke, 45, Frank Sprogell, 16, John Budd, 6; treasurer—Willie Maguire, 36, Jack Mackie, 31.

14

The PGA Looks to It's Homework, Tries to Make Better Golfers, and Another War for PGA Veterans

[1940, 1941, 1942]

AT the twenty-fourth annual meeting of the PGA, held at the Morrison Hotel, Chicago, November 11 to 14, 1940, President Tom Walsh and his fellow officers enjoyed the novelty of a tranquil gathering at which PGA business was routine and the greater part of the proceedings devoted to planning the extension of professional services.

Twenty-nine sections were represented, and only one veteran was among the vice-presidents. He was Alex Cunningham, who'd come from Scotland and served at clubs in West Virginia and Ohio before coming to the North Shore Country Club in suburban Chicago and being Illinois PGA president for several terms. Other vice-presidents were Howard Beckett, Charles Congdon, Johnny Farrell, Ed Gibson, Wendell Kay, Joe Smith, Frank Sprogell, and Joe Novak, who was to become a PGA president.

With a war raging in Europe and many professionals leaving their American jobs to go into the British military service, there was no disposition among American pros to engage in small domestic wrangles. Although the attack on Pearl Harbor was more than a year away, the PGA had already raised over $50,000 in Red Cross matches.

The PGA treasury needed fattening despite the rigid economy of Jack Mackie's years in charge, so another ball-promotion scheme was hatched. This time the PGA was to be sole distributor of the coreless ball, a sphere made of rubber thread wound upon itself to the cover. Of course the ball was supposed to have more distance and putt truer than any other ball and outsell all other balls. It didn't. As a consequence, the dues of the 1,900 members of various classes constituted PGA revenue in 1940.

The Benevolent, Relief, and Unemployment funds were reorganized on the advice of attorneys, because the PGA had failed to take advantage of allowable tax exemptions. A sum of $4,662 was paid to members unable to work and $1,085 to members who couldn't get jobs anywhere in golf. The PGA War Relief Fund paid out only $62, and that was for part of the burial expenses of a member who certainly didn't get a state funeral. Whether the lost comrade was American or British, the records don't show. The War Relief payments were to formerly active PGA members who'd gone into military service.

A high percentage of the older British-born members of the PGA had been in World War I; some had even served in the Boer War. Big Bob Macdonald of Chicago, in his later days, and little Tom Clark, many years pro at the Blue Hills Club, Kansas City, used to do an African war song and dance they'd learned while serving Her Majesty the Queen.

In 1939 and 1940 there was a great deal of buying of golf clubs and balls by large corporation purchasing departments to be resold to employees at cost plus a small handling charge. There had been considerable increase in fee-course play in the 1930's, and it was estimated that approximately 60 percent of the rounds of golf in 1939 were played on the public courses. Naturally, a low price was the first and often the only factor controlling the purchase of golf equipment, so the purchasing agents as competitive retailers were killing club, ball, and bag business at public-course pro shops and cutting into pro-shop business at many private clubs.

This competition was halted by PGA sections in the Southwest, where oil companies in Kansas, Oklahoma, and Texas had been particularly active in allowing their purchasing departments to operate as cut-price golf goods stores. An Oklahoma advertising man wrote a letter for the professional at his club that served as a model for other requests that the oil companies sell their own products and allow the golf professionals to make a living selling golf goods. It was sent by PGA sections to presidents of offending companies and to officials of retail merchants' associations so they'd know what was going on. The letter said that the professionals presumed that the companies were paying employees enough so that there was no reason for company purchasing departments to get into cut-price golf goods retailing. After all, the professionals and their customers paid established retail prices for petroleum products and other merchandise, so the function of a purchasing department was to buy for the company's operation, not to sell in a way that ruined a small retailer who was giving expert, individualized service. And it was suggested that company executives review a purchasing department practice that was injuring the company's public relations.

Some professionals were afraid the PGA stand was too strong and could cost pro jobs at good clubs. It worked out the other way, though, and soon quashed the company-store idea. Other small retailers backed up the pro protest and added the prospect of legislative action compelling corporations to stay in their own retailing field.

This sectional PGA experience in the limited area of unfair competition reflected a merchandising and public-relations strength that pros never used again by collective design. However, during the civil-war split years later, home pros spontaneously refrained from selling clubs bearing the names of tournament pros they thought were in favor of dividing the PGA.

These examples of club-pro marketing strength, about a quarter of a century apart, were recalled more by veteran executives of golf manufacturing companies than by PGA officials. The cheap clubs bearing the names of pros all too often were shoddy implements that could be made in a backroom by sticking a head, a shaft, and a grip together and boxing the assembly. There wasn't enough profit per club to worry a manufacturer. And eventually the PGA quit bothering about cheap pros' names on cheap clubs. The reasoning was that those clubs sold to a part of the market in which stores were cutting each other's throats. Those who should be worrying, the pro merchandisers concluded, were the reputable big-name pros whose market value sank every time a playing professional's name went on inferior golf merchandise.

The merchandising lessons of 1940 had little general impact on the pro field, but they were elemental and significant. They accelerated the growing collective effort of professionals to make themselves successful in specialty-shop operations.

The collegiate and high school golf educational work of the PGA suddenly burst into full bloom at Purdue in the spring of 1940, when professionals and other authorities on golf presented demonstrations, lessons, and lectures in the university field house. More than two hundred professionals, mainly from the Midwest, attended, and hundreds of university students came into the classes for lessons from noted professionals.

Purdue's research and advisory work in golf turf and its golf course management short courses had been valuable to golf in Indiana, Illinois, Kentucky, and Ohio for several years, but the 1940 venture into golf-playing instruction was new to the game. The schooling was not repeated. It was highly popular with students who cut other classes. At that time Purdue did not have its two attractive golf courses, and only a few of its students had attained distinction in Big Ten golf competition.

Golf instruction in high schools and smaller colleges got more attention than ever before. The junior promotion at private and public courses was also stepped up by PGA members. The Junior Committee, headed by George Lake, professional at the Long Beach, California, municipal course, issued diplomas and Junior PGA membership cards to youngsters who completed the courses, usually a series of six free lessons.

It was beginning to be difficult to find caddies. With the improved economics of the nation, as well as the fact that many potential caddies lived so far from courses that transportation was a problem, thoughtful pros decided to do something to provide golf with millions of young recruits as the caddie field diminished. The junior program was the answer, and it worked especially well in the South, where blacks supplied most of the caddie requirements, and in sections of California, where thousands of vagrants began to tote bags. These adults crowded the kids into junior classes, where the youngsters learned so soundly that when they grew older they established standards of golf play higher than usual in other parts of the country.

The benefits of the junior project were immense and lasting beyond expectations, but the pros' work was handicapped by regulations of the schools and the United States Golf Association. Schools prohibited instruction by individuals not having a teacher's license, and the USGA had a rule excommunicating as amateurs teachers who taught golf among other subjects. These official restraints were discouraging, but eventually were corrected when professionals were paid to teach golf to physical education instructors. Then, after due deliberation lasting almost thirty years, the USGA revised its ruling to agree with the far more realistic approach of the Royal and Ancient toward the promotion of golf in the schools.

The Tournament Bureau situation was quiet in 1940, giving Fred Corcoran a chance to arrange and develop the schedule instead of having to spend so much of his time with argumentative players before he could get a good show ready for the road. That year there were twenty-six tournaments and purses of more than $160,000.

The PGA Seniors had sixty players in their championship, which was won by Otto Hackbarth, first of the home-breds to win the title. The Seniors scheduled their 1941 tournament at Sarasota, to observe the twenty-sixth anniversary of the PGA.

There was talk at the annual meeting about limiting the president to two terms, with the idea of reducing PGA internal politics and the wheeling and dealing so prevalent during the Jacobus administrations. Another reason for the proposed limitation was that the PGA needed as president a man so valuable to his club that he couldn't afford to divide his abilities and time between his club job and the PGA for more than two years.

This move was only adopted years later, after the 1942–48 terms of Ed Dudley, who was anything but a politician but got along with everybody and was a fine player. He knew many professionals and amateurs well and was liked by every one of them. He was professional at the Augusta National Golf Club, which was closed summers and didn't have its Masters tournament during the war years. Dudley was too old for active military service but ideally qualified by temperament to help fit professional golf into a useful program of rest and recreation for military personnel and civilians in war and normal work.

The educational interest of pros in their business picked up in 1940 following the opening of Purdue University golf clinic. The Heddon Company, makers of steel golf shafts, offered a $650 prize for answers to the question of "what we need for progress and service." The contest was repeated from the previous year when returns were moderate, but in 1940 there were more than 140 answers from pros and their assistants. One of the judges was J. Leslie Rollins, who as dean of men at Northwestern University devised the basis for the Western Golf Association's Chick Evans caddie scholarship selections and supervision.

The educational session that completed the 1940 PGA annual meeting was in itself a review of the high spots of professional golf business for the year. George S. May, the business management consultant who became the first sponsor of big-money golf tournaments as corporation advertising, talked to professionals on the urgency of applying business principles to the pro shop in ordering stock and in display, advertising, and record keeping. Dr. Robert Dyer spoke on certain medical aspects of golf, reporting interesting statistics involving the higher scores on the second nines of a large number of club tournament results reviewed by a California physician. These were believed to be caused by fatigue and a reduction in blood sugar.

O. J. Noer, noted turf expert, cited problems of golf turf maintenance with which the club professionals and the tournament specialists should be acquainted, lest they expose themselves to embarrassing disclosures of ignorance of an essential of their game and business.

Glenn Morris, executive director of the National Golf Foundation, related how professionals and golf course superintendents had worked in helping small towns to get golf courses built. Herb Graffis, in commenting on golf's growth without such publicity as had been given baseball and football, said that newspaper advertising of golf merchandise would get more sports-section space for the game.

Stores were increasing their golf goods advertising in newspapers, but manufacturers had discontinued sending their tournament headliners into stores to promote sales in competition with pro shops.

The formalities went on as usual at the 1941 PGA annual meeting. There was surprise that no Tournament Committee fuss was bubbling, and Fred Corcoran reported that the thirty-two tournaments of the year had a new high of $185,000 prize money and an estimated 500,000 in the galleries. Ed Dudley, head of the Tournament Committee, had appointed a Sponsors' Advisory Committee, which was intended to help players get tournaments on a business basis. Its members were Bing Crosby, Elmer Ward, Russell Gnau, Adolph Bremer, Cloyd Haas, Maynard G. Fessenden, John B. Kelly, and Thomas McMahon.

PGA internal affairs were in good shape, with a roster of 2,015 members. A PGA Hall of Fame Committee was formed with Grantland Rice as chairman, and it was reported that a Red Cross benefit match had been played in Nassau by American professionals with the Duke of Windsor presiding at the ceremonies. Progress was also beyond expectations in the PGA program for golf education in high schools and colleges, in employees' recreation at numerous industrial plants, and at YMCA's and YWCA's. There were problems in this educational work, but it was giving professionals more of a chance to test teaching ideas.

Teaching was the first reason for golf pros and for the PGA, in the judgment of many professionals. These men considered instruction the foundation of the pro job and were worried that the PGA had been making tutoring a mere sideline of the pro job; they also worried about the generally unimproved standards of golf play. They couldn't understand why such nice, intelligent people as their members played such bad golf.

It seemed to older professionals that the lesson tee had failed to produce the results of the playing lessons, which were getting scarcer because professionals and their assistants lacked the time for them. During the playing lesson the pupil had to learn and accept responsibility for absorbing and effectively applying the instruction under playing conditions, while on the lesson tee the pupil listened to the instructor and hit shots, but how much he or she actually learned, nobody knew. The idea that the pupil had responsibility for learning and that the lesson was a partnership hadn't been put across.

The background of discontent with the lesson situation accounted for the instruction topics' running away with

Joe Novak. PGA

the 1941 program. There were signs there might be a revolution in golf instruction and that golf's teaching professionals might become as famous as football coaches, and as well paid, too. But that apparent breakthrough lasted only a few weeks. On December 7, 1941, came the attack at Pearl Harbor, and the pros' plans for a brilliant teaching revival were put aside.

As the war continued, golf instruction became important and popular in the recreation and physical condition programs at military stations in the United States, and numerous golf professionals were assigned to teaching jobs at the military courses. There was no coordination in nationwide instruction. However, the prospect of cooperative work in a teaching job that was definitely individualistic, which had been envisioned by a few enthusiasts at the 1941 PGA lesson instructions, succeeded with millions of young men in the armed forces.

This outburst of concern for the customer's game marked the twenty-fifth annual assembly of the PGA, which was held on November 10 to 13 at the Medinah Club in Chicago. Tom Walsh was president, and there were twenty-nine sections represented. The calm and knowledgeable veteran Frank Sprogell was secretary, and the treasurer was Willie Maguire, who with Jack Burke, Sr., Sid Cooper (Harry's father), Graham Ross, George Aulbach, and a few others, had brought along a galaxy of golf's younger stars. Former president George Jacobus attended as honorary president. The vice-presidents were Howard Beckett, Charles Clarke, Charles Congdon, Alex Cunningham, Jimmy Hines, Larry Nabholtz, George Schneiter, Ernest Smith, and Eugene ("Skip") Wogan.

In a brief talk to his brother professionals, Wogan warned that their clubs were going to be in increasingly serious trouble unless some concerted effort was made to present the case of the golf course as the best tax bargain for a community. He pointed out that whenever a golf course was built the value of the surrounding property was raised. The golf club did not send children to school, required little or no street construction, maintenance, or street lighting, required only one-stop garbage collection, was not a fire hazard to adjacent buildings, needed only moderate sewerage facilities, provided a scenic area, and if it did use city water, it used the water mostly when other demands were minor. Further, Wogan remarked, the golf club provided caddying work that in every way was desirable employment for youngsters.

Officials and delegates failed to see how or why the PGA should concern itself specifically with a club's tax problems, and new ideas on instruction that promised to help the pupil to learn golf better never got beyond the discussion stage. These ideas were presented by Joe Novak, chairman of the Teaching Committee, and Professor John Anderson of the University of Minnesota, who was a consultant for General Motors on educating men in motor skills. His observations and recommendations on golf instruction had been effectively applied by Les Bolstad, a golf professional at the university.

Novak, who had won a number of sectional championships before specializing in instruction, had worked out a system of rating golfers on features of their styles—address, forward press, footwork, pivot, control, and hand action. Along with Novak, Tom Walsh, Frank Sprogell, Willie Maguire, and Ed Newkirk had made ratings at the first tee during the 1941 PGA Championship at Denver, and using the system's appraisal of form, had picked the final four finishers, five of the last eight, and twenty-one winners of the first-round matches. The system made a similar good showing at the 1941 National Amateur Championship at the Omaha Field Club, with four other professionals as examiners in the first round.

Novak wrote helpful articles and books about his research into golf form as a reliable indicator of playing success, regardless of deviations from what he believed to be the most dependable procedure. At the Bel Air club he had several motion picture stars as pupils, and they learned quickly and well because, he explained, Hollywood notables had been conditioned to respond to movie directors in getting satisfactory results. They'd learned how to learn, which is something other adult golf students hadn't mastered.

Novak's pro listeners knew what he meant. They also had been frustrated and discouraged by pupils who were physically and mentally adept, but simply couldn't learn golf. Hence, when the practical psychologist, Professor Anderson, told them about the teacher-learner relationship in what he called the motor skill of golf, the pros heeded every word. Several who became excellent instructors attributed it to their use of Anderson's advice on how to get the pupil conditioned for learning and how to present the lesson.

Anderson explained why golf resort professionals often have success with pupils who haven't improved after lessons with their home club pros. A lesson every day for six days, with time in between to work out the answers in practice and play, was far more sensible timing than six lessons a week apart, as the home club pro generally had to schedule them.

Almost thirty years after Professor Anderson suggested revisions in the pattern of golf instruction, Claude Harmon jarred pro golf and its amateur students by saying the set half-hour or hour lesson time was a heavy handicap to golf instruction. He recommended a short, clear, basic lesson, then allowing the pupil to learn for himself in supervised practice. Anderson had advised such a program, and the pros agreed he made a lot of sense, but with the war coming on, there was no inclination to make golf experiments.

Anderson went to the roots of instruction—something the pros had never heard of before and have not heard much of since. He showed why and how teaching is a professional job that is often beyond the capacities of some extraordinarily good athletes.

"In every kind of learning," he said, "the final outcome is a very, very simple performance, much simpler than the performance with which the individual starts. Fifty years ago the common method of teaching reading was to teach children the letters of the alphabet, then words, then sentences. A series of brilliant investigations showed that if you started with words or sentences, you got an excellent result, and the speed of instruction was stepped up sixty to seventy-five percent."

The pros who heard Professor Anderson translated his remarks in terms of their own children and the youngsters of other pros who began by hitting a ball, then backed up into grip, stance, and pivot. The professionals wondered; they continue to wonder. Teaching golf is a puzzling business. As Professor Anderson saw the golf instructor's job, "The problem of the teacher is to guide and direct the learning process rather than to assume that he does the teaching."

The Minnesota teaching expert intrigued his audience as he told of the application of compensating errors, such as teaching the chronic slicer how to hook and helping the learner to discover the happy medium, the straight ball. In describing something about what he'd had to learn in qualifying himself as a teacher, he noted, "There is amazingly little research—almost none—of the sort which would describe the manner in which a human being acquires control over a golf stroke." Unfortunately, nothing ever happened to Anderson's suggestion of golf instruction research along the lines teaching specialists in other fields use.

The meeting also heard talks by experts in accounting and on education in golf course maintenance and merchandising. Several delegates suggested the PGA employ an educational director, but that had to wait till the mid-1960's. At the moment the PGA was

faced with the urgent problem of keeping clubs alive during the war years.

Ed Dudley was serving his first term as president when the PGA held its 1942 annual meeting on November 9 and 10 in the Medinah Club, Chicago. Tom Walsh had become the honorary president, Frank Sprogell had been re-elected secretary, and Willie Maguire was treasurer. Vice-presidents were James Beirne, Alex Cunningham, Jimmy D'Angelo, Eddie Duino, Ben Lord, John Manion, Walter Mund, Dave McKay, and John Watson. The Pacific Northwest section did not send a delegate to the meeting, but the other twenty-nine sections were represented.

With a war being fought and not looking bright for the Allies, PGA members did what they could to raise funds for the Red Cross and military sports programs, provide recreation and physical training at military installations, keep their clubs from going under so golf would be ready to swing ahead when peace came, and provide entertainment in championships.

Of the association's 1,824 members, dues were waived on 201 who were in the armed services. Nearly 900 of the PGA's Class A members were veterans of World War I, according to careful estimates. Each delegate was given a copy of the PGA's audited financial statement. (It was, of course, a sketchy one, and it would be years before the association opened its financial books as widely as the USGA. And even today, despite its involvement with tax-exempt hospital and benevolent institutions and the sponsors' concern with the division of television revenue, the Tournament Players' Division of the PGA seems to retain the old PGA uneasiness about revealing financial statements.)

The PGA was proud to disclose that

more than $25,000 had been raised by PGA members for the United Service Organization (USO), Red Cross, Army, and Navy relief, and similar operations. Furthermore, the PGA had bought two ambulances for the Red Cross, and thousands of clubs and balls had been collected by pros and distributed for use at military establishments.

The rubber shortage necessitated a campaign to collect used golf balls at pro shops, then to send them back to manufacturers for reconditioning and resale. New golf balls were at a premium, and the pro or other retailer who had a supply of them had only his conscience to guide him in pricing them. With few exceptions, pros rationed their new golf balls until the supply was exhausted.

Gasoline was rationed. There was little demand for golf clubs, so production was limited, using materials manufacturers had in stock, and the market was supplied mainly by prewar inventories of manufacturers, pros, and sporting goods stores. Many professionals were working in factories producing war matériel and were at their clubs only on weekends. Their wives ran the pro departments the other days and helped out in the clubhouse operation, and wives of the older professionals made the discovery that when new clubs, balls, and bags weren't available, golfers spent their money for apparel. Thus the pro-shop apparel business, which was to become a large part of shop revenue, got its initial impetus.

In addition to doing a considerable job in keeping pro shops operating, wives of the veteran professionals were busy in the Red Cross, USO, and kindred wartime jobs that engaged energetic, patriotic women. Wives of British-born pros remembered the days of World War I when they'd been stars of

a popular song, "Sister Susie's Sewing Shirts for Soldiers." So they were back in wartime action again. The click of knitting needles in American pro shops warmed many lads serving on sea, land, and air.

The 1942 PGA Championship was the only national golf championship of the year, and a large percentage of the field consisted of pros on leave. Seaman First Class Sam Snead defeated Sergeant Jim Turnesa 2 and 1 at the Seaview Country Club, Atlantic City. Jim defeated Harold ("Jug") McSpaden, Ben Hogan, and Byron Nelson in succession. There were thirty-two starters. That title was worth $1,000 and was good for two years, since there was no PGA Championship in 1943.

Twenty-six tournaments were played that year on the PGA circuit. Prize money slumped from the preceding year for one of the few times since the PGA began developing the tournament circuit. The $155,000 was paid in war bonds.

A Hale America tournament for the Navy Relief Society and the USO, sponsored by the USGA, the PGA, and the Chicago District Golf Association, was played that year, with 1,560 entries playing thirty-six-hole qualifying rounds at twelve locations and the seventy-two-hole final at the Ridgemoor Country Club, Chicago, on June 18 to 21. Ben Hogan won with 271, leading Jimmy Demaret and Mike Turnesa by three strokes. Captain Robert T. Jones, Jr., was in a group at 290, in what was to prove the last national event in which he played. The tournament raised $20,000 for Navy Relief and the USO.

Objections were raised to scheduling any professional tournaments for 1943, and several sponsors wanted to be released from their agreements. Maynard

Craig Wood, Robert T. Jones, Jr., and Ed Dudley at the Hale America Open Tournament. PGA

G. Fessenden, an official of the Western and Chicago district golf associations and a veteran of World War I combat, together with L. B. Icely, Wilson-Western Sporting Goods Company president, offered to underwrite any tournament abandoned by sponsors. The public seemed to need the escape and restoration the tournaments supplied.

The PGA Seniors, recalling that criticism of recreation during World War I had come from those who showed no eagerness to be exposed to enemy fire, continued with their annual tournament. They played January 15 to 18 on the Fort Myers municipal course, and the small field gave $125 from the top of the prize money to the Red Cross. Eddie Williams won the championship.

Alex Cunningham was elected the new Seniors' president. Captain Charles Clarke, another veteran of service in the British forces in World War I, and limping from combat wounds, became vice-president; W. H. Way, of the Mayfield Country Club in rural Cleveland, was second vice-president. Eddie Williams, of the Bryn Mawr Country Club, Chicago, was elected secretary; and David Ogilvie, of the Oakwood Country Club near Cleveland, was made treasurer.

U.S. Ryder Cup team chosen in 1941—competition canceled because of the war. GH

Since the Ryder Cup international match had been canceled, a Ryder Cup match between teams of American-born and British-born pros was played at the Oakland Hills Country Club in suburban Detroit and raised another $25,000 for the Red Cross. Bob Hope and Bing Crosby began playing exhibition matches with prominent pros and amateurs and raised millions through golf for military relief and recreation organizations. Bing and Bob drew what veterans still believe were the largest galleries in golf history. One exhibition that Crosby, Hope, Tommy Armour, and Chick Evans played at the Edgewater Golf Club, Chicago, for the Fort Sheridan athletic fund attracted a multitude that the police couldn't control. One youngster was impaled on the club's fence, and a fire department ambulance crew had to unhook him. The crowd was too tumultuous to permit the players to swing freely and safely, so the exhibition was called off after nine holes. Of course only a small number of the spectators paid.

Along with other sports, golf was rapped for continuing its activities during the war. John D. Kelly, director of physical fitness, Office of Civilian Defense, told the PGA annual meeting he thought golf was valuable in helping to keep some citizens well conditioned, although he did not think there should be competitive golf tournaments. But he also believed there would not be voluntary enlistments much longer, so everybody who was physically and mentally subject to being drafted ought to stay in the best shape possible. He added that there was too much hysterical scolding of Americans who weren't carrying guns, and in reference to remarks Senator Harry F. Byrd had made about Kelly's office of physical fitness being a playground operation in wartime, said "I can roll in the political gutter with Senator Byrd anytime and come out with less mud than he can."

James Cady Ewell, the Wilson Company's advertising manager, in describing "The Case for Golf" to PGA officials, said that of the 132 million U.S. population, 9 million would be in the armed forces. He estimated there would be 3 million golfers among the 124 million nonuniformed population, that these golfers would have an average of about nine clubs to a bag, and in a normal year would use about 2.5 million dozen golf balls. Of these balls, about 75 percent would be available for recovering. He also estimated there were about 2.5 million clubs in manufacturers' carry-over stock, and material stocked for making 30,000 to 40,000 dozen balls for 1943. He figured that golf was in fairly good condition to make a contribution to the physical fitness and morale of its players in wartime.

It was also announced that Fred Corcoran, the Tournament Bureau manager, was given six months' leave of absence with pay by the PGA to go overseas for the Red Cross and that Clifford Roberts and Henry Hurst had been added to the PGA Advisory Committee.

15

The PGA Carries On in Wartime

[1943, 1944, 1945]

NO championships, PGA or Seniors, needed reviewing at the twenty-seventh annual meeting held at the Medinah Club, Chicago, November 15, 16, and 17, 1943. Twenty-nine sections were represented, and Ed Dudley again was president. With him, Frank Sprogell was reelected as secretary and Willie Maguire as treasurer. The vice-presidents were James Beirne, John Budd, Tom Mahan, Walter Mund, Joe Novak, Leo O'Grady, Ernest Shave, and William Wotherspoon.

In such troubled times the delegates were principally concerned with keeping private and public golf clubs in operation and at the same time continuing the tournaments and exhibitions that were such effective morale boosters in an America at war. The PGA also solemnly noted its losses. Its first combat fatality was Johnny Shimkonis, who had been professional at the Andover (Massachusetts) Country

Club. Then came A. F. Drake of the Ohio section, William Harmon of the Southeast section, and John Gerlings of the Pacific Northwest section.

By November 1, 1943, there were 350 PGA members in military service, and the association sent each member a carton of cigarettes as a Christmas gift. When reports were presented at the 1943 annual meeting, the association's membership in all classes had dropped by 126. Although no PGA Championship was played in 1943, there were events on what remained of the tournament circuit, and usually about 120 professionals showed up for them. The PGA Seniors' Championship was canceled, saving $2,500, and the USGA played none of its championships in 1942, 1943, 1944, and 1945. But a number of exhibitions were played by professionals for bond drives and other fund-raising involved in the war effort. At the annual meeting, twenty-two sec-

Fund-raising for the Red Cross. GH, photo by Stanley Toogood

tions reported their exhibitions had sold $6,674,354 in war bonds and had collected $96,315 as gallery fees, which were passed along to war relief organizations.

In mid-April Bob Hope and Bing Crosby took to the road for six weeks of exhibition matches with pros and amateurs. They started at the Dallas Country Club with a gallery of about 5,000 who bought $4.5 million in war bonds and an ambulance for the Red Cross. Playing with Hope and Crosby were PGA President Ed Dudley and amateur Jack Munger. Then came a performance at the Colonial Country Club, Fort Worth, where Hope and Ben Hogan, who was an Air Force rookie, Colonel O. E. Henderson, and Dudley had a gallery of 4,000 who bought $1.5 million in war bonds. Next stop was at the Shreveport Country Club, where 3,000 spectators bought $2.5 million in war bonds and an am-

bulance for the Red Cross. Hope and Dudley were paired with Louise Suggs, then Southern women's champion, and Merle Israel, Louisiana state women's champion. At New Orleans City Park a gallery of 8,000 bought $4.5 million in bonds. Miss Israel and a Mrs. Kostenmayer each played nine holes while Crosby, Hope, and Dudley went eighteen. Then Hope and Crosby played at the Mobile Country Club with Miss Israel and Miss Suggs as partners before a gallery of 4,000 paying for war bonds.

Matches at the Memphis Country Club, the Belle Meade Country Club at Nashville, the Llanerch Country Club at Philadelphia, the Capital City Country Club at Atlanta, and the Edgewater Golf Club at Chicago completed the tour. Hope and Crosby paid their own expenses throughout the tour, and the PGA gave them money clips as tokens of appreciation. Sam

Byrd, Byron Nelson, Joe Kirkwood, and Harold McSpaden were also among other professionals who were in the exhibitions. The recreation funds of the Army Air Transport Command and the Air Force were increased by the golf shows, as were operations of the Navy League and the Red Cross Motor Corps.

There were innumerable fund-raising matches at golf courses in which professionals were involved. They were small affairs but collectively raised millions for armed forces recreation and entertainment at military hospitals.

Jimmy Hines was chairman of the PGA Tournament Committee. All prize money was in war bonds, and there were no problems with the players.

Golf was becoming popular at military bases. The lesson tees and such courses as were available saw considerable action when the officers and enlisted men had time available. It has been estimated that at least 200,000 young men were introduced to golf while they were in the armed forces during World War II.

With no tournament problems to distract it, the PGA had a chance to take a good, cool look at itself and determine what needed to be done to make it function as a business. Somehow the PGA had never been able to knit itself together as an efficient organization. Perhaps the individualistic nature of its members prevented cohesion; perhaps the frequent change of officers hurt, just as personnel turnovers at golf clubs explain why so few are successful business operations.

At any rate, the PGA couldn't seem to make up its mind what it wanted to be. Was it a group to protect, enlarge, and make more useful and profitable pro employment at clubs? An outfit

booking and managing tournaments as a show window for golf? Or a social and benevolent association?

The PGA's brief experience with Albert Gates as its "commissioner" was principally to obtain for professional golf the same prestige baseball received when it hired Commissioner Landis. It was an effort to have a head man with experience and business knowledge managing the main office. But it didn't work out, because money was short, for one thing, nor were the problems of professional golf similar to those of professional baseball. And it was at this low point that Thomas W. Crane became executive secretary, and turned out to be the best bargain the PGA ever got. He handled small but troublesome and potentially dangerous cases for the association for years. Then came actual or threatened litigation involving the PGA initials and trademark, overtures to get the PGA into real-estate promotion, and now an offer by F. C. O'Keefe to take over the PGA Tournament Bureau with O'Keefe paying expenses and supervising and conducting operations. O'Keefe was to get 75 percent of the net, and the PGA 25 percent. The PGA was "guaranteed" a minimum of $1,000 annually. (Some years later, Crane was to see a somewhat similar offer made by J. Edwin Carter to take over the Tournament Bureau.)

At the 1943 meeting, some members of the PGA Advisory Committee recommended that the offer be seriously considered. The tournament situation had been expensive and troublesome ever since the PGA had begun to develop a growing market for the services of playing specialists. Besides, the majority of the Advisory Committee thought the PGA would be better off concentrating on its service to the golf-

At an exhibition of golfing technique: Gene Sarazen, Horton Smith, Kay Byrne. PGA, photo from AAFTC

ing public, instead of dividing its resources in building a business for men who had never been particularly concerned about the progress of the Professional Golfers' Association and its work for golf in general.

Naturally, the talk backstage was hot over this endless running controversy. On top of that, the PGA, rather than the tournament players themselves, had been severely criticized for continuing tournaments after the USGA had discontinued its national championships. Since the PGA probably had a higher ratio of World War I veterans among its members than any other American professional sports organization, its men could take a realistic rather than emotional view of tournament activities during wartime, but the accusations stung. In any case, Crane was among those realists. He knew the tournament players needed the PGA and

would be going nowhere without it; so he gently eliminated the proposal to sell out the tournament golfers.

Crane's wise and prompt action on the matter has meant millions to the PGA and has proved the foundation for the rich tournament circuit. In all tournament deals involving sponsors and players Crane had also inserted a clause identifying the PGA's participation in "all radio rights and broadcasting privileges," and such rights in connection with the PGA Championship, Ryder Cup matches, and other special events were "expressly reserved" for the PGA. Crane's foresight was the guide in all wireless negotiations, and when television replaced radio as an important medium of sports news information, the "broadcasting" term covered the shift.

There was a sidelight to the broadcasting rights clause. When Fred Corcoran, as Tournament Bureau manager, was dealing for tournaments, radio revenue sometimes was a subject of trading. To give Corcoran leeway in closing, the PGA gave him all broadcasting rights for $1 with the "gentlemen's understanding" that if he could get anything from radio he was to give it to the PGA. Revenue from that source was then meager. But when Crane recommended that the root of potential evil might also be eliminated, Corcoran cheerfully relinquished his ownership of a revenue producer that has become immensely valuable to the PGA and tournament players. He was too deeply involved in his overseas tours for the Red Cross, entertaining the armed forces with sports celebrities, and in arranging war relief golf exhibitions in the United States to worry about who in golf got what out of broadcasting.

The Athletic Institute, composed of leading manufacturers of sports goods, had voted $8,600 to help the PGA continue golf tournaments as wartime entertainment. Maynard G. ("Scotty") Fessenden and Thomas McMahon of the PGA's Advisory Board were hopeful that the institute might underwrite tournaments to the extent of $19,000 to $20,000 for a year, and L. B. Icely, a major factor in the sporting goods group, assured the Advisory Board and the PGA that in a pinch such underwriting probably would be available, but not if the Tournament Bureau was turned over to O'Keefe. However, no underwriting was needed under the cautious plan of tournament presentation that was conducted.

Records of the PGA do not identify the "young lady" who applied for membership in that year. No action was taken on her application at the 1943 annual meeting.

The Michigan section proposed an amendment to the constitution, which was adopted, then revised years later. The Michigan amendment stated: "Professional golfers of the Caucasian race, over the age of eighteen years, residing in North or South America, and who have served at least five years in the profession (either in the employ of a golf club in the capacity of a professional or in the employ of a professional as his assistant) shall be eligible for membership."

The racial clause was a subject of routine question rather than controversy and was adopted when one delegate, who expressed the collective view of the meeting, said, "Show us some good golf clubs Negroes have established, and we can talk this over again." Some black caddies had developed into good players, especially in the Southwest, and there was a national black golf association holding annual championships at public courses. There were also black professionals at a few Southern courses who had earned their jobs after long experience on course maintenance crews, then as greenkeepers. But the restrictive and exclusive nature of the "Caucasian race" stipulation was to become increasingly controversial in the years to come.

In 1943, the PGA worried about members who had been unemployed for some time and was equally concerned about golf courses wanting to employ professionals returning to golf after military service. Cooperation with the USGA was sought in getting jobs for pros, and the PGA Employment Committee, headed by William Wotherspoon, worked out a "Professional's Record" form that proved helpful in screening job applicants.

George Hall, professional at the Cornell University course, and Jimmy

D'Angelo of the Baederwood Golf Course, Philadelphia, proposed that the Executive Committee investigate the advisability of building a PGA golf course in Florida where members could play in the winter as club members. Pros had experienced increasing difficulty in being accepted as guests for winter rounds at desirable private clubs in Florida, especially since the war had begun, and veteran professionals, a number of whom had been at clubs for about forty years, were beginning to wonder where they would go with their wives when they became too old to handle jobs at big clubs.

The suggestion became one of the multitude of crucial questions facing the newly hired Tom Crane. He let word get around that the PGA *was* interested in Florida, and the arrangement that eventually took the PGA to its National Golf Club and offices at Dunedin developed from the key 1943 discussion. And, looking ahead, when the PGA's move from Dunedin to Palm Beach Gardens was being considered, George Hall was treasurer of the PGA and as cautious as the canny Scottish-Americans who had preceded him. Hall got the advice of Cornell University officials and lawyers, and even under heavy pressure from fellow PGA officials, he wisely backed away from letting the PGA in for a $2 million loan to finance courses and a clubhouse as a promotion for a real-estate development in the dreary Florida boondocks. Imagination, the selling and traffic value of the PGA name, and millions of the developer's cash and credit converted the cheap land into expensive real estate with everyone coming out reasonably happy.

Nothwithstanding the war, apparently a fair amount of golf was played in the United States in 1943, as 1,100 applications for Hole-in-One awards were made to the PGA.

Fitting golf into hospital and rehabilitation programs for physically and mentally wounded military personnel got much attention at the PGA's twenty-eighth annual meeting on November 12 to 15, 1944, at the Continental Hotel, Chicago, where the association had its office.

Twenty-nine sections were represented. Ed Dudley continued as president. Also remaining in office for the year were Secretary Frank Sprogell and Treasurer Willie Maguire. Vice-presidents were C. V. Anderson, Robert Barnett, John Budd, Tom Mahan, Walter H. Mund, Joe Novak, Leo O'Grady, Ernest Shave, and William Wotherspoon.

Three more PGA members had died in military service during the year: William A. Francis of the Tri-State section and Stanley Porkorski of the Philadelphia section had been killed in action, and Milton Trish of Western New York was a noncombatant fatality.

A total of 436 PGA members had entered the armed forces since the war had started. Four had been killed in combat, and three had died in other military service. Four PGA members were in Red Cross service overseas, three of them veterans of World War I —Harold Sanderson, Fred Moore, and Robert Smith. Fred Corcoran, Tournament Bureau manager, had been making USO appearances with former heavyweight champion Jack Sharkey and baseball pitcher Lefty Gomez in 1944, following his 1943 service with the Red Cross in Sicily, Italy, and Africa. Corcoran ran into numerous PGA members overseas, among them former sectional PGA officials Lieutenant Joe Davis and Sergeant Dugan Aycock.

In 1944, membership increased

Tom Walsh, PGA President 1940-41, conducts a golf program at Hines Veterans Hospital in Chicago. PGA

slightly for the first time since 1941, when it had been at a high of 2,035. In 1944, paid membership was 1,321.

At a dozen or so military hospitals where land was available, local professionals and greenkeepers cooperated in building practice putting greens and practice ranges and professionals provided instruction. The PGA Rehabilitation Committee, with Frank Sprogell as chairman, had difficulty organizing and coordinating golf installations and entertainment at military hospitals, partly because the success of the venture depended on the interest of high-ranking hospital officials in golf and partly because PGA sections often were careless about the paperwork necessary

for official military approval and also about reporting and "communications" to PGA headquarters.

Among the military hospital entertainment and rehabilitation programs in which PGA members were active with personal and financial support were those at Fort George Wright AAF Convalescent Hospital and Baxter General Hospital at Spokane; Ashburn General Hospital, McKinney, Texas; McCloskey General Hospital, Temple, Texas; Dewey and Hines hospitals in the Chicago area; Valley Forge General Hospital; the Naval Hospital in Philadelphia; Halleran General Hospital, Staten Island; Lyons Veterans Hospital in New Jersey; Thayer General Hospital, Nashville; Percy Jones Hospital, Battle Creek; Deshon Hospital, Butler, Pennsylvania; Crile General Hospital, Cleveland; Snelling Hospital at St. Paul; the Danville, Illinois, Veterans Hospital; and hospitals in Denver.

A complete list of military hospitals with golf services supplied by pros was never compiled. Some of the golf programs for military hospital patients were handled at nearby private and public courses with pros as unpaid instructors.

The Philadelphia section raised $65,000 for its hospital golf projects. Of this sum, $20,000 was spent in building the nine-hole course at Valley Forge General Hospital, of which $13,000 was paid to working convalescent veterans at $6 a day. With the PGA on the Valley Forge job were the Golf Association of Philadelphia, the Women's Golf Association of Philadelphia, and the Philadelphia Greenkeepers' Association, which had Joe Valentine, Leonard Strong, James Conway, and Benjamin Mantell heading the force of course maintenance experts who built the layout. J. Wood Platt and Samuel Phillips, president of the Aronomink Club, were named by the PGA members as also having been especially helpful. PGA members also raised prize money and put on competitions at Valley Forge. Marty Lyons sponsored a putting contest with $150 prize money. Six of the contestants were in wheelchairs.

Eleven sections reported that their exhibitions and tournaments in 1944 raised $130,000 for golf at military hospitals. California sections staged tournaments at which were sold $6,440,000 in war bonds.

Frank Sprogell's Rehabilitation Committee officially included Leo Diegel of the Philmont Club, Robert Barnett of Chevy Chase, Alex Cunningham of North Shore in suburban Chicago, George Norrie of the Mobile Country Club, James Thomson of the Mohawk Club in Schenectady, and W. H. ("Bert") Way of Mayfield at Cleveland. Unofficially but actively it included about a third of the PGA membership, with the members paying the promotion and operating expenses of the many fund-raising affairs in which they were involved. PGA headquarters got $1,000 from the Chicago District Golf Association as its share of the Victory Open revenue after the USO and Navy Relief received their contributions. This was about the only expense money the pro organization got from the tournaments themselves.

Military hospital services associated the pros with women's organizations busy with hospital work. The women gave a great deal of time and effort to making use of golf for wounded servicemen and had well-organized programs. They kept the golf professionals very much on the job. The American Women's Voluntary Service, headed by the vigorous Helen Lengfield, continued its golf work at hospitals, blossoming out into Swing Clubs of able and admirable women who continued with golf and other valuable free work at hospitals after World War II ended, through and after the Korean War, and are still at it today, with the PGA, through its National Golf Day, making substantial contributions to finance military hospital golf projects sponsored by these women.

Lowell Thomas, the war correspondent and broadcaster, and Grantland Rice, the noted sportswriter, along with Clarence Budington Kelland, Robert Goldwater, John Foresman, Harry Todd, and other members of the PGA Advisory Board, were active in planning and conducting many events for the PGA hospital jobs and the Red Cross. Most successful of these affairs was the Red Cross benefit at the Wyka-gyl Club in the Metropolitan New York district, which raised $65,000.

Numerous professionals were being assigned to physical training duties, and in the process golf was getting a lot of recruits. For years you would notice a somewhat familiar flailing swing on courses all around the United States, then you would learn that the man with the distinctive swing had acquired his golf stroke at the Norfolk Navy base when he attended golf classes conducted by Paul Runyan, a PGA Champion with a swing all his own.

Outside of hospital and Red Cross work the PGA did little wartime business. Tournaments were booked by request, and there were no personality problems because the Navy admonition, "Shape up or ship out," was generally heeded by participants. Playing pros also spent much of their off-time in demonstrations at camps and visits to military hospitals.

The Athletic Institute gave the PGA $20,000 to finance tournament operations in 1944, and twenty-five tournaments were played, with $300,000, all in war bonds, as prize money. The PGA Championship resumed with the Spokane Athletic Round Table as sponsor. It was played at the Manito Golf and Country Club, August 14 to 20, and prize money was $14,500. The winner, Bob Hamilton, got $3,500 for defeating Byron Nelson, 1 up. Nelson received $1,500, and the first-round losers got $200 each. Sam Snead, who had last won at Seaview in Atlantic City in 1942, did not defend his title. He was in the Navy, then at the Sail Ho Golf Club near San Diego, and the skipper of the base didn't have a policy of

leaves for the asking. Fort Wright and Baxter General hospitals got $25,013 from the Spokane Round Table as tournament profits, and the money was used for the hospitals' rehabilitation programs.

From November 1, 1944, until April 1, 1945, nineteen tournaments were scheduled, with $70,000 in war bonds as prizes. Civilian wartime play was down to a rest-and-recreation level. Getting out to the clubs was usually a car-pool performance, and there seemed to be many more caddies than golfers. Few complaints were heard about clubhouse service, mainly because there was little service. Some motion picture theaters accepted a used golf ball and 15 cents as admission and sold the balls for reprocessing. The National Golf Foundation also conducted a campaign to collect used balls for reconditioning at pro shops. Since the rough at golf courses was long, and rough areas at some clubs were used as victory gardens, the risk of losing balls made the price of reconditioned balls attractive.

Only 835 holes-in-one were recorded for the PGA prize. Caddie programs at clubs got more than normal attention because pros had more time for the job, and many boys were developed as good golfers. Naturally, the financial condition of many country clubs was shaky in 1944, and the task of the professionals as specialists in golf was to keep them going on meager revenue. The job was simplified by play being mainly on weekends.

Tom Crane and Irene Blakeman had their own problems trying to keep the PGA office operating on a small budget with such a heavy work load. The offices in the Hotel Continental were small, and a move was arranged to the Metropolitan Building, 134 North La

Salle Street, Chicago at the end of the year.

Hope Seignous, secretary-treasurer of the Ladies' PGA, requested membership or a working arrangement of the LPGA with the PGA, but the PGA Executive Committee turned that down. F. C. O'Keefe withdrew his proposal to operate the Tournament Bureau, so that subject was closed. Percy C. Pulver, who had been editor of the PGA magazine, *The Professional Golfer,* since it started, retired in July, 1944, after twenty-five years at that post. He'd been in bad health for a year. Tom Crane took over Pulver's editorial job in March, 1944.

With the PGA's operations mainly geared to wartime demands, everyone looked ahead to peace and a surge in golf comparable to that which followed the end of World War I. This vision framed the picture of the PGA's own golf course, which had been talked about for several years. Now, in 1944, the PGA treasury was very low, according to Treasurer Maguire's report at the annual meeting.

Nevertheless, Florida real-estate promoters were inviting the PGA to come in to revive projects that had wilted when the famous Florida land-speculation bubble burst, leaving (without owners or residents) potential dreamlands with adequate if not impressive golf courses. Air Force training installations were bringing some money into the state in exchange for land, but that situation wasn't going to last long, so real-estate men, recalling that golf had been instrumental in establishing Florida as a winter resort, had big ears for any PGA chatter about its own longed-for course.

Sarasota and Fort Myers, where PGA Seniors Championships had been played, showed interest in the PGA in-

tentions but didn't come forward with definite proposals. In 1944, the idea of a PGA National Golf Club with winter and retirement homes of professionals surrounding the course was a concern mainly of older members. On the other hand, there was PGA interest when Dunedin, a pretty, neat little village on Florida's Gulf Coast north of Clearwater, came up with a specific offer. Dunedin was a promotion of Cleveland interests. The course had been designed and built by Donald Ross, it was about a mile from the Gulf, and an orange grove bordered several holes.

The clubhouse was simple and small and set in a grove of several large trees that shaded it from the tropical sun and allowed comfortable drinking and lunching in the little barroom where air conditioning was entirely by windows and nature. However, the locker room and showers provided sharply limited conveniences, the lounge was about the dimensions of a small trailer and modestly furnished in wicker, and the pro shop was a wing on the clubhouse about fifteen feet wide and thirty feet long.

When a few veteran professionals inspected the Dunedin property, they saw it not as it was but as they were confident it would become in the golden times of peace and prosperity. It never did become the dream that some old pros had for the Dunedin Isles Club, but it was a lot of fun as well as a lot of headaches for PGA members before the association moved out and the club returned to private status in richer times, built a new clubhouse, and rehabilitated the course. It became an attractive club among those in the pleasant towns of the strip of Florida's west coast called the Hoosier Riviera. And the PGA did well by Dunedin and Clearwater in bringing in the winter golf money of professionals and their families and guests, and PGA tournaments and business schools. Some pro families remained as residents of the community that the PGA National Golf Club had restored to life.

Action on the Dunedin-PGA deal was taken after Dunedin officials proposed a ninety-nine-year lease at $1 a year, with the privilege of cancellation on six months' notice. The PGA was to maintain the course and clubhouse. PGA Vice-President Joe Novak, Al Nelson, George Hall, and Fred Haas, Sr., made up the PGA committee recommending that the city of Dunedin offer be accepted. Those PGA investigators, plus President Ed Dudley, George Aulbach, Alex Cunningham, Eddie Kuhn, Marty Lyons, Wally Mund, and Bill Wotherspoon, with Tom Crane as their lawyer backstop, met at the Medinah Club, Chicago, November 11 and 12, with Dunedin City Attorney Kerr and W. Owens of Clearwater, and arrangements were completed for converting Dunedin's city course into the PGA National Golf Club. Part of the transaction was that the PGA had the option to buy 250 lots adjacent to the golf course for $250 a lot.

Fred Haas, Sr., was named chairman of a PGA-appointed Management Committee, whose duties were not sharply defined, although it was broadly responsible for putting the course into good playing condition as soon as possible, using whatever money could be spared for the purpose. Under the circumstances, it was not surprising that the other phases of the project were dreamy and vague. There was to be a model pro shop with leading manufacturers cooperating to present and test their lines in the shop and on the model teaching area that was to be constructed. The greatly enlarged clubhouse was to include a big golf library and a motion picture theater, which could be used for pro schooling and conferences in the daytime and for the entertainment of pros and their families in the evenings. It was all a beautiful idea. Part of somebody's dream about the PGA club did come true, though. Those lots adjacent to the course are worth far more than $250 today.

In an exchange of teaching, pro business, and club survival ideas at the annual meeting, a pro named Eddie Bush said he'd had a tag bearing the member's name, the club name and address, and the PGA emblem made and attached by a small strap to every member's bag. He said it was good advertising and identification all around and might be a good thing for other professionals and the PGA. Thus did the golf bag tag, which has been used by the million, make its debut before a national group.

With the war ended, the PGA tried to get its affairs back on the fairway at its twenty-ninth annual meeting at the Bismarck Hotel, Chicago, November 12 and 13, 1945. About 20 percent of the association's membership had served in the armed services, and around 15 percent in war production jobs. Eleven PGA members had been killed in action, and three more had died while in the armed forces, but the minutes of the PGA meetings do not name all these men.

Since the hotel meeting place and the PGA headquarters were in connecting buildings, the delegates from the twenty-nine sections represented were able to work long hours at the gathering. Ed Dudley again was president, and Secretary Frank Sprogell and Treasurer Willie Maguire had been reelected with him. The vice-presidents were Robert Barnett, Walter Mund, Joe Novak, Harry L. Moffitt, Leo O'Grady, James K. Thomson, and William Wotherspoon. Tom Walsh continued as honorary president. As the only national PGA official with a job in the Chicago district, Walsh had been carrying a heavy association work load, and Tom Crane as executive secretary usually also had a twelve-hour workday during the war years.

A few pros were discharged from military service shortly after VE Day, May 4, but they didn't get back home in time to begin looking for club jobs, nor did the pros who were quickly separated after VJ Day, September 2, have much more luck. In one sense, with part of the war over, the clubs and fee courses had had a good part of the summer to get back into the swing, but the postwar adjustment was to be a slow business, and the shortage of members and money was to prove an increasingly severe handicap for the next two years. There had been 5,209 private and public courses when Pearl Harbor was attacked in 1941; now there were only 4,808. As of September 30, 1945, 468 PGA members had been in military service and 377 were still in uniform. That meant a lot of professional men to find work for, and there were heated discussions at the annual meeting about the problems of the tournament circuit, and in particular, locating jobs for the returning pro veterans.

Through the distributing agency of the Athletic Institute, golf-playing equipment manufacturers granted $25,-000 to the PGA to get the Tournament Bureau back in action again with a peacetime program. This was an increase over its previous yearly grants, and older delegates who remembered World War I wanted the money used for a PGA employment fund, or at least split between the tournament-promotion and job-getting problems. They insisted that the tournament players ought to be able to finance themselves, while the pros who'd been away fighting should have first call on any relief money for pros, especially since they had to rebuild the golf market.

The arguments were acrimonious and emotional—not unusual between playing pros and home pros—but things cooled off later, when Lloyd Mangrum, a tough professional with four Purple Hearts for wounds incurred in combat as a foot soldier, won the 1946 National Open, the first one held after the war.

In 1945, dues-paying membership of the PGA was down to 1,565, which was 570 fewer than when hostilities began, but pro golf could look back on its war record as admirable in every respect. While PGA hospital work usually was carried out on a sectional basis, PGA members had been involved in constructing, equipping, and operating practice putting greens, practice tees, courses, and indoor nets at more than sixty-two armed services hospitals. Professionals and superintendents often got together and built small golf installations at hospitals, and the pros kept going back to instruct patients and maintain the golf playgrounds. Some of this work went on several years after World War II ended, and much of the continuing work in instruction, exhibitions, and tournaments at hospitals was done in association with the Swing Clubs of women golfers.

Tom Crane had been seriously wounded as a Marine in the Argonne during World War I. As chief operating executive of the PGA, he'd seen to it that the PGA war service work was followed through, especially visits to patients at the request of relatives of the injured soldiers or when the wounded men happened to have worked for the visiting pros.

No record was kept of the amount of war bonds sold through PGA activities. Tournament circuit prize money during the war was the least of the departments in volume, although all prizes were in government bonds—one of the reasons why the circuit was kept alive. In the forty-two tournaments of 1945, prize money consisted of approximately $500,000 in war bonds. That year exhibitions by PGA members in and out of military service raised over $100,000 for hospital, USO, and Red Cross work.

Those wartime tournaments and exhibitions had a great deal to do with establishing the pattern of today's tournament circuit, since most of the events have hospitals, boys' clubs, and other welfare operations as promoters and beneficiaries. The vast amount of unpaid labor involved in these enterprises, their tax-exempt feature, which provides advertising bargains for companies sponsoring tournaments, and the celebrity drawing power that Hope and Crosby displayed during wartime PGA events, all directly account for the business procedure in most of today's rich tournaments. And it should be added that Crosby and Hope, working along with the PGA in wartime golf performances, led to the multitude of pro-celebrity and actor-sponsored tournaments that now enrich pro golfers.

When the officers and delegates had appraised reports on the PGA's war service and gotten down to business, their new baby, the PGA National Golf Club, gave them a shock. It was the same sickening discovery that often confronts officials of new clubs: No provision had been made in the budget for the maintenance equipment needed to get and keep the course in even a mod-

erate standard of wartime condition. What mowers, tractors, and other equipment were scattered about the Dunedin barn were rusty and dilapidated. The greens, tees, and fairways hadn't been fertilized for years. There were weeds in profusion. Fresh paint, new boards, and hard work with broom, soap and water, and rake in and around the clubhouse might make the structure acceptable by old-country, small-town standards, but the course needed major rehabilitation, including rebuilding, if money were available. But none was for a new course.

Authorities like to say that a Florida golf course can be built so that it is in as good condition as it ever will be in its first year after completion. But there wasn't enough money to build the Dunedin course well when it began as a real-estate sales attraction; there never was an adequate amount at any time for doing what needed to be done on the PGA course. Time, money, and griping would probably have been saved by plowing up the course and starting all over. The watering system was poor and ineffective. Drainage was fair. Greens were sandy and were playable quickly after thundershowers. Ball washers, tee markers, flags, and tee benches were in shabby condition when such accessories were available. This was the initial condition of the golf course that the PGA hoped to present as its model and on which PGA members and their guests were to play pleasant rounds.

The layout did improve slowly, despite heavy handicaps. It received ample expert advice from the noted turf expert O. J. Noer, the famed architect Dick Wilson, and countless others. After his retirement from the professional job at North Shore in suburban Chicago and the quiet of his farm on the Mississippi Gulf Coast, Alex Cunningham, a veteran of pro-greenkeeping work at several fine clubs, took on the PGA National Course management job, following other good men the job had defeated. He was able and explosive and soon had had all he could take. "Too many experts," he explained. "I've had men who couldn't raise a weed in a window flower box at tenements where they lived when they were caddies try to tell me how to run this golf course. I tell them they're lucky to be on the course with golf clubs instead of with picks and shovels!"

The course-maintenance equipment problem was further complicated by a fire that burned the storing shed and most usable machinery. Insurance was $2,000, and the city of Dunedin added $1,500, but even with that money little course machinery was available at the time and the grass grew long and ragged.

Fred Haas, Sr., George Hall, Eddie Kuhn, and Al Nelson inspected the Dunedin plant and reported it had to be viewed as it might be rather than as it was. The brightest picture of the PGA National Golf Club was presented in *The Greener Pastures* a booklet, on which Maynard G. Fessenden of the PGA Advisory Board and Joe Graffis of *Golfdom* and the National Golf Foundation collaborated. It sold memberships in the PGA National Course to the PGA's pro members, and brought in $5,000, which meant a good net profit.

Another nice little thing happened to the PGA at Dunedin. The city deeded free to the PGA eight and a half acres, including a grapefruit orchard. Then someone sold the pro shop a lot of little tubular gizmos that you stuck into oranges and grapefruit and sucked out juice. With all the citrus

bordering the course, players came staggering onto the eighteenth green carrying loads of orange and grapefruit juice, beverages unimagined in the land of golf's birth. The PGA was also offered an option to buy ninety acres at one edge of the course for $50 an acre, but said, "No thanks." That was one of those might-have-been things that happen to all of us except the rich.

With all the complaining about the Dunedin layout, it was a lot of fun—just simple country fun—with fine Gulf fishing sandwiched between rounds of golf. There were motel rooms and houses to rent at moderate prices. Otto Hardt, a veteran professional, built a deluxe motel, and the winter guests had to reserve early. And there were excellent and moderately priced restaurants at Clearwater Beach and across the bay in the Spanish section of Tampa. To sum up, the PGA spent $25,000 in 1945 at Dunedin, and progress was made.

Affairs at PGA headquarters were going along smoothly since Tom Crane had had a chance to get them organized. The group insurance policy sold by Edward J. Riley was now a satisfactory one, and this was long before fringe benefits. Of course, no pro died rich, and the PGA policy helped a widow until her tears dried and she could get work or go to live with the children. Approximately a third of the money collected from PGA members went for insurance premiums.

Nearly twenty-five years would pass before a pension plan that would share the premium cost could be worked out between the PGA and employing clubs. The annual turnover in private club membership was a major reason why pro job security was nothing to brag about, although in 1965 there were an estimated 125 professionals who had been with their clubs for twenty-five years or longer.

Pro-shop burglary insurance was re-examined after experience had shown that top-quality unused golf bags and balls had a ready black market. The remote and unprotected location of pro shops and the shops' usual deficiency in burglary prevention made them attractive targets. Along with this, fire insurance was another rising cost. The pro stored the bags and clubs and some golf balls of his members, and there was no uniform practice on coverage. When a pro shop burned and the pro's insurance wasn't included in the cost of club storage and cleaning, the pro often lost his job. Moreover, even if pro-shop merchandise and the contents of the club-and-bag storage section were insured, how could they be replaced if they were destroyed by fire in wartime?

The PGA Championship was played July 9 through 15 at the Moraine Country Club, Dayton, Ohio, for $15,-000 in war bonds. Byron Nelson won the title—his second—and $3,750, plus $125 as one-half the medalist prize he shared with Johnny Revolta. The defending champion, Bob Hamilton, went out in the first round. Ticket sales, programs, and concessions brought, in addition to prize money, $51,515 to the Wright Field and Patterson hospitals at Dayton and a $5,000 profit to the PGA.

S. C. Allyn and H. S. Mead were co-chairmen of the event at the Moraine, which was the most financially successful PGA Championship yet played. Allyn, the National Cash Register chief, a brilliant and tireless executive, known worldwide as "Chick," was on the PGA Advisory Board. (It took a long time before the PGA learned how to inform and use this board.) Allyn had golf courses built for the NCR employees at Dayton, and it was there that Ray Floyd won the 1969 PGA Championship.

There was good news at the 1945 meeting, in that *The Professional Golfer* had made a profit of $700 for the fiscal year. It was a bookkeeping profit, with subscription revenue coming out of dues and minimum expenses being charged to the magazine.

In 1945, George Aulbach, chairman of the PGA Educational Committee, worked on getting job training for professional golf as one of the business courses financed by the GI Bill of Rights plan. Aulbach had discussed with the faculty members and officials of several universities the prospects of schooling for potential golf professionals on the order of college training given to potential club and hotel managers and to golf course superintendents. College people thought well of the idea and its practical application by specialists in golf, but the career educational notion was knocked out of bounds by the USGA amateur status ruling that declaration of intention to turn professional excommunicated one as an amateur.

The Manufacturers' Relations Committee requested golf club makers not to use the names of professionals on any clubs retailing for less than $5. That proved to be just another of many futile efforts over the years to prevent the use of pros' names on cheap, inferior golf merchandise that damaged the pro name as an indication of quality.

The teaching program that Joe Novak had been developing during the war was applied to golf at military hospitals. Interesting exercises were presented, but the program never really got organized on an extensive basis. Novak had heard how Tommy Armour, languishing in the severely injured section of a British military hospital in World War I, blind in one eye, one lung gas-burned, bones broken, and otherwise hopelessly battered, had thought and dreamed of how he would play golf when he got well. Novak felt that Armour could give the casualties some idea of how to win the National Open, the British Open, the PGA, and other championships just as he had when he recovered from his wounds.

It didn't work out quite as Novak had planned, but the men in the wards enjoyed Armour's visits, even though he hated going there. Armour was a peculiar combination of the sentimental and brutally realistic. He disliked the hospital visits because he kept wondering, "Why should that kid be there instead of me?" Tommy himself had gone into a Highland regiment as a freshman collegian and amateur golf champion, and after battlefield promotions came out as a major. He was marvelously gifted with his hands and had some sort of a record for assembling and repairing automatic weapons in the field. He tried to get into World War II as an instructor, but he didn't make it.

Tommy's brother Alexander ("Sandy"), also a veteran of World War I, tried to help in the hospital service. Sandy had been wounded, then captured in World War I. Before enlisting he had been a concert violinist. He used to tell a few of his close friends how, when he was in prison camp, he'd dream about being a soloist in Edinburgh or London, and he'd name his selections. A few times Sandy took a violin into hospitals where there were boys who knew music. Some brother Scots said Sandy was a better violinist than golfer, but he was a good amateur.

Another veteran pro who took a few swings on the military hospital circuit was Bobby Cruickshank. Even the men who didn't know the first thing about golf, and were not in the mood for caring, felt Bobby was a buddy. He was one of the most colorful men in American golf and narrowly missed a championship when Bob Jones beat him in the 1923 National Open. He was close a lot of times for other titles, but for laughs and excitement and competitive thrills, veteran golf spectators learned that Cruickshank was the most reliable entertainment in golf.

Cruicky was the GI's kind of guy in any war. As a POW he got the Jerries thoroughly confused by sneaking into a burial detail and getting German soldiers stinking when they and their captives liberated a saloon on the way back to the prisoners' corral. The also-stewed Scots had to carry their guards back to camp, and the CO practically broke out in tears.

Cruickshank made several unsuccessful attempts at escape. Then came his triumphant venture. He escaped and went cross-country, navigating by the stars and hiding in haystacks from his captors. Then one extremely hungry and thirsty evening he crawled out of a haystack and hunched his way across the fields. Eventually wee Robbie Cruickshank skulked his way to a small French village and found the house he entered was a saloon operated by a friendly fat lady. He also learned to his delight that the war had been over for two days. He and the friendly fat French lady came to peace terms.

Golf professionals may not have been well organized in their military hospital jobs, but they seemed to have the temperament to brighten spirits. Take, for instance, Harry Pezzullo, for many years president of the Illinois section, who was a dependable man on hospital calls around Chicago. Harry was an excitable man but always in a happy mood without being goody-goody. Sometimes his discussions with a roomful of mental patients at the Great Lakes Naval Training Station seemed to take an ominous turn as talk grew loud. But all ended calmly.

"Pezzullo's great for those fellows," a doctor commented. "Apparently he understands them and goes along with them and lets them ease themselves by winning arguments from him. He says he knows how they feel—he's punchy himself from three-putting."

Harry had the PGA spirit at its very best.

16

Golf Was Gospel to the Old Pro –
The Story of the PGA Seniors

IN 1931, when elders on the PGA roster conceded they were indeed no longer threats in the National Open and the PGA Championship, they decided to do what older amateur golfers had started doing in 1905—establish a Seniors' Championship.

The U.S. Seniors' Golf Association Championship was first played in the autumn of 1905 at the Apawamis Club in Rye, where the organization's tournaments are still played annually by congenial golfers of varying degrees of competence who are fifty-five or older. U.S.-Canadian Seniors' amateur team competition began as early as 1918. State and sectional Seniors' championships sprang up with practically juvenile vigor among amateur golfers, but somehow the Senior professionals didn't have the organizing urge and were content until 1931 to have competitions as incidents of gatherings of the patriarchs. Then, at Philadelphia, Charles

Mayo and Freddie McLeod tied for the Senior Pro Championship, which had no official blessing, and Mayo defeated McLeod in the play-off.

Nobody got swept away into the formalities of organizing, so the Seniors' Championship didn't come into the PGA program as a fixture until 1937, when the PGA Executive Committee authorized $2,000 for prize money and expenses of a championship for PGA members of fifty or older. The competition was under the jurisdiction of the Seniors' Committee of the PGA, with Grange Alves as secretary. From the start, some veteran professionals wanted their organization to be a coordinated associate of the PGA, as it later became. But PGA officials had so many urgent duties they were content to have the Seniors' Division spin off and mind its own business, barring main-office help in financing the Old Boys' championships.

Duncan McInnes was referred to in minutes of early PGA Seniors meetings as "historian" of the group, but he was inactive in that capacity because of his involvement "in City of New York work." The McInnes chronicles, if such were put onto paper, have vanished from the ken of posterity, but the somewhat sketchy minutes of the first few meetings of the Seniors' group and the clear reports of Eddie Williams, a winner of the Seniors' Pro championships in 1942, '45 and '46, show how the old pros of golf regarded the spirit and service of the game as a sacred trust they never were to take lightly. And they didn't, either.

At the first meeting of the Seniors' Division, in the fall of 1937, George Sargent, second president of the PGA and later to become the Seniors' president, said to his colleagues of fifty or older, "We owe a debt of gratitude to golf and to the American public which holds us in esteem. The player who scores from 85 to 100 is the backbone of this country and of golf. We professionals at fifty are more understanding of these men than we were before.

"The pictures we see in the papers are of the tournament stars. Our purpose now is to improve the games of our members, and for that we can't expect to become prominent in the press."

Sargent knew both sides of the pro career from experience. As the winner of the 1909 American National Open and of the 1912 Canadian Open he'd had the glory, or such of it as there was in the growing-up days of tournament golf in North America. Then came the problems and the long hours of trying to teach others how to work their wonders.

Sargent was an excellent instructor, and he stirred embers of the vanishing art of bench clubmaking when he said,

George Sargent. PGA

"I feel we should work on a type of club easier for the multitudes to use than the present type. The present type is far from being the most scientific tool."

Val Flood, a sprightly ancient from the Shuttle Meadow Club, New Britain, Connecticut, followed through on the Sargent swing into club design. Flood was called by his fellows "The Senior of Seniors." He was well into his seventies and had the freshness of a high school cheerleader. "George is right," he said, "and we all know it after years of teaching and playing with members. There should be bigger heads on women's clubs. Manufacturers ought to make implements more helpful for the poor player instead of making clubs for a few hundred fellows who don't do anything else but play golf and ought to be able to use any sort of a stick."

That statement by Brother Flood was not endorsed unanimously. Not many expressions allowing conflicting judgments ever rolled smoothly through meetings of the venerable professionals.

The spirit of those early meetings in which the Seniors volunteered to answer many questions on golf was emphatically voiced by Alex Cunningham when he was president of the Old Boys. "Good, sensible discussion is healthy for us and for golf," said the sturdy Cunningham at one heated stage of a Seniors' annual meeting, "but I don't want any of you wasting our time in arguments."

Alex was the executive type. "You're out of order" was his ruling of parliamentary law—which took care of those who disagreed with him. He was a kindly man, when not crossed, and an excellent professional at fine clubs.

The Senior professionals always regarded the Rules of Golf as they did the Ten Commandments, but where they might forgive someone who broke a Commandment, he who cheated at golf was forever damned. As Flood put it to the group that organized the PGA Seniors:

"We have a responsibility in guarding the moral side of golf. Golf to me and most of you always has been almost a religion. I can put up my right hand before God and honestly say I never in my life have consciously broken a rule of golf.

"We always have the duty of reminding the boys around us of the great good they can get from golf. I have systematically given talks two or three times a week to my caddies showing them the right way to live, to carry themselves, to be honest with everybody, and how all that fits in with golf and is a part of golf."

Then, after practically opening as a prayer meeting, the gathering got down to business and split sharply on how much the competitive angle of the meeting should be accented or whether it should be incidental to the fraternal spirit. A satisfactory compromise was worked out for age grouping, with the fifty- to fifty-four-year-old men playing in what generally was regarded as the championship. Class B comprised the fifty-five-to-fifty-nine bracket; and Class C, those sixty and over. The route was fifty-four holes. Prize money was $2,000 for the first several years, and the Seniors had a battle getting that away from the PGA's treasury. After financing the Tournament Bureau in developing a tournament circuit and a source of wealth for the young playing experts and paying the expenses of the Ryder Cup team, the PGA didn't have much money left for its old pros.

However, the Senior professionals were playing for more than money; at heart, they were the truest of amateurs. Their criticism of courses was based on the most enjoyable test of golf for their members and other paying golfers. While they were damning PGA officials for not freely providing cash for their own tournament, the Seniors endorsed the association's hiring of A. W. Tillinghast to make courses more fun to play.

The veterans had witnessed members hacking in traps that shouldn't be where they were, adding strokes and subtracting fun and paying far too much money for the construction and maintenance of the needless bunkers built at a time when acres of sand were the fashion on newer American courses. That constructive protest of Senior professionals against an architectural excess exercised a beneficial influence for years. And the tone was set for the PGA Seniors' policy in its organizing session when Charley Hall, a former PGA president, asked, "Will young men coming along in golf become as fine Seniors as we have seen?" The question was significant. From the earliest days the ethical values in pro golf were decidedly high. Playing ability was high, too, especially considering the equipment and course conditions. The Old Boys could really manipulate the ball around the course.

The first championship of the formally organized PGA Seniors was played in 1937 at the Augusta National Golf Club, at the invitation of Bob Jones. Jock Hutchison won the championship with a 223 that included a finishing 72, a round as good as many of the recent winners of the Masters. Dave Ogilvie, of the Augusta Country Club, and Freddie McLeod, of the Columbia Country Club at Washington, D.C., tied at 234, in the middle-aged Class B of players from fifty-five to fifty-nine years old. George Low, of Huntington Valley, was the initial sixty-and-over winner with 80–86–82–248.

So the Seniors' show opened its long run with an all-Scots quartet of headliners. Hutchison and McLeod were long-time troupers in championships. Jock's 1921 British Open and 1920 PGA titles were dim enough when he teed up at Augusta, but Freddie, with his 1908 National Open title, seemed to belong to the dawn of history. He'd weathered well, though. In 1938, McLeod was back in his age class (fifty-five to fifty-nine) at the PGA Seniors' thirty-six-hole event and got 154 to tie with the younger Class A winner Otto Hackbarth. Hackbarth won the play-off. There's nothing else in sports like the PGA Seniors to exhibit durability of contestants. Bertie Way, who'd played in his first American championship in 1896, was playing more than forty years later in the Seniors.

The progress of the PGA Seniors was marked by the same feverish differences of opinion that cropped up so fre-

quently during the growth of the PGA. How many holes the competition should be in age classes was a sticky point from the start. It sounds odd today when so much play is from golf carts, but some Seniors insisted that their championship in all groups be at seventy-two holes. They compromised on that issue without acknowledging any lack of stamina among the ancients; it was agreed that the older men would play eighteen holes a day for four consecutive days.

But there was one suggestion that came close to wrecking the PGA Seniors as a young organization: That was that the older Seniors play from the ladies' tees in the championships. Perhaps the proposal was a deliberate job of ribbing, but its reception wasn't in jest and the man who advanced the notion during the heat of a planning session didn't answer when, after the storm had abated, the secretary of the meeting asked, "I didn't get the name of the gentleman who made the suggestion. His name, please?"

A regrettable split between the Seniors' founders occurred when the organization expanded. Jack Jolly, a St. Andrews boy who'd been one of the early U.S. professionals, then a successful golf ball sales executive, got Alfred S. Bourne, a retired capitalist, golf enthusiast, friend and playing companion of many veteran professionals, to give a large and beautiful championship trophy to the Seniors. Jolly certainly had no selfish motive in wanting the gift he'd solicited to be the perpetual top prize of the Seniors. Bourne did come through generously at the right time, but Jack didn't like it one damned jolly bit, as his comrades said, when the Bourne trophy was demoted and the Teacher's Cup was introduced as the top ornament of Seniors' competition.

The Teacher's Cup was accompanied by considerable cash and guarantees that changed the unique sports event from an informal affair to a nationwide competition with sectional qualifying rounds and expenses paid to the finals, including an international showdown between the winners of the PGA Seniors of America and the PGA Seniors of Great Britain.

The personality of Ronald Teacher, the Glasgow distiller who sponsored the tournament and put up the money, and the pleasant nature of "Tex" Bomba, the sales chief of Schieffelin, Teacher's American distributor, and a deft public-relations man, quickly healed most of the scars of the Bourne trophy battle.

The mating of the PGA Seniors with Teacher's seemed ideal because there never could have been a more compatible association than that of a Scottish game and Scotch grog. Then, after Teacher's signed off, the Ford Motor Company began sponsoring the event, and again the elderly pros were well matched. The Old Guard really got golf going in the United States about the same time that Henry Ford's Model T was demonstrating that the suburbs with their fancy country clubs and cow-pasture playgrounds were easily accessible to city folk.

The records of the PGA Seniors' tournaments are the same as any other sports scores; they show what's past. But these items in the scorebook pass in review the eras of the famed Hutchison, Watrous, Sarazen, Mortie Dutra, Goggin, Metz, Runyan, Snead, Bolt, and Boros. They also reveal that lesser-known aging professionals stepped up and knocked off the proud ones. Hackbarth, Eddie Williams (a three-time winner), McKenna, Crichton, Newham, Schwab, Pete Burke, Barron, Chandler

Harper, and Freddie Haas, first of the collegians to go far in pro competition, enjoyed winter vacations from their club jobs by showing in the Seniors what might have happened if they had been playing rather than teaching pros.

Foresighted professionals knew there'd come a time when age would creep up on the 365 professionals who were members of the PGA in 1916, its first year, and they weren't figuring on curling up and getting lost in the rough of the years. The PGA had 1,814 members in 1937 when Mickey Gallagher, pro at the Forest Hills Hotel course at Augusta, Willie Kidd, pro at Interlachen at Minneapolis, Grange Alves of the Acacia Country Club, Cleveland, Captain Charles Clarke, a crippled British war veteran who was pro at the Mayfield Heights Club in suburban Cleveland, and a few others realized that the time had come to get the Seniors' Division off the ground. They didn't need or want a sponsor. Gallagher got them a room where they could call a meeting to order, and that was it. The initial meeting began November 28, 1937, at the Forest Hills Hotel, and the fifty-four-hole first championship began November 30 at the Augusta National course.

At the second meeting, held at the Partridge Inn in Augusta, on December 6, 1938, Alves, who'd been promoted from chairman to president of the new outfit of Old Boys, was sick and absent, so George Sargent was elected president and took over. Dave Ogilvie, who was pro at Cleveland's Oakwood Club in the summer and the Augusta Country Club in the winter, was voted vice-president, and Clarke was made secretary.

That December, Augusta wasn't as balmy as usual, so the tournament was only thirty-six holes. In 1939, the Old

Boys couldn't get organized or find a host for their tournament, so George Jacobus helped out. He had been president of the PGA at the time the Seniors organized, had a winter job with the Sarasota Chamber of Commerce, and got the Seniors an invitation to hold their 1940 meeting and tournament at Sarasota. Everybody was happy about the party, especially with the city boosters paying for a program of entertainment for the professionals' wives and picking up other tabs. Dave Ogilvie was elected the Seniors' president that year, and Alex Cunningham became vice-president. And in 1941, with a beguiling offer of $300, the Seniors returned to Sarasota.

In 1942, Fort Myers and Ponte Vedra in Florida invited the Seniors. Fort Myers emphasized its invitation with $250 to be spent on entertainment of the Seniors and their wives, so Fort Myers was the spot—on a municipal course Donald Ross had designed. That was where Eddie Williams won the first of his three consecutive Seniors' championships, defeating Jock Hutchison in a play-off. Like so many other professionals, Williams had a youngster who was a talented golfer. His daughter Ella Mae won a number of amateur titles before she majored in a career of family life.

W. C. Sherwood was the Seniors' president in 1942, when he was professional at the Memphis Country Club. He had been there for many years and in the old days was responsible for getting Memphis's factories active in supplying hickory shafts on a worldwide scale.

The 1942 Seniors' tournament was played in mid-January, and winners in each class got war bonds as prizes. Only $75 of the Fort Myers entertainment fund had been spent, so the remaining $125 was given to the Red Cross by the Seniors' men and women.

In 1943 and 1944, gasoline rationing, war work, and the shortage of genuine rubber balls left the Seniors in no mood for a tournament of their own. A majority of the home-bred and foreign-born Seniors had served in World War I, and they appreciated the talk of golf's being vital to the national health and morale. British-born professionals were sending food packages to Scotland and England, and few of the British families with sons who had come into pro golf in the United States between 1896 and 1921 escaped fatalities. United States professional golf seems to have contributed possibly more than its due share of combatants to World War II.

When the PGA Seniors' Championship was renewed in January, 1945, it was practically an unveiling of the Dunedin Isles Country Club course, rechristened the PGA National Golf Club. The long search of the PGA for a home began during the revival of the Seniors' Championship, with Alex Cunningham as the Seniors' president. Ernest Anderson, the third secretary of the PGA, recalled that, years back, in the PGA's magazine, he had suggested a community to which professionals could retire. And several Seniors, remembering their own dismal experiences after being mustered out of World War I, believed the PGA should try to provide a building of hotel type for "the boys back from the war and not connected with jobs," as well as residential sites and a country club for retired professionals.

Reviewing discussions of a PGA National Golf Club in the minutes of the annual PGA Executive Committee meetings, as well as in the Seniors' concise minutes, it is plain that the Seniors made valuable discoveries about the ownership, management, and operation of a PGA golf course and residential development. So PGA Seniors actually functioned as an experimental and advisory committee on the PGA National Golf Club. Unfortunately the lessons were not brought to the direct attention of the younger PGA officials, nor did they examine the precedents for which PGA members had been paying. Then, as almost always, "next on the order of business" at the 1945 meeting of the PGA Seniors at Dunedin was the condition of the course. It was well designed but badly built, as was the case with numerous courses in Florida and elsewhere. Construction was based on sketchy information and limited backing, with the developers invariably running out of money before revenue started coming in.

Alex Cunningham. PGA, photo by D. Scott Chisholm

Al Nelson early had the job of conditioning the PGA National course at Dunedin for the Seniors' championships. He was a competent pro-green-keeper and had the right answer for all complaints: "Want this job? And right now?" When Alex Cunningham took charge as the Seniors' president, he blew up when anyone who had a few three-putt greens blamed it on the course: "I'll not be put on the defensive by any man's bad golf! Shoot yourself a few strokes under par, then I'll listen to reason!"

When the Seniors discovered that Dunedin wasn't destined to be the eternal home of a PGA course, they began casually shopping around for a new site, although the job was officially a PGA responsibility. The southwest coast of Florida pleased them. There was an atmosphere of serenity in this area, known to sophisticates as the Hoosier Riviera. Prices were moderate, most of the towns were quiet little Kokomos with palms, and Tampa was the

Big City, perhaps a combination of New York, London, Tokyo, and Madrid. But the Gulf towns of the Florida peninsula didn't come up with the big money and the high-powered real-estate promotion to attract the professionals —old, middle-aged, or young.

In 1945, when Bertie Way was president of the PGA Seniors, Dunedin developers Owens and Knight gave $500 for the PGA Seniors' tournament. Then Willie Ogg, the Seniors' first vice-president, and George Morris and Eddie Williams, also Seniors' officials, teamed with Way to get $3,000 from the PGA as Seniors' tournament prize money. This caused a ruckus among the younger tournament players, who wanted the money for the PGA Championship purse and tournament circuit expansion. But that $3,000 a year was about the top from the PGA, although half the members of the association in 1945, and for the next twenty years, were fifty years old or more. Until

Teacher's whisky and Ford automobiles and tractors began sponsoring the PGA Seniors' tournament, paying substantial prize money and the expenses of the qualifiers, the PGA veterans were actually playing their championship for a moderate percentage of their PGA dues.

In 1946, the Seniors decided they'd have to make more plans for their wives' enjoyment of the veteran pros' annual conclave. So, the Ladies' Auxiliary of the PGA Seniors was organized at Clearwater in 1952 and quickly became a lively, entertaining element of the annual reunion. The wives kept the thoughts of pension plans and a retirement community stirring. Retirement on pension was the comfortable destination of a number of the professionals, but it was a forlorn hope under the employment conditions of most pros. Occasionally a club of gentlemen sportsmen would arrange a pension payment for a good and faithful servant who'd been on the club pro job for thirty-five years or more, but that was the exception. The pro on the job often outlived most of the members who had belonged when the professional was young on the job, and the younger members were not especially concerned with what happened to Old Faithful.

So for some years the PGA National Golf Club at Dunedin was a dream the Senior professionals tried to keep alive. Theoretically, there never was a more promising setup, but the old pros were unable to find a substitute for money—and money was all that the Dunedin establishment needed. There was a lot of ability and experience available, but very little money for course rebuilding and maintenance, and for building a satisfactory little clubhouse. Alex Cunningham and Fred Haas, Sr., made slight improvements in the course.

Bert Way. PGA, photo by Larry Shafer

Frank Sprogell was becoming active in Dunedin management, and O. J. Noer, the golf turf expert of the Milwaukee Sewerage Commission, came to give expert help and found he was one expert among many.

Willie Ogg became the Seniors' president in 1947. George Norrie and Eddie Williams continued in office, and Henry Williams was elected second vice-president. Then the job fell to an administration headed by George Norrie, with Charley Mayo as first vice-president and Charles Lorms as second vice-president. Eddie Williams continued as secretary and treasurer.

The members complained that the manufacturers had contributed $25,000 to the Tournament Bureau but had given nothing to help Dunedin, which by then had become virtually a PGA Seniors operation. More than a hundred entered the 1947 Seniors' Championship, then most of the field moved on. It was difficult to get enough professionals for a pro-amateur event at Dunedin because so many of the professionals wintering in the area had good jobs at the dog track.

In 1948 the officers moved up in the customary way, with Charley Mayo becoming president and Mike Brady coming in as second vice-president. Brady, among the first of the great home-breds, still was hitting the ball long enough to keep up with the young boys, but his putter suffered the infirmities of age. By now, the PGA was taking little more than a formal interest in the Dunedin course and showed no more concern about the location of its offices at Dunedin than it had when the offices were at New York or Chicago. The Seniors' Championship prize money was divided so that most of the starters (all of them in the higher age classes) got a share. The older contestants laughed about the pittance and called it their "appearance money."

Although there was the same growl at every annual meeting of the PGA Seniors about the work being done by a few and the criticism piled on by many, the truth was that the PGA never had enough to build or maintain a first-class golf course. The visions of big money, publicity, and sales-promotion rewards shining before the PGA Seniors began to fade when realistically examined. The meetings resounded with cries of: "The greens still are lousy!" "Who calls this a clubhouse?" "Our fairway mowers were old when I left Scotland!" and "Why should this course get so little and the Tournament Bureau so much?"

When Joe Donato, Hugh Bancroft, Bill Gordon, Stanley Davies, Phil Turnesa, and Frank Sprogell, along with Mike Brady, got into the Seniors' administrative act, it was one happy family of the Scotch, English, Italian, Irish,

Willie Ogg. PGA, photo by George A. Spencer

and just simply American blends united by golf. The PGA National Golf Club with the Seniors running the show wasn't a place to brag about or to attract people who wanted to trade money for fancy living. The golfing retirement home they enjoyed at Dunedin certainly wasn't pretentious, but they owned their golf club (at least under a ninety-nine-year lease), and it didn't own them.

Dunedin also saw the beginning of the PGA educational program. Emil Beck headed the committee that got the PGA winter schools established and that knitted together the loose ends of the sectional educational efforts. The entire educational operation at Dunedin was a pioneering job in all sports. There'd been baseball schools in Florida to develop playing talent, but the PGA schooling program at Dunedin was far, far ahead. The golf professionals directed their schooling as a public service, with the students getting training in playing, teaching, programming for player interest, participation in club management, and the operation of golf shops as golfers' service stations.

The Merchandise Show was another multimillion-dollar operation that began at the PGA National Golf Club at Dunedin and that the PGA let the Seniors handle by default. When Frank Sprogell was running Dunedin for the PGA, he saw that the salesmen had a preview service for pro-shop merchandise buyers, and he made arrangements to bring the professionals and buyers closer together. And from those small bazaars came the huge tent shows at Palm Beach Gardens, an 8-iron shot from the PGA offices.

The PGA was going through the change of life at Dunedin, but the menopause was pleasant while the Seniors were being phased out. About the

Charlie Mayo. PGA, photo by Sun Photos

last of the top champions to bridge the gap from earlier PGA championships to the Senior title was Paul Runyan. In 1961 and 1962, Runyan became PGA Seniors Champion at Dunedin, and the old boys marveled that "Little Poison" could still work magic with a 4-wood and a putter. Runyan joined Hutchison, Sarazen, Snead, Bolt, and Boros as national champions who also won the PGA Seniors' title.

But as the 1940's faded, so did the power and the glory of the PGA Seniors. The PGA could no longer afford to put on a tournament for the fellows who built it, and commercial sponsors took over. In 1947, Old Pro Jock Hutchison won by three strokes over Ben Richter, the St. Louis lefthander, then the winners of the PGA Seniors were often the forgotten losers of the bigtime events. Charlie McKenna won in 1948. (He was pro at the Oak Hill Country Club in Rochester in 1959 when the National Amateur was played there. Someone asked him whether the big event had proved good business for his pro shop. "Never had such a boom in the free tee business!" Charlie snapped.) Other pros who never quite made it but got their names in bronze as champions of the Seniors included Marshall Crichton, Al Watrous, Ernest Newham, Harry Schwab, Mortie Dutra, Pete Burke, Willie Goggin, Dick Metz, Herman Barron, Fred Haas, and Chandler Harper.

At the 1950 Seniors' meeting, Bill Gordon moved up to the presidency. Joe Donato became first vice-president,

Paul Runyan. PGA, photo by Jimmy Dale Photo Service

and Eddie Williams, for years the organization's secretary and treasurer, and tired of the job, was relieved by John Manion. Williams was elected second vice-president. Donato was made head man in 1951. Jim Wilson was brought on as second vice-president, and Matt Jans, who had started in golf as one of the Chicago district's early caddies, became a vice-president. Hugh Bancroft became secretary-treasurer. Otto Hardt and George Ferrier became Seniors' officials about that time, and eventually, presidents.

A number of the PGA Seniors were dapper individuals at work and play. Jim Wilson, a tall, handsome veteran, always wore a rather high collar and a tie carefully chosen to coordinate with his sports coat and slacks, whether in his shop, teaching, or on the course. Ferrier looked as though he'd just come from his tailors. Bancroft and Hardt were dressed as business executives. Good grooming was something the successful pioneer professional considered essential to the job. Without realizing it, the deans of professional golf and their protégés, such as Al Watrous and Frank Walsh, and others of the third generation of American professionals, and in the 1950's the Senior pros themselves, definitely had an immense influence on golf's being a game to be played in comfortable, casual clothes. Today's gigantic sports apparel business in golf pro shops and a multitude of other retailing establishments stems from the example set by the pioneer golf professionals.

A goodly number of the pioneer pros were also active in church affairs, although at the crest of their business on Sunday mornings the wives of the Protestant pros voted the family proxies from the pew. The Catholic pros attended dawn Mass.

When he was at Louisville, Eddie Williams conducted an early Sunday school class for caddies. It certainly was nonsectarian, although many caddies eventually entered holy orders. The Beverly Country Club on Chicago's South Side several years ago counted twelve of its former caddies who had become priests.

Religion also figured in one National Open Championship—in 1929 on the West course at Winged Foot in suburban New York. Bob Jones, after taking two 7's in the fourth round, holed a twelve-foot putt to tie Al Espinosa at 294. Jones, always a tough competitor but doing nice things when he didn't think he would be caught at it, asked

Joe Donato, Bill Gordon, Eddie Williams. PGA

Otto Hardt. PGA, photo by Sun Photos

George Ferrier. PGA, photo by McCombs
Photo Service

the USGA to delay the starting time for the Sunday play-off for an hour to give Espinosa time to attend church. Jones still won the thirty-six-hole Open play-off by twenty-three strokes, but Espinosa got the first $1,000 professional prize.

Golf's old pros established a code for the game's showcase players that was so outstanding that it meant millions for the young men who followed the pioneers. Of course, there were a few heirs to the paradise of opulence and social acceptance that the pioneer golf professionals had opened, who seldom made themselves look at home. At bottom, they were only lucky caddies. Nothing could elevate them—surely not money.

Then there were the "nice kids" on the golden circuit who never quite understood the beautiful, old-fashioned picture of top quality that brought the big money into tournament golf. One of the boys, who couldn't quite catch up mentally with the show, criticized a golf course that was host to the National Open. He said that the real-estate advertisements bordering the course distracted him. An old pro laughed when he read that rap by a young pro looking for excuses, then apologized on his behalf to his companions: "The boy hasn't sense enough to appreciate that it's those real-estate signs that raised him from being a caddie at $1.25 a round to playing for $125,000 a year. What can you do for the bubbleheads?"

Nothing. That was the answer, according to the veteran professionals, but their expert appraisal changed as they looked at a new generation of players. Outside of Nicklaus, a genuinely great all-around shotmaker who knew how to play courses, Palmer, a strong slasher who was next to Hagen

as a scrambler and second to none as a
putter, and Player, who was like Sarazen in his prime, playing better critical
shots than he knew how to play, the rest
of the winners lacked the approach
shot in close enough for one putt.

There were a few exceptions. Tommy
Bolt was one of the finest sharpshooters
ever on a golf course. If he had been
able to control himself when he was
strong and keen, he would have won a
dozen major championships. Sam
Snead? The most magnificent swinger
and stroker golf had ever seen—more
beautiful than Vardon, Jones, and Hogan, but when he had a putt less than
six feet, where he had to think, an utterly bewildered, frozen, and frustrated
competitor.

Television never made the most of
golf coverage, according to the veteran
pros, even though it hired a few genuinely competent playing-lesson teachers to assist its routine commentators.
While these gentlemen could and
would tell you where the ball was, how
the putt should curl, and how the contestant let his right elbow get away
from his body, accounting for a poor
shot, something was still missing.

TV never came close to telling the
thrilling sort of story the old pros told
as they watched the picture on the
screen. The television comment was
uniformly dull compared to the observations of the Senior pros watching and
listening. You have never seen a golf
tournament television program that's
worth your time unless you've been in
a room with two or three old pros.

However, when TV golf was coming
in, the old pros were going out. As the
transition was occurring, the PGA Seniors were invited to participate in a
National Open Seniors' Championship
promoted by Joe Mozel, an ingenious
professional in Oregon. Joe had in-

Carroll McMasters. PGA, photo by Sun
Photos

vented a gimmick for practice ranges
that teed balls up quickly and gave the
customer a lot of whacks without back-
aches. The PGA Seniors never joined
hands with the playmates Mozel assembled, but Joe got a fat piece of the prize
money and a lot of fun for his Open
Seniors' group.

The drastic change in the PGA Seniors came when a beloved old Scottish
influence, Teacher's Scotch Whisky,
came into the program with money
needed to bring Senior professionals
from the far boundaries of the country
to Dunedin for a golf championship. It
was far too good to last. Ronald
Teacher, the personable surviving head
of the house, and "Tex" Bomba, the
charming pusher of Teacher's Scotch
for its American distributors, did wonderfully well by the Seniors. But Amer-

ican merchandising bewildered the respectable Scotch distiller, so Teacher's signed off.

But a resilient reserve corps was coming in: Alec Watson, Harry Schwab, Marion Askew, Carroll McMasters, Art De Mane, Lou Galby, and dozens of others arrived at the fifty-year post when the PGA Seniors seemed to be getting tired. They enlivened the whole outfit for a gala exit from Dunedin and a triumphal entry into the MacArthur Holy Land at Palm Beach Gardens, where there was pie in the sky, even in fine print, for the worthies who would shill for what soon was developed into the most glamorous real-estate golf pitch on Florida's east coast.

17

The Tournament–Home Pro Hassle Flares Up Again, the PGA Stresses Teaching, Dunedin Becomes Home Base

[1946, 1947, 1948]

WITH a big war out of the way, the PGA quickly came to grips with its own smoldering civil war at the 1946 annual meeting at the Bismarck Hotel, Chicago, November 18 to 20, with delegates from thirty sections attending. (A new one, the Southern Ohio section, had just been added to the association.) The preliminary skirmishes were argued on November 15 and 17 between the Executive Committee and Ben Hogan, representing the tournament players who had held several meetings at tournaments and favored breaking away from the association.

The PGA had kept the tournament circuit alive during the war, dipping into its shallow treasury and getting help from the club and ball manufacturers. It hadn't been either an easy or a popular job, inasmuch as the USGA, the Western Golf Association, and other amateur bodies had discontinued their championships in wartime. Only

Nelson, McSpaden, Ed Dudley, Harry Cooper, Joe Kirkwood, Gene Sarazen, and a few other pros who had not qualified for military service, plus those who took time off from club jobs or war plant work, had maintained public interest in tournament golf. In 1946, there were 4,817 courses in the United States and about 2,250,000 golfers, few of whom had been developed as tournament spectators.

There probably weren't a dozen pros in the country who did nothing else but play in tournaments. A few were manufacturers' representatives, but most tournament players depended on club jobs for a living and took time off for tournament play.

Ed Dudley, serving another year as PGA president, had two pro jobs—one in the summer at Broadmoor at Colorado Springs, the other in the fall, winter, and spring at the Augusta National Golf Club, where the Masters tournament was resumed in 1946. He had a swing Bob Jones declared was the most graceful he'd ever seen, but he couldn't bear down enough to be a successful competitor. Still, that easygoing temperament was ideal for his job as PGA president; the other fellows argued and stormed, and Ed serenely let them talk themselves out.

That year, Dudley had Joe Novak as secretary, Willie Maguire as treasurer, and Tom Walsh as honorary president, still minding the main-office chores. Vice-presidents were C. V. Anderson, Robert L. Barnett, George L. Hall, John R. Inglis, Harry L. Moffitt, Gordon Richards, George H. Schneiter, James K. Thomson, and William W. Wotherspoon.

At this meeting the Advisory Board stepped forward as the association's business mentors instead of being merely the PGA's Important People and window dressing. S. C. Allyn, the National Cash Register executive, had been made chairman and insisted that the PGA get the time-wasting haggling settled in preliminary conferences, so that the delegates could act on vital matters that had been screened and summarized by competent associates. He told the home pros and the tourney travelers frankly that they had a lot of growing up to do before they could be rated as businessmen qualified to run a business as big as pro golf.

As usual it was many years before the PGA followed Allyn's sensible advice. Whether the delay was because of the professionals' inability to communicate on a business plane, or because of a failure to outgrow cliquish "secret" meetings, or because parties with selfish mercenary interests wanted to keep the members apart, are matters that baffle even the pros themselves.

Ben Hogan was more hard-boiled

than the other playing professionals. He objected when they talked about cutting the prize money so it would work down to the boys who hadn't scored well; he insisted that the way for a pro to make money in a tournament was with his clubs, not through any easing of the regulations. And that was the hard way he had had to make it. His attitude didn't endear him to the less proficient of his colleagues, but they had to admit Ben Hogan was a realist who would stand up and be counted anywhere, so he was their man when it came to telling the PGA they wanted an organization of their own. They were vague on the why, how, and what of their plans, but it looked as if, now that the PGA had saved tournament golf and might turn it into a profitable show business, the aspiring Hagens and Sarazens and Armours were ready to take over on their own.

The PGA made a counterproposal, giving the players' group virtual autonomy, although Hogan had not revealed how the tournament players were planning to finance their organization. And PGA vice-president George Schneiter, who later became manager of the tournament circuit professionals, was appointed to work out an agreement with the restless players.

Conditions change, and so does one's position, as Ben Hogan learned years later when he became an affluent golf club manufacturer. When the division between the home pros and tournament travelers finally occurred, Hogan was a consultant to the buyers of his golf club company. He knew by then that the boys to play with for profit were the home pros who bought and sold clubs for cash. The playing pros wanted special clubs without paying, but their names as tournament winners were valuable only to the extent that paid ad-

Ben Hogan. PGA

vertising in newspapers and magazines identified the clubs with the players and built up a case for the clubs doing for the ordinary hacker what they had done for the experts who wielded them. That's quite a case to build up!

Hogan was a shrewd businessman and had acquired for his company a consulting staff of veteran home pros who were experienced clubmakers and knew how to fit clubs to their users. So, as a result of conferences between these experts close to the buying users and Hogan as the thoughtful originator of new design ideas for the talented playing specialist, the brand sales picked up smartly.

The popularity of Hogan and Hagen pro-only club sales, while the clubs of pro stars splitting from the PGA were slipping, was a lesson that club-manufacturing sales executives and treasurers learned before the pros did. But that lesson was only learned about twenty-five years after Ben Hogan had met with PGA officials to separate the tour-

nament pros from the home pros. And all the time it was these same home pros who had a strong command of the quality market and the endorsements that determined whether a particular pro had the character, skills, and reputation that warranted association with the maker of first-class merchandise, or was just a greedy guy whose hungry manager would sign him into any kind of junkman deal.

When Hogan left MacGregor to go into clubmaking on his own, he had prominent and substantial financial backing. After trying to get his sales force going, he tied up with the organization of Ernie Sabayrac, a rotund ex-caddie of Basque parentage who had a staff selling mainly Footjoy golf shoes and apparel. But Ernie's men found the pros were much too interested in seeing what new ideas Ben Hogan had in his line and didn't spend enough time buying clubs, shoes, or clothes. So the sales deal was amicably ended, and Sabayrac's organization, free to concentrate on golfers' wear, soon built up an annual sales volume exceeded by only four—maybe five—of the other companies selling to pros.

Tournament sponsors fretted as bigger purses were being asked without the PGA Tournament Bureau's guaranteeing a first-class field or, in the opinion of the sponsors, providing adequate service in the operation of a tournament. Nor had the players reached the point of assessing themselves for paying the expenses of their proposed organization.

Fred Corcoran had returned to the PGA as tour manager and was operating an office in New York that was getting the circuit management reorganized. He spent much of his time at the tournaments, and George Schneiter as chairman of the Tournament Committee also was playing in a number of them. Now there was talk of establishing a second circuit, a junior league, to answer the conflicting dates problem, but there weren't enough players of the type to attract a profitable gallery to a minor event, so the idea was laid aside to be used almost twenty years later in what were then called "satellite" tournaments.

In 1946, the PGA Executive Committee met with representatives of tournament sponsors for the first time. The chairman of the sponsors was Maynard G. Fessenden, and others on the committee were S. C. Allyn of Dayton, Fred Dowd of St. Louis, Marvin Leonard of Fort Worth, Tom Utterbach of Richmond, Virginia, and Robert Jordan of Los Angeles. In business standing, the sponsors' group was as high as could be assembled to serve a professional sport voluntarily and without pay. But it got nowhere in getting the tournament players to give assurances they'd cooperate fully with the people who were putting up the money.

Eventually the high purses made possible by television advertising, tax-exempt organization sponsorship and free work, and companies promoting and operating tournaments changed the picture. Money, and only money, became the rule in tournament golf operation, and the old-fashioned practice of thinking about what's good for golf didn't count for much. There were three exceptions: the National Open, the Masters, and the Westchester Classic (for that New York county's hospitals). These happened to be probably the three most successful of the year's tournaments, in prizes as well as in prestige.

The manufacturers kept the tournament players in line after the war by continuing an annual contribution of

$30,782. With the PGA absorbing a sizable portion of the Tournament Bureau's office expenses, the cost of running the bureau in the fiscal year 1946 was $28,985. That year there were forty-one tournaments, with prize money of $454,200 in cash (the war bond payments had been discontinued), and all that money went to PGA members. The sponsors had informed the PGA that no pro tournament entries other than those of PGA members would be accepted.

The minor-league or "satellite" tournaments, which were Ed Dudley's idea, were to have a minimum purse of $5,000, and the suggestion brought on sharp comment when it got out of committee and before the delegates. "We ought to be having state PGA championships for $5,000 instead of talking about that amount for seconders," said an irate sectional officer. He and his colleagues at the 1946 meeting never dreamed of the years to come, when PGA sections would have annual tournament schedules with prizes of from $50,000 to $100,000.

An offer was made by S. C. Allyn to finance the 1947 Ryder Cup matches at the Moraine Country Club in Dayton, but Robert Hudson of Portland, who had been the angel of the 1946 PGA Championship, again spread his golden wings and flew the Ryder Cup event to the Portland Golf Club. Hudson again was the angel of the Ryder Cup matches in 1955 at Thunderbird in Palm Springs and in 1959 at El Dorado in Palm Desert, California.

Hudson was a champion at picking up tabs. He met the British teams in New York, was host at big welcoming parties, then paid a considerable share of the travel and living expenses of the visiting teams. Hudson was joined in the California desert by other wealthy men who enjoyed being hosts to the Ryder Cup teams in a swanky area where the galleries weren't large but the golf shows were exciting. Hudson also accompanied American Ryder Cup teams to Britain and became internationally famed as the eager and generous golf professionals' host. He was in the business of producing choice canned fruits and other foods, and this qualified him as an expert on cuisine. For one of his golf parties he even flew a chef from New York to Portland.

Tournament matters had always taken over PGA annual meetings. Even in the infant stage the tournament circuit gave the most trouble, while the association's other activities were handled with a minimum of confusion and complaining. And it turned out that pro tournament golf had developed more during the war than had other PGA departments. As the books were closed for the fiscal year 1946, the PGA had 2,168 dues-paying members. Final figures showed the PGA recorded 480 members as having served in World War II, and at the time of the 1946 meeting, 339 were back in active PGA status.

Employment was still a problem. Any sort of a good golf job opening had from 75 to 120 applicants, the majority of whom were PGA members. Although the GI Bill of Rights gave financial aid to a veteran training as an assistant to a professional, and the USGA announced it wouldn't take amateur status from a veteran in such training, there were few—probably fewer than 20—men working as assistants.

Purdue University proposed a professional golfers' business training course that could have changed and made more profitable the business history of professional golf. Purdue's faculty and athletic department had queried golf club and municipal officials on

Robert A. Hudson. PGA

the need for the school, and the reaction of pro employers was highly favorable.

The pro golfers' school curriculum as outlined by Purdue was as follows: Fundamental Learning Processes; Art of Teaching; Analysis of Golf Fundamentals; Teaching Techniques; Golf Market Analysis; Buying, Display, and Merchandising; Business and Accounting Methods; Shop Management; Assistant Training and Supervision; Repairing Equipment; Preparing Reports to Club Officials and Talks at PGA and Other Meetings; Golf Course Design, Construction, and Maintenance; Rules of Golf; Planning and Operating for and with Committees; Practice and Lesson Tee Management; the Professional's Own Game; Class Instruction; Promotion of Women's and Junior Golf; Club and Pro Business Publicity, In-

formation, and Advertising; Programs
and Operation of Club Events; Golf
Literature; Handicapping; Cooperation with Other Department Heads;
Caddie Management.

Crowding such an ambitious program of pro business training into
about a week of long days and assembling teachers for the subjects was a
big job that Purdue was prepared to
handle for the PGA, but the idea never
advanced past the outline stage because
PGA officials, delegates, and members
indicated little interest, so the entire
matter was dropped. Purdue later built
its own courses and has had a brilliant
showing in Big Ten golf championships. Several of its graduates became
tournament professionals, then went
into club jobs.

There had been previous brief educational sessions in pro golf business at
the University of Minnesota as well as
at Purdue, with sectional PGA cooperation, but the PGA did not get into
business schooling on a national basis
until it started its weeklong winter
school, mainly for assistants, at Dunedin.

The Dunedin project was coming
along slowly, but as fast as limited
money would allow. Jack Ford had
been hired on a two-year contract at a
salary of $2,400 a year, plus food and
pro-shop concessions and 20 percent of
the net bar profit. He was to be general
manager of the whole place, but there
had been little play during the hot
summer. Most of Ford's time had been
spent in trying to get the course ready
for the winter and working with carpenter tools and a paintbrush around
the clubhouse. Mrs. Ford had been
readying the kitchen, bar, and small
dining room for the fall and winter
visitors.

A committee of amateurs, including

Bob Jones, Bing Crosby, Scotty Fessenden, Chick Allyn, Joe Dyer, Al Lam-
kin, Bill Rector, Frank Stranahan, Dick
Snideman, and Ross Sawtelle, was
formed to enlist amateurs as members
of the PGA National Golf Club at $100
per year. The committee got 43 charter
members out of 219 invited.

Seven exhibition matches were
played during the summer to help finance the PGA club. Bob Hope played
with local pros and amateurs in
matches at Houston, Portland, Denver,
Dallas, Spokane, Tacoma, St. Paul, and
Tulsa. Green fees in the 1946 fiscal
year at the PGA club were $11,000, and
the grapefruit on the course brought in
a few hundred unexpected dollars.

Byron Nelson, Harold McSpaden,
Sam Snead, and Ben Hogan each were
presented with a lot in Dunedin for
their exhibition on January 7, 1946,
prior to the PGA Seniors' Championship. And Norman Clark, Alex Ross,
James Herd, Robert D. Pryde, Jack
Campbell, and George Christ, who had
joined the PGA in its first year, were
made life members at the 1946 annual
meeting.

It was discovered that Robert White,
who had been the PGA's first president,
back in 1916, had been dropped from
membership in 1946 because of nonpayment of dues, but it was a clerical
error. He hadn't been getting PGA
mail, and the PGA constitution and bylaws provided that dues of past presidents be waived. White, now about
seventy-two, was living in a beautiful
home at Myrtle Beach, where he owned
a golf course and had extensive property interests.

Leigh Metcalfe came into the PGA
in 1946 from National Cash Register's
advertising department to revitalize the
association's magazine. He had been
editor of *Club Management* magazine

Lew Worsham. AG

prior to joining NCR, and even on a part-time basis did the PGA a great service in improving communications among headquarters, officials, and members. The association got another good man in Gerry Moore from the *Boston Globe* to handle tournament publicity. With Fred Corcoran and George Schneiter the Tournament Bureau was well satisfied.

It was a fairly good year financially for the PGA as it recovered from the war. The PGA Championship prize money was $17,950, the largest ever given, and the championship at Portland yielded a net $2,259. The club- and ballmakers gave the Tournament Bureau $30,000 for 1946, and the PGA National course expenses exceeded income by $15,990.

Nearing the close of a year of comparative tranquillity, the PGA held its thirty-first annual meeting on November 17 through 19, 1947, at the Hotel

Morrison in Chicago. Membership had started to pick up, with 2,395 paid. Ed Dudley continued as president, Joe Novak as secretary, and Willie Maguire as treasurer, although the latter had been ill for months and missed the annual meeting. George M. Corcoran, Alex Cunningham, and L. J. McClellan were freshmen on the Board of Directors.

Cunningham was also serving as professional, greenkeeper, and manager at the PGA National Club. For that job he got a salary of $3,000 a year for the pro-greenkeeping work and a guarantee of $2,000 from the food concession.

The nationwide teaching program was coming along very satisfactorily, and much interest was expressed in the PGA junior golf program conducted by a committee headed by George Lake, pro at the Long Beach, California, municipal course and recreation park.

There was no more than the usual heat in the Tournament Bureau's squabbles within its own ranks and with sponsors and PGA officials. It continued to amaze golfers in general how tournament players, usually quite congenial, personable fellows, managed to get themselves into so many mercenary arguments in which they never mentioned the good of golf as a major reason for their status. Yet their earnings were being steadily increased by PGA promotion efforts, by tournament sponsors usually helped by unpaid workers, and by payments of bonuses and contributions to the Tournament Bureau. But the tournament players were not alone in whining, "What's the PGA doing for me?" Some club pros did the same crying. At the 1947 annual meeting, Secretary Joe Novak displayed charts telling the story in cash of the PGA's services to its members. On a percentage basis, the figures showed an annual prize-

money increase that, barring the war years, compared with the increase in tournament purses during the previous decade. Novak added that the brothers who were doing the most complaining about the PGA were those who had done nothing for the association save pay their dues, often tardily.

The 1946 agreement between PGA officials and the tournament players, which gave the "tourists" autonomy in their operations, had had a full season to be tested. It had been an interesting test, marred only slightly by a hasty-tempered playing star's hitting a Tournament Bureau official with a sneak punch, confusion about depositing Tournament Bureau funds, and the normal differences with sponsors.

The hard-knuckled player apologized to his target, and both parties, neither one a stranger to alley arbitration, laughed it off and made up. But it took PGA headquarters somewhat longer to get the tournament funds back into one channel where they could be audited, reported, and protected. The reports contained the honest but restricted information long common to PGA tournament and general financial statements.

The arrangement for self-government of the Tournament Bureau never was abrogated. Apparently it was never read either, at least to the extent that it would have prevented the PGA civil war thirty years later. That fight was settled by an agreement almost identical with the settlement of differences in 1946. However, the second time around, the agreement for self-government of and by the Tournament Division was made in expensive lawyers' language.

A "clinic," which was an exhibition, lecture, and question-and-answer session, became the curtain raiser of many tournaments. It was held on the day preceding the first round of the tournament. For this event and assistance in conducting the tournament, the Bureau received $1,500 from the sponsor. Participants in the clinic were generally the stars. They received fees for their work, and the added money was an inducement to enter the tournament. "Appearance money" had been ruled out by the Tournament Bureau, and the few under-the-table payments to stars by sponsors were becoming more infrequent. However, the problem of getting the leading players to enter any one tournament besides the Open, the PGA, and the Masters remained unsolved. Those who didn't enter those three tournaments when they were eligible simply were not rated as "leading" players by the public. In time, the clinics were displaced as tournament preliminaries by pro-amateur events, with substantial prize money for the professionals and usually high entry fees for the amateurs because the events were being played for beneficiaries that had tax exemptions.

Jim Ferrier. AG

A minimum of $10,000 was set for the winter events. The 1946 prize money was reported as "around $508,-000," and the 1947–48 tournaments up to the 1948 Masters would exceed that amount. Tournament Bureau income from sponsors in 1947 was $20,750, and players got $7,000 of that amount in payment for performances at clinics. The manufacturers contributed $17,-500. The General Fund of the PGA, which consisted almost wholly of dues, didn't pay anything in 1947 to the Tournament Bureau, nor did it charge the bureau anything for expenses that the PGA incurred.

Among the plans the Tournament Bureau announced to assist sponsors was the updating of the tournament operating guide, the tournament record book, and other statistical material that had been assembled in the first *PGA Official Record Book*. That was the 1940–41 book that included events played up to April 15, 1941.

The 1947 PGA Championship at the Plum Hollow Country Club in suburban Detroit proved to be profitable, even though the experiment of having a program that carried the matches past a weekend resulted in an absence of big names still being in competition after Sunday. Ben Hogan, the defending champion, went out in the first round to Tony Penna. Jim Ferrier, who had gone extra holes in two earlier matches, defeated Chick Harbert 2 and 1 for the title. The final match drew surprisingly well, with total attendance at a new high of 53,000. The 1948 PGA Championship was awarded to the Norwood Hills Country Club in suburban St. Louis, May 19 through 25, with a record $30,000 guarantee.

David Griffith of Plum Hollow was elected to the tournament sponsors' advisory committee and was to remain active as a useful counselor of the PGA for years. Sponsors' fears about the gate at a PGA Championship flopping following elimination of established stars in the earlier rounds had been eased by large galleries in the later rounds at Plum Hollow. It was a case of "The king is dead! Long live the king!" Golfers wanted to see the youngsters who had knocked down the rulers.

The Ryder Cup date remained a problem. Dayton wanted the matches, but the British team refused to play in the United States during the summer. One reason was that British tournaments were reviving in interest and paying bigger prize money; another was that the heat at Columbus, Ohio, where the 1931 matches had been played at the Scioto Club, had been so fierce that members of the English team still claimed it was like playing in fur coats somewhere east of Suez.

Leigh Metcalfe had the magazine situation straightened out, convincing officials that any effort to use *The Professional Golfer* politically would be the end of the publication. Metcalfe did so well in this direction that the policy prevailed for years. There were vague references to hostilities within and around the Tournament Bureau, but factions within the PGA could be fighting tooth and nail and not a word appeared in print. As the magazine grew in its service to members, Metcalfe returned to his job with National Cash Register, and Bob Husted, a capable young reporter, was hired as editor. The PGA magazine made $8,244 in the fiscal year 1947.

As preparations were made to move headquarters to Dunedin, there was discussion about an office building's being constructed for the PGA. That ended when attention was called to the privilege the PGA had of canceling its lease on the course and clubhouse in five years. The staff at headquarters consisted of Executive Secretary Tom Crane and Office Manager Mrs. Irene Blakeman, who cared for all the routine PGA paperwork, including membership and insurance records, magazine subscriptions, Tournament Bureau records, and much of the correspondence. Bob Husted, the magazine editor, also had his office at headquarters.

No satisfactory answer had been found for job-hunting members, and a letter was sent to the presidents of all golf clubs, describing the qualifications of PGA members for pro jobs. The association also tried to stiffen its membership requirements with a five-year apprenticeship leading to a Master Professional rating and with other educational preparation of assistants.

At the annual meeting, the educational session reflected the interest and work being done in the thirty sections. Ben Hogan, Frank Walsh, and Vic Ghezzi headlined the instruction demonstrations. President Marshall Farnham of the Greenkeeping Superintendents' Association spoke of the mutual interests of the pros and superintendents and urged that tournament players acquire at least some primary knowledge about golf turf so they'd know what they were talking about when they criticized playing conditions.

Caddie welfare and junior golf development received studious and extended attention, and there was much talk about effective use of the Western Golf Association's caddie recruiting and training program and the caddie work of the Massachusetts Golf Association.

Another effort was made to get the

Vic Ghezzi. AG

Ladies' PGA accepted as a branch of the PGA, and Patty Berg, a charter member and ex-president of the LPGA, made an earnest sales talk but got nowhere. The gentlemen's PGA apparently had more than enough of its own problems, even though Miss Berg, one of the most effective salespersons ever working in and for golf, reminded the meeting that there were more than two hundred young women physical education instructors teaching golf in schools and colleges, and in a few years the students of these teachers and the families of those grown-up and married students would be immensely important to every phase of the golf market.

Delegates from all thirty sections got to see the PGA National Golf Club and the association's new offices when the 1948 annual meeting was held at Fenway Hotel, Dunedin, December 1 through 3. It was the first visit for most of them to the quiet little town on Florida's west coast. Some delegates found the site too far away from metropolitan excitement and the club and course incompatible with their dreams of grandeur. On the other hand, delegates and officials from the Rockies and the Far West said that it was apparent the PGA wanted to get headquarters as far as possible from Pacific Slope members, but it didn't have to hide the main office altogether!

The realists countered criticism by pointing out that the costs at Dunedin for the PGA and its 2,594 individual members were moderate. Work could be done more easily and less expensively in offices at Dunedin, and as most PGA main office service was by mail or telephone, the location just north of Clearwater was practical. Clearwater and neighboring Tampa were two of Florida's earliest golf resorts, so the area was accustomed to making golf history. They'd had courses there in the 1890's, before California.

Ed Dudley served his seventh term as president in 1948. At the thirty-second annual meeting, nearing the end of 1948, Dudley had with him Joe Novak of the Bel Air Club at Los Angeles as secretary, and Bill Wotherspoon of Southern Hills, Tulsa, as treasurer. Quiet, reliable Tom Crane, of course, continued as executive secretary. Vice-presidents and members of the Executive Committee were George Corcoran, Joe Donato, William Gordon, George L. Hall, Martin Lyons, L. J. McClellan, Gordon Richards, George Schneiter, and John Watson.

Wotherspoon, who added Yankee business caution to his management of the PGA treasury, showed charts of PGA revenue and outgo to the delegates. Wotherspoon's graphic presentation of the association's finances was something new, but did not become established procedure. This came some twenty years later when Bill Clarke and President Max Elbin explained the complexities of PGA finances in *The Professional Golfer*. The traditional policy was for the delegates to take a PGA financial statement home and explain it to association members, instead of having the statement printed in the PGA magazine, thus making it a matter of public record.

George Schneiter, as Tournament Bureau chief, had been on the tour as a player until there was a question of his playing interest disqualifying him from making impartial decisions. The question was hypothetical; Schneiter had the circuit operating smoothly. The few cases of misconduct reported involved a few tourists who departed without observing the formality of paying their hotel bills, or those players whose checks did not show the mathe-matical genius they had exercised in keeping their scorecards. Schneiter was a cattleman as well as a golf professional. He learned by experience that although a club job was no royal road to riches, it was less precarious than tournament business and stock raising.

There were forty-one tournaments in 1948, with prize money of $541,025. The Tournament Bureau received a fee of $1,500 from nineteen sponsors and smaller service fees from five other sponsors, for a total of $27,717. The bureau also had $11,000 from a Bing Crosby and Bob Hope exhibition. Fred Corcoran's salary as tournament publicity director was listed as $5,000. The bureau finished the fiscal year with profits of $18,891, the first time it had ever been in the black.

The general fund of the PGA had a balance of $14,023 after spending $86,-662 in the fiscal year of 1948. The Magazine Committee reported a profit of $14,152 for two years. The subscription price was subtracted from each member's dues, and magazine expenses were absorbed to a considerable extent as part of PGA office overhead, so the publication did not have to be heavy with advertising to be on the profit side.

Moving PGA headquarters from Chicago to Dunedin meant *The Professional Golfer* had to get a new editor, the industrious Wilbur Skourup, to replace Bob Husted. The two of them decidedly improved correspondence from the sections, although in some areas there was a chronic shortage of news cooperation with headquarters.

Close teamwork between the sections and headquarters during the year was in keeping with the association's campaign to make its membership requirements more stringent. Five years' service as an assistant was set as the basic requirement for PGA membership. Membership applications, channeled through sections, were expertly examined, with a six-month waiting period between amateur status and eligibility for sharing in purses on PGA cosponsored tournaments. In accepting the responsibility for tournament players and backing up the rules the Tournament Committee had made for discipline, the PGA helped to stabilize the tournament situation.

The PGA's leadership got it into a lawsuit for $315,000 filed by the attorney for three black golfers who claimed they had been denied entry to the Richmond, California, tournament because of color. After the customary fussing around and publicity, the case was settled out of court. It cost the association $2,100 in legal fees, and if it proved anything, it demonstrated that the PGA could maintain the status quo by insisting that its regulations be followed to ensure orderly development of the tournament business.

The campaign for high membership qualifications was beginning to help the PGA secure better jobs for its members. Club officials conceded that an applicant for a pro job who had received adequate training and had been screened by a jury of his peers was a logically desirable candidate for a first-class professional job. Word got around that it was getting tougher to get into the PGA, and the publicity of the association expanded. Fred Corcoran took care of the tournament side, while a bright young collegiate publicity man, Mark Cox, was hired on a part-time basis to get more newspaper space for the PGA on its membership requirements, its junior golf promotion, its caddie welfare program, and its participation with the National Golf Foundation in getting more courses built.

Cox began showing home professionals how to get more newspaper and radio publicity for their clubs and themselves. The education was immediately and extensively effective and brought Cox to the attention of L. B. Icely, president of the Wilson Sporting Goods Company. Thus began the successful career of Mark Cox as an executive of golf manufacturing companies.

The first national Junior Golf Week of the PGA was one of the most popular low-cost sports promotions ever conducted. PGA members gave out about 20,000 membership cards in the PGA Junior Golfers' Association and issued 6,000 diplomas to youngsters who completed the course of free lessons given by pros in twelve PGA sections. *Golfdom* magazine paid for the membership cards. Diplomas and other costs to the PGA were $77.

Junior golf got a tremendous boost in 1948 from the Junior Chamber of Commerce of the United States, which worked with the PGA in running the Jaycees' annual National Junior Championship, with 10,000 young people qualifying in thirty-nine states for the championship at the Country Club of Omaha. It was the world's largest golf championship. The USGA also started its Boys' Championship that year and the USGA Junior Girls' the next year. George Lake, Harry Moffitt, and Bud Williamson were the PGA officers who headed the junior program.

PGA officials ran the National Caddie Championship for Mayor James Rhodes of Columbus, who later became governor of Ohio. He had started in golf as a caddie and sponsored the National Caddie Association tournament, which offered college scholarships as prizes. The Hearst newspapers also had a national caddie championship. These caddie affairs faded, then vanished as the Western Golf Association's Chick Evans Caddie Scholarship Program developed.

In 1948, the PGA was active with the National Golf Foundation and the *Athletic Journal* in getting professionals to serve as teachers for limited periods at schools for high school and college coaches. Football, basketball, track and field, baseball, and tennis were sports usually taught at these summer schools, but golf was left out until practically shoved in by the professionals volunteering. Basic golf instruction became highly popular, even in the sketchy pattern of the 1948 summer teaching.

Progress was slow, quiet, but obvious at Dunedin. The PGA National Golf Club now had 142 charter members, including 60 members of the former Dunedin Golf Club, who rarely used the course. Manufacturers had rejected an offer to rent space in the pro shop, and while clubhouse business was sluggish, during the winter months the place had a simple, congenial atmosphere reminiscent of the small clubrooms and taverns that served as clubhouses in Scotland. The wives of the Senior professionals clicked their knitting needles and chatted in the small main room of the clubhouse and on the porch, and the men, generally older pros, home-bred and foreign-born, laughed as they replayed contests of years before.

Green fees at Dunedin slumped $2,000 from the 1947 fiscal year. Sales in the clubhouse of sandwiches, Scotch, beer, and tea were up to $11,500, about $3,000 over the preceding year. Mrs. Alex Cunningham, who ran the clubhouse while her husband took care of the rest of the place, reported a $3,216 profit, almost $2,000 more than the previous year.

Between 700 and 800 PGA members played the PGA National Course that year. The PGA Seniors' tournament in 1947 had been won by Jock Hutchison. A left-handed St. Louis pro, Ben Richter, was three strokes back of Jock's 145. Richter was an unusually good teacher. As a lefthander he could have a pupil look at him and mirror his swing.

The PGA Seniors asked for $5,000 for their annual tournament. There was a minor dustup about the need to develop the tournament circuit, an old and familiar complaint over the years. After a few indignant questions about how long the PGA Seniors were expected to baby-sit for the tournament players, the $5,000 for the Old Boys was budgeted.

The PGA treasury had again been fattened by a $5,000 gift from the Masters tournament. That gift went into the Education and Benevolent funds, but with the output of the Benevolent Fund now light, the Education Fund was financing a growing program of schooling. There was a great deal of golf instruction by motion pictures in 1948, including a film of the Masters and of Harold McSpaden, Patty Berg, Sam Snead, and Lloyd Mangrum, who was second to Ben Hogan in prize money that year.

Some delegates talked about appointing a tournament players' "czar," with Maynard Fessenden and Robert Hudson being mentioned for the spot. These two hastened to announce that under no circumstances would they take the job. Furthermore, they emphasized that since the Tournament Committee had been given a free hand in running the circuit, the seven-man committee had done a thoroughly satisfactory job, handling such matters as placing five tournament players on probation and questioning Chairman

Joe Novak. PGA

Schneiter about his expense account with admirable discretion.

Charles Bartlett, secretary of the Golf Writers' Association, presented to the Tournament Committee an urgent request for adequate weekly releases of statistical material on tournament performances, including scores, money winnings, exceptional play, Ryder Cup points, data on courses, scoring averages, and other information giving the reader a picture of tournament play. He also asked for more biographical material on the players.

The PGA had just about ignored tournament information since the publication of the *Official Record Book* of 1940–41, but it decided to do something about the matter after Bartlett told the Tournament Committee it was far behind other major professional sports, even the fairly new business of pro football, in public relations. Bartlett called attention to the fact that golf tournament stories were written mainly for readers who played the game and wanted some detail to let them know

what happened. The courses all differed. The situation wasn't as in Britain, where most golf readers knew the courses on which events were being played. Bartlett, the *Chicago Tribune*'s golf writer for many years, explained to PGA Tournament Committeemen and other officials that tournament news was often put on the wires by reporters who knew little about the game and needed expert guidance.

Bartlett wrote vivid and accurate stories that contained the kinds of technical references golfers enjoyed. He had a special "box score" that took a lot of figuring on his part, but it revealed whether the leading rounds were played in a conventional manner, by lucky or adept scrambling, or by unusually good putting and bunker shots. He also gave the reader an idea of the nature of the course. Bartlett's box score, an idea he shared with cooperative fellow workers, was dropped after his untimely death. Unfortunately, the PGA Tournament Players' Division, with its large organization and control of players, has not seen fit to meet the information standards of professional baseball, football, basketball, and hockey by making available something either on the order of the Bartlett box score or a standardized performance rating.

By 1948 the PGA was able to breathe easily on its championships for the first time. It had them booked for 1949 at Richmond, for a $30,000 guarantee, for 1950 at Columbus, for $40,000, and for 1951 at Pittsburgh, for $45,000. It was a happy change from worrying about who'd be host next year.

The annual election was a peaceful affair, with Joe Novak becoming the first PGA president from west of the Rockies, thereby easing the pain of the loyal brethren of the West, who were doing a notable job of developing and serving golf and had the feeling they were being treated like stepchildren. Novak was a sound and diplomatic administrator who believed that a professional's raison d'être, or justification for existence, was teaching, and if that were well done, other things would take care of themselves. Novak got forty-seven votes for the presidency.

Horton Smith, who'd become very active in PGA affairs as president of the Illinois section and on various committees since returning from war service, got twenty-six votes. He was the first of the younger tournament players to take an intense and diligent interest in the PGA. He had enlisted for military service, taken officer candidate schooling, expected combat service, but was assigned to Special Services in the European Theater of Operations. Smith handled that job as he did every other —with thoroughness, care, and good judgment. When he came out of the Army, he realized his tournament days were over except for winter junkets, and he became professional at the Oak Park Country Club in suburban Chicago. As an Illinois PGA official, he gave the section a lot of the Army organization method, which of course was not appreciated by a quorum of his fellow members, who had had all the Army SOP they wanted. But the discipline was good for the PGA in Illinois and for its members' clubs.

Horton Smith also received twenty-six votes for the PGA secretary spot in the 1948 election, but again lost—to Marty Lyons, an able veteran from the Philadelphia district who won with thirty-seven votes. John Budd, another veteran, got nine. William Wotherspoon was the unanimous choice for re-election as treasurer.

18

The Cocky Little Champion
in the Bloomers—Gene Sarazen

PERHAPS the most famous of the youngsters who came out of the Westchester County golf nursery, and certainly an inspiration to hundreds of caddies with similar backgrounds, was Gene Sarazen. As legendary a golf figure as Walter Hagen in his own special way, the spunky, stocky Gene seems to have stalked the fairways forever and ever in his unmistakable knickers. They became his trademark long after the vogue for plus fours had died unlamented. Just like other caddies of Italian origin, though, he had to struggle while getting started in golf. In and around the New York, Boston, and Philadelphia areas, the rough, tough boys of Irish parentage had clearly staked first claim to the available caddying jobs, and other kids encroached at their peril.

However, the home professionals, almost all of whom came from Scotland and England, wisely refrained from taking sides in the caddie rivalry. They were more than willing to give a break to any boy who looked, listened, and performed well. One of them was Fred Biscelli, who was the Larchmont Country Club pro, greenkeeper, and caddie master when eight-year-old Eugene Saraceni took that forty-minute trolley ride from Harrison to Larchmont and made his debut as a caddie in 1910. The little boy was introduced by Danny, Fred's younger brother—Gene wisely began knowing the right people early in the game.

Caddying at the nine-hole Larchmont course was dull and financially unrewarding because there wasn't enough play. After three years when his talents hadn't filled his pockets, in 1913 Gene switched to the busier Apawamis Club at Rye to give its members the benefit of his services. Golf clearly fascinated the boy; he'd practice swings and hit a ball on that four-mile walk from Harrison to his new job at Apawamis. The caddie master at Apawamis was George Hughes, a descendant of a long line of Irish kings and not the first and most fervent of the Sarazen fans. Gaelic kids like the late Ed Sullivan were his pets. It is funny to think of little Eddie Sullivan, his bright and smiling face charming one and all around the first tee, growing up to work for years as the awkward, heart-of-gold ringmaster of the longest-running television vaudeville show on record.

As a fifteen-year-old, Gene went into factory work during World War I under plenty of family economic pressure. His father was a scholarly man, displaced and soured and a loser in a new land; his mother was one of those endearing women whose skillet and smile shine through the ages. An overworked teenager in a factory job, Sarazen took sick. When he beat pneumonia after receiving the last rites prematurely, he regained enough health and drive to get a job with Al Ciuci, then pro at Beardsley Park, a nine-hole pasture course at Bridgeport, Connecticut. He received no wages. The pay consisted mainly of what Gene could hustle from other golfers, and no doubt the brash, personable, highly competitive youngster more than held his own.

Al Ciuci helped Gene work out a fundamentally sound golf game, although Sarazen's grip and other elements of his technique weren't orthodox in the Scottish manner. But Gene was an experimenter from the beginning. As might be expected, Italian-Americans stuck together and Al Ciuci soon pushed his young friend onto George Sparling, a big, taciturn Scot who was pro at Brooklawn, the top club in Bridgeport. Sparling, a rather good player, wasn't eager to hire the Sarazen kid as an assistant, but when

two of the club's leading members, the twin brothers Archie and Willie Wheeler, showed a favorable interest in the lad, Sparling did the discreet thing and took Sarazen on as a shop boy. The big Scot soon became impressed by Sarazen's play and mentioned it favorably, but not to Gene. That was not an uncommon attitude in those days; the pro wanted to hold his job, and eager youngsters wanted to get it. Who could blame either one? In the case of Brooklawn, Sparling knew the Wheeler brothers carried weight, and Gene also sensed that.

The kid had to do plenty of infighting to get ahead, but he knew that the odds didn't favor the nice little "pardon-me" boys in his league. He showed that understanding again when he got a job as assistant to Ramsey Hunter, professional at the Fort Wayne Country Club, after his first winter in Florida where Bill Goebel, pro at the Charlotte (North Carolina) Country Club, and Alec Gerard, winter professional at the Lake Wales (Florida) Golf Club befriended him and gave him the chance to improve his game.

Flocks of pros went South for the winter, depending on free playing privileges at private and public courses. They hustled members for bets and playing lessons, beat the pros at host clubs out of business, and so often conducted themselves crudely and rudely as club guests that they wore out their welcome. Few of the young migrant pros were educated in the amenities—nor were they even average at reading and writing—but they were fond of playing golf in the Southland's winter sunshine instead of having to contend with hard work in the Northern winters. Besides, back home, jobs for fellows who wanted to quit as soon as spring arrived weren't easy to get.

Older professionals to whom good manners came by early training or instinct were embarrassed by the winter visitors who called themselves professionals. As a result of their thoughtless actions, what had been hospitality was replaced by limitations on the pro tourists at private clubs down South. The restrictions were undeserved and humiliating for the majority of experienced professionals who went South in the winter and whose personalities and conduct contributed to the enjoyment of the club's members and their amateur guests and pleasantly extended the service of the resident professional. And they were undeserved in the case of Gene Sarazen as well. Public relations as such wasn't stressed then, but while the screening of youngsters most likely to succeed in pro golf was taking place in the 1920's, the bright Sarazen kid was doing something to distinguish and advance himself. He was writing thank-you letters and postcards.

Sarazen was the first, and possibly still the champion, at writing to influential people who had been gracious to him. They might be amateurs who were successful businessmen, important club officials, or sportswriters he'd met here or there—all of them rated a pleasant acknowledgment. Gene was his own best press agent, and no other celebrated professional golfer ever had a busier or better one. His paperwork went ahead of him in getting pro jobs at Titusville, Pennsylvania, at the Highland Country Club, Pittsburgh, at the Fresh Meadow Country Club on Long Island, at Lakeville, and at other clubs where he has been pro in residence. The Highland job was his first big break, and he got that by showing appreciation by mail to Emil ("Dutch") Loeffler, the pro-greenkeeper at Oakmont who was the top sergeant of the

noted W. C. ("Bill") Fownes, Jr., the 1910 National Amateur Champion who became president of the USGA.

Always a realist, Tommy Armour observed that he'd never seen Gene spend more than five minutes with somebody who couldn't do him some good. "And that's no sin," Armour added. "I wish I were that way myself."

Young Sarazen's capacity for identifying himself with the right people was again in evidence when some members of the Fort Wayne Country Club who'd been impressed by his scoring paid his way to the Open at Inverness in Toledo in 1920. Inverness that year was possibly the greatest debut party in the history of American tournament golf. Playing in the National Open for the first time were Sarazen, Leo Diegel, Bob Jones, Tommy Armour, Bill Mehlhorn, and Johnny Farrell. Ted Ray of England won with 295, one stroke ahead of his traveling companion from England, Harry Vardon. Leo Diegel, of the Lake Shore Club in suburban Chicago, tied for third with Jack Burke, one of the young Irish professionals from Philadelphia.

Sarazen should have been the first of the millionaire pros. He was willing to work for money and play all the possible angles. His club jobs weren't the sort he thought would make him rich; they demanded that he work too hard on the members' games instead of on his own. That was not for Gene. Or for Walter Hagen. It was deadly boring work. The only one of the famous playing professionals who ever did brilliantly well at a club professorial job was Armour. He found teaching—for a few hours a day—a challenge and a stimulation. Tommy was fond of both.

Gene was driven by bossiness and

Gene Sarazen and Joe Novak at the Masters. PGA

ambition, and a club pro job is no place for those traits to flower. So, after his victory in the 1922 National Open at the Skokie Country Club, where he registered as pro from the Highland Country Club at Pittsburgh, it was inevitable that the Sarazen career as a club professional was mutually less than agreeable. He was not yet America's Sweetheart. When he'd beaten John Black, a rather elderly Scot, and Bob Jones, pride of the newborn South, by a stroke at Skokie, there were mutterings about a drive at the seventy-first hole that wasn't decisively within the premises. In 1922, when he beat Emmet French, 4 and 3, in the final at Oakmont, Sarazen began to register as a young man who had really arrived.

In 1923, when he won the PGA by defeating Hagen in two extra holes, there again was a question of an out-of-bounds shot. He was really one of the greats then, but the narrowness of his wins and his disposition to regard himself as "picked on" instead of glorified was a soft spot in his acute sense of public relations. That was corrected eventually, when he won the British Open decisively in 1932 at Prince's Sandwich, over Macdonald Smith, by five strokes.

Then came a spectacular finish at Fresh Meadow in the 1932 U.S. National Open, when he beat Bobby Cruickshank and Phil Perkins by three strokes. His victory in the 1933 PGA against Willie Goggin, 5 and 4, was colorless. Both finalists were good golfers, but Willie was a "Who's he?" and Gene had finally arrived at the top. He had mastered himself as well as the other fellows.

Mechanically, Sarazen wasn't a stylist. Psychologically, he was in command of the golf ball. In a crisis he could play better than he knew how. He had the rare quality of learning from mistakes, and he seldom made the same error twice. He was eager for publicity. Golf writers used to say that Gene would jump naked off the torch of the Statue of Liberty to get his name in the papers. He'd get an idea about an eight-inch cup for a golf tournament. That was something to talk about in the winter, but in effect, the idea was to make golf so easy that any one of a myriad clumsy slobs could win. The big cup idea was used in a Florida tournament one winter. It was a very dull bust in publicity, and Gene, a bright lad who didn't want to ride a loser, got off that hunch.

Gene was the first of the champions to criticize the architecture of a golf course. Previously, professionals had accepted courses as fields of competition they all had to play, and if any contestant thought the course had him licked at the start, he could jolly well stay away and keep his mouth shut. Gene popped off about a National Open Championship course and was knocked right out of bounds by the late Westbrook Pegler, then a hard-hitting sports reporter. Pegler wrote one of his classic barbecue columns, in which he remarked that, if the ex-caddie didn't like the course on which he was being allowed to play, with an opportunity of far higher reward than was possible by genuine work, why didn't he have the decent manners *not* to play on it, but to join the club, pay his dues, and dig into

his pockets to provide money for remaking the course the way he wanted it? "Otherwise," said Peg, "why doesn't he shut up? He is boring." That devastating observation ended all Sarazen criticism of championship courses. Here Gene displayed better judgment than has been shown by latter-day professionals whose snide comments on course conditions have accounted for the reluctance of first-class clubs to be hosts to tournaments.

Sarazen seemed to enjoy playing with businessmen golfers and quickly and comfortably getting them over their stage fright, regardless of what scores they were making. That valuable quality and the business sense he acquired as he grew up led him into profitable connections as a contact man for industrial organizations. Gene would play with executives of companies his employer was trying to sell, and run interference for sales engineers who were carrying the ball.

He got the itch to travel and made a couple of tours of South America and the Orient with Joe Kirkwood, the famous trick-shot artist. And he had more than the customary excursions of American professionals after their British Open working trips. His double eagle at the Masters followed by his win of the play-off against Craig Wood could have been just another one of those lucky things. It happened late on a Sunday afternoon, and the comparatively few writers covering the 1935 event, the second Masters, had virtually finished their stories when Sarazen holed an incredible 220-yard, 4-wood shot after his drive at the par-5, 485-yard fifteenth, then went on to finish in even par. The tournament itself wasn't much to write about. Without Jones playing spectacularly as the host, the competition was pretty much a

Jones social affair about which the general golfing public couldn't have cared less.

Instead of the Sarazen double eagle's being given quick treatment as a substitute lead by sportswriters unhappy about having to stay through a Monday round at Augusta, it was given a big play by Alan Gould, sports editor of the Associated Press. Gould, a skilled worker, realized there was no big sports story for a Monday at that time of the year, so he made the spectacular Sarazen shot the topic that called for a ribbon head across the page. When the other reporters—a dozen or so of them —saw Gould working hard, they shrewdly guessed that Alan was building up a story that might have their editors asking, "How come the AP made a big story out of what you handled as just another tie to be decided later?"

Gould's decision to grab the Sarazen exploit as a feature for an otherwise dead Monday, plus the continued astute plugging of Cliff Roberts, the Masters Tournament Committee chairman and the canniest planner, manager, and publicist tournament golf has ever had, gave Sarazen a tremendous boost. For years he had the asset of the top ballyhoo of any one circus shot in the game.

That one stroke was the richest in golf, not only in the news space it got through the years, but in the way it kept Sarazen qualified for profitable sidelines. With only his 1958 PGA Senior title identifying him as still swinging, Gene was brought back to golf's spotlight by his job with Shell's "Wonderful World of Golf" television series. This TV golf show was the most attractive and durable golf entertainment ever aired. It combined international golf competition, scenery, close-ups of exclusive clubs all over the world, golf instruction, and even commercials that

were fascinating travelogues. It was the idea of the then president of Shell Oil, and it sold the company's products. It had the rare value in television advertising of making people remember who had paid for the program presented and what it hoped to sell.

The debonair Tommy Armour was asked to be the master of ceremonies, guide, and tutor of the deluxe golfing tour, but when he learned how much hard work, routine, and inconvenience were involved, he bowed out and said there was only one man who'd go the distance and finish chatty—that was Sarazen.

The Shell TV show brought Sarazen back to life in golf. The chunky, sunny-faced veteran in the old-fashioned bloomers was unique and delightful in a simple, friendly way—not trying to be too smart, talking as though he were walking along with a rich friend, and making some mistakes that the TV producer was bright enough to leave in the picture, so that Sarazen would be going along in a living room just as sociably as in a locker room.

Later, when a strenuous schedule had Sarazen showing signs of weariness and wear, Jimmy Demaret was brought in to pep up the act. Jimmy was smooth and dapper and cute to the correct degree. He kept attention on the play. The affable Demaret was known as the Bob Hope of pro golf's show business. By all accounts Sarazen and Demaret made the most entertaining, interesting, and informative sports team TV has ever offered.

Gene Sarazen, on the Shell golf show, conducted his Second Coming as a public sports favorite. He'd had his moments when he was downright rude and abrupt, although possibly amply provoked. He was credited with the classic retort to a nuisance who hailed him

Gene Sarazen and Walter Hagen (1948). PGA, photo by Boice Studios

just when he was about to make a shot in a tournament. "Hey, Gene!" the man shouted. "I'll bet you don't remember me!" Sarazen walked away from his ball, looked at the fellow, and shook his head. "No, I don't!" he snapped. "Why the hell should I?" Which is exactly the reply most of us would want to come back with in a similar situation.

But then there is the classic story of how another formidable golf professional put the brusque Sarazen firmly in his place. It happened when the equally hard-nosed and outspoken Lloyd Mangrum, a relative unknown at the time but clearly a comer, was playing a practice round ahead of Sarazen's foursome. Gene was often an impatient and impulsive player, and he

Ken Venturi. *Golf Guide,* photo by Joe Gambatese

kept driving into Mangrum and his friends up ahead on the fairway. Mangrum stood it as long as he could, then, after either he or one of his friends had barely escaped getting beaned by one of Sarazen's powerful drives, he stalked, enraged, back up the fairway. "Mr. Sarazen," he said, glaring, "if you do that once more, I'm going to hit a ball right down your [expletive deleted] throat!" Gene's reaction is not recorded, but it's safe to say that he knew Mangrum meant what he said and acted accordingly. However, when Gene was on the Shell TV show, he was the most gracious of sports heroes. And that job brought him a connection with a Florida real-estate organization where he's probably doing more useful sales work than any other ancient athlete.

In his extraordinarily successful public relations, Gene had a genius counseling him backstage—his gracious and charming wife Mary. He had the sub-

lime good sense to pay attention to her judgment and advice. He never was a play-around boy, and after he married his Hoosier small-town girl, Mary, he was the best of the lot, as husbands go. Sportswriters, for one reason or another, or even for no reason, were often prepared to belt Sarazen in cold type, but when they met Mary and she smiled, the hostilities were over. In his mother and his wife, Gene Sarazen had all the fan club he needed to make him great, in his own opinion. And he gradually earned a valid rating of greatness as greatness goes in sports.

Best of all, on the way he was an inspiration to hundreds of youngsters of Italian ancestry, admirable, ambitious working kids who were eventually to do golf and golfers a great deal of good. Consider just a small part of the endless Latin roster: the Turnesas, the Maneros, Johnny Revolta, the Fords (Fortunatos), the Penna brothers—Toney and Charley, Tommy Lo-

Presti, the Bontempos, Ken Venturi, Vic Ghezzi, Sam Bernardi, the Pezzullos, Jimmy D'Angelo, the Ciucis, Felix Serafin, Perry del Vecchio, the Baronis, the Nordones, Tony Longo, the Gianferantes, the Circellis, Joe Belfore, George Fazio, the Commissos, Frank Strafaci, Sam Urzetta, the Addesos, the Barbaros, the Tisos, Frank Strazza, Louie Galby, the Steppos, Mike Bencriscutto, the Biancos, the Biagettis, the Boninos, Dan Galgano, the Catropas, the De Manes, Joe Capello, the Caparellis, Mike Serino, the Chiapettas, the Columbos, Bob Saielli, Dom Salerno, Johnny Raimondi, Louis Quarandillo, the Morescos, Alex Antonio, the Bellinos, the Perellis, Jack Patroni, the Martuccis, the Marcos, the Lombardis, Frank Cormaci, Vic d'Alberto, Sal Di Buono, Eddie Duino, the Espinosas (and there was another pro golf family of that name, with a Spanish, Mexican, and Portuguese background), the Farinas, Fred Canusa, the Roccos, the Palettis, Gene Marchi, Dave Trufelli, Mike De Massey, and Frank Rodio.

Certainly many more deserve mention, for in their own ways and in their limited fields, they served golf and golfers every bit as well as their illustrious trailblazer, Gene Sarazen. Or—in many, many cases—even more valuably than he. Like Hagen, Armour, Hogan, and Snead among the older star players, Sarazen took little interest in PGA politics, and outside of participating in its championships, he deliberately did little to develop the association. But that's not to disparage Gene. After all, champions and top contenders have been few among PGA officials. Besides, he did his stint as a club professional, and that is where the golf professional definitely and personally contributes to the advancement of this intensely individual game. The tournament and exhibition performer has a secondary entertainment rating with the golfing public, which, basically, is selfish itself. That blunt fact of golfing life emerged during the civil war between the playing specialists and the club professionals. The amateurs who pay the bills were not impressed by the glory and glamour of the stars. Their complaint was always: "What have any of the rich heroes done for me?"

Like the judge who was honest even when he was a young attorney and could hardly afford to be honest, Sarazen had an ethical attitude toward the game. He felt he owed it plenty. Gene has never been a blushing violet, but he has always been quick to ask, "Save for the grace of God and golf, where would I have been?" The clothes show is probably the only bet that Gene Sarazen ever blew in the golf business. Professionals have been paid big money for endorsing slacks, but never a nickel for modeling knickers. Just as Nicklaus was once known as "Fat Jack," it's a wonder Sarazen never had to worry about eating. Anyone who has ever sat down to a good, hearty two-hour Italian meal knows what I mean.

But Gene was always careful of his physical condition, nor did he ever drink too much or forget his good manners. Any way you look at him, Gene Sarazen was a fine, clean leader of the young men of Italian-American stock who constituted perhaps 30 percent of the membership when the PGA was growing up.

19

The PGA Looks at Its Bookkeeping, PGA Angel George May Advises a Split, The PGA Meets with Its Super Santas

[1949, 1950, 1951]

THE division of PGA expenses occupied delegates from the thirty sections at the thirty-third annual meeting, held at the Mid-Pines Hotel, Southern Pines, North Carolina, November 28 through December 1, 1949. President Joe Novak, Treasurer William Wotherspoon, Secretary Martin Lyons, and the Executive Committee had decided the budget had grown more as a matter of expediency and compromise than of balanced judgment. And the vice-presidents in office—Ted Bickel, George M. Corcoran, Joe Donato, Eddie Duino, William C. Gordon, L. J. McClellan, David McKay, William Suchart, and John C. Watson—had also been hearing plaints of: "Where does the money go and why?"

Expenses were running 40 percent for the general office, including the salary of Executive Director Tom Crane, 30 percent for the Tournament Bureau, and 15 percent each for the association magazine and the PGA National Golf Club. Ryder Cup expenses came out of the general fund.

It was estimated that only about 15 percent of the members participated in circuit tournaments, hence the Tournament Bureau was getting a generous cut of the PGA members' dues without showing any eagerness to support itself. The customary debate followed about the comparative advertising value to golf of tournaments as compared to market development, instruction, and other services of the home professional. Television was a babe in the woods, its days of paying big money for sports programs still years ahead, but the Tournament Bureau had already tried unsuccessfully to sell the 1949 PGA Championship and other tournament radio broadcasts to a network or local station for a piddling $300.

Harry Wismer, then attaining prominence as a radio sportscaster, had introduced the PGA Championship to nationwide radio in St. Louis in 1948. The facilities were provided at the Norwood Hills Country Club by a local station, and although the PGA got no money for the broadcasting, it didn't have to pay anything either, so all concerned were happy. To show its appreciation to Wismer, the PGA offered him the rights, without cost, to a national broadcast of the 1949 PGA Championship at the Hermitage Country Club, Richmond, Virginia, May 25 to 31, with local radio rights open to any station wanting them. But nobody went for the national broadcast of the championship, which was won by Sam Snead, succeeding Ben Hogan, who was still in precarious condition from his automobile accident the previous February.

The advertising value of the tournament circuit to golf had again been reviewed at a meeting in Chicago earlier in December between Joe Novak and Bill Wotherspoon of the PGA, L. B. Icely of Wilson, Henry Cowan of MacGregor, Dave Levinson of Spalding, and Maynard Fessenden of the PGA Advisory Board. And it was an uncontrovertible fact that the leading manufacturers' financing of tournament players was the key factor in keeping star players on the circuit.

Spalding had started the star exhibition tours with Harry Vardon at the turn of the century. Icely, as Wilson's president, came strongly into the star system with Sarazen and Snead among his early headliners, then later Palmer, who left to head his own company, Boros, Casper, and others. Patty Berg went on the Wilson staff when she turned professional, and made friends all over. Manufacturers and home pros said that if all others, male and female,

in the manufacturers' pro corps worked as hard and as effectively in promoting golf as the brisk and beaming little redheaded girl did, the golf business would be vastly increased.

MacGregor got actively into the star plan of publicity and promotion with the colorful Tommy Armour. It also had, at times, Byron Nelson and Ben Hogan (before he started his own company). Tony Penna, an Armour protégé, was a valuable member of the MacGregor staff until he, too, started his own club manufacturing company. And when Jack Nicklaus turned pro, MacGregor signed him.

As makers of the Louisville Slugger baseball bats, Hillerich and Bradsby were far into the star system early and carried the plan over into golf with Bill Kaiser, a widely liked former professional as the H & B talent scout and pro sales manager. Other golf manufacturing companies signed players whose fame, the clubmakers hoped, would help sell clubs.

Spalding added Bob Jones to their big names when he left the amateur ranks, and continued to enlist stars, including some like Al Watrous and Paul Runyan who had become home pros. The Spalding road show of Horton Smith, Jimmy Thomson, Lawson Little, and Harry Cooper, in addition to starring in tournaments, did perhaps the most extensive missionary job ever done in American golf promotion. They played exhibitions in the metropolitan areas and in the backcountry, often on nine-hole sand-green courses where a club had forty or fifty members and the gallery was a hundred. The Spalding Flying Circus, as Charley Bartlett, the *Chicago Tribune* golf writer, called the travelers, made many converts.

Home pros were making armies of

converts, too, with their programs of group instruction at clubs, fee courses, and schools, and their trade-in allowances on used clubs that provided thousands of low-priced clubs for beginners. The home pros protested *they* were making the market while the show-business boys were getting the big payments from the manufacturers, but then a number of the home pros were on manufacturers' payrolls as "staff members" themselves.

It had been customary to supply some balls without charge to professionals who were especially good customers. Ostensibly, the balls were for "sampling," but that was poetic license. Trade practices involving the tournament professionals and home professionals had grown to be curious and costly, besides having dangerous tendencies in the rapidly expanding golf trade.

In this regard, at the meeting of the PGA and manufacturers' executives, Maynard Fessenden, as the PGA Advisory Committee official, said that the PGA's failure to inform the committee of developments in which the advice of experienced businessmen might be useful continued to nullify the Advisory Committee's potential value. PGA officials admitted the Fessenden charge was valid and again promised to inform the Advisory Committee before acquainting the membership with unfavorable developments. But again little was ever done in this direction for about twenty years. Then Lloyd F. Lambert, executive secretary of the PGA, summarized PGA Executive Committee meetings and major news of the annual meetings and provided these digests to Advisory Committee members.

For years the Advisory Committee

knew very little of the business of the PGA and professionals. The committee was excellent in theory, but not much use in actual practice, since it usually got information when it was too late to be of any use. As late as the negotiations for moving the PGA National Golf Club and the association's offices to Palm Beach Gardens, and during the series of meetings that resulted in the division of the PGA, committee members commented that whatever advice they might possibly be asked to give would have to be based mainly on what they'd read in the papers. Things reached a point, prior to the Lambert briefings, when members suggested that the Advisory Committee be ended.

One member of the Advisory Committee, Allyn of National Cash Register, was aware of one urgent need of professionals. He had some of his company's experts prepare a uniform pro-department accounting system, which was first made available at the 1946 national meeting and was extensively used.

Professionals were getting into sales tax and internal revenue tax trouble. Those at the larger jobs hired accountants, who often discovered that the pros were not taking advantage of allowances due them according to Internal Revenue Service regulations. The Allyn idea also showed numerous professionals and club officials how pros frequently were netting very little out of their jobs because they carried more inventory and took more risks in a short-season and limited-customer business than they or their employers realized.

This contribution from a member of the PGA Advisory Committee was an unrecognized historic milepost in pro-golfer business progress. The uniform accounting gave professionals a basis for evaluating and comparing their jobs and specific figures to show their employers when they wanted a better contract. Private club officials and members almost invariably thought their professional was making at least $25,000 a year or more in a six- or seven-month season. The misconception was heightened when, say, a professional got himself a Cadillac with a good down payment and neglected his golf-shop merchandising bills. Members who owned cars in the moderate price range liked the pro but didn't relish being reminded that a man working half a year for them was doing better than they were working the year round.

At the 1948 meeting, the pension and insurance problems came up again in realistic appraisals of the pros' job insecurity. But no progress was made in adjusting the pro golfers' situation to that of empolyees in other fields.

The PGA's war service interests were dimming, of course, but the association members still kept on the job. In Minnesota Wally Mund, an aggressive section official, got a congressman named Hubert Humphrey to say that he would seek a congressional appropriation for ranges, practice greens, and nine-hole courses at Veterans' Administration hospitals. Nothing seemed to come of it.

The tournament situation for 1949 had been about as usual, but the PGA Championship at Richmond had lost about $10. In what was to become an oft-heard complaint, the USGA implored the PGA's Tournament Bureau to do something about slow play. It was retarding the growth of golf by limiting the capacity of golf courses and also alienating the interest of

young men with families who wanted recreation that didn't drag its feet.

Manufacturers were in keen competition about supplying free golf bags to the Ryder Cup team, and George Schneiter, chairman of the Tournament Bureau, and the irrepressible, handsome Dick Metz got into an altercation over the matter. This got Metz another official scolding for doing the laundry out in the open, but he continued to maintain that everything, *absolutely everything*, about PGA tournament operations should be as public as a scorecard. Schneiter took the position that if the players knew what was happening, there would be a big argument at the first tee of every tournament. He censured his colleagues for wanting everything and wanting to give nothing. And he was getting more than fed up with his job, which carried responsibility but no money.

Schneiter forecast what eventually happened when the tournament players got in another room of the PGA house. He said they'd have to get somebody detached and superior who could scare them, run them, and keep them in line. He didn't think much of the power of the Tournament Committee or Bureau. They were too close to the players. "Familiarity breeds contempt," he asserted, and in other comments uncannily forecast the arrival of a commissioner like Joe Dey. George Schneiter saw it all coming. He was a tournament player with ambition and a pretty fair talent for character analysis.

The labor pains of the 1949 annual meeting were somewhat eased by the Cosgrove family of Southern Pines and Richard Tufts, president of Pinehurst, Inc., each of whom contributed $1,000 toward meeting expenses. The PGA National Club was going along as a fine small-town course; nothing fancy, but reasonably satisfying to those who paid for it and used it. Fred Grau, director of the USGA Green Section, suggested improvements for the greens, fairways, and tees. A few minor design changes came from golf architect Dick Wilson at the request of the Dunedin committee, but he said the Donald Ross design generally provided a good test of golf. Pinellas County, Florida, was asked to allot money to improve the PGA course as a tourist attraction, but the county officials said "No."

The Quarter Century Club was being formed, as it had been noted that more than half the PGA members had been in professional golf for more than twenty-five years and were older than fifty. In making Richard Clarkson a life member of the PGA, it was stressed that he was one of more than a hundred former residents of Carnoustie, Scotland, who had come into golf jobs in the United States.

The golf ball situation disturbed the government; it required a gambling tax on the golf ball slot machines that had been disposing of many thousands of dozens of balls. Estimates of slot-machine ball sales were as high as 20 percent of all golf balls sold through pro shops. The pros said they had to try some trick merchandising to compete with the cut-price ball advertising of stores. And the ball-selling battle got close to court and legislative action when a PGA sectional official said that he hoped a certain drugstore chain was more accurate in filling prescriptions than it was in its golf ball advertising. PGA members wanted the association to have the government prevent the use of playing pros' names on cheap balls that they didn't use themselves. PGA members claimed this deceived

the buyer and was in violation of several laws. Nothing happened.

There was a minor storm when Edwin Carter, the energetic PGA tournament director, proposed to add the lease of a Monterey Peninsula pro shop to his personal operations, while the PGA was strenuously campaigning to get all pro-shop concessions for its members.

Bobby Locke of South Africa, who had been profitably campaigning on the PGA tournament circuit, was suspended for not complying with regulations that PGA of America members had to obey. The South African professional and amateur bodies immediately countered with rulings that would have restricted Yankee ventures for tournament money in South Africa. No hearts were broken. Locke had his winnings, and no tempting golf loot was waiting in the diamond-mining country.

Other noteworthy items in international golf included the "challenge" match of the 1949 U.S. Ryder Cup team against other American professionals at the Belmont Club in suburban Boston, which raised $5,000. When the U.S. team went to Britain, it took along for entertainment of the hosts $1,349 worth of prime American beef. The edible stock was the gift of the Wilson Company and was questioned by competitors but not by the lip-smacking Britons. The U.S. team defeated the British, 7 to 5, at Ganton in 1949.

The year was a busy one for PGA members cooperating with newspapers in golf promotions. The *Chicago Tribune* golf school, the *New York World-Telegram* hole-in-one competition, and numerous smaller newspaper promotions had golf professionals active in building the golf market. And a survey of the PGA's business was made by the George S. May Company, the business-management engineering operation of the premier fiscal sponsor of tournaments. May made the investigation without cost to the PGA. It was sunk without trace.

Membership in 1949 reached 2,716, which was 344 off the previous year's final figure, and the Tournament Bureau reported a loss of $18,563. There were thirty-three tournaments in the fiscal year 1949, paying $474,672, including prize money for eight professional-amateur events. And twenty-eight sponsors paid the PGA Tournament Bureau service fees of $30,000.

Tom Crane and his assistant Vic Trauscht at PGA headquarters seem to have kept the sponsors as happy as they'd ever been with the high command of tournament operations. Normal complaints were heard about stars not appearing for tournaments, but that problem was solved on paper and didn't seem to disturb the players who had been doing well in collecting along the road.

Recommendations that the PGA separate from the Tournament Bureau and permit sports reporters coverage of PGA annual meetings provided mild jolts but no surprises at the thirty-fourth annual meeting of the association at the Sheraton Hotel, Chicago, November 13 to 16, 1950.

Joe Novak presided as president. Horton Smith was secretary, and Harry Moffitt was treasurer. Vice-presidents were Ted Bickel, George Calderwood, Joe Donato, Eddie Duino, Dave McKay, Graham Ross, Harold Sargent, Bill Suchart, and John C. Watson. All thirty sections had delegates attending.

The recommendation that the PGA and the Tournament Bureau be di-vorced, with both parties continuing to have loving, helpful mutual custody of the PGA Championship and the Ryder Cup competitions, came in the report of the George S. May Company's business engineers. They had been examining PGA operations for months, and May himself was chairman of the PGA Advisory Committee when the report was presented. No doubt about it—George S. May was an extraordinary figure on the American golf scene. He was the man who got pro tournament golf into the big money with his All-American Open tournaments begun in 1941. He also staged All-American men's and women's amateur championships and a women's professional championship as sideshows to his All-American golf show at his Tam O'Shanter Country Club on the northwest suburban rim of Chicago. May also had an invitational championship at thirty-six holes for a dozen professionals with a winner-take-all purse of $10,000.

In 1948, Lloyd Mangrum got a check for $22,500 for the two victories, breaking the course record with his 63 in the second round, and a bonus of $5,000 for twin wins. First prize in the All-American Open was $5,000. Up to that time, the $22,500 the dashing Mangrum got was the largest check a pro had ever collected. In addition to that record for a week's play, Mangrum collected pleasantly otherwise from the spectacular and canny May. Mangrum was Tam O'Shanter's touring pro and a very good advertising and customer relations man for his friend George.

Bill Gordon was Tam O'Shanter's club professional. His pro shop was no merchandising showplace by any standards, but May shrewdly moved it around to a clubhouse corner hard by the first tee. Though still rather dark and crowded, the shop did big business because of its location, especially during the All-American tournaments. Location also played another remunerative role. Play was heavy at Tam O'Shanter, and a branch of the Chicago River that twisted lazily through the course swallowed up thousands of golf balls from erring shots. Bill Gordon promptly collected the balls and reconditioned, repainted, and sold most of them to used-ball retailers and ranges. That sideline was O.K. with May and added substantially to Gordon's annual income.

May certainly was a valuable, foresighted friend of pro golf. In addition to spending his own company's money to boost tournament prizes, May pioneered television coverage of golf tournaments. He had local coverage for several years and arranged for the first nationwide telecast of a golf competition to show his Tam O'Shanter World Championship, which Lew Worsham won by holing a 110-yard pitching wedge on the seventy-second hole. In pioneering a World Championship that attracted stars from other countries as well as U.S. major tournaments, May paid richly without TV help. The World Championship winner also got a highly lucrative booking of exhibitions as May Company advertising.

In any case, the May report pointed out what a much later survey by business-management consultants also observed: The PGA was basically for the development of golf and profit to professionals by their service to golfers and golf clubs, while the tournament activities were for competition between pros with an entertainment value that had only a slight relationship to actually playing the game.

This cold appraisal, which had cost the PGA nothing, was accepted in a "so-what" way, as were the suggested revisions in PGA business procedure at headquarters, in sectional coordination, and in administrative practices. The report also stated that the PGA Advisory Committee should be reorganized (a recommendation George S. May obviously was qualified to make), and President Novak again urged that information for the Advisory Committee be brought up to a business level.

Mayor James A. Rhodes of Columbus told the convention that the PGA quarrels over tournament matters, which so frequently resulted in unfavorable newspaper publicity for the association, could be interpreted much more sympathetically if golf writers were admitted to the annual meetings. Rhodes went on to say that he never had known of an instance when the PGA, as an organization of golf professionals working at private clubs and public courses, hadn't worked earnestly for the betterment of golf and the increased enjoyment and proficiency of players. But almost every time he had seen the PGA mentioned in the sports pages for the previous several years, it was involved in some controversy or with the waywardness of tournament players in not meeting responsibilities to a public that was doing quite well in patronizing tournaments, which, after all, were not among life's necessities.

Rhodes had the sense and feel for effective publicity in politics and went to the top in Ohio. He was pro-minded from his days as a caddie and club official and on into his public life. He reminded pros at the PGA meeting that they, too, were very much in public life, closer to their public than pros in baseball, football, and boxing, yet they didn't seem to show the slightest interest in developing their advantages and actually were careless about this.

He proposed a National Golf Day with charities sharing in tournament and exhibition gallery fees and events conducted by pros at their clubs. He suggested governmental proclamations of National Golf Day and other circus promotions that eventually became standard practice after National Golf Day was started by *Life* magazine with the PGA, a few years after Rhodes had addressed the annual pro meeting.

Rhodes's suggestion for PGA public-relations promotion got backing at the 1950 meeting when the PGA approved "kickers" tournaments with pro cooperation with the National Foundation for Infantile Paralysis prevention and cure. This was the first association of this sort the PGA ever had made, although they had often been solicited. Club pros were frequently under pressure to conduct tournaments for health and welfare organizations but cautiously decided such arrangements were house matters. However, the Infantile Paralysis golf fund-raising plan never panned out because the promotion crew of the organization was dead on the job.

In caring for the PGA's own business, the officers and Executive Committee announced that Dave Elphick had been hired as professional, superintendent, and manager of the PGA National Golf Club. The doughty veteran Alex Cunningham told one and all in blazing detail that he had had all he could take of the Dunedin problem, adding that the job should be one of the best-paying in pro golf, inasmuch as the PGA was trying to raise all golf salaries, yet it was paying in miserly fashion for one of the most difficult

tasks in the business. Then he gave them his fiery lecture on the PGA's spending freely on tournament promotion for a minority of its members but parsimoniously for something that the majority of the PGA membership could enjoy.

Alex Cunningham was one of those grand old gentlemen to whom golf was a religion to be enjoyed by the anointed, and any sacrilege had him storming. He also was a genial, generous man, and a round of golf with him drove care away. Cunningham's kind— from five hundred to a thousand of those old pros—wrought the wonders of golf in the United States. The rest just followed through.

Another change in PGA personnel in 1950 was the hiring of Bob Gibson as editor of *The Professional Golfer*. He'd had newspaper experience and had been an assistant professional; he soon learned that if there were two sides to a PGA magazine subject, skip it. Tom Crane had set a sound example. The quiet Crane's observations were clear and prescient. He was asked to direct policy for the PGA but refused to do so, knowing that the popularity of a policymaker was fleeting. Vic Trauscht also came to the headquarters staff as assistant to Crane and to give a hand on the PGA magazine. He was a bright, versatile youth who'd been a naval officer during the war, then became a sales executive with a big household appliance company in Chicago.

The big change in the PGA roster was the departure of George Schneiter as head of tournament operations. Schneiter had been getting service fees from tournament sponsors and depositing them in a Salt Lake City bank. This money was meant for the PGA, President Novak told Schneiter in reclaiming the payments for the association and cutting him loose as tournament-circuit head man. The Tournament Bureau cost between $50,000 and $60,000 a year, and the purses were about $600,000.

With Schneiter gone, Terry Malan and his wife, who had been in charge of scoring, the scoreboard, and to some extent statistical compilations and starting times, were also out. They'd done well, but reorganization was in order. Mrs. Malan left a bright mark in tournament development by organizing scoring by women of the host and neighboring clubs. There'd been a little of this done before, but Mrs. Malan worked out the procedure that became general with women at clubs. As one considers the tremendous number of scores the women have recorded and the exceedingly few errors, a lot has to be said for the competence and carefulness of women scorers in tournament golf.

Howard Capps followed Schneiter as tournament supervisor, with Mrs. Capps as field secretary. Again a woman contributed greatly to establishing tournament operations. Later Mrs. James Gaquin worked with her husband when he was directing the tournaments. As Lois Hayhurst she had been on the Wilson Sports Goods staff. The two of them were a highly effective publicity and management team for the PGA's tournament golf. Later they went with the USGA and with the Royal Canadian Golf Association.

When Capps came in from his pro job, the veteran "Spec" Hammond joined him as a field assistant and announcer at tournaments. Hammond had started as a caddie when the tournament circuit was beginning in Southern California, then went with Walter

Hagen as a caddie and chauffeur, and was with Bob Harlow for a while, when Harlow was nursing the infant circuit. Capps came in at a troublesome time, but then the tournament circuit was always troublesome.

Horton Smith reported to the 1950 meeting that the tournament players had attempted to organize their own department with Frank Walsh as an Executive Committee member-at-large representing the tournament players. This arrangement went on for a few years, but the tournament players seemed to forget that it existed, so again, after having been given autonomy, they continued to talk about forming their own group separate from the PGA.

Smith told how twenty players at a tournament in Long Beach held a private meeting at which George Schneiter was chairman and a paper was signed forming a new tournament organization. Smith said he was staying at the same hotel with the men who attended, but that the meeting was kept secret from him as a PGA official. And some players later admitted that they signed only because they were afraid they would be denied entry into tournaments if they didn't.

The ink was still wet on the tournament insurgents' declaration before second-guessing was in order. Clayton Heafner, Chick Harbert, and Lawson Little suggested that instead of going off the deep end by starting a competing circuit, someone ought to find out the specific differences the rebels had with the elected officials of the PGA and try to settle them. Eventually, though, they agreed that regardless of how many headliners one circuit might have, if there were two tournament circuits, the resulting conflict would kill tournament golf. (The same situation existed almost twenty years later when the compromise that maintained major tournament golf was reached.)

In 1950 manufacturers' support was essential to a tournament player. And any tournament player who was trying to wreck the PGA would cost his manufacturer-sponsor severely in sales to home pros. Jimmy Thomson and Lawson Little pointed this out to their colleagues. They were on the Spalding staff; so was Horton Smith, but he was careful about not getting involved where his commercial ethics could be questioned. His colleagues on the tournament circuit were, of course, equally honorable, but they didn't think far enough ahead to consider the conflicting elements. So the Professional Golf Players' Association died while being born.

It seemed to make no difference that what the tournament players wanted had been given to them in 1946. Although nobody seemed to know exactly what was needed for the tournament players and the home-club service professionals to be one big happy family, another effort was made by naming to a Board of Governors for the tournament circuit Bob Hamilton, Lloyd Mangrum, John Palmer, Sam Snead, and Ellsworth Vines, the tennis champion who had turned golf pro. This board was intended to function in place of the group that had been appointed after Ben Hogan had talked at the 1946 annual meeting and asked that tournament players be given greater control over the Tournament Bureau. That request had been granted, and a control board was appointed at a Harlington, Texas, tournament in 1948. At the Masters in 1950, PGA officials tried to get the

board of tournament players to try again, but the request was turned down.

The difficulty lay in getting the tournament players to decide on what they wanted. Tournament professionals seemed to think that the rising salaries of baseball players were in some way the result of the commissioner control that had started way back with Judge Landis. George Schneiter sincerely believed this was the answer and desired to be the commissioner. He didn't make it.

Clayton Heafner, one of the talented tournament professionals who fell short of the peak, was a big, laconic fellow who, other tournament players said, was remarkably even-tempered—always angry. Heafner lost interest in the tournament players' controversies and with a characteristic lack of diplomacy told them: "You don't need a commissioner—you need a caddie master!" His observation was good for laughs for many years.

The Tournament Bureau didn't do badly financially in 1950. It got $25,000 of golf-playing equipment manufacturers' money, which enabled it to operate at a profit of $9,473 against the previous year's deficit of $18,563.

Tournament stars and top players among home professionals played in exhibitions for two headliners who needed help. Leo Diegel was dying of cancer, and "Skip" Alexander was long hospitalized in critical condition as a result of a plane crash. Both had played in many benefit matches. A PGA exhibition event in Southern California raised $2,900, and other sections raised about $1,400, but the Diegels didn't want to accept the money. Alexander waged a magnificent battle in getting back into working condition.

Horton Smith, Clayton Heafner, Dugan Aycock, and others of Alexander's fellow members of the Carolina section played matches to help lift the heavy load of hospital and surgical expenses.

Members of the 1949 Ryder Cup team complained that the PGA hadn't paid them enough with the $1,750 it had given each of them for the matches at Scarborough, England, so $250 per man was added. The bright notes on the financial side were 1950 dues of $110,320 and a record guarantee of $25,000 for the 1951 PGA Championship at Oakmont.

The PGA Educational Committee, headed by Eddie Duino, and the National Golf Foundation published a book on pro-department operations that reflected the pro shops' arrival at a merchandising position comparable to that of the better specialty shops in the suburbs. A *Teacher's Guide* was also issued by the Teaching Committee, headed by Harold Sargent.

The junior golf program had another good year. Again the PGA cooperated with the Junior Chamber of Commerce in staging the nationwide Jaycee Junior Championship, which had nearly 10,000 entries. Contestants screened by state qualifying play took part in the championship at the Iowa State University course at Ames. Gene Sarazen and Johnny Revolta conducted brief training schools for the youngsters.

During the year a concerted effort was made to establish standard allowances for used clubs when applied on the purchase of new clubs. The campaign, which continued for several years, was not successful. Pros often learned that some members were better traders than the professionals and that the pro had to take the member's deal

—or else. Used club sales were good in some industrial areas with good public courses. Buyers were rather good judges of materials and workmanship and had friends who were dependable advisers on club design. Hence clubs of top quality, used and restored by the pro to fairly good appearance, were more desirable than new clubs of inferior grade at the same price.

Around 1950 it was estimated that the typical golf club member bought a new set of irons about every six years and new woods every seven years. In materials, design, and workmanship, the clubs improved noticeably faster than every seven years, so the pros had a problem enlarging the market. Trade-in deals got to the stage where about 75 percent of clubs sold meant selling two sets—the new one and the set it replaced. This killed the profit in the club business, so after giving their stock of used clubs to caddies or veterans hospitals, many pros refused to accept used clubs from members.

As had become customary, the final day of the meeting was a school day, presenting highlights of the work in various phases of the pro golf business. George S. May spoke on the business management of the PGA and pro departments. O. J. Noer described what pros ought to know about developments in golf course maintenance. Eming Stumm, head of sales training for National Cash Register, outlined the NCR training of salesmen and how the plan could be adapted to the training of professionals. Earl B. Fox talked about "The Value of Golf in Academic Training for the Future." Herb Graffis described the coordination of National Golf Foundation activities with the PGA. He stated that the foundation's operations definitely had accounted for the building of a considerable number of clubs and forecast that the foundation's job in promoting more golf and more golf courses would be the biggest specific factor in increasing pro employment.

After the complaints about the Advisory Committee's not being told what the score was, the Advisory Committee's sighing that the PGA home and journeyman pros were hopeless as subjects for business education, and President Novak's considering tossing the Advisory Committee out of the picture, it turned out that the committee had its biggest meeting. Of its twenty-four members, there were present, on November 11 to 12, George S. May, S. C. Allyn, Robert Hudson, Maynard Fessenden, Emile Collette, Robert Goldwater, David Griffith, Robert Jordan, William May, Thomas McMahon, Clifford Roberts, Thomas Utterback, and James A. Rhodes.

At its thirty-fifth annual meeting, the PGA seemed again to be taking a good look at itself and asking the old-time politician's question: "Whither are we drifting?" The meeting was held at the Sheraton Hotel, Chicago, November 26 through 29, with Joe Novak serving his last term as president. Horton Smith was secretary, and Harry Moffitt was treasurer. Tom Crane continued as executive secretary. Delegates came from thirty sections, and Dave Douglas was the Tournament Section delegate. Vice-presidents present were George Calderwood, Joe Devany, Eddie Duino, Lawson Little, Dave McKay, Tom Mahan, Maurie O'Connor, Graham Ross, Harold Sargent, and Bill Suchart.

An Executive Committee meeting and a joint meeting of the Executive and Advisory committees were held on November 25. The Executive Commit-

tee session produced nothing significant. For years, only rarely were these meetings much more than formalities, with the few differences of opinion or unorthodox proposals being rapidly smothered. The committee was a long time learning to communicate with the PGA members and amateur golfers, if it had anything to say to them.

In contrast, the Advisory Committee was very much coming to life and from that one meeting got more newspaper space than the PGA sessions. Not that that was hard to do. The PGA had lost its chance to make its annual meetings newspaper stories of interest to the golfing public it was serving and never had learned how to regain the lost opportunity. Golf had become a national sport without the kind of fond publicity baseball and football had received. By 1950, golf writers were an energetic, competent group greatly interested in promoting their favorite sport and having important readership, but they still had to beg for space from insensitive editors who were still unaware of the progress in social and economic conditions that made golf lively news to influential readers of their sports sections. Along with being shut out by the PGA at its annual meetings and having trouble getting ordinary golf news into print, except for local and pro tournament competitions, the golf writers gave up trying to make the pros' annual meeting a big sports story on the order of the major and minor baseball leagues' annual meetings or the football coaches' and the early pro football club owners' meetings.

Hugh Dean, a dynamic little Chevrolet executive from Detroit, Hugh Rader of Detroit, Cliff Roberts of New York and Augusta, who was chairman of the Masters tournament committee,

Hord Jardin of St. Louis, who later became president of the USGA, George S. May, business engineer and tourney impresario, and Robert Hudson, internationally known producer and distributor of food products, were among the nationally prominent businessmen at the Advisory Committee meeting. They didn't exactly advise the PGA; they told the PGA what should be done. Hudson, as committee chairman, spoke to the sportswriters.

The committee was to be enlarged by the addition of John Jay Hopkins, head of General Dynamics; Harry Radix, executive of a Chicago precious metal company and an official of American and Olympic figure skating associations as well as a golf club and association official; B. H. Ridder of St. Paul, top executive of a nationwide chain of newspapers; and Robert Stranahan, head of the Champion Spark Plug Company, an enthusiastic and gifted amateur golfer. Stranahan and Ridder had sons who became prominent in golf. Frank Stranahan won amateur and professional championships before retiring to the investment business, and Bernie Ridder, Jr., an excellent amateur golfer, became a member of the Executive Committee of the USGA and one of the top command of the vast Ridder interests in newspapers, television, sports, and other enterprises.

That committee presented an array of super Santa Clauses. What they said got news space. George S. May announced he was raising his 1952 World Championship purse to $75,000, with a first prize of $17,500, plus fees from a rich string of exhibitions sponsored by the May company. The May purse was to be more than 10 percent of the 1952 prize money.

John Jay Hopkins was sponsoring a team match between U.S. and Canadian professionals for the Canada Cup and a fat purse and expenses. Canadair was one of Hopkins's General Dynamics properties. As tournament manager for Hopkins, Fred Corcoran had developed the Canada Cup tournament into an annual international professional event of national team and individual competition, later known as the World Cup tournament. Because of geographical and personnel restrictions, the World Cup competition could never become one of the big-money tournaments, but in paying players' expenses and good prize money, usually at a time when football was taking U.S. sports section headlines, the tournament did well in serving its original purpose of international friendship through golf. It was played in many countries of the golfing world and had as its sponsors prominent international businessmen who were directly and indirectly valuable to professional golf.

Clifford Roberts, with his companion, Bob Jones, had started the Masters, and his management genius soon made the Masters the best-operated tournament in world golf. It long has been directly and indirectly a gold mine for professionals, and the Masters for many years has annually given $5,000 or so to the PGA Educational or Benevolent Fund.

At the 1950 Advisory Committee meeting, Roberts said that the PGA should play its championship at the same place every year. The trouble, of course, was in getting a sponsor to take the PGA title event for more than one year. The PGA felt fortunate to be able to have the 1952 Championship at the Big Spring Country Club, Louisville, for a $40,000 guarantee. The alternative was a $25,000 guarantee plus half the gallery revenue, half the net profit of the program, and half the radio and television revenue. Television was coming in, but not generously or eagerly.

Southern Florida hadn't proved to be an area that attracted big galleries; residents and guests appeared to prefer playing to watching. But the Roberts recommendation that the PGA Championship have a steady home was recalled when the 1971 PGA was played on the PGA National East Course in the winter, five weeks ahead of the Masters, thus ensuring the publicity it needed to be successful. The galleries weren't exceptionally large, but the event was highly profitable from the television and program advertising point of view. Later in the year, the World Cup tournament was played on the same course. The glamour of the two events was very pleasant to John MacArthur, landlord of the PGA, and twenty years after the Roberts suggestion and for different reasons, he wanted the PGA Championship to be a fixture on his premises.

High on the PGA's Santa Claus roster and enjoying every minute of it was the free-spending, ebullient Bob Hudson, the wealthy groceryman who instituted the warmly approved habit of presenting U.S. Ryder Cup team members with $750 and the British players $500 in 1947 when they met at Hudson's home club, the Portland Golf Club.

In his Advisory Committee report, Hudson told the PGA to quit giving so much time to friction between home professionals and the traveling performers and to pay more attention to the pros' services to customers and mar-

ket development. "There's always some trouble in business," he said, "and the star is the man who can handle it. Otherwise, if everything ran smoothly, any bum could be boss." He counseled tournament players not to get selfish and cocky, because they were in a trade where skill was comparatively short-lived and hungry young competition always was pressing. "People forget a golf champion's record quickly, but remember his personality," Hudson noted. "Good business manners are one of the best investments for a tournament professional as well as for the home professional."

To show PGA officials they didn't have a monopoly on headaches, Hudson related that one of his salesmen had been making "about $300,000 more than the head man and thinks Hudson House should be turned over to him. That happens with a different man every year. Wait until I get home, and I'll figure out some way to make him happy and making more money for himself than he does for me. Tournament professionals are making more money than they ever dreamed they would have, and you can't blame them for not knowing how to act. They need foresight and sound judgment to help them as there may come a day. . . ."

In an unexpected way, Hugh Dean turned out to be one of the greatest Santa Clauses for tournament golf. Little Hughie, without realizing it, made the tournament program an immensely rich lode for promoters. Prior to Hughie Dean, those who sold advertising in tournament programs pretty much followed the well-worn path of the programs for aldermen's picnics and union balls. This gave birth to the golf tournament program as a means of hustling, in a refined way, those with whom the program sponsors were doing business. Some who realized the small circulation, high advertising rate, and small readership of the tournament programs put in the usual formal anonymous "Compliments of a Friend" ads. But for years the golf club and ball manufacturers had refused to advertise in any of the tournament programs, frankly declaring them a shakedown.

In some way the word circulated around Detroit that pleasant little Hughie, a *big* man with Chevrolet and General Motors, was a sort of godfather to every golf tournament program ad-peddling and ticket-selling operation, and contributions would at least not be frowned upon by purchasing agents and others whose reciprocity was desirable. Perhaps Dean didn't know what was going on, but those big programs, reputedly having automotive associations in and around Detroit, provided samples and guidance that tournament program and ticket pushers used effectively all over the country, frequently with the warning that the big companies putting on the show expected every supplier to do his duty—or else.

In contrast, this left the Masters as the only tournament at which customers were informed without getting the bite put on them. The Masters has program information, starting-time sheets, and parking included in the price of tickets. It sells all the tickets it desires and probably makes more net than any other tournament.

In attending to business for the general good of the order, the 1951 meeting reported and made haste slowly, as was PGA custom. A financial report was given to delegates to transmit to their members. It was in the usual state of honest confusion and really meant nothing. But that was the condition of most private golf club financial statements, and so the procedure continued. One delegate, after listening to a reference to the PGA annual financial statement, called, "Move it be accepted!" and another voice out of the fog said, "I second it!" Carried.

Harold Sargent, head of the teaching campaign, showed an interesting motion picture film of men and women stars. *Life* magazine paid for the movie, which was titled *Keep 'Em on the Fairway* and was extensively shown at clubs. The stars cooperated enthusiastically and without complaining about the inconvenience, and the film was a useful contribution to the education of golfers. Harold's father George had been a pioneer in teaching such significant things as the steady head of young Tom Morris, the balanced grip and handiwork of Harry Vardon, the footwork of Hagen, and the Jones straight left arm.

The elder Sargent had the feeling that much could be done to improve golf instruction by developing a more receptive and responsible attitude on the part of the pupil. As a Vardon assistant he had become a good learner or he wouldn't have held his job. The expert players and effective teachers all have been apt and dedicated learners. But the relationship of the usual club member as employer and the teaching pro as employee never favored cultivation of a favorable attitude for learning.

By insisting that the pupil accept responsibility and work in an orderly way at the lesson, Tommy Armour conspicuously and consistently showed the way to the revolution in golf instruction: Awaken the pupil to his responsibility for learning.

Harold Sargent sensed that development and tried to put it across in the PGA schooling of teachers. But like other high ambitions of the PGA, the switch from teaching to consideration of the learner was a tough job. The annual teaching seminars at PGA national and sectional meetings continue to have stars demonstrating how they make their shots and very little on *how* to get the pupil to learn and *what* to learn so it will stick.

As a member of the Tournament Committee, Lawson Little said that television, which was getting to be an important factor in sports, would bring golf into every American home. He, Chick Evans, and Bob Jones were the only collegians to win the U.S. Open title up to 1940, when he beat Sarazen in a play-off. Jones had been the only graduate of the three. The Little sweep of U.S. and British Amateur championships in 1934 and 1935 was a showing of supremacy nobody has come close to equaling, and his victory in the 1936 Canadian Open also made it plain that nobody awed the colonel's son who'd picked up his golf game around Army posts. Little was also outspoken in telling his fellow tournament players that they'd better think hard about their obligations as gentlemen sportsmen, as good businessmen, and also their obligations to golf and the PGA, or they'd slide down to the level of preliminary boxers in the public eye.

There were complaints about demands for "appearance money" from several tournaments, including the St. Paul Open, which had been a lifesaver in rough times. PGA officials were shy about this matter, but not Little, who used some biting adjectives—of which "ungrateful" was the softest—and remarked that tournaments had nothing

Tommy Armour. PGA

to worry about until the people who sold tickets demanded appearance money.

The routine business of the PGA was brightened by raising the salary of Dave Elphick, pro-greenkeeper-manager of the PGA National Club, from $3,000 to a guarantee of $5,000. President Novak reminded the delegates that the PGA was not out to corral golf, nor had it been formed to tell tournament players what to do. It had spent a great deal of money to establish the tournament golf business and did not regret the expense or having to assume the responsibility when tournament golf got into trouble financially or with the public. "What all of us must remember," Novak said, "is that there are the USGA and many regional, state, and

Lawson Little, Jr. GH

local amateur associations, women's seniors, and intercollegiate associations, to whom we all have a great obligation. They are paying us."

There were complaints about manufacturers giving too many balls to leading amateurs. Pros at clubs where the National Amateur was played had commented that about the only thing the better amateurs had to buy was wooden tees. There was also discussion with manufacturers about who was qualified to sell pro-only clubs. A considerable number of the pro-only clubs were on sale at stores and driving ranges where there were no PGA members.

Another year had been given to upgrading membership in sectional business meetings. The results were beginning to show in improved credit ratings and in applications for jobs.

The Seniors had continued to keep the PGA Club at Dunedin in business. The PGA had 765 Class A members over age fifty, and some elderly members or former members were in bad health and indigent. Maurie O'Connor, an official of the New Jersey section, had tried to promote an all-star exhibition match for the PGA Relief Fund but couldn't get stars interested. Amateurs and some lesser-known professionals contributed $2,830 to the Relief Fund. There was plenty of thinking and talking about a pension fund, but its realization was far in the future. The turnover of officials at private clubs, the instability of pro employment at any course, and the cold commercial fact that the pro usually had to make his own living income beyond a minimal guarantee brought a pension plan no closer. Things didn't come easy to the men who were building the PGA.

Bob Jones was the honored guest at the PGA annual dinner. He told the concluding session that, as near as he could remember, he had had a very enjoyable evening. Therefore, it seems certain that he did.

Horton Smith was elected president, polling fifty-seven votes, and Harry Moffit got nineteen. Smith quickly prepared for business. The evening following his election he announced committees for the coming year.

20

Versatile Horton Smith Takes Over, the PGA Bears Down on Homework, the Golf Cart Makes the Scene

[1952, 1953, 1954]

HORTON Smith, the new PGA president, was the first tournament star of the modern era who became a successful home professional. He quit touring as a regular to become professional at the Oak Park Country Club in suburban Chicago but still played in major championships in the summer and went on the circuit in the winter. He was active in Illinois sectional PGA work, filling top offices in a manner that brought business methods into operations that had been casual and probably inadequate. Assigned to Special Services in the European Theater of Operations during World War II, he used golf as a means of rest and recreation for soldiers training for combat or getting their second wind. There were other well-known tournament professionals on this assignment, among them Chick Harbert.

In the Army, Smith performed according to regulations and expected everybody to work as ordered. Others didn't like his way of thinking regulations were made to be obeyed with a war going on, but that was their tough luck. Horton Smith couldn't have cared less; he'd experienced unpopularity with the hard boys before. He had been a nonsmoking, nondrinking, nonswearing, twenty-four-hour-well-behaved young man winning or finishing high in golf tournaments, and it hadn't bothered him to be called a Boy Scout on the tournament circuit.

When Smith came back from the war to become professional at the Detroit Golf Club, he continued a distinctive standard of pro service that had been established by men like the venerable Alex Ross and Ernie Way. Horton was an organizer. Soon everything in the shop, on the lesson tee, and elsewhere in the pro department was operating according to plan and with carefully selected and trained men. And there

Horton Smith. PGA

was a profit-sharing incentive to keep the young men looking for every chance to encourage spending by members without resorting to high-pressure selling.

The contents of the bag racks in the pro shop were inventoried and each member given a record of his clubs with the name of the manufacturer and year of manufacture. The make, material, and condition of the bag and its approximate age were recorded. The number of balls and accessories were also listed. Smith said that the records were for insurance purposes as well as for keeping an inventory of members' property in the pro department. When members realized the age of their clubs and bags, some of them were in the mood for new equipment.

Smith brought a similar new attitude into the PGA. He thought the association could stand some of the practical business ideas he'd learned in Detroit. He also thought the Army had a good thing in its assignment of responsibilities. When after he'd been elected president, he promptly shook up committees and seemed to have chairmen and members aware that their appointments were not formalities—they were expected to work. And there had been a year to review results when the 1952 annual meeting was held November 7 through 11 at the Hotel Sheraton, Chicago.

With Smith as president were Harry Moffitt as secretary and Harold Sargent as treasurer. Thirty sections and the Tournament Division were represented. Dave Douglas and Al Zimmerman were cochairmen of the Tournament Committee, and Jack Burke, Jr., and Jim Turnesa also represented the tournament players. Jackson Bradley was delegate-at-large. He was the tournament players' selection.

All committees had been unusually active that year because Smith had prodded them. Except for the war period, the Teaching Committee had for years received more interest than any other committee. Rarely, though, was it able to make much of a public showing except on one afternoon of the annual meeting. All committees were handicapped by small budgets and the lack of stenographic service in pro shops. Sectionally, the Tournament Committees were most active, since it was the Monday tournaments in the summer that kept the members together.

The PGA National Golf Course Committee, with Emil Beck as chairman, was able to assure members that by winter they would find the Dunedin golf course in fairly good condition and with a clubhouse that was clean, convenient, and adequate, if by no means fancy. Only about 700 PGA members out of a total roster of around 2,600 played Dunedin in a year, but it showed an operating profit.

Smith was an ideal president for inspiring committees, and he knew what the chairmen were up against. He'd been a tournament player when the winter tour had been developing into the tournament circuit; he knew most of the tournament sponsors and USGA and Western GA officials personally. He'd grown up with the problems of operating a tournament and with the players' troubles. He had the reputation of being closer than 99 is to 100, but he'd loaned much more money than any other player to golfers who either had to make a touch or go down the back stairs from a tournament hotel.

As a successful club professional at the Oak Park Country Club and the Detroit Golf Club, and from his ob-

servations when he was on the Spalding exhibition tour with Cooper, Little, and Thomson, Smith was more
familiar with home-pro jobs than any
other professional. That Spalding connection had also given him a sound
understanding of the pro-manufacturer
relationship.

Al Houghton, an able professional
who'd come up from the caddie ranks
around Washington, D.C., and was a
friend of many congressmen and government officials, was now chairman of
the PGA Manufacturers' Relations
Committee. Houghton believed that
golf professionals, more than any other
small retailers, had made a huge market that was becoming a price-cutting
field with stores being favored by manufacturers who were unloading their
bad guesses at prices murderous to the
pros' markets.

The Federal Trade Commission and
other agencies formed to protect smaller
retailers received plenty of attention
from Houghton. He turned out to be
an adept lobbyist for the PGA and its
members and showed a picture of
sports goods merchandising that was
entirely new to legislators and admin-
istrators in Washington. But he had
more effect on the golf goods manufacturers and sports goods dealers in general than he did on the PGA.

The PGA didn't know the golf-
marketing score in dollars, cents, and
percentages, nor has it learned since. In
recent years, only after the PGA and
manufacturers got kicked around in a
lawsuit concerning pro-only marketing
competition with the low-price retailing of other outlets were there indications of interest in marketing statistics
involving pros.

Houghton had Smith's support in his
inquiries concerning protecting professionals in the market they had de-

Al Houghton. PGA, photo by Hessler Henderson

veloped. However, the subject was too abstruse for the PGA membership at the time, and Houghton's committee report was put to sleep. But he did stir up manufacturers' interest, and they began to pay more attention to Washington.

Houghton had caddied for Presidents Wilson, Taft, and Harding. He'd seen President Wilson slip down a hill on the Presidential backside, laughed, and been reprimanded by Secret Service men. He became a PGA sectional and national official, and his club members loved him. He retired free from financial worries. He was the pro who pointed out that pro golf was a significant though not huge element in the nation's business. Smith also tried to get professionals and the public to realize the home professional's unique position in business but wasn't able to excite much interest among his colleagues.

Harvey Raynor had been hired as tournament supervisor to succeed Frank Caywood. Raynor had been a home professional and a good one. With him on the tournament staff were Ray O'Brien as Raynor's assistant; Betty Raynor, Harvey's wife, as field secretary; and Milton ("Zip") Davis as official scorer. The Tournament Committee had engaged Fred Corcoran as promotional director.

The players were getting themselves organized for business—the Tournament Committee listed eighty-nine as "approved tournament players." These men paid dues of $5 a tournament, up to $35 a year, and the books were kept separately from the PGA accounts. Arguments with sponsors were easing. During his presidency Joe Novak had smoothed away rough spots in sponsor-player relations. Horton Smith in his first year as president made good use of

his tournament experience by showing the players how to grow up as businessmen by cooperating more with sponsors who often had difficulties among themselves, especially on dates and appearance money. Ten or twelve of the sponsors formed an organization with the vigorous M. R. ("Monk") Wilson of San Antonio as chairman of the group.

There'd been a highly successful tour of U.S. pro stars Jimmy Demaret, Lloyd Mangrum, Ed Oliver, and Jim Turnesa to Australia arranged by the PGA, and the U.S.-Canadian pro tournament that began the Canada Cup international competition had received much favorable publicity. It cost John Jay Hopkins of General Dynamics plenty, but he was happy.

Through their Athletic Institute, club and ball manufacturers had given the Tournament Bureau $25,000 for "promotion" during the year. The Tournament Bureau had spent $63,358 during the year, and by the accounting then in fashion, PGA operations showed a net operating profit of $1,472.

There had been forty-eight tournaments and programs in 1952, with $675,000 prize money. The top event was a $75,000 purse for May's World Championship. Only twelve tournaments were for purses of more than $10,000, and fewer than fifty players won any money.

The 1952 PGA Championship at Big Spring in Louisville had made $13,000, and the Ryder Cup matches at Pinehurst early in November, 1951, had made $16,000 because Pinehurst President Richard Tufts minimized expenses and substantial income from the program. Ampol Petroleum Company of Australia had given $5,000 for the Australian trip to play for the Lakes Cup at Sydney. The Masters had given

Julius Boros. AG

$2,500 to the PGA, of which $1,500 went to the Tournament Bureau and the remainder was split between the Educational and Teaching and Relief committees as the PGA decided.

PGA membership had increased by 160 to 3,078 during 1952, and expenses had been reduced by moving the offices of the association to Dunedin in January. Two valued members of the staff didn't go along. Vic Trauscht, who had been with the association for four and a half years as Tom Crane's assistant, stayed in Chicago, as did Bob Gibson, editor of the association's magazine. Trauscht was succeeded by Harold Adams. Gibson also prepared and published the Tournament Bureau's new edition of its annual of tournament records and players' biographies, a service that had been begun by Bob Harlow and developed by Fred Corcoran. Although no one was ever able to compile statistics and other information on the professionals' important marketing operations, the tournament players seemed to involve no problem at this time.

Gibson offered to publish *The Professional Golfer* and pay the association $5,000 a year. The proposal was declined. An offer by a concessionaire who wanted the food and beverage outdoor sales at tournaments was also turned down. It had called for 5 percent of the gross on sales to go to the Tournament Bureau and 15 percent to the sponsors.

Outdoor pro-shop sales were growing at tournaments. Hats and caps, periscopes, seats, and rain garments were the items mainly in demand. Tournament matters that forecast important changes in operations included the offer by Bus Ham, sports editor of the *Washington Post,* to sponsor a PGA stroke-play championship for five years.

(The PGA changed its championship to stroke play in 1958.) Julius Boros, National Open Champion in 1952, wasn't eligible to play in the PGA Championship because he hadn't been a professional enough years to be eligible for PGA membership. That rule was changed, as was the practice of allowing numerous exemptions for tournament qualifications. Boros was elected by 90 percent of the PGA members and golf writers as the Professional Golfer of the Year for 1952.

Pabst raised prize money for its Open tournament at Milwaukee, charging the increase to its television advertising, and the tournament was televised locally. The next year the World Championship at George S. May's Tam O'Shanter Country Club was televised on what then passed for a national network but had only a few stations in the cities of the major Central states. In 1952, Fred Corcoran was trying to sell golf tournaments to television stations and advertisers, but they weren't ready. They liked the quality of the golf atmosphere and market but didn't have the equipment to cover more than a couple of holes near the clubhouse.

One unpleasant international development turned up in the tournament field. Jimmy Demaret was fined for accepting an invitation from the Mexican Golf Association and playing in the Mexican Open, thus skipping a conflicting U.S. tournament, and the resulting newspaper publicity was unfavorable to the Tournament Committee. Pedro Suinaga, president of the Mexican Golf Association, in an expression of regret so polished it was embarrassing to our side, offered to pay the Demaret fine. Jimmy wasn't one to stay sore, so he wrote a check and laughed the whole thing off. The incident was just one of those things. A party of Texas and Mexican golf enthusiasts honored Jack O'Brien, the San Antonio newspaperman who'd started the Texas Open in 1922 and began what changed the "winter tour" into the tournament circuit. The Texas PGA gave O'Brien an award.

In the home work during 1952, much had been accomplished at Dunedin. Leo O'Grady was hired as the pro-manager of the PGA National Club at a moderate salary and given 15 percent of the net of the dining room and bar, the total hardly affording him a chance to become pro golf's first millionaire.

National Golf Day, which Craig Wood and Horton Smith had arranged with officials of *Life,* got a good start, with $80,000 being raised. The choice of play day—Memorial Day—was bad, as too many other events were going at pros' clubs. But there is no other welfare and educational fund-raising operation in professional sports quite like the PGA's National Golf Day. The home pros themselves do the work of collecting from members or fee-course players, and although the entry fee is only $1 for playing in a nationwide net competition against the lowest score in the "Round of the Champions" (the PGA and National Open of that year), that dollar is not always easily given.

The first year's proceeds were divided half to the USO, half of the remaining $40,000 to the American Women's Voluntary Services, then $3,000 to the Swing Clubs of women golfers working at veterans' hospitals. The USGA Green Section got $3,000; the PGA Benevolent Fund, $1,000; the PGA Relief Fund, $4,000; the PGA Educational Fund, $3,000; the National Junior Chamber of Commerce junior championships, $3,000; the National Caddie Association scholarships, $1,500; and the caddie scholarship funds of the Western Michigan, New England, Rhode Island, Michigan, and Pacific Northwest golf associations together got $1,500.

Fred L. Riggin, Jr., Michigan industrialist and prominent in senior golf, was president of the National Golf Fund, which screened applications for National Golf Day funds. Tom Crane was secretary-treasurer. The directors were J. E. King of *Life* magazine, Milt Woodard of the Western Golf Association, and Herb Graffis of *Golfdom* and *Golfing* magazines.

Later distribution went mainly to the caddie scholarship funds of the Western and twenty-six other golf associations, coordinated nationwide golf turf-grass research according to the expert recommendations of the USGA Green Section, the scholarship fund of the Golf Course Superintendents' Association, the American Women's Voluntary Services, the National Amputee Golf Association, and the Relief, Benevolent, and Educational funds of the PGA. The PGA's members and the officials of the distributing organization, the National Golf Fund, insisted on this unselfish policy. Of course they never got credit for this sportsmanship.

Until recently, playing professionals never showed a willingness to share in the PGA's fund-raising other than sometimes having the PGA and National Open champions contribute their services and expenses in playing in the Round of the Champions. The playing stars missed a bright chance for favorable public relations by not making much of a move to contribute tax-free checks until club pros had raised about $2 million on National Golf Days, an annual pro-public goodwill event originated by the high regard the public held for Horton Smith and

Craig Wood, tournament stars of their times.

At the 1952 annual meeting, a pension plan with professionals and their clubs sharing payments was discussed for the first time. Almost twenty years later, such a plan was put into effect at some clubs on a basis worked out by PGA advisers. The subject was brought up by Robert Hudson, who said that, considering the data easily available from PGA Seniors and the Quarter Century Club, it seemed as though professionals at private clubs, public courses, and privately owned fee courses were actuarily well qualified for the sort of equitable pension plans that industry had been compelled to put into effect because of union demands and the competitive labor market. Considering their uncertain duration of employment because of the vagaries of club politics and changing membership, plus the fact that they had no job protection other than satisfactory service and personality, members of the Advisory Committee concluded that home professionals deserved a pension plan.

Two additions were made to the Advisory Committee that year. One was Waco Turner of Ardmore, Oklahoma, an oil producer who'd built a course on his ranch and who, with his wife, put on lucrative and entertaining tournaments. The other was A. T. Jergins of Los Angeles, another wealthy oil man and pro golf fan.

The Advisory Committee seemed to be a bit snoopy in its 1952 meeting with PGA officials and the Executive Committee. "We suggested that the PGA might retain its national headquarters in a central location," said Hudson, "and several of us believed that real-estate men could be interested in building a course, clubhouse, and office building free for the PGA in suburban Chicago as the main feature of a golf residential development. Was that possibility ever explored?"

It wasn't. Years later, the PGA was offered almost the same sort of arrangement in Florida. Only by luckily and suddenly awakening did it save itself from paying out $2 million or more for developing the property that, without the PGA headquarters and courses that added a vast premium to the project, would have been just another subdivision.

The last-day session focused on pro business education as usual, and Julius Boros talked on the mechanical aspects of tournament play as distinguished from everyday play. Marilynn Smith spoke on teaching women. Al Ciuci, Bill Gordon, and Joe Jemsek expressed their thoughts on the training of assistants. A panel of instructors traded ideas on how to give playing lessons. The old playing lesson seemed to develop golfers more effectively than the now-customary, timesaving teaching-tee method. Harold Sargent, chairman of the Teaching Committee, had the hunch that the playing lesson was effective because it put responsibility for learning and demonstrating results on the pupil, while lesson-tee instruction had the pupil expecting to be taught without too much effort on his part.

There were talks on merchandising and a report by Herb Graffis on how professionals and superintendents were collaborating with the National Golf Foundation in getting more courses built. Lou Bola, an official of the Indiana section, described effective section work in promoting golf and the PGA in all thirty PGA sections.

Norman Butler, chairman of the Public Relations Committee, said that while the PGA sections were increasingly successful in getting across stories of their service to golf and golfers, he found it puzzling that PGA publicity on a national basis was almost exclusively devoted to the fifty or a hundred members who didn't give a hoot whether a member scored 70 or 170, or whether that same member bought a set of woods, irons, a bag, two dozen balls, or even as much as a single package of tees a year. "We've got the most useful business organization in sports, but who knows it?" said Butler.

Tom Crane got the PGA out of a troublesome spot when he discovered the Perfumers' Guild of America was using PGA as its insignia. Friendly neighborhood lawyers settled the situation easily and forever.

For years the PGA had been evolving in about the same way and experiencing the same problems without coming up with any answers. At the 1953 annual meeting, November 6 through 13, 1953, at the Sheraton Cadillac Hotel, Detroit, the association's thirty-seventh, officials and delegates gave the PGA a critical examination. The findings revealed that a great deal of revision was needed in operations and possibly even in the organization's basic structure.

Horton Smith was president; Harry Moffitt, secretary; Harold Sargent, treasurer; and Thomas W. Crane continued as executive secretary. Vice-presidents were Dave Bonella, Joe Devaney, George Lake, Tom Mahan, Henry McGarvey, Wally Mund, Maurice O'Connor, Charles Vittitoe, James D. Fogerty, and Cary Middlecoff, who was also cochairman of the Tournament Committee with Jerry Barber.

Delegates from the thirty sections and association officials were jolted by the report of business engineers of the

George S. May Company who had studied the workings of the PGA and found it deficient as a first-class business—mainly because of outgrown procedures or methods that had been poor to start with. It was urgently recommended that PGA paperwork be reduced and simplified; that a system be devised to eliminate the high peak load in the headquarters section; that headquarters business be coordinated so that work could be more effectively handled; that bank accounts be consolidated; and that accounting and payroll be simplified.

The May analysts concluded that PGA headquarters office personnel seemed competent and diligent, although both salaries and offices were rather unattractive. The tenor of the report was that the PGA business methods had not kept pace with its increased membership and responsibilities or with the growth of golf in general.

There was some improvement when the offices were moved from Chicago to Dunedin, but the Executive Committee couldn't decide whether to give Tom Crane authority to modernize the PGA's office work. The professionals' own business was not the kind to make them sensitive to the developments and demands of office work for a nationwide organization of over 3,000 members with activities spread widely in character and geography.

Attention to the headquarters office was diverted by sharp differences of opinion regarding the PGA form and policy of government. Horton Smith and others believed that the PGA was becoming too centralized. They thought that the original plan in which sections had responsibility for their regional problems was the primary practical function of an organization of professional golfers; and they felt that

collective attention should be given to matters of nationwide or international interest such as the PGA Championship and Ryder Cup competitions, insurance, relief funds, manufacturers' relations, credit rating, and golf market competitive conditions.

The trouble with this view was that the sections lacked the organization or facilities to handle the business. Few pro sectional officials were letter writers or office men who could care for their sections' business during part of the Mondays away from the club. Eventually a few PGA sections hired full-time executive secretaries in the person of bright young businesswomen or keen young men who knew golf. The acquisition of such energetic and informed personnel was possibly one of the most valuable, though little considered, elements in the development of the PGA as a business organization. Headquarters had to be coordinated with these alert people and communications kept open or questions would be asked by sectional officials and members. Besides, sectional and national officials of the PGA changed every few years, as did officials of private clubs, and that was why defects in management had cost clubs and the PGA ill-afforded time and money.

The debate about revising PGA organization policy had thoughtful delegates on both sides of the subject in a quandary. The Tournament Bureau had grown into such a big, worrisome, and expensive operation for the PGA that the May Company business engineers and prominent members of the Advisory Committee suggested that the PGA abandon it. The Tournament Bureau was concerned with a relatively small part of golf business and often was in difficulties for which the PGA in general was blamed as inconsiderate, greedy, and ungrateful. The PGA had experienced a near replay of the trouble pro golf had had in the first decade of the century when too many professionals in tournaments were regarded by amateurs as undesirables and club professionals had difficulty in getting their clubs to host Open tournaments.

There were able, thoughtful tournament professionals who'd tried to get their fellow players to share in financing and managing the show business part of the game, but they were unable to get tournament golf on a steady business basis. The Tournament Bureau was in bad shape financially. Manufacturers were withdrawing the $25,000 yearly support, and sponsors were displeased.

Horton Smith realized that the tournament players were as much a part of golf as putting was a part of the game. Fundamentally, the popularity of tournaments depended on how successful the club pros were in developing interest in golf. After his tournament years were over, it was the usual practice for a touring pro to get a job at a private or resort club while a new generation scored in the sports headlines. And this was why Smith insisted that the tournament circuit's growing pains could be amicably worked out within the PGA family.

Jerry Barber and Cary Middlecoff for the Tournament Committee reported that on November 6, "We met all day and all night, it seemed, with all of our committee and twenty-two summer tournament sponsors and eleven winter tournament sponsors in an effort to establish policies and procedures and to get organized together." No agreements seem to have been put in writing.

The Tournament Bureau ended the fiscal year with revenue of $72,143, of which $25,000 was from the club and ball manufacturers' Athletic Insurance and $35,300 was sponsors' fees. The deficit for the year was $3,607. The bureau had enough money on hand to operate for two months, then again would have to borrow from other departments of the PGA treasury.

It certainly couldn't be said that any phase of the PGA operation was extravagant. Tom Crane as executive secretary carried a heavy work load for $15,000 a year. Fred Corcoran as Tournament Bureau promotion director had been hired at $12,000 a year, but when funds got slim, Corcoran volunteered to work for $1 a year plus a commission on new tournaments, television, and radio. Television was beginning to look more promising, but a great deal of selling remained to be done. (It was discovered some years later that Corcoran still had television rights on PGA cosponsored tournaments because of his 1953 $1-per-year deal, which was still in existence. Corcoran laughed and told PGA officials to forget it and quit worrying. They don't come like that in sports anymore.)

William Rach was hired to edit *The Professional Golfer*. He was paid $6,500, plus 25 percent on any increase in advertising revenue over the preceding year. There was no increase.

Leo O'Grady as pro manager at Dunedin was paid $250 a month, plus dining-room concessions and a split of the bar profit with the PGA. He hopefully stuck at that for about two years, then concluded he could no longer support the PGA on his savings and credit, and got himself another job.

Horton Smith's own extensive travel supported his contention that the PGA needed to revise its operations drastically because too few men were expected to do too much. In 1953, Horton had made fifteen trips to various sections, one into Mexico on PGA business, and numerous trips from his Detroit job to PGA Chicago offices. It was tourist-class air travel and no luxury suites on PGA money for the thrifty Smith. He saw too many other places where the PGA needed to spend money —if it had money to spend. He also discovered one case that especially distressed him.

It concerned Alex Pirie, a founding member and the fourth president of the PGA. Pirie, a kindly Scot who became an American asset, had spent his own money on PGA business when the organization was young, and now, at the end of the course, he was slowly dying of a brain tumor. This was before hospital insurance and benefits were commonplace, so here was a proud old gentleman, who'd thought of obligations to unfortunate brother professionals when the PGA was established, callously left to his own devices by the men he had helped so much. Something certainly had gone wrong in the insurance and relief planning of the association.

When the 1953 meeting convened, the PGA had 3,213 members. Harold Sargent had the association's financial statement consolidated and printed in the proceedings of the 1953 meeting. This was in line with the May business management experts' suggestion that PGA finances be simplified for easier handling and so members could understand what was happening. The PGA general fund receipts for the fiscal year 1953 were $135,391, about twice the Tournament Bureau's intake, and the PGA finished the year with $21,883 over expenses. The PGA Championship at the Birmingham (Michigan) Country Club, July 1 through 7, had no difficulty meeting its guarantee, with 35,-000 tickets sold and a program with a record 314 pages of advertising sold. The program advertising gross was $107,000 and firmly established Detroit as the Klondike of the roving prospectors for lodes of what has been laughingly called "courtesy" advertising.

An embarrassing problem arose in reorganizing the Advisory Committee, which had grown to twenty-nine members. Many of them were inactive, and the active ones were constantly remarking that their advice was sought too late and considered too rarely. George S. May was appointed chairman of the 1954 Advisory Committee. Harry Radix was made secretary, and David Griffith of Detroit was vice-chairman. Hugh Rader and Arthur Zebedee of Detroit and James Bowes of Chicago were added to the committee. Several other members were quietly dropped.

While President Dwight D. Eisenhower was proposed by Ed Dudley as honorary chairman of the PGA and elected unanimously, few other matters were unanimously decided. Dunedin was getting to be as much of a headache as the Tournament Bureau, though not so costly. The proposal in 1952 to move PGA headquarters from Chicago to Dunedin had a vote of seventy-two against the move and thirty-three for it. At the 1953 meeting, the Central New York section proposed that headquarters be moved from 134 North LaSalle Street, Chicago, to Dunedin, and lost by a heavier margin than was polled against the move the previous year.

Tom Mahan, a New England veteran, told the officials and delegates: "We are fighting a losing battle at Dunedin. The course has been in horrible shape for years and is getting progressively worse." Denny Shute took a

Irvin Schloss. PGA, photo by Roger Luce

more optimistic view: "Greenkeeping is a long-range program. We have had five or six greenkeepers in a few years, and none of them had enough money to take care of a course."

The new man in charge of the PGA National Course that winter was Hugh Moore from Albany, Georgia. Moore had a high reputation for getting Southern courses rehabilitated, but the starved, sandy situation at Dunedin was to defeat him, too. Nevertheless the club was busy in the fall and winter, mainly with Seniors, and a vote to abandon it, taken at the 1953 meeting, lost by a big margin. The PGA National Course picked up in favor when Teacher's, distillers of Scotch, began sponsoring the PGA Seniors' Championship in 1953 on a basis that paid the expenses of sectional qualifiers to Dunedin and eventually the expenses

of U.S. and British Senior champions to international competition. In any case, all PGA of America Senior members were eligible to compete at Dunedin, and there were large fields and pleasant rivalry in all age classes.

Irv Schloss had organized and conducted the instruction groups at Dunedin with professionals comparing their experiences in teaching. This was the beginning of Schloss's long service, which was to win him a Horton Smith prize for usefulness in improving golf teaching. The Smith award was established almost twenty years after Schloss's work began at Dunedin.

A new award was established in 1953 by the Special Awards Committee headed by Dugan Aycock. It was the Robert E. Harlow trophy given to the Golf Professional of the Year, for outstanding service to his members (or fee-course players), to his profession, to his community, and as a professional who in his public and private life exemplified the high standards to which the PGA was dedicated. The award was the suggestion of Richard Tufts, president of Pinehurst, who believed the PGA had been neglecting its obligation to recognize highly admirable members. The choice of the Golf Professional of the Year was much more difficult than selecting the paid player of the year.

Class A membership standards and performances among the PGA's home pros were so high that actually two hundred or more might have qualified for the Harlow award. At first, selections were made by sectional committees of men and women amateurs, golf writers, and PGA members; eventually selections were made by sectional committees of PGA members, then by national officials. Although the award has never received deserved national publicity, it does demonstrate that the character of PGA personnel serving the public is probably far above that of most other professional sports and surpassed by none.

At the 1953 meeting, the PGA again tried to further upgrade its membership classification. A proposal was made that Master Professional rating eligibility require ten or more years of service at a first-class place, private or public. The motion failed. In 1972, the Master Pro class was established by factors of years of excellent service at a first-class club, service to other professionals and the PGA, playing proficiency, and a written examination. James D. Fogerty of St. Louis became the first man to earn the Master rating. In 1953, he was serving his first term as a PGA national vice-president.

The PGA Hall of Fame Committee chairman, Tom Walsh, announced the first group of choices: Willie Anderson, Tommy Armour, Jim Barnes, Chick Evans, Walter Hagen, Ben Hogan, Robert T. Jones, Jr., John McDermott, Byron Nelson, Francis Ouimet, Gene Sarazen, Alex Smith, Sam Snead, Jerry Travers, and Walter Travis.

An offer was made by a Yonkers, New York, group to build the PGA a hall of fame, but the proposal was declined. The PGA didn't want to "commercialize its choices of American golf's most illustrious ones."

In 1953 the PGA was asked by the USGA to work out free admission for PGA members to PGA championships and to help speed up play in tournaments. Some delegates said that the USGA slowed play with long rough and no fore-caddies.

In its home work for 1953, the PGA extended its group life and accident insurance and arranged for more coverage on liability, accident, robbery, and fire insurance. Robbery of pro shops was

James Fogarty. Photo by Bill Knight

rapidly increasing. Pension plans were again discussed with insurance companies, but again the lack of security in many pro jobs was the hurdle that couldn't be jumped. (Years later, of course, insurance companies devised pension plans for pros and other club employees who took work at other clubs.) And a resolution to restrict membership in the PGA to those of the Caucasian race was thrown out as being a subject primarily of interest to employing clubs.

The closing session, as usual, reviewed highlights of the year's golf instruction and business education. This program marked the debut of Ernie Sabayrac, a former caddie and assistant pro and now a salesman of apparel to pro shops, in a merchandising expert role. O. J. Noer, Milwaukee Sewerage Commission agronomist, again spoke on what was new that the pro should know about golf turf. Gordon Leslie of American Fork and Hoe described developments in steel golf shafts. Warren Orlick, who much later was to become PGA president, and Thomas McMahon, Chicago District Golf Association former president, discussed correct handicapping in developing competitive interest in golf. John Walter of the *Detroit News* and Bill Rach of the PGA outlined what the professional could do to increase local publicity for his club and himself. But just as always, the annual PGA meeting failed to come up with a newsworthy story about helping golfers that would receive sports-page space all over the country.

Education of PGA members and assistants and of the average golfer was a feature of the thirty-eighth annual meeting of the PGA. The sessions were held at the Hotel Lowry, St. Paul, November 27 through December 3, 1954, with Horton Smith as president, Harry Moffitt as secretary, and Harold Sargent as treasurer. Thirty sections and the Tournament Bureau's delegate, Cary Middlecoff, attended.

Reports were given on the spring business schools conducted by eleven sections. Professionals and their assistants attended these seminars. The sections holding the business schools were Philadelphia, Pacific Northwest, Western New York, Indiana, Illinois, New Jersey, Tri-State, Middle Atlantic, Northeast New York, Southern California, and Minnesota. Golf enthusiasts who were authorities on merchandising, advertising and publicity, physiology and psychology, and teaching, and experts from the professionals' own corps and from the manufacturers of golf goods and the course and clubhouse management departments, served as instructors.

There were at least two so-called clinics for assistants during 1954, one in the Illinois section, the other in Indiana. Many of the assistants needed clinical instruction. Some eager youths had never even been told how to clean clubs. When it came down to repairing a grip or some little trouble with the sole plate or other minor repair, the boys were helpless. So factories of leading manufacturers were jammed with clubs needing simple repairs that took as long as three months when the work could have been done in three days at golf shops.

Keeping shops clean and smartly arranged was another subject that assistants had to master mainly on their own. They got a bit more teaching technique from their Master pros because they wanted to learn the answers themselves, but all too few of them knew how to teach, and members complained when they had to take lessons from assistants. And as for fitting clubs, assistants who had never known the trial-and-error method of bench clubmaking to fit clubs to members were at a complete loss. And yet every successful veteran professional admitted that a pro was only as useful as his assistants. These sectional assistants' schools became the kindergarten for the PGA's most profitable education effort—the business schools that began at Dunedin and spread to many sections.

The teaching job of the PGA, according to experienced professionals, was the most frustrating of all the association's hopes. The PGA's initial aim had been to achieve deserved respect for the professional, then to provide a living income that would attract desirable men to responsible jobs, then to develop players with instruction that would have them playing more and better and bringing others into the game.

PGA professionals were making progress everywhere except in lower-average scoring by amateur golfers. Despite far better playing equipment and courses, as near as could be figured, that average had shown little improvement in the past fifty years. The statistics, of course, were difficult to compare, but to the credit of the PGA professionals, they were far more dissatisfied with the scoring standard of amateur golf than the amateurs were.

Professional golf's first educational objective in the United States was teaching. The pioneer pros reasoned that the better one played, the more one played. As far as anyone has been able to learn since, the old boys were right. The next educational target of the founding pros was proficiency in course maintenance. A better course invited more play.

The pioneers got fairly good results in instruction. They taught mainly in playing lessons, in which they shared the responsibility for the lesson with the pupil. If a shot was misplayed in a playing lesson, there was a chance for instant expert tuition and a quick examination of the pupil's attention, concentration, and capacity to learn. When players became too numerous for the time required for the playing lesson, the lesson tee was substituted. The time between the lesson on the tee and the execution of the shot allowed too much margin for error, too many opportunities for blaming the professional for what the pupil didn't do.

During 1954, the problem of getting assistants accepted as competent instructors received considerable attention. Male club members refused to take lessons from assistants. Women didn't mind. Many professionals admitted that women pupils made more progress than the men. Why? It took a long time for PGA pros to figure out the answer. Women realized they had to learn; men expected to be taught.

During winter discussions on the practice tee at Dunedin, the old-timers debated for hours about how to fit clubs as keen assistant pros asked questions. Manufacturers had devised formulas that theoretically "perfectly matched" sets. But to whom were the sets *matched?* Expert players and veteran masters of bench clubmaking described their experiences with clubs that felt as though they were natural projections of the hands. They told of impressive results obtained by ordinary pupils of theirs, using different clubs. Willie Ogg, one of the older masters of bench clubmaking, and Al Watrous, who sold an exceptional number of steel-shafted clubs in seeking the ideal ones for his members (clubs that would save four or five strokes a round), were leaders of those exploratory sessions. All the professionals in those researches knew that one of the greatest ways a professional could help his players was with *precision* club fitting. But how to master it?

The relationship between their members' requirements and the pro-shop stocks of clubs was a topic that affected buying by pros. Previously they had bought mainly what they liked. Another phase of the club-fitting study concerned the extent to which the desires of the expert players should dictate the design of clubs for the ordinary golfer, who needed help from clubs that the experts refined by their own dexterity. That debate, fired up in 1954 business schools, still continues. An amusing sidelight is that the experts have many variations in the lofts, lies, and other specifications of their clubs.

At the 1954 PGA meeting, one section hoped to limit the use of noted professionals' names on cheap clubs. It asked that manufacturers put star players' names only on clubs that were the same in every respect as those the players used in tournaments. The stars wouldn't stand still for that. The next PGA move was to be a request for some action on the matter in Washington, either by new legislation or by existing regulations enforceable by the Federal Trade Commission or some other body.

Then it was discovered that the Washington and Chicago bills of the PGA included $30,000 for lawyers' fees in 1954. This brought loud cries of pain from PGA members and officials who'd never thought of the PGA in any legal jam more serious than parking too close to a fireplug. The PGA was learning that the law was all part of its program of education.

A lesson boom was reported for 1954 —all the result of National Golf Day, on which *Life* magazine had spent $60,000, and the previously mentioned film, *Keep 'Em on the Fairway,* which was directed by Harold Sargent and others on the Teaching Committee and showed most types of men and women players and pointed out differences in their styles. Featured in the film were Ben Hogan, Sam Snead, Bob Jones, Horton Smith, Byron Nelson, Cary Middlecoff, Lawson Little, Pat Abbott, Louise Suggs, Fred McLeod, Lloyd Mangrum, Ed Oliver, Jerry Barber, Lew Worsham, Walter Burkemo, Shelley Mayfield, Jimmy Hines, Johnny Dawson, Bing Crosby, and Bob Hope.

The film was made in Palm Springs, Atlanta, and the Dallas Jones studio in Chicago, and there were about 3,000 showings in the United States, in servicemen's recreation centers overseas, and in Canada, Mexico, and Britain.

Golf club parties and luncheons of businessmen's organizations also used it to draw attendance. In hundreds of instances local pros were commentators. The film was valuable public relations for the professionals and introduced many of them as entertaining and instructive luncheon club speakers.

The film was shown in installments on one hundred television programs. Much discussion about golf technique was started, and the businessmen who saw the film expected it to do wonders for their golf. It didn't because they wouldn't stay at their lessons long enough to learn.

National Golf Day, 1954, had 133,-000 golfers at 2,600 courses. Of those who paid the Golf Day entry fee, 9,488 were women and 1,643 were caddies. Not many of them beat the 64 that Ben Hogan shot on the par-72 Baltusrol Lower course where the 1954 Open was to be played later in the year and was won by Ed Furgol. Hogan, who had won the 1953 Open at Oakmont and had been the PGA's Professional Golfer of 1953, played the Round of the Champions with the resident pro, Johnny Farrell, Claude Harmon, and the New Jersey Junior Champion. The Baltusrol Lower course for Hogan's Golf Day round was 200 yards shorter than for the Open, but the way Ben had been playing, 200 yards longer or shorter didn't make much difference.

That year Hogan received the largest amount ever paid for a golf instruction article. *Life* paid him a reported $10,-000, then *Life*'s companion magazine *Sports Illustrated* doubled the amount by reprinting the article before getting a clearance from Hogan. The "secret" of his winning game, as might have been expected, was declared by veteran professionals to be a "wristy" performance—as favored by James Braid, winner of five British Opens, and developed further by George Duncan, another British star of long ago. Hogan was now and here. His revelation did not revolutionize golf or golf instruction, but it did show there were not many techniques of smart business Ben Hogan needed to be taught.

Another conflict that popped into the open in 1954 pertained to golf course superintendents, who had organized as the National Association of Greenkeepers of America ten years after the PGA was established. They complained that they were doing the work and applying the latest developments in golf course management and distinctly improving the standard of golf course condition but the professionals were getting all the public credit. The superintendents' irritation was further aggravated by the remarks tournament players made about courses.

Most of the pro jobs had been pro-greenkeeper work until about 1910, when course maintenance became too much for one man who also had pro responsibilities. State agricultural experiment stations and schools and USGA Green Section research and field services, as well as the services of agronomists and salesmen of golf course fertilizer, chemicals, and machinery, had advanced golf course management to a level with the educational requirements and responsibility of other golf club department heads.

The explosion came when the Northeastern New York Golf Course Superintendents' Association declared pro-superintendents were ineligible for membership. Some clubs in the area, who couldn't afford two good men, had been compelled to have combination jobs. There was much controversy not on a plane of sweet reasonableness, but

the examination of the business education of the superintendents, professionals, and clubhouse managers possibly did some good all around. Tempers cooled. Understanding and cooperation improved all the jobs and the financial picture of the clubs and fee-course operations.

Instruction from various viewpoints was featured in the meeting's education program. Les Bolstad, an excellent amateur before he became a professional, had been highly successful with innovations he'd devised for group and individual instruction at his alma mater, the University of Minnesota, where he was golf instructor. He demonstrated those methods with university students as his subjects. John P. Hawley, Jr., president of a large pump manufacturing company, next gave an astonishing exhibition of approaching and putting. Twin City professionals had said he was the best they'd ever seen at the short game on a course or indoors. He certainly didn't get stage fright. His system was the simple one of a steady head and a grip and stroke that kept the putter face straight across the line of the putt.

Others who lectured on the techniques of playing and instruction were Ed Furgol, Jackson Bradley, Cary Middlecoff, Joe Novak, Harold Sargent, Jerry Barber, Lloyd Mangrum, David Lilly, and Willie Kidd. George Edmond of the *St. Paul Pioneer Press Dispatch* and J. E. King and Hudson Stoddard of *Life* spoke on pro public and press relations and on National Golf Day. Joe Dey of the USGA talked on rules. James Watson of the Toro Manufacturing Company outlined new methods in golf course maintenance. The differences between superintendents and professionals, which had been bitter earlier in the year, were soothed by diplomatic addresses by Norman Johnson, president of the Golf Course Superintendents' Association, and Tom McGuffey, president of the Club Managers' Association.

Rex McMorris, executive director of the National Golf Foundation, described how the foundation went about getting new private and public courses built and how employment of pros, superintendents, and managers had been increased. That situation could stand a great deal of improvement, as the PGA Employment Committee reported it had an average of between 250 and 300 members looking for jobs, and only 27 openings, according to PGA files. McMorris urged that the PGA Employment Committee keep a close watch on National Golf Foundation information concerning courses being planned or under construction. His advice was never taken by any organized campaign, by a PGA Employment Committee, or by the employment committees of the GCSA and CMAA, although the foundation's frequent reports noted where competent men were needed.

Dr. Howard Longstaff of the University of Minnesota talked on the "Psychology of Selling," and Herb Graffis of *Golfdom* and the National Golf Foundation introduced a slide film, *Par for the Pro Department,* which explained studying the pro's market from records readily compiled, setting up sales quotas and buying, then arranging displays to accelerate buying. Graffis pointed to the contrast between pros' playing a course on which par was a reasonable, definite, helpful objective and doing business in a market where sales par based on number, character, purchasing capacity of members or course patrons, volume, character

and display of merchandise for sale, traffic in the shop, selling expenses, and overhead should establish a business par for the job but rarely did so.

The *Golfdom* magazine editor reported that pro salesmen had told him that about 90 percent of the dollar volume done in pro shops was buying and the remainder was selling done as a result of the initiative and energy of the pro and his staff. With possibly the most successful real selling campaign in sporting goods marketing history under way at pro shops, Herb Graffis was reminding PGA officials that pros seldom did a first-class selling job.

Joe Graffis, *Golfdom* publisher, had the conviction that an immense market for Christmas gift golf goods could be developed by professionals. He devised *Christmas Shopping at Your Pro Shop,* a colorful booklet showing a fascinating array of golf goods as a guide to the gift shopper. The professionals' names, clubs, addresses, and telephone numbers were on the shopping guide cover.

Christmas Shopping at Your Pro Shop put a lucky thirteenth month into the pros' business calendar and in a few years became so effective in sales promotion that for numerous professionals December was the biggest selling month of the year. Gift givers and receivers both welcomed the golf suggestions. Many shops sold their inventories instead of carrying them over until the next year. Manufacturers stated that the gift booklet was the best one thing that had happened to improve the pro credit situation, as it converted inventories into money and sold members much that they might have bought from other retailers. However, the booklet involved serious production problems because manufacturers did not have their next year's merchandise ready in time for the publication's deadline. The booklet had an increasing number of users each year, until nearly 700 pros were using it the last year *Golfdom* published it.

Harold Sargent, treasurer, tried to get across a picture of PGA revenue and expenses plain enough for the delegates to explain to the PGA's 3,386 members, 2,559 of whom were Class A. Sargent noted that the Tournament Bureau service fee had been increased so that sponsors now paid $2,000. The general fund had an income of $158,-535; there was net income of $9,739; and tournament income was $63,906, with a net loss of $3,462.

The Relief Fund paid $60 a month to any indigent professional and $40 a month to an indigent PGA member. Eddie Schultz, a Northeastern New York delegate, proposed that the amounts be increased and the increase be taken from National Golf Day proceeds, but no increase was voted. It was discovered that the professionals in need must be a proud lot; their requirements had to be discovered by others.

Sargent listed as percentages of the PGA income during the previous year: members' dues and initiation fees, 31.24; Tournament Bureau, 20.36; PGA National Golf Club, 16.32; magazine, 16.32; PGA Championship, 11.82; Benevolent and Relief funds, 2.08; and other sources, 1.86.

The treasurer accounted for the year's dollars in the following percentages: Tournament Bureau, 21.31; magazine, 16.25; PGA National Golf Club, 15.74; Chicago office, 11.51; members' life insurance, 8.61; PGA Championship, 8.22; excess of income over expenses, 8.18; annual meeting, 3.65; Ryder Cup (1953), 1.65; Seniors'

Championship, 1.06; Benevolent and Relief funds, .34; and all other expenses, 3.48.

No money was spent in a Horton Smith administration without a double-take at the bills. The 1953 annual meeting cost a tight $14,000, and the rental of the Chicago headquarters at the Loop was $7,000 a year. Until the PGA moved its offices to Dunedin, Smith argued, if the PGA stayed in or near Chicago, it would get better quarters for less money in a suburb.

All forty-two committees had a busy year with Smith and Tom Crane crowding them. The Hall of Fame Committee got offers to have a building in Dunedin. Greensboro, North Carolina, also offered the PGA a headquarters building, but the officers weren't interested.

The tournament situation had been in a rare condition of peace and progress during the year. Smith knew the tournament picture from all angles better than anyone else in golf, and he continued to travel widely as a PGA official and player in the United States, Canada, and South America. The 1954 fiscal year of the PGA had forty-six tournaments, with $854,500 in purses. Bob Toski, with $65,891, was the leading money winner and was assured of that distinction by winning George S. May's World Championship. Money was spread around fairly well, with thirty-four players each winning more than $6,000 during the year.

Professional tournament golf was lucky to have Robert Leacox of Kansas City appointed coordinator of schedules in 1954. Leacox, a wealthy tire dealer in Kansas City, took the difficult assignment on terms that might accurately be described as "just for the hell of it." He got no salary,

Bob Toski. PGA

and he loved golf. Because of his interest in local tournaments, he was familiar with scheduling problems from the viewpoint of the sponsors, the players, the Tournament Bureau, and the PGA in general. Even at that date, schedules were somewhat complicated by such foreign events as the Ryder Cup, the Australian Lakes trophy, and Mexican and South American competition. Australia was developing fine professionals, and W. G. Walkley and W. M. Leonard of Ampol Petroleum, Limited, helped build the show and the players with prize money. Walkley later became a director of the International Golf Association and arranged for two of the Canada Cup tournaments to be held in that country.

Leacox devised the schedule so there would be a minimum of travel between tournaments. He tried to get the program set well in advance, and in a few cases was so successful that sponsors who didn't decide promptly about their dates were disturbed by the possibility of tournaments crowding them. That

happened when Leacox signed William McDonald, the trailer magnate, to sponsor the 1955 Pan American Open at the Ingleside Club in Los Angeles and infuriated the Los Angeles Junior Chamber of Commerce.

The Palm Beach tournament was a bright spot on the circuit, with Elmer Ward, head of the sponsoring company, giving the Tournament Bureau 20 percent of the gross. The PGA Seniors got their championship award problem settled by deciding to have each yearly winner's name engraved on the Bourne trophy, which was given by Horton Smith's father-in-law when the Seniors' event was started, and having the Teacher's trophy awarded yearly.

There was talk about a trophy to be given annually to the winner of the driving contest at the PGA Championship, but the talk vanished in air and the driving contest was eventually discontinued. At the 1954 Championship at Keller Park, St. Paul, Roberto De Vicenzo won the event with a drive of 301 yards. He got $75. Second for distance and accuracy was Ed Furgol, with 297 yards for his longest shot. Chick Harbert beat Walter Burkemo, 4 and 3, for the title. The 1955 Championship was going to the Meadowbrook Country Club in suburban Detroit, with a $41,500 guarantee.

Frank Stamburger, a delegate from Kansas City, Missouri, brought up for the first time a subject that was to have a wide effect on golf business history —the golf cart. Golf carts had been in use for a few years, and daring professionals had been buying and renting them when caddies weren't available. In the autumn, when caddies were back in school, the golf carts were godsends. They brought much business to the clubhouse, and as leaf sweeping was standard operating procedure, the cars meant much more play. For the older players the carts were the answer to much more golf, but in the spring, with the course still soggy, the superintendents complained about the damage done by cart traffic.

Stamburger discussed whether clubs or members should own the carts or lease them, how they should be rented, and where the pros figured in the picture. He talked about insurance, the cost of operation and repairs, the possible profits and risks, and damage to courses. When Stamburger seemed to be running out of breath, Leo Fraser told how a pro got $7 a round and a nice storage profit if a member owned a car. Then a Southern professional said that good black caddies were hard to get, and the carts were going to run the caddies out of business. Then some-

body mentioned clubs in the South that were kept going by the cart revenue.

There was a great deal of talk but no agreement about what action the PGA might take if the golf cart developed into a profitable item. But the subject was dragged out into boring detail at the meeting, and this was regrettable because in less than twenty years golf cart revenue was so big and so vital to golf that, in comparison, tournament players' purses shrank to nothing. Forecasts were made at the 1954 meeting that golf cart revenue would be high in the millions, but no one ventured the fantastic guess that in the coming years golf cart revenue would be more than a quarter of a billion dollars a year and exceed pro-shop income.

21

A Quiet Year of Growing Up,
PGA Headquarters Moves to Dunedin,
PGA Headaches in Merchandising

[1955, 1956, 1957]

HARRY L. Moffitt completed a quiet year as the eleventh president of the PGA at the finish of the association's thirty-ninth annual meeting at the Ritz-Carlton Hotel, Atlantic City, December 3 through 9, 1955. Moffitt, long the professional at the Heather Downs Country Club, Toledo, was a soft-spoken, methodical man. He'd listen, as though in deep thought, while both parties to an argument talked themselves out and peace returned.

Moffitt's first year saw the debut of Florida as the PGA's thirty-first section. The new section spun off from the Southern section because there was too much action for one area.

Tournament circuit prize money in 1955 passed the $1 million annual mark for the first time, and during the year twenty-three players won more than $10,000 each. Julius Boros was the year's top prize winner with $61,151,

which included the $50,000 first prize of George S. May's World Championship at Tam O'Shanter in suburban Chicago. May had a bonus of fifty exhibitions at $1,000 each that tied the World Champion in with the May Company's sales promotion and customer goodwill campaigns.

Jerry Barber, chairman of the Tournament Committee, told the delegates that he'd had sponsors gladly volunteer to raise prize money if the Tournament Bureau elevated the standard of conduct of players and recognized that its business was based on the good conduct and sound occupational sense of pro golfers. Ray O'Brien, a tough, shrewd man who was the field director of the tour, had to contend with malcontents who naturally wanted to blame their failures to score on somebody other than themselves. He disciplined a few of them and did a good job of training

Harry Moffitt. GH

younger men on the tour to behave as sponsors had told Jerry Barber they wanted them to.

O'Brien was a good salesman who sold sponsors and golf writers on an understanding of his problems in trying to help them and also to build the tour. He was no flannelmouth. With him there were two camps—the Good Guys and the Bad Guys, the "For Me's" or the "Ag'in Me's." Host club officials, members, or sportswriters who complained about unpleasant performances of players supposed to be representing the high standards of the PGA were quickly disarmed by Ray O'Brien. He'd say something like, "I'm glad you came to me. You think you have troubles with that bum? Listen to me. This thing would run itself if we didn't have that bad-mannered, muscular halfwit and a few more like him lousing up the deal for the respectable, intelligent

guys in the field. He puzzled me, but he isn't as mean as he acts. That's his inferiority bubbling out. His main trouble is that he is just simply stupid. Have you ever had to deal with a guy who has almost nothing in his skull?"

His listeners would then nod in agreement; they'd had just that sort of trouble and they could sympathize. Then O'Brien would sigh and hope the unpleasant tourist would win some money in this tournament. "Although the bum is cheap and tight, I'm always hoping he gets enough to send a couple of bucks to his mother and father for a marriage license." Then he'd add brightly, "Now about some of the really great, nice guys in this tournament. . . ."

Bob Leacox had improved the tournament routing so that the tourney tourists were happier than they'd been, but not overwhelmed to the extent of giving a percentage of their purses to pay the salary of the Tournament Bureau manager. In the first $1 million-plus prize year, the sponsors paid $8,000 more in service fees than in the previous year. Incidentally, the PGA was seventeen years ahead of the Ladies' PGA in passing the million-dollar post in purses, proving that the sports world is just as male-oriented as the business world.

Midland, Texas, and Long Beach, California, wanted PGA championships, but the travel-time element, when many players traveled in their own cars instead of by planes as now, ruled out locations such as Midland and Long Beach.

Horton Smith had successfully negotiated a series of tournaments in the Caribbean zone. They were to develop into a minor league of winter events, profitable and pleasant as winter swings

Jerry Barber. AG

for a number of professionals not quite up to big-time play. Most of these men were primarily club pros.

The overall picture of the PGA looked good. Treasurer Wally Mund reported income of $185,774 and expenses of $146,641 for the year. However, the Tournament Bureau was in the red by $5,123, even with an income of $69,350 for the year.

The PGA's dues-paying membership was now 3,517, and members were having only the normal troubles and triumphs of men in a growing business. One unexpected backlash of increasing prosperity was criticism of the pros' addiction to fancier automobiles than their members seemed to be able to afford. The gripe had been heard before, but there were just enough of these cases to cause a sweep of locker-room jests, which, of course, perplexed some pros of fine credit standing. As always, they wondered why they should be censured for doing as well at their business as members did in their own fields.

Leo Fraser, owner of the Atlantic City Country Club and an official of the Philadelphia section, had arranged for the meeting in Atlantic City. His Scottish-born father had been a professional at that club and elsewhere in the area for years, and a brother, also deceased, had been a high-ranking amateur and a New Jersey state legislator. Leo and the Philadelphia section picked up $2,500 of the cost of the annual dinner.

Insurance salesmen again tried to work out a retirement plan for PGA members with employing clubs dividing the cost, but they had difficulty getting information for such a contract. To secure the basic data needed, 3,000 letters to club officials were mailed, but only 523 answers were received.

The Executive Committee had been under pressure on a decision to move the PGA headquarters from Chicago. Then its members—President Moffitt, Secretary Harold Sargent, Treasurer Walter Mund, and Vice-Presidents Dave Bonella, Al Ciuci, Charles Congdon, James D. Fogerty, George L. Hall, Fred Hawkins, Gene Marchi, J. M. Riley, Edward Schultz, and Charles Vittitoe—finally recommended the move to Dunedin in order to save money. Most of the PGA business was by mail. If people who wanted to sell the PGA something couldn't get to Dunedin, which was near the Tampa airport, then it was just too bad for them. So the move was put up to the delegates at the 1955 meeting. The vote was 54 to 4 in favor of the move.

Mund continued the practice of Treasurers William Wotherspoon and Harold Sargent in presenting the delegates with charts showing where the PGA dollar came from and where it went, so they could pass the information along to their sectional members. It was a muddled picture because, as the May experts had pointed out and PGA executives were to observe years later, the association had accounts that played all over the course and only a specialist could tell the true financial score. Dividing the time of the PGA headquarters' seventeen employees into the various accounting brackets was like playing a course with eighteen mulligans at the tees.

Mund's treasury box score showed on pennies of each dollar coming in: members' dues and initiation, 31.07; magazine, 16.71; Tournament Bureau, 16.86; PGA National Golf Club, 17.37; PGA Championship, 13.04; Benevolent and Relief funds, 2.50; educational, 1.46; and other, .99.

It was interesting that the revenue from the PGA National Golf Club, which the famed tournament players regarded as an old folks' home, was paying into the PGA more than the tournament players, and taking out considerably less.

Where the pennies of the PGA dollar went in 1955: Tournament Bureau, 18.10; magazine, 15.76; PGA National Golf Club, 14.19; Chicago office, 10.93; PGA Championship, 8.77; members' life insurance, 7.02; annual meeting, 3.30; all other, 3.96; Benevolent and Relief funds, 1.36; educational, .58; Seniors' Championship, .34; and income over expenses, 15.69.

The Seniors' Championship was so big now that the annual meeting resolved to prohibit display of merchandise at the PGA National Club during the competition. It was felt that such exhibits were "rather unbecoming to the dignity and the stature of the event." That resolution seems to have rested in peace in the PGA's vast burial ground of resolutions because, during the PGA Seniors' the next winter, the pro salesmen were again making their brisk pitches in the shade of the spreading trees around the little clubhouse, showing samples in hotel and motel rooms at Clearwater, and hustling a goodly volume of preseason orders. Pros had enough to do when spring came to the Northern clubs without having to attend to salesmen and the shop buying needs. The pro golf version of county fair week and Oriental bazaar the salesmen started at Dunedin grew into the biggest business operation of the PGA.

It was a sensible combination with the Seniors' Championship, since the buying trips to the Merchandise Show were tax deductible as business expenses and one of the best answers ever devised to the difficult problem of

Ed Furgol. PGA, photo by Kuehn

pro buying of seasonal merchandise. With members always needing attention in the shop, on the lesson tee, or elsewhere, the professional couldn't arrange his time for buying as other merchants were able to do. In time, the Merchandise Show, brainchild of Frank Sprogell, grew so big that it became confusing to many professionals, yet it was a tremendous improvement over the former buying, which was without much of a plan.

Jack Moon, a successful sales manager who had lately completed organizing a large fruit-juice firm in Florida, had been trying to sell the PGA on a strong campaign of merchandising numerous golf products under the PGA label. Moon's idea was not to license various manufacturers to make a prod-

uct bearing the PGA label, as the PGA ball arrangement had been for a while, but to restrict the label to one manufacturer of each product. He worked out an attractive plan, which was presented to the Executive Committee. The PGA officials were fascinated but wary. In the past, they had received too many confusing and expensive opinions from their lawyers in Washington and elsewhere concerning PGA involvement in contracts that might be in restraint of trade or contrary to some other laws.

Officials and delegates had listened to a great deal of discussion about PGA members in a complex situation as merchants. It seemed that the pro's customer often complained seriously if a pro used a private club shop to push some lines strongly and ruled out others. But there were two sides to the question. The professional was the authority on what clubs, balls, bags, and possibly other equipment were best for the player. His judgment was usually extraordinarily fair in a highly competitive, small-store market, especially considering that he might have a staff relationship with some manufacturer. The pro usually had too many lines of clubs and balls in stock, whereas the other golf goods retailers who were in business for profit and had a minimum of responsibility toward the user who bought the goods usually had no more than three lines of clubs.

The pro was handicapped by the reputation of being high-priced. This was because he refused to handle clubs that were slapped together with a cheap head, a low-priced shaft, and a bottom-grade grip. But he made that handicap an asset by insisting on top quality, and that was the reason for Moon's program for PGA lines.

The manufacturers were also concerned. The pros' credit position was improving, and Jack Moon might make banking connections that would allow a good production program, selecting the most desirable pro accounts as outlets.

The pro club, ball, and bag business always has had an incentive and reward for a manufacturer of quality golf merchandise. Jack Forester, a Texas delegate, set the matter straight when he told the 1955 gathering: "I ask the salesmen: 'Would you rather sell $300,-000 worth of goods on which your company makes some money and gets a reputation for quality or make a $30,-000 sale where you have to compete with somebody who'd beat you out with a price of $29,999?' "

At that meeting, there was talk about the urgent necessity of schooling assistant professionals and about requiring inexperienced tournament contestants to qualify by some examination. *Life* retired as cosponsor of National Golf Day. The USGA was asked by the PGA to come in, but declined, so the PGA decided to go ahead. Golf Day grants had already become substantial factors in welfare and education programs. The veterans' hospitals had made nearly 1,000 requests during the year through the Swing Clubs for golf programs, many of which were answered by PGA sections through a committee headed by Harry Obitz.

Ed Furgol got 72 against the 77 of Patty Berg and the 78 of Babe Zaharis in the Round of the Champions on National Golf Day at the Olympic Club in San Francisco. The Red Cross got 40 percent of the gross of $158,017 that was raised at 3,004 clubs.

The British Ryder Cup team, which was defeated 8 to 4 at Palm Springs on November 5 and 6, played pleasant warm-up matches at Atlantic City and Tulsa, en route to the competition at the Thunderbird course in the desert wonderland.

Doug Ford made his first start in a PGA Championship at the Meadowbrook Country Club and was medalist at 135 and the winner by 4 and 3 over Cary Middlecoff. A bunker play and an approaching contest were added to the driving contest. Leon Pounder, who holed out from the sand, gave an unbeatable performance.

Fred Hawkins was elected chairman of the Tournament Committee, which at that time saw no more than the ordinary problems ahead. One of them was changing the PGA Championship to stroke play, as clubs didn't want to tie up their courses for a week of medal play competition.

Doug Ford. GH

The Golf Business School session began with Jack Lust of Di Fina talking on the responsibility of golfers as influences on fashion. Ben Hogan spoke on "Competitive Golf as I See It," telling of psychological factors that require a shockproof swing. George Dochat, pro at the Rutgers University course, talked on the psychology of teaching. Mrs. Dorothy Germaine Porte commented on women's instruction. The 1940 Women's National Amateur Champion said that she'd been informed that about 65 percent of pro golf lessons were given to women. If pros thought the same type of instruction given men was equally effective for women, they were making a big mistake. Ernest Jones, the famed one-legged teacher who stressed "the swing is the thing" and warned against detailed technicalities as more confusing than helpful, spoke on "How I Teach Golf." He had at one time been especially successful in teaching women outdoors at the long-defunct Women's National Golf Club on Long Island, where he was professional, and then at his "studio" on Fifth Avenue. He did well there, getting men students to swing so they scored in the low 80's. The strenuous "hit" effect at the bottom of the swing was something Jones's advanced male pupils picked up for themselves. Jones had such a high percentage of successful pupils with his simple way of teaching that other professionals were interested in learning from him.

The 1956 PGA Championship was awarded to the Blue Hill Golf and Country Club, Canton, Massachusetts, which guaranteed a $40,000 purse. The club was overly optimistic at that stage because the PGA was delayed in getting its "guarantee."

Bob Kay and Tony Patricelli asked the PGA for authority to use the association's name in starting a PGA Golf College at Hartford to train youths as assistant professionals. The request was denied after a discussion that concluded, "Somebody's going to do this someday. Why not us?"

Robert Goldwater of Phoenix and Sidney Solomon of St. Louis were named to the PGA Advisory Board. Both had been enthusiastic and proficient amateurs; they were prominent businessmen and helpful to pro golf.

The PGA had signed a one-year lease on an office at Dunedin, beginning October 1, 1956, and the move had been completed when the fortieth annual meeting of the association was held at the Fort Harrison Hotel, Clearwater, November 29 through December 7. Tom Crane, executive secretary, and cheerful, energetic Mrs. Irene Blakeman, who had been the entire PGA headquarters staff until the move to Chicago, got the organization's records packed and shipped and set up on the second floor of a two-story building.

The offices were air-conditioned and cheerful, and there was no rush-hour jam getting to work or going home. Nearly all the employees at the Dunedin office were new, but they easily adjusted to the job. When the officers and delegates checked on operations, they were more than contented with the results.

Harry L. Moffitt continued in the presidency, Harold Sargent was secretary, and Walter Mund was treasurer. The roster of vice-presidents remained the same. In changes made in the tournament management, Harvey Raynor was appointed tournament supervisor, and J. Edwin Carter was put in charge of the Tournament Bureau, with salary and travel expenses for the year to be $21,000. For taking charge in the

Jack Burke, Jr. AG

field, Harvey Raynor received $510 a week as salary, "living," and travel expenses.

Contracts with Ray O'Brien as tournament supervisor, Fred Corcoran as tournament publicity director, and Robert Leacox as tournament schedule coordinator were terminated. None of the three was brokenhearted at being cut loose. They believed they'd done their work well in improving the acceptance and the purses and performance of the tournament players. They'd been in wearing jobs and needed a rest.

Shortly after the appointment of Ed Carter, the Executive Committee questioned what part of Carter's time and attention was being given to the Tournament Bureau. He was in the business of publishing programs for national Open and Amateur championships and had started in this business as a committeeman at Baltusrol. He was a personable and dynamic man who had the hunch there was a lot of gold in those golf hills, and he discovered it in tournament program advertising. Carter felt that club tournament officials were great businessmen in their own precincts, but knew nothing about golf tournament programs. He believed they needed a nurse, a teacher, a big, strong, smart man to protect them and take care of their money.

The astute J. Edwin Carter was also exploring other commercial phases of golf. He was a good man for the PGA at the time. He was doing business at a period when people were forgetting about the question: "Is it good for golf?" but saw the game strictly as a business, just as the tournament players did. Eventually Carter went into the tournament management and program business and did very well at it, giving his trade expert services. In that department of commerce he was much better off than as Tournament Bureau director. As a tournament promoter, manager, and program publisher, he got first grab at the big money.

Bill Rach, editor of *The Professional Golfer* and publicity director, asked the association to change his title to promotional director and to authorize him to sell television rights to National Golf Day, the PGA Championship, and other events in which the PGA was cosponsor. The PGA said "No." Television was beginning to look like big money.

John Caswell was hired as administrative assistant to the overworked Tom Crane. In the new offices at Dunedin, the PGA saved $4,200 a year in rent and got 500 square feet and John Caswell too. It also got more work for Crane and his staff, as the association's forty-some committees piled up paperwork, which generally meant urgent recommendations for somebody to do something. The duties were not always clear, but the buck stopped with Crane.

That didn't mean that the president's load was lightened. Moffitt had been away from home on PGA business forty-eight days during the year. Membership in 1956 was 3,790 in all classes, including 2,754 in Class A, and there were still thirty-one sections.

Dave Hendry had been hired as superintendent at Dunedin. A veteran pro-greenkeeper, he came confidently into a job that had been the graveyard of reputations for course management. In a few years the job did Hendry in, too. The PGA was never able to find a substitute for money in course maintenance at Dunedin. In 1955, it spent $39,000 on maintenance of the PGA National Golf Club course, at a time when the national average for eighteen-hole course maintenance was $43,000.

What apparently hadn't been considered was the longer growing period, the summer and winter grasses, the fertilizer requirements of the sandy soil, inadequate equipment, the neglect of years, and the demands for first-class metropolitan course condition at what was essentially a good small-town course. Actually, a thrifty and effective job was done on the Dunedin course under the circumstances.

Some PGA members were irate when asked to pay a green fee for play on the course at Dunedin. They regarded it as their own private club course, with all costs being included in their dues. When Tom Mahan, a New England delegate, noted that a number of courses in the Tampa Bay area were generous in allowing recognized professionals to play a few rounds free as guests in the winter, the PGA National rules were relaxed to permit any PGA member to play the course free three times a year.

The top tournament of the winter at the PGA course was the PGA Seniors, sponsored by Teacher's on January 25, 26, and 27, 1957. The PGA was paid $8,000 for prize money, plus $1,000 for the championship promotion expense. The defending champion and each sectional PGA champion (or alternate) was given round-trip air fare from his home to Tampa and $15 daily expenses. The winner, in addition to getting the Teacher's trophy, got $1,500 for a trip abroad to play the British PGA Senior Champion.

The Seniors' Championship ran smoothly, which couldn't be said of the PGA's thirty-eighth Championship at the Blue Hill Golf and Country Club, Canton, Massachusetts, July 20 through 24, 1956. Jack Burke, Jr., defeated Ted Kroll, 3 and 2, after both men had survived tight, tough competition. The course was part of a real-estate project and was not in good condition. The clubhouse had burned the previous New Year's Eve, the new building was unfinished, and the New England PGA was sore about the whole thing, since it had not been consulted when the championship was awarded. Nor did Blue Hill have a PGA member as its professional. Julius Boros and Cary Middlecoff passed up the championship for exhibition matches, and this cost them their places on the 1957 Ryder Cup team. The Blue Hill $25,000 guarantee wasn't paid until after legal action, and a rules controversy delayed play. The championship lost the PGA $2,900, and the New England section got a Blue Hill bill for $28,600 for unsold tickets.

Other tournament affairs had been quiet. The sponsors recommended that the PGA Championship be changed to stroke play. Paul Runyan, speaking for a group of tournament players, suggested that the PGA Championship be made a national match-play championship with all professionals and amateurs being eligible to qualify.

The Sponsors' Association proposed that the top ten professionals of the year be selected on a point-system plan to help sponsors present "the most attractive field" at a tournament.

At the meeting there were more complaints by the home professionals about the names of prominent playing pros on cheap clubs. The public thought they were bargains because of the star players' names, but they were merely the usual shoddy clubs made even shoddier than usual because of the royalty paid the pro whose name was stamped on the flimsy tool.

If the PGA had had any marketing and research department, it would have known that the cheap pro-name clubs sold poorly. They were mainly irri-

tants because pros saw the cut prices in store ads and so did some of their members who were unaware that there was no comparison between the value of the inferior store clubs and the high-quality pro models. While the cut-rate clubs presumably brought millions of golfers into the game who would have been kept away by the price of quality equipment, PGA club pros maintained that the use of playing stars' names on poor equipment was an unnecessary and wasteful deceit. But the only figures they got on their case were on a lawyer's bill.

Eventually the practice proved self-defeating because the poor stuff just did not sell. Stockholders of companies selling such equipment also objected when they learned that clubs and balls bearing the names of professional stars only sold in proportion to the amount of advertising money spent on them. The Hagen and Hogan lines had been kept pro-only and at the highest manufacturing specifications. The Nicklaus line by MacGregor was an initial casualty of the home pro–playing pro civil war, but eventually sold well. Arnold Palmer's line, which was pro-only, was a similar casualty in pro-shop sales, then it went to Sears when the aluminum-shaft rush was on and sold nicely for a while. Sears knew how to sell clubs better than any other outfit and had already sold thousands of clubs bearing the name of J. C. Higgins, who was not of this world, pro or amateur.

Generally, the leading manufacturers confined themselves to advertising their own brand names, using pro names only when a pro playing with their clubs happened to win a major tournament. (This might possibly impress some trusting party who hoped to win a Class D championship at his club.) Thus were fortunes in merchandising money and club pro goodwill lost in what might have been a legitimate source of playing pro income. The warnings at the 1956 meeting and other PGA gatherings that confidence in pro testimonials was being destroyed went unheeded. All of which proved what other businesses had found to their sorrow: That Elbert Hubbard was right when he said, "American business now is learning that honesty is the best policy, having tried everything else."

The PGA got a welcome bonanza from a veteran tournament player when "Jug" McSpaden, now out of tournament golf and working for Elmer Ward of the Palm Beach Company, gave the association's Relief Fund $8,461 as a gift from the Palm Beach Round Robin tournament. National Golf Day had also done well in its maiden flight under PGA auspices. It brought in $80,000, but had to pay out $17,000 when Jack Fleck, 1955 National Open Champion, and Fay Crocker, Women's Open Champion that year, played the Round of the Champions at Oak Hill, Rochester, and got 69.

The Assistants' Training Program was started at Dunedin by a staff of instructors headed by Emil Beck. The assistants' fees were low, so were those of the instructors, but it was a distinctly successful beginning for the PGA's organized educational campaign. The fundamental concept was that a pro handles his job according to the competence and spirit of his assistant. It wasn't possible for the Master Professional, with all he had to do, to devote the attention he desired to the education of his employees. The school at Dunedin and Clearwater hadn't been operating long before it had as students successful pros who admitted

that the refresher courses would help them.

The educational program was organized and operated in a remarkably effective way, considering that its instructors were not professionally trained as teachers. The superintendents had the experienced professors of the agricultural colleges and the scientists of the manufacturing companies running the schools. Club managers had hotel school faculties as specialists. The PGA business schools were pioneering. Emil Beck was chairman of the Professional Training Committee. George Aulbach, one of the first university graduates to get into professional golf, was on the committee, as were Joe Devaney, Bill Hardy, a veteran club designer and maker (his colleagues said he could make a club so that it felt as though it were part of the player), and Arthur B. St. Pierre. There were informal, practical postgraduate sessions of veteran professionals at the practice tee under the casual direction of Irv Schloss and such knowledgeable helpers as Willie Ogg, Al Watrous, Frank Walsh, Willie Hunter, and scores of others whose explorations and appraisals of instruction, playing technique, and equipment comprised a wide range of experience.

Those schooling sessions at Clearwater and Dunedin had a positive effect on employment. A young man who could say he had been at winter school at the PGA National Golf Club had an advantage in getting any assistant's job that was open. A high percentage of these youths quickly got pro jobs and are now doing well at first-class clubs.

The educational portion of the 1956 meeting presented the same old stuff on display of merchandise in the shop and the psychology of instruction. There were enviably effective strokes exhibited by Sam Snead, Bob Toski, Jack Fleck, Jay Hebert, and Jack Burke, Jr. They told how they thought they operated, but again, not how they'd learned or been taught. Bill Strausbaugh, Jr., discussed "Practice Drills in Teaching," a routine that was to make Strausbaugh a notably effective teacher. Conrad Rehling, golf coach at the University of Florida, in speaking of "Group Golf Instruction in Schools," stressed the problem of making the fundamentals so clear that pupils would know how to work out their individual methods.

Reporting as treasurer, Wally Mund interested the delegates with the innovation of disclosing the Tournament Bureau figures. The finances of the Tournament Division before 1956—and generally since that time—were regarded pretty much as hush-hush. Nobody knows why.

The income for the fiscal year 1956 was as follows: sponsors' service fees, $84,709; PGA Tournament Sponsors Association, $7,274; Masters' tournament, $1,000; percentage of purses, $1,200; players' assessments, $6,025; and non–PGA member approved-player dues, $4,885.

The outgo: field salaries and expenses, $39,710; salary and expenses, Tournament Bureau manager, $4,083; internal publicity and public relations, $4,964; coordinator of schedules, $3,251; proportion, Chicago office salaries, $4,885; and other expenses, $18,890.

Two things were perfectly clear about that statement. One was that it was honest; the other was that absolutely nobody—repeat, nobody—knew what it meant.

The schedule coordinator was getting $1 a year and expenses, but the Tournament Bureau manager's salary and expenses didn't quite jibe with the budget figures agreed on at the 1955 meeting. "Proportion of Chicago office salaries" was O.K. That was anybody's guess. "Other expenses" were from looseness, not larceny, as expense accounts sometimes are. The May organization's auditors and other CPA's who had urged that the PGA simplify and consolidate its accounts had made no impression whatever. They left the PGA playing with numbers in the deep rough. The procedure eventually was corrected as a matter of public record, except that the Tournament Players' Division accounts, until lately at least, have not been so open as the financial statements of the USGA, the Western Golf Association, the GCSA, the CMAA, and other departments of the PGA that handle money.

Why the Tournament Bureau never divulged its whole story in black and white for delegates to take home from the 1956 meeting escapes the memory of the tournament representatives who at that time were operating the tournament circuit autonomously, as had been and continued to be the case for years. In 1956, the Tournament Bureau profit was $23,159, against a loss of $5,123 the previous year.

The PGA general financial showing was good for 1956, with income of $186,116 and expenses of $163,436. The PGA Benefit Fund received $12,600 from the Palm Beach tournament. The pie chart on income showed: members' dues and initiation, 28.33; Tournament Bureau, 22.36; PGA National Golf Club, 17.14; magazine, 14.07; PGA Championship, 10.06; Benevolent and Relief funds, 4.52; education, 2.54; and other, .98.

Where the outgoing dollar went, in pennies: Tournament Bureau, 17.45; PGA National Golf Club, 14.85; magazine, 14.70; Chicago office, 10.57; PGA

Championship, 7.50; members' life insurance, 6.20; all other, 5.40; annual meeting, 3.57; Benevolent and Relief funds, 1.59; 1955 Ryder Cup matches, .85; education, .67; and excess of income over expenses, 16.65.

Pros west of the Rockies were not happy about the PGA's leaving Chicago for its new Little White Home in the Southeast. The Western Slope was rapidly increasing in golf courses, and the Southwest had started the winter tour—as the tournaments were then called when sponsors were few. The area had produced a very liberal angel, Bob Hudson, for Ryder Cup matches and a PGA Championship, and had started the Junior Chambers of Commerce as the sponsors who put on the tournaments when it was difficult to arouse interest accompanied by money. The principal recognition the Western members had received from the PGA was the election of Joe Novak of Bel Air at Los Angeles as the association's president in 1949, 1950, and 1951. Southern California pros had brought Bing Crosby and Bob Hope in to star every time the PGA needed the invaluable help only they could give. All the pros owed bows to Crosby and Hope. And still do.

To quiet the Pacific Coast members, as well as to give itself wide expression, the PGA held its 1957 annual meeting at the Lafayette Hotel, Long Beach, California, November 7 through 15. Harry L. Moffitt presided as president. Harold Sargent was secretary, Walter Mund was treasurer, and Horton Smith participated as honorary president. Tom Crane continued as executive secretary. Delegates from thirty-one sections attended, and Jackson Bradley represented the Tournament Bureau as its delegate. Vice-presidents at the meeting were Charles W. Congdon,

U. C. Ferguson, Jr., George L. Hall, Henry G. Poe, J. M. Riley, Leonard Schmutte, Lou Strong, and Willie Whalen.

The association had 3,979 members of all classes. Treasurer Mund's long report showed all was well with the cash register. One printed copy of the lengthy and complex report was given to each delegate, so he could take it home to his section's members and go over it in detail. Criticism was voiced that the method was not businesslike, but the complaint was quickly skipped as the meeting had to give much time to the merchandising plan for PGA products. The plan had been developed by Jack Moon and, it was hoped, would develop into such a huge, multimillion-dollar operation that current finances were routine.

Jack Moon's idea was a combination of cooperative buying and a voluntary chain of stores. For two years he'd worked on the PGA brand merchandising and now had it going so well that he could report that twenty-five manufacturers were associated in the operation. Like everything else in which the PGA was involved, the PGA brand was a complex job. With the Jack Moon plan, the home pros were promised an increase in profit at their shops that might ease the strains of the twelve-hour days and the worries of buying for a limited market and a short season.

Always careful about tax and legal matters, Tom Crane had established the Professional Golfer's Foundation for Education-Service. Crane's attention to the organization of a channel through which the PGA's share of the expected revenue was to flow had been strongly influenced by the government's seizure of PGA files.

The PGA's Washington lawyers, Arnold, Fortas, and Porter, had drawn up the PGA-Moon contract, and distribution of the PGA products was through nine franchised wholesalers. The PGA was to average about five cents on the dollar, which was the usual royalty rate pros got for their names on clubs. The total sales of the PGA lines during the first nine months of 1957 exceeded $1.5 million. That wasn't bad, but the painful thing was that $300,000 accounts receivable were on the books shortly before the PGA meeting. Especially disturbing · about the slow accounts was that a substantial percentage represented closeouts, mainly clubs that were being eliminated from a line at cut prices because of model changes due the next year. These closeouts indicated that no effective sales push was being applied to the PGA clubs.

Franchise owners had more than half a million in inventories and accounts receivable, and as independents who were financing themselves, they were cooling on the PGA deal and had begun looking for other lines. The New York district PGA distributor said he had to sell $350,000 a year to break even; the Chicago agency had to go $400,000 before making a profit. The distributor had to have at least 15 percent margin before he could make money. Etonic, which made PGA golf shoes, wouldn't tie in with PGA distributors and the Burke Golf Company, which made the PGA line of clubs. The account was good in volume, but Moon had intended to put on a strong advertising campaign for the PGA lines financed by 1 percent paid by each manufacturer on his PGA brand volume and 1 percent by each distributor. The campaign didn't get far. Moon advanced $5,000 of his own money, which he didn't get back. The others paid nothing. It became plain

that too many professionals actually were losing money providing clubs and public courses with pro-shop merchandise and services.

A PGA golf cart contract was made, and there were early promises that professionals might sell or lease many of these carts to their clubs, but an inability to finance the project accounted for cancellation of the arrangement before any carts were delivered.

There were differences of opinion between the manufacturers and PGA committeemen on designs of clubs and bags, and when these groups compromised, some PGA members were critical of the designs that were accepted. The headaches of the previous PGA club and ball deals were multiplied by the distribution plan, which put another element between the manufacturer and the pro. When reports of the first year of the PGA merchandising plan as devised by Moon were made at the 1957 meeting, it became plain that the operation wasn't going to last long.

The Dunedin situation was going along smoothly, but without any showy progress. A resolution was presented to build a PGA office building at Dunedin, but it was defeated. Frank Sprogell was hired to be the general manager of the PGA National Club, and the selection of this widely experienced and resourceful man was fortunate. He improved the club in every way until the decision to move to Palm Beach Gardens was made. He was a veteran pro-greenkeeper with a pleasing personality and the sound financial judgment needed to stretch the small budget. Bob Lee was hired as pro to succeed Leo O'Grady, and Dave Hendry continued as superintendent.

The winter business school was getting about as many students as could be handled. The educational and pro-

fessional training budget was cut from
$4,400 to $3,300, but most of the men
working on the program were not discouraged by losing money. As instructors at the school, Eddie Duino, Joe
Devaney, George Aulbach, and Bill
Hardy were given $500 a week for
travel and living expenses at the Dunedin school, and Willie Ogg was given
$300. The PGA was giving all profes-
sionals a thoroughly well-rounded golf
education. It typified what Findlay
Douglas, a former USGA president,
had meant when he told Alex Pirie,
another golfer of Scottish origin and
PGA president in 1929: "If I want to
know anything about golf, where do I
go? I come to you fellows. You are the
sole source of information on golf, and
if you lose that position it is your own
fault."

Professionals didn't appreciate it at
the time, and not many have since, but
the Douglas credo: "If I want to know
anything about golf . . . I come to
you fellows," should be on a bronze
tablet over the entrance to the PGA offices. The elder Sargent also told those
at the 1957 meeting that the PGA
magazine had been started with money
from former president Alex Pirie, and
he reminded his brother professionals
that Pirie would not knowingly accept
anything from the PGA funds during
his long and costly terminal illness, although small amounts were sent to his
family from the PGA Relief and Benevolent funds. The reference to the
demise of the beloved Pirie led to the
usual discussion of the pension plan
hopes to ease the exit of fine old professionals who had done much for
golfers and for golf.

This time consideration was given
an insurance company proposal of
$3,000 a month, offered with the pos-
sibility of several changes of pro job

locations being offset by a higher premium to be financed by a nationwide
"Birdie Battle" or All-Member Best
Ball Championship. Two imaginative
pros, Al Houghton and Lionel Callo-
way, figured out a tournament with
collective entrance fees that could go
well past $1 million, return a rich prize
to the winning club, and leave enough
over to pay for a pro retirement program. It was another of those meet-me-
tonight-in-Dreamland ideas that never
got off the ground.

One important detail of PGA home
work was accomplished when Bob Russell was named PGA magazine editor
and public-relations man, succeeding
Bill Rach. Russell was an experienced
man from the *Chicago Daily News* who
wanted to get out of the big-town rat
race, and Dunedin suited him perfectly. Russell gave the PGA good coverage of its inside affairs, organized sectional reporters, and stayed out of
PGA politics.

The meeting was enlivened by emotional remarks about money from Joe
Donato and Jim Warga. Donato, a
generous fellow himself, said he
thought it disgraceful that professionals had to keep practically begging for
a dollar once a year for the National
Golf Day educational and welfare
work. He said he saw more reason for
alarm at clubs' being reluctant to put
a dollar a year on members' bills for
National Golf Day than in being afraid
that the National Golf Day contribution might establish a precedent. He
thought any club member or fee-course
player who could not afford to pay a
dollar annually for golf's only public-
service fund ought to get out of the
game.

Warga's remarks came in a discussion on whether a good credit rating
should be considered a requirement of

a candidate for PGA office. Warga said he was tired of having pros' credit so often questioned in PGA meetings. He maintained that pros generally had credit records superior to those of other smaller retailers of sports goods and not infrequently were using their own money when their members and clubs were slow in paying. The resolution requiring a satisfactory credit rating was defeated.

Affairs of the Tournament Bureau, the PGA Championship, and the Ryder Cup matches were normal in their persistent problems. Ed Carter was Tournament Bureau manager. The bureau's publicity service was improved decidedly by hiring Jim Gaquin, who went to the tournaments carrying his office equipment in a station wagon and ground out daily releases during the major tournaments. A rating arrangement called the TTT plan and involving tournaments played, position of finishes, and other elements was devised as an incentive to replace the appearance money sponsors had had to pay. New distribution of prize money was worked out by the players so the twentieth finisher in a tournament would have ample expense money.

What was taking place within the PGA was minor in its effect on tournament golf compared to what was decided by Associated Press officials after conferences with newspaper sports editors, managing editors, and business departments. Some tournaments sponsored by commercial interests to get sports-page publicity were not getting the desired results. The Associated Press sports policy, which the United Press had also tacitly adopted, was to avoid mention of the commercial sponsor's name, but to refer to the tournament by city or course. The reasoning was that, if the manufacturer wanted advertising in the newspapers, he should pay for it just as the newspapers and their employees had to pay for what the manufacturer was selling. "We'll call it the Buick Open free when we get free Buicks," one sports editor decided.

Television was cutting into the advertising appropriations of tournament sponsors, yet television was unable to make an established success of any sports event by itself. The newspapers had to do that. Advertisers weren't getting the free newspaper publicity they had expected from golf tournaments and were wavering on the tournaments as advertising that didn't sell.

Advertising agents for Carlings, the brewers, brought the tournament sponsor identification issue before newspaper and Associated Press executives. The AP eased its attitude on free publicity and so did the United Press. That was the point at which the tournament circuit got adopted by big business and didn't have to depend on the energetic free work of Junior Chambers of Commerce for promotion.

Later, when it was discovered that in addition to getting free newspaper publicity, the commercial sponsor could get tax deductions and local goodwill by having tournament work done free for hospitals, boys' clubs, or other noble projects qualifying as tax umbrellas, golf tournaments began to beat out keno and bingo as fund-raisers for holy causes.

However, local sponsors still couldn't solve their problems on dates and assurances that stars would play. Paul Ridings, who handled publicity for the Colonial Invitational, was hired as the PGA's publicity man to backstop the vigorous Gaquin in the field. All the same, publicity wouldn't solve such problems as the Tournament of Champions at Las Vegas, with its limited field, murdering a tournament scheduled elsewhere on the same days.

In other business, the delegates defeated a motion to have sponsors represented on the Tournament Committee, and George Hall was engaged to supervise the Caribbean tour. Jay Hebert was named chairman of the Tournament Committee, and Dow Finsterwald, Bob Toski, Jack Fleck, Fred Hawkins, and Bo Winiger were also appointed to that group. Warren Orlick and Jackson Bradley were the PGA officers on the committee.

Although the British had won the Ryder Cup matches at Lindrick, they'd lost money on the event. The American team had played a match with a team of pro challengers at the Wanakah Country Club in suburban Buffalo for a guarantee of $12,900, with the PGA Ryder Cup fund getting $3,000 and each Ryder Cup player getting $600 added to his expense money. Manufacturers equipped and clothed the American team. It had been costing each PGA of America member about $2 to maintain the Ryder Cup matches, but the British had no such financing. Leo Fraser bid for the 1959 Ryder Cup matches at his Atlantic City Country Club, but the competition was awarded to the Eldorado Country Club, Palm Desert, California.

The Tournament Bureau was high out of the red with a year's record income of $123,524. Of that amount $23,000 was paid by players at $5 each for every tournament entered. The Teacher's Scotch sponsors of the Seniors' tournament raised prize money from $8,000 to $10,000 and increased the PGA payment for tournament expenses from $1,000 to $1,500.

A seldom-mentioned asset was received by the PGA in a collection of rare golf books bequeathed by Judge Earle Tilley of Chicago. The collection included a copy of the first golf book published in the United States, *Golf in America—a Practical Manual,* by James P. Lee, published by Dodd, Mead, & Company on May 25, 1895. That book, which was mentioned earlier, and others of the Tilley bequest are in a locked case at PGA headquarters.

Arrangements with the Llanerch Country Club, Havertown, Pennsylvania, were all set for the 1958 PGA Championship. The PGA was to get 60 percent of the gross ticket sales after 10 percent was deducted to pay J. Edwin Carter for tournament management services to the club. The PGA was also to get 12.5 percent from program advertising revenue after paying 15 percent of the gross to Carter. In addition, the PGA was to get television and radio income, and after paying selling expenses on this revenue, pay the sponsoring club 20 percent.

The 1958 Championship was the PGA's first at stroke play and at seventy-two holes over four days. Finsterwald's 276 beat Billy Casper by two strokes. The gallery paid $95,000 for admission.

Help was needed by the Ladies' PGA. They offered the PGA 5 percent of the LPGA prize money and a minimum of $5,000 a year for scheduling events for the girls' circuit. The PGA had made no progress in its endeavor to establish a minor league, and the women thought they could put on a more attractive show than the men who hadn't been able to make the big time. The LPGA proposal was turned down. And no action was taken on the suggestion that George Meany, head of the American Federation of Labor, be invited to be a member of the PGA Advisory Board.

Harold Sargent. PGA

An all-star array of experts addressed the business education session. Russell Peterson of Douglas Aircraft talked on "What to Look for in Hiring"; E. W. Elliot, buyer for the May Company, on "Merchandising Men's and Women's Wear"; Morgan Aldrick of Munsingwear on "How to Buy Men's Clothing"; Paul Sprinz of *Esquire* on "Fitting the Fashion to the Golfer"; and S. C. Bilheimer of Silverwood's on "How to Be a Buyer." The headliner of all speakers on women's golf wear at a PGA annual meeting was Eleanor Phillips, West Coast editor of *Vogue,* who discussed "How Fashion Sells Women." Other speakers were Kenneth Lake, CPA, on "Taxes at the Pro Shop"; Ted Dexter of Denny Class Service on "How to Display to Sell"; Bob Wolcott on "Public Relations of the Pro"; and a dynamic used-car salesman on "How to Close the Sale."

PGA insurance was becoming a fac-tor of considerable expense and extent and was paid for rather than understood and used correctly by most PGA members. This was one of the few times at a PGA annual business education session that an explanation was given by an authority, Joe Dennis, who sold the PGA most of its insurance for members' coverage.

The teaching session presented Olin Dutra, Bud Oakley, Guy Bellitt, Jerry Barber, Dale Andreason, Paul Runyan, Paul Hahn, Shirley Spork, and Dick Mayer, the 1957 Pro Golfer of the Year. They spoke on many phases of individual and group instruction.

Before the election that brought Harold Sargent in as PGA president in 1958—pretty much of a routine promotion of a man who had demonstrated his good judgment and competence—there were evidences of a shakeup in the changing of the guard down the line. Leo Fraser was nominated for the presidency by New Jersey. He'd been in Michigan before, and his father had been a pro and owned the club in Atlantic City that the aggressive young Leo was running. His amateur brother "Sonny" was a state legislator, and Leo had his backers. But it was the quiet Sargent, son of the PGA's third president, who won the election, 62 to 14. After three ballots Lou Strong, a pro from the Chicago district, was elected secretary, with 40 votes. Wally Mund got 23, and a quiet pro from Michigan, Warren Orlick, got 9.

In the voting for treasurer, Warren Cantrell from Texas got 52 votes, and Emil Beck of Michigan, who established the PGA educational program, got 22. Neither was an eager candidate.

Fraser, Cantrell, and Strong were to become PGA presidents in the most clamorous years of the association's history.

22

George S. May Gives Up the Golf Show,
TV Deals Threaten a Split,
the PGA Gives Up on Dunedin

[1958, 1959, 1960]

THE Colorado and Southwest (most of them members in Arizona) sections made their initial appearances at the PGA's forty-second annual meeting, bringing the section total to thirty-three. The meeting was held at the Fort Harrison Hotel, Clearwater, Florida. President Harold Sargent started the proceedings on November 6 with a report that proved that the PGA's top man lived on the run to accomplish his job.

Secretary Lou Strong and Treasurer Warren Cantrell also had their burdens for the cause, but they were mostly occupied with paperwork and headquarters routine. With Executive Secretary Tom Crane being the man for a hundred jobs, it was the president who had to be the association's road show.

The PGA was growing bigger and more complex and had a public-relations problem more delicate and difficult than any other pro sports or-

ganization because of the close contact between the golfing public and PGA members. No other professional sport had such intimacy, and other professional athletes were employed by comparatively few team owners. In contrast, golf professionals in 1958 were employed by the club officers and owners of public courses in 5,475 locations. Few of these employers were concerned with what the PGA did nationally. Most of them thought of the PGA as a vague organization that conducted a championship and had matches with British pros now and then and had players who were always arguing with one another or somebody else about something and were overpaid. These employers generally considered the PGA locally as a pleasant group of men whose officers included "our own pro, and you can't find a finer fellow anywhere."

Sectionally, most of the pro associations were in good standing and were operated in a businesslike way. The PGA of America actually had begun as an assembly of pro golfer organizations in the New York metropolitan area, the Chicago district, New England, and the Philadelphia and Virginia territory. The actual founding of the PGA of America only crystallized a sentiment that had been expressed for years. Only geography and money had delayed the sections getting together as a body.

At the 1958 meeting, Harold Sieg, pro at the Golden Valley Golf Club, Minneapolis, stated that the PGA originated in Minneapolis during the 1916 National Open at the Minikahda Club, June 27 through 30 inclusive. This was in conflict with the record showing that on January 17, 1916, Rodman Wanamaker's checkbook spanked the infant organization into loud, yelling life at a dinner as reported in an earlier chapter.

A search of Minneapolis newspapers has disclosed nothing to confirm the statement. Sieg was a youngster in pro golf when Chick Evans won the Open with a scoring record that stood for twenty years. At Minikahda the Open was beginning to be more than merely a jewel in the crown of a professional. The prize money had been increased to $1,200 even though it was divided only among the first ten, but first place got $500 and a gold medal. Imagine, $500 for playing four rounds of a game you and millions more would love to play for fun. And with factories then paying skilled workers little more than $1 an hour—$500 for four rounds of golf! That was better pay than Tris Speaker got, and he batted .386 for the Indians that year. And those golfers only had a working day of about three hours!

That was the situation when Willie

Kidd, George Sargent, Jock Hutchison, Will Reid, Gil Nicholls, Herbert Strong, Jim Barnes, Carl Anderson, Tom Boyd, W. C. Sherwood, and others, including Sieg, according to what he remembered, held the first PGA meeting. It could have been the first meeting outside of New York and really got the PGA operating by enlisting men from regions remote from Manhattan, such as Tom Vardon, Walter Fogargue, Herb Largeblade, J. B. Simpson, Bob Peebles, Jack Croke, Arthur Clarkson, John Gatherum, Jim Wilson, Norman Clark, Otto Hackbart, George Turnbull, George Simpson, and Jimmy Donaldson.

Minneapolis also figured in the cradling of a chapter of the PGA that had a pleasant influence on the fame and fortune of veteran pros. According to the recollections of George Sargent, a PGA pioneer, in 1936 a Chicago brewing company offered to sponsor a Senior PGA tournament, making the proposal to Willie Kidd, who had been the pro at Minikahda for years. The easygoing Willie was all for the idea and passed it along, but the brewery people went flat on the financing. Ultimately George Sargent got several veterans who were wintering in Augusta, Georgia, to organize the PGA Seniors, which played its first championship in 1937 with the PGA putting up $3,000 prize money.

The story of these pioneer components of the PGA of America has been pieced together from brief references in old golf magazines which were widely scattered in single or bound copies and usually related scanty details of the associations, which were conducted more on the order of lodges than of men in the same business. No secretarial records of these early sectional PGA meetings have been discovered. Such records must have been kept, as the secretaries usually were men who had been well schooled in Britain and must have absorbed the habit of the British amateur and professional golf organizations of keeping careful and informative records.

Early records of the PGA and its sections are few. Sectional records of the earlier years exist mainly in the memories of veteran members. Later records are rare. When research for this story of the PGA was begun, sectional secretaries were written to for information on their sections. This is the kind of background that would normally be available in a business organization, but only a minority had records. The majority of sectional secretaries didn't reply to three inquiries. They probably had three good excuses: (1) they didn't have records, (2) they had more urgent things to do, and (3) writing was a lot of trouble for a man without a secretary. Some may have been in the class of a genial PGA sectional official who, said R. W. ("Doc") Treacy, PGA national secretary, read only two kinds of letters, those starting politely: "Undoubtedly you have overlooked," and the following one that began: "Unless we receive a remittance from you promptly . . ."

The sectional business operations of the PGA have improved greatly during the past decade with the employment of business managers and secretaries who care for the inevitable load of association arrangements and paperwork. The professional rarely can handle such details. On Mondays in the summers, the professionals' days off, they have their own sectional tournaments and business meetings, and the officials have more than enough to do that day.

Like his father, Harold Sargent was meticulous in attending to correspondence as a sectional PGA official, then national committeeman and officer, and as president. After his club job at East Lake was finished, he worked late into the night on PGA business. He had recruited and trained a staff of assistants that insured his club against any loss of Sargent's expert attention when the pro was on his PGA job.

The PGA president partially logged his time away from home on association duties up to convention time in 1958: he traveled seven days, primarily on PGA National Golf Club business; he spent twelve days away from home on the PGA merchandising program; and he had thirty-four days away from home on PGA general business. Altogether, on matters involving the PGA, Sargent had logged 124 days away during the year, and his wife had typed 325 PGA letters. A PGA president's wife isn't elected to her tough job.

Every PGA president had added to his regular work an out-of-town schedule much as Sargent set forth. Despite a better headquarters system and more personnel, the president's duties have increased. Warren Orlick, as PGA president, detailed a schedule of seventy-three days entirely, or in part, on PGA assignments from November 22, 1971, to April 28, 1972. Only the dedication of the Eisenhower College and Hospital, which involved the PGA as cosponsor of the "Golfers for Ike" campaign, and the Golf Course Superintendents' convention and banquet weren't important PGA affairs. The planning of the 1972 PGA Championship, Tournament Policy Board meetings, sectional and business school meetings in wide-apart locations, committee meetings at various spots, sessions with amateur as-

View of the bleachers, Tam O'Shanter course. PGA

sociations, and discussions with the landlord about the lease at Palm Beach Gardens were some of the subjects on the Orlick docket as another roving president of the PGA.

In 1958, the PGA hired a young man who was to greatly ease and simplify the executive operations of the PGA at headquarters and in the field, when Lloyd F. Lambert came out of the offices of Arnold, Fortas, and Porter to be aide to the seriously overworked Tom Crane. A quiet, efficient man with a genius for boiling down the reports of innumerable PGA meetings so that only the essentials took up time and space, Lambert quickly proved himself invaluable to Executive Secretary

Crane. The two strengthened PGA operating management even more when Crane was made executive director and Lambert was named executive secretary.

Affairs were as usual in one respect at the PGA National Course in 1958—there was another superintendent. The brave new man on the job was Carl Dilsaver. Complaints of the pro winter visitors about the course were not shared by the few resident professionals, all of them retired from pro jobs, and members of the Dunedin Isles Country Club who'd bought memberships when the PGA Club had been a local private operation. However, the amateurs protested they weren't getting much of a chance at starting time in the winter.

Then George S. May, whose golf show had made playing professionals rich, announced that he was through with golf. The pioneer of tournament golf, who showed business how to get cheap advertising to the right people with a purse that made the peasants' eyes pop, had had enough. He told Lou Strong, professional at his Tam O'Shanter Country Club on the northwest rim of Chicago, "I'm just tired of fighting the whole thing." Strong, Illinois PGA president and later to become national PGA president, couldn't get the tournament professionals to cooperate with the man who raised purses for his All-American and All-World championships for men and women professionals until the winner of George's World Championship was top prize money winner of the year.

May paid his company's money for full-page ads in newspapers inviting to the tournament thousands in and around Chicago who had never seen golf. He also gave away free tickets by the thousands (and discovered he had to pay a tax on them). He was the first to erect bleachers at the sixteenth green and other vantage spots at the course. His press room in the clubhouse, overlooking the eighteenth, sixteenth, seventeenth, and first greens and much of the fairways, was so much better than the press facilities at any other tournament that golf writers thought they were in another world when they came to the May events.

May had plenty of free parking space for members, players, guests, and press near the clubhouse and acres at $1 per car per day bordering the course. He had his tournament on network television as a "first"; he had moderate prices for hot dogs, hamburgers, and other food and drinks on the course and in the clubhouse during his tournaments. He was the first to require tournament players to have identifying numbers of their caddies and gave away free starting-time sheets carrying the players' numbers. He declared that anybody who paid to get in deserved to know who was playing.

May refused offers to sponsor a tournament program, saying that as a business management authority he'd decided that putting money in a slot machine was a much better investment than a golf tournament program. He certainly qualified as an authority in this department, since his organization had made an extensive study of golf tournaments, perhaps the only one ever made, and one that dug into details not usually loosely revealed. He also had a number of slot machines and wheels of chance in his clubhouse, and the Chicago mobsters had had the ax over him and many other private clubs and fee courses around Chicago. But George S. May was the first one to stand up when the mob was bearing down. The Chicago area golf courses were exposed to corrective measures if they didn't let the crooks run the clubhouse slot machines and other gambling devices. With guts and high-priced lawyers, and Joe Jemsek, a tough ex-caddie who owned fee courses and who knew who was taking what and from whom among fellows laughingly called "law enforcement" personnel around Chicago, May stood up and fought back.

May was a historic character in a lot of ways. He certainly made American business aware of the publicity and sales potential of golf tournaments. With his remunerative competitions he shook big business and made it realize that a company could make the right contacts with golf publicity. He was the daddy of all corporations that wanted publicity cheap.

He had also done tournament golf a great service by showing clubs how to conduct tournament business at a profit, providing prize money was a good normal sum for those times, if considerably short of what May gave as an advertising expense for his company. May owned Tam O'Shanter. He bought it when the course and clubhouse were unfinished, members were few, and creditors were pressing. He made his clubhouse thoroughly modern, with enough dining rooms and bars to care for a heavy volume. The outdoor food and drink stands were attractively operated. The word got around that clubs needing money should be host to a tournament in the May manner. With a share of television revenue in prospect, the tournament looked even better. Hence, clubs that were not qualified for the National Open or Amateur, or didn't want these events, saw a chance of substantial profit in a tournament and had members willing to work free to put the tournament across.

And with all this, possibly Arnold Palmer, Jack Nicklaus, Billy Casper, Lee Trevino, Johnny Miller, and the other boys who hit the golden goose for over a million dollars worth of feathers have only the faintest idea who George S. May was.

Treasurer Warren Cantrell reported that the PGA had operated with $8,601 more revenue than expenses for the fiscal year 1958. Income had been up $41,471 over the previous year, and expenses had been $24,490 greater. The Tournament Bureau had registered a net income of $32,814. Despite the complaining about the PGA National Golf Club, General Manager Frank Sprogell

George S. May. PGA, photo from *Professional Golfers* magazine

had followed the 1957 net profit of $15,524 with another year in the black, with a profit of $8,137.

For the second consecutive year the Relief Fund showed a loss of $2,000. Members were getting older, and clubs were far behind other employers in fringe benefits. The fault wasn't altogether that of the clubs. Many professionals didn't stay too long at their jobs for the simple and sufficient reason that they couldn't make a living at many of the clubs and pay-as-you-play courses.

The association broke about even on the PGA Championship at Llanerch. The club made about $30,000. Ticket sales were $90,000, and the program revenue was $45,000.

A new type of contract was made with the Minneapolis Golf Club for the

1959 PGA Championship. The PGA would get the first $40,000 of admission revenue and split following sales fifty-fifty with the club. The program advertising arrangement was continued, with 12.5 percent of the net going to the PGA.

Television revenue was a foggy factor. There'd been good televising of the championship at Llanerch, as televising of a golf tournament was done in those days—a two- or three-hole job of coverage and the prize money presentation. But the PGA got nothing out of that air show from suburban Philadelphia.

An agency offered to buy television rights to the PGA Championship and PGA cosponsored tournaments, but was turned down. Marty Carmichael, a bright young lawyer at the Columbia Broadcasting System, discovered the PGA was an innocent in the TV woods and snatched it by the hand as adviser, representative, and what-all on the medium to the PGA. The PGA's tournaments got only a few choice advertisers for several years and used cheap copy better suited to commercials for a crap game than for tournament golf's quality market.

With baseball switching from afternoon to night games, there was a lot of air time available to golf. Perhaps golf lacked the action to contend with other TV sports, but it had scenery, an association of social prestige, the fine play of experts, and the drama of a lot of money hanging on one putt. In the earlier years, televised golf was relatively inexpensive to produce. People didn't expect much. Then competition between the networks expanded both the area of coverage and the expense. The Masters provided camera platforms, underground wiring, and other facilities possible for a fixed event and gave TV preference over the press in

interviewing the winner. This infuriated golf reporters, who felt they were being downgraded by the tournament they'd made into a classic. And soon television managed to do what the press had never been able to do—it commanded pairing and starting times for easy coverage on the last two days of a tournament. The USGA and the Masters had to accommodate themselves to TV or lose a trainload of fiscal gravy.

Steadily the prize money increased, with the 1958 figure passing $1.5 million. Every phase of tournament golf was bustling, and opportunities for development and exploitation were so profuse that J. Edwin Carter, manager of the Tournament Bureau, was asked to discontinue his representation of the Ladies' PGA and curtail other activities to concentrate on his PGA job.

The PGA had ninety-one events, including pro-am, on its calendar for the year. There was considerable turnover in the schedule, and twenty-three of the 1958 events were new. The sponsors couldn't get together. About half the tournaments were sponsored by members of the International Golf Sponsors' Association, and half by unaffiliated sponsors. Jay Hebert of the Tournament Committee told a meeting of the Tournament Advisory Committee that professionals were controlled and penalized by their own members now, but if anyone else told them what to do, the players would "walk out." Walk out to where? sponsors wondered, and asked the Tournament Committee to spell out what rights sponsors had in return for putting on an expensive tournament.

The PGA had appointed a Tournament Advisory Committee, consisting of Advisory Board members Harry Radix, Glenn Sisler, and Bob Goldwater and representatives of the International Golf Sponsors' Association and of unaffiliated sponsors. Bo Winiger, Dow Finsterwald, and Bob Rosburg represented the players, with the PGA entitled to vote in case of a tie. The Tournament Advisory Committee was similar in purpose to the Tournament Policy Board, named to keep the peace after the PGA civil war had been settled and the Tournament Players' Division formed. The earlier group never managed to become effective.

The PGA Seniors' Championship had made a nice little profit of $2,000 at their competition and merry gathering of the clans, foreign and domestic. National Golf Day took in $82,000, compared to $70,000 the previous year, and the Tournament Bureau reported a surplus of $90,000.

Money was easier all around with the PGA. The PGA Foundation announced a grant of $2 per member to each section for educational programs, although the PGA contract with Jack Moon wasn't paying as had been expected and Moon had indicated he wasn't going to renew the sales contract that was to expire June 30, 1959.

Thurman W. Arnold of the law firm representing the PGA reviewed the foundation's financial situation and said it was deteriorating rapidly. In the first twenty-one months of the PGA contract with Moon, sales were $2,260,000. In nine months of 1958, sales dropped to $650,000. Arnold told the meeting that the PGA and the Burke Golf Company had negotiated a ten-year contract, with Burke guaranteeing to sell $1.5 million worth of PGA-brand clubs the first year and to increase sales by 10 percent each of the following ten years.

Other manufacturers to which PGA-brand licenses had been granted were Eaton shoes, Perella gloves, Stein belts, Aristocrat headcovers, Lissner slacks, C. M. Hill headcovers, Plymouth golf balls, Manhattan shirts, shorts, and sweaters, Camelia Mills hosiery, Fran Noseworthy jackets, MacNeill golf spikes, Esquire Sportswear slacks and shorts, Westchester Luggage carryall bags, Fountain Hill sports shirts, Old Colony Knitting Mills sports shirts, Herschel caps, Brass Ram putters, Truly Lee hats, Fred Matzie putters, Nadco Sporting Goods Company seat canes, Haas Jordan Company golf umbrellas, and Pittsburgh Fabric Products carryall bags.

The sales brains and marketing power of those organizations, plus Jack Moon's distributors and the PGA's own efforts, should theoretically have made that PGA-brand campaign a great success, but it flopped and was wilting away to dust with only the Burke club business remaining as a skeleton in the dream.

Eventually, control of what was left of the Burke Golf Company, with its PGA contract, was acquired by Jack Schram, a Chicago financier and golf enthusiast. Then Schram and A. C. Buehler, principal owner of the Victor Comptometer Company, were involved in a deal to absorb the older and decidedly substantial Worthington Ball Company, which had been making golf balls since 1904. Along with the Worthington and Burke companies, Buehler got Robert F. Smith, who'd been with the golf ball department of United States Rubber, then with the L. A. Young Golf Company before going to Worthington. Buehler and Smith were not the kind to ride losers, and they immediately began to take charge of the golf goods manufacturing and wholesaling situation with which PGA officials had had no luck at all.

Smith brought out of retirement Eddie Rankin, who'd been general manager of the Hagen company and then with Ben Hogan, and the revival of the PGA line was on. Then Smith became ill and retired, but not until he'd worked with his successor, Mark Cox, who'd been with Wilson, Golfcraft, and MacGregor, and Jim Butz, who'd been a companion sales executive with Cox at Wilson and MacGregor. With the new lineup, the PGA brand in a little more than three years achieved a sales volume exceeding that of all previous PGA brands, going way back to the PGA balls of the 1920's.

The substantial revenue from PGA-brand sales was channeled from the Educational Fund to the Pension Fund even before the association could work out a pension plan with clubs and some fee-course owners, with the employer contributing in a manner compatible with wage and tax regulations. For a long time, kinks in the laws precluded a pension plan for club professionals, and a pension plan for playing professionals was delayed by the inability of players to agree on a method of assessment.

The PGA annual winter business school continued its short course at Dunedin with a continuing increase in enrollment. The educational session at the convention was brief. The golf cart continued to concern professionals, who worried about what effect it would have on their earnings. William Freund, of the Victor Golf Cart Company, forecast that the electric golf cart would increase play when caddies were not available and would produce revenue that would enable many golf clubs to operate at a profit. But obviously, financing, management, maintenance, course construction, and course wear problems were going to be

numerous and complex before the golf cart became standard equipment. Some of these problems became too much for the Victor company's golf cart department, which was a hobby of the company's president, so its manufacture was discontinued.

Milt Woodward, executive vice-president of the Western Golf Association, talked about the golf cart in its relation to the caddie and the caddie master, foreseeing that the three factors could be coordinated for the good of golf, profitable operation at the majority of metropolitan district clubs, and retention of caddie interest in golf. Paul Stephens of the Pinellas County, Florida, School System spoke on "Psychology of Learning as Applied to Motor Skills." It was too postgraduate for most of his listeners.

The Georgia-Alabama section, the PGA's thirty-fourth, was the new geographic element at the association's thirty-fourth annual meeting December 3 through 10, 1959, at the Fort Harrison Hotel in Clearwater. First attention was given to the affairs of the touring specialists, which were even more tangled and contentious than usual.

For seven years the Tournament Bureau had been operating and voting as a section virtually independent of the PGA, but closely allied with it because of mutual benefits to tournament and home professionals. The parent organization also helped provide the financing needed to get a tournament circuit established, and it also helped defend tournament activities against a number of parties craving to take over what obviously had become a rich and growing sports field. In this connection the meeting heard partial disclosures of proposals made by individuals and corporations desirous of taking over pro tournament golf. Some of the calculating citizens involved had devious commercial reputations.

Harold Sargent continued as president at this gathering, with Lou Strong as secretary and Warren Cantrell as treasurer. Tom Crane stayed busy in the background as executive seretary. Again the constitution was altered to spell out in sharp detail the effective autonomy of the tournament section. The result was to set the Tournament Division in the position it is in today. (When the PGA civil war broke out and the Tournament Players' Division of the PGA was formed, the brawling, attorneys' fees, office expenses, and salaries greatly increased without any significant alteration in the type of management and promotion, except that Joseph C. Dey, Jr., was brought in from his post as executive director of the USGA to handle the PGA tournament management job done by J. Edwin Carter.)

Treasurer Cantrell presented the PGA financial picture as a scorecard should be: simple and accurate. Cantrell was the most experienced businessman the PGA had had as a national officer—he and a brother had built up a large engineering and contracting company. But Warren Cantrell preferred a career as a professional golfer. He was an ideal club professional at Lubbock, Texas, and an outstanding official of the PGA in that state before being elected to PGA national office where, among other services, he saved the PGA from becoming indebted for millions in a real-estate promotion that would have held it captive in a business it didn't know. Already the bloom was off the rose in Dunedin, and city officials as well as PGA members and officers were looking for a way to get out.

In 1959, about 80 percent of the

PGA membership was located east of the Mississippi. The association had, as of September 1, 1959, a total of 4,257 members, of whom 3,142 were Class A. Dues income was $199,005. Net income of the PGA for the year was $32,814, after caring for a Tournament Bureau loss of $16,288. Tournament circuit, PGA Championship, and Ryder Cup figures were all in the report but rather scattered.

Bob Rosburg replaced Bo Winiger as chairman of the Tournament Committee. With him on the committee were Art Wall, Julius Boros, and Don Fairfield. Rosburg said he'd been trying to get the Tournament Committee settled in profitable coordination with the rest of the PGA and now thought the situation was better than it had been for ten years, but he was having trouble finding out what was going on in his own part of the job, as J. Edwin Carter didn't seem to be eager to take the committee into his confidence. The oversight was excusable. J. Edwin possibly was the busiest man in golf.

In addition to being the manager of the Tournament Bureau, an assignment that had kept industrious predecessors fully occupied for the PGA, he was managing a group of tournament players he'd signed for Screen Gems, a subsidiary of Columbia Pictures. There were, eventually, a reported fifty-five of the players signed for $500 each for a competitive series that was to be televised. Avoiding the yowls of players who weren't cut in for the $500, selling program advertising, promoting ticket sales, and planning recruiting and employment of free labor in the operation of the forthcoming National Open and PGA championships were some of the matters that filled his day. Also engaging the attention in leisure moments of the vigorous J. Edwin were the overtures of the Music Corporation of America, the leading talent booking agency in the theatrical business, agents for several leading golfers who wanted their cuts first, and if possible, exclusively, on revenue accruing from the golf talent of their clients. And there were merchandising opportunities in professional golf that also fascinated Carter, who also represented thirty-five players for television appearances.

Carter overlooked no bets. Eventually, though, he saw that the best, the easiest, the surest, and the most lucrative department of golf show business was that of organizing and conducting major tournaments. In that work you dealt with experienced businessmen who were out of their respective fields and needed the specialized knowledge Carter had. He'd seen from the way the Junior Chamber of Commerce had enlisted volunteer workers—young businessmen and their wives—that tournament golf had the biggest and best pool of free labor that possibly could be used to make a tournament pay.

Consequently, he virtually quit herding the tournament players and competing with numerous other managers and went after the big money of a few big tournaments a year. So when a pro star was worrying himself about top money in one of the major tournaments, there was a chance that J. Edwin already had the top money made through the program, the tickets, and some of the fancy trimmings. And if a player didn't like that, he might be told that Carter was smarter and worked harder. In tournament management Carter had been preceded by Fred Corcoran from the Tournament Bureau, who made the Westchester Classic and the Canada and World Cup international professional tournaments brilliant successes.

J. Edwin Carter. Akron *Beacon Journal*

The tournament confusion, deficit, and hopes, as outlined to the PGA's 1959 assembly, were about as always, but one aspect of PGA club-pro business reflected in the treasurer's report astonished members. That was the sale of products bearing the PGA label in the few years of the current arrangements. The totals through June 30, 1959, were: shoes, $823,806.77; clubs, $778,586.39; balls, $330,331.14; gloves, $159,340.15; and other products, $395,600.85. From that $2,524,665.30 of PGA-brand merchandise the association received a royalty of $108,760.16.

The Ryder Cup fund got $30,000 from the Eldorado Country Club at Palm Desert, California, where the cup matches were held on November 6 and 7, 1959. Expenses were considered too heavy, and Cantrell and PGA President Sargent inaugurated an economy program. The May Company engineers had studied the PGA office and urged a revision of methods involving modern equipment instead of additional personnel. The investigation had taken eight weeks.

The British politely suggested that the Yanks might be somewhat too hospitable for a team that was supposed to be hungry—hungry for victory and not hungering to eat itself out of shape at American welcoming parties. There had been a fine party and an informal exhibition at Leo Fraser's Atlantic City Country Club and another round of play and a dinner given by members of the Burning Tree Club in Washington, where Max Elbin was pro. And in the California desert the exuberant Bob Hudson was host every time a visiting player or British journalist felt hunger or thirst.

American team expenses could have been reduced somewhat if all the free offers of apparel and trimming had been accepted. Ernie Sabayrac, an ex-caddie who became an extensive distributor of golf-playing equipment and apparel, offered to equip the team with everything except the clubs and balls the players had been signed to play, if he were allowed to advertise that he'd uniformed the team and supplied the bags. But the PGA turned down the offer of cosponsorship of the Ryder Cup matches by his suppliers. It was a far cry from the time when the dapper Hagen, as captain, sent Ryder Cup team members to the most expensive sports tailors in New York to get correctly outfitted, with the bill dispatched to the PGA.

Sargent believed that the PGA and the host club should share fifty-fifty in the profits of a PGA Championship. It would be foresighted for the players to request this, Sargent declared. The Association of PGA Tournament Sponsors and the International Golf Sponsors' Association had combined and

were campaigning to prove that the absence of Snead or Hogan didn't reduce a tournament's profit.

Players were complaining about the way the National Open was run. It was too tough for the stars. They wanted more prize money. The USGA was having its own difficulties then in getting desirable clubs willing to undertake the work of putting on a National Open Championship. Meantime, the young professionals whom Carter had overlooked in picking the talent for the Screen Gems films were now talking about a circuit of three-day tournaments and a junior PGA of their own, while the Masters, still the best-run tournament of them all, had pros as invited guests, well pleased and honored to be invited.

A settlement had been made with the Blue Hill Country Club of suburban Boston about the 1956 PGA Championship. Instead of the $25,000 the PGA claimed was due it, the association got around $20,000 minus lawyers' fees.

Another embarrassing complication occurred when it was revealed that the promotion and program commission paid J. Edwin Carter had been deducted from the gross before the PGA began dividing the proceeds according to its agreement. Otis Dywick, University of Minnesota athletic press agent and long an indefatigable press agent for pro and amateur golf, had produced the program, so the club naturally wanted to get his cut from the gross before the split, but it was slow on the trigger, and J. Edwin, who had also worked hard, was out of range. This didn't make Wally Mund and Gunnard Johnson, veteran PGA officials who had prevailed upon the Minneapolis Golf Club to take the championship, look unblushingly at their neighbors. But at the annual meeting it was all settled happily with the PGA making the requested financial adjustment and saying to the boys and girls at Minneapolis, "Sorry, good folks, you guessed the peas were under the wrong shell."

Harold Sargent saw the policy of the PGA in a different light. Young Sargent was a prescient professional and had the good luck to be aligned with club officials and members who saw the future in golf as he did. Sargent and his employers had a far better working arrangement than possibly 80 percent of the other clubs in the world. And Sargent was strong on the National Golf Day operation as a way of identifying golf players and pros as the most generous persons in all sport. But he could never get across his idea of generosity as a golfer's trademark.

National Golf Day income went up to $82,000 from the $81,000 of the previous year. Few clubs were represented, and it puzzled pros that tournament players should be so tight. But pros were frank enough to ask if it might not be their fault for not going about the game's nationwide benefit day in the right way. They agreed that women at clubs were far more important than men as unselfish and useful fund-raisers.

The pros have always worried about the future of golf but seem to have Providence protecting them. There was plenty of talk at the 1959 meeting about not having PGA tournaments played at clubs where PGA pros didn't have full concessions. But just when somebody jumped up to say, "I move the motion be seconded," another man arose and said, "I haven't got them and am with a good club and making more than anybody else in our neighborhood." Although a resolution was passed to prohibit tournaments at

courses where pros didn't have the shop all the way, it was never taken too seriously.

The PGA Business Training School at Alameda, California, was inaugurated with a faculty headed by Jimmy Thompson of the Rancho Golf Club and Guy Bellitt of Altadena. Jimmy Thompson (not the old long-driving Jimmy Thom—no "p"—son) was a young man who combined the first principles of golf business: instruction and selling. Pacific Coast amateurs said that only Willie Hunter's wife was better at selling golfers the supplies they really needed, although Larry Lamburger at the Portland Golf Club might be the champion. But in working out agreements with municipal and private club officials so their people and the pro came out happy, Guy Bellitt was proclaimed the champion by all concerned.

Professional golfers had to have a quick sense of humor to survive. One of their laughs came at the 1959 meeting when several earnest professionals petitioned that the manufacturers advertise "pros" only as "professionals," that no "pro" shop should be designated as such, but as a "professional" shop—all the familiar "pro" stuff being dismissed as beneath the dignity of the PGA member. The matter was given profound thought, then somebody addressed the officials and delegates to demand a change in the method of selecting the Golf Professional of the Year in various sections. The selections had sometimes missed the target, as prominent women golfers and golf writers in some sections had voted in pros who were minus several zeros in credit ratings, not PGA members, and just simply didn't rate officially. Dedicated to progress and with enough headaches over trying to make the journeyman playing specialists rich, the delegates laughed and concluded that nature would take its course—which nature did, and all worked out satisfactorily for the clubs and gypsy pros concerned.

CBS had bought TV rights to the next two PGA championships, with the PGA getting 80 percent of the TV revenue and the host club 20 percent. The Firestone Company's Number One course was to have $100,000 spent on it for the 1960 Championship. Firestone unquestionably got far more valuable publicity over the years from golf tournaments on. its primary course than any other industrial course owner. It also had a bright public-relations staff and had everything going for it in pro golf until somebody put on a television plug for Firestone store sales of a cheap putter and three cheap golf balls. It took years for Firestone to regain a quality rating with golf pros.

With television money coming in, there was a feeling among tournament players that they'd be in pictures and get rich, so never mind the PGA. Bob Rosburg said at the 1959 meeting that four or five men had signed between sixty and seventy professionals to television contracts, and that the situation could wreck the PGA tournament schedule, the PGA Championship, and the Ryder Cup competitions. That threat vanished in a couple of years when so many pros and their managers, in addition to the ubiquitous J. Edwin Carter, got into the act, that the expected TV bonanza all but fled over the horizon in the rush.

The salaries disclosed at the meeting again reminded the delegates why club pro members always complained that the PGA was being run for the tournament players. Carter got a salary of $20,000 a year, plus $16,800 for ex-

penses, in what was a part-time job for the association. Harvey Raynor, the tour supervisor who really operated the pros' road shows, drew $18,200 as salary. Frank Sprogell got a salary of only $4,200, plus pro-shop and cart concessions. Carl E. Dilsaver, the course superintendent, got $7,000 a year.

Sprogell had done something that was to produce a large revenue for the PGA and become one of its valuable services to home professionals. He'd noticed several energetic salesmen exhibiting their lines at tables around the PGA National Course clubhouse and in the pro shop, and he got the idea of putting on a Merchandise Show during the PGA Seniors' tournament. He sold the notion to PGA officials and took on the job of getting a big tent erected on ground cleared back of the little clubhouse. Bad weather and every other setback handicapped Sprogell, but he kept taking abuse and bellyaching, and he was the one who thought up and sweated out the right answers that the eventual cooperation of astute PGA committeemen and exhibitors made a tremendous success.

With some imagination about Merchandise Show possibilities and immense work, Frank Sprogell brought more money than any other man to the PGA and the community that received the buying pros and salesmen. And all this for a salary of $4,200 as PGA National Golf Club general manager.

The club was due to move. Offers were coming in—from Naples, Florida, which proposed giving 400 acres to the PGA, and from Fort Lauderdale and Southern Pines, North Carolina, with no details attached.

In a summary of PGA problems, President Sargent remarked, "During the life of the Advisory Committee we have taken very few of its suggestions. Later on we have found the committee has been right."

Proposals to get the PGA heavily involved in a real-estate promotion in Florida and to sell out the tournament operations for 3 percent of the gross of all income involved in the show business section of the PGA took up most of the association's forty-fourth annual meeting at the Valley Ho Hotel, Scottsdale, Arizona, November 10 through 18, 1960. There was no change in officers from the previous year. Harold Sargent was president, Lou Strong was secretary, and Warren Cantrell was treasurer. Present were delegates from thirty-five sections, the added section being the Tournament Committee, which voted as did other sections. The association reported a high of 4,624 paid-up members, of whom 3,303 were in Class A.

Since PGA-cosponsored tournaments were being made promotions—generally for local charities in which a substantial promotion fee came off the top—a group of amateurs suggested that the PGA protect professional golf against a possible charge of complicity in the promoters' misuse of the charity and other worthy cause aspects. Carlton Blunt, who'd been active as a Western Golf Association official in building the Evans Caddie Scholarship operation, James Clark, and John Pounders proposed that a nonprofit organization, Golf Tournament Charities, be formed, staffed, and operated in an expert manner, applying the highest type of forceful business methods and conforming to the PGA's Code of Ethics. There was eyebrow lifting as the subject was discussed briefly, then dropped. Under existing conditions and with enough Tournament Bureau problems already,

this was not a matter of public service to be handled in haste.

More pressing was the problem of the PGA National Golf Club at Dunedin, which had not been the utopia some pros expected. Many weren't sure what they did want—maybe something like Seminole, Indian Creek, Lake Wales, or Palma Ceia with no dues, or something like the Old Course at St. Andrews or Carnoustie with starting anytime you wanted to. The beautiful plan just hadn't worked out for the wintering pros, the local real-estate people, and other businessmen.

President Sargent told the meeting: "Last year we received a mandate from the membership to give up the Dunedin course." City officials of Dunedin were in rather enthusiastic accord with the PGA's decision to move, because the PGA hadn't brought many residents to the pretty little place. Irv Schloss was one of them, and he doubted that more than twenty PGA families had moved in. Tom Crane and a few others came with the PGA offices. Mike Brady and his wife Grace lived on the border of a fairway. Mike was one of the truly great pioneer stars. His mementos would have been prized on the walls of exclusive golf clubs in the North; down there, they were stuff Mike and Grace could keep at home.

Johnny Inglis, the little man who as caddie and professional in the early 1900's had made celebrated fine citizens out of little dirty-nose kids, was another quiet and beloved unknown at Dunedin. Frank Sprogell, who brought thousands of dollars to the Clearwater area by working up the PGA Merchandise Show, was just another nice, civic-minded resident in Dunedin, but he made history in the billion-dollar golf business.

However, moving wasn't easy. Where to go? Why? What was it going to cost now and all the tomorrows? Was the PGA in the real-estate business? Shouldn't members join clubs where they lived in the winter as men in other businesses did? There was no end to the questions, but now the hunt was on.

Paul Erath, a delegate with successful pro-superintendent experience who had also been a club owner in western Pennsylvania, reminded fellow members that: "At a PGA National Golf Club you've got about a four-month operation for most of us and twelve months' expenses for all of us. We've got the PGA Seniors, the Quarter Century Club, the Club championship now, and will have more events when we can get sponsors, and may have the PGA and other major championships in the winter, if we can get other people to put up the money. We've gone into one deal on a shoestring and expected the superior club we didn't get. What we want is going to cost a lot of somebody's money. And the course is just a part of the proposition. You may have a clubhouse that will cost you about what the association costs in dues. Then there is office rent and a convenient location. This is not a deal for amateurs."

There were abundant warnings not to play the other fellow's game. Bob Hudson voiced the opinion of the Advisory Committee: "If somebody wants to give you something for nothing, look at his financial statement and find out what he's given away before."

The Lefcourt Realty organization offered to build the PGA a course in its development and to build a clubhouse at a cost of $1,450,000. The course was to be located in a project that would have 2,000 homes in time. It was the consensus of the meeting that the Lefcourt people were pleasant but long on real estate and short on cash, so the proposal died.

General Development Corporation, which was active in Florida real-estate promotion and had a former PGA champion, Chick Harbert, as an executive, lost interest in the PGA proposition, as did other companies that had discussed building a PGA winter home. General Development had several good courses in its operations on the eastern and western coasts of Florida.

Several delegates argued that Arizona would be the best place for a PGA National Course. The Executive Committee didn't present a building and operating budget for the proposed club, and such details as who'd pay the taxes, and who'd get the green fees, and how much the annual interest would be on the proposed course, clubhouse, and office building were not mentioned. From the character of the discussions, it did not appear to Treasurer Cantrell that the PGA was qualified to be engaged in an enterprise of this sort. Cantrell, later a PGA president, never could sell himself on the idea of the PGA's using its members' money to sell real estate for somebody else.

Delegate Terry Malan remarked that some members seemed to have the notion that they were going to have a fine playground in the winter at the expense of the PGA but should snap into reality and be businessmen figuring dollars and cents. Max Elbin, later to become a PGA president, also counseled less loose talk about money. He said that at the 1959 meeting, delegates had voted to buy ground and build a course but had not mentioned money. Now the PGA had neither the ground, nor the course, nor the money, but at least it should be reminded that the

Executive Committee couldn't do the impossible and wouldn't do the impracticable.

There was confusion about J. Edwin Carter's offer to buy the PGA's tournament business, not for cash but for 3 percent of certain limited income from the tournaments and the players. Just what Carter *wouldn't* deduct 3 percent from was not specified. President Sargent clarified that matter somewhat by remarking, "J. Edwin is very frank. He wants everything."

The situation was often amusing. At a meeting of tournament players at Fort Worth, the players wanted to know if Carter was representing Screen Gems, the eighteen players Screen Gems had optioned at $1,000 each for the coming season of its television exhibitions, and the PGA as its tournament director. To the bewildered journeyman pros, whose guardian he was believed to be, J. Edwin was one of those East Indian idols that have arms reaching in every direction. When bluntly asked whom he was representing, he made it plain to any except the incurably obtuse that Mr. Carter was representing Mr. Carter, period.

It proved to be a pretty good thing for the commerce of golf, for although J. Edwin Carter was not one of those old-fashioned, romantic types who remained sleepless, wondering: "Is it good for golf?" he was convinced that noble character is the best business policy and involves less strain on the memory.

Bob Harlow had seen the possibilities of the Junior Chamber of Commerce members and their wives giving PGA tournament circuit promotion the vast amount of free labor needed. Then came Fred Corcoran to get tournament planning, facilities, and operation well organized on a basis that has remained

substantially the same. Corcoran's imagination and lawyers and the generosity of Bing Crosby, plus the business and publicity savvy of Bing's brother and business manager Larry, brought the charity angle with its broad tax exemptions into the tournament business. Tournament program advertising was a hit-or-miss deal, calling for deft and relentless use on everybody in the line of fire of what in the lower levels of commerce is called "muscle."

Bing Crosby wasn't aware of what he was doing in contributing the net of his annual tournaments to boys' clubs and other welfare causes. The charity tax deductions with the players' purses and the tournament promoter's bill and other operating expenses getting priority didn't invariably confirm the New Testament line: "And the greatest of these is charity." But the exemptions did allow corporations and individuals sponsoring big-money golf tournaments to get extensive advertising and stars in their crowns with low net cost, and what could make good works more popular?

The change of life of tournament golf from a traditional sport to a trade was puzzling for a while to professionals and older amateurs, but the change was clear to J. Edwin Carter. He'd learned the curves and the angles and was the only one with the experience, temperament, and energy to move into the mercenary tomorrow of the ancient and honorable game.

Corcoran was content with his top class and successful tournament promotion accounts, with his consultant work with golf and other sports organizations in the United States and abroad, and with advertising agency work as a sports consultant. He needed no more money or ulcers. Fred Corcoran had steered Sam Snead, the first pro golfer to score a million at the bank. This record needs the confirmation of the Almighty and the IRS but is validated by substantial evidence and authoritative snitches. Corcoran never did take a percentage of the prize winnings of his clients and thought managers who did that were pickpockets, but different times seem to require different morals.

Carter saw the brilliant financial prospects in the phony testimonials of pro athletes and was not horrified by the promise of sharing a cut in the loot. He had been around. But when he saw Hollywood talent agents trying to take over the management of pro golfers, he got out of that end of the business, and by directing tournaments with free labor doing the work that brought in the money, lived happily ever after as golf turned from a nice old game into a rough grand racket. Carter was a realist and deeper on the reach than other Tournament Bureau directors had been before, so when he announced he wanted to take over tournament golf, that was the end of an era.

At the 1960 meeting, the fundamental division between the home pros and the tournament players once again became apparent. It was a realistic split with malice toward none. The home pro had to think of his members and his club or fee-course employers and golf in general; the touring pro didn't think of anyone except himself until his money competition days were over and he had to make a living.

In 1960, there was a surplus of almost $90,000 in the Tournament Bureau funds. The PGA Championship was getting to be a solid moneymaker, and the Ryder Cup had acquired so much prestige that if a tournament player didn't make the team he was just another guy swinging a club. So, as

before, if now even more heatedly, pros discussed how much more the PGA had spent since its formation in 1916 on building tournament golf than on developing the game for the home professionals and their amateurs.

Television revenue and the income from tax-exempt tournaments, charities, and advertising meant big money for the journeymen, while the home pros were taking a beating from competing retailers selling golf goods. In preparing for the inevitable, a tournament player was defined as one who played in more than ten major tournaments a year. The Caribbean winter circuit tournaments were not rated as major events. And now that the Tournament Section was practically autonomous, the leading players wanted to reduce the number of playing specialists voting on tournament matters.

Carter offered a $300,000 tournament from the Seagram whisky people, with $175,000 for home-pro competition in fifteen sectional events if he were allowed to run the event for the distillers. Seagram's had put up the trophy and prize money for the Canadian Open and was also the main sponsor of the Caribbean circuit. Teacher's distillers had been financing the PGA Seniors for years, so there was hardly the public-relations problem that would have existed had a whisky company shared billing with pro baseball or football as a partner. But the transaction was turned down because of the home pros' reluctance to be identified with liquor distributors in localities where unsavory characters were believed to have too much of the action. The PGA had already been criticized for being too clubby in tournaments with Las Vegas characters who were no doubt charming parties and engaged in some legal enterprises, but were hardly

America's landslide choices as Scout-masters.

Eight players had made over $80,000 each in prize money and endorsements, according to J. Edwin Carter—and you may be sure that with his 20/20 cash register vision Carter was not given to making fanciful statements about money in his department. Carter's remark jarred the PGA's home-pro membership, none of whom had done any too well in profits in 1960. There was a revival of the query: "What's the PGA doing for me?" And the answer was that home pros were paying to make the show business pros rich, and that the insurance, educational programs, and employment aid provided by the PGA for the home pros were not exceptional benefits.

Figures on the percentage of PGA operating costs devoted to tournament professionals were not accompanied by figures on what the tournament players paid. The tournament players continued complaining, while demands and trouble with sponsors, collectively, were getting to the stage where many club pros were fed up. They had not had a satisfying business year, and that left them frustrated and impatient.

The PGA educational program for the year had been about as usual in the marketing and instruction areas. Manufacturers and salesmen of golf apparel and increased employment of saleswomen in pro shops were strong factors in the development of pro merchandising. Better accounting and closer inventory control made it easier to keep better records for local, state, and federal taxes. Formal business schooling in short courses in Florida and California trained assistants much better than the catch-as-catch-can methods of the old apprentice way.

Sales volume at hundreds of shops

was increasing to the extent where many professionals were financing their spring inventories at banks. That gave the pro an adviser who could help him a great deal, as the banker was often a member of the borrowing pro's club. And the Christmas golf gift sales campaigns of virtually all of the alert and capable pro merchants turned their end-of-the year stocks into cash.

Yet there were many soft spots in the pro-golf merchandising situation. The pros continued to have control of the high-quality market for clubs, balls, bags, and shoes, but there was apprehension that pro-quality golf goods were getting so expensive they were pricing the pros out of a large dollar sector of the business.

When it began to look as though the PGA might plan marketing development for its members that could succeed as well as the PGA's promotion of the tournament business, nobody knew where to begin. A wealth of statistical and operating information on tournament golf had been collected over the years by the Tournament Bureau, but when it came to the marketing part of the pro business, which was about forty times the dollar volume of the playing activities, facts and figures were non-existent.

There was talk about the PGA's establishing itself as a business power with the same sort of marketing research and services other modern businesses have, but outside of expansion of the Tournament Bureau formation, nothing happened. Before definite action could be taken on the marketing bureau matter, the PGA found itself involved as the shill in a real-estate promotion, and although hooked by cunning and powerful interests, this time it luckily escaped the problems and expenses of course and clubhouse operation. All the same, the lesson of Dunedin, if any, had been quickly forgotten.

It had been plain for some years to thoughtful professionals that teaching methods had not kept pace with the improvement in scoring of playing specialists. However, the condition of instruction was difficult to determine because of lack of data on the number of lessons to men and women and the general handicap ratings of golfers. The PGA had absolutely no figures on this important phase of pro business. *Golfdom* made surveys on the number of lessons, but the response was small and did not justify a nationwide estimate by the men most experienced in golf business statistics. Some professionals reported what appeared to be an abnormally high number of lessons a year, and it was learned that they'd counted in the instruction given to classes of juniors and women as individual lessons.

Around 1960, individual lessons to women accounted for about 65 percent of all lessons. Scoring averages as determined by handicap records of sectional amateur associations indicated that approximately 90 percent of male private club members scored 90 or higher. Professionals at public and other daily-fee courses said that 95 percent of their golfers scored over 95.

This was sorry news to earnest, competent professionals. They had been doing everything possible to increase the effectiveness of instruction and had tried to make golf instruction programs a big feature of PGA meetings, national and sectional, but at the annual national meetings interest in the teaching program ran far behind tournament affairs.

Presidents George Sargent, George Jacobus, Joe Novak, and Horton Smith, especially, had always stressed instruction as the basis of the professionals' service and business growth. There had been several revisions of PGA instruction manuals, differing from each other in details and ramification rather than in development or discovery of elemental technique. The situation was baffling. Many intelligent, capable teachers knew about all there was to be taught about golf. They were good observers and analysts. But they weren't making the progress their qualifications and efforts merited in this field of adult instruction.

Professionals continued to agree that successful golf instruction was about 25 percent teaching and 75 percent learning. It was often noticed that the pros at colleges were more effective than those teaching at private clubs or ranges. Several professionals believed that not only did the more favorable muscular and nervous condition of college-age pupils, male and female, make them more responsive to instruction than adult club members, but also that their psychological condition was an important contributing factor in successfully absorbing the elements of the game.

It was also noticed that lessons meant more when a strong and exciting personality, such as that of Tommy Armour, or a quiet and intense attitude, such as that of Harvey Penick, impressed upon the pupil responsibility for learning. Then, for a brief period, there was self-examination and lively discussion concerning the possibility that golf instruction focused too strongly on the professional and too lightly on the pupil's learning attitude and capabilities. When it seemed that the PGA might come to grips with a possible breakthrough in golf instruction, the chance was again shoved aside to take another swing at the PGA National Golf Club development of a real-estate project.

During 1960, PGA finances had been satisfactory, in line with the expansion of the game in general. The general fund had $53,097, up about $14,000 from the previous year, and the Tournament Bureau net was $29,410, against a loss of $16,288 for the previous year. The magazine showed a profit of $943, against the previous year's loss of $1,957.

The 1960 PGA Championship at the Firestone course in Akron made a net profit of $43,425 for the PGA, and prize money was a high of $63,000. The beneficiaries were the Akron Junior League, the Junior Chamber of Commerce, and the Akron Beacon-Journal Charities, which split about $50,000. Firestone spent almost $250,000 in revising and reconditioning its championship course for this championship, and the course was later used for the World Championship of Golf, a television production, and the Akron Classic, an annual circuit event. Because of top-management foresight and money and the sparkling publicity team of Brubaker and Connor, Firestone got more out of golf as corporation advertising than any other company with a course, although its neighbor, National Cash Register at Dayton, which also had two courses for employees, seemed perfectly content with having one championship, the PGA of 1969, at its course.

A minor embarrassment of a type not unusual in the world of sports was treated frankly by PGA officials at the 1960 meeting. In several sections, members chosen as Golf Professionals of the Year by boards of men and women amateurs, sportswriters, and other professionals, did not get votes from man-

Jay Hebert. AG

Lou Strong. PGA

ufacturers' credit departments. Consequently, the method of choosing sectional candidates for the annual national award of the Bob Harlow trophy was altered and voting was confined to professionals who had the responsibility of getting themselves thoroughly informed.

There was mild political campaigning prior to the 1960 annual meeting. The Southwest continued to complain about taxation without representation, but the South had had Charles Hall in 1931 and 1932, and the West got Joe Novak in 1949, 1950, and 1951. Florida got the PGA National Course at Dunedin, and that was trouble and expense, so that was nothing for the Southwest to be eager to get.

On the evidence of the many mutually approved details at the annual meeting, it appeared that at last the club pros would mind their own PGA business and the journeyman pros their own affairs, and that the service professionals and playing pros were just one happy PGA family after all. Moving the PGA course wouldn't be much of a job. Dunedin didn't want it, and the PGA didn't want Dunedin. Florida real estate had hundreds of thousands of acres for a PGA home course, so there was really no problem there.

Hence, with the delusion of peace and happiness forever and evermore, the delegates voted as follows: president, Lou Strong, fifty-seven votes, Warren Cantrell, thirty; secretary, Wally Mund, fifty-one votes, Dugan Aycock, thirty-five (Warren Cantrell and Leo Fraser both were nominated for secretary, and both withdrew); and treasurer, George Hall, fifty-three votes, and Warren Orlick, thirty-two.

23

Real-Estate and Show Business Headaches,
the MacArthur Deal Puzzles Members,
the PGA Builds the House Divided

[1961, 1962, 1963]

THE forty-fifth annual meeting of the PGA, held at the Diplomat Hotel, Hollywood-by-the-Sea, Florida, November 2 to 10, 1961, was a long and tedious conclave that again proved that nothing came easily for the PGA. The year before it had appeared that the journeyman professionals had been taught at great expense of PGA time and money how to mind their own tournament business. And the experience at Dunedin, it was believed, had given the trusting PGA at least elementary lessons in the real-estate business. Hence, the association would be able, at long last, to concentrate for a time on rewarding the club professionals who worked hard to serve golfers who were paying their money to develop golf as a game and as a business. It didn't work out that way.

The vice-presidents at the meeting were Dugan Aycock, Frank Commisso, Don Fischesser, Leland Gibson, Don

January, Tom Mahan, Jack Mitchell, Bud Oakley, and Don Waryan. And no sooner had President Lou Strong pounded the gavel and Secretary Wally Mund and Treasurer George Hall begun pawing over papers, than the delegates of thirty-four sections and Don January and Lionel Hebert as Tournament Section delegates began wondering whether the PGA was in the pro golf business or the promotion of Florida subdivision sales.

They were somewhat confused and concerned at the pace at which the PGA was tying itself to the MacArthur interests. Some members of the Executive Committee thought the "understandings" and agreements should be spelled out and decisions made on advice of competent counsel. The proposed transaction was one between real-estate experts and a group of men who were experts in professional golf, but not experienced in real estate or office building construction and management. Experience apparently told; the PGA paid in litigation costs for playing the other fellow's game.

It became obvious, too late, that much of the trouble between the PGA and MacArthur could have been avoided by more frankness on both sides. PGA members, of whom there were 4,826 (including 3,384 Class A members) in 1961, felt they weren't told what was happening about negotiations for a new national golf club and that Executive Committee meetings were usually confined to "matters of a confidential nature." The ordinary member paying dues into a "Building Fund" was beginning to think he wasn't to be trusted with full information about his association. It was an unfortunate situation, resulting from poor communications rather than lack of confidence.

A strange little thing, quickly forgotten, happened at that meeting. In the usual annual fussing about how many clubs there should be legally, it was agreed that the number-two wood was obsolete. The delegates were thinking of the better players, but the finding, really, was that drivers, instead of having ten or eleven degrees' loft, should be laid back more, and the gap between the lofts of drivers and number-three woods for the immense market of people who paid for their clubs should be sensibly adjusted. It took some manufacturers almost a decade to revise loft specifications to the 1961 PGA recommendation.

But that delay was not unusual. Club manufacturers continued to consider primarily the wishes of playing specialists who did not pay for their clubs, instead of the home professionals who were teaching and testing clubs for players who paid cash. Hence, so

home professionals said, the purchase of golf clubs was being retarded by the failure to give primary consideration to the requirements of 95 percent of their market.

There was the customary hassle between the PGA and manufacturers about playing stars' names used on some clubs and balls of low value, and the annual complaint about manufacturers offering "closeout" clubs in midsummer through cut-price stores, thus reducing the value of pro-shop inventories months before the next year's models were available. Manufacturers claimed that television was bringing people into golf who could only afford the cheapest in clubs, balls, and bags. Buying by retailers in this cheap market was too close to allow more than precarious pennies of profit for manufacturers. However, the PGA couldn't devise a way to take advantage of the situation by campaigning on the quality merchandise platform.

The PGA Business School program was progressing steadily. The graduates were getting good pro jobs and handling them well. It wasn't spectacular and fast work, so it didn't get much publicity. Horton Smith was a leader in that schooling, and his work has been recognized with the Horton Smith Award, given annually to the PGA member who has aided pro business schooling especially well. The salary of instructors at the PGA winter school was raised to $500 for the two weeks of the terms.

At the Clearwater winter schools, the faculty included Emil Beck, Horton Smith, George Aulbach, John Budd, Bill Hardy, John Watson, Bill Hook, Don Fischesser, and Irv Schloss. At the school at the Ambassador Hotel, Los Angeles, the instructors were Dick Boggs, Bud Oakley, Guy Bellitt, Harry

Bassler, Jimmy Thompson, Joe Novak, Len Kennett, George Lake, Mac Hunter, and Olin Dutra. The schools and the educational sessions that sprang from them proved to be by far the most productive investment that the PGA ever made for golf in general. A review of the results over the years shows that the business schools alone made the PGA immensely valuable to golf clubs and public courses and to all golfers and golf goods manufacturers.

Keeping financial score for the PGA —its general and Tournament Bureau funds, the Benevolent Fund, the PGA Championship and Ryder Cup, and other items of income and outgo—made the bookkeeping a complex affair. CPAs and the stout honesty of officials and headquarters staff kept the accounting precise but rarely understandable to members.

PGA funds accumulated in several bank accounts without drawing interest. An official had observed that the PGA had money "all over: in regular banks, piggy banks, and between pages of the family Bible" and had suggested concentration and sounder management of the association funds, but no action was taken for years by the PGA, and banks weren't going to suggest they pay interest.

At the 1961 annual meeting, the breakdown was as follows: general fund income, $218,465; Tournament Bureau, $229,911; sponsors' service fees, $210,699; non–PGA member approved tournament players dues, $12,652; Tournament Bureau field, salaries and expenses, $81,172; tournament director salary and expenses, $44,733; total net income of the PGA year, $72,411; general fund net, $22,957; and Tournament Bureau net, $43,801.

Television was beginning to pay golf well. CBS had bought PGA Champion-

ship telecasting from 1958 through 1962. Sports were heavensent to television networks, since a sports telecast required no costly creative writing or planning, could be adequately produced by ordinary competent mechanical operation, and called for conventional comment on what had already been seen and heard. Televised golf, although abbreviated to the last four or five holes, showed enough of the play of the top contenders for prizes to satisfy the audience, and still allowed considerable time for commercials.

Televised golf benefited immensely at the time from a program called "Shell's Wonderful World of Golf," a series of contests at famous courses of the world between American professionals, including a few women pros, and professionals of the host countries. Although the competition wasn't the most exciting in golf, the program had everything else. It had far higher class than most televised sports events. The man who had the idea for the program was a high official of Shell so well connected and so devoted to the best interests of golf that the finest clubs in the world willingly cooperated in staging the program.

In addition to being a pleasant sports competition and a travelogue devoted to interesting and exclusive golf clubs, "Shell's Wonderful World of Golf" also presented unusually effective playing lessons by the contestants, with Gene Sarazen and Jimmy Demaret as discerning commentator-companions. There was also an excellent merchandising tie-up in the program, with the lessons being compiled in an attractive booklet in annual editions distributed through Shell service stations. The entire campaign, worked out by the Kenyon and Eckhardt advertising agency, was said to have been the most profitable selling campaign in television for service station and industrial accounts. It put golf in the big time as a TV attraction.

The show business part of professional golf was changing in personnel. J. Edwin Carter had asked and received permission from the PGA as its tournament manager to manage tournaments for sponsors as well as to run the affairs for the PGA and players. The days of commercial golf as a lovely sport were gone; it was now a business. Commercial golf was long past the years of evangelism, and J. Edwin would have no part of managing pro golfers. He'd seen them grow to distrust, then hate, managers who had several players and had the impossible problem of treating all of them equally despite differences in talent, personality, and public appeal.

So, after playing both ends (the PGA and the sponsor) against the middle (himself), Carter plainly saw that the surest path to the big money lay in getting the first bite by directing operations for tournament sponsors who didn't know what it was all about. They needed management, and Carter needed them for one of the most profitable performances in sports promotion.

Jim Gaquin, who'd been the Tournament Bureau's field publicity man, succeeded Carter as the PGA's tournament manager. He had been doing an extremely difficult job and getting no recognition for it. He was creating personalities in print and in the public mind for young tournament players so deeply overshadowed by Arnold Palmer's engaging charm that they and the rest of the field might just as well have been office clerks, truck drivers, factory workers, or farmhands.

Even Jack Nicklaus was then a solemn and distant second to Palmer in

Gene Littler clasps the World Series of Golf trophy he captured in 1966. AG

popularity, although knowledgeable golf reporters were saying among themselves that the powerful young pro was a fine news source for a competent interviewer. He gave thoughtful answers to questions and didn't get itchy and edge away when a business manager came into the locker room with a bulging briefcase of urgent mercenary concern. Palmer was in a class with Hagen and Jones. Charm came naturally to him. He'd inherited good manners, and he was a good-looking youth who smiled easily and liked people. He had excellent judgment in handling himself in public and was helped and aided decidedly by a pretty wife with all the social graces and a marvelous memory.

Gaquin had to supply golf writers with material that gave color and character to such amiable young men as Gene Littler, Bob Goalby, Billy Casper, Bob Nichols, Jackie Cupit, Dave Marr, Dave Ragan, Doug Sanders, Gay Brewer, and others who usually were there as chorus boys while the stars put on the show. Tension eased between the PGA and sponsors with Gaquin managing the Tournament Bureau. There were no angles in his relations with anybody involved in tournament golf business. He was direct and frank. Prize money increased, of course, and the free advertising, free labor, and tax exemptions of golf tournaments made them certain and substantial fundraisers.

The Tournament Bureau now acquired Jack Tuthill as tournament director. Tuthill, formerly employed by the FBI, was and is a fine golfer. He gave the tournament operation the expert supervision, sound judgment, quick decisions, knowledge of rules, and authority needed in the field. Tuthill many times took command of explosive situations and proved to be one of the best investments in men the PGA ever made. At headquarters the self-effacing and efficient Lloyd F. Lambert served as backstop to its executive directors. The PGA's operation basically works through more than thirty committees and thirty-seven sections, plus the Tournament Players' Division. Lambert is the one who keeps the committees informed, coordinated, and functioning with more life and effectiveness than might be expected from an organization of this scattered and voluntary nature.

In 1961, the PGA had forty-five "official" tournament events and nine more that didn't meet big-time standards. Total prize money was $1,792,330. Sponsors were given options on their 1961 dates for the next year, providing they increased the purses at least $5,000, with a minimum of $40,000 a tourna-

Dave Marr. AG

John MacArthur. PGA, photo by Clark's Photography

ment. The Caribbean tournament circuit in the winter of 1961 paid out $55,000 in prize money.

Bob Rosburg proved to be an invaluable member of the Tournament Committee. He was tough, blunt, knew the facts, and spoke out. He was not in favor of underground meetings. Rosburg warned there was getting to be too much gambling at tournaments. He frankly stated that some players didn't enter tournaments because the courses were inferior and in bad condition. He believed a few alterations in the Rules of Golf should be made to fit tournament circuit conditions. In that he clashed with the PGA Executive Committee, which maintained that if the circuit players got rich playing a different kind of golf game from that played by those amateurs who paid the tournament players, then tournament golf would lose its popularity.

An agreement with the British PGA

to add a third day to the 1963 Ryder Cup matches was announced. The added competition was to be in four-ball foursomes and would be inaugurated at Atlanta in 1963.

An indication that the business of playing golf was a lot of hard work came in a report from Joe Black, tournament supervisor. He said the field staff would like to work 300 days a year, then take a vacation, but the schedule wouldn't allow that, so they had to keep toiling more than 300 days a year, but without overtime pay.

The situation at the PGA National Golf Club at Dunedin was grim. When winter was over, there wasn't much play at the course. A loss of $10,000 was budgeted for 1962, and the annual meeting listened to part of the story on the move of PGA headquarters and golf course to the Promised Land, wherever that might be.

De Soto Lakes, Lehigh Acres, Fort Myers, Port St. Lucie, Sarasota, Royal Palm Beach, and Fort Lauderdale in Florida and a Del Webb project in Arizona had lost interest in becoming the home of the PGA. The remaining prospect was Palm Beach Gardens, a development on some 15,000 acres of gaunt boondocks a goodly distance northwest of Palm Beach. This area of scrub vegetation was owned by John MacArthur, a daring and entertaining party who'd brought a questionable insurance company through precarious periods of publicity and investigation in Illinois, and having attained a comfortable position, began buying cheap land in Florida. John MacArthur was one of four dynamic and imaginative brothers. The youngest was Charles, the playwright and husband of Helen Hayes. Another was Telfer, who became rich publishing suburban newspapers around Chicago, and the eldest was Alfred, a colorful insurance millionaire and patron of the arts.

John MacArthur was ingenious, imaginative, and was to become talked about as a near-billionaire in Florida land investments. His Palm Beach Gardens dream was Nothingsville until RCA located a moderate-sized plant in the subdivision, and with that came some residents. The development was dragging, but MacArthur wanted to have the whole place first class, and a shop with its workers wouldn't do it. He didn't play golf, but his adviser on this real-estate job, Jerry Kelly, came up with the PGA as the window dressing that could give the subdivision instant national class if well handled. He let the PGA nibble for a while, then got down to business with Lou Strong, PGA president. Understandably enough, Strong wanted to have a palatial playground for the PGA as a monument to his administration, and having known MacArthur as owner of a small bank in northwestern Chicago, was not averse to being taken into the confidence of a banker.

Lou did his best to play it safe for the PGA, although the details of the negotiation at times were regarded as hazy by Strong's fellow officials. Judge Arnold of the PGA's law firm was at a meeting between the Executive Committee and Kelly, the first of a great many meetings that were to have lawyers earning a considerable sum trying to establish a happy home for the PGA at Palm Beach Gardens.

The difficulty was not uncommon in

PGA National Golf Course, Palm Beach Gardens, Fla. PGA

matters involving the PGA as a tenant and as a guest at Palm Beach Gardens. Few were told all the facts about the PGA's debut in a multimillion-dollar real-estate transaction. Lou Strong told the 1961 annual meeting he'd frequently talked with Jerry Kelly about the courses, clubhouse, and office building that were to be features of a community that would have 70,000 population by 1970. But the Executive Committee and membership generally

Strong informed the delegates that on September 21, 1961, at Dunedin, Wally Mund, Harold Sargent, George Hall, Tom Crane, Lloyd Lambert, Bob Goldwater, and he had had lunch with Jerry Kelly. Kelly had proposed that the PGA should buy the land for the golf section of Palm Beach Gardens, sell the lots, and build the courses and clubhouses. After the work was done, the PGA would make money.

The delegates did not thrill to a project that only promised profit but did not guarantee it. Bob Goldwater, sitting in as a longtime member of the PGA Advisory Committee, wondered out loud why he'd traveled from Phoenix merely to listen to the PGA's being invited to finance and sell lots in a subdivision. However, by the time of the 1961 annual meeting, negotiations between the PGA and MacArthur had advanced almost to the point of signing the papers. "I want to make one thing perfectly clear," Strong told the delegates. "We are not being given anything. They have certain assets which are advantageous to us. We have certain assets that are advantageous to them. We are merely exchanging assets."

What the "assets" were and what was "advantageous" were not mentioned.

As questions continued, details of the "understandings" gradually became public. Strong informed the delegates that there had been some changes in the original agreements, but the "original agreements" themselves were never clarified. MacArthur and Kelly wanted to choose the architect for the golf courses, but the PGA wanted and got Dick Wilson of Delray Beach, Florida, one of the foremost course designers of the time, to be the architect. From 900 acres, he was to select the land he thought best suited for at least two eighteen-hole PGA courses. MacArthur agreed to pay the cost of the course maintenance buildings.

Delegates persisted in asking: "What's it going to cost us?" Max Elbin, who later was to become PGA president, insisted, "Tell us what assets we are trading." To which Strong replied, "Our financial obligation is to construct the clubhouse and office building. We, of course, will have to operate the entire project. We must provide memberships available to residents who have homes abutting the golf courses. We will have the opportunity to screen who owns the property. We have an obligation to accept daily fee play of residents of Palm Beach Gardens." And he added that the assets to be exchanged were "intangibles," such as use of the PGA's name in promotion and PGA members who "will come down and play and get their club members to come and maybe buy lots."

As far as printed records are available, the factors of PGA championships and the PGA Merchandise Show, which was to become a substantial business producer for MacArthur's Colonnades Hotel, were not mentioned in the negotiations. As to the cost of the Palm Beach Gardens PGA commitment, Strong said, "Our decision is that we

Bruce Herd (at right). PGA, courtesy of Louis Burton

might be committing ourselves to as much as $700,000 or $800,000. But it might be done for $400,000 or $500,000. We don't know."

The PGA was to get a sharper idea soon, as have many others who've built their own homes. Not many months after the 1961 meeting, Lou Strong was shopping among Chicago banks for $1 million for the PGA. The bankers were polite when they considered the odds on a real-estate promotion deal be-

tween the golf professionals and John MacArthur. But Strong's expert caution saved the PGA a great deal.

California delegates continued to ask questions about the location of the PGA National Golf Club and headquarters. As with Dunedin, Florida didn't strike them as being located in a nationally convenient spot for PGA members. "How are we going to pay for it?" delegates persistently asked. "In three years the PGA Building Fund will be $300,000," Strong told them. "Then we ought to get $75,000 from Dunedin." Delegates weren't confident they could get that much from a course that had a $10,000 operating loss budgeted for the coming year. It was also learned that PGA headquarters had been moved to a building six miles north of the Dunedin club where the rent was to be $10,500 a year for three years.

Thus it went. The PGA thought it was getting its show business headaches cured so it could devote its major efforts to helping its home pros and their members or daily-fee players, and it walked smack into a new and bewildering array of problems and mismatched itself against shrewd real-estate promoters. It was to worry through some expensive landlord and tenant conflicts before it got settled in its beautiful location at Palm Beach Gardens.

For the first time since 1941, the PGA annual meeting, November 23 through 30, 1962, was open to all PGA members, members of the Advisory Committee, and executive personnel of the organization.

There had been mild complaints, then a mounting protest about PGA members knowing too little of what was going on, especially about the dealings with John MacArthur and his employees concerning the prospective PGA courses, clubhouse, and office building. Members who didn't want the PGA in debt for millions were concerned about the "secret meetings" and "confidential" negotiations, and muttered of a revolt against the high command.

Again the good luck of the PGA and the good humor of its members prevailed, and peace was restored by putting on a show in the open at the Palm Beach Towers Hotel, Palm Beach. Talk

about private meetings being conniving rather than constructive quieted when the arguments and confusion between MacArthur and PGA officials were aired. But delegates and the few general members were astonished when Vice-President Wally Mund proposed that John MacArthur hire PGA President Lou Strong to run the new course that association members were not even clearly aware they had agreed to have built. Strong would be available. Like other PGA presidents, he had been devoting a great deal of time to his unpaid job, and officials at the Oak Hill Country Club where Lou Strong had been hired were not happy about the absence of a man who had demonstrated high competence and character as a professional. A divorce of Strong and Oak Hill was readily arranged.

Strong did become MacArthur's man, running the PGA golf operation at Palm Beach Gardens, and it was a good arrangement all around. MacArthur hired himself a competent professional, Strong got a good job, and the PGA got itself a winter playground that was far superior to the facilities provided on the tight budget at Dunedin. With Strong were Robert Thompson as clubhouse manager and Robert C. McKinney as superintendent of courses and grounds. The three made a team of superior abilities. Thompson had been in the hotel business in Detroit, then manager of the exclusive Detroit Golf Club. He came to Florida expecting to retire but was brought back into club management by MacArthur. Thompson not only ran the clubhouse, restaurant, and bar business in a remarkably satisfactory way in the winter, when business was heavy during the various PGA tournaments and the big Merchandise Show, but also built up a substantial volume of summer business.

McKinney, primarily a tree expert before he took charge of MacArthur's outdoor plant, was extraordinarily successful in beautifying the MacArthur barony. The golf courses were in excellent condition despite the vagaries of weather in the winter. Professional golfers from all over the world remarked they'd never seen courses in better condition for golf and in grooming than the PGA layout.

Strong and his staff operated a beautiful and useful pro shop, took fine care of cart assignment and maintenance, and handled playing-time bookings with expertise and diplomacy, which was often needed when PGA members came to what they thought was their own course and had the same difficulty in getting starting times that members of their own clubs experienced on Saturdays, Sundays, and other holidays during the summer.

These demonstrations of ability in operating the PGA courses and clubhouses were to come much later than the 1962 PGA meeting. The Mund recommendation of Strong as MacArthur's man was badly timed, considering the delegates' lack of information about how far the PGA had gone in its commitments to MacArthur, and George Hall, as treasurer, listened intently. He had had advice of counsel to sharpen his own ideas as the watchdog of the PGA funds.

There were thirty-four sections, with the Tournament Bureau, in effect, the thirty-fifth section, attending. The vice-presidents were Frank Commisso, Dave Bonella, Don Fischesser, Dick Forester, Lionel Hebert, E. E. Johnson, Tom Mahan, Jack Mitchell, Bud Oakley, and Don Waryan. Past Presidents Harold Sargent, George Jacobus, Joe Novak, Harry Moffitt, and Horton Smith were present at the sessions, as were

Robert L. Russell, assistant executive director, and Lloyd Lambert, executive secretary. Tom Crane, executive director, was absent. The additional work and complications of the Palm Beach Gardens negotiations hadn't done Crane's health any good.

When it was announced that John MacArthur was to meet with the Executive Committee, the news of another closed session didn't sit well with the delegates. So they were later advised that John MacArthur would appear before all sectional representatives at a session of the annual meeting.

The PGA was through with its National Golf Club at Dunedin. Transfer of the property was made on August 31, 1962, and the PGA got $50,000 for its holdings from the Dunedin Isle Golf Club as assignee of the city of Dunedin. The association had made a profit its last year at Dunedin, mainly from the Merchandise Show. The PGA's winter tournaments and its growing Merchandise Show were to be held at Port St. Lucie, Mahan announced.

Financially the PGA had a good year in 1962 with a gross income of $1,-221,700 and a net of $243,191 over expenses. The Tournament Bureau income was $244,582, with a net of $72,-035. Evidently the Tournament Bureau was being efficiently operated by Jim Gaquin as director, the Tournament Committee, the PGA headquarters, and the field staff, which certainly was working more than most of the players. It asked for and got a reduction of its annual working days from 300 to 295. Why not? Purses had increased to $2,084,170, and fifty-nine players topped $10,000 in winnings.

As of September 1, 1962, the association had 5,001 members, 3,568 in Class A. It had thirty-four committees. Comparatively little was recorded in the

Executive Committee meetings and the annual meeting of 1962 concerning matters of immediate interest to the majority of PGA members, their employers, and the traditional good of golf as a game. Tournament Bureau subjects had been taking over much of the association's meeting time for the past few years, and now the confusion of the MacArthur deal took most of the officers' and delegates' time. They had the help of a new attorney, Madison Pacetti, who had been hired to see that the PGA got a fair deal playing against big-time real-estate promoters.

As usual, the PGA high command did not seem eager to get expert advice, and the Advisory Committee was kept in the dark regarding the Palm Beach Gardens negotiations. Glenn Sisler of Detroit was chairman of the committee, Bill MacDonald was vice-president, and Harry Radix was secretary. It also included Dick Irwin, and as recent additions, Curtis Person, an active senior amateur from Memphis, and Francis W. Sullivan, a distinguished lawyer from Philadelphia who successfully represented large corporations.

Delegates asked what had happened before Dick Wilson was engaged as architect for the PGA courses on the MacArthur property. Tom Mahan, Mac Hunter, Bud Oakley, and Horton Smith spoke of the difficulty they'd have as delegates in trying to explain to the members at home how the PGA happened to get its golf course and clubhouse. Mac Hunter protested that the Southern California section hadn't been advised of what had happened. He added, "And we're Class A members in the dark." Tom LoPresti, a Northern California delegate, exclaimed, "I think this whole deal is being slipped in over our heads!" Warren Orlick of Michigan said he was confused about dates. He hadn't learned when construction of the course and clubhouse was to be started and finished. Nobody appeared to have the answer.

Paul Erath, a delegate from western Pennsylvania, in the Tri-State section, said to the meeting, "I read the minutes of last year. There was nothing in them, or in information since, about the deal with Mr. MacArthur or the progress of the work."

Gene Mason, from the Pacific Northwest section, stated his position: "I feel like I was about to go out and play Palmer a seventy-two-hole match, winner to take the $11½-million and the loser go home with a nickel. There are a hundred percent of our section's members who feel we should not be in the business of running a golf course for a small percentage of our members. It looks at present that I will have to go back and tell our boys they are in the business up to their fannies. They don't want it no matter how much it will cost, no matter how fine it will be. We have paid $7,800 in assessments. I don't know how much we paid for Dunedin. We will continue to pay, but for goodness' sake, let's put this project on a businesslike basis, with contracts."

Warren Cantrell, a Texan who later became PGA president, advised: "Take a hardheaded look at the cost per member. What will the income be, and the expenses? How much will television income help? I have been at some Tour Committee meetings, and they haven't been as pleasant as Jay Hebert [Tournament Committee chairman] is. We are going to have to finance this project with more money from tournament players."

Cantrell proved to be foresighted. The tournament players got the notion that too much of their money was going into the PGA National Golf Club. The idea was never corrected and was ultimately one of the factors in the tournament players' split from the PGA.

The polite term "lack of communications" often was used in an effort to explain why few, if any, of the delegates knew how the PGA had gotten into a deal for a golf course that was under construction and already had two blunt individuals, John MacArthur and golf architect Dick Wilson, clashing head-on. In a way, they were kindred souls, both of them having whimsical and stubborn natures. Wilson had what MacArthur wanted and needed and possibly got temperamental just for the hell of it, but MacArthur laughed off the lost rounds. MacArthur is rare as a fabulously rich character with an alley fighter's sense of humor. There are indications that he enjoyed and aggravated the bewilderment of the PGA representatives.

That bewilderment could hardly be magnified, according to existing records. When delegates charged that officers had held back information on details and status of the course and clubhouse project, Secretary Mund replied that the officers knew nothing about them themselves.

President Strong denied that the MacArthur arrangement was being railroaded through, and in answering Paul Erath's statement that the 1961 minutes hadn't stated the terms and acceptance of the MacArthur proposal, declared, "We're not considering at all the agreement we entered into. That is a firm agreement. We are proceeding on the contract, and any action should have been taken by the delegates at the last meeting. This action and contract we have insofar as the golf courses are concerned, and our obligations have already been approved."

Seemingly Erath and Strong had read different minutes, and the delegates expressed the sentiment that somewhere along the line someone had blundered or failed to read the fine print. With Tom Crane ill and Lloyd Lambert and Bob Russell, Crane's assistant, present, the executive director's office wasn't called upon to look over the minutes and come up with the correct answer.

When John MacArthur took the microphone to lull apprehensive delegates, he assured them that: "You can get a million dollars from John MacArthur. You will have good title and any damages you incur of my failure to make my gift perfect. . . . I'll put my companies—every one, and I've got fifteen—on the hook. I am not selling you this land. I am giving it to you. For the past several years my tax contributions to the government have exceeded a couple of million. I thought it would be great to get some credit on my tax and give it to the PGA, a nonprofit organization. Then lawyers said, 'It won't work; you can't give it to the PGA.' Then I said, 'I'll give it to the city, and the city can do it.' "

Later there were questions about the city of Palm Beach Gardens being legally able to give the PGA the property. There were also questions about title on part of the land. The PGA and John MacArthur were good news to lawyers. And among the numerous controversies between MacArthur and the PGA on building the course was who was to pay the cost of a "fully automatic watering system." MacArthur demurred at paying for what he called "this gold-plated feature as the same work could be done just as well with four automatic boys."

The 1962 annual meeting proceedings, from page 45A through 103A, are devoted to discussion of the PGA National Golf Club project, with John MacArthur and PGA President Lou Strong on one side and Horton Smith, Harry Moffitt, Leo Fraser, Warren Cantrell, Gene Mason, Bud Oakley, Harold Sargent, Mac Hunter, and others imploring that financial and other figures, facts, and dates and legal commitments acceptable to authorities be made plain. The result of the storm and fury about the PGA National Golf Club at Palm Beach Gardens was that the delegates went back to their sections in confusion, bewilderment, and disarray.

By good luck, by being wary in the right places, and by having good lawyers in others, the PGA got itself two splendid, beautiful golf courses, with a third course projected for an entirely private club adjoining, and an attractive combination clubhouse and office building that a member proudly described as looking like the grandstand at Arlington Park, the handsome horse-racing plant in northwest Chicago. The PGA also got excellent facilities for its big yearly tent show of golf merchandise.

And John MacArthur got a golfing establishment that gave him a great deal of print and air time free and was the nucleus of a valuable residential community that had been a wasteland a few years before. However, it was hardly a case of the PGA and John MacArthur walking hand in hand into the sunset. Even after the PGA moved into its offices, there were angry flare-ups. When MacArthur failed to execute legal formalities at the time appointed, Leo Fraser, the association president, ordered PGA furniture and files moved out of the clubhouse. Agreement was reached, and the trucks returned and unloaded before the PGA got a new address. But for many months the PGA and MacArthur or his representatives had their lawyers arguing before judges.

There was one bright period of peace, if not understanding, during the controversy and confusion about the new PGA National Golf Club. At the 1962 meeting, Lou Strong was re-elected president, Wally Mund, secretary, and George Hall, treasurer. The voting was unanimous. No one else volunteered for the jobs.

Tournament Bureau matters were handled smoothly except for a flap over the television debut of the old World Series idea that U.S. and British National Open champions used to put on as road shows. A Chicago promoter signed the American and British National Open champions, the Masters and PGA winners, for a match at the Firestone course. There was fast talking on this affair, which sold the PGA into approving the televised exhibition on dates conflicting with the Denver Open, in which the Rocky Mountain section was strongly interested as civic advertising and to some extent financially. Naturally, with the year's outstanding champions absent from the Denver tournament and playing competitively in an air show, there was a roar of complaint at the prospect of the section's being made to look like country boys trimmed by the wily city slickers.

It was a mess. The World Series TV was blacked out in Denver. The Denver dealers of the sponsors, Zenith and Amana, who'd been sold by the promoter, complained that they were hurt in more ways than one. The purported world-title play was talked about among pros as one of those things where competition was on the level, but the split of the money was equal, as the last-place money itself amounted to a substantial "appearance" fee. The promoter offered to increase the PGA's fee from $7,500 to $32,500 if the onus of "exhibition" would be taken from the deal and the show given some "official status."

Of course, the television feature never got "official status" with the USGA, the R & A, and the Augusta National Golf Club, but because it was the end of the customary season for golf and the televised contest was being pushed out by baseball's World Series and pro and collegiate football, the golf World Series eventually was built by newspaper publicity into good acceptance as the last of the year's TV golf programs. And the Canadian Open winner was brought in to complete a foursome if needed because other contestants were multiple-title winners. In time, because of the retirement of the promoter, Chicago advertising man Walter Schwimmer, the PGA became heir to the show.

Jay Hebert told the meeting that the tournament players felt that the PGA was cramping the Tournament Bureau and grabbing too much when it took the television income from the golf World Series. They complained it was getting too involved in tournament affairs, especially the television side, which the players considered the big source of their revenue. The players didn't like the tournament sponsors cutting in on the TV money but were informed that there wouldn't be many big-money purses unless the sponsors had their load lightened by television as well as by tax exemptions. Treasurer George Hall suggested that PGA participation as a not-for-profit organization receiving considerable TV show business revenue might call for study by tax experts.

NBC, ABC, and CBS were all negotiating for the PGA Championship television rights. Marty Carmichael of CBS, who became the PGA TV counselor, urged that CBS, which had been given the PGA Championship rights five years before, continue to receive the contract, as it had learned how to handle the show. Again, the uninformed delegates discussed possible conflicts of interest in selling the PGA TV rights, and again, as usual, the PGA was in the middle. CBS wanted to renew with the PGA for $30,000 a year for the championship, but when NBC and ABC each bid $55,000 a year for two or three championships, the PGA didn't need any expert to tell it to take the $75,000 per year offer that Bill McPhail of CBS raised to beat the competition.

Jim Gaquin had the PGA's road show operating more smoothly than it ever had before. Donald ("Doc") Griffin had come from the *Pittsburgh Press* to join the tournament field staff as press secretary. (The affable, able Griffin later went with Arnold Palmer.) Gaquin recommended an increase in pay for Jack Tuthill and others of the field staff. The pay boost wasn't much —$10 a week for the invaluable Tuthill being the top, and the total making no appreciable dent in the $72,305 the Tournament Bureau netted out of its 1962 fiscal year revenue of $244,582. The tournament players were not going to spoil their employees by overpaying them. The bureau staff did become eligible for PGA employees' pensions in 1962, and Gaquin, the bureau's director, got a bonus of a week's vacation in August.

It was announced that Billy Booe, a former Yale football player who had been unable to take satisfactory samples out of tournament circuit purses, would be Caribbean tour supervisor, beginning in 1963, succeeding George

Hall. That first of the minor-league schedules was doing nicely, with five events and around sixty contestants from the United States. Purses weren't high, but neither were expenses.

Leo Fraser pleaded that the PGA enlarge and accelerate its educational program. The same brief and limited winter schooling by the national body and the day or two-day spring educational sessions of the sections were inadequate to train the type of professional needed by a business that was in a critical period of change and growth. He added that a professional giving fifteen lessons a day had no time to educate properly a young man to meet the demands of a first-class professional's performance and to protect the position of professional golf generally.

Jay Hebert observed that the tour was overcrowded with young professionals who didn't have a chance to make expenses and who were moving on without paying caddies and leaving bouncing checks. He said many of them belonged back in the shops. Then there was the usual exchange of comment about assistants who hoped to get rich on prize money and wanted to spend their time at the club practicing their own games instead of learning to be fully qualified professionals.

Horton Smith questioned the PGA's group medical insurance. He told them that his own check was returned because his medical history was unsatisfactory. This was the first that Smith's friends knew that he, who'd always taken good care of himself, was ailing with the disease that caused his death a few years later.

The manufacturers' relations matters and the employment situation, usually topics of extended discussion at the annual meeting, were mentioned with no progress reported.

Sectionally, there was decided growth in the junior programs and in pro-amateur tournaments that bettered relations with women and senior golfers especially, but nationally the PGA was too tangled in the real-estate business of the PGA National Golf Club to register any advance in the golf business of its home professional members.

At the PGA's forty-seventh annual meeting, held November 28 through December 6, 1963, at the Palm Beach Towers Hotel, delegates hoped to get a good, clear look at what was going on and where the association stood. Real-estate business connected with the PGA National Golf Club, its courses, clubhouse, and headquarters office had been a source of concern and confusion for many PGA members for almost two years now. What PGA progress had been made in the period, they said, was almost altogether on the sectional level and with the Tournament Bureau, which had more business than it could satisfactorily supply with dates and players.

Hence, the immediate problem that confronted President Lou Strong, Secretary Wally Mund, Treasurer George Hall, and the Executive Committee was to show restless delegates and members how the PGA was operating as a business. There were delegates from thirty-four sections and the Tournament Committee, represented by Dave Marr, Jr., Jay Hebert, and Johnny Pott, listening for the answers.

The policy of having the annual meeting open to any member, which had been declared in effect for the 1962 meeting, didn't work out agreeably. So that open-meeting experiment was concluded. At the 1962 meeting, a delegate from the Rocky Mountain section had brought a tape recorder into a session with the intention of securing for his neighboring fellow members an authoritative report on what had happened when PGA national officials sold dates and television rights to the World Series of Golf exhibition, which conflicted with an Open tournament at Denver. For unexplained reasons, the introduction of the tape recorder caused some protest. Lou Strong announced at the 1963 meeting that the only recording equipment permitted would be that of the official reporter.

The members continued to be curious about how their association was being run and how it might be operated in an efficient and open business way. They got so restless and vocal about this that the Executive Committee appointed a Management Plan Committee to investigate and make recommendations. Its chairman was Jack Mallon of the Wheatley Hills Golf Club in the New York Metropolitan district, and others on the committee were Dick Forester of the Houston Country Club, Don Fischesser, professional at the Evansville Country Club, Arnold Palmer, representing the tournament specialists, and Richard D. Irwin, head of a large book-publishing company and for some years a member of the PGA Advisory Committee.

Three firms submitted bids for the job of examining the PGA business operation and advising changes in management. Booz, Allen, and Hamilton was the company chosen, and its report after a six-week study of the PGA was given to the Executive Committee well in advance of the 1963 annual meeting. (This wasn't the first survey of PGA business methods that had been made. The George S. May Company had made one several years earlier as another example of May's numerous services to professional golf. It had cost the PGA nothing and soon became merely

more paper in the bales in the offices.) With one annual meeting providing about nine hundred pages of typed reports for each delegate, it can be realized that the PGA was buried by paperwork. The office had to handle reports of every sort—on the PGA Championship, the Seniors' and other championships on the Florida winter entertainment program, Ryder Cup matches, dues collection, coordination of sectional affairs, planning and operation of the business schools, the Merchandise Show, much of the Tournament Bureau and Tournament Committee paper, publicity, group insurance in several areas, an organization magazine, a tournament players' school, the annual meetings, Executive and other committee meetings, National Golf Day, relations with other golf associations, legal matters, accounting, projects such as proposed pension and retirement plans, and the details and entanglements of a PGA National Golf Club. As a consequence, the PGA headquarters staff of twenty-seven was constantly busy and Tom Crane, executive secretary, was working himself into the breakdown that eventually claimed him. As the number-one employee of an organization dependent upon recreation, Crane had little time to play.

Lloyd Lambert, who came from a large Washington, D.C., law conglomerate to be executive secretary and backstop for Crane, had promptly proved himself to be the most valuable rookie of the year ever to be associated with the PGA. He continued to be a remarkably versatile counselor to the PGA, screening the inside chores and getting them out of the way and correctly directing the high-priced outside legal minds the PGA hired.

Bob Russell handled PGA general publicity and edited its monthly magazine, and John Hubbard was the magazine's advertising manager. None of the staff ever had a chance to be accused of spending too much time on golf courses.

The Booz, Allen, and Hamilton study concluded with the observation that the PGA needed a competent business manager with an able staff large enough to care for sharply defined duties promptly. In 1963 and in years previous, the PGA had a table of organization pretty much like that of a private country club, with unpaid officers and directors making policy in a rather casual way, then turning over the tasks of execution to Tom Crane, who was, in effect, pro-manager-superintendent of the outfit. The PGA negotiations for the national golf clubs at Dunedin and at Palm Beach Gardens were cited as examples of what a well-run business *shouldn't do,* according to the management experts.

The report failed to receive unanimous endorsement because its references to the Palm Beach Gardens National Golf Club suggested that examiners might find more than met the eye in the transaction, and that additional information should be brought out and evaluated. There was some official resentment of that expert comment, and the business consultant firm was told to stay away from this territory. The part of the report dated June 25, 1963, which was disclosed in minutes of the 1963 annual meeting, included, among other recommendations, one reducing the size of the Executive Committee and realigning its functions. This suggestion was tossed out because of the geographic factor. PGA sections west of the Rockies saw golf courses and PGA members in their areas growing rapidly, but they believed their influence in PGA management was diminishing. They'd had only one representative in the high command—Joe Novak, who was president in 1949, 1950, and 1951, and treasurer in 1946, 1947, and 1948. The Westerners understandably were not happy about their money being used to construct the PGA clubhouse, courses, and office building in Florida and being involved in commitments that were not clear to them.

The report said: "The present size (fourteen members) of the Executive Committee creates a cumbersome structure for the management of the association," and added that decision making and action would be facilitated by an Executive Committee of seven members—the president, secretary, treasurer, chairman of the Tournament Committee, executive director, and two vice-presidents-at-large.

The Executive Committee did not endorse the study's recommendation about changing the use of funds from the PGA merchandising of products bearing its label, saying that the present allotment was the legally sound one in protecting the organization against higher taxation.

The report also questioned the budget for the proposed construction and operations at Palm Beach Gardens. The Executive Committee believed the budget was as close as estimates could be made, considering the indefinite character of the project, but the study went on to stress the PGA's "primary administrative need": strengthening the position of the executive director, giving him full authority and responsibility to act as chief administrative executive officer for the association. A qualified business manager was urgently called for, especially since Tom Crane had toiled himself into poor health and because Lloyd Lambert was serving competently in guiding and supervising the legal aspects of the PGA operations, as far as he was allowed to function.

To get the man the PGA needed, a substantial salary would have to be paid, and Crane was to be retained in a consulting and advisory capacity until his appointed retirement in May, 1966. The report commended the work of Lloyd Lambert as counsel and executive secretary and of Bob Russell as assistant executive director and director of public relations, and included a job description and statement of qualifications of the proposed executive director, who was to report to the president. Discussion about establishing a paid presidency was revived briefly by Booz, Allen, and Hamilton experts, who said such a position was neither necessary nor desirable. They also urged that a qualified business manager be hired to relieve executives of detail and routine.

The duties and salary of the Tournament Bureau manager were "appropriate," it was noted, and a salary increase of 11 percent was recommended for the clerical staff of the PGA when the move was made to the new offices at Palm Beach Gardens.

The forty-page report suggested that much of the travel being done by PGA executives should be the function of the executive director. It added that: "In view of anticipated tight cash position of the PGA over the next several years, the association should encourage travel by its officers, executive staff, and delegates by air coach. This would result in significant saving in the present total travel cost of $90,000 a year, the majority of which is made by first-class ticket."

After getting what information they could on the PGA real-estate commitments and the operating budget for the

PGA National Golf Club and PGA headquarters, the experts went on to say: "In view of the heavy financial commitment for the PGA project at West Palm Beach Gardens . . . it is essential that any excess cash or restricted funds not available for this project be invested to return the maximum yield. . . . To obtain sound investment counsel on the use of its funds, assistance should be obtained from competent banking sources, trust departments, or investment advisory service."

It took unduly long for this simple and obvious move, but nobody could ever explain why. The PGA high command was eager to borrow a million or more for a real-estate venture but didn't appear to feel sure of itself in getting its complicated funds untangled so their utmost safe earning power could be utilized.

In some ways the report was prophetic, such as when it urged that "greater effort is necessary to foster stronger unity between the club and the playing professionals as both groups have fundamentally the same long-range goal and objectives. A unified association is essential and must be preserved." Looking at the PGA financial statement, the business management men observed: "While merger of the Tournament Fund into the General Fund would have certain accounting advantages, such action is not considered opportune because of the objection and possible loss of the tournament players."

Digging further, the study found that: "Further divergence and possible separation would result in two weak groups instead of one strong association representing all professional golfers. During his professional career a PGA member may earn his living as a touring player and later as a club professional."

This was a realistic transition for pros, and Jay Hebert of the Tournament Committee spoke of several players who had been on the circuit ten or twelve years and had now turned to more settled work at clubs.

Later events showed that the Booz, Allen, and Hamilton investigation and recommendations would have fitted the PGA into a program of effective operation and would have relieved officials of much of the detail, travel, and fence building that heads of other professional sports organizations were able to avoid without neglecting any responsibilities. It was obvious to the business management authorities that PGA officials needed to have their loads lightened for their own good and for that of their families and the organization.

But now or next year wasn't the time to settle PGA business management problems once and for all. The complications and mysteries of the real-estate deal with John McArthur were delaying the organization in its decision to locate a new headquarters office. Many businessmen among the PGA membership believed this was more urgent than getting a golf course for some pros to play on during the winter.

President Lou Strong was trying desperately to get the real-estate deal explained and signed. He told the 1963 meeting: "Our understanding at the outset of this project two years ago was that they [MacArthur] would build two golf courses according to our plans and specifications and give us the land and courses and maintenance building they would build.

"We would be obligated to build a clubhouse and office building and operate the club in a first-class manner. We have to operate it for a minimum

of ten years. At the end of twenty-five years we would be free to sell the club.

"We have first commitment of $1 million from the First National Bank of Chicago, at an annual basis of 5½ percent."

There was question about the title, and Strong assured everyone that the Lawyers Title and Insurance Company and the First National Bank of Chicago had issued a title binder for $1.5 million to the PGA, and as additional protection on title problems, the PGA also had coverage by the Bankers Life and Casualty Company, a MacArthur operation.

Butler and Penbrink made the low bid on construction of the PGA clubhouse. MacArthur told the PGA: "We'll build the building. You pay for it on conclusion of the job." That's what was done. The budget for the PGA National Golf Club as submitted at the 1963 annual meeting estimated a total of $173,000 in golf fees, breaking down as follows: PGA members, $24,500; other members, $19,000; and daily green fees, $129,550. Golf cart income was estimated at $46,330, and total course income at $219,380.

There was a difference of $2,660 between the detailed budget of cart operation and the figure in the overall budget, but the guesses seemed reasonable enough to the delegates. The golf cart rental estimate was: golf cart rentals, $90,000; pro supervision at $1 a round, $15,000; maintenance and salaries, $7,000; power, parts, and supplies, $5,000; and depreciation, $16,670—for a net from carts of $46,330.

Golf course annual maintenance expense was estimated at $145,000, including a superintendent's salary of $14,000. The golf professional's "retainer" was set at $10,000, and the club manager's salary at $12,000. Considerable clubhouse revenue was also expected from the restaurant and bar during the big week of the Merchandise Show, from local club members who didn't belong to the PGA, and from parties of industrial concerns in the vicinity of the PGA clubhouse. So those guesses were dependent on a yield to the PGA of a yearly net of $75,000, payable on principal, interest, taxes, and contingencies of the association's participation in the development of Palm Beach Gardens.

The estimates were optimistically imaginative, but PGA officials were hardly to blame. Their employers in private clubs had made even wilder guesses. To backstop the budgets it had accepted, as well as the honest-to-God statements it had received from various parties involved in the negotiations for its new home, the PGA Executive Committee hired two more lawyers. They were Madison C. Pacetti of West Palm Beach and Robert McDonald of the New York law firm of Sullivan and Cromwell, who brought along a teammate, Ed Bremfohr, who was to help study the tax status of the PGA and its pension plan and other matters that overtake a group that has money and is too trusting.

Although PGA delegates and officials alien to the area that was to be the association's new home only suspected what their association's legal bills were going to be, they were lionhearted and laughed about the PGA's getting to the point where it would have more lawyers than members. At that time the association had a membership of 5,090, of whom approximately 1,800 were in the Senior group of fifty and older.

The lawyers and everybody else were trying to figure out what had happened to the original contract for the office and clubhouse, to which was added the cost of parking lot and locker rooms, running the bill up to $1,534,914. Architect Dick Wilson definitely was to get $30,000 as his designing fee as well as compensation for the superintendents building the courses.

On December 7, the Executive Committee considered applicants for the professional–managing director job at the PGA National Golf Club. Lou Strong, the PGA ex-president, didn't contest for the position but was given the job at the club he had worked so determinedly to establish on the MacArthur premises. All informed parties agreed that Strong, regardless of his methods, had turned out to be the most effective golf director MacArthur and the PGA could have chosen.

Getting around to the home professionals' business, the PGA honored one of the great pioneer names in American and English professional golf by naming Bruce Herd as Golf Professional of the Year. One of Bruce's uncles, Fred, had won the fourth USGA Open in 1896 at Shinnecock Hills while he was a professional at the Chicago Golf Club. Another uncle, Alexander ("Sandy"), had triumphed in the 1902 British Open. He was the first champion to win with the new American-type thread-wound ball.

Julius Boros was named the PGA's Player of the Year, and Ralph Guldahl and Johnny Revolta were elected to the association's Hall of Fame.

There were discussions about tightening membership standards, disciplining those who had violated the PGA Code of Ethics, and making an excellent credit standing a requirement for delegates to the annual meeting. The association also established a pension plan for its employees, paying half of the pension premium; took out Blue Cross and Blue Shield insurance for its employees, paying all the premiums; and bought a group life insurance policy that covered each member for $1,000.

Financially the PGA was very healthy, with $604,229 in the general fund and $164,282 in the Construction Fund. George Hall freely admitted that after three years as treasurer he wasn't clear about the accounts but depended on the auditors. The PGA National Golf Club accounts were, in some respects, bewildering but amply checked. Many figures were coming to light. A total of $60,000 was to be spent for golf course equipment, and the clubhouse was to cost $850,000, plus 8 percent for the architect.

The PGA's magazine, *The Professional Golfer,* was doing nicely with Bob Russell as editor and John Hubbard as advertising manager. The magazine's advertising revenue in the 1961–62 fiscal year was a twelve-month total of $94,442, with a net profit of $11,421. The circulation to PGA members was 5,091, and other paid circulation was 2,868. PGA Class A members were obliged to pay for *Professional Golfer* subscriptions. The March issue usually carried the largest amount of advertising, although once in a while April would be the top month.

Although they tried intensively, John Hubbard and advertising managers of other golf publications rarely could awaken golf-playing equipment manufacturers to the realization that golf was becoming a twelve-month buying business. Winter golf resort and other Southern winter play was increasing so much that it accounted for almost 30 percent of the year's total. The pros were aware of that and were working and making money, while the majority of golf goods manufacturers continued to put their big selling effort

on during March through June, then relaxed into the custom of feeling that the year's selling show was over.

Growth of the annual Merchandise Show continued steadily. The show at Port St. Lucie rented 131 booths at $150 each and made a profit of $15,431. A winter program for the PGA National courses began to take shape at the 1963 annual meeting with Lew and Dan Oehmig and Jack Harkins of the Professional Golf Company and First-Flite agreeing to sponsor a 1964 club championship for $25,000. Bill and Beverley Dolan of E-Z-Go Golf Cart became sponsors of a $10,000 match-play tournament. Those events, with the Seniors' Championship, provided an attractive opening schedule for the PGA courses that were being built under confusing circumstances.

The Booz, Allen, and Hamilton investigation, which cost the PGA approximately $15,000, had been steered away from the Palm Beach Gardens transaction, which President Strong kept reassuring PGA officials was not a real-estate sales-promotion operation, but which MacArthur representatives continued to underscore in connection with selling lots. Executive and annual meetings had authorized President Strong to borrow $1 million for building and furnishing the clubhouse and headquarters offices, but delegates weren't clear whether the loan covered both the offices and clubhouse. Then the city of Palm Beach Gardens, a MacArthur project, revised its arrangement with the PGA. Lou Strong offered to settle the controversy about installing a fully automatic watering system by paying the substantial difference himself. Strong had been selected over twenty-three other candidates for the PGA National Golf Club director job, but there were at least twenty-three questions about that choice, plus doubt on the part of some PGA officials and members that Strong had truly defined his own position as to a possible conflict of interest in being president of the PGA and engaged as an employee of a MacArthur auxiliary enterprise.

Strong said he had been reluctant to take the pro job because of "possible criticism," but since he had made statements as to how the new club should be operated, he was greatly interested in seeing that it followed his own guidelines. That's what happened, and the operation was generally very satisfactory. Professionals continued to call the establishment "MacArthur's club," instead of thinking of it as PGA property. This feeling was best expressed when renewal of the office lease was being considered and a Texas professional interested in a real-estate development near Houston offered to make one of the company's courses available to PGA members as a PGA National Course at the "same fees as Mr. MacArthur's course."

Tournament player representatives at the 1963 meeting said that the older professionals at clubs seemed to be against them and were carelessly using the money of touring PGA members in a golf course and real-estate proposition that nobody was able to describe clearly. The PGA National Golf Course transaction was yet another reason for pushing a split with PGA headquarters so the tournament professionals could keep tabs on their own money.

Probably no two other golf courses in the world were built with such complications, confusions, mysteries, suspicions, legal, financial, and personal controversies as plagued the PGA National establishment. But the finished product had superior course design

and construction and an ideal clubhouse for its functions, plus the integrated PGA offices thronged by visiting professionals during the winter.

The green, tree-spotted acres, with their blue pools and patches of white bunker sand, and the beautiful clubhouse stretched on a mound in pool-table-flat country, were eye-catching. John MacArthur was proud of his PGA National Golf Club, and well he might be. It was a miracle in the ugly Florida boondocks, an awesome achievement of the type the country boy described as showing "what a wonderful job the Lord can do if He gets money enough."

John MacArthur's acquisition and use of money had yet to win the cheers of the millions for him—not that he ever gave a damn—but what he accomplished with his cash did earn him favorable mention this time, and he appreciated the novelty. And his delight was further heightened because the PGA golf layout increased the value of the surrounding property tremendously.

When the local club members who used the course and clubhouse presented MacArthur with a tall and costly flagpole, he greatly enjoyed the change in sentiment, remarking that after he'd been called every dirty name in the book, he'd finally been recognized as one of nature's noblest works.

There was little reason to expect that 1963 would be much of a year for the general business advancement of PGA members. The committees, with the exception of the Tournament Committee, functioned pretty much as orphans, and sectional contact with the upper echelon was usually devoted to trying to explain and sell the PGA club operation. And it is strange that in view of the PGA's functioning by committees, the association has never been able to adopt the USGA's informative and convenient manner of presenting its annual scorecard on what it has experienced and done. For example, at the time of its annual meeting the USGA distributed an attractive twenty-eight-page booklet to all member clubs, committee members, other association officials, and the press.

In recent years, the PGA had presented a 220-page *Report of Officers and Committees and Proposed Resolutions.* Not all of the PGA committee reports were included in this heavy collection, and the edited minutes of the annual meeting ran to far more than 100 pages in the past decade. It was punishment to read them, as one tired researcher can attest, and he probably is the only mortal to have read the proceedings in their entirety.

In recent years, Lloyd F. Lambert, executive secretary, has prepared a *Summary of Actions and Important Matters Considered* at the annual meetings. Although this does not have a digest of committee reports, it has been far more useful than the bulk of type long given to officials and delegates that has partially accounted for the PGA's deficiency in communications. (The expense of all this voluminous annual data, mostly unread, was noted as wasteful in the Booz, Allen, and Hamilton reports.)

National Golf Day in 1963 wasn't up to standard, as a producer of only $77,-000. This unique pro sports fund-raising in the public interest, mainly for caddie scholarships, was not being thriftily managed. Some pros further declared that with $20,000 in medals given out when total revenue was only $70,000, a tightening of PGA management was called for.

The Advisory Committee, which had shrugged off its figurehead status and

had been kept ignorant of the PGA real-estate deal, now came forward with two trophies announced by William McDonald, the committee's chairman. McDonald had been a bus conductor in Chicago, made millions in the trailer business, and was an active golf fan and frequent sponsor of other sports events when the tax conditions were favorable. He donated one trophy as a memorial to Ed Dudley, who originated the Advisory Committee, and another in memory of Horton Smith, to be awarded annually to the professional doing the most in professional business education.

A review of the minutes of the annual meeting and the reports of the Tournament, Executive, and Advisory committees showed the tournament players' situation in 1963 closer to the inevitable division between the journeymen and the home professionals. It was becoming clearer that they were in two different businesses. The home pros were in the business of serving golfers and enlarging the roster of golfers; the playing professionals were in an acutely self-centered operation of working in a market that had been created for their personal profit. Not that the latter were to be censured, for they were in a trade where a short putt meant a small check—or possibly none. It was dog-eat-dog, with television offering a juicy mess of bones for the winner.

The tournament sponsors were hungry for a larger share of the money because the sponsors took the risk and did the work of putting on the shows. The Tournament Advisory Committee had met twice, and spurred by the International Golf Sponsors' group, asked for 25 percent of the television revenue. John Monfrey of the sponsors' association asked that the tournament sponsors be present at all meetings of the tournament players. Lionel Hebert and Bob Goalby of the players' committee agreed, then the idea seems to have been forgotten.

Jim Gaquin, the tournament manager, opposed the sponsors' group's "getting into the scheduling act," saying it would further complicate an already difficult problem. It was Gaquin's recommendation that the circuit be limited to forty-three events, because with fifty tournaments scheduled, those later in the season did not include most of the stars and these minor-league tournaments had a limited gallery.

The Tournament Bureau had its biggest year to date in 1963, with $2,-349,000 prize money and income over expenses of almost $87,700. The PGA Championship had been quite profitable, being $63,000 in the black. The Ryder Cup matches at Atlanta about broke even.

The Caribbean tour for early 1964 was set up solidly, with $62,500 prize money for five events and a prospective field of about sixty. Billy Booe succeeded George Hall as director of the tour, and Hall retired. His sideline work as PGA treasurer during the mysterious proceedings of arranging the PGA National Golf Club real-estate transaction with John MacArthur had been wearing on Hall, a careful fellow who considered himself bonded in every way in handling the PGA finances.

A Tournament Committee meeting was held at Akron in 1963 with Jay Hebert, Dave Marr, Johnny Pott, and Bob Goalby responsible for thinking up the right answers to the problems of invitations and exemptions of foreign players at the rich U.S. tournaments; to the many conflicts between the players, the sponsors, and the PGA

on television revenue; to the sponsors' demands for greater rights in running the shows they put on for the enrichment of golf professionals; to the beguiling exploitations of TV networks; and to the wily promoters who were not thinking about what was good for golf but only of what was good for them.

Internal difficulties were many and embarrassing now that golf was strictly a cash business. The stars had to show or the gate was diminished and the TV value was reduced as a salable product. Numerous television offers came into the PGA. CBS wanted its "Classic" to be filmed on tournament off-days. Headliners such as Arnold Palmer and Gary Player had their own filmed TV "contests" going. The PGA had rules against splitting purses in television, but no more attention was paid to that pronouncement than to the Ten Commandments.

Each player individually had about as much team spirit as an opera star, and the force that really held the PGA road show together was the tough, super-hardboiled letter-of-the-rule management of Jack Tuthill and his staff at the tournaments, and Jim Gaquin, manager of the Tournament Bureau.

Meetings like the one at Akron started after the committee members had finished their rounds and ended in the early morning. Committee members wondered how they could play competently after the frequent and confusing meetings on tournament affairs, but they did. Johnny Pott, for instance, won that tournament at Akron.

Never has any professional sport presented a more attractive, conscientious, and competent group of young businessmen under less favorable circumstances than the PGA Tournament

Committee did when pro golf was changing from a paid sport to a cold, cold business. The young men on the tournament circuit and the boys aspiring to get instant wealth and fame weren't impressed by what Texan Earl Stewart told the annual meeting about the truly great Ben Hogan's going broke four times, then coming back to the tour, before he made the grade to glory. They didn't want to have to pay the price of Hogan's guts. These were different and easier times.

The background of tournament circuit and TV development, to which the PGA's Tom Crane referred as the sound legal basis for the PGA's getting repaid on its investment by first reach at tournament circuit television income, meant nothing to the newer players. They couldn't have cared less about the high percentage of PGA dues spent to switch golf from a participants' game to show business.

Naturally, the unpaid PGA committeemen were reviled as money-hungry, overpaid caddies with absolutely no regard for the good of golf and the future of their own trade. Yet they were doing an exceptional job that couldn't be accurately evaluated until years later, when the PGA had split into two divisions. The paid executives of professional baseball, football, hockey, basketball, and horse racing never had to contend with the baffling situations of pro golf as it was suddenly emerging into big business.

Golf tournaments with their tax-exempt advantages provided profitable fund-raising attractions. John Ames, a former president of the USGA and a director of the Children's Memorial Hospital in Chicago, got the tax-exempt angle working in attracting a fine field of socially and industrially

important amateurs to team with pros at an annual event the Monday following the Western Open. The tournament was played at the exclusive old Onwentsia Club in Lake Forest and used the Bing Crosby pro-amateur formula. For a short time, headline professionals played in the event, but they soon had "other urgent interests." Or so they claimed.

With the wrench between the vanishing sentimental period of golf and its current commercial exploitation, something would surely have to give. It was a year of divisive elements, with explosions of economic and social factors beyond the realization of earnest professional sportsmen who thought they were in a simple, straightforward business.

Before the PGA finished its 1963 annual meeting, it elected Warren Cantrell of Texas as its president, succeeding Lou Strong. The most experienced businessman yet to head the PGA, Cantrell was a successful engineer and contractor and figured prominently in building the Houston Astrodome. He loved golf, and it was a service to his fellowmen and a release from the heavy and often ridiculous demands of business for him to get back into the game as a professional. His fellow professionals in Texas recognized his merit, and his rise in PGA official ranks was rapid.

Now he faced the almost insurmountable task of untangling the dark and devious procedures that had made the PGA National Golf Club a highly profitable real-estate development and of somehow putting them on a sound, understandable business basis.

Cantrell didn't last long after he became PGA president. The job had become murderously difficult.

24

A Las Vegas Meeting Raises Eyebrows, Problems When a Sport Becomes a Business, the Old Separation Blues

[1964, 1965, 1966]

WHEN it was announced that the 1964 annual meeting of the PGA was to be held at the Sahara Hotel in Las Vegas, sportswriters were astonished. They couldn't believe that with professional football severely disciplining players for association with notorious gamblers, professional baseball carrying for years the stain of a gambling scandal, collegiate basketball shocked by disclosures of gamblers reaching players, and all professional sports expected to be vigilant in protecting its public regard, a professional sports organization would hold its major meeting of the year in the green-felt jungle.

Between "Sure Thing" John MacArthur making his real-estate pitch on the Florida coastal plain and the adroit speculators in the Wild, Wild West of Las Vegas, the PGA seemed to be placing its trust in a kindly Power Above. And Divine Providence, or a reasonable facsimile thereof, brought the earnest professionals through the dangers unscathed. Of course, the PGA annual meeting never was much of a sports-section story; the association simply could never get across to millions of golfers the immensely valuable work its members were doing for the golfing public.

While the PGA should have been making itself an authority on the golf business and golf marketing, it was mainly concerned with routine organizational matters, along with getting in over its head in real-estate deals. Meantime, the National Golf Foundation was steadily growing as an outstanding practical and helpful sports promotion operation. By following in the spirit of the pioneer professionals who founded the PGA, and by extending its services, the National Golf Foundation has figured usefully in hundreds of millions of dollars' worth of golf projects, and has been the most effective producer of jobs for golf professionals.

During the Las Vegas lull after the storm over the Palm Beach Gardens operation, the PGA renewed its efforts to get back into the golf business for the profit of its members and their employers. Warren Cantrell, president, had with him Max Elbin as secretary and Leo Fraser as treasurer. Cantrell reported fully on the closing of the lease with John MacArthur. One section—not identified in the edited official report of the 1964 meeting—questioned the handling of the PGA National Golf Club deal, and the new administration went to work with a policy of making the best of the situation, forgiving and forgetting. It paid the clubhouse architect, Al Parker, and arranged to move PGA headquarters to Palm Beach Gardens on or about March 15, 1965.

The PGA was studying a standard employment contract for professionals. The hiring of professionals had been

Warren Cantrell. PGA

unsatisfactory in the past because, more often than not, neither the professional nor his employee understood the scope and responsibilities of the job. It had also been learned that the pro's credit difficulties were often the result of his carrying too much of a financial burden for his club. Another problem was the willingness of too many applicants to take a pro job under any conditions; they were eager to be accepted by employers who didn't know how to evaluate applicants for the pro vacancy.

With the PGA's getting back to the primary work of improving the occupational status of its members, it was again appreciated that the PGA Advisory Committee had a wider influence than had been previously regarded and employed. Members of the Advisory

Committee had been effective in getting PGA members into desirable jobs, and that factor, among others, caused the 1964 delegates to give members of the committee "full information on matters affecting the PGA." Possibly it was this action that kept the Advisory Committee alive.

The committee had been amused rather than miffed by being detoured from significant and prompt information on the PGA's real-estate promotion with John MacArthur. It had considered advising the PGA that the Advisory Committee be eliminated, which, of course, would have been a most embarrassing withdrawal of ex-

Martin Carmichael. PGA, photo by Clark's
Photography

pert advice, when the association officials were engaged in the big-money
negotiations with John MacArthur.
The committee was composed of businessmen who had negotiated successful,
complex deals with adroit parties on
the other side; it was amused, as one
member put it, by "finding out what
had been going on late enough to be
pallbearers."

Lou Strong announced that he had
been hired by John MacArthur to be
golf professional and managing director at the PGA National Golf Club and
was authorized to make agreements for
tournaments and would be glad to
work with the PGA in arranging for

winter tournaments at its National
Golf Club. The information was
scarcely earthshaking, but it did bluntly
remind PGA members who was running what they had thought was
"their" club.

Tom Crane was breaking in Joseph
R. Ewers as his successor in the executive director post. Ewers had been assistant to the president of Indiana University, but his connection with the
PGA proved to be a case of miscasting
that was corrected by mutual consent
after a few months. Ewers learned to
his regret that the PGA and Indiana
University were educational institutions of varying characteristics. He was
quickly introduced to the tournament
problems, and no student of that subject of the PGA curriculum could be
blamed for quickly deciding to become
a dropout.

In the tournament department Jack
Tuthill succeeded Joe Black as tournament supervisor, and the Tournament Committee set his salary at $20,-
000 a year. The cool, competent Tuthill
had kept the journeymen well under
control, but additional confusion was
introduced to the PGA tournament
operations when Tuthill and the field
staff were made responsible to the
Tournament Committee instead of to
the tournament manager, Jim Gaquin.
And on "policy matters" Tuthill was
responsible to the Executive Committee.

Marty Carmichael had been hired on
the simple basis of representing the
PGA on television deals.

A few worldly-wise PGA officials protested. They realized that the PGA had
been giving away enough of its television and other tournament assets to
make it a tremendously rich professional sports organization. While the
professional baseball, football, hockey,

and basketball leagues and club owners were hardheaded about trading those assets, the PGA had behaved like a gullible plowboy at a county fair. A maverick in PGA politics who was not easily influenced by others, President Cantrell knew that the PGA was the last rich lode of professional sports to be mined by television and the tournament concession operations.

So he tried to jar his associates awake after they'd been stumbling into real-estate deals, getting deeper into the tournament scheduling of shows with stars of operatic temperament, and in other ways deviating from the fundamental principles of the PGA in considering service to the golfing public as its reason for being. Besides losing millions, Cantrell told his colleagues the PGA had also forever lost a trading position in television and other markets by depending on advisers whose attitude was that the PGA should be regarded lightly. Tournament sponsors were too busy jockeying dates and purses and headline players to have much of a voice on television revenue. So, almost every way you looked at it, the PGA was prey to the sharpshooters. Cantrell jabbed his companions Elbin and Fraser into awareness of what had been happening to the PGA. But with the sports boom on, and golf leading by a long way as the nation's favorite participating game, the PGA was sure to do well and carry along with it those who had "cut themselves in" good and strong when PGA officials failed to understand that the association owned a gold mine.

The energetically and efficiently managed PGA Championship at the Columbus (Ohio) Country Club had paid nicely for the PGA and had also earned the club $143,000. The PGA got another good break from its burgeon-

ing show business in the person of Walt Schwimmer, the advertising man who took the old World Championship exhibition series and put it on television. With only four contestants, the event was ideal for television presentation. But it got the PGA into trouble by making a loser of the Denver Open, which had been scheduled for the same weekend as the golf TV World Series, and by guaranteeing the year's four leading golfers good purses that kept them out of other tournaments, thus downgrading those affairs. Schwimmer raised his payoff to the PGA to $35,000 for the next two years, and eventually the PGA was to become owner of the TV property. Ed Carter also got into the act with Schwimmer on a promotion involving an automobile company that was to give $500,000 in cars to professionals and assistants in a lottery deal. It was a sweet proposition for club pros, but it didn't go through.

Another project for club pros that got nowhere was Sim Bows's plan to offer script that would be good nationwide for golf lessons. The idea had a tie-in as a premium on merchandise widely sold, but the PGA ruled it out because parties who held the lesson tickets might show up at exclusive private clubs to get their coupons redeemed for golf instruction by the resident professional. It was not an idea that assured such professionals job security.

Another sign of the booming golf market was evident when Ed Carter, who had signed the Laurel Valley Club near Ligonier, Pennsylvania, to promote the 1965 PGA Championship, predicted that program advertising might reach $300,000, of which the PGA had a good chance of getting $35,000.

Dan Bernheim, a whisky salesman,

wanted permission to transfer the Haig and Haig tournament, a men's and women's professional tournament, from Florida to Las Vegas. The tournament had drawn small galleries in mid-Florida and prize money was minimal, but it was good golf entertainment in a period when pro football was holding the most spectator interest. However, Bernheim's application for the transfer was denied because officials considered that it continued to make the PGA appear too closely connected with the nation's gambling capital.

As it was, PGA officials and members sensitive to public reaction had been jarred by criticism of the annual meeting at Las Vegas. Golf writers and sports editors had sneered at what they regarded a juvenile eagerness to go on an expense account to Las Vegas and get rich by scoring new course records with dice, slot machines, cards, and wheels. And amateur golf officials and amateur golfers in general thought the location of the PGA's annual meeting indicated either immature judgment or irresponsibility, and in either case, disqualified the association as a ruling body of golf.

From a public-relations viewpoint, then, the Las Vegas annual meeting was the costliest single mistake the PGA ever made. The split between the home pros and the journeymen was widening, and the journeymen, who'd been around quite a little, felt that those lured by the green felt and the other seductions of Las Vegas were not exactly the right kind to nurse along the show business branch of the PGA, which had already been deeply infested by slave traders and sharpshooters.

To the credit of the Cantrell administration, it gulped and faced the facts. The 1964 annual meeting report was merely a routine matter, but important in pinning down what had been swept under the rug when the PGA's attention had been monopolized by the real-estate business at Palm Beach Gardens.

Warren Cantrell was a sick man, but a wise one dedicated to the cause of professional golf. He listened coldly and decided with foresight. He was a leader without parading his leadership. The ailing Tom Crane came back into action when the shooting got too heavy for Ewers, and the always reliable Lloyd Lambert kept score. There wasn't much for him to write about in condensing the story of the 1964 PGA annual meeting.

It was dawning upon professionals of business training and temperament that the PGA had to modernize itself for the sake of its members and for golf. With Cantrell were Max Elbin and Leo Fraser, men of different dispositions and backgrounds, but both equally devoted to professional golf and golf in general. They brought the PGA through for itself and golf after a civil war that, like the Civil War itself, was bloody, tragic, and futile.

Looking back at the 1965 meeting of the PGA at the Palm Beach Towers, November 4 through 12, it is now clearer than ever that the split between the home professionals and the touring pros was inevitable. Jim Gaquin resigned as tournament manager because of "developments which had eroded his authority." The Tournament Committee simply wouldn't back up its manager, the PGA officials didn't take a clear, strong stand on debatable issues, and the tournament sponsors were unhappy about the difficulty of getting stars to come to help attract large gates and take money away.

Nobody appeared to be satisfied about the television revenue and the way it was split. Goodyear refused to

renew its sponsorship of the PGA television package deal, which didn't include the PGA Championship. The
PGA contract for the World Series of
Golf called for the event to be played
on the Firestone course, a proposition
that did not enhance the PGA's charm
for Goodyear.

Golf's tournament journeymen kept
reading about the big money paid for
television rights in baseball, football,
and boxing and got fanciful ideas
about what Palmer and Nicklaus were
picking up as TV side money. They
thought Marty Carmichael was treating
the collection for the pro-golf interest
indifferently and repeated their complaints about J. Edwin Carter's being
a Tournament Bureau manager reaching in too many directions.

Carmichael didn't have a signed contract with the PGA and wasn't especially interested in a sideline of collecting commissions from players for
getting them into television sidelines,
including the CBS Classic, a match-
play competition filmed on tournament
off-days by Marty's ex-employer. But
considering the loose arrangement between Carmichael and the PGA, the
harsh fact that only the Bing Crosby
tournament, the Masters, and the National Open had TV ratings that were
particularly attractive to advertisers,
and the reality that Carmichael was
competing in a hard-nosed field, the
PGA was perhaps doing as well as
could be expected on television.

Nobody in television could figure
out a presentation that had the class of
Shell's "Wide World of Golf" shows,
in which viewers had the atmosphere
of exclusive clubs and clubhouses and
the feeling of association with quality
people. The Masters had that air. But
many of the other televised golf tournaments had the tone of places where

anybody could pick up a fast buck—
and that was the lowest, most integrated plane in this critical period for
professional golf.

Warren Cantrell was president, Max
Elbin was secretary, and Leo Fraser
was treasurer. Warren Orlick of Tam
O'Shanter in suburban Detroit was to
be elected treasurer late in the meeting
when Cantrell finished his term and
others moved up.

Elbin was professional at Burning
Tree, the exclusive, men-only club on
the fringe of Washington, D.C., and in
that position ran what amounted to a
sanitarium and sanctuary for President
Eisenhower and others in the Potomac
squirrel cage. He was a handsome,
earnest young man ardently devoted to
golf in the same spirit as many of the
pioneer professionals who regarded the
game almost as a religion. As a businessman he also rated high.

Warren Orlick of Michigan was
elected to the PGA hierarchy in 1965,
as treasurer. He had suffered combat
injuries in World War II that had
seemed to doom him to living as a
paraplegic, but he had conquered that
threat and had become distinguished as
a professional who trained numerous
assistants to be excellent professionals.
He was also the first professional to be
an active member of the USGA Rules
of Golf Committee. Elbin, Fraser, and
Orlick were all to follow Cantrell as
PGA presidents.

The Advisory Committee suggested
that PGA officials review the Booz, Allen, and Hamilton study as a possible
source of valuable suggestions. The Advisory Committee was all too plainly
aware of the widening gap between the
home and touring professionals and believed some organizational revisions
might restore the unity valuable to
both sectors, especially at a time when

$32,000 had been budgeted for the Tournament Bureau operating deficit in 1966. And H. Franklin ("Bud") Waltz, chairman of the Advisory Committee, got an appeal from Marty Carmichael to have the committee help sell the PGA television package.

The Tournament Committee, headed by Tommy Jacobs, was having difficulty in learning what the players wanted other than more money. Billy Casper, who enjoyed high public regard as a player of sound judgment and was devoted to the broad interests of golf as a game and business, resigned from the committee and was succeeded by Gardner Dickinson.

Private meetings of players continued around the circuit without any definite demands being made of the PGA officers and the Executive Committee. Since the tournament players had operated on a practically autonomous basis for years and had been supported by funds provided to a major degree by home-pro PGA members, the one viable complaint that could be imagined by PGA headquarters concerned a possible readjustment of the Tournament Bureau's share of general expenses.

Golf writers around the circuit paid little attention to the players' informal meetings, as the sessions usually were organized by players whose names didn't mean much to the golfing public. But the discontent of some tournament players who were far from being in the Palmer million-dollar class was noted in a *Sports Illustrated* article that discussed a revolt the players were planning.

The PGA had contracts with the sponsors of most of the tournaments scheduled for 1966. The National Open, the Masters, and the Western Open were not PGA cosponsored tournaments, and the PGA Championship would not be played if the dissenters pulled away from the PGA.

Paul Warren, a Cleveland advertising man, had gone into tournament promotion along the lines developed by J. Edwin Carter when he was with the PGA and continued when the PGA decided that Carter had the association working for him. Warren started with the Cleveland Open, and in the six years before he died suddenly, had built up a string of six tournaments. When the player revolt was budding, he said he'd go with the new association, if it was formed, as it probably would have most of the star players. A few other tournament sponsors made indefinite commitments of the same nature. In several instances officials and members of clubs that had been hosts to circuit tournaments declared they would be closed to tournaments not cosponsored by the PGA.

Lawyers were warming up on both sides. The PGA, which had never done a strong public-relations job for home professionals and their contributions to the game, was not prepared to jump into a campaign telling its story. The PGA had spent a considerable amount of home professionals' money over the years building up the tournament circuit and in publicizing tournament players, but when there was a need to keep the house from being divided, the association was at a complete loss.

The majority of amateur golfers couldn't have cared less about what happened to tournament professionals discontended with winning $25,000 for four rounds of play. In locker rooms, when there was any mention of the tournament players' unhappiness, the reaction was, "So what have any of them done for me? Our pro here at the club is the one for us." And with indi-

Harold Sargent. PGA

cations of two camps of pros playing in 1966 or 1967, there was no eagerness to make fat television deals. The tournament players thus lost critical momentum that might have been devoted to increasing TV revenue.

The Advisory Committee believed that a division between tournament and home professionals was inevitable and urged that a strong tournament director's office be established, coordinating with the PGA. Since it was composed mainly of leading businessmen, the committee based its recommendation on the economic and social changes that had made tournament golf professionalism a trade and not the competitive pastime it had been when the older pros were making golf the nation's most popular participating game.

The change was evident in the Ad-

visory Committee's personnel, information, and function. For the first time since the committee had been formed, PGA officials were telling committee members what was going on involving the association, even though such information was limited because there were so many secret meetings of the tournament players and so many clashes of personality.

The Advisory Committee functions were divided, with Richard Irwin as chairman and George Chane as chairman of the Finance Committee. Chane, once a caddie and clubmaker in New England, had worked his way through college, become an executive with one of the nation's largest accounting companies, then formed his own consulting service, which was employed by as many large banks and corporations as were able to get his time. He has been called the nation's foremost authority on seeing the stories behind corporation financial statements, locating the sick spots, and pointing to the cures.

Francis Sullivan of Philadelphia was chairman of the legal and taxation group, and with him was Senator George Smathers of Florida, another eminently astute and well-connected gentleman who'd grown up in the is-it-good-for-golf? spirit.

The chairman of the Advisory Committee's tournament group was Curtis Person, a wealthy, retired automobile dealer of Memphis, who rejoiced in his recovery from a crippling illness by making a happy career of playing in Senior golf tournaments and winning a lot of them. He knew so many influential Seniors around the country that he was a very good man to have on the team. With him were William Black, son-in-law of Bob Jones; Giles Crowell, another man of broad acquaintance among Southeastern tournament sponsors; and Bob Leacox of Kansas City, who'd solved tournament scheduling problems of the PGA as coordinator in putting the circuit on the sports calendar as a business instead of as the hop-skip-and-jump operation it had been. Also on that committee was Clifford Roberts, who, with Bob Jones, had made the Masters the most successful of the world's golf tournaments without the circus sideshow tricks of squeezing the customers with the program racket, costly and remote parking, and high drink and food prices at the concession stands. Roberts had the know-how to give a tournament top class.

So with the PGA having a free array of all-star advisory talent, for which other businesses would have paid millions, and finally learning how to make use of an asset unique in pro sports, it was supplied with heavy intellectual artillery in case the journeyman pros declared war. And when Advisory Committee businessmen finally got a close-up look at the PGA operation, they advised that the load be eased on the Executive Committee at the PGA Championship meetings. There was the question of too much detail taking time that should be given to policy matters. Relieving the president of his heavy travel schedule was also suggested by the Advisory Committee.

As president Harold Sargent had kept an accurate log of the time he'd been away from his club on PGA service, and Advisory Committeemen wondered whether he was overtaxing himself. The PGA couldn't expect its president to be away from his home and club on an unpaid job for more time than a club member could afford to give free to his own industrial or professional association affairs.

A comparison was made between the PGA operation and the way the USGA

Tom Crane. PGA, photo by Dunedin Studio

officials delegated Executive Director Joe Dey to fill in at numerous public appearances where a USGA head man was expected. Dey handled those assignments to the decided satisfaction of all concerned. However, Tom Crane had neither the time nor the temperament to substitute as the PGA's front man in pictures or at microphones. Others were welcome to that publicity, fun, and glory while Crane worked on PGA unfinished business.

With Crane retiring as executive director because of illness, the Executive Committee considered as his successor his next-in-line, Lloyd F. Lambert, who'd come from the PGA's Washington lawyer corps to become PGA executive secretary. Other applicants were also screened until Robert F. Creasey was named to the post.

Creasey had been a lawyer in Washington and on the Labor Department staff during Harry Truman's presidency, and he was a member of the Burning Tree Club in Washington, where Max Elbin was professional. Creasey served seven somewhat stormy years as executive director before being replaced. He was caught in the PGA civil war, and being a representative of parental authority, was not loved by the separating journeyman professionals. As an appointee of the Elbin administration, Creasey was caught in the fussing and feuding between the Elbin camp and the adherents of Leo Fraser as president. The leasing arrangement with John MacArthur and negotiations for a possible new location of the PGA National Club presented other difficulties, to which were added complaints of "poor judgment." So, even with golf courses outside the office door and $50,000 a year, Creasey's lot was not a happy one as PGA executive director.

Robert Creasey. PGA, photo by Clark's Photography

Despite the imminent division within the PGA and the continued practice of devoting major attention to playing activities, the 1965 meeting increased the association's focus on its educational function. Gene Mason, chairman of the Education Committee, asked that an educational director be employed, but it took several years before his request was answered. Meanwhile, sections were energetically pushing their own school programs. The national body budgeted $12,000 for 1966 miscellaneous expenses over the entrance fees the sections received for their educational programs.

The contract that had been signed with the Victor Company of Chicago for royalties on the PGA-Victor line of clubs, balls and bags, and other playing equipment and apparel also provided a substantial sum. This was distributed through the Professional Golfers' Foundation for Education-Service, which had been formed to use the tax relief granted for educational operations. Among those appointed to the Board of Trustees of that fund were Franklin Waltz, Richard Irwin, and Curtis Person of the Advisory Board.

The Western New York section asked for five business schools to be held annually in different localities by the PGA, and the proposal was adopted. Another sign of the keen interest in the business education of PGA members came from the Dixie section. It recommended that the educational background of officers, delegates, and committee appointees be stated when these names were presented to the entire membership. One reason this suggestion was advanced was that numerous officials of the Golf Course Superintendents' Association and of the Club Managers' Association had college degrees. Almost all of the younger superintendents had attended agricultural colleges and had graduated with degrees, and the successful younger club managers also had degrees from the hotel and restaurant schools of universities. The professionals, who were specialists in golf, had no special schooling for their business but generally had good basic backgrounds through high school.

Efforts had been made to have the college education of students on golf athletic scholarships directed toward preparing these young men for careers in the golf business. George Dawson of Spalding, winner of the USGA and other Senior Amateur championships, was especially active in trying to get colleges and universities to organize golf business education, but nothing was accomplished, as the career schooling was contrary to USGA amateur status regulations.

Later, the National Collegiate Athletic Association Championship, in the opinion of many, outranked the USGA Amateur Championship. And after graduation the NCAA stars quickly enlisted for the PGA tournament players' tests to qualify for the tournament circuit. The PGA eventually got Patrick Williams, then Gary Wiren, as director of its business schooling, and got a national program coordinated.

Another indication of progress in PGA business operations came at the 1965 meeting when the Southern California section requested that its executive secretary, Mrs. Marilyn O'Pace, be admitted to sessions as a spectator. Mrs. O'Pace was a pioneer among able paid executive secretaries, women and men, who got sections operating as efficient businesses and accounted for a mod-

ernization of PGA headquarters operations and its relations with the sections. The request to admit Mrs. O'Pace was denied as a "dangerous precedent." Women's Lib might easily have claimed that the precedents of women as observers and helpful recorders and secretaries could be cited in the cases of the daughter of Herbert W. Strong, first secretary of the PGA, and Mrs. Irene Blakeman, who was the PGA's first office employee and was secretary to Herbert Strong and to Jack Mackie when he was president in 1920, continuing with the organization for many years through its moves to Chicago and Dunedin. Miss Strong's writing preserves the authentic early records of the PGA.

The employment of a public-relations director was again discussed, and no action was taken. Home professionals were irate about being blamed for the misconduct of tournament players and for the journeymen's disregard of their obligations to their supporting public. Home pros said that the higher the PGA raised tournament prize money, the lower tournament golfers in general stood in their consideration of the good of the game and the golfing public. All professional golf was being rapped for the greed and bad manners of a few conspicuous tournament players, and the home professionals complained that they were getting no publicity to offset this.

It was suggested by Leo Fraser that the association magazine, *The Professional Golfer*, increase its circulation, and although it was losing money, extend its circulation to club officials at no cost to them as an educational and propaganda medium. That was done for a while until postal regulations limited the free circulation, but even so, the promotion was ineffective.

PGA officers and the Executive Committee were unable to formulate a policy for the guidance of a public-relations director. It hired several public-relations men but never defined their function, so their work was limited to preparation of releases on routine matters. The job was long a waste of competent personnel and of the opportunity to publicize the PGA's authoritative position in golf and its helpfulness to amateur golfers.

The annual meetings of professional baseball and football organizations, which are really businesses that affect relatively few people, regularly received extensive coverage in sports sections, while the annual meetings of the PGA, which was the biggest business in American sports and involved about 10 million people a year, received only casual coverage. Generally, only the election of officers made the wire service news, unless there was major warfare, such as when the home pros and touring pros split, which, as sports news and information in moderate depth, was the most poorly handled big sports story in many years. Sports editors and writers were having difficulty adjusting themselves to the TV sports era and with very few exceptions missed the significance and possibilities of the story.

Not realizing that it was in a business as well as in a sport, the PGA was completely at a loss on how to get its side of the story into print and on the air. Long before the civil war in its ranks, the PGA's public-relations problem was already apparent in the preparation and building of its National Golf Club. That small part of the golfing public belonging to the PGA had incomplete information about what was going on. This was the biggest business transaction that the PGA had ever

been involved in, yet there was no such indication in any story in *The Professional Golfer*. Nor was any information forthcoming from Executive Committee members; most of them admitted they didn't really know what was going on either.

John MacArthur later said that his understandings and agreements with PGA officials had not been passed along to the membership as news, but then MacArthur himself was not a frank and cooperative news source on the matter. With both sides deficient on information policies and procedures, the arrangement was doomed to become a source of frequent haggling, requiring the services of expensive lawyers, and a needless waste of time and money.

But during the lulls in the brawls, winter was fun at Palm Beach Gardens for PGA members. There were nine tournaments scheduled and also the big Equipment Show at the PGA National Golf Club during the 1964–65 winter months.

Peace prevailed temporarily in the tenant-landlord relationship between the PGA and John MacArthur when the 1966 annual meeting was held at the Palm Beach Towers Hotel. After all the strife and convulsions within the PGA, it was hoped that the association could get back on its original track of making more money for the majority of its members, as well as improving and extending its services for the good of their employers and golf in general. But then again, as might have been expected, things didn't quite work out that way.

The annual meeting of delegates, officers, and the Executive Committee ran on October 28 and 29, but committee meetings extended from October 28 through November 4. Max Elbin was

Dan Sikes. AG

president, Leo Fraser, secretary, and Warren Orlick, treasurer. In the usual manner, the immediate past president, Warren Cantrell, was now honorary president. The new vice-presidents were John Conley, succeeding Lew Adesso, Bob Popp for Gene Mason, and Noble Chalfant, replacing Terry Malan. Dan Sikes, Jr., replaced Tommy Jacobs on the Tournament Committee, and the revered and admired Robert T. Jones and Walter Hagen were on display as honorary vice-presidents.

The annual meeting and the Executive Committee worked at length on a new constitution. So many revisions had been made in updating the original working papers of the organization that drastic updating and simplifying were necessary. The revised constitution was to become effective on January 1, 1967.

The first shock came following a request from the Tournament Committee for the delegates to approve PGA payment of a bill for legal services entailed in splitting the organization. Up to this point most PGA members—home pros and journeymen alike—were convinced that the differences were minor, since the Tournament Committee had been operating efficiently as an autonomous section of the association, and that they could still be amiably settled so that professional golf could present itself as a body unified for service to and the entertainment of the paying golf public.

But that one bill to pay the legal fees that resulted from the secret meetings of the PGA player dissidents made the majority of PGA members feel as if they were being charged for both the gun and bullets to be used in killing them. Not only did it end all hopes of a separate players' section's being established within the PGA framework, but it also polarized points of view. The loyalists, as it were, now believed that the sooner professional golf was rid of the characters who regarded such an outrageous proposition as sound business ethics, the better the status of professional golf with the amateur golfers who supported it.

In the discussions that followed presentation of the bill for approval, both sides objected to everything that was proposed for unifying the PGA as the voice of the commercial phase of golf. A demand was then made for a separate players' section, inasmuch as the proposed new constitution provided that a quorum for a tournament section meeting should consist of two PGA officers and two tournament players, instead of simply four PGA members.

Unfortunately, the successful business executives who were serving on the

PGA Advisory Committee because of their dedication to golf had been unable to confer with the rebellious players because they held secret meetings at which discussion was limited. And, revealingly enough, although a few had done unexpectedly well financially on the PGA tournament circuit, the leaders of the breakaway movement were not prominent players nor publicized for their winning personalities.

Cynical realists—and there were plenty around—saw the oncoming split as an inevitable development of the times. The exhibition sector of professional golf had become merely another moneymaking trade similar to professional football, baseball, basketball, horse racing, boxing, wrestling, or even the roller derby. Led by the incomparable Walter Hagen, American professional golf had brought wide social acceptance to professional athletes. Of course, the road had been prepared for Hagen by golf's estimable old pros, the pioneer members of the PGA, who were so highly valued in their communities. But that cycle had definitely ended. The distinction of being a performing pro golfer was being dimmed by a small, vocal group powerful enough to tarnish the "image" of the tournament professional.

In public esteem Arnold Palmer and Jack Nicklaus were the Number One and Number Two pro golf performers. The experienced Palmer had the record and personality; the younger Nicklaus was winning and blossoming, so he was plainly going to be top man. He didn't sparkle with the Palmer charisma, nor even have the interviewing touch of Gary Player, but Nicklaus was a young man of candid, honest answers and 100 percent quality of character. Now he was being taught in an uncomfortable way the difference between grabbing

for every loose penny that meant managerial percentage and a business reputation as sound as his golfing status.

The Nicklaus name on the cheapest sort of golf balls came in for criticism at the PGA meeting. It was out of character with the Nicklaus label on high-grade sportswear or a first-class real-estate development. Palmer tried to be a peacemaker. He saw the damage that could be done to playing professionals' earnings and their identification with a big, top-quality market of personalities and products. The quality that was associated with the names of Ben Hogan and Walter Hagen on golf goods was established when the PGA was unanimous in rating a member's name as being of higher value than money. The member whose name was on inferior stuff was scorned or laughed at. He didn't belong to the elite.

The split in the PGA cost Palmer and Nicklaus money from the home professionals who directed the quality golf goods market. What a store said about a club or ball didn't mean much to a knowing buyer; the home pro was the authority. Palmer's attempt to maintain PGA unity included a discreet approach to the Golf Writers' Association officers, but the reporters were usually closer to the home professionals than to the journeymen and believed that much of the tournament players' unrest was the result more of jealousy of Palmer than of mishandling of the tournament situation by the PGA.

The shock waves from the blast over the disputed lawyers' bill quickly divided the PGA into several camps. Probably most of the members were for separation, including the discontented minority among the tournament professionals who wanted the bill paid— but not by them. Then there were the belligerent home professionals who wanted the discontented playing professionals thrown out of the PGA and prohibited from playing in the PGA Championship, the Ryder Cup matches, and participating in the PGA tournament circuit. The dissidents were threatening to form a new tournament circuit and to take the stars with them, and they claimed they had the support of the majority of tournament sponsors. However, a check by reporters and several PGA officers did not confirm the strength of the rebels' position. In fact, enough tournaments were divided in sentiment to make the future of the circuit itself precarious.

There was a group in favor of compromise—continuing the autonomous operation of the Tournament Division exactly as it had been for years under the PGA roof. Further, a considerable number of PGA members didn't care whether the tournament pros stayed on or cut loose. Perhaps that still is the situation, since the impact of tournament professionals as market influences on the purchase of the smartest apparel, the finest clubs, and other playing equipment is not strong at the private clubs from which golf market tastes radiate. For all purposes, however, the bill for legal services marked the end of PGA unity. The awakening and the wrap-up followed.

All the same, the shake-up proved healthy for the PGA. It brought a realization that there were two parts to professional golf: first, the section that developed and served the amateur players; then, second, the showcase professionals who provided the entertainment when golf's participants were sightseeing.

After the officers, Executive Committee, and delegates had awakened to the dismal fact that the PGA was being torn apart internally, attention was given to professional golf as a service and development factor of the game. The winter schools for assistants were attracting and effectively training desirable young golf businessmen to the extent that head professionals were warned about overeager recruiting at the schools. Pros were hiring away from previous employers assistants who showed superiority in the schools. Delegates listened to debate on whether the youngsters' opportunities for advancement could be controlled. The discussion indicated that the training program was succeeding.

The qualifying and educational sessions for young men seeking tournament playing cards were valuable in screening new talent for the circuit and reducing problems of fields having too many pros deficient in the type of golf needed in Open tournaments. (The Approved Tournament Player pattern has continued.) Some were underfinanced, and bad checks were not uncommon along the tournament route. Bob Creasey said the applicant for a tournament card should have enough to meet expenses of $250 a week for six months. Tommy Jacobs thought that figure might be too high.

Plans were made at the 1966 meeting for hiring an educational director and for having a correspondence course for professionals and assistants. Patrick Williams was employed to direct the educational program, and eventually home-study material on professional department business was made available.

Apparel selling, with its sudden fashion changes and impulsive ordering to suit the members, had increased pro-department inventories to the point that overstocking and slow-moving items made the pro shop a risky business. In the pro shop everyone had to be a merchant as well as a teacher, plus a starter, a cart dispatcher, and a publicity man or woman. The sportswear business was becoming so important that effective saleswomen could determine the difference between profit and loss for a professional in a year. Yet the PGA business schooling hadn't figured out how to use the abilities of saleswomen in pro-shop merchandising, even though it had been the wives of the old professionals who had put golf shops into the apparel business in the first place.

The PGA was getting around to the point where it recognized its members would slump or progress on their merchandising ability. William Clarke of Maryland told his colleagues to quit spending so much time on the details of constitutional amendments that any lawyer employed by the PGA should be able to work out satisfactorily. Walter Nagorski of Hawaii pleaded with the PGA to get merchandising improved on the local level. In Hawaii, inferior-quality golf clubs, balls, and bags were being sold by stores as first-class products. When the misrepresented stuff was shown by golfers to professionals, the pros agreed that the buyers had been stuck, but they didn't know how to protect themselves and the market against the costly deceit.

For almost seventy years American golfers had learned that the pro standard of golf merchandise was top quality, and "pro only" on a line of golf goods had become consumer protection. Variation in materials and workmanship of the cheaper goods was extensive, being limited only by the trading shrewdness of the retail buyers in cutting down the manufacturers' profits. "For sale at professional golfers' shops only" became a buyer's protection line often seen in magazine advertising and heard in television commercials of first-

class golf merchandise. The "pro-only" selling point had to be stressed in a way that would bring buyers into pro shops, as the Hawaiian delegate and other pros knew. How to do that job was a big problem for the PGA.

There was no doubt that the professionals had created and built the golf market, while the stores had done nothing in this development except collect by selling cheaper goods. That was a service of a sort in extending the golf market, but even there, professionals at public courses supplied consumer protection by offering expertly chosen values in the lower price ranges. The professionals' service was so good that stores claimed it was unfair competition, but a few years after the PGA assembly worried about how to make "pro only" a service to the golfing market, the courts declared "pro only" illegal.

Pro-shop business was getting to be about 50 percent apparel—possibly a little less where the pros directed the proper compression of golf balls for their individual customers and consequently were qualified to order shop inventories and special clubs were better suited to the needs of the individual buyers. In any case, the PGA felt that the golf professionals who had built the golf business and risked their own money in serving it well were to be denied by the courts the right to acquaint the public with professional superiority in golfer service.

The 1966 meeting also discussed and approved a revision of a standard professional employment contract with private clubs. The previous suggested form had been helpful in defining the professional's duties and responsibilities and in clarifying what the professional was to get from the club. With the variations in private club conditions, contracts had been pretty much a matter of trial and error, but arrangements usually favored the club. A professional who'd had a bad season at a club could be discharged a month or so before the opening of the next season and thus be caught with heavy inventories of new and leftover merchandise and not have much time to find himself a new job.

The professional's own payroll was considerable. Pay, meals, insurance, hours, and duties of shop and teaching assistants, and federal, state, and other tax involvements of the employees, concerned both the pro and the club, but how far such responsibilities extended was vague.

Supervision of caddies and of golf and bag carts was also an area requiring clear definition. Customarily, the professional got the shop "concessions," lesson income, and income from club cleaning and storage. Usually, the club also guaranteed payment of members' accounts due the pro. Gross and net revenue from golf cart rental was about evenly divided when cart use was new, but the expense of building and maintaining cart roads and bridges, and the cost of the carts themselves, soon had the clubs taking the gross cart revenue. Often the pro department was allowed $1 a round for cart assignment, supervision, and bookkeeping. The pro got the abuse when the machine went dead on the course. And when soaked turf made the course officially unsuitable for carts, it was usually the superintendent who had the responsibility of making the decision. However, when the superintendent wasn't close to the first tee, the pro had the job of enforcing the ruling to protect the course.

Pensions, insurance, and other fringe benefits were slow coming into the golf club employment picture. Public

courses, because of civil-service or union operations, frequently did better by employees than private clubs, although numerous pros went broke bidding too high for concessions at public courses.

Competition for professional jobs was so keen that there always would be some professionals who would take jobs at any terms offered. On that account, well-qualified professionals and good clubs could not get together readily. Club officials were not experienced employers of professional golf workers, and as a rule, they changed annually or every few years. Trusting and kindly personalities were responsible for most of the satisfactory pro-club working agreements. Times were changing, and the old pros who'd been valuable and loyal for years were now working for new members who wanted new faces in the pro department. As a consequence, competent, faithful veterans were turned out with sweet words and lovely farewell parties but little in material wealth as evidence of the club's appreciation. Some clubs, though, took seriously the traditional obligations of gentlemen sportsmen toward the old family retainer, but sentiment was surely running a poor second to a modern pension system in the new look of pros and their employers toward the job.

Although not too widely applicable among golf's approximately 9,000 possible places of pro employment in 1966, the standard pro employment contract was a sound basic proposal that provided a practical working overture for mutually satisfactory agreements. Some private clubs and privately owned fee courses wouldn't subscribe to the policy of giving the professional full shop concessions but paid a salary that, according to employers, netted the professional more than was netted on a concession basis by comparable private clubs.

The full-concession basis of pro employment has long been so generally satisfactory to pros and employers that the PGA Tournament Committee agreed to play tournaments only at courses where the professional had the shop concessions. This was perfectly satisfactory to clubs and pros where the professional was on a salary basis. But there were few of these clubs, and they were usually wealthy, exclusive ones that positively didn't want tournaments. So there was only a faintly remote chance that a club professional who didn't have all shop concessions but was making money and was happy with his job would demand that his club open its books to the PGA.

Some delegates also feared that the PGA proposal of shop and other concessions for the pro as essential to a tournament arrangement might be another one of those issues that could mean more litigation for the association. So the demand that tournament circuit events be played only at private clubs and fee courses where the pro has shop concessions continues as a pleasing formality with a do-not-disturb sign on the door.

President Elbin had rightly guessed that the secret meetings of the tournament players would threaten PGA unity, so he asked that the press be admitted at the 1966 annual meeting in order that the association might get some sympathetic publicity about its problems with dissidents. The few golf writers who had suspected what was going on at their undercover sessions regarded them as juvenile affairs and unlikely to derail the gravy train the PGA conducted for its tournament player passengers. But the golf writers

seemed unaware that they were at the end of an era themselves. Their words in print had built up the National Open, the PGA Championship, the Masters, the Crosby and Hope invitational affairs, the Colonial, and the Firestone World Championship, while television had only Shell's "Wonderful World of Golf" as its outstanding tournament production. Yet who got the big money? Not the golf writers who made the event, but the television boys who traveled on the free air.

Print had also made the World Series, the Kentucky Derby, the Indianapolis 500, the boxing championships when the fighters were fighters, the Olympic Games, the collegiate bowl games, and then had built pro football until it saved television from the deadly boredom of most of its programs. The change was sweeping, but managing editors, sports editors, and the specializing sportswriters had trouble adjusting.

The golf writers saw little copy in the PGA annual meetings—when they were finally admitted to proceedings that the association officials thought of great news value. Their reaction was: "What should be kept private about these meetings? Who cares?" More plainly than ever, the PGA had never been able to get across the news that it was one of the world's largest sports businesses, with a $250 million annual volume and with its circus side alone bringing in about $9 million a year.

The annual meeting story, and most of the other nationwide news about the PGA, was that the association was primarily a business having a tremendous effect on real-estate values, apparel merchandising, and social developments instead of just another sport like, say, cockfighting. How to give that news the same treatment a tournament got, baffled sportswriters and was beyond the PGA. The simple fact that golf had become a bigger and more exciting business than it was a sport was slow in getting through to the writers and the PGA. A husky ex-caddie of Russian ancestry named Joe Jemsek was far ahead of Arnold Palmer, Jack Nicklaus, Bill Casper, Lee Trevino, and other tournament circuit winners in financial rating. He had acquired a fortune by owning and operating golf courses.

Major residential developments in the United States and practically all popular foreign resorts were to a large extent dependent on golf for their attractiveness and success. And famous players were of minor value as drawing cards compared with the thoroughly first-class management of the golf facilities by a competent professional. Domestic and foreign golf resort play also made golf a year-old business, with charter flights of vacationing golfers accounting for thousands of dollars of increased pro-shop purchases by the travelers.

The names and picture in the paper of the couple that won Sunday's mixed foursome at the Bear Trail Country Club will sell additional papers, which is more than can be said for print about who is third in the National Open Championship. Publishers and editors noted the influence of local golf news on circulation that was definite and different from other sports news and kept newspapers in a position television couldn't occupy. These experts in communications recognized the unique public-relations function of golf publicity far more quickly than did the PGA or sports departments.

Certainly the PGA, whose members provided the organization with the most extensive, intimate, and effective public-relations contacts in all sports, was blindly and inexcusably slow in learning the difference between the organized promotion of immensely valuable human-interest public relations and the sort of crass publicity that gave sports-page headlines to a trained chimpanzee matching drives with a golf pro.

25

Modern Club Design and Ball Development

ABOUT the time bench clubmaking for the individual was nearing its end, American merchandising and factory quantity production began experimenting with marketing clubs purporting to be identical with the implements of famous professionals whose names the clubs bore. The experiment was based on sound psychology and was intended to influence the ever-hopeful and -gullible golfer, although a rational child would reason that if certain clubs were precisely what the expert player needed for his almost daily use, they were not necessarily suited to the golfer of limited ability who played far less frequently.

When assistants were trained in clubmaking, they usually also devoted enough time to teaching to see what kinds of players needed what kinds of clubs. If a man or woman wanted one or more new clubs, the man who was to make the clubs generally took a few clubs out to the lesson tee and studied the player as he swung the test models. Then there were discussions, followed by trials of the finished clubs. Even then there might be some alterations.

The experienced professional of the hickory-shaft days could watch a player make a few shots with various clubs, then go into the pro shop and tell a clubmaker exactly what was needed. The pro's education in the precision fitting of clubs was aided by shaft breakage. Fairways, rough, and the bunkers were often hard and spotted with stones, and the generally observed rule was to play the ball as it lay. That practice, strangely enough, was neglected as the playing conditions improved greatly.

The popular imported iron heads were from Stewart, Nicoll, and Forgan. American forged iron heads for bench-made hickory-shafted clubs didn't rate high with British-born or home-bred pros who were the expert hickory-shaft clubmakers, but the story was the other way on wood head blocks. A Jack White model, which needed only shop shafting and finishing, was the one driver head that was imported in appreciable amounts.

Much of the winter factory production went to store outlets at lower prices than the custom-made pro-shop clubs with their hickory shafts screened by experts. The master clubmaker would carefully examine a shipment of a gross of seasoned hickory in his shop and find perhaps a dozen he regarded as workable for his masterpieces. The customer had to pay for this premium material.

Bruce Herd, long the professional at the South Shore and Flossmoor clubs in the Chicago district, and one of a family of famous British and American clubmakers, tells of his uncle, Fred Herd, who worked with Herd and Yeomans. He had learned clubmaking in his hometown, St. Andrews. He knew how to use clubs, too; he won the 1889 USGA National Open. He worked at Chicago clubs and made that area a center of fine clubmaking.

Herd always kept looking for prize shafts in seasoned rough material he received from Tennessee. In one instance he put his selections into two woods and four irons that he crafted with superb workmanship for a prize customer who was one of Chicago's wealthy golfers. Herd charged the man a dollar or two over the going price and the robber baron complained, since the price at that time for a clubmaker's work of art was $5 or $7. Shocked by the response to his effort to make the finest clubs possible for the rich man, the Scottish artist exploded: "If ye can't afford the best, don't come to me! Get your clubs elsewhere!" Fred Herd kept

his job and the respect of his club members.

In learning the whys and wherefores of golf club construction and design, earlier American golfers also learned about the golf stroke. Maurice McCarthy, for years pro at the Nassau Shores Country Club on Long Island, used to give Lesson Number One by putting a ball in the palm of his left hand, then taking the head of an iron or wood club in his right hand and showing how the leading edge of the club was expected to get through the grass under the ball so the "sweet spot" of the club face met the ball precisely.

While materials used for making golf clubs have varied through the years, it's somehow reassuring that "wood"—at least for the club head—still remains a "wood." Of course wood does stretch, warp, and expand, and here lamination of wood strips to prevent climatic deviations from the original have proved successful. On the other hand, aluminum and plastic have proved unsatisfactory substitutes for wood in club heads. The sound of solid contact with the ball and the feel of a good wood shot have not been produced by other materials.

Expert players and clubmakers have said that in striking the ball, wood has the distinctive quality of maintaining contact just long enough to allow maximum reaction of the rubbery ball material. This is one of the mysterious areas of golf club and ball performance still to be probed, and this factor in the resilient performance of the golf ball has not been mentioned in information the USGA has made available concerning its golf ball tests.

Although numerous experiments with steel and other metal rods and tubes were made during the hickory-shaft period, it wasn't until the late

1920's that any steel tubing proved satisfactory. By 1929, steel-shafted wood clubs were being used by many professionals who continued to play with hickory-shafted irons. The year of Bobby Jones's immortal Grand Slam, 1930, marked the last general use of hickory-shafted clubs, although hickory-shafted putters continued to be popular for another decade.

Every sort of variation genius could devise has been employed in the development of the steel shaft. Differences in alloys, thickness, taper, steps of different diameters and location of those steps, weights, and manufacturing processes have been tested by millions of strokes in actual play as well as by laboratory and machine examination. But the arrival of the steel shaft meant new and serious problems for the PGA. To maintain professionals in their authoritative position as providers of correct equipment for players, a great deal of education had to be done among some of the younger professionals and almost all assistants.

The steel shaft also meant inventory problems for the professionals expert in club fitting. The flexes and stiffness of shafts, the overall weights, lofts, and lies, the set of club faces for slight hooking, length of shaft, and swing weight were provided in enough range in various manufacturers' lines so that the professional who knew club fitting and how to order for his potential customers was in a position to give them very valuable service. With expert fitting and a practice tee convenient for testing the feel and performance of the clubs, the pro was in the ideal selling and service position.

The shafts of fiberglass, aluminum, and graphite threads that followed steel seldom had breakage problems. The glass shafts promised a springiness

that would snap more distance into the ball; also, they were said to be virtually free from torsion, thus assuring a more accurate performance. The glass shaft was slightly larger in diameter than the steel shaft, and this size was visually magnified by the shaft's being black. The clubs had an appearance of clumsiness that they did not have in "feel." Black was unconventional for a shaft. There were sheaths to give a hickory appearance over early steel shafts, but these coatings were soon abandoned. The glass shafts did not catch on with tournament players, and Gary Player was the only one who won championships with them.

Then aluminum shafts came in briefly. These lightweight shafts were presumed to add a highly desirable head heaviness to the club because of the light weight of the shaft and also to have a "kick" in the shaft low and effectively close to the club head. The theory of more ball distance from the higher velocity of the club-head mass enchanted a multitude of golfers who had been eagerly looking for the answer. Still, tournament players' trials of aluminum-shafted clubs didn't make converts. The average player's reception of the aluminum-shafted clubs was like a gold rush, but in three years aluminum-shafted golf clubs were a ghost market and some makers were unloading their inventories at less than cost.

Then came the shafts of graphite thread, which were introduced by a few tournament players. In addition to lightness and strength, the shafts could be made in many degrees of flexibility. They were said not to have the torque of the steel shaft, and not having the club head twisting as it came into the ball, kept the shot on the line.

The introductory price of the graphite-shafted clubs was as high as $135 for

Gary Player. GH

drivers. Purchases were so large they jolted professionals into realizing that players were eager to spend a lot of money for clubs if they promised improved results. Some good amateurs and a few tournament professionals boasted of better-than-average performances with graphite shafts. Responding to the alarms of extraordinary distance from the new shafts, the USGA considered testing them as a potential menace to the traditional values of the game, but quickly cooled off.

As shafts changed from hickory to steel, with glass, aluminum, and graphite figuring in the story, the search for the ultimate in golf club shafts was prominent, but the changes in golf-head design went about almost unnoticed. An Americanized Scot named Willie Ogg got the idea of adding weight to the toe of the club, thus balancing the weight of the hosel and extending the width of an iron club face on which a ball could be struck in a straight line to the target. Ogg had worked on a Scottish idea that nobody had paid much attention to because the hunch was that extension of the "sweet spot" of the iron was to be accomplished by lessening the weight of the hosel or neck of the club. The Ogg weighted-toe idea, first called Ogg-mented, didn't catch on quickly. Now it is basic in club design.

Lowering the center of gravity or effective weight of the iron club so it could get the ball airborne properly was slower to arrive. A Texas amateur named Smith got the idea of putting a slight flange on the bottoms of irons so more weight would get under the ball and propel it in the desired trajectory. The Burke Golf Company bought Smith's idea and made a line of iron clubs that were used with satisfaction by ordinary golfers but were not well publicized or merchandised. Burke was not particularly strong with the pro trade, so the Smith irons never sold well. But whether it was the flange or a well-placed wide sole, the Smith iron idea eventually had a tremendous effect on iron-club design. The newer designs of iron heads not only got the ball up better than the old models, which had weight higher from the sole, but usually gave the average player more distance.

Notwithstanding advertising emphasis on the brands of clubs used by winners of professional championships, there was significantly increasing mention of club-design features especially useful to the typical golfer who lacked the finesse and strength of the playing specialist. Considering the variations the experts had in their own clubs, it is surprising that more of a selling point has not been made of clubs designed with the needs of the multitude of club buyers and users in mind, rather than the wishes of the tournament specialists who often are supplied with virtually custom-made clubs.

Wood-head design has not given evidence of as many developments as the iron heads have shown. The club designers continue to try to get weight in

wood heads toward the front and at the angle that will most efficiently get the desired trajectory for the energy applied. There has been no material change in the slight but effective curvatures of wood club faces. From time to time, there have been slight changes in the tops or soles of wood clubs with the hope of some superior aerodynamic performance, but usually these changes have not been for long and have had no appreciable effect on performance or sales.

The golfing public's ability to make good use of a 5-wood and the infrequent use of the 2-wood by most amateurs accounted for the big change in wood-club production in the 1960's and thereafter. As club heads, shafts, and grips improved, some thoughtful professionals wondered if the selling and fitting of clubs had improved proportionately. But it began to be clear to the best businessmen in professional golf that clubs were being bought rather than sold. The old custom-fitting advantage of pros was being lost. However, one veteran clubmaker, Ken Smith of Kansas City, and a few of his aging bench clubmaking colleagues, continued to do a big custom-made club business by mail and through old friends in pro jobs who knew how to order clubs to fit the individual.

With the passing of the hickory shaft, clubmaking in the pro shops became a lost art. The supply of skilled clubmakers for winter work in old golf club factories also vanished quickly and had to be replaced by men and women with new training in the manufacturing techniques. New production methods had to be worked out and new standards of suitability for the market had to be determined. No longer was every club practically a custom job as in the days when the pro and his clubmaking assistants fitted each club to each buyer.

The only way the early steel-shafted clubs could be designed and made was for the expert players. Hence, the manufacturers hired expert players as consultants, and the field staff idea grew. Many of the younger playing stars certainly weren't stars at clubmaking, and the veteran pros didn't take kindly to manufacturers paying the tournament headliners for advice on making clubs. The names of playing experts on clubs assembled cheaply and sold at low prices in stores only further irritated the older pros who really knew how to make and fit clubs.

It used to burn up home professionals to have so many of the newer tourists "high-nose" the local professionals, except when the traveling men wanted to do a bit of benchwork on a club, then come into the pro shop, acting as though they were sliding down from heaven and doing the resident laborer a great favor.

What made the older professionals, who were clubmaking experts, bleed internally were inept jobs of trying to twist a 3-iron into a 1-iron or set it for a hook or a slice. The home pros snorted that, if the wandering Wonder Boy was good enough to be worth a lot of any manufacturer's money, why didn't he come into the shop and help the local pro sell a set of woods or irons in person, or show that he knew enough about clubs to take care of a minor repair on a grip? All that's gone now. Arnold Palmer may be the only playing specialist who knows anything about benchwork in adjusting clubs for the individual.

During the early 1930's, professionals on the Spalding staff came to the factory once a year to voice their observations and opinions on club design

Macdonald Smith. GH

and construction. This was all part of an attempt to get clubmaking out of the arts-and-crafts stage and onto a scientific basis, but there were frequent clashes between the experienced bench clubmakers and the playing specialists. They simply did not operate on the same wavelength, and their requirements were quite different—all of which led to confusion as to what kind of club should be manufactured.

Those working on Spalding club design at this· time included Ed Dudley, Al Watrous, Harry Cooper, Horton Smith, Henry Ransom, Ralph Hutchinson, Jimmy Thomson, Paul Runyan, Harold Sargent, Wiffy Cox, Lawson Little, and Mike Turnesa. Among these, Dudley, Watrous, Cooper, Ransom, Hutchinson, Runyan, Sargent, Cox, and Turnesa had done a limited amount of clubmaking and repairing as assistants.

Paul Runyan was especially profi-

Paul Runyan. AG

cient, good enough to have the great
Macdonald Smith ask him to change
the grips on clubs. Runyan recalls that
Mac Smith asked that no listing be
wrapped under the leather of the grips.
The work was done, but it didn't feel
right to Runyan, so he put a thin listing
under the leather. Smith picked up a
club, and because of the tiny difference
in diameter and weight, he literately
ate young Runyan's ears off. It was a
reminder of the exquisitely sensitive
touch of the old masters. The newer
player experts also have the delicate
fingertip feel that is perhaps too sensitive to be much of a factor in golf club
design and construction.

Paul Runyan was a small fellow and
not especially strong, so he had to have

all the help he could get from clubs.
His case underlined what Tommy Armour said about ideal golf clubs being
the only part of a good golf game a
player can buy. Howard Nannen, who
became Spalding's vice-president of
sales, says that when he was a young
pro golf salesman Runyan was a strong
advocate of large pear-shaped heads for
woods and of shorter grips than were
customary. The combination made for
a swing weight that gave the clubs a
head-heavy zip.

At the time Spalding was studying
Jones as the perfection of all golf, their
research and development staff included Milton B. Reach of the Spalding family and an intense golf scholar,
along with John Dickson and Victor

East. They spent many hours studying high-speed photographs of Jones, and studious professionals and club designers still say those pictures remain basic material. When he was designing the irons that first bore his name, Ben Hogan thought it tremendously significant that movies showed the club smashing into the ball and the flattened contact side of the ball being squeezed onto the upper edge of the iron.

"I need all the club face I can get to move and control the ball," Hogan said when he went into the clubmaking business, with such notables as Bob Hope, Bing Crosby, Marvin Leonard, and several other millionaire golfers as his partners. Hogan's first irons were not lovely works of art, and he spent a lot of time in his small factory grinding the irons to suit his feel and sight. Before he got the design and finishing done to his satisfaction, he had to throw away a ton of the heads, but apparently he figured the value of his con-

science as a clubmaking expert was worth more than his wealthy associates' money. It also cost him plenty of his own money while he was learning to make clubs that would be common denominators between his game and that of his customers.

Toney Penna had come up from the clubmaker's bench, working for Joe Sylvester and then with the brilliant Cuthbert Butchart as mentors. Then he went (along with Toney's astute brother Charley) as assistant to Tommy Armour at the Congressional Country Club, Washington. Clarence Rickey, who brought Armour as professional to the Medinah Country Club in suburban Chicago and to the MacGregor staff where Rickey was the top golf executive, encouraged Penna to continue playing tournaments, working as a pro salesman, and teaming with the shop designing staff of Clarence Custenbord, Leon Nelson, and Robert Nysgart.

Toney was a valuable addition. He

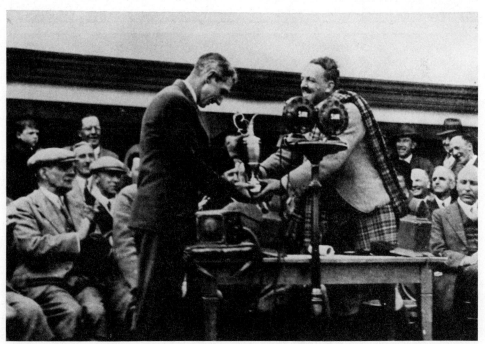

Tommy Armour accepting the British Open trophy in 1931. AG

knew enough to make use of men who knew more than he did; he was investigative and resourceful; he'd been fervently impressed by Armour to stay close to the basic essentials. He had made clubs for Leo Diegel back in the days when Diegel carried several drivers —one hooked, another straight or angled a trifle for a slice, one almost vertical, being about nine or ten degrees in loft, and another about fourteen degrees. Diegel knew that his clubmaker had put something into the shot, and regardless of his jumpy nerves, he had faith in his clubs.

The association of an expert in execution and an expert in club design was brought to the attention of seasoned playing and club-designing professionals when a tournament headliner wailed that he couldn't get the ball high enough off the tees to play in the Masters. The old fellows, who knew all of golf and had won championships and worked on their own clubs and those of other champions, rolled their eyes and exclaimed, "Migod, don't tell me the guy didn't know enough to get a little more loft on his clubs!" And to confuse the veteran experts still more, there was advertising of the complaining journeyman telling about his driver having a ten-degree loft, which, for the average golfer, would get them drives about like deliveries on a bowling alley.

Walter Hagen was also a master clubmaker. He had a touch and eyes that made a club a precision instrument. Wilson and its Hagen division had design control under Mike Behrendt, his assistant and successor, Joe Wolfe, and Dick Ling along with The Haig. Eddie Rankin, general manager of the Hagen company for a while, went to the Hogan company as an executive, then to the PGA-Victor company with Mark Cox and Jim Butz as design consultant.

Rankin said that Hagen and Hogan as artists had the same sort of feeling about club lines and distribution of weight, shafts, and grips. The Sure-Out sand wedge is a blend of Hagen and Hogan by Rankin.

Hagen had the basic idea of the leading edge and the flange of the wedge head, but it didn't get into the line because the Wilson Company, which owned Hagen, had such an effective sand wedge that pros who were on other manufacturers' staffs had a Wilson sand wedge in their bag. So when Rankin, one of the golfers who plays more in the sand than a little kid with a bucket and shovel, brought the no-no head to Hogan at Fort Worth, Ben, with the keen Hogan perception, figured out alterations to suit the club to any sort of sand, and regardless of the change of style in clubs, that wedge has remained in style.

Gene Sarazen was another who made money out of what he learned at bench clubmaking. The flattened small area on the grip of a club that was known as the "reminder grip" was Gene's idea to get the ordinary golfer's hands over a trifle more to the right side of the grip. And it worked.

Sarazen also did well for himself and golfers with the sand wedge. The flanged sole club was an old, old idea, as exhibits of irons fabricated by Scottish blacksmiths show in museums. The notion had been almost forgotten until a Texan had flanged-sole irons made, and through Horton Smith got the Burke Golf Company pushing them. They were of effective design, as later developments showed, but didn't sell.

Sarazen saw that the wedge, with alteration of the angle of the sole, would cut in under the sand instead of burying into it and would bump the ball out with a cushion of sand. He came up with the right answer. Previously there was a flanged-sole sand club with a concave face that Hagen made. It was a magic club. Jones used it for only one shot in making his Grand Slam. At Merion in 1930 when Jones was completing his Grand Slam, George Sayer, the club professional, had the Hagen wedges in his shop and sold hundreds of them during the week Jones was en route to glory everlasting. That was probably the only time a National Amateur Championship made much money for a club professional. Then, a year or so later, the USGA discovered that the wedge might hit the ball twice on its way up and out, and declared the club illegal.

Tommy Armour, an artist at selecting clubs, never had much of an idea how to make them. When he went to MacGregor, their design staff worked up clubs that Tommy considered suitable for his pupils and himself. But before they could all agree on particular models, everybody was abusing everybody else, and preliminary costs soared. In contrast, Bobby Jones, who was an engineering student as well as a master golfer, devised the Spalding models and even would make slight changes for the top men on the playing payroll.

Dunlop and Hillerich and Bradsby had veteran clubmakers designing their equipment with a few slight changes for the individual player. Everybody made some sort of a putter. Northwestern Golf Company, which was started by Natale Rosasco, Sr., who had been a clubmaker with Wilson, had ninety-two kinds of putters. John Reuter, Jr., with his Bull's Eye putter, had only a few variations of the basic design of his original blade putter and sold more of that type than any other putter ever made. Reuter, so some say, was responsible for knocking out the old idea that

John Reuter, Jr. PGA, photo by Clark's Photography

thirty-six putts per round was formal. He gave plenty of his clubs to tournament stars, and they found that by stroking the ball about under the place where the shaft came onto the head, they had either good luck or precision. Anyway, by the time there was any doubt, experts using the Reuter putters had won so much money on the long-stroking putts and the short taps that John was rich and didn't mind when the style changed in putters again, just as it always does.

Plenty of poetic license has been taken in comparing the golf clubs of the hickory-shafted times with today's production. The forging and finishing of the old iron heads, the beauty in de-

Bob Jones and his Calamity Jane putter. GH

sign and finish of wood heads suited to the old turf and ball conditions, and the shaping, finishing, and fitting of hickory shafts that remain in excellent condition—these are still works of art although made forty or more years ago or longer. Modern steel- and graphite-shafted quantity-production clubs, with assembly frequently and carefully checked, continue improvement of the clubmaker's art.

But just how effectively the new implements are suited to their users remains debatable. The earlier golfers found by trial, error, and revision with many clubs just what felt best and worked best for them. Bob Jones, after trying countless clubs, got a mashie that was perfect for him. That was the key club of the Grand Slam "matched set" he had made. His famed Calamity Jane putter, which was a magic wand for him, was a patched-up job, using a head that had been pro-shop junk. But it gave Jones the fingertip sensitivity of the old-time safecracker who could feel a safe combination lock falling into gear.

Even with the production control and uniformity of steel shafts, cases occur such as that of Sam Snead and the driver he had for seventeen years. It

Sam Snead. GH

had a battered head and a shaft that looked like a roughly used lightning rod. Since he was the star of its staff, the Wilson Company begged Slamming Sam to use a new driver and made him duplicates of the worn weapon, as identical as humanly and mechanically possible. Wilson is in the business of selling new clubs, and the shabby antique that Snead used so effectively on the tee seemed to put off golfers from buying nice, fresh drivers. Then one day the old driver was lost or stolen. Wilson rushed Snead a replica, and the first time he used it the club shot like a rifle, but Sam still growled he could

have done better with his old favorite. It took him a long time to be convinced that the modern club was an improvement.

"Nipper" Campbell was an accomplished player, teacher, and clubmaker of yesteryear who finished a colorful career in Ohio in the early 1940's. His finale at Dayton had him professional at the Miami Valley Golf Club, then designing the Moraine Country Club course and becoming its pro until his death. Tommy Bryant succeeded Nipper as pro at Moraine and stayed there for twenty-eight years until he retired. Bryant gave to Bob Kuntz, a collector

Typical pro shops. PGA, photos by The Commercial Photographers; Jorge L. Cuadrado

of rare golf clubs and books, the clubs Campbell had selected out of the thousands he'd made, and had used for about twenty-five years. And despite the years' wear and tear on the muscles, the clubs (hickory-shafted) continued to be just right for Nipper. He'd spent many hours on the lesson tee, at the clubmaker's bench, and with his shop stock of factory-made clubs, trying to fit others with as satisfactory a set as his own.

Club fitting, the companion art and science of clubmaking, was a tremendously important factor in putting the professionals into the development and control of a growing business, and it continues to be a difficult subject for the PGA educational efforts, men's and women's.

There are extensive stocks of clubs in pro shops; they usually carry a far more comprehensive inventory than the golf departments of stores. Now, when the fully trained, experienced professional sees a pupil's problem that he suspects may be with clubs as well as technique, he has to go back to the method successfully employed by his astute predecessors who were golf pros in the building decades of the early 1900's. He supervises the player's shot-making with clubs of different weights and balances and shaft qualities. In the opinion of numerous successful club fitters, the swing weights are only general guides, as swing-weight physics can be and is changed considerably by a slight difference in placing the hands on the grip.

Beyond the wide range of clubs the pro shop has in stock or available, leading manufacturers have their own custom-club departments, and there are other custom clubmaking specialists such as Ken Smith, Stan Thompson,

George Sayers, Irv Schloss, and the father-and-son teams of Bert Dargies and Toney Penna. A few others are veterans in fabricating golf clubs for individuals, and there are also pros in several areas, such as Chuck Tanis, one of the last of the artists of the bench club-making days, retired as Olympia Fields's pro after many years. And with his small and expert staff kept busy, he has the pleasant experience of the guy who made better mousetraps.

Tanis wants to see his clients hit some shots before he prescribes. So does "Hubby" Habjan, a protégé of George Smith, long professional at Onwentsia, who was once a brilliant tournament player, then decided he enjoyed himself more and could do better for all concerned by helping others enjoy golf. That was the spirit of many of the admirable veterans. The club-fitting phase of a genuinely expert professional's qualifications is one of the very valuable services bequeathed by the pioneer pros who made golf in the United States.

Stores have complained about "pro only" as limiting the local retailer's scope of service to the golfing public in the area where golf goods can be sold most cheaply. Not the most useful playing equipment, necessarily, but the *cheapest*. There has even been litigation about the possible legality of professionals of specialized training, point-of-use supply, and testing facilities, taking undue advantage of merchants whose main, and in its way commendable, objective is to sell anything to anybody cheaper. There is no law against that, but American professional golfers have done their work for the public so well that the courts had to decide whether or not it was illegal for them and manufacturers to use their expertise to determine how the golfing public could best be supplied with what was needed.

Certainly the pioneer American professionals never dreamed that they had established such a high standard of individual service that those inheriting that obligation would be brought before a court on the charge that "pro only" was the identification of a customer service so superior that it was unfair to competition. This growing-up phase of golf involved knowledge of club designing, construction, and fitting that was considerably beyond the PGA business schooling. There was a hunch that quite a few of the fellows who flunked the PGA Players' School courses actually didn't know Lesson One—what clubs to use.

Maybe it all narrowed down to putters, but what clubs to use came earlier in getting the ball within a one-putt radius of the hole. This called for a wide choice in the selection of clubs by men unable to select clubs either expertly or judiciously and who therefore could not be confident that they had been truly educated as Master Professionals.

The growth of the club business with its manufacturing, distribution, and inventory complexities has delayed the golf club business in adjusting to the vast multitude of golfers. Experts, whose dexterity should enable them to effectively use eight or ten clubs, kept crying to the USGA as though pros had been handcuffed if they were not allowed to use sixteen clubs. Which sixteen they didn't say. That didn't make them appear to be authorities, but then the playing pros generally didn't pay for clubs; they were manufacturers' staff members.

While the USGA was being entreated and abused regarding the four-teen-club limitation by the experts who were supposed to be able to manipulate a club, nobody mentioned the ordinary men and women amateurs who paid for clubs and weren't any too adept with what they had. That's one place where the journeyman experts cut themselves off from the amateurs whose money supported them.

The tournament professionals were playing with a 1- or 3-wood and an assortment of irons depending on how consistently they performed with certain wedges in putting the ball within a one-putt radius. Walter Hagen played that sort of a game, and his followers who sprayed shots all over the country got fat by following his departure from the orthodox game. But whoever gave a thought to the different requirements of men and women who paid money for clubs? Drivers continued to have about eleven or twelve degrees' loft, although you could stand by a first tee any Saturday or Sunday afternoon and see most drives were as low as line shots. At one time, a prominent manufacturer got big sales on his irons by pointing out that they were stronger than the rest of the brands. The answer was that the manufacturer made his 4-irons with 3-iron lofts, and so on down the line.

But somewhere along the line the intimacy of use and design of clubs was lost, although a few pro clubmakers could blend club face and weight, shaft length and flexibility, and grip size, weight, and location into a useful implement for a golfer who surely needed help. The PGA and the manufacturers, as progressive as they were and with the millions they had in the game, were needlessly slow in responding to what was happening.

The professionals, therefore, lost a tremendous advantage in this change of life in club merchandising. Probably a big percentage of all golfers today are playing with clubs that handicap them several strokes a round. A man or woman will go into a store and buy a set of bargain clubs that in actual play will cost him or her more than a dollar a round if he or she wagers modestly. But what does the store salesman who sells the clubs know about how the particular buyer plays?

The PGA has plenty to do in continuing its educational program, for, without any doubt, on the basis of club fitness, a PGA pro ought to be able to fit clubs immensely better than a store clerk. An interesting thing about the vital business of club fitting is that the older professionals who can see players swing and who select clubs for the individual are still doing helpful work for their pupils.

As golf club design achieved refinements that were of dubious value to many golfers, some features—generally picked up from early Scottish designs instead of being innovations—worked out well under American turf and wind conditions. In the first issue of the PGA magazine when Jack Mackie was the association's president, club prices of leading manufacturers' lines were about 50 cents to a dollar under what it cost to have clubs benchmade to the player's needs at his club's pro shop. The manufacturers' prices in 1920 were $5.50 to $6.75 for woods and $5 to $6 for irons. The juvenile market began getting attention, with manufacturers advertising junior woods for $2.25 and junior irons for $1.75.

By the time the PGA was three years old, there was plenty of discussion among pros, manufacturers, and amateurs on golf market development. The PGA notes as "trade problems vital to the welfare of our calling:

"Clubs selling balls and other supplies (with the professional being denied this potential revenue for service useful to the player);

"Manufacturers selling to department stores and others at prices under prices charged professionals;

"Preparation of a minimum price list on clubs, repairs, etc., for guidance of pros in general."

The PGA was never able to do anything definite on the price control of anything—clubs, balls, club repairs, trade-in allowances on used clubs, lessons, or club storage and cleaning. Probably the failure avoided trouble with the law. For a few years, a professional compiled and sold a book giving reasonable trade-in allowances for used woods and irons of various manufacturers and even in some instances listing clubs over eight years old. But the book didn't prove practical—even as evidence to a customer that the professional was making more of an allowance than was warranted.

From 1950 to 1965, there was a fairly good market for used golf clubs, especially in metropolitan areas where factory and office workers were thronging to the public and daily-fee courses. Many of them hesitated to buy a first-quality new set of woods and irons and bags without being sure they would like the game and play often and long.

The mass production of cheap clubs reduced the market for first-grade used clubs to the extent that professionals, fed up with having to make two sales to make one slim profit, practically stopped making trade-in allowances and advised buyers who proposed the trade-ins to give the clubs to caddies and others and to check on what gift-tax allowance might be approved.

When the aluminum-shaft flood came, steel-shafted clubs in manufacturers', professionals', and stores' stocks were nearly dead. They had to be moved at price reductions that virtually eliminated the used-club market. So that was one problem of pro-shop merchandising that dwindled from being a menace to becoming a minor nuisance.

Prior to the formation of the PGA Tournament Division, the PGA had discreetly handled demands by some of its touring members wailing for an easing of the Rules of Golf. The complaints of the playing specialists, reputedly of superior proficiency, that they were operating under conditions too severe for their talents, amused millions of golfers who had the idea that prize money of $100,000 or more for a four-day tournament should be as strict as regulations for amateur competitions.

PGA policy was to screen and pass along tournament players' remarks about rules. A few of the comments suggested improvements in playing conditions that may or may not have helped scoring but at least softened the psychological strain. Over the years a plea for smooth putting surfaces, undented by approach shots dropping onto the greens, had removed restrictions on repairing the ball pockmarks and established the practice of lifting every ball on the green and tossing it to the caddie for cleaning. So the quality of putting surfaces was immeasurably better than when professional tournament golf was growing up.

Complaints about unsatisfactory greens seemed to get worse as greens got better, according to veteran players, but that was the nature of golf. Of course the greens, not the player, were to blame when more than the normal number of "makeable" putts were missed. When a player is virtually a subject for locker-room intensive care because of bellyaches about the greens, some sadistic questioner is bound to ask: "Well, how come so-and-so went around with twenty-nine putts? Did he play the same course?"

Very much to the credit of the better-scoring tournament contestants, they did excellent jobs of repairing ball marks on greens and provided television lessons for multitudes of amateur golfers who don't repair damage they've done to greens, don't rake bunkers after their shots, or replace divots. In this delicate matter of rules, tournament professionals were probably conspicuously superior in intellect and game morality to the vast number of professional and so-called amateur athletes in other sports.

We have tried to cover the development of golf clubs from the Year One to today in this and preceding chapters, and we will now go on to round out the development of the golf ball. The big thing now is that they're tough, they last, and they go. From 1930 until almost 1960, the number of American golfers could be rather closely estimated by the golf ball production. There were sound reasons to believe that the golfers averaged a dozen balls bought per year. Then came tougher covers and more durable white paint on balls, chemical weed control that made it easier to find balls in the rough, shorter cutting of the rough to speed play and make the game easier, and large numbers of balls reclaimed from water holes, reconditioned, and resold at low prices.

Now, with the golf ball's extended life, it is estimated that the players' purchase of balls per year has been reduced from the former average of a dozen to 10.5 balls a year. Although the initial "PGA" were copyrighted in

1921, it was some years before deals were worked out between ball manufacturers and the PGA to license "PGA" on one pole of balls with the name of the manufacturer on the other pole. The arrangement was made with leading ballmakers, and in 1930 the PGA got a $36,000 refund to be split between the association and its members who had bought golf balls bearing the PGA pole imprints. The licensing arrangement never was completely satisfactory to manufacturers or professionals, even though retailers other than the pros sold comparatively few top-quality balls. In 1934, there were 45,546 dozen balls sold, most of them Spaldings.

One reason the PGA balls didn't sell better was a bonus system of rewarding pros for their work in selling balls and to some extent because of their credit rating. Spalding, in particular, paid pros with extra balls for their ball sales performance, and naturally the pros wanted to convert these balls into cash before pushing the PGA or other, less-popular balls.

Leo McNamara, the golf executive whose father was an early pro star and golf sales executive, retains a list of one of the ball manufacturer's payments that shows just about how pro-shop volume was distributed nationally at the time of the PGA deal with the golf ball manufacturers. Eventually the ball-licensing arrangement with several manufacturers was discounted, as PGA officials believed they could get a better deal from makers of coreless balls. The ball never became a success, the licensing was discontinued, and no further such deals were made.

With the invention of elastic plastics, there began attempts to make a molded solid ball like the gutty ball, but these solid balls were unsatisfactory, even

though production costs were low. The cored, thread-wound and covered golf ball, with its precision requirements, is difficult and costly to make. However, in its comparatively small increase in price since it first came onto the market, it is a manufacturing, distributing, and merchandising phenomenon.

In the 1970's came molded plastic golf balls with covers of another plastic. These balls, of course, met the USGA standards of not less than 1.68 inches diameter, not greater than 1.62 ounces in weight, and not greater than 250 feet per second muzzle velocity when tested on the USGA machine with the ball at 75°F.

The Royal and Ancient specifications require weight not greater than 1.62 ounces (45.9 grams) and a diameter of not less than 1.62 inches (41.2 millimeters). Royal and Ancient specifications do not include ball velocity. Metric specifications, parenthetical in the Royal and Ancient description of the official ball, indicate the vast international scope of the Royal and Ancient authority. The R & A ball specifications do not have a testing machine initial-velocity restriction. The USGA deemed that the initial-velocity restriction would keep the ball distance controlled so that the ball distance would not exceed reasonable limitations of ground area for golf courses. In Britain, with less area available for golf courses, the R & A didn't seem to worry about the ball's getting so long it could be knocked off the tight little isle.

In international professional events not sponsored by the USGA or the R & A, players usually were allowed to use either the R & A or the USGA ball. But the R & A and USGA worked together consciently and expensively in an effort to decide upon a ball that would be ideal for use in any country and by every player. Golfers generally couldn't have cared less about the intense effort the golf ruling bodies devoted to seeking a ball that would provide uniformity in golf-playing conditions in Kokomo and Calcutta, St. Andrews and Hong Kong. That universal wonder ball would also correctly evaluate and reward or punish the skill of the highly paid playing specialist or the uncounted happy and hopeful hordes praying for a ball that would enable them to break 100.

Whether under R & A or USGA jurisdiction, the golfing public was little concerned about the search for a uniform ball being conducted mainly with the consulting services of the pro stars, who differed from the gigantic majority of amateur golfers in that they (1) did not pay the manufacturers for the balls they played, and (2) had the skill and finesse to play either the R & A or the USGA ball effectively or should not be regarded as properly qualified champions. However, in 1974, the USGA and R & A search for a ball that would make the Rules of Golf universally uniform was abandoned.

A major factor in the decision to discontinue the uniform ball specifications was the complaints of American and British ballmakers that a change in size and weight would require a large investment for new manufacturing equipment. The next step would be an increase in the price of the first-grade ball. That development would place the blame on the USGA and R & A for ending the remarkable record of the golf ball in keeping the price of a quality product practically the same for more than half a century.

The PGA advocated a golf ball of standard weight and size years before the USGA and R & A. The wide variety of specifications for all balls was, to some extent, caused by difficulties in making balls uniform. The small, heavy American ball became popular in Britain, although the Royal and Ancient officials were against it. In 1919, the R & A Rules of Golf Committee, making its first postwar report, recommended that the distance of the ball be limited to preserve the balance between the power of the ball and the length of the hole.

After the USGA was consulted, there was agreement that "the players and not the inventors should guide the development of the game," but no action was taken until meetings between USGA and R & A committees in June, 1920, at Muirfield and in London, brought the proposal that "on and after May 1, 1921, the weight of the ball shall not be greater than 1.62 ounces and the size not less than 1.62 inches in diameter."

There had been warnings that a standard ball would weaken the professional's position in the ball market. His advice guided buyers in obtaining a ball best suited to their games and playing conditions. His authority in this area was considered to be of mutual value to his customer and himself, just as his recommendations and supply of fitted clubs was a decidedly useful factor in the development of golf's popularity.

The cored, wound, and covered golf ball remains one of the most complex of the precision items involved in playing games. However, whether the PGA's early urging to adopt a worldwide standard ball was sound continues to be debatable. Extensive variations in turf conditions are cited as a reason for making a uniform ball impractical. And manufacturers who have huge investments in ballmaking equipment wryly laugh off references to a one-world ball's making international competition equitable. They say that professional experts competing internationally usually get their golf balls free from manufacturers, who charge the cost to "promotion," and amateurs who can afford enough time from work to qualify for international competition won't have to drop out of golf because of the expense of practicing and playing with a ball of specifications differing from those to which they are accustomed.

The PGA wisely took only a small listening part when the Joint Committee on a Uniform Ball engaged in technical tests and studies. Possibly the ball-testing apparatus used in the process resembles a standard brainless golfer. The human golfer rarely has the ability to distinguish between two- or four-hundredths of an inch in diameter or of a half-ounce in weight, and according to the testimony of such gifted artists as Ben Hogan, seldom strikes more than five perfect strokes during a wonderful eighteen holes. Hogan had such a round in his magnificent 67 in the fourth round when he won the 1951 National Open on the 6,927-yard par-70 course at the Oakland Hills Country Club, Birmingham, Michigan.

Prior to the introduction of golf ball specifications by the USGA and R & A, professionals recommended to their customers the ball that in size, weight, cover, and resilience seemed best suited to the buyer's game. The first ball standards were determined by experiment rather than by science, and general turf and wind conditions accounted for the variation between the USGA and R & A standards. The two

sets of specifications have not been unreservedly endorsed. Golfers in many countries prefer the USGA ball, although otherwise playing by R & A and USGA rules, and a goodly number of American golfers prefer the smaller R & A ball, which the Americans believe goes farther.

The USGA introduced the "balloon ball" in 1931, and there was a period of three years when it had three different golf balls. Golf ball specifications by years are as follows: 1930—diameter, 1.62 inches, and weight, 1.62 ounces; 1931—diameter, 1.68 inches, and weight, 1.55 ounces; then in 1932—diameter, 1.68 inches. But 1.62 ounces became the legal ball weight, and the USGA and R & A have been cautious ever since about ruling a different ball into being.

During the USGA and R & A discussions about ball specifications no reference was made to what may account for considerable differences in ball specifications—that is, the compression. This is chiefly a factor of the resilience of the ball and its sound from impact with the club head swinging at various speeds. The compression rating originally was determined by a device an inventor got the PGA to endorse and which, for reasons forgotten, leading ballmakers of the time adopted.

The device was based on tests made for publicity by the Packard automobile company in which Gene Sarazen was shown to be swinging a club head at an impact speed of 115 miles per hour; the ball, after compression, left the club head at 130 miles an hour.

Figures have also been published on club-head speed per hour of men and women with handicaps of 18 or higher of around 75 miles an hour. But the relationships of the speeds of club heads, ball compressions, and distances have never been determined scientifically by the USGA, the R & A, the Golf Ball Manufacturers' Association, or the PGA.

Consequently, the typical golfer, whose money makes the golf market, often is psychologically overlooked. So say the experienced home professionals who are in ideal positions to observe the golf market and who occupy an authoritative position unique in marketing. They add that too many of their ball buyers ask for balls with too high a compression to make their swings effective. These professionals state privately that they have no difficulty switching brands of balls requested by the players, who haven't the slightest idea of what compression ball fits their games—and neither do their pros, often because of the absence of scientific information.

But when you consider the history of the golf ball from the viewpoint of the professional, as one who plays a ball as an expert or recommends a ball to a man or woman player whose game he knows, you get a different picture of ball specifications in relation to the individual golfer's requirements. In the first issue of the PGA's *The Professional Golfer*, May, 1920, Spalding advertised the Spalding 30 and the Spalding 50 as "quite alike except that the '50' is a little heavier." That difference gave the professional leeway to recommend the ball best fitted to the customer's swing and general type of game, the turf and wind conditions, and the clubs that the professional had made for the customer. The 30 and 50 both retailed at $1. The Silver King, another top seller in pro shops at that time, was $1.05 for the American-made ball and $1.10 for the British-made product.

Even so, the advertising of golf balls continued to stress professional victories. Spalding advertised in the initial *Professional Golfer* that "Every professional tourney in the south with the exception of St. Augustine and Augusta the last winter was won with a Spalding ball."

Distance doesn't seem to have been altogether the major consideration in golf ball selection in the United States prior to World War I, or in the spurt after that war, until the USGA and R & A got involved with specifications. In the pre-fairway-watering period, winners of driving contests often got well over 300 yards' carry and roll on the baked fairways. What was an important factor with the multitude of amateurs was cover durability—balls that stood up against the hacking of the sharp-edged irons and the abrasion of the rocky rough or bare spots in fairways. Even the 110-shooters were expected to play the ball as it lay, instead of moving it so that it was virtually teed up.

Hence, the professionals took a dim view of the USGA's effort to control ball specifications. The professionals believed that practical experience, manufacturers' competition, and pro-shop merchandising would provide the right answers. The pro position was confirmed by the brief but unsatisfactory experience with the USGA's larger and lighter balloon ball.

Of course, much of the objection to the balloon ball was psychological because of the inability of most players to get strokes uniformly adjusted to tiny variations in diameter and weight. The psychological element continues to figure importantly in golf ball sales. Manufacturers go to considerable trouble and expense to control the production of top-grade balls in various classes of compression suitable to the speeds and firmness of different swings, but a player with a swing that couldn't make a dent in a soap bubble often will insist on a ball of tight winding. The swift, powerful swing of the expert is required to compress such a ball enough to take full advantage of its resiliency and to control it.

Until the 1920's, most golf balls were floaters. Now few of them are, and naturally a tremendous business has developed in repairing and repainting balls reclaimed from water holes. Although the covered, thread-wound, and cored golf ball is one of the most difficult of manufacturing jobs, involving rubber and kindred materials and cores, the price of golf balls themselves has been kept so low that it is a unique example in modern merchandising. The standard top-quality ball that was about $1 in 1914 is generally only $1.25 more than half a century later.

To sum up modern developments in golf clubs and balls in terms of the great golfing public at large, it is interesting to listen to the older professionals with extensive experience in observing and fitting the needs of those who make up probably 95 percent of the golf market. They are outspoken in saying that the failure of the national standard of golf scoring to improve is not so much the result of deficiencies in instruction as it is a lag in equipment design and information. These practical market authorities believe that irrational stress has been placed on what the highly talented stars play and that not enough attention has been paid to the needs of Mr. and Mrs. Average Golfer, the buyers who support the market.

They cite the frequent cases of ordinary golfers, who don't hit a tee shot quail-high, being sold drivers with only 11 percent loft, or the same players being sold irons that don't get the weight low enough and the leading edge under the ball so that it will get into the air. And they add that these ill-suited sales to ever-hopeful customers have been enriching the showcase experts. They also feel that there has been too much focus on the flex of shafts rather than on compression of the golf ball in the practical but unplanned effort of some professionals to improve the ordinary golfer's score.

A good word certainly should be said for that vital facility, the pro shop. Naturally, at many private clubs and pay-as-you-play courses, gross bar and restaurant revenue is considerably higher than the gross revenue of the pro shop, where today apparel sales often bring in as much as sales of clubs, balls, and bags. But the pro shop does contribute a bright side to private club and public course accounting: Because the professional usually operates the shop as a concession, it is in the black.

In particular, the pro shop at a private club is an exceptionally good example of a small retailing business that supplies many services, along with making expertly selected merchandise available at point of use. The pro's merchandising position at a private club usually involves a fairly short active buying season (seven months and Christmas gift sales) and a limited market. At clubs with 300 members, of whom about 225 men, women, and juniors are fairly frequent golfers, members like to think that the professional nets around $25,000 a year. These optimistic parties do not appreciate that such a net income to the professional would call for a per-member expenditure in the pro shop of about $300 a year. That's high for the customary figure at good clubs. Even at the prevailing prices of woods and irons, the pro profits are offset by the life of the implements. The woods, market figures indicate, usually remain with the owner for nearly eight years, and the irons for six, despite the manufacturers' efforts to improve the clubs and promote style changes.

But then psychology has a lot to do with golf ball and club marketing. The typical golfer is inclined to use a ball of higher compression than he can hit effectively, and just like the seasoned tournament stars, to hold onto a favorite club, especially a driver, sand wedge, or pitching wedge, because he's had good luck with it through the years. Today, the pro shop is expected to be a deluxe sports retailing establishment out in the sunny country far from worldly cares. While the shop has built up a big, dominating position in sports merchandising, its development has meant a new responsibility for the PGA. With their influential status and their specialized services, the pro shops have been recognized as vital to golf's continuing growth and prosperity. The PGA must reorganize and research, educate and establish itself as *the* authority on golf merchandising.

26

Time for the Showdown, The Old PGA Ends–the New Begins

[1967, 1968]

AT the 1967 annual meetings of committees and the general meeting of delegates and officials held in the Palm Beach Towers Hotel, November 10 through 16, there was more talk about the possibility that the PGA needed immediate reorganization and modernization. Those who urged an overhauling of PGA operations said that golf had changed tremendously since the PGA was founded back in 1916, but that the association had failed to keep pace.

First off, the delegates from the Carolinas pointed out that the annual meeting was being smothered by resolutions from various sections. They complained that these were all matters that could better be handled by a mail vote from sections, after arguments pro and con had been presented by an executive director who ostensibly had been employed to do just that sort of a job. A considerable number of the resolutions involved membership classifications and sectional boundaries, which the majority of PGA members considered merely operating details.

The 1967 meeting also exposed the positive reaction of the home pros to the journeymen's endless faultfinding, which ended in a threat to boycott the 1967 PGA Championship at the Columbine Country Club in Denver. Everything was wrong—the prize money, the course, the Rules of Golf, the television split, the PGA's management, and the Tournament Committee's own rules. By that time many PGA members wanted to kick out the tournament players, most of whom, the home pros declared, were playing golf only because they could make more money at it than by working.

The Northern California section exploded with a resolution moving that the president dissolve the Tournament Committee and appoint a new one.

The section asserted that the committee had done nothing to stop the almost continuous carping of the tournament players. They felt these rebels were destroying the goodwill built up for the PGA and were chronically dissatisfied even though the association had always spent a disproportionately large share of its income and time in building the tournament circuit. They also believed that the surreptitious meetings and agreements of the tournament players were seriously damaging all professional golf.

Northern California's move for a showdown evoked vigorous debate. Tournament Committee Chairman Sikes said that if the resolution were adopted, he had several tournament contracts for next year that would have to be canceled. Proponents of the move to appoint a new Tournament Committee asked for details on the contracts: With whom? Accepted by what party for the PGA? And didn't the PGA have legal rights to have the contracts fulfilled? Discussion was vague, but the intent of Northern California and other sectional members to reform the tournament section without the dissidents was clear. However, after an informative battle, the resolution was withdrawn.

Instead of alarm that the tournament players might leave the fold, there was growing concern that the majority might simply excommunicate the malcontents. It seemed that the bad manners and thoughtlessness of too many tournament players were being blamed on the home professionals, who were held accountable for the PGA's reputation by the public that supported it.

Complaints about courses and demands for treatment that paying members of clubs would never expect, plus too-frequent churlishness in pro-amateur events where amateurs paid $200 to $1,000 (tax-deductible, of course!) to play with supposedly gentlemen professionals, were seriously injuring golf as a whole. In the view of the home pros, by exhibiting such bush-league behavior the journeymen were reverting back to the callow stage when the PGA was organized to get playing professionals trained and disciplined to acceptability at first-class clubs.

On the other hand, the threat of discontented tournament professionals to withdraw from the PGA and ruin the tournament circuit drew differing reactions, none of them good for pro golf. Some tournament sponsors said they'd go along with the new circuit to be formed by the PGA rebels, but their assurances were promptly weakened by members of the quasi-sponsors' clubs who didn't want circuit events at their clubs. This somewhat unexpected development menaced the continuance of tournaments other than that of the USGA and Western Opens, the Masters, and a few other events, including the PGA, at first-class private clubs that were in solid financial position.

The aroused home pro members of the PGA then took the position that, just like themselves, the journeyman players owed primary consideration to the amateur golfers who paid money to the tourists. This led to talk about another tournament circuit, minus the discontented leading money winners. After all, there were plenty of youngsters who were beginning to show color, class, and talent, and who were hoping that a new PGA circuit would give them their big chance.

The trouble was that there had been too much gossip and publicity about the millionaire status of Palmer, Nicklaus, Player, and a few others to make the golfing public sympathetic to the

PGA rebels. So, suddenly, the tournament circuit rating, which the PGA had built at heavy expense over the years, had reached the flash point of the long-brewing civil war that would surely hurt all concerned.

Max Elbin took the position that all elements of the PGA owed amateur golfers primary consideration. The PGA president maintained his position staunchly and openly and had the endorsement of the home professionals and a few of the tournament professionals who enjoyed warm public esteem. But all this time, unknown to most of the PGA officials, meetings were being held for the purpose of breaking the tournament players away from the association. A few efforts at compromise were made. Yet, despite frequent indications that the amateur golfing public regarded most tournament pros as spoiled rich kids pouting in their easy prosperity, the cleavage within the PGA was obviously spreading beyond control.

The formalities of unity in meetings of the Tournament Committee and the Executive Committee continued. At the annual meeting, Dan Sikes, who'd been in the thick of the bitter arguments, including the threat of some tournament players to boycott the PGA Championship unless it was altered to suit them, was publicly thanked by President Elbin. He told professionals that he "wished it to be known that while there had been some hectic, unpleasant, and bad moments during the past year for which Chairman Dan Sikes had taken some abuse, PGA officials respected him as a gentleman and were aware that he had made a very generous contribution to the success of the PGA."

With Sikes on the Tournament Committee at that time were Max Elbin,

Max Elbin. PGA, photo by Clark's Photography

Leo Fraser, Warren Orlick, Jack Nicklaus, Doug Ford, Gardner Dickinson, Jr., and Harry Pezzullo.

Despite their rebuffs and disdain, the PGA official family continued to defer to the headline-grabbing tournament rebels by trying to establish a minor tournament circuit. Don Clarkson was appointed chairman of a Second Circuit Committee, which arranged a few events for less than major-tournament prize money and which did not conflict appreciably with the big circuit events. A loss was budgeted by the PGA in promoting the secondary competitions with their purses of $25,000 or even less.

The PGA high command of Elbin, Leo Fraser as secretary, and Warren Orlick as treasurer had some new vice-presidents: Richard Beckmann replacing Jamie L. Jackson, Dick Drennen replacing Harry Pezzullo, and Joe Walser, Jr., replacing Don Clarkson.

Warren Cantrell of Texas, who had preceded Max Elbin as PGA president, died in 1967 following an illness of almost a year. Lou Strong then returned to the PGA official roster as honorary president, following the customary procedure of retaining the most recent president in an advisory capacity. Strong was now working for John MacArthur as general manager of the PGA National Golf Club and luckily didn't have time to get involved in the home pro–journeyman controversy.

The failure of the Ryder Cup competition to arouse the interest, draw the galleries, and invoke the spirit that the skilled competition and international character of the event warranted continued to bother the U.S. and British PGA officials. Harold Sargent suggested additional experiments in the format to develop excitement.

Another section was added when Texas was divided into Northern and Southern sections, and getting down to business for the good of most PGA members and golf in general, the 1967 meeting adopted regulations tightening membership eligibility and extended the pro business schooling program.

Executive Director Creasey reported definite progress on a proposed pension plan. Clubs and other employers of professionals still showed little interest in participating in a pension plan similar to those in businesses other than golf, and the tournament players again failed to agree on a way to take pension payments out of purses.

Group insurance of every sort—life, accident, liability, theft, fire, etc.—received the usual attention with very little change from the pattern of years. Some delegates and officers said that the PGA should be in the position of buying insurance with expert advice in doing its insurance shopping instead of always merely being sold policies.

Several sections had paid executive secretaries who were effectively handling their operating functions, and they now proposed that their secretaries be admitted to the PGA delegates' session. But the suggestion was turned down after a brisk debate during which it was said that the paid sectional secretaries could bind the PGA together nationally and make it a modern power in the golf business.

The feeling that the PGA spent far too much of its time and money on the tournament circuit minority, which had been building for more than a decade, was again strongly expressed by Frank Stamberger of Kansas City, a delegate from the Midwest section. He proposed that the association establish a home professional department to improve the business methods and standing of the professionals who stayed on the job caring for amateur golfers. His suggestion was approved vocally, but there was no official or operative follow-through other than the established educational program.

George Alexander of the Texas section asked for PGA aid in financing shop operations. He claimed it was easier to get financial sponsorship for a beginner on the tournament circuit than it was to get needed financing for pro shops on many new jobs of PGA members. Alexander summarized an interesting contrast between the home and journeyman pros in noting that if a promising young amateur hustler could get a tourist ticket, he could easily get backing for a circuit try because he was such an ideal house-odds man for a professional gambler. Besides, the touring pro's net loss couldn't be too much, since there were plenty of pro-amateur events and opportunities that rewarded hustling in pro golf's fiscal ghetto, while the home club professional was strictly on his own in supporting and developing the game and business.

In stocking his shop at a new job, Alexander added, the home professional was often forced to obligate himself financially for a larger amount than most of the money-winning pros spent in a year on the tournament circuit. Furthermore, the new pro often followed in the footsteps of another hopeful who had gone broke and received a bad credit rating for trying to finance merchandising and other services to club members who failed to spend enough to justify his risk.

Alexander was given understanding and sympathetic attention, but there was no definite action on his plea, although it helped accelerate formation of the PGA Credit Union several years later. The Credit Union took care of loans to professionals of good character who didn't have the background for a local bank loan to finance a new job inventory or for emergency needs that might be satisfied only by paying a high interest rate. The PGA Credit Union was an indication of the improved credit rating of professionals. Manufacturers didn't ship desirable goods to slow-pay accounts with the speed required to get a pro-shop business started and to keep it going.

Apart from the inevitable split between the home pros and the show business golfers, it was clear that PGA operations demanded extensive overhauling in specific areas. In this regard, Leo Fraser urged that instead of the annual meeting's talking about "what to do tomorrow," the PGA formulate a foresighted progress schedule, get busy on it, and report definitely and

frequently on the program. This resulted in the formation of a long-range Planning Committee that put the PGA in line with numerous private clubs that had established committees to tie together the objectives and work of administrations that changed every year or so. However, just as with other new PGA committees, this one was handicapped by a simple and fundamental deficiency in the professional's own business setup. The pro didn't have a stenographer and secretary, hence communications were limited between PGA officers and committee chairmen and members. There was no prod of urgency when committee reports were made only annually.

John MacArthur, landlord of the clubhouse, office building, and courses at Palm Beach Gardens, which the PGA proudly called its own PGA National Golf Club, then caught the PGA long-range Planning Committee unprepared. He canceled the PGA lease as of the end of February, 1973, a year before its expiration date, and hit the association for $30,000 as the final payment of rent on the original terms.

Other real-estate developers were negotiating with the PGA for a new PGA National Club, but a considerable number of PGA members—certainly most of the members west of the Rockies—again doubted the association's need for a "national" golf club in Florida. Whether Florida was really a strategic location for the PGA national offices was quite another matter.

In truth, it would be years before the long-range Planning Committee provided PGA presidents with surveys and forecasts that proved helpful in setting administration policies and procedures. In its business schooling program, the PGA needed authoritative data on professional golf marketing, which it didn't have. Nobody had this basic information, and the PGA was in the best position to learn the answers. Eventually PGA President Warren Orlick appointed a Research and Marketing Committee to obtain the facts the PGA needed to identify itself as the primary authority on merchandising material to golfers. But it would be a long time before that committee had the authority to stamp the PGA as a basic source of guidance in the golf business.

Advisory Committee members expressed the opinion that the tournament operations were halfway between costly and comical. By its loss of standing with sponsors and advertisers, the Tournament Committee was costing playing professionals a bale of money each year. Men with extensive experience in handling tax deductions as foundations for pension plans wondered why the tournament players and their managers would want to pass up an industrywide pension plan that would cost the professionals very little, net, and be far preferable to the pension plans for which professional baseball and football players were striving.

The Advisory Committee was pained to see the complaining tournament players making themselves merely professional athletes. The loss of distinction also meant loss of market value. The slump of consumer acceptance of Arnold Palmer— and Jack Nicklaus— brand clubs during the PGA civil war must have impressed these two bright, distinguished golfers. Palmer, with a family background in the valuable public service essentials of earlier pro golf, tried to bring the touring and home pros together, but it didn't work. Nicklaus, who had never known much about business, learned quickly after some embarrassing mistakes. He was

growing up in other ways than golf. From being a big, strong, fat, withdrawn, rather arrogant, one-putting boy—"Fat Jack" or "Jack Nicklouse" as some labeled him—he suddenly got the message, went on a diet, and contoured himself physically and mentally to fit his glamorous new label as the "Golden Bear."

Unfortunately, there were many personable youngsters on the tour who were not properly presented to the golfing public in the Palmer and Nicklaus mold and spirit, but as mercenaries in an irritable group who were extremely well paid for playing what amateur golfers paid for playing. Pro golf's showcase was getting a shabby look. It wasn't selling the merchandise well, and pro-shop sales figures showed a consistently higher annual rate of increase than tournament purses.

The Advisory Committee was aware of the deteriorating favor of the tournament players in general and suggested that the PGA reorganize to exercise control over the policies and business operations of the tour and its players, with the field staff having responsibility only for planning and conducting the tournaments.

Arguments continued among the players, the Tournament Committee, and the sponsors about the split of television receipts. A little more care was taken with commercials on the tournament shows, but outside of the Masters and the National Open, golf tournaments were not impressively associated with a quality market. All the same, Marty Carmichael's contract as the PGA television representative was renewed for another year at the same figure of $50,000.

Notwithstanding dissatisfaction with tournament circuit business, the PGA tournament field staff performed with such expertise and sound, firm judgment that there was rarely criticism of Jack Tuthill and his men who were actually running the events. The field men were given increases in pay—not enough to make them fiscally fat for the season's long grind, but at least as an indication of appreciation for staging the show for the stars, the chorus boys, the sponsors, the gallery, TV, and the PGA.

Expectancy filled the air as the PGA held its last annual meeting as a house undivided at the Palm Beach Towers Hotel, November 8 through 15, 1968. The officers, delegates, and committeemen gathered there all felt they were involved in a crisis in American professional golf history, one that had been coming to a head for many years.

Max Elbin was in the second and last year of his hectic administration. Leo Fraser was secretary, and in the course of PGA routine promotion, was to succeed Elbin as president. Warren Orlick was treasurer, and he, too, was to get his turn at the burdens of a PGA presidency.

Lou Strong was honorary president. The vice-presidents were Joseph R. Aneda, Jr., Richard Beckmann, Noble E. Chalfant, William Clarke, John P. Conley, Richard N. Drennen, Bob Popp, John Reuter, Jr., Wendell V. Ross, James D. Rudolph, Joe W. Walser, Jr., and Lyle O. Wehrman. Past presidents, in addition to Lou Strong, present at the final annual meeting of the unified PGA, were Tom Walsh, Joe Novak, Harry Moffitt, and Harold Sargent. There were 109 at the 1968 annual meeting, and the count included members of the Tournament Committee but not the Advisory Committee members.

Instead of leaving the final decision to the journeyman pros themselves, the debates over ousting them from the PGA had degenerated into a blazing family quarrel. It should be emphasized, though, that with few exceptions the journeymen were pleasant, honorable men who were rather embarrassed by the furtive strategy of their colleagues engineering the Tournament Division split. The differences that had finally come to a climax were primarily a matter of simplified bookkeeping that the PGA should have been able to solve with good business management. The tournament players thought they should be allowed to handle their own money to make sure they weren't being charged too much for administration. But most probably the PGA division was caused by the inevitable clash of the long tradition of pseudo-holy public service of the club pros and the new dollar economics of the tournament professionals built by the PGA and the changing times.

But the new economics also controlled the more solid, conservative home professionals and suggested that they, too, might be financially better off without carrying the tournament professionals. Yet the first thought of division within the ranks shocked them. All the same, the revolt of the home pros against the priority given the playing pros in PGA procedures was ultimately strengthened by their realization that they commanded a market of almost $400 million annually, while the tournament specialists, both on the PGA circuit and sectionally, were only going for $7 million. And during the hottest part of the PGA civil war the home-club pros were delighted to discover that they far outweighed their starring counterparts in sales influence.

The close association of the home professional with his members or patrons at his fee course gave him confidence in his capacity to do what was best for them. The club pro was realizing that he was not destined to be a second-class citizen in a sport he had made big. Therefore, most home pros were willing, maybe eager, to have the fewer than 200 complaining tournament specialists go their own way, while the 6,500-and-some other pros continued to flourish in the business.

The PGA was at the stage where it was scared to move without asking a lawyer's permission. Suffice it to say that the association was the ideal client—rich and scared. The minutes of the Executive Committee meeting prior to the 1968 annual meeting contained a deletion because of "legal matters of a confidential nature." The printed report noted: "Details with respect to this discussion are not included in these minutes." So the PGA couldn't tell its members or the golfing public what was doing at the top PGA level.

Advocates of compromise at the 1968 meeting were unable to sell their story to the delegates and the Executive Committee. They had to wait until the new ticket headed by Leo Fraser came into office and with the new members of the Executive Committee got a peace agreement by a margin of one vote. But the PGA officials who objected to a compromise maintained that it had been and would continue to be impossible to please the tournament corps, whose personnel changed far more frequently than that of the home pros. Meantime, they added, the tournament players' demands and quarreling were retarding the PGA's obligations and efforts at service to all golfers.

In presenting its case about the futility of trying to please the hard-core separatists, the PGA brought up and refuted the points Alfred Wright had raised in his article "The Revolt of the Pros," which appeared in the August 9, 1966, issue of *Sports Illustrated*. The major objections of the tournament pros to their relations with the PGA and the reactions of association officials and members were as follows:

1. *"We want our own boss."*

This didn't seem much of a problem to the home pros, since they regarded the tournament operation as nearly autonomous. The Tournament Committee, then headed by Dave Marr, was not being overruled in any decisions by PGA officials or the Executive Committee. In the field Jack Tuthill, the ex-FBI man, was boss and doing so well that PGA officials, sponsors, the players themselves, spectators, and reporters hardly heard a whisper of disapproval. The management and operation of the PGA field staff was one of the most difficult and best-handled jobs in professional or amateur sports. A better "boss" for this task couldn't be imagined.

Nor was Joe Ewers, then executive director of the PGA, in any way the tournament players' boss. When he was hired by the PGA away from Indiana University his work instructions were vaguely catchall, except that he was told not to intrude on the tournament players, whose own committee was in charge of their program.

Ewers knew something of the problems of athletic management from his university administration experience. He quickly learned that the situation of the tournament pros was unique and was glad to be officially advised to stay away from tournament problems. This he did and was blamed for undefined errors by leaders of the rebel tournament group. The same vague sort of blame for mishandling the tournament players was placed on Robert

Creasey, Ewers's successor with the PGA. Creasey, formerly a labor lawyer, thought he had seen everything in organized and disorganized labor disputes, but the PGA tournament wrangles were new to him.

When the journeyman golf pros voiced their need for their own boss in 1965, they had no idea they were rapidly losing face with the public. A golf tournament is a very difficult and costly operation to stage. The free work of hundreds of women and men over many months, often the sacrifice of playing time by members on a course that costs them heavily to play on, and many other factors explain why only the hardy and enthusiastic put on the circuit events. And these unselfish workers who supported pro tournament golf were getting fed up with the complaints of men who were known as players, not workers, in a business that paid as much as $35,000 for four days' work.

The intelligent players sensed that mounting resentment and had the fuzzy hope they could find a leader who could bring them back into good standing with the public and protect the pleasantly remunerative careers the PGA had built up for them. They needed a front man—and they knew that he must come from the outside. It was then, in 1965, that Joseph C. Dey, Jr., was among those first mentioned as a tournament players' commissioner. He had been executive secretary of the United States Golf Association for thirty-four years and was an able and effective representative of that august ruling body, accurately reflecting the admirable spirit of that organization through many changing administrations.

2. *The tournament professionals wanted no more than thirty tournaments a year and no more than six big-money events close together in midseason.*

Complaints about the tournament schedule were eternal and actually had brought the tournament circuit into being. Now the problem was complicated by the fortunate players' having all the money they could stand at midseason without having to borrow for the tax man, while the insolvent unknowns were sweating out qualifying rounds for the next big-money event. In truth, tournament scheduling was one of those things that never could be satisfactorily settled for all concerned.

Nor did the money of the Oriental circuit in the fall or the increased revenue of the European tournaments in the summer help matters. The "satellite events" were not profitable enough to count, and while the "minicircuit" tournaments did flourish for a time, all they amounted to was a group of contestants hustling each other for their shares of the entry fees. These events folded when the promoters took too much too soon. The "mini" tournaments were a good education for players who could get $5,000 to $7,500 for an entry fee but who either weren't good enough or lacked the funds for the $25,000 required for a year of tournament circuit expense.

The Oriental tournament circuit became attractive to American pros in the early 1970's when Japanese golf was booming. Long forgotten was the genesis of that rich development when, more than thirty years earlier, Bob Harlow got the PGA to finance a cheap tour of the United States by six Japanese pros who returned home as golf missionaries. Australia was also to present prize money that made transpacific travel profitable in the fall and early winter for able American pros.

A tournament circuit began to build in Europe as well in 1970. With the dollar dropping in foreign exchange, the European affairs kept the younger British pros, who might have become serious contenders for American prize money, content to play nearer home.

While it was in the nature of the game that all major events should be crowded into midsummer, this presented the journeyman pros with a difficult, if not unanswerable, problem, but there was nothing either the PGA or the players themselves could do about this competitive fact of golfing life. As for golfers and fans of the game itself, nationwide they probably remembered the winners of such summer tournaments as the National Open, the PGA, the British Open, the Western Open, and the Westchester Classic. To this list could be added the men who won the Masters and the Crosby. The winners of the Bob Hope Desert Classic, because of Hope's TV showmanship, and the Colonial at Fort Worth, which had been striving for years to be a Texas Masters, might be recalled without consulting the records.

In all fairness, then, the tourney pros had no basis for blaming the PGA for either the perplexities or the complexities of their scheduling. The PGA was more than eager to have the journeymen handle their timetable for themselves, so that was no cause for a split in the pro family.

3. *The journeymen "wanted no more than thirty tournaments a year, spaced to give rest to the golfers and cut down travel time."*

That was all right with the PGA. However, the majority of the tournament pros wanted more than thirty tournaments a year. It was only the boys in the big money who wanted rest; the hungry boys wanted more work.

4. *The journeymen wanted the roster of approved players to be "cut by almost a third."*

No problem there with the PGA, as the Tournament Committee was in charge of the eligibility tests for players' cards.

5. *The specialists also demanded "emphasis on a training program to develop new players."*

Nothing to fight about here either. The PGA had been trying to do just this since it was formed in 1916.

6. *The players also wanted "a looser affiliation with the parent PGA, which has outlived its usefulness to them,"* adding that they were being administered by *"a badly out-of-date organization."*

While there was plenty to be said on both sides about these charges, even the home pros agreed that the PGA hadn't adjusted to the times. As to the demand for "a looser affiliation," the home players were divided. One camp believed that the tournament malcontents were hurting pro golf; they were due for a day of sorry reckoning, so they should be left to shift for themselves. The other group maintained that if the PGA didn't reassert and strengthen its control, the tournament organization would fall into the hands of promoters and television interests only concerned with exploiting golf. Naturally enough, the older professionals were far more aware of the comparatively short competitive life of most big-money playing specialists than were the rebels themselves.

Immediate repercussions followed the outbreak of civil war within the PGA. When the leaders of the breakaway group made statements that offended amateur golfers, Robert T. Jones, Jr., American golf's great, almost legendary figure, said in an interview that golf was fundamentally a game for participants rather than for spectators. Therefore, its character and appeal should not be destroyed by men intent on making golf a trade for themselves and a few others. The Jones observation drew a nationwide roar of approval that amazed sports editors. They thought that Jones, who won his unequaled Grand Slam way back in 1930, would have been nearly forgotten by golfers, old and new. Plainly, though, Jones represented the true and enduring bright spirit of the game.

Another blistering barrage came from the Burning Tree Club in Washington where Max Elbin, PGA president, was professional. When the leaders of the separatists rapped Elbin in an ill-considered public statement, club members promptly retaliated by issuing a tribute signed by nationally known statesmen and businessmen. These influential people hailed Elbin as a bright example of the professional golf sportsman who has contributed both generously and greatly to the health and happiness of the nation's men, women, and children.

The Burning Tree endorsement of the home-pro position was extensively printed and echoed loudly in locker rooms at private and public golf clubs. The amateurs' reaction was that the tournament players were led by men who did not understand the true situation.

The 1968 annual meeting of the PGA was the last time PGA officials and delegates devoted their attention to the tournament-playing minority. Most delegates went home feeling relieved that they had completed their terms as baby-sitters for pampered and petulant tournament pros. Now their successors could get back to the job of aiding golf and golfers as the association had

always intended. This was why the PGA had been organized.

Their relief was to be short-lived, since the new administration called a crucial Executive Committee meeting within a few weeks. However, as always, the PGA had again completed an annual meeting with a routine that had become tiresomely customary and outdated. It finished by attending to matters that involved the majority of PGA members and their relations with amateur golfers. Most urgent and important of the slighted home work of the PGA was its educational program.

When the distorted tourney picture was corrected and the PGA was able to look at itself accurately, it became clear that coordination on a national scale was essential. No longer was business education in golf a matter for the elementary grades of apprentices and assistants. Now the head professionals had to be made executives. Extensive use of golf courses as features of real-estate developments and the importance of golf as a resort attraction called for management and responsibility beyond that of the usual pro job. Men qualified for the expanded positions, usually called golf directors, were hard to find.

Mail instruction courses for assistants and examinations for membership gave emphasis to the PGA educational program. The educational work was also supplying a stronger tie between the sections and the national organization. Most sections were quick and constructive in their comments on the PGA schooling. In fact, the New Jersey section had noted at the 1968 meeting that the examinations for assistants were "too vague."

Year after year, the delegates at the annual meetings had had to spend many hours on resolutions dealing with classifications of membership and sectional boundaries. Invariably they had come to the businesslike conclusion: "There must be a better way of doing this." But they were operating under a patchwork constitution that had been the casual effort of a law clerk to begin with. And a member of the PGA Advisory Committee, who headed one of the nation's most successful large businesses, had read the PGA constitution and exclaimed: "The PGA might be better off to throw this antique out and start all over!"

This was why the function of the delegates was unclear beyond voting on constitutional matters, mainly resolutions submitted by the sections. And these resolutions mainly involved membership classifications and sectional boundaries, all of which resulted in more rhetoric and parliamentary procedure than improvement of pro golf business. In this sense, the annual meeting had become something of a meaningless ritual, which was aptly summarized by a Palm Beach writer who had been one of the first reporters allowed to sit in on these heretofore sacrosanct sessions. He emerged numb and confused after listening to hours of aimless talk to ask: "Do you mean to tell me that's the kind of meeting the PGA thinks should have been kept a deep, dark secret?" And by 1968 the secrecy of the PGA annual meetings had become the subject of jokes because it was common knowledge that the dissidents were holding their own private hush-hush meetings to break off from the parent association.

But the 1968 meeting did bring forth news of further limited progress on a PGA pension plan. There were explanations that the tax laws prevented a master professional pension plan that would apply to clubs and fee courses. At that time a pension plan would have had to include home pros and journeymen, but there weren't enough financially successful tournament players to make a pension plan actuarially sound. Eventually, however, there was a breakthrough on a pro pension plan financed by clubs and with the professionals paying their share. The plan was a good beginning, but it required strong selling to club officials, and the PGA didn't get operating any too quickly on that sales campaign.

The PGA's own praiseworthy National Golf Day also came in for discussion at this annual meeting. Noble Chalfant, professional at the Denver Country Club and chairman of the committee in charge of the countrywide campaign for the event in 1968, lamented that with around 5,000 PGA members only a third managed to have their club or course members take part. Naturally, Chalfant, with a free-spending club membership, wondered why the 9,000 golf clubs in the country couldn't raise a million dollars for golf's own charities and welfare funds, when golfers had kicked in vastly more to other charities, educational funds, and welfare funds.

On National Golf Day, usually a Saturday, players who were agreeable to paying the minimum of a dollar for a net-score contest against the better ball of the National Open or PGA winner generally rebelled at adding another dollar as a minimum for the National Golf Day entry fee. PGA members didn't know how to pass along what they had to sell. A lot of pros acted as though they actually were afraid to push National Golf Day with its bright message, "Golfers Give," to their players. A professional at one of the richest clubs in the Southwest vividly expressed his bewilderment: "I rattle the National Golf Day tin cup until my arm is sore and my club gets famous for giving $2,000, but a few members lean on the others for a cancer-fund donation and get $10,000, and other people say, 'Why, the cheap bastards!' "

Prominent businessmen who were members of the National Golf Fund, the agency that evaluates and distributes the National Golf Day receipts, also wondered at the inability of the PGA headquarters to get National Golf Day well organized, especially since the association was supposed to be working with the advertising geniuses of some of the country's biggest businesses.

The Merchandise Show for the next year was reported at the 1968 meeting as a complete sellout, with 226 booths assigned. Here was a business that was growing, well handled, and not publicized to the degree of its influence on all pro business and as a barometer of golfers' business.

It was decided that all applicants for PGA membership must attend the association's business schools, and that applied to the tournament stars as well. An effort was also being made to make better use of incoming PGA officials by conducting seminars for elected vice-presidents. Sectional seminars were also arranged to help other officials in their work. Don Fischesser had been assigned as coordinator of the 1968–70 winter educational program at the PGA National Club. Colleges and universities made proposals for seminars for those who taught golf in schools. There was an educational surge, but the instruction of PGA officials plainly needed to become more cohesive.

The usual alterations to the group insurance plan were made at the 1968 national meeting. There also was the customary report of losses on the association's Book of Golf, a beautiful promotion job intended to educate amateur golfers, but which conflicted with many PGA sectional publishing enterprises. Government wage-and-hour regulations were discussed as another worry and thrown into the basket of "unfinished business." The PGA was finding that as big business it needed trained businessmen to conduct its operations, nationally and sectionally.

General Development proposed to build a PGA Hall of Fame at Port St. Lucie, but the offer was not accepted because of a deferred plan to build a Hall of Fame in the National Golf Club building. Several Golf Hall of Fame projects were being considered, the latest being a Hall of Fame at Pinehurst, which has since been constructed and is open to the public.

There was talk about big expenses of the PGA being approved without having all Executive Committeemen polled (the committeemen wanted time for a second look at costly projects), and last, the usual formalities involving the PGA Seniors' tournaments were approved. Thus ended the routine of the 1968 annual meetings of the PGA, but the big question—the split with the tournament players—hadn't been met head-on. This was to be handled at the first meeting of the new administration of the PGA, which consisted of Leo Fraser, president; Warren Orlick, secretary; and R. William Clarke, treasurer. Max Elbin followed the usual pattern of retiring presidents by becoming honorary president. Past presidents who continued to have a voice in PGA affairs were Harry L. Moffitt, Joe Novak, Harold Sargent, Lou Strong, and Tom Walsh.

Elected as vice-presidents were Dugan Aycock, Richard Beckmann, John Boda, Sr., Noble E. Chalfant, John P. Conley, Richard N. Drennen, Howard E. Morrette, Bob Popp, John Reuter, Jr., Joe W. Walser, Jr., James L. Warga, and Lyle O. Wehrman.

Since the Declaration of Principles had been discussed at fever pitch during the 1968 meeting, then left up in the air, it was not surprising that the carry-over factor was strong enough to ensure some immediate action. As noted, the comment in the official summary of the meeting was that the tournament players' rebellion was a matter of "confidential nature" and should not be made public—something like saying gravity was a confidential matter between God and Isaac Newton! Not until after the annual meeting, when Leo Fraser became president, were the lawyers' papers dividing the association brought before the PGA Executive Committee when it met at the Safari Hotel in Scottsdale, Arizona, on December 13, 1968. Fraser was out there, a sick man, but determined to keep the dissidents allied to the parent body in some way so that eventually, when "cooler heads prevailed," there might once again be unity and concord. Elbin was present at the Executive Committee meeting as honorary president.

PGA members in the Elbin camp maintained that everything imaginable had already been done to appease the fewer than 100 journeyman pros among the association's close to 7,000 members. They believed that if one group of players were allowed to dictate to the entire PGA, then in a few years another new group of tournament specialists would come along and want something else. There would be no end to it. Therefore, since a showdown was inevitable after years of attempted ap-

Leo Fraser. PGA

peasement, it might as well be handled firmly at this time, once and for all.

Proponents of the Fraser policy, which called for some division of the home and touring PGA members, agreed that there had been far too much of the tail wagging the dog among the tournament and home pros. However, they thought that a separation would give the PGA far more time to apply itself to the needs of the home pros and their employers, as well as give the tournament players responsibilities that could no longer be escaped or avoided. They believed that after a few years the young men who qualified in the tournament player schools established by the PGA would become students at PGA business schools and rated as competent to handle home professional jobs.

The two sides clashed head-on at Scottsdale just when the Club Professionals Championship was being played at the Century Country Club and Road Runner resort courses. The stormy session concluded when the Executive Committee (two of whose members were absent) ratified the Declaration of Principles agreement drawn by William Rogers for the PGA and Sam Gates of the Tournament Players' Division by a vote of 6 to 5. The formation of the official Tournament Players' Division meant that the house was finally divided—the same house of professional golf that had been created through the years even before the PGA was founded during World War I. The Professional Golfers' Association, which had led all professional sports into first-class social acceptance, and which had become pampered, glorified, and made rich, was practically back where it had started—working primarily for the amateur golfers' pursuit of happiness.

Professionals who were not intensely interested in the PGA civil war forecast that in not too many years the two groups would be back together. They felt that, by minding its own business and developing itself as an authority in golf, the PGA would be far better off than ever before and would qualify home pros for much higher incomes on the basis of what they were doing for their employers.

Professional golf was far different from the time when Walter Hagen was building a reputation that was to pay him over $100,000 a year as the nominal head of a clubmaking organization. Now there wasn't an angle that a golf pro's manager didn't exploit to the limit. And the exploitation was becoming worldwide. In Europe there were complaints that pro golf with increasing purses as advertising was mak-

ing an American racket out of what had once been a pleasant sport. And the move was spreading. There was already a golf tournament circuit building in Asia, especially in Japan, and paying big purses as advertising.

Pro tournament golf shouldn't get too proud and forget its working professional allies at many of the nation's almost 11,000 golf courses, the forecasters warned. Although baseball sometimes appeared to be a dying sport, pro football, basketball, hockey, and automobile and horse racing were increasing the annual earnings of their professionals at a tremendous rate. And with the national mood inclining more and more toward physical fitness and fast-moving "action" sports, tennis was beginning to experience a resurgence as an inexpensive, popular game for all the people. Its professionals, both men and women, were also coming into a financial bonanza with a big assist from TV.

Those who were convinced the journeyman pros would be coming home to the PGA before long included men who thought the charity-sponsored tax-exempt sports promotions were headed for a day of financial reckoning. Too many sports events and dinners with tax-exempt charities as sponsors were yielding so little to the charities that there were demands that promoters and participants in the affairs be compelled to make public financial statements of the "benefits" as a requirement for receiving tax exemptions. And there was no doubt that most of the circuit tournaments and many exhibition golf matches were sponsored by charities.

To get back to the details of that crucial Executive Committee meeting at Scottsdale, it appears that the Tournament Players' Division originally was called the American Professional Golfers. The initials "APG" were promptly identified as standing for "Arnold Palmer Golfers," and Palmer was not amused. Nor were others in the group. In any case, questions now arose about the validity of the contracts already signed by both groups. The problem had already been foreseen by Curtis Person, chairman of the PGA Advisory Committee and a prominent senior golfer who got around and met people from many clubs. He had warned the Advisory and Executive committees during a meeting at the Palm Beach Towers earlier in November that some clubs were sharply divided about being hosts to circuit tournaments.

Now the possible legal strength of the 1969 tournament agreements seemed to be as vague as the public-relations status of the camps in conflict. Obviously, the PGA was going to miss some of the big names for a while if it cosponsored tournaments. That deficiency would hurt the gates at a period when young players were building up playing reputations and personalities.

The journeymen had done a poor job of handling public relations while conducting their rebellion against the PGA. Their case had been based on money, and they were not like the usual professional athletes with their annual noisy, well-publicized salary arguments with club owners. The tournament players simply had too many people working for them for nothing to justify their whining about money. It only drew more attention to the embarrassing fact that a woman club member driving a courtesy car at a tournament and working for nothing was doing more for golf than a player who was getting paid $30,000 for four rounds. So their insistent charge that

they were being shortchanged by the PGA hardly moved the golfing public and sportswriters to tears.

In Fred Corcoran and John Ross the PGA had two of the most adept public-relations men in sports. The veteran Fred Corcoran, who'd been a builder of the tournament circuit, was planning long-term PGA policy in case there were to be two circuits; now he predicted that the early rounds would go to the headliner rebels. And this was just what happened, as the Sunol, California, tournament, which was played about the time of the Los Angeles Open, cost the PGA about $100,000 as cosponsor because it had been scheduled too late to be called off when the PGA-journeymen agreement was signed.

On his part, the astute Ross, who had wide experience as a sportswriter, golf editor, and promoter, had planned a campaign for home-pro public relations that would emphasize the home pros' service to golfers and shrewdly contrast it with the playing pros' position. So it quickly became plain that the tournament pros and the PGA would have to carry their fight into the courts to determine who was to conduct the tournament circuit.

If this happened, everybody would lose. The PGA's work of years in building the tournament circuit could be destroyed; nor would sponsors want to be caught in a legal crossfire. The PGA was in business to encourage fun and health, not lawsuits, and lawyers for both sides saw a long, costly battle ahead in the courts if the home pros and journeymen failed to get together on their own.

It was obvious to others in the golf business that the tournament players were benefiting from a bull market in tournaments and that they would foul their nest if they fought with the PGA, which had members who were closer to tournament supporters than the journeymen were. Tournament prize money was also increasing yearly. Inflation, tax-exempt charities and other benefit tie-ins, free advertising in print, and television's desperate need of programs made the picture so rosy for pro tournament golf that it would seem incredibly stupid to risk wrecking everything.

The PGA was aware of criticisms that tournament players were the primary beneficiaries of the tournaments and accused of getting far more hard cash in purse money than the sponsoring charity organizations. Then a cold-blooded look was taken at the costs of raising money for charities. It apparently varied from 35 to 85 percent in most of the major operations and appeared to be one of the country's biggest rackets. And to think that the PGA worried when its operating costs for National Golf Day once ran as high as 19 percent, including prizes for the entrants who beat the champion's score!

At the climactic Scottsdale Executive Committee meeting with the players' representatives, Leo Fraser had despaired of making the two groups cooperate. When it looked as though everything was set, there was a move by some players to go along with the promoters of a Frank Sinatra tournament at Palm Springs that was scheduled close enough to the Bob Hope Classic to threaten the revenue of the Hope affair, which benefited a Palm Springs hospital. The Hope tournament had been played for some time now, and Hope himself had worked willingly, cheerfully, and often through the years to help golf and golfers. On the other hand, Sinatra seemed to have done nothing in that direction. How-

ever, the Crosby and Hope sponsorship of benefit golf tournaments had made these events attractive, tax-exempt publicity gimmicks for actors who badly needed the lift of the good publicity associated with golf and charitable causes. But when some prominent pros, who had been in favor of breaking away from the PGA, didn't go for the Sinatra ballyhoo, the singer wisely backed off. The matter did arouse second-guessing by tournament players and the PGA to the degree that it made them listen to their lawyers.

William Rogers, who helped work out the agreement for the PGA, was associated with a big Washington legal firm that had been representing the association for years. Samuel E. Gates, the journeymen's counsel, came from a big New York City law firm, and his company had been hired after a lawyer specializing in union-management disputes had rejected a chance to represent the dissidents.

Rogers and Gates were quick to see the home pro–journeyman's wrangle as one of those dangerous and extravagant exercises in futility that might foolishly cost both sides so much they wouldn't be able to pay their lawyers' bills. This was a calamity to be avoided by all means. So Rogers and Gates carefully rewrote the agreements between the PGA's home pros and the journeymen that had been made many times before at PGA annual, Executive, and Tournament Players' Committee meetings. Evidently no one had bothered to read them. Now Rogers and Gates, by the simple process of reading the minutes of meetings, settled the PGA civil war.

The Declaration of Principles signed at Scottsdale December 13, 1968, ended a war that, like most wars, had been unnecessary, unwise, and expensive.

The peace treaty split the PGA into two divisions but left a passage open between the PGA and the dissidents. The tournament players would continue to pay some dues into the PGA, and at the time a player reached the stage when he could no longer win big prize money on the tournament circuit, he was eligible and qualified to anchor safely in a snug harbor as a club professional and, it was hoped, make a fine, comfortable living for his family and himself.

Not only had the tournament pros questioned the expenses of operating with PGA management for their own office in New York, thereby increasing their expenses over $150,000, they had also exhibited themselves as perhaps the least capable businessmen in sports. Their cry for their "own boss," when they were lost in the tall fiscal rough needed to be answered as an essential of the peace settlement.

The peace settlement had been approved by the PGA Executive Committee by the extraordinary margin of one vote and thus was by no means a stable agreement. It needed someone with the character of an honest, hard-hitting house detective to maintain law and order. The journeymen also needed a new and much prettier image. And this was why Leo Fraser, pleased by the settlement but still worried at the prospect of the PGA's being torn asunder forever, came up with the idea that Joe Dey, for thirty-four years the USGA's invaluable Man Friday, would be the ideal front man for the Tournament Players' Division.

Dey, who became known as "Mr. Golf," had lived through the Jones-Hagen-Sarazen years, taken charge of any number of big tournaments, and been familiar and worked with thousands of golfers, the famous and the un-

known. He began as a sportswriter in New Orleans and Philadelphia. His biggest story was perhaps his stroke-by-stroke report of Bobby Jones's last round in the United States Amateur in 1930, completing his never-to-be-equaled Grand Slam. As executive director of the USGA, among many other noteworthy accomplishments, Dey codified the Rules of Golf, added five national championships to the competition schedule, and formed the World Amateur Golf Council.

Probably no other figure on the national or international golfing scene had the outstanding reputation and the wealth of golf administration background possessed by Joe Dey. Further, he had a deep, old-fashioned love of the game, a vital spiritual asset that might well rub off on the tournament players. After all, it was all too easy to censure the younger players for living by the computer instead of the heart. They were lashed by managers who were their masters and eager to exploit golf.

The Declaration of Principles gave Dey clout on a Tournament Policy Board with "complete and final authority" that was entirely separate from the PGA Executive Committee. The board consisted of ten members: four voting members of the Tournament Players' Division elected by the voting members (these were the player directors), three elected officers of the PGA, and three "independent public figures with a demonstrated interest in golf." One of these independent directors was elected as chairman of the board, and the agreement provided for the independent directors to choose their successors.

The first Tournament Policy Board had as independent directors: J. Paul Austin of Atlanta, a Coca-Cola executive who was made chairman; George H. Love, chairman of the board of Consolidated Coal Company and former chairman of the board of Chrysler Corporation; and John D. Murchison of Dallas. The PGA officers were Leo Fraser, Warren Orlick, and William Clarke. The four player directors were Gardner Dickinson, Jr., Jack Nicklaus, William Casper, and Dan Sikes, Jr.

After the Declaration of Principles was signed, the tournament contracts of the two groups were consolidated. The agreement had among its connections between the two divisions the automatic appointment of all player directors as members of the PGA Rules Committee. Samuel E. Gates for the TPD and William D. Rogers for the PGA were made nonvoting advisers to the Tournament Policy Board, which was empowered to appoint a tournament director "to carry out its policies, rules, and regulations."

The administration of financial matters, discipline of players, and negotiations with sponsors and networks were duties formerly handled by the PGA Tournament Committee and turned over to Dey by the PGA-TPD peace treaty. All pending litigation involving the PGA and TPD was dismissed, and both parties pledged that no new litigation would be instituted or punitive action be taken against any sponsor, player, or the TPD. All tournament players became members of the PGA subject to the primary control of their division. Everybody trusted each other, but just to make sure, lawyers Rogers and Gates were authorized to review all contracts before execution.

Commissioner Dey was given the authority to hire and fire all office and field employees of the players' division, but neither he nor his successors would have any authority over the PGA Championship and the Ryder Cup matches. The qualifying schools for tournament players were to be continued by the TPD in the pattern established by the PGA Tournament Committee. There was no problem in revising the PGA constitution to adjust the old organization to the breakaway of the players who'd been brought to riches. To all intents and purposes, the working points of the agreement had been in effect for years. The weak point continued to be getting a field of players that would satisfy sponsors. Perhaps that was why no reference was made to the matter in the document.

One enduring weakness in the PGA's administration of Tournament Committee and Tournament Bureau affairs came from the tournament players' insistence on running their own business. But when they elected members of their own group to be policy and operating officers, the job turned out to be a nuisance. Along with repeated personality clashes, considerable detail was involved, and it was essential that this should be handled just as any growing and intricate business demanded. Of course, when anything went wrong, PGA headquarters was blamed. However, the marvelous thing about the PGA troubles with its gifted lads was that eventually everything seemed to work out well, even in the split.

One of the amusing sidelights of the PGA division was supplied by the Golf Writers of America. The writers were close to golf fans but not so fervently devoted to the game's current stars as veteran golf writers used to be. To the younger golf writers, Palmer was the one pro star with color; the other gentlemen of the ensemble simply did not know how to combine a theatrical performance with the right dramatic telling of a round. But all the journeymen pros were "nice fellows," even when the sources for stories about them were no better informed or reliable than the man who owned the laundromat where the players' wives took the wash. So the writers didn't get too excited about a pro golf civil war that perhaps did not show much sense or gratitude.

After the PGA hostilities ended, the Golf Writers of America gave their top award for service to the game, the William Richardson plaque, to Max Elbin, the PGA president who had tried to keep the PGA unified all the way. A few years later, the writers voted their Richardson award to Leo Fraser, the PGA president who had left the doors open after the PGA and the tournament players had decided to live separately.

By the time of the split, the PGA had grown from a gathering of a few groups of pros joined in 1916 to an organization that included thirty-seven sections when the Georgia section was formed in 1969.

Fundamentally an organization for the benefit of amateur golfers teamed with their professional mentors, the PGA had actually become the mightiest operation in the world of professional sport. Although it didn't realize it for a few years, the peace agreement would enable the PGA to get back on the track of primarily serving people who

needed golf. For far too long the PGA had been dithering over about fifty men who were making immensely more money out of golf than they'd have been able to acquire by any other conceivable means.

All of golf needed a revival of the spirit of those good men and true who had founded the PGA. Perhaps no other group in sports had ever approached the valuable character of the work done by professional golfers, and it was fitting that it should not be ruined by a small group of prize-money-greedy characters.

The PGA began as more than a group of men wanting money. It was unique and historic as the gospel of sports evangelists who foresaw their fellowmen in peril of being crushed by concrete, machinery, clocks, and avarice. They envisioned an escape from the furies of the world to a quiet spot where man could examine himself on the grass that is nature's comfortable carpet. It was a retreat, relaxation, and treatment.

There is a rare quality in golf, far too precious to be sacrificed for merely that stuff anyone can make any way. The pioneer professionals accepted the responsibility of being guardians of that treasure. It was a glorious heritage the old pros passed along to all of their successors.

27

The PGA Fills in Some Divots on Its Fairways

THE USGA National Open Championship was started in 1895 with a field of ten professionals and a Canadian amateur who tied for third. It was played October 4 in four rounds on the Newport (Rhode Island) Golf Club's nine-hole course and was a sideshow to the USGA's National Amateur Championship. Prize money was $336, with the winner, Horace Rawlins, a nineteen-year-old assistant at the host club, getting $150 and a gold medal. His club also got the championship trophy because the USGA wanted to reward clubs for having their professionals play in the American Open Championship.

The USGA definitely had in mind a vacation trip to the Open competition as a reward to professionals who attended to their business. It couldn't have cared less about the best hired golf player in the United States. This was a matter to be settled by contests between pros in which the competitors were backed by the betting money of amateur golfers. Exhibition matches played at private clubs or summer and winter resort courses were good sources of pro income until about 1915. They were regarded as tests of championship caliber equal to the National Open, which had the primary rating because it consisted of four rounds and had a more extensive field than the Western, Metropolitan, and North and South seventy-two-hole Open championships. So actually it was the business background of the National Open that made it a premier playing event.

The PGA of America itself and its championship grew out of the business rather than the playing of professional golfers. Rodman Wanamaker, son of the famed merchant, John, was host to the luncheons and dinners that resulted in the union of the Metropolitan New York, New England, Eastern, and Cen-

Bob Charles. AG

tral professional golfers' organizations into a nationwide association. And the PGA's only team championship, the Ryder Cup matches against the British PGA team, was a commercial development starting with a pro-shop circulation promotion operation of *Golf Illustrated* magazine.

While coldly commercial factors, rather than any surge of colorful players, accounted for the sudden spurt of tournament circuit purses, little publicity has been given to the contributions star golfers have made to charitable and educational causes. Tournament pros have been among the most generous of all professional athletes in sharing their wealth. Because they participate in so many tournaments and exhibitions for charitable causes, the stars are in a position to be helpful. Granted that many of these events have tax-deductible aspects and that the big money winners are advised by expert tax counsel, they still give liberally off

the top. And these donations usually get limited local notice.

Gary Player gave his 1965 National Open first-prize money to the American Cancer Society and the Boy Scouts. Chi Chi Rodriguez has contributed generously to the families of needy pros and to organizations that aid poor children. And these are only two well-known examples of a common practice among the pros.

The always-boyish Palmer, the ageless Snead of the perpetually perfect swing, and the affable Boros, who was admired and envied because he had a swing that made him look as if he were thoroughly enjoying himself, were pro golf's foremost exhibits of the character the prizefight fans used to call "crowd pleasers." Golf writers regarded Jack Nicklaus as an earnest young man with innate class and a game that would put him in the historic category with Jones and Hagen and as a man who was easy to get to for a straight-answer interview without sparkle. Lee Trevino was thought of as refreshingly unpolished. His short game was spectacular, and he was anything but solemn in his relations with the gallery and golf reporters. And lately it has been Johnny Miller who has taken over the limelight and the purses. (We'll talk more about them further along.)

As it was, the writers looked in vain for colorful characters among the other able pros on the circuit. Some, like Casper and Rosburg, said they had neither the temperament nor the type of game to be theatrical. Most of the pros were diligent, undramatic golfers trying to make a good living in a pleasant way that called for spending about $25,000 a year competing in a high percentage of the tour events.

As for showmanship and pleasing the gallery, Roberto De Vicenzo of Argentina was the most colorful of the foreign players in his appearances at the Masters, World Cup tournaments, and a few other prominent competitions. He was a big, cheerful latecomer. Before him the Australian Joe Kirkwood was the most colorful importation. A pioneer in the trick-shot field, Kirkwood did rather well in championships during his playing prime. With the exception of a fiery little competitor called Norman Von Nida, the other Australians and the personable left-hander from New Zealand, Bob Charles, were not showy types, but rather competent, well-mannered young men pursuing a lucrative trade in the public eye. Tony Jacklin from England

Tony Jacklin. AG

distinguished himself by refreshingly good manners when he was an Open winner in the United States, and so did Gary Player of South Africa at all times and under difficult circumstances when there were political demonstrations on golf courses. Apart from his days as one of the Big Three with Palmer and Nicklaus, Player was and remains an extraordinary and dedicated golfer in a class all his own.

But the color of the days when Hagen, Jones, Sarazen, Lawson Little, Bobby Cruickshank, Bill Mehlhorn, Leo Diegel, the younger Sam Snead, Olin Dutra, Lloyd Mangrum, Ben Hogan, Porky Oliver, Clayton Heafner, John Rogers, Jimmy Demaret, and their ilk brightened the golfing landscape is gone. Even the quiet fellows, Nelson, "Doc" Middlecoff, George Fazio, Horton Smith, Billy Burke, Craig Wood, handsome Dick Metz, small but mighty Paul Runyan, big Frank Walsh, Billy Burke, Vic Ghezzi, Harold McFadden, and the skillful and quiet Henry Picard had magnetism that brought spectators into play as partners.

Big and stooped Ralph Guldahl had the mannerisms of an actor. He could make a critical situation look easy or a simple shot seem difficult. He would adjust a glove as though he were a surgeon getting ready to operate. Ambling along while flanked by a large gallery, he would take a comb out of a hip pocket and carefully arrange his thick, curly thatch.

In the days before galleries began to grow, Wee Freddie McLeod, Jock Hutchison, Tom McNamara, and Mike Brady, and of course the amateurs Francis Ouimet and Chick Evans, were idols of the few but intense rank-and-file golfers. Ouimet and Evans even drew nongolfers to competitions to look at the game in which American

Ed "Porky" Oliver. AG

boys were starring. There were no gallery fees in those days and very little marshaling. The gallery could get close to the players and talk to them between strokes.

Television never has been able to develop a colorful athlete. Ink alone has done that creative job with the sportswriters finding, discovering, and entertainingly reflecting the exciting elements of the character and performance of the athlete. The performer's conduct in his public life by no means had all the color; his private life, or what might have been his private life, certainly was a matter of interest, amusement, admiration, envy, emulation, or criticism. Certainly Hagen and Ruth and lesser lights of their era were distinguished by their enjoyment of life as well as by the fun they obviously had making a living at a game they loved.

The falling tide of color in sports in the 1950's began to be a matter of concern to experienced sportswriters. They

Ralph Guldahl. AG

wondered if they themselves were losing the zest they'd had in their jobs or actually being thwarted by a scarcity of colorful characters. Prior to Pearl Harbor, in almost every city large enough to be called a "reading center," morning and evening newspapers and their readers boasted a potential shining talent in sports departments. In fact the sports sections were bright entertainment with close-up reporting and conceived in the spirit of high fun. Even the fight news, which had become the sewage of the sports desk, was amusing and exciting. And a women's city or sectional golf championship was given a crisp, newsworthy treatment superior to that of the men's or women's professional tournament circuit events later on.

Time was when the New York newspapers alone could boast of an all-star array of sportswriters that included Grantland Rice, Westbrook Pegler, Joe Williams, John Kiernan, Henry McLemore, Paul Gallico, Bill McGeehan, Jimmy Cannon, Bill Richardson, Alison Danzig, Jimmy Powers, Dan Parker, Jack Miley, Frank Menke (who ghosted for four or five players in several World Series), and a dozen more who were versatile although primarily hired as specialists in boxing, yachting, tennis, baseball, horse racing, or football.

By the mid-1960's the roster of the nation's scintillating sportswriters had dwindled to a precious few. The new crop was small for the simple reason that there were no longer any colorful characters in sports to write about. The sports story was merely another commercial item that might fit under the heading: "What's Going On at the Meat Market."

After Arnold Palmer, no exceptionally fine professional golfer with show-

Lee Trevino. PGA

manship has come along the fairway. Doug Sanders, a good fellow and a proficient golfer, appeared with a rainbow wardrobe and a somewhat playful nature after working hours. A few big wins and he might have made it—become colorful despite his distracting tendency to dress like golf's sartorial answer to Liberace.

There there was Lee Trevino, the onetime caddy from El Paso, a glistening diamond in the rough with more rough than diamond visible and audible. When he started winning, Trevino had the good fortune to come under the management of Bucky Woy, an assistant professional under polished professionals at fine clubs and a successful professional at an excellent club. He knew class and had it, and as a starter, applied as much polish as possible to his charge. Trevino's native good sense and geniality, plus his growing awareness of the blessings he'd received from golf, made him an amusing and attractive personality within limits. Trevi-

Doug Sanders. AG

Johnny Miller. GH

no's backers on the tournament circuit apparently owned more of Trevino than did Super-Mex, as he called himself, and the majority stockholders were unhappy about the quick financial returns of the Woy management. So the two parted company, but some of the Woy polish in the gracious old tradition of golf stayed on. But so did the Super-Mex brashness.

Some of the Trevino color faded at a National Open Championship when he pulled a trick snake out of his bag and brandished it at Nicklaus while they were at the first tee. It was a more or less impromptu confrontation, a performance without malice, a joke to relieve tension. Anyone with even the slightest acquaintance with Trevino would have conceded that. But in a game that has etiquette as a preliminary and integral part of the rules, the snake-charmer act was out of place. USGA officials raised their eyebrows while Nicklaus, no stranger to psychological warfare, grinned a what-the-hell grin. Comparative newcomers were delighted at what they considered a cute hustler's trick. But veteran spectators and golf writers felt that Hagen, Armour, Sarazen, and other earlier matchplay warriors could have achieved the same effect far more subtly and artistically.

Trevino's color was kept bright because he liked to be interviewed and was not eager to dash off after his rounds. He spoke honestly and spontaneously, behaved the same way on the course, and generally came out ahead. When he did make mistakes, the golf writers just shrugged and said, "Well, what else did you expect?" The timing was right for Super-Mex. He shone in the twilight of the caddie champions. After him appeared a long line of intense young men who had been in college on golf scholarships and had acquired a campus air. They had been in golf for business from their days in knee pants, and there was no reason to expect the old sports color from confirmed businessmen. Unlike Trevino and those before him who played golf because it was fun with eating money, instead of something resembling work, they, and the baseball, football, and basketball pros in the same category, had never done anything else but play their game. And a benign destiny, helped along by scholarships and advanced professional payments, shaped their ends on a high financial plane.

However, just as in every other professional sport a new personality always seems to come along to take over the game, the 1970's in pro golf seem to belong to the skilled, handsome, and exemplary Johnny Miller, who could come back to win the big tournaments after long periods away from the game when he hadn't so much as picked up a club. He is something special, a truly extraordinary, spectacular, and record-breaking player.

Money, the root of all other evil, was responsible for forcing the separation of the PGA into the service professional and the playing specialist groups. The annual purses were increasing steadily at a rate far higher than common in commercial play. In 1967, the year before the PGA civil war erupted, Jack Nicklaus was the leading winner in tourney prize money with $188,998, and further was rewarded in the show business the PGA had built up over the years by a bale known only to the Internal Revenue Service, his tax lawyers, and the Almighty, in the order named. Next year, when the split came, quiet Bill Casper collected $205,168 from purses. Sponsors' commitments for 1969

PGA tournaments, even with war clouds hanging over the negotiations, assured still another record year of purses.

Yet a major problem of tournament sponsors remained to be settled—how to make certain all the gallery-drawing stars would be in a field. That problem remained unsolved long after the split, although the years have proved that rarely do more than six stars have much strength in drawing spectators.

Three men have made tournament players wealthy. No doubt few have heard of the golden trio of Jerry Rideout, Ted Smits, and Bob Leacox. Leacox, a Kansas City tire dealer, became interested in the tournament schedule and entry problems as a member of the PGA Advisory Committee. He took time off from his business to work free for the PGA.

Guarantees of appearance money and bonus payments for tournament participation did not draw fields that pleased the sponsors. Frequently they were unhappy about dates given them, so Leacox readjusted the tournament procedure by declaring that the sponsors putting up the most money got priority in everything, including dates and players. By making the arrangement that simple, Leacox took the abuse that had been going to players for their ingratitude to sponsors who had put up money when the pros desperately needed purses.

When Leacox completed his campaign, present and potential sponsors of golf tournaments had been distinctly informed that tournament golf had no place for love, but was solely for money. The purses increased—and so did the abuse Leacox received. The records fail to show that Leacox got any official appreciation from the tournament players via their committee.

Dave Stockton. AG

The Leacox program eliminated some sponsors who had been conducting lower-purse tournaments as community publicity, but their place was taken by a rich and ready group when Jerry Rideout created the tournaments as corporation publicity. He got the Associated Press to call the "Flint Open" the "Buick Open" at a time when newspapers refused to give golf tournament sponsors a free ride instead of their having to pay for the advertising.

Rideout knew that underpaid sports department workers weren't any too happy about fat weekend purses for men playing the golf that they had to buy for cash. So he exercised his persuasive talents and charming personality to establish a situation in which bright guys working fifty weeks a year for $8,000 were to write reports about men who worked thirty weeks a year, at most, and got well over $100,000 per annum. Rideout had been with United Press International when the realistic sports editor "Pete" Peterson asked, "What makes golf pros different from guys in any other business? The pros get paid plenty when they win and go broke when they don't. If they are in the advertising business, they're for the newspaper ad men, not for the sports department."

Rideout went to work on Ted Smits, sports editor of the Associated Press, which had a policy strongly established by publishers and managing editors of having businesses pay for advertising instead of getting free publicity. Smits had ruled against mention of the Miller and Carling brewing companies as golf tournament sponsors in AP stories. The sportswriters paid cash for plenty of the Miller and Carling products, as Smits and his literary colleague Rideout argued about the Flint Open. The

Flint Open was called the Grand Blanc Open because Grand Blanc is the name of the suburban Flint, Michigan, real-estate development owned by Buick officials.

Rideout worked through automobile editors of newspapers who often handled auto advertising as well as publicity. He was also "hospitable" to publishers and managing editors by having Buicks freely available when these executives were on vacation. Thus he had the AP commanding powers taking a second look at the mention of Buick as a tournament sponsor. By then, Smits was ready to give up because stock car races were getting sports-section space in which the names of the makers were mentioned as well as the drivers. So it became the Buick Open.

The Buick Open was purely a sales and publicity promotion, but when Buick's man Rideout opened up the sports-page publicity lode as an incentive to tournament sponsorship by commercial firms that could associate with tax-exempt operations of public concern, Buick became one of the most bountiful contributors to a very worthy cause—the tournament golf professionals.

Tournament golf was a happy home for television money, and sports programs were increasingly valuable to networks. They had a lot of advertising time to sell at high prices. At last, all the time, money, and headaches the PGA had devoted to building tournament business, often at the expense of the needs of pro golfer public service, was beginning to pay off richly. Then, after long, bitter rumblings over the years, came the civil war and the split.

It took the PGA a long time to realize that as a business it needed a well-qualified business manager, whether he was given that title or called executive director. It eventually seemed to get the ideally experienced man in Mark Cox. He came into the business sector of sports from the sports departments of the *Minneapolis Tribune* and *Chicago Tribune,* then went with the Wilson-Western Sporting Goods Company to become advertising and sales promotion manager. He also served in a similar capacity with the Golfcraft Company, then with the MacGregor Golf and other departments of the Brunswick Corporation.

Cox was also president of the Park Ridge (Illinois) Country Club and of the Western Golf Association, was an official of the National Golf Foundation and the Golf Club and Ball Manufacturers Associations, and was president of the Golf Division of the Victor Comptometer Corporation. In the latter connection he handled the manufacture and distribution of the PGA line of golf clubs, balls, and bags, which paid substantial royalties to the PGA Corporation. Cox's future with and for the PGA appeared to be largely a matter of what the PGA Executive Committee would do in allowing a business manager to manage PGA business.

After the division in 1968, the PGA began afresh in more areas than many members realized. It was entering a new era of responsibility in the golf business, and only the years would tell how the different and tougher test would be met. But reconstruction after any war is slow and difficult. In his two years as PGA president beginning in November, 1968, Leo Fraser served boldly, wisely, and well during a period jammed with critical developments. He had been blamed for meetings with the rebel players that were unknown to others in the Elbin administration, but he stood up and

Jerry Heard (playing with Arnold Palmer). AG

slugged it out toe to toe for the PGA when he was president. His battles included moving the PGA offices away for a brief period from the MacArthur building, the large PGA National Clubhouse and office building some PGA members naively considered their own. Entering the arena with John MacArthur was risky business for Fraser, who had rather extensive personal interests that might come under fire.

Satisfying the demands of the rebels had taken all the attention away from the promotional, educational, and sectional coordination requirements of the PGA. Fraser wanted to handle these vital tasks but believed he was handi-

capped by what he called the "Palace Guard," the supporters of the ex-president, Max Elbin. It was taking far too long for combat nerves to be tranquilized after the controversy dividing the PGA.

Veteran PGA members and others in the golf business agreed that the PGA never had two more capable, dedicated, and unselfish men working as presidents in trying times. The esteem they were held in and their high service to the PGA was acknowledged by the Golf Writers of America's Richardson awards to both men.

Elbin stood strongly for preserving golf as basically the nation's most popular amateur participation game. He showed professional golfers in their traditional role as champions of golf as the game of a lifetime for millions instead of a field of exploitation by the talented few and their directors. Like Elbin, Fraser shared the service spirit traditional with club professionals, and because he didn't want the PGA to engage in a ruinous, destructive battle, worked out the compromise that produced the Tournament Players' Division. He saw the sponsorship of tax-exempt tournaments by corporations as blatant advertising, and this, along with the management of players by men whose interest in golf was purely financial, constituted a clear and present danger to the PGA. Nobody seemed to care about the possibility of shattering the organization and permanently destroying a valuable service to all golfers.

Fraser's attempt to modernize the PGA and put its headquarters operation on a businesslike basis closely integrated with sectional business, his action in trying to shake loose from the unsatisfactory clubhouse lease with John MacArthur, his contribution in adjusting PGA and TPD financial arrangements and in making a TV contract for almost $1 million on PGA championships for the near future also qualified him for the Richardson award. The writers were ahead of the association's membership and its Executive Committee in balancing the qualities and performance of two exceedingly personable, honorable, and valuable pro leaders.

Nevertheless, the embers of controversy continued to smolder among the devoted adherents of Elbin and Fraser. Even after Warren Orlick succeeded Fraser as president in November, 1970, and during his two terms as president,

his serenity and constructive plans were ruffled by rear-guard feuding between Elbin and Fraser partisans. Not until William Clarke was elected president in November, 1972, did the former combatants forget what they had been arguing about.

Senior members doubted that even the poise and foresight of Clarke would maintain the PGA calm of the first year of his administration. Clarke and his Executive Committee had Lloyd Lambert on the job again as executive director between Robert Creasey and Mark Cox. Tom Boyle continued as comptroller, Bud Harvey as editor of *The Professional Golfer,* and Larry Null handled public relations.

After the separation of the home professionals and the journeymen, it became plain to the realists that the PGA had a big job of rebuilding. The connection between the two branches was too thin to be of much practical working use. Still, payment of nominal dues by tournament players to the parent body kept a line open for professionals who planned to get club jobs after their playing days were ended. And the PGA continued to have strong and mutually useful connections with amateur golf association officials, club officers, and other employers. A man who claimed to be a professional but did not have his qualifications validated by the PGA was considered unable to handle a club or pay-play course pro job competently.

In actual fact, while some had feared that the home pro–playing specialist split might wreck the association, one big change had been making it stronger as a federation of the sections than it had been as a national body with branches. The closeness of sectional officials to their pro employers was a major reason for the strength of the sec-

Gay Brewer. AG

tions. Another was that the sections had been improving in operation as golf business enterprises simply because paid secretaries did the work promptly and effectively that been left for PGA sectional officials to do nights or on Mondays away from the job. In most cases the paid secretaries were business managers of the sections, and in following the PGA headquarters practice, the sectional paid secretaries were sometimes designated "executive directors."

A few sections, especially Michigan, collaborated closely with the state amateur organizations and other regional golf business groups. One of the Michigan PGA's most impressive and pleasant public-relations affairs is the annual National Golf Day Dinner, which brings together many of the foremost golf figures. Michigan has frequently led all other sections in the sum raised

for the PGA's nationwide fund-raising for education, golf turf research, veterans hospital golf therapy, and additional areas where golf can serve.

And the Michigan PGA showed its business capacity in making the 1972 PGA Championship at Oakland Hills in suburban Detroit the most profitable by far of all PGA championships to date. Warren Orlick, then national PGA president and former Michigan sectional president, led the campaign. He felt that the PGA had to work more strongly and closely through the sections in expressing itself and its service to all golf. He tried to accelerate the sectional liaison but was handicapped by indifference in some sections and the smoldering resentments of the civil war.

Eventually it was all too obvious to national and sectional PGA officials that the PGA might as well realize that it was in a new game after 1968 and the division of the home and touring professionals. Fraser had to do a great deal of the cleaning up after the battle. He no longer was in a situation where negotiations with dissident members might be conducted backstage, so by a head-on attack with the arguments brought out into the open, he began to direct the development of the association's modern program.

Max Elbin in his role of honorary president was a constructive force instead of being in the customary formal capacity of an ex-president. He realized what Fraser was up against in trying to reconstruct the PGA so it could improve the home pros' financial status and serve as a beacon to all golf business confronted by perplexities. And Fraser also saw that the Executive Committee would have to think and act more openly as a policymaking group and eliminate politics. After all, the PGA was dedicated to the good of all golf, and what was there in that which required any more secrecy than in any sensible, common-good business discussions and decisions?

The PGA pension plan had been dragging, partially because of Internal Revenue Service positions, partially because the dreams of television revenue hadn't come true, but mainly because the PGA couldn't move to enlist private clubs and other employers of professionals. The clubs were notoriously poor employers of pros, superintendents, and managers, as rated by the standards many club officials were compelled to observe in the pension plan requirements of their own private businesses. The PGA insurance plans were also due for revision, as they'd been handled year by year on a selling, not a buying, basis.

Warren Orlick. PGA

Where the PGA headquarters should be located and whether there should be golf courses adjacent to it were other pertinent subjects that had to progress beyond the meaningless discussion stage. The Merchandise Show, which had begun as a few tables in front of the little clubhouse at Dunedin, had become big business but was still inadequately exploited as a public-relations asset. The annual show in Florida was a big selling operation—mostly to professionals east of the Mississippi—but there was a management problem in dealing with the general golfing public, which came in such numbers that it interfered with quantity sales to professionals.

In looking for headaches, the PGA was certain of finding more in real-estate transactions following the Dunedin and MacArthur arrangements. The

Herb Graffis (left) with Freddy Corcoran. AG

arrangements did not last long and did not sell homes to many PGA members, and the sites were remote from locations where PGA national publicity and other business could be conducted easily and conveniently. According to numerous PGA members, they were places for brief winter vacations instead of for the headquarters of a sports business with more than $250 million in sales volume annually.

In surveying the needs of the PGA after the shakeup, the Fraser administration realized that the affairs of the association had not been conducted in their order of importance. As owner of a club in Atlantic City and with financial interests in other clubs and operations, Fraser had more financial background than any other PGA president.

Like Arnold Palmer, he flew his own plane and said with a laugh, "I have spent many hours in the air on PGA business." Fraser worked so hard at his unpaid PGA job that doctors ordered him to slow down.

Despite their differences about handling the tournament pro demands for a split, regardless of the autonomy under which the journeymen had been operating, Elbin and Fraser were agreed that the tournament affairs had for far too long been taking an unbusinesslike share of the PGA's time. Out of approximately 7,000 PGA members in 1968, only around 200 were particularly interested in tournament affairs. Yet nearly half the time of the officers and the Executive Committee was devoted to tournament circuit matters, the PGA Championship, and the Ryder Cup and the Club Professionals' Championship. The Seniors pretty much ran their own championship. The Quarter Century Club and other tournaments played as entertainment sideshows around the time of the Merchandise Show were merely matters of getting sponsors in the golf business. Running the championships themselves was routine.

Once relieved of the tournament circuit load, the PGA was free to concentrate on its home work, and the administrations of Fraser and Orlick put increasingly strong emphasis on the educational program. Orlick's experience in the Michigan section included participation in one of the nation's most successful free-golf-lesson, public-service programs cosponsored by a newspaper. He and other professionals in the Detroit area saw what the lessons did to give golf professionals a close, authoritative relationship with amateur golfers that was unique in sports.

Orlick and the Education and Teaching committees got Gary Wiren from the University of Oregon to succeed Patrick Williams as PGA educational director. Williams was strong on the merchandising and schooling needs of PGA members, and Wiren, although not an expert in pro-shop management, had sound experience as a club professional. As a golf instructor at a private club and a member of the physical education staff of a large university, he met the PGA needs enthusiastically and well.

In the early 1960's, the golf business picture was generally satisfactory, although there was a slowdown in building new private clubs. Costs were getting too high to encourage many desirable younger family men to join the socially high-class clubs that needed them. Golf club taxes in most areas became prohibitive; the clubs asked and got little in return for their tax payments. Starting in 1964, labor and material costs for course and clubhouse operation in metropolitan districts increased nearly 10 percent annually.

Country clubs in the smaller towns also had costs that prevented much headway. Clubs that were financed by long and low-rate loans guaranteed by the Farm Home Administration were falling behind on their easy payments. Although these clubs were needed to provide social and recreational facilities comparable to those in larger communities, the idea was incompetently and extravagantly handled. Eventually the FHA was to engage the services of the National Golf Foundation field staff in efforts to correct errors made when the government agency was careless and quick in tossing around taxpayers' money.

Privately owned courses operated on a daily-fee or private-club basis were still growing solidly, and increasing land prices and the tax positions of the owners of the courses made a golf operation an attractive long-term deal. Resort and retirement projects of the better class had also determined that a golf course was an essential. The so-called short executive courses of par-58 to -64 length were proving decidedly effective in selling condominium residences to retired people. At these short courses, whether connected with residential projects or independently operated, those in charge reported the pleasing and unique story of many women taking up golf in their mid-sixties to play with their husbands and keeping up a lively pace of play, although their scoring was considerably less than sensational. Retired married

couples were also getting fun and exercise and fresh air in a much more delightful way than they had anticipated.

Management of the residential and
resort golf facilities meant jobs for professionals qualified beyond the customary experience in teaching and shop
operation. The professionals who satisfactorily handled these golf-residen-
tial resorts were now termed "golf
directors." They were definitely instrumental in bringing to their places of
employment golfers who spent $20,000
to $100,000 for a building site, then a
larger amount for a home.

The value of the well-qualified golf
director was noted by a Southern California real-estate developer who pointed
to a lesson tee at which his golf man
was engaged with a pupil. "There is
one of my best offices and best men," he
said. "He has them selling themselves."

Max Elbin and Leo Fraser as PGA
presidents sensed that great changes
were inevitable in the golf professionals' business. Employment conditions
and responsibilities of the home professionals differed greatly from those
when the PGA was young, yet there
had not been much change in the PGA
plan of operation. There were such
new questions as local, state, and federal taxes, wage and hour legislation's
application to assistants, increased business education of professionals, vast alterations in the range of pro employment conditions and problems, heavy
investments in merchandise, problems
of golf cart operation, broadened public-relations needs, and the need for
overall improvement in instruction—all
these, plus the old questions of getting
jobs, insurance, and other necessities
increased by the tremendous enlarge-
ment of the golf business since the
PGA's founding.

The number of sections had been in-

Don A. Rossi. AG, courtesy of National
Golf Foundation

creased to thirty-seven. The Tournament Players' Division had been
formed, and the constitution had again
been revised and patched in response
to the need to bring the organization
up-to-date, but this was still not enough.
Elbin and Fraser and their companion
national officers agreed that to become
most effective for its members and golf
in general, the PGA had to devise policies and procedures for operations that
would have all the sections doing what
they could do best and the national
body coordinating the sectional work
and directing it to achieve a beneficial
effect on all golf nationwide. The function of the national PGA as an authority strengthening the influence and status of all professionals could then be
attended to energetically.

Appointment of a sectional liaison
officer was about as far as the Elbin and
Fraser plans got. The business schools
and seminars, visits of national officers,

and the annual meetings continued to be the routine contacts they had been for years. But when Warren Orlick became president, he realized that the modernization of the PGA as a business organization was probably coming from the sections into headquarters. Half the sections had their own executive directors, who were practically business managers working full time and in closer contact with officers and members than the PGA national organization had with its components.

Orlick struggled with the problem of modernizing the PGA nationally on a par with sectional developments, but the job was too much for a lone missionary. Orlick spent a great deal of time away from his club on PGA duties and for Rules of Golf educational sessions, public-relations talks, the PGA Championship, and Ryder Cup matches. Robert Creasey, then PGA executive director, was a lawyer experienced in labor relations but with no business background qualifying him for the reorganization the PGA needed quickly, smoothly, and diplomatically. The prospects for modernizing the PGA brightened when William Clarke became president and Mark Cox was hired as executive secretary.

A progress report on the PGA from its founding to the end of the home pro–tournament journeyman civil war in 1968 generally showed that the PGA had become an influence if not a power authority in golf. It had served all golf well by educating and controlling its members and accepting responsibility for their conduct.

Employers of home professionals had learned that identification as a PGA member was the primary qualification of a man to handle a job satisfactorily. The professionals themselves knew more about what it took to do the golf

job than did the club officials or other employers. That was one area in which the PGA did have considerable authority, but even so, the PGA did not have the weight to recommend selections among its members within sectional boundaries.

Before its division, the PGA had also become pretty much of an authority on controlling and disciplining tournament players for the simple reason that if and when tournament players were guilty of conduct unbecoming gentlemen sportsmen, sponsors lost interest in financing the competitions.

Officially, the PGA was not an authority in the golf business because it didn't have even elementary information about the golf market and the extent of the professionals' domination and leadership in the top-quality element of the market. Unofficially, of course, the association was a strong influence in improving pro credit as a factor in membership qualification.

In the instruction sector, there was the puzzling failure to reach the PGA founders' objective of having most of the nation's golfers score well. Again, the problem was complicated by the lack of definite figures that the PGA as the authority on golf teaching and learning might be expected to collate from the sources of club handicap data and educated estimates on the public course play.

It began to occur to pros that the teachers might be competent but the system could be wrong. The teachers had been discussing the science and mechanics of the golf stroke in depth but could perhaps have been missing education and application in the art of their vocation. The facet of personality and the other conditions affecting reception of the instruction hadn't been adequately considered. Lesson revenue was steadily diminishing, and most of the lessons were given to women because most male golfers didn't have enough time for lessons. And even men who did take lessons were often those who were reasonably apt pupils, not the ones in dire need of basic instruction. Thoughtful professionals discovered that for golf instruction to be effective, far more attention had to be paid to conditioning learners. The slump in the number and results of golf lessons came not so much from deficiencies in teaching as from the failure to develop able learners and present a system practical for instruction other than the obsolete half-hour lesson pattern.

It was becoming apparent to realistic male professionals that women were effective teachers. Male professionals frankly acknowledged that female assistants were getting results with women pupils who had baffled them, and with the junior classes as well. Johnny Revolta, acknowledged by male and female professionals to be one of the most resourceful teachers, had the proud and astonishing experience of having people tell him that his wife Luraine got them learning better than Johnny did. Johnny had taught her. She had the learner's attitude.

The Ladies' PGA was naming its Teacher of the Year annually, and like the PGA, was collaborating in the instructional program the National Golf Foundation was putting on at colleges. The LPGA was paying more attention to instructing women students than the PGA was paying to men. So, suddenly, the PGA, which had been somewhat haughty toward any sort of alliance with the LPGA, began to think that maybe it had better modernize itself and to some extent go coeducational.

When the PGA was finally able to shake itself free of the burden of being minority-ridden by the showman pros and to devote itself to the mighty millions of amateurs, other urgent problems came into sharp focus for constructive attention. A refresher course on the mechanics and art of club design was long overdue. Knowledge of this basic training in the pro job began to vanish when bench clubmaking no longer was part of the pro job. Something had to be done to educate professionals in the reasons for club design and construction and in the application of this information in correctly fitting clubs to the users.

There was no difficulty in getting highly reputable sponsors for the PGA's Quarter Century Club Championship and other competitions for members that were usually run around the time of the association's Merchandise Show early in the year and at courses close to the golf merchandise exhibit. The Club Professionals' tournament was established as a movable event to give all sections a chance to stage the event, although the Southern sections got preference because the home professionals had to conduct their competition in the winter when most pros could conveniently get away from their clubs. And the annual prize money was substantial for the PGA sectional and national tournaments presented for members who were not tournament specialists and who in only a few cases had eligibility cards in the Tournament Players' Division.

Most of the sectional tournaments were played with civic, charitable, or hospital associations as beneficiaries getting what was left after the distribution of prize money. Purses were provided by sponsors under the same tax-exempt arrangement usually made by sponsors of tournament circuit events.

While the association had made real the dream of its founding fathers in establishing a high character rating for men in the golfing profession, the PGA as a group did not rate as high as its members did individually. It was always blamed for the bad manners and avarice of its most favored members, a rather small number of tournament specialists reaping rich harvests from the PGA's tournament development work but markedly failing in the social graces. To avoid this kind of thing, the club managers' national association and the golf course superintendents had adopted programs of "certifying" the competence of their members. The qualifying procedures were not entirely popular with the members of those organizations and in some respects were questionable as practical appraisals, which all such certification must be, but the effort served to upgrade the certified men to their present or possible employers.

Under the presidency of Warren Orlick, the PGA's own plan of rating the qualifications of its members began to make some headway. It proved difficult to get a comprehensive method of evaluating the PGA members' qualifications because of the more than half dozen classes from apprentices to experienced head professionals and the various sources of credit information in qualifying the men. And delegates to the annual meetings always said there must be a better way to spend time than by hashing over the tedious technicalities of sectional resolutions proposing changes in membership classification. However, no specific suggestions were ever presented.

Orlick thought his administration had succeeded in disengaging the PGA from the real-estate business and heading it toward a concentration on the golf business, but the temptation to get a winter wonderland with golf courses and offices at virtually a gift price through the generosity of real-estate salesmen remained strong. Yet conditions had changed greatly since the PGA had conceived of the pleasant hamlet at Dunedin, Florida, with its Donald Ross course and small clubhouse, as a retirement community for thrifty senior pros let go from their club jobs with not much more than a farewell dinner.

The PGA hadn't been able to get an extensive pension plan, but the pro-department business had progressed to the point where the professional who had been at a first-class club for years was able to take care of his wife and himself in retirement. Social security payments certainly helped.

While it was evident that management and operations were more modernized and efficient sectionally than at PGA national headquarters, there were encouraging signs that official personnel, sectionally and nationally, were being selected on the basis of sound business qualifications. No longer were elections mere popularity contests or political maneuvers. Work as a PGA officer or Executive Committee member took a lot out of a man. He had to have considerable ability, as well as luck to start with.

When William Clarke became president in 1972, there were still many loose ends to be tied together. National Golf Day, unique among sports welfare funds, needed businesslike examination rather than the casual treatment it had generally been getting from the PGA.

The Western Golf Association's Par Club, which supported caddie scholarships, reported that while some members questioned the need for caddie

scholarship money, 868 scholars were en-
rolled at twenty-nine universities across
the country and 6,089 members of the
Par Club were paying $100 a year or
more and thousands of club members
$5 a year or more to finance these schol-
arships.

Max Elbin had recognized that
golf was growing faster than the PGA
was developing as a golf business organization. Caught in the home pro–
journeyman hurricane, Leo Fraser saw
the PGA business lag keenly. As a
progressive golf businessman, he knew
he'd have gone broke if he'd been as
tardy as the PGA to adjust to the new
conditions. The necessity for modernization became more acute to Warren
Orlick, but he was straitjacketed by the
old routine. When William Clarke
came in as president with Mark Cox as
business manager, it appeared that the
bright new day of the PGA in the golf
business had at last arrived.

Overhauling the PGA educational
program was continued by Mark Cox
after he became the association's executive director. The requirement that
members be officially certified as being
qualified to hold professional jobs
meant that training and periodic examinations be formal and comprehensive from the apprentice stage on up.
Credits were given on the usual scho-
lastic plan.

In addition to the business schools,
executive management seminars were
scheduled to deal with the enlarged
area of opportunities for professionals
handling general-management club positions and the broad duties involved
in the operation of golf facilities at resorts and residential developments.

The new policy was to tell the PGA
business training story as news that
would show pro employers how their
men were taught the answers to golf

business problems. The Club Managers' Association had been keeping club
presidents well informed of the educational program for managers. The sectional golf course superintendents' associations had also kept green chairmen
and other officials of clubs and fee
courses aware of the extensive educational work in which the superintendents were involved, together with state
agronomists, USGA Green Section experts, and other authorities. And Gary
Wiren, the PGA's director of education, planned a new schooling curriculum with which golf writers as well as
PGA members were kept acquainted.

The new PGA Business School curriculum follows:

I. *Rules and Etiquette*
    a. History and Principles Behind the
       Rules
    b. Definitions and Use of the Rule
       Book
    c. Marking the Course—Situations and
       Decisions
    d. Rules Changes
    e. Golf Etiquette (*Courtesy on the
       Course* Film)

II. *The PGA Businessman*
    a. Buying and Inventory Management
    b. The Professional's Relationship to
       the Supplier
    c. Bookkeeping and Accounting—
       Taxes and Insurance
    d. Contracts and Job Arrangements

III. *Teaching the Teacher to Teach*
    a. Psychological Factors in Motor Skill
       Learning
    b. Priorities in Developing a Teaching
       Method
    c. *The Evolution of the Golf Swing*
       Film
    d. Recognizing the Laws of the Golf
       Swing
    e. Club Teaching Techniques
       1. Individual Techniques for Stage
          1 Players

2. Individual Techniques for Stage 2 and 3 Players
   f. Station Practices—Putting, Chipping, Woods, Irons, Sand Play
   g. Record Keeping
   h. Use of Audiovisual Aids
   i. *Swing Analysis* Film
   j. Corrective Teaching

IV. *The PGA Professional Dedicated to Service*
   a. Public Speaking Film
   b. Toward PGA Membership—Ethical Conduct in the Profession
   c. Club and Course Programs—Tournament Management, Handicapping, Juniors, Caddies, Ladies' and Men's Associations

There were some differences of official opinion about many of the policies and procedures of PGA progress but practically unanimous approval of the reorganization, nationally and locally, of the golf pros' schooling plan. In the extensive revision of PGA operations that followed the division of the home and touring professionals, public service became more than ever before the association's dominant theme.

28

The Era of Commissioner Dey
and a Summing Up

THE Tournament Players' Division continued to operate about the same as when its connection with the PGA was integral rather than nominal. TPD headquarters were changed from Florida to New York because New York was a far more convenient and logical location for conducting most of the division's business. Commissioner Dey resided in suburban New York and had established many contacts in the New York metropolitan area when he was working for the USGA as its executive director. Jack Tuthill stayed on the job as tournament director, heading the field staff. Tuthill and his men speedily handled any brushfires that blazed among nervous players, so there were rarely any cases requiring authority on high that got to New York. George H. Love, John D. Murchison, and J. Paul Austin, with Samuel E. Gates as counsel, rounded out the im-

pressive roster that would ride herd on the TPD prize stock and its yearlings.

Expenses were higher with the TPD than before the split, but the increase was well justified as the price of peace under the new arrangement. Despite their popularity and their attractive personalities, the prominent tournament players had experienced a dizzying slump in public favor when they found themselves put in the position of greedy complainers careless of the good name of tournament golf that had been built for them by the PGA. Joe Dey soon proved his worth in restoring the quality note lost during the split. The favorites were favorites again. It was obvious that the television revenue of tournament golf depended chiefly on a quality market appeal. It was just as obvious that it had taken the earlier golf professionals too many years of dedicated service and conduct to establish acceptance of the professional golfer as a paid athlete of a superior sort, and that it would be idiotic to risk defiling that image.

All the tournament stars had to do was behave and hold the place won for them. Maybe nobody saw the picture clearer than Joe Dey, who had been close enough to the later social and financial powers who had developed golf for the American populace to learn what the story was in making golf move. But nobody was sure which side had won the PGA's civil war. Neither had, really.

To backtrack a little and to recapitulate as well, after the cease-fire of legalities, lawyers, and fine print, the tournament players were in the same position as they'd been in under the PGA that had built the circuit. They had Joe Dey to make them look good for golf. They had a New York office because Joe lived in suburban New York. And they had three big business names on a nicely labeled Tournament Policy Board, which was in a way the counterpart of the PGA Advisory Committee, an asset the PGA hadn't learned how to use.

By a narrow and lucky margin a bond was kept between the journeymen and home professionals when the Tournament Players' Division was identified as a division of the Professional Golfers' Association of America. The president and secretary of the PGA were made members of the TPD Policy Board, and TPD members were also required to qualify as members of the PGA. In any case, the "division" satisfied both camps. Actually, the two PGA elements were no farther apart than they'd ever been.

Dey's reputation was what tournament golf needed. He didn't believe

in exploiting golf just because there was a fast buck in it for the hustler. He was a reminder to the tournament pros to be careful about their own reputations, and that made him worth more than the money that was paid him.

When Dey was hired to be the house dick and model of deportment for the tournament professionals, the Articles of Agreement that restored peace called for him to be called the "tournament director." Lawyers who drafted the agreement had overlooked the fact that the PGA already had an outstanding tournament director in Jack Tuthill, who had left the FBI in 1960 to go into the golf job.

He had been tournament director of the PGA since 1964. He and his nine-man staff had done a more competent job of smoothing out difficulties than any other professional sport's field operation. Certainly they never have been given recognition by the competitors they have helped to make rich. The public doesn't know them.

But when the title of tournament director was to be bestowed upon Dey, it was discovered that the dignity, accompanied by less pay, had already been bestowed upon Jack Tuthill. Now there was a delicate decision confronting the touring players. They wanted a boss who wouldn't boss too harshly but who would make them look superior to the common run of professional athletes.

There were exceptions, of course. But to be wide-eyed about it, Dey had to replay Walter Hagen in getting the playing professionals of golf back into the parlor. And he had to keep them there because the general public reaction to the professionals' rebellion was that money hadn't given manners to all too many prize winners. And, again, there came the age-old reminder: There is no substitute for class. And Dey had, and has, class. The word that went with Dey's class—and his job—was "commissioner." Hence, designated by the masterminds to be "tournament director," but following the ancient and honorable billing of the baseball housecleaner, Joe Dey became "commissioner."

When the PGA had its family brawl and the issue was between well-timed normal avarice, the table of organization, and last but not least, acknowledgment that the amateurs were those from whom all blessings flowed, it became obvious that Joe Dey, for years executive director of the USGA, was the man to bring to all parties the peace that passeth all understanding.

Joe Dey was transferred into the commissioner's spot from unquestionably the most tranquil, most respected position in sports. The United States Golf Association is the smartest, most honored sports ruling body in the United States, and Dey was the number-one employee of the astute sportsmen who finally got amateur golfers to agree that the best government was by the consent of the governed. Of all executives in amateur and professional sports, Joe Dey, then approaching retirement at the USGA, was the only one who had been in a sustained crossfire for years and come out unpunctured.

So when the arguing between PGA presidents Max Elbin and his successor, Leo Fraser—both of whom were primarily concerned with the greatest good for golf and the association—subsided, they agreed on Dey to end the war and relieve the shocks that professional golf had suffered. And he was eagerly accepted as den mother of the playing pros.

Still, many people felt that Joe Dey was a much better boss than his wayward charges deserved. And he was no loner on the job. He had Joe Schwendeman, a Philadelphia golf writer, as public information director virtually from the formation of the Tournament Players' Division. Schwendeman knew the players about as well as any golf writer and is highly regarded by his colleagues for his ability and judgment. He was just the sort of a man to have backstage for sound counsel in situations inevitable to a development of the Tournament Players' Division type. Dey also had John Ross, a veteran newspaper and magazine editor with extensive golf experience, as a public-relations counselor.

All the same, the younger players grumbled. They expected that the breakaway of the playing specialists from the overall golf professionals' association would immediately result in easier and more money for them. But there was no way in which Commissioner Dey could invent a substitute for the scorecard. So there were quite a few complaints about "satellite" tournaments'—especially in Florida—not giving enough money and not dividing it to the complete satisfaction of the secondary players. However, since the satellite tournaments usually lost money and in the winter were played on courses where paying customers wanted to enjoy vacations as golfers rather than spectators, the growling failed to arouse any deep sympathy among those who finance golf.

The lower-rated players also resented being labeled "rabbits," a term imported from Britain where it was applied to the young professionals who had not been able to demonstrate by club and ball their right to be classified among the top-class "tigers." The cubs were fortunate that Schwendeman and Dey understood the limitations of their charges in the public-relations field. Accordingly, they protected the boys against being "minor leaguers" or "bushers" or some other such designation of inferior playing talent that would have knocked down the promise of satellite tournaments and the dream of two "major-league" tournaments in widely separated spots during the summer.

Dey behaved like a college president and gave the rebellious juveniles whatever it was they wanted. They weren't sure what it was, but they got a committee and quieted down. So Commissioner Dey got over that problem of budding delinquents with no trouble. Besides, the kids themselves had been getting solid basic training in the PGA schools qualifying them as Approved Tournament Players.

Another threat came from some younger journeymen who were beginning to show promise of becoming winners whose names the public might be expected to remember for a few weeks. They wanted more to say about the way the TPD was being run. They were not specific, just restless, as their predecessors had been in storming up the PGA split. At that time, only one precious vote in the PGA Executive Committee, which was balloting on whether to toss out the dissident players or retain them as a "division" pretty much in the autonomous situation they long had been in, had prevented a disastrous open break between the home pros and journeymen.

Dey got rid of the juniors' questioning of his authority by the cute Machiavellian method of having the more annoying disbelievers collected in a committee to settle their own grievances, real or fancied. As noted in an earlier chapter, this is a cunning and useful practice in golf club politics. It accounts for the man who has complained most about the clubhouse operation or the course being made the chairman of the house or course committee. Cruel and unusual punishment? Maybe. But it teaches the victims not to speak out of turn.

The older tournament professionals, who'd been eating their pie in the sky, couldn't think of anything to moan about. But there was a trifling thing when Commissioner Dey wanted the journeymen to use local caddies instead of the wandering caddies who also served as chauffeurs, valets, club cleaners, alarm clocks, laundromat errand boys, club counters, deep students of the ABC's of the Rules of Golf, travel agents, and otherwise showed their versatility toward their employers.

That rumpus was settled quickly and easily. The rich, veteran journeyman pros, who had their own caddies as expert bricklayers used to have their own hod carriers in the good old days when trades were growing up into big money, told Commissioner Dey to forget it, be himself, and not mess around with a matter primarily concerning his employers. So Dey wisely backed away but got the last laugh when the professional caddies forgot to show up with their journeymen's clubs on time and were otherwise guilty of derelictions of duty that would have embarrassed a fifteen-year-old Class B caddie at any country club.

Anyway, being overruled on the touring-caddie situation by the friendly giant intellects who were making more money per annum than he was gave Dey balm for his soul. And as far as the knowledgeable golfing public was concerned, who cared? It was getting fed up with the prima-donna pronounce-

Larry Hinson. AG

Johnny Miller. AG

Bobby Nichols. AG

ments of journeyman professionals. Sure, it was an era of anything goes, but solvent amateurs couldn't help wondering what kind of character would want to be a traveling caddie.

Dey probably found that his sense of humor, more than his experience with the administration of America's most popular participating sport, was going to keep him of sound mind and in command of the situation. There had been far too much ballyhoo about the millionaire golf pros, too many reminders about who was making $100,000 or more a year out of a game where 100,000 or more ordinary golfers had to get up before daybreak and await starting time at public courses. Besides, unemployment, a slump in Wall Street prices, and other indications that the nation's business wasn't in a flush period called for a reappraisal of tournament golf. Dow-Jones, which of all tournament sponsors was in a position to read the signals, put on the biggest of all money tournaments up through A.D. 1970. The purse was $300,000. Expenses were murderous. The tournament was reputed to have cost the *Wall Street Journal* publishers approximately $500,000 and established, according to a practical authority, a bear market for tournaments.

Union-management controversies and the salary hassles of professional baseball and football players and the club owners did not make professional golf with its big purses for four days of play look any more beautiful to people who paid to see the shows. And there was an added warning for golf in a Miami tournament sponsored by National Airlines while the company was being cramped by a strike. Pickets patrolled the course, but the small gallery for this big-money tournament failed to give the pickets much of an audience.

The Westchester Classic, a hospital benefit involving the unpaid help of about 1,200 women and men, and the genuine "classics," such as the Masters, the Colonial, the Crosby and Hope tournaments, the National and Western Opens, were standing steady. But the Texas Open gave up. Too much money was demanded by the players. And when anybody can demand more money than Texans are willing to pay, it's a sure thing that the Tournament Players' Division had something to learn from Neiman-Marcus about merchandising.

It began to get clear to tournament golfers who could read beyond the sports pages that the commissioner had far bigger problems than settling nursery quarrels between players guilty of conduct unbecoming to grown-up gentlemen sportsmen. The kid stuff got so bad that players conspicuous for bad manners cried about each other for being discourteous. Certainly Dey was earning his money—and more—for having to put up with that sort of alley circus after his association with the gentlemen and ladies of the USGA.

As might be expected during a slump in business, professional golf tournament financing by merchandisers got a cold, clear-eyed examination. To advertisers planning to sell a market, golf was merely an instrument to be used in making money. And it was the same for managers of professional golfers who were milking the game and not contributing a thing to golf as a game or business.

The Alcan affair, paid for by the Aluminum Company of Canada, was another tournament casualty of this period. Stockholders and executives asked whether it sold enough to be worth the money. The answer was no, despite the affair's having a cute promotion angle of qualifying contestants by their showing in several important tournaments in the United States and elsewhere.

Naturally, the difficulties and problems of professional tournament golf increased as the business got bigger. British tournaments benefiting advertisers were being pushed by promoters who realized they'd better hit and run. Worldwide tournaments, especially in Australia and Japan, were also offering tempting prize money. So after the civil war in professional golf in the United States, there was an international stage of readjustment. Businessmen who supported professional golf were being reminded to think about the game as a strictly commercial factor. True, the home professionals and the journeymen were friends again and taking a forward look, but the construction of new courses was slowing. The costs of private club operation were getting so high that desirable young men and women were excluded from membership. It appeared that the legislative and tax climates were simply averse to private clubs as private clubs.

The prize money that Gary Player, Bob Charles, Bruce Camption, Bruce Devlin, Tony Jacklin, and other foreign players had taken out of American purses was no painful loss to the American pros, as European and Far Eastern events were beginning to give Americans chances to get even. Exhibitions in Japan were decidedly profitable for the leading American professionals.

Numerous pros with several championships to their credit had tie-ins with American golf architects. Japan was figuring on between 300 and 500 golf courses to add to its 500, so the guessers said, and those architectural advisory services with good advertising names meant more foreign money for the American playing pro stars. There are but few indications that the playing stars showed any marked golf architectural talent, but they were flashy window dressing for men who were competent course design specialists.

Taking the long view, it is apparent that pro golf never had it so good as when Joe Dey was hired as the TPD commissioner. As *vox dei* when he was working for the USGA and backstopped by the Power and the Glory, Dey was able to keep amateurs behaving. With the golf tradesmen paying his salary, it was a different situation, but Dey kept growing up to it and warranting the good judgment of those who'd hired him. Even so, his five-year contract with the Tournament Players' Division of the PGA was enough. He had done well as a sort of a mother hen to the journeymen; he had made far more money than he'd ever expected to make out of golf and was well nested for old age.

Away from the USGA he was no longer a member of golf's Holy Family. That loss of prestige, if any, was amply blamed on payday. But Joe Dey was highly regarded as possibly the most competent of the pro sports commissioners even though he did not have to deal with the kind of experienced and wealthy businessmen who seemed to own such sports as baseball, football, hockey, and basketball outright.

Most of the pro golfers were bright young men and had been shocked to learn that the golfing public had an utter and cold minimum of compassion for the fiscal miseries of the Gypsy golf players, whatever the miseries of these playboys. The "millionaire" tag attached to Palmer, Snead, and Nicklaus was backfiring on all pro golf, although they were three of the brightest, most affable sports headliners, and the galleries and reporters were fond of them.

Dey had a clearer fix on the glamorous publicity picture of his stars and the ordinary gentlemen of the golfing ensemble, the promising hopefuls, than anyone else in the golf business. His association with USGA executives gave him Phi Beta Kappa rating when he began the TPD commissioner's job. He also clearly understood that the beautiful job had been promoted for him by Leo Fraser, PGA president during the reconstruction period, because Bob Creasey, the PGA executive director, simply did not have the temperament to walk hand in hand into the golden sunset with the tournament players from the seventy-third hole in the old, loving, sentimental, silent-picture way.

A skilled labor-relations expert, Creasey had been a private club member who couldn't get the problems of the tournament specialists into sharp focus. He thought that if there were to be any complaints about golf tournament prize money they should come from the people who were paying. Consequently, the players knew that they needed Dey's good name and trusting friends. And Dey found his new employers very reasonable. They knew they couldn't risk more public questioning of the players' complaints. The PGA tournament operation in the field with Jack Tuthill in command was satisfactory to all concerned and a model for a professional sports operation. Dey wisely let Tuthill alone, and Tuthill settled situations that could have caused trouble under a less competent man.

A major reason for the tournament players' unhappiness with the PGA was that the arrangement was costing them too much for administration. Yet, after the split, the lawyers' bills, Dey's salary and fringe benefits, the cost of operating a New York office, and other new charges, it turned out that the Tourna-

ment Players' Division was costing nearly $300,000 a year more than under the previous PGA arrangement. Other than having Dey as commissioner and a New York office, the tournament players' business went on in the same way.

Although the PGA civil war turned out to be a rather silly and extravagant argument that nobody won, it probably was a good thing for both sides. The PGA home professionals began to get the benefit of the golf business management for which the PGA had been organized. The association had been weakened because its officials and Executive Committee fell into the habit of devoting more attention to the whines, demands, and problems of the tournament players who comprised about 5 percent of the membership than it had to the business interests of the majority of its members and their employers.

As we have seen, undue emphasis on tournament circuit matters had cost the PGA a good deal of its rating as an authority in the golf business. The association was losing the capacity to coordinate its thirty-seven sections as a strong national influence in golf. Its educational program was getting challenging competition from the programs of the Golf Course Superintendents' Association and the Club Managers' Association of America. Like other important matters in professional golf, the educational program lagged because the tournament players had to be given such priority.

With the Tournament Players' Division splitting, a side block to PGA progress was removed. Mark Cox, an experienced and successful golf business executive, was hired as the first businessman to work as executive director of the PGA. With Cox on the

Mark Cox. Moffett Studio

job, the PGA began to make up for lost time and opportunity at a period when the golf business in general urgently needed competent management with imagination and guts. And the association's educational service was intensified and broadened with Gary Wiren hired to formulate and direct the new program.

Cox promptly applied himself to the task of coordinating PGA national headquarters with the thirty-seven sections. Some sections had been quicker than the association nationally in adjusting to the new conditions of pro jobs. In many respects the PGA needed to make a clearer showing of unity, strength, and service to all golfers. Therefore, a revision of public-relations operations was effected to bring the PGA and its members' employers to

a position of mutual understanding and helpfulness.

There had been a great deal of talk by PGA officials concerning the need to modernize the organization's platform and performance, but energetic and informed PGA management plans for a new day never seemed to get past the talk stage. Cox changed that, and without the problems of the tournament players to distract its attention, the PGA began to show a new confidence. Golf was changing socially and economically, and the PGA seemed to be preparing itself for leadership.

The Tournament Players' Division was in excellent operating condition when it left home. The agreements with sponsors, the television contracts, the qualifying schools for players hoping to participate in circuit events, the prize money distribution, the tournament staging procedure, and a multitude of details, even down to recommendations concerning caddie fees, had been worked out over the years. The PGA Tournament Committee had been blessed with good judgment and good luck in the field. And in Jack Tuthill it had a star.

Hence, Joe Dey's job was that of improving the looks of the players to their public and to the sportswriters, who had begun to class the journeyman pros as spoiled by too much money and too little work and responsibility. All in all, Dey had very little trouble with the employers he'd restored to public grace. As a matter of fact, they were young men of engaging personality and far higher intelligence than the usual professional athlete. They had made themselves look bad while they were getting considerably more money than they'd ever expected.

Dey had learned from the USGA how to work with big men and make

Deane Beman. AG

good use of their prestige and superior business capacity for the benefit of all concerned. With the big-business names he had on the TPD Policy Board, along with the PGA president and secretary and the representatives elected by the players, Joe Dey really had no worries that his authority might be questioned. And he was able to make far better use of the big business Advisory Board of Love, Murchison, and Austin than the PGA ever has with its own Advisory Board.

As the finale of Dey's employment by the TPD approached early in 1974, it became obvious that he could bow out gloriously by exercising his experience in the choice of his successor. There were a number of candidates for the TPD commissioner's job. The pay and the pleasant nature of the job were attractive, especially to retired military men who enjoyed golf. But while he

was with the USGA, Dey had had called to his attention the very practical merits of Deane Beman of Washington, D.C., who combined a great deal of amateur golf with his partnership in a sound insurance business.

Beman turned professional in 1967 after a busy and successful amateur career. He had won the USGA Amateur Championship in 1960 and 1963 and the British Amateur in 1959. He had been on five Walker Cup teams, four World Cup teams, and four America's Cup teams. He had a growing family in Washington, and notwithstanding business interests that would finance his amateur career, according to his brief biography in the *TPD Tour Book,* he hankered to test his talents against the pros by really settling down and playing tough competitive golf. How he could play more golf as a professional than as an amateur is puzzling.

Beman is not a long hitter. With the tendency to stretch out golf courses to such gigantic lengths that they could be played with a driver, another long wood, a wedge, and a putter, as the veteran Toney Penna remarked, it didn't appear that Beman would make a profit on the tour. However, there were many distance hitters among the amateurs when Beman was competing, and he managed to do well at getting the ball in the hole in the fewest strokes. In his seven years on the tour he was first in four tournaments, which did not include any of the top events, and won around $370,000 and the respect of his fellow contestants, so he was elected a player director on the Tournament Policy Board. He left that post to become the commissioner on March 1, 1974.

Of course the first thing he inherited from Dey was the chronic problem of trying to get the big names to show up for all the big tournaments. The National Open, the Masters, and the PGA always get the stars with good sense as entries, although now and then the Masters scared away a few who wouldn't be missed. But other events that were putting up top prize money and deserved encouragement by players in the trade for money continued to have trouble getting an all-star field.

In the early days of organizing the circuit, the stars were paid "appearance money." It was this guarantee, added to the money the star might win, that made the event quite attractive. Usually the appearance money was paid surreptitiously and was a matter of bargaining. If one star discovered that another shining light had got a better deal, there were petulance and other displays of temperament. Then methods were devised to give bonuses for entering tournaments to players with out-

standing records, but nothing seemed to satisfy both the sponsors and the tournament headliners.

However, assurances to sponsors that players would appear in tournaments as planned continued to plague the TPD. Dey had suggested that there be fifteen tournaments annually, each with prize money of $260,000 or more. The outstanding players were expected to be in all of these events or be ruled out of that top-money category. Two lower-prize-money groups of tournaments were also proposed, but the prominent players did not favor the idea. Then, in 1973, when the requests for tournaments and the projected annual prize money fell under the figures for the preceding year, Dey and the Policy Board formulated the "Designated Tournament Plan" as a guarantee that the richer players would enter the richer tournaments or be penalized.

Again there were complaints from wealthier players who might have other golf business engagements that made the Designated Tournament appearance inconvenient. And sponsors protested that the Designated Tournament rating made other tournaments second-rate affairs. Players also objected to the idea on the grounds that since they had already given the tax man too much, it was unfair to schedule one of the Designated Tournament events late in the season.

For a professional golfer to have won so much money that he did not want to play was far too wild a dream ever to have been imagined back in the old days when the PGA first began to build a tournament circuit. But that was exactly what had happened. Prosperity had separated the tournament players from the PGA that had created the solid-gold course expressly for them—and prosperity was the problem Commissioner Beman inherited from Commissioner Dey as the wealthier playing pros wanted fewer competitions for more money.

If a business has to have a problem, certainly prosperity is one of the best to have. It was much better for a tournament pro to have to pay the Internal Revenue man than it was in the nursery days of the tournament circuit, when ambitious young players had to sneak out of tournament-city hotels, leaving behind checks having more rubber than the golf balls in their bags.

The golf prosperity had spread abroad, too. Prize money on the European and Asiatic circuits was being increased to the point where foreign players could do well without coming to the United States, and American players were being attracted abroad. Taxation of winnings figured strongly in the tournaments with international fields. British and Continental professionals and tournament sponsors muttered that American professionals and their managers were making the European events an "American racket." One new development was the way managers cut themselves into tournament money, but the demands of American professionals for appearance money was an old custom that tournament sponsors in the United States had complained about in vain for years. Nothing could be done about it until the ordinary names on the circuit got the PGA to control the star's demands for such fees.

European complaints of American exploitation of the substantial and growing overseas circuit merely reflected American protests over British, South African, Australian, and New Zealand professionals' taking home heavy hauls of American tournament prize money. That situation was brought into balance by the PGA Tournament Committee, which placed moderate restrictions on the entries of foreign players in American events. So far as prestige that could be converted into testimonial revenue was concerned, only winning the British Open meant anything to an American professional. But clearly the tournament development the PGA of the United States had originated, financed, and made big advertising had spread internationally. There was no question that the PGA of America was the source of this multi-million-dollar miracle in modern sport.

When they got stirred up by American tournament promotion, the Scots put on bigger and showier golf circuses during the British Open and the Ryder Cup matches than anybody else. A unique holiday spirit pervades the many thousands who seat themselves on the rolling sandy rises to watch the play in the tufted-heather-and-gorse grassy amphitheater below as the surf breaks languidly on nearby shores. Exhibitions of golf merchandise and other goods are held in the canvas cities that fringe the clubhouse, and plenty to eat and drink is provided in other colorful tents close by. The first big exhibition tent at a major British golf event was put up by *Golf Monthly* to promote British golf-playing equipment, apparel, and sundries. It became a popular feature of the Open Championship, served British professionals buying for their shops and themselves, and was also open to the public. *Golf Monthly*'s tent at the British Open was doing volume selling long before the PGA Merchandise Show was begun.

The World Cup international professional tournament of the International Golf Association, when played at Buenos Aires in 1970, also presented gallery sideshows in attractive small tents of uniform size where makers of golf

Cliff Roberts. PGA, photo by Hal Swiggett

term a colorful character, but he is so great at running a tournament that he doesn't need to be showy. In various other activities, mainly that of running his investment business, he is also highly successful. In no respect is he deliberately conspicuous. Roberts and Bob Jones were strong among the earliest evangelists of Dwight D. Eisenhower for President, and Eisenhower died a rich man, probably due in no small degree to investment advice given him by Roberts. He is a canny, cautious party not addicted to bubbling over with confidences, as golf writers are reminded every year when they try to learn the attendance and financial score on the Masters.

The Augusta National Golf Club's course was born of a desire to have a club for congenial amateur golfing notables who'd be hosts to a major tournament annually. Hence, the course was designed to be pleasant for members, adjustable to testing expert professionals and amateurs, and, uniquely, as a course that gave spectators better opportunities and better treatment than they had ever had at a big tournament before. The small clubhouse couldn't handle many guests, but outside facilities for food and drink service were provided, and the toilets are considerably above the general standard. The prices for food and drink at stands outside and in the clubhouse during the Masters are moderate, and the conveniently located large parking areas are free.

The annual spring flower show is also free. The Masters, on the site of a famed horticultural nursery, is an unusually beautiful course with superior design and layout of the holes. The mounds and stands as comfortable observation points are also superior to those anywhere else. And it all stems

goods and other merchandise of interest to free-spending golfers was displayed.

In the United States the closest approach to the happy sporting air of a British Open played on the grand if somewhat bleak courses of Scotland is at Augusta, but the Masters is a far cry behind. It's played on a magnificent course, usually perfectly groomed, and staged in a garden. The Masters spectators—even the children—are the most knowledgeable of American galleries. And there is no denying that Clifford Roberts is the most successful golf tournament planner and manager of all time. He is hardly what anyone would

Lee Trevino. AG

Bobby Mitchell. AG

Tommy Aaron. AG

George Archer. AG

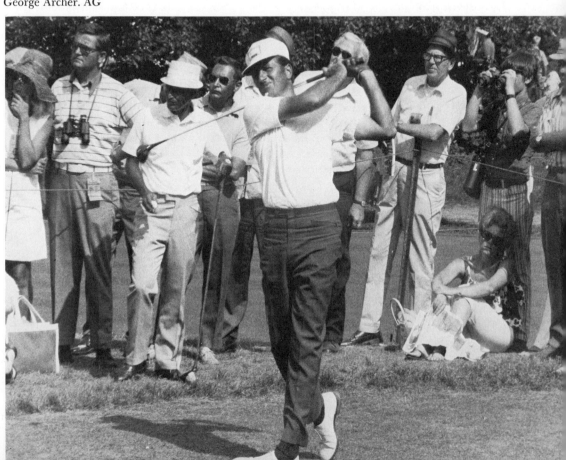

from the foresight of Jones, president of the club, and Roberts, chairman of the Masters tournament committee, with the collaboration of architects Dr. Alister Mackenzie, Robert Trent Jones, George Cobb, and George Fazio.

Even with this consideration the Masters' tournament attendance was getting jammed until Roberts decided that not many more than 20,000 people a day could be handled, so series badges (now at $25 each) and daily tickets on sale at the gates for $10 each, are limited. Those who haven't got tickets are out of luck, but those who have get the same sort of treatment Roberts himself expects for cash, and if that isn't acceptable, then they can see part of the beautiful show on television, since, beginning in 1969, the local TV blackout on the Masters was lifted.

The curtain raiser of the Masters—the field's competitive play on the interesting par-3 course designed by George Cobb—for years has replaced the instruction exhibition and clinic formerly presented the Wednesday before the Masters starts. It gets more of a gallery than many tournament circuit events get on a good day.

Statistics also attest to the Masters's impressive credentials. PGA championships in five cities during 1966 through 1970 averaged 66,000 attendance for the four-day affairs, even with all the high-pressure ticket-selling drives that could be devised, but the USGA's annual report of Open admission revenue indicates that the Masters, which puts on no ticket sales campaign—merely a form letter advising that tickets are available—is the biggest money show in golf.

On the basis of "class," in every way there's no doubt of the Masters's priority. Even the Masters TV commercials —owing to Roberts's standard of quality and possibly his muscle with big-business connections—are on a considerably higher financial, social, and intellectual level than is normal for television sports programs.

Despite Roberts's control over television at the Masters, it certainly was TV's demand for attention that accounted for the hurry up—hurry up—hurry up that stampeded Roberto De Vicenzo away before he was able to check his scorecard carefully in the 1968 Masters, which resulted in the clouded victory of a very able golfer, Bob Goalby. After that lamentable mishap, which was caused by the television boys' taking over a tournament that the press had nursed into its elevated rating, Roberts got back on the job of allowing an even break for the reporters, whose copy was remembered long after the television commercials were forgotten.

Roberts and Jones had supplied at the Masters the most convenient, practical, and pleasant press facilities for coverage of any major sports event, and the TV crowd had it better than at any other golf tournament. They figured that Roberts was part of the package deal, so they didn't refer to him in the classic case of the regrettable De Vicenzo blunder. But nobody makes that mistake twice, especially Clifford Roberts.

Japan Golf Association officials, other prominent businessman golfers in that nation, and veteran Japanese professionals admit that the tremendous golf boom in that country is the direct result of the PGA's American promotion. That push started in 1935 when Robert E. Harlow, then the PGA's Tournament Bureau manager, got the organization to finance a series of coast-to-coast

Fred Corcoran. PGA, photo by Hal Swiggett

ment prizes as big as the United States, Japanese men and women professionals are factors in worldwide competition, and Japanese manufacturers are selling balls and other golf equipment in the United States and Europe.

Fred Corcoran, who succeeded Harlow as the PGA Tournament Bureau manager, was also a power in the promotion of golf in Japan. When he became tournament manager of the International Golf Association, he awarded two of the IGA professional tournaments to Japan, with pros from thirty-eight nations competing. And Japan's victory in the first of these gave golf another terrific boost there.

In any case, the influence of those pioneer missionaries—the immigrant Scottish professionals we described earlier who made up the dedicated, benevolent, and clannish groups that eventually evolved into the Professional Golfers' Association of America—extended into the farthest reaches of world golf. Even in that stately old cathedral of the game, the clubhouse of the Royal and Ancient Golf Club of St. Andrews, whence issued the holy writ accepted as law by golfers (barring a few exceptions in the United States), the observation and counsel of the PGA of America were heeded.

exhibitions for six Japanese professionals. Bob Harlow never got to see Japan, but because of his imagination, persistence, and energy, on top of the golf promotion techniques he'd learned as Walter Hagen's manager, the American PGA can take bows for the fantastic growth of the game in Japan. And he also made it possible for American professionals to take large sums from Japan in tourney purses, exhibition money, and architectural fees. Today in Japan golf club memberships at top clubs can cost as much as $25,000, Japanese tournaments are offering tourna-

Because of its members' close contact with all golfers and its own religious regard for the traditionally high principles of the game, through the years the United States Golf Association found that the PGA was of great help in getting the right answers to golf's problems of self-control. Right from the professional organization's founding, the USGA relied on it to develop the National Open into the ideal example of Open championship competition in any sport. For helpful com-

Al Geiberger. AG

Julius Boros accepting the World's Championship trophy after defeating Cary Middlecoff (right) in 1952. AG

Art Wall, Jr. AG

Billy Casper. PGA

Palmer, and Jack Nicklaus in taking courses as they come and how this can favorably direct the futures of younger tournament professionals.

The story concerns Tony Lema, whose bright career was tragically cut short in a plane crash. He had the right idea about course criticism. After he had listened to his manager at the time, Fred Corcoran, describe the Old Course at St. Andrews prior to the British Open of 1964, he said, "Why tell me all those things, Fred? I'm a player, not a golf course architect." Then Tony Lema went on to win that championship. He knew what even the average golfer seems to be aware of early in the game—it's the nature of golf to have courses differ. They are not standard, as are baseball diamonds, football fields, basketball courts, ice hockey rinks, or distances in track, field, and

ment on the rules of the game and the complex subject of a possible uniform ball for worldwide use by amateurs and professionals, the PGA also proved to be a valuable preliminary research group. However, the tournament specialists in the United States had not qualified themselves as experts on all phases of the game for the amateurs whose money supported them. Yet the amateurs presumed that the tourney journeymen were so proficient they could play on any turf of local standard and with any ball of specifications acceptable to the resident amateurs.

Which brings to mind an appropriate story about a famous golfer with color, charm, and the right attitude. First, since we've mentioned professionals who want the course either to suit or favor their games or particular whims, we want to cite the excellent examples of Bill Casper, Arnold

Arnold Palmer.

Jack Nicklaus. PGA

teurs played the same game. If the journeyman pros played one game, and the amateurs another that was based on stricter requirements, then they would lose the common denominator that joined the specialists with the many millions of amateur participants who'd made golf tournament play richly rewarding to the professionals.

Neither professional nor amateur golf organizations have ever made any scientific studies on the relationship between the time the golfer takes on varying lengths of putts and the accuracy of the putting itself. The few and rather casual investigations that have been made indicate that most of the preventable loss of time that decreases the popularity and increases the cost of golf occurs on the greens. Experienced amateurs say that the slow putting procedure of playing pros misleads ama-

swimming competitions. It's not *where* you play but *how*.

Although slow play was a problem in golf long before the PGA built the tournament circuit, television seriously aggravated the offense in the United States and presented a bad professional habit around the golf world. Attempts to make play less tedious were resisted by professionals who claimed their livelihood depended on a pace of play slow enough for their temperaments. The proposals of American tournament players to change the Rules of Golf were advanced on the same grounds—that golf was a business to them and not the pleasure it was to amateurs. After all, a missed putt could cost them thousands of dollars!

But the amateurs and some clear-sighted tournament professionals recognized that tournament golf differed from other pro sports in that millions of ama-

Tony Lema. PGA

teurs who are betting more than they can afford on their "friendly" games. Hence, they are psychologically compelled to be fanatically careful, and only succeed in being all but inert.

Since we've dwelt at length on the history of the Professional Golfers' Association and professional golfers themselves, both the specialists and home pros, it's only appropriate to give their amateur counterparts their due. It's no exaggeration to say that the extent, accomplishment, and efficiency of amateur association work in golf are unequaled by anything comparable in other sports. The United States Golf Association and the Western Golf Association are the major amateur bodies, with men's, women's, and seniors' amateur organizations active in many states and larger territories. There is remarkably close and practically spontaneous cooperation between sectional groups, and the USGA and the WGA are probably the best operated of all nationwide organizations in amateur sports.

While there are no conflicts between them, it wasn't always peaches and cream. What differences there were mainly involved rules; the WGA abolished the stymie and accepted the steel shaft before the USGA. And there was what could be called a feudal period when the Westerners (as people west of Pittsburgh were termed in the 1890's when the USGA was a pup) felt they were being patronized by the USGA's Eastern collegians. But it was an unfair charge. The time, expense, and responsibility involved in being a member of the USGA Executive Committee eliminated many candidates for the positions. If a socially prominent member of the Championship Committee was accused of being a Grade A snob of the USGA hierarchy, he must have cringed at man's inhumanity to man and fel-

low golfer. This same committeeman probably had to participate in a meeting that dragged on until midnight just to satisfy the demands of some faraway golfers, then perhaps belted down a couple of nightcaps and left a 6:00 A.M. call so he could go out on the course with the superintendent to set the cups in positions that were sure to be violently criticized by some contestant who arose at a leisurely hour to meet an 11:00 A.M. starting time. An official's life is ever thus.

Obviously the sniping between the West and East persisted, with the latter having the upper hand in the USGA hierarchy, because not until 1911, when Silas J. Strawn, a Chicago corporation lawyer, was elected as the ninth president of the association, did the USGA have a head man outside of the New York City and Boston areas. Strawn served in 1911 and 1912; then Frank L. Wood of the Denver Country Club was president in 1915 and 1916. The next "Westerners" to head the USGA were J. Frederick Byers of Pittsburgh, 1922–23; William C. Fownes, Jr., of Philadelphia, 1926–27; and Melvin A. Traylor, a Chicago banker, 1928.

Then not until 1942–43 was there another USGA president elected from the Indian country far west of Wall Street. He was George W. Blossom, whose family had been active in golf since the game had been introduced in the Chicago area. Blossom was an Ivy Leaguer and a member of Onwentsia, one of the oldest clubs around the Windy City. He launched an effective soft-sell campaign to persuade the Nominating Committee to unknot the old school ties and to identify the association as nationwide in every way. Soon the USGA began to broaden with the geography and the times. In 1948–49 the president was Fielding Wallace of Augusta, Georgia; in 1950–51, James D. Standish, Jr., of Detroit; in 1952–53, Totton P. Heffelfinger of Minneapolis; in 1956–57, Richard S. Tufts of Pinehurst in North Carolina; in 1958–59, John D. Ames of Chicago; in 1960–61, John G. Clook of Long Beach, California; and in 1962–63, John W. Winters, Jr., of Tulsa.

It wasn't until 1964–65, when Clarence Benedict of Winged Foot was elected, that the presidency returned to New York. He was followed in 1966–67 by William Ward Foshay of Greenwich, Connecticut. Then Hordon W. Hardin of St. Louis was elected for 1968–69. Philip H. Strubling, who was USGA president in 1970–71, was the second USGA head from the Philadelphia area. He was followed by Lynford Lardner of Milwaukee, who died in 1973 while USGA president and was succeeded by Harton S. Semple of Pittsburgh.

Harton S. Semple, USGA President 1974-75. GH

The appointment of USGA Nominating Committee representatives from all parts of the country (men who are experienced with golf affairs and the private, daily-fee, and public courses in their areas) assures members that the USGA concerns itself with the National Open championships for men and women, the National Amateur championships for men, women, boys and girls, and senior men and women. The Walker Cup Championship between U.S. and British men amateurs, the Curtis Cup matches between U.S. and British teams, and international contests between American men's and women's teams and those of other nations are also handled by the USGA.

The Rules of Golf are made and administered by the USGA in almost complete agreement with the Royal and Ancient Golf Club of St. Andrews, which is the rules authority for the rest of the golfing world. Only one major difference exists between the USGA and the R & A about the rules—this concerns the specifications of golf balls. The R & A ball shall weigh not more than 1.62 ounces, and the size shall be not less than 1.62 inches in diameter. The USGA ball's weight is the same as that of the R & A's—"not greater than 1.62 ounces." The USGA size specification is "not less than 1.68 inches in diameter." The American ball also has a velocity restriction when tested on a machine the USGA had engineers devise.

In recent years, contestants in international competitions have been allowed to play either the USGA or the R & A ball, and there has been no significant effect on the results. Considering the wide variations in turf and climatic conditions of golf play and the wide range of abilities of players, it is remarkable that golf's top authorities should come so close to agreement on a universally acceptable ball. The main fear of the ruling authorities is that perhaps 5 percent of the world's players may hit the ball so far that the cost of real estate required for the long hitters' games might retard the growth of the game. On the other side are the 95 percent of golfers who wish they could hit the ball farther.

The official worry about the danger of long hitting of the golf ball has aroused discussions about the potential-distance factor inherent in varying shaft materials: hickory, steel of various alloys, aluminum, and graphite. Watering of fairways and rough has had more effect on the distance of golf balls than any other factor, but that isn't mentioned because it reduces the roll of the ball. The achievement of the USGA and the R & A in codifying practical and acceptable rules that preserve the harshly self-disciplined nature of golf is almost miraculous when you consider the difficulty of determining rules for fair play when the courses and weather conditions vary as much as they do in golf.

The fundamental philosophy of golf rules is that you are playing against yourself. If you are tough enough to want to play a tough game, then you've won something. Cheat and you cheat yourself, first and foremost. However, Hord Hardin, for thirteen years on the Executive Committee of the USGA and eventually its president, said that in all his years of service with the association he had never heard even one request to make golf *harder*. The complainers always wanted to make the game *easier,* a pretty good indication that the rules made it a challenging game.

During the tournament-pro restless-ness that brought on the PGA civil war and the division of the tournament and home players, several attempts were made by the tournament specialists to ease the rules. These efforts were regarded unfavorably by the amateurs, who argued that for the big purses the tournament pros were getting, they ought to be willing to play by the same strict rules amateurs observed (or agreed that they should) when they got up before daybreak and stood in line at public courses on frosty mornings. Further, many public-course amateurs say the television tournament pros play a soft game and are allowed to lift the ball from tough spots, whereas two gentlemen sportsmen playing for money on a public course play the ball as it lies —or else.

The rules, tournament, and general public service work of the USGA are enough to identify it as a great body of sports public service, but it does even more. Within the USGA is a department that has had a stronger effect on American living than any other operation in world sports. This is the USGA Green Section. Not only does every fine golf course in the United States owe something to the USGA Green Section, but so do those in other countries. Thanks to the Green Section—for keeping down dust and repair costs—are due from every owner of a beautiful lawn, from people who play on the grass of parks, from those who, perhaps unthinkingly, enjoy the beauty of the grass that borders industrial areas and roadways and airport runways—even from those who get some heart's ease in seeing the green grass blankets of cemeteries.

It was probably in the early 1900's that men looked out at their yards and asked themselves: "Why can't I have a lawn that looks like a golf course?" At that time, the golf course was established as the top quality of American turf and was given and accepted responsibility of doing more for the beautification of the United States than any other sports endeavor. As a consequence, the Green Section sprang up from an idea of the green chairman of the Inverness Club, Toledo, where the 1920 Open was played. The green chairman and the greenkeeper were seeking advice on how to prepare their course for the foremost national championship. They called upon the USGA (which didn't have the answer), and a member of the USGA Executive Committee got interested.

The result was that the U.S. Department of Agriculture was brought in; then the Green Section was formed and hired its own men and women, starting with John Monteith. On a small budget, which never has been increased in proportion to their service, the Green Section men coordinated state agricultural college experts, greenkeepers (later called golf course superintendents), and manufacturers and their scientists and turf nurserymen in a job that has no parallel in sports or industry in the far-reaching aesthetic and practical effects of their united efforts. New strains of turf grass developed while John Monteith, Fred Grau, and Alexander Radko were Green Section technical heads and have improved golf-playing conditions and the beauty of the American outdoors far beyond the comprehension of city men who don't know the finer points of agriculture. Surely golf grass must be one of the most intensively cultivated and harvested of all crops. And the prominent businessmen on the boards of the National Golf Fund, the PGA annual fund-raising operation, and members of the PGA Advisory Committee have

said they wished their own industries showed the research coordination between sectional and national authorities reported by Alexander Radko, the Green Section research coordinator.

The Green Section operates for around $330,000 a year in a normal year like 1973. In that year, most of the expense was paid for by subscribers to the Green Section consulting service, which had its men traveling 360,000 miles to care for the 950 subscribing clubs and to attend sixty-nine golf turf conferences. The Green Section's net cost to the USGA in 1973 was about $40,000, or a little less than $10 per club member of the association. Not only has the Green Section served a great purpose in the United States, it has also done the same in Scotland, England, Japan, Canada, Mexico, and Argentina.

Another golf organization within an organization shares its revenue with the Green Section. This is the National Golf Fund of the PGA. In twenty-one years the National Golf Fund has raised about $2 million for education, Green Section research, veterans' hospitals, amputees' therapy, and other charitable and welfare causes, with only a minor fraction of the grants going to PGA educational or relief funds. And within golf there are also associations of daily-fee-course owners, the associations of golf ball and club manufacturers, and the American Society of Golf Course Architects.

The Golf Course Superintendents' Association, which began to develop as a greenkeepers' organization after golf course maintenance became too much of a job for one man, has been enormously valuable to this country. It has established standards of turf grass and home landscaping with the beautiful exhibits that golf course superintendents have provided in the grass, flowers, trees and shrubs, and roads around golf courses. These men are probably the foremost "business poets" expressing themselves today. Their association, the Golf Course Superintendents' Association of America, has chapters in every major golfing area in the United States. On Mondays, about once a month, the superintendents meet at various clubs, give the host club superintendent the benefit of their experience frankly (and free), play golf, listen to authorities lecture, then go home. It's been a day on their own time and often at their own expense. What else in American business can compare to this self-help and employers' service program of the superintendents? But very few golfers, club officials, and owners know about this program, which has improved golf course conditions tremendously and also saved millions in golf course operating expenses.

From its beginning, the Club Managers' Association had managers who had received sound basic training at the early hotel and restaurant schools, especially at Cornell and Michigan State. Today, the managers' organization has a broad and effective educational program that features a series of workshops conducted in various areas so that managers can bring their own problems for consultation. The Club Managers' Association was the first to have its classroom, correspondence, and on-the-job training correlated for examinations that would certify adequate, experienced club managers. The superintendents' and professionals' organizations followed in formally certifying competent specialists.

As for golf itself, it is so much a microcosm of life that the home professional naturally gets blamed for what isn't his fault. A member comes in with a score much higher than it should have been, and in some mysterious way the fault often is vaguely supposed to be that of the pro. Perhaps that is one of those things best explained by the remark of a loser who confessed, "I took that beating as a man should—I blamed it on my wife."

The home pro can also read about one of his associates in the show business department of his profession winning a $40,000 first prize for four days' work and still take pride in being one of the dedicated thousands in professional golf who created and kept thriving the opulent trade of golf tournaments. And there may come a day when today's winner has three-putted himself out of the headlines and had enough of the rocky path of glory. Then the faded star will also be content to worry about a member's duck hook instead of his own, and feel as though he has been crowned with high praise when he hears a member say, "This guy is the best pro the club has ever had."

For the weary home professional, there is always home work to be done. He gets out a correspondence file and begins his unpaid job as a PGA sectional official. He telephones amateur friends and golf writers about the PGA Junior Championship, or the PGA Ladies, or the PGA Seniors, or some other pleasant pro-am service he has been assigned to manage. He smiles as he looks at the stack of papers and recalls how he used to ask himself: "What has the PGA ever done for me?"

The years have taught the observant and thoughtful golf professional that the PGA, somewhat like Providence, works in mysterious ways its wonders to perform. Yet the topflight pro who gets testimonial money from a sportswear manufacturer is totally unaware that it was the infant PGA that insisted on a high standard of grooming among its members. When there were complaints that some of the first American professionals were attired in a manner unbecoming to ladies and gentlemen prominent in American society and business, correction in the ranks was prompt. Soon the American professionals, foreign-born and home-bred, were wearing clothing made by the smartest British sports tailors and outfitters. And pretty soon the club members found themselves following the professionals' fashion lead.

But the imported tweeds proved too heavy and bulky, so textile manufacturers in the United States started to make lightweight materials for men's and women's wear at country clubs. From that time and those places, the new sun of American sports fashions began to rise. "What's the PGA done for me?" is a question that the textile makers and the men's and women's clothing manufacturers never ask, but an accurate answer could be given: "The PGA members revolutionized your materials, designs, and colors."

Road builders, automobile manufacturers, and real-estate men, of course, would never ask: "What's the PGA done for me?" Looking backward to the first decade or so of the twentieth century, there were summer residences out in the country where active, forward-looking citizens established golf courses with simple little buildings that passed for clubhouses. Golf was a fad that might easily have passed, but the enthusiasm and personality of the young professional on the job made the club a fixture in the community; and with the club there to stay, people built homes near it, good roads were built, and club members bought the most desirable automobiles to travel on those roads.

Golf's professionals probably exer-cised an influence in American life far surpassing the effect that paid or unpaid sports personnel elsewhere had ever achieved. But the American golf professional himself never realized his indirect influence on better living in this country. He was content to mind his own business, which was that of helping others to enjoy their lives more. And that's a grand career.

Cold analysis, then, shows that the PGA has been an astonishing successful exhibit of self-government in a huge and peculiar business run by men not particularly trained or experienced in extensive commercial responsibilities. The American golf professional is a free soul and a free agent. He doesn't need or want the sort of regimentation and command endured by the professional baseball, football, basketball, and hockey player. His PGA is of the golf professionals, by the golf professionals, and for the golf professionals in a field of sports public service unique in all this world.

The PGA keeps fresh the spirit and the work of a glorious little group of sports evangelists of yesterday. Those pioneers brought from the shorelands of home a gift of health and delight and escape from the sorry scheme of things. They gave the game of a lifetime to the land of their adoption. These missionaries of a sport were a rare breed of men. They inspired and taught and led the younger men who honored golf by serving it well.

The founding fathers of the PGA did many things no others in professional sports had done. Among these exceptional contributions was a term describing them that has become an accolade of the highest order. It is a term given with respect and affection to a man in any field of human endeavor. It was first an honor paid by golfers to a veteran whose able and faithful service year in and year out had made him one of the family. He was a man who went into the American lexicon as an "old pro."

In other sports, professions, trades, arts, and sciences, the tribute to the pioneer golfer is echoed and a man stands high among his fellows when he earns the title of nobility in golf, "old pro."

APPENDIX

I. A Summary of the Aims of the PGA

The objects of the Association shall be to elevate the standards of the Professional Golfer's vocation; to promote interest in the game of golf; to protect the mutual interest of its members; to hold meetings and tournaments for the benefit of its members; to assist deserving unemployed members to obtain a position; to institute a benevolent fund for the relief of deserving members; and to effect any other object which may be determined from time to time by the Association.

Code of Ethics. The name of "Professional Golfer" must be a synonym and pledge of honor, service, and fair dealing.

His professional integrity, fidelity to the game of golf, and a sense of his great responsibility to employers and employees, manufacturers and clients, and to his brother Professionals transcend thought of material gain in the motives of the true Professional Golfer.

In the fulfillment of the purpose to which it is dedicated, the Association enjoins its membership to rigid observance of this Code of Ethics.

APPENDIX

II. Requirements for Membership in the PGA, 1975

Section 1. DEFINITIONS

(a) The term "recognized golf club or course" shall refer to a golf club or course which has at least nine holes and which is fully equipped to teach or demonstrate the use of all types of golf equipment and includes a golf shop adequate for the display and sale of golf equipment and apparel.

(b) In order to be considered recognized, a Par 3 golf course must consist of no less than nine holes and a driving range, have a minimum hole length of 55 yards and have a total yardage of at least 1,000 yards for nine holes or 2,000 yards for eighteen holes, have at least fourteen acres in total course area exclusive of the clubhouse, golf shop and parking areas, be entirely planted in grass except that it may provide artificial tee mats, and have a professional golf shop located on the course.

(c) The term "golf professional" shall apply to a person who owns and operates or supervises and directs a golf shop at a recognized golf club or course and engages in or supervises the teaching of golf at such facility.

(d) The term "assistant golf professional" shall mean a person regularly employed by a golf professional in the category of teacher or shop assistant.

(e) The term "Tournament Player" shall refer to those members of the Association or Approved Tournament Players who have participated in the minimum number of tournaments to quality for Voting Membership in the Tournament Players Division, or have been among the 25 leading players as determined by the Association in such Tournaments in the preceding calendar year; or who have been members of a PGA of America Ryder Cup Team, PGA, U.S.G.A., British Open or Masters Champions, current or former leading money or point winners or Vardon Trophy winners.

(f) The term "Approved Tournament Player" shall refer to persons who are not members of the Association but who have been granted permission to participate in PGA co-sponsored or approved tournaments.

(g) The Board of Control, which shall have control over all membership matters, shall be composed of the Secretary of the Association, who shall be Chairman, and two members of the Association appointed by the President who are not members of the Executive Committee.

Section 2.   ELIGIBILITY

In order to be eligible to apply for, or be reelected to, membership in the Association an applicant must:

(a) Be a golf professional or be employed as an assistant golf professional to a Class "A" member who is a golf professional as hereinabove defined in Section 1(c), or an Approved Tournament Player.

(b) Have accumulated at least 32 credits, which shall be awarded in the following manner;

(1) One full credit for each month of employment as an assistant golf professional to a Class "A" member.

(i) Experience as an assistant golf professional gained prior to January 1, 1967 may be counted even though the assistant was not in the employ of a PGA member.

(ii) Experience as an assistant golf professional gained between January 1, 1967 and September 1, 1970 may be counted only if it is gained while in the employ of a Class "A" member who is employed at a recognized club or course.

(iii) Experience as an assistant golf professional between September 1, 1970 and November 16, 1972 may be counted only if it is gained while in the employ of a Master Professional, Head Professional or Associate Professional.

(iv) After November 16, 1972 experience as an assistant golf professional may be counted only if it is gained while in the employ of a Class "A" member who is a golf professional as hereinabove defined in Section 1(c).

(v) Credit for experience gained either as a golf professional or an assistant golf professional after May 1, 1970 will be given only for time served after an application for Apprentice status has been filed.

(vi) Credits toward membership may not be gained as an operator or supervisor of a driving range or as an assistant to an operator or supervisor of a driving range.

(2) One credit for each month of employment as a non-member golf professional prior to November 16, 1972 and also after that date if such professional has 18 or more credits. After November 16, 1972, one-half credit for each month of employment as a non-member golf professional with less than 18 credits; however, non-member golf professionals who work a full season in golf, as defined by their respective Sections, shall earn a minimum of six credits annually until they attain 32 credits toward membership.

(i) Those registered in the Apprentice program prior to November 16, 1972 shall receive one full credit for each month of employment as a non-member golf professional regardless of the number of credits accumulated.

(3) For Approved Tournament Players, one-half credit for playing at least 36 holes in a PGA co-sponsored or approved tournament (including tournaments on the Latin American and Caribbean Tours).

(i) No credit shall be given for participation in qualifying rounds only of such tournaments.

(ii) No person shall accumulate more than 12 credits in any 12-month period of time.

(4) Six credits for successful completion

of an approved PGA training course held prior to November 15, 1967.

(5) Eight credits for having a Bachelor's Degree from an accredited four-year college or university and four credits for having a degree from an accredited two-year college (the latter to be applied to those who subsequently are awarded a Bachelor's Degree but not to be counted twice).

(c) Be a citizen of the United States of America.

(d) Be over 21 years of age.

(e) Have a high school education or its equivalent.

(f) Have demonstrated that he can play a creditable game of golf by making no more than the score indicated below for 36 holes on a course rated as shown (effective April 1, 1974):

Score	Course Rating
151	68.0
152	68.5
153	69.0
154	69.5
155	70.0
156	70.5
157	71.0
158	71.5
159	72.0
160	72.5
161	73.0

(g) Have successfully completed a PGA approved training course.

(h) Pass a standardized written and an oral examination.

(i) Not have been eligible for PGA membership more than five years, unless such time limit is waived by the Board of Control.

(j) Otherwise fully meet the terms and conditions of this Constitution.

Insofar as experience requirements are concerned, the following additional rules shall apply:

(a) Experience may be cumulative over a period of years, but no experience may be counted unless it is on a full-time basis and unless the person claiming such experience is engaged in the golf profession as a major occupation at the time the experience is gained.

(b) No person shall be eligible for membership in the Association while a member of the military service on a career basis, and experience in golf activities acquired during military service shall not be counted toward membership requirements.

(c) Any golf professional or assistant golf professional who applies for reinstatement to the status of amateur, or who participates in any amateur events shall lose all service or experience credit acquired previous to such application or participation.

(d) Under no circumstances shall any person be eligible to apply for membership in the Association in less than 40 months after he first becomes employed in the golf profession or is granted the status of Approved Tournament Player, except that applicants who have a Bachelor's Degree from an accredited four-year college or university may apply after being employed in the golf profession for 32 months or having been an Approved Tournament Player for 32 months and applicants who have a degree from an accredited two-year college may apply after being employed in the golf profession for 36 months or having been an Approved Tournament Player for 36 months.

(e) Anyone who has been employed in the golf profession but has had a break in such employment for a period of five years or more during which he was not employed in a capacity for which his experience could be counted toward membership in the Association (except for breaks in employment resulting from attending school on a fulltime basis or being in the military service) must meet all current requirements for membership and must have attended all approved PGA training courses after returning to the golf profession following such a break in employment.

APPENDIX

III. Officers of the PGA

A. Officers 1975

Executive Director
MARK H. COX

President
William Clarke
Hillendale
Country Club
Phoenix, Maryland

Treasurer
Donald E. Padgett
Green Hills
Golf & Country Club
Selma, Indiana

Secretary
Henry C. Poe
Vanity Fair Golf Club
Monroeville, Alabama

Honorary President
Warren Orlick
Tam O'Shanter
Country Club
Orchard Lake,
Michigan

District No.	Term Expires in Nov. of	Vice-Presidents
1	1974	JOHNNY GAUCAS Van Schaick Country Club Cohoes, New York
2	1974	FRANK CARDI The Apawamis Club Rye, New York
3	1976	HARRY A. BERRIER Gatlinburg Country Club Gatlinburg, Tennessee
4	1975	FRANK SOCASH Elmira Country Club Elmira, New York
5	1974	DON SOPER Royal Oak Golf Club Royal Oak, Michigan
6	1976	HUBBY HABJAN Onwentsia Club, Lake Forest, Illinois
7	1976	AL CHANDLER Columbia Country Club Columbia, Missouri
8	1975	JOSEPH AUGUST Elmwood Country Club Marshalltown, Iowa
9	1975	JOHN DIFLOURE Las Vegas Municipal Golf Course Las Vegas, Nevada
10	1974	GORDON W. LEISHMAN Idle Hour Country Club Lexington, Kentucky
11	1976	LYLE WEHRMAN Sunol Valley Golf Club Sunol, California
12	1976	DICK FORESTER Bear Creek Golf World Houston, Texas
13	1974	CHARLES E. FICKER Tequesta Country Club Jupiter, Florida
TPD	1974	LIONEL P. HEBERT 301 White Oak Drive Lafayette, Louisiana

515

B. History of the Officers of the PGA

Presidents of the PGA
(by Section)

1917–1919	Robert White, Metropolitan
1920	Jack Mackie, Metropolitan
1921–1926	George Sargent, Southeastern
1927–1930	Alex Pirie, Metropolitan
1931–1932	Charles Hall, Central New York
1933–1939	George Jacobus, New Jersey
1940–1941	Tom Walsh, Illinois
1942–1948	Ed Dudley, Colorado
1949–1951	Joe Novak, Southern California
1952–1954	Horton Smith, Eastern Missouri
1955–1957	Harry Moffitt, Northern Ohio
1958–1960	Harold Sargent, Southeastern
1961–1963	Lou Strong, Illinois
1964–1965	Warren Cantrell, Texas
1966–1968	Max Elbin, Middle Atlantic
1969–1970	Leo Fraser, Philadelphia
1971–1972	Warren Orlick, Michigan
1973–1974	William Clarke, Middle Atlantic
1975–	Henry Poe, Dixie

The First Officers

The first PGA slate of officers, elected at the first annual meeting held in the Radisson Hotel, Minneapolis, June 26, 1916, included Robert White, President; James Maiden, Vice-President; George Fotheringham, Vice-President, and Herbert Strong, Secretary-Treasurer.

PGA Seniors' Presidents

1937–1938	*Grange Alves
1938–1939	*George Sargent
1939–1940	*Dave Ogilvie
1940–1941	*W. C. Sherwood
1941–1945	*Alex Cunningham
1945–1946	*W. H. (Bert) Way
1946–1947	*Willie Ogg
1947–1948	*George Norrie
1948–1949	Charles H. Mayo
1949–1950	Charles Lorms
1950–1951	*William C. Gordon
1951–1952	*Joe Donato
1952–1953	*Eddie Williams
1953–1954	Otto Hardt
1954–1955	Hugh Bancroft
1955–1956	Marty Cromb
1956–1957	*Carroll T. MacMaster
1957–1958	*John C. Watson
1958–1959	*Willie Whalen
1959–1960	George Ferrier
1960–1961	Jack Ryan
1961–1962	Ralph E. Beach
1962–1963	*Horton Smith
1963–1964	*Bill Mitchell
1964–1965	Leonard Schmutte
1965–1966	Cliff Good
1966–1967	Harry Moffitt
1967–1968	Paul Erath
1968–1969	Johnny Gaucas
1969–1970	Johnny Vasco
1970–1971	Denny McGonegal
1971–1972	Harry Pezzullo
1972–1973	Frank Socash
1973–1974	Ray Hill
1974–1975	Don Soper

*Deceased.

APPENDIX

IV. Growth of the PGA Membership 1929-1974

1929	2,022		1952	3,076
1930	1,100		1953	3,213
1931	1,363		1954	3,400
1932	1,228		1955	3,598
1933	1,009		1956	3,798
1934	1,216		1957	3,979
1935	1,516		1958	4,200
1936	1,800		1959	4,500
1937	1,818		1960	4,670
1938	1,736		1961	4,807
1939	1,813		1962	5,050
1940	1,900		1963	5,124
1941	2,041		1964	5,300
1942	1,824		1965	5,500
1943	1,685		1966	5,837
1944	1,723		1967	5,926
1945	1,850		1968	6,272
1946	2,236		1969	6,451
1947	2,400		1970	6,641
1948	2,594		1971	6,779
1949	2,716		1972	6,946
1950	2,869		1973	7,176
1951	2,916		1974	7,392

APPENDIX

V. Summary of PGA Prize Money Over the Years

A. Leading Individual Money Winners 1934–1974

Year	Winner	Amount
1934	Paul Runyan	$ 6,767
1935	Johnny Revolta	9,543
1936	Horton Smith	7,682
1937	Harry Cooper	14,138
1938	Sam Snead	19,534
1939	Henry Picard	10,303
1940	Ben Hogan	10,655
1941	Ben Hogan	18,358
1942	Ben Hogan	13,143
1943	(None compiled)	
1944	Byron Nelson	*37,967
1945	Byron Nelson	*63,335
1946	Ben Hogan	42,556
1947	Jimmy Demaret	27,937
1948	Ben Hogan	32,112
1949	Sam Snead	31,594
1950	Sam Snead	35,759
1951	Lloyd Mangrum	26,089
1952	Julius Boros	37,033
1953	Lew Worsham	34,002
1954	Bob Toski	65,820
1955	Julius Boros	63,122
1956	Ted Kroll	72,836
1957	Dick Mayer	65,835
1958	Arnold Palmer	42,607
1959	Art Wall	53,168
1960	Arnold Palmer	75,263
1961	Gary Player	64,540
1962	Arnold Palmer	81,448
1963	Arnold Palmer	128,230
1964	Jack Nicklaus	113,284
1965	Jack Nicklaus	140,752
1966	Billy Casper	121,945
1967	Jack Nicklaus	188,998
1968	Billy Casper	205,169
1969	Frank Beard	175,223
1970	Lee Trevino	157,037
1971	Jack Nicklaus	244,490
1972	Jack Nicklaus	320,542
1973	Jack Nicklaus	308,362
1974	Johnny Miller	353,021

* Computed in War Bonds.
(Note: Until 1966 computed totals based on "Official Money" only.)

B. PGA Tour Prize Money

(*Compiled from Tournament Bureau records, PGA annual reports, and records of the PGA TPD*)

These winnings include the full year's playing schedule of tournaments approved and co-sponsored by the PGA for migrant players. This does not include PGA winter activities, the Club Professional Championship, or the Ryder Cup biennial matches.

1935	$ 134,700
1936	148,945
1937	163,350
1938	158,000
1939	174,000
1940	160,000
1941	185,000
1942	155,000
1943	No tour
1944	No tour
1945	No tour
1946	454,200
1947	466,000
1948	541,025
1949	474,642
1950	564,372
1951	555,715
1952	654,514
1953	687,316
1954	746,359
1955	930,504
1956	987,632
1957	1,064,420
1958	1,316,015
1959	1,354,597
1960	1,527,849
1961	1,791,816
1962	2,087,770
1963	2,349,102
1964	2,743,465
1965	3,631,301
1966	4,149,991
1967	4,650,661
1968	5,559,097
1969	6,041,697
1970	6,751,523
1971	7,242,976
1972	7,596,749
1973	8,631,205
1974 (Preliminary)	8,111,225

APPENDIX

VI. Summary of the Trophies and Awards of the PGA Over the Years

A. PGA Professional-of-the-Year Award

This award is made annually by the PGA of America in tribute to the working club professional whose total contribution to the game best exemplifies the complete PGA golf professional. Originally suggested by Richard S. Tufts of Pinehurst, N.C., former president of the United States Golf Association, the award embraces a wide range of service including promotion of junior golf, encouragement of ladies' play, service to his club, devotion to the game itself, concern for caddie welfare, promotion of public relations, and service to his community. The winners have included:

1955 BILL GORDON
Tam O'Shanter C.C.
Chicago

1956 HARRY SHEPARD
Mark Twain Community G.C.
Elmira, N.Y.

1957 DUGAN AYCOCK
Lexington C.C.
Lexington, N.C.

1958 HARRY PEZZULLO
Mission Hills G.C.
Northbrook, Ill.

1959 EDDIE DUINO
San Jose C.C.
San Jose, Calif.

1960 WARREN ORLICK
Tam O'Shanter C.C.
Orchard Lake, Mich.

1961 DON PADGETT
Green Hills C.C.
Selma, Ind.

1962 TOM LoPRESTI
Haggin Oaks G.C.
Sacramento, Calif.

1963 BRUCE HERD
Flossmoor C.C.
Flossmoor, Ill.

1964 LYLE WEHRMAN
Merced G. & C.C.
Merced, Calif.

1965 HUBBY HABJAN
Onwentsia Club
Lake Forest, Ill.

1966 BILL STRAUSBAUGH, JR.
Turf Valley C.C.
Ellicott City, Md.

1967 ERNIE VOSSLER
Quail Creek C.C.
Oklahoma City, Okla.

1968 HARDY LOUDERMILK
Oak Hills C.C.
San Antonio, Texas

1969 A. HUBERT SMITH
       Arnold Center C.C.
       Tullahoma, Tenn.
1969 WALLY MUND
       Midland Hills C.C.
       St. Paul, Minn.
1970 GRADY SHUMATE
       Tanglewood G.C.
       Clemmons, N.C.
1971 ROSS COLLINS
       Dallas A.C. C.C.
       Dallas, Texas
1972 HOWARD MORRETTE
       Twin Lakes C.C.
       Kent, Ohio
1973 WARREN SMITH
       Cherry Hills C.C.
       Englewood, Colo.
1974 PAUL HARNEY
       Paul Harney's G.C.
       Hatchville, Mass.

B. PGA Player-of-the-Year

Until 1969, this award was based on a ballot of PGA members and the golf writers and sportscasters on the PGA mailing list. Winner now is determined by a vote of the PGA Executive Committee, which evaluates the nominee's playing record, scoring average, and character. Past winners:

1948 Ben Hogan
1949 Sam Snead
1950 Ben Hogan
1951 Ben Hogan
1952 Julius Boros
1953 Ben Hogan
1954 Ed Furgol
1955 Doug Ford
1956 Jack Burke, Jr.
1957 Dick Mayer
1958 Dow Finsterwald
1959 Art Wall
1960 Arnold Palmer
1961 Jerry Barber
1962 Arnold Palmer
1963 Julius Boros
1964 Ken Venturi
1965 Dave Marr
1966 Billy Casper
1967 Jack Nicklaus
1968 No award made
1969 Orville Moody

1970 Billy Casper
1971 Lee Trevino
1972 Jack Nicklaus
1973 Jack Nicklaus
1974 Johhny Miller

C. PGA Hall of Fame

The PGA Hall of Fame grew out of a discussion among golf writers at the 1940 Masters Tournament. The first twelve nominees, selected at that time, included four amateurs. Several voting formulas have been used and abandoned. After five years of inactivity, the Hall of Fame was revitalized in 1974 with voting privileges extended to a panel of golf writers and others closely identified with·the game.

1940 Willie Anderson
       Tommy Armour
       Jim Barnes
       Chick Evans (am)
       Bob Jones (am)
       Francis Ouimet (am)
       Walter Hagen
       Johnny McDermott
       Gene Sarazen
       Alex Smith
       Jerry Travers (am)
       Walter Travis
1953 Ben Hogan
       Byron Nelson
       Sam Snead
1954 Macdonald Smith
1955 Leo Diegel
1956 Craig Wood
1957 Denny Shute
1958 Horton Smith
1959 Harry Cooper
       Jock Hutchison
       Paul Runyan
1960 Mike Brady
       Jimmy Demaret
       Fred McLeod
1961 Johnny Farrell
       Lawson Little
       Henry Picard
1962 Dutch Harrison
       Olin Dutra
1963 Ralph Guldahl
       Johnny Revolta
1964 Lloyd Mangrum
       Ed Dudley

1965 Vic Ghezzi
1966 Billy Burke
1967 Bobby Cruickshank
1968 Chick Harbert
1969 Chandler Harper
1974 Julius Boros
      Cary Middlecoff

D. Vardon Trophy Averages

The Vardon Trophy, named in honor of the great British golfer Harry Vardon, recognizes the player whose superior consistency is reflected in the lowest strokes-per-round record for the tournament year. A minimum of 80 official tournament rounds is required for eligibility. Previous winners and averages:

1937	Harry Cooper	(Points)
1938	Sam Snead	(Points)
1939	Byron Nelson	(Points)
1940	Ben Hogan	(Points)
1941	Ben Hogan	(Points)
No award made during World War II		
1947	Jimmy Demaret	69.900
1948	Ben Hogan	69.300
1949	Sam Snead	69.370
1950	Sam Snead	69.230
1951	Lloyd Mangrum	70.050
1952	Jackie Burke	70.540
1953	Lloyd Mangrum	70.220
1954	Dutch Harrison	70.410
1955	Sam Snead	69.860
1956	Cary Middlecoff	70.350
1957	Dow Finsterwald	70.300
1958	Bob Rosburg	70.110
1959	Art Wall	70.350
1960	Billy Casper	69.950
1961	Arnold Palmer	68.859
1962	Arnold Palmer	70.271
1963	Billy Casper	70.588
1964	Arnold Palmer	70.010
1965	Billy Casper	70.586
1966	Billy Casper	70.276
1967	Arnold Palmer	70.188
1968	Billy Casper	69.821
1969	Dave Hill	70.344
1970	Lee Trevino	70.642
1971	Lee Trevino	70.275
1972	Lee Trevino	70.891
1973	Bruce Crampton	70.576
1974	Lee Trevino	70.5

E. Ed Dudley Award

This award is made annually by the PGA of America to the low qualifying player in the PGA Tournament Players' Division qualifying test tournament. Winners have included:

1965	John Schlee	(144 holes)
1966	Harry Toscano	(144 holes)
1967	Bobby Cole	(144 holes)
1968 (Spring)	Bob Dickson	(144 holes)
1968 (Fall)	Grier Jones	(144 holes)
1968 (Fall)	Martin Roesink	(144 holes)
1969 (Spring)	Bobby Eastwood	(72 holes)
1969 (Fall)	Doug Olson	(72 holes)
1970	Bob Barbarossa	(72 holes)
1971	Bob Zender	(108 holes)
1972	Larry Stubblefield	(108 holes)
1973	Ben Crenshaw	(144 holes)
1974	Fuzzy Zoeller	(144 holes)

F. Horton Smith Award

In 1964, the Horton Smith Trophy was donated by the PGA National Advisory Committee. It was left to the PGA Executive Committee, acting in conjunction with the screening services of a special Awards Committee, to determine the annual winner after first establishing a basis for the award in 1965. At that time it was decided the award should be made in recognition of a professional whose contribution in the field of professional education is outstanding. Winners include:

1965 EMIL BECK
    Black River C.C.
    Port Huron, Michigan
1966 GENE C. MASON
    Columbia-Edgewater C.C.
    Portland, Oregon
1967 DONALD E. FISCHESSER
    Evansville C.C.
    Evansville, Indiana
1968 R. WILLIAM CLARKE
    Hillendale C.C.
    Phoenix, Maryland
1969 PAUL HAHN
    Miami, Florida

1970 JOE WALSER
    Oklahoma City C.C.
    Oklahoma City, Oklahoma
1971 IRVING SCHLOSS
    Dunedin, Florida
1972 JOHN BUDD
    New Port Richey, Florida

1973 GEORGE AULBACH
    Pecan Valley C.C.
    San Antonio, Texas
1974 BILL HARDY
    Chevy Chase Club
    Chevy Chase, Mayland

APPENDIX

VII. History of PGA Tournaments and Championships

A. The Masters Tournament

Year	Winner	Score	Runner-Up
1934	Horton Smith	284	Craig Wood
1935	*Gene Sarazen (144)	282	Craig Wood (149)
1936	Horton Smith	285	Harry Cooper
1937	Byron Nelson	283	Ralph Guldahl
1938	Henry Picard	285	Ralph Guldahl
1939	Ralph Guldahl	279	Sam Snead
1940	Jimmy Demaret	280	Lloyd Mangrum
1941	Craig Wood	280	Byron Nelson
1942	*Byron Nelson (69)	280	Ben Hogan (70)
1943–1945	No tournament played—World War II		
1946	Herman Keiser	282	Ben Hogan
1947	Jimmy Demaret	281	Byron Nelson
1948	Claude Harmon	279	Cary Middlecoff
1949	Sam Snead	282	Lloyd Mangrum, Johhny Bulla
1950	Jimmy Demaret	283	Jim Ferrier
1951	Ben Hogan	280	Skee Riegel
1952	Sam Snead	286	Jack Burke, Jr.
1953	Ben Hogan	274	Ed Oliver
1954	*Sam Snead (70)	289	Ben Hogan (71)
1955	Cary Middlecoff	279	Ben Hogan
1956	Jack Burke, Jr.	289	Ken Venturi
1957	Doug Ford	283	Sam Snead
1958	Arnold Palmer	284	Doug Ford
1959	Art Wall, Jr.	284	Fred Hawkins

Year	Winner	Score	Runner-Up
1960	Arnold Palmer	282	Ken Venturi
1961	Gary Player	280	Arnold Palmer, Charles Coe
1962	*Arnold Palmer (68)	280	Gary Player (71), Dow Finsterwald (77)
1963	Jack Nicklaus	286	Tony Lema
1964	Arnold Palmer	276	Dave Marr, Jack Nicklaus
1965	Jack Nicklaus	271	Arnold Palmer, Gary Player
1966	*Jack Nicklaus (70)	288	Tommy Jacobs (72), Gay Brewer (78)
1967	Gay Brewer	280	Bobby Nichols
1968	Bob Goalby	277	Roberto de Vicenzo
1969	George Archer	281	George Knudson, Tom Weiskopf
1970	*Billy Casper (69)	279	Gene Littler (74)
1971	Charles Coody	279	Johnny Miller, Jack Nicklaus, Gene Littler
1972	Jack Nicklaus	286	Bruce Crampton, Tom Weiskopf, Bobby Mitchell
1973	Tommy Aaron	283	J. C. Snead
1974	Gary Player	278	Tom Weiskopf, Dave Stockton
1975	Jack Nicklaus	276	Tom Weiskopf, Johnny Miller

* Winner in play-off. Figures in parentheses indicate play-off scores.

B. The U.S. Open Championships

Year	Winner	Score	Runner-Up	Played at
1895	Horace Rawlins	173-36 holes	Willie Dunn	Newport G.C. Newport, R.I.
1896	James Foulis	152-36 holes	Horace Rawlins	Shinnecock Hills G.C. Shinnecock Hills, L.I., N.Y.
1897	Joe Lloyd	162-36 holes	Willie Anderson	Chicago G.C. Wheaton, Ill.
1898	Fred Herd	328-72 holes	Alex Smith	Myopia Hunt Club Hamilton, Mass.
1899	Willie Smith	315	George Low, Val Fitzjohn, W. H. Way	Baltimore C.C. Baltimore, Md.
1900	Harry Vardon	313	J. H. Taylor	Chicago G.C. Wheaton, Ill.
1901	*Willie Anderson (85)	331	Alex Smith (86)	Myopia Hunt Club Hamilton, Mass.
1902	L. Auchterlonie	307	Stewart Gardner	Garden City G.C. Garden City, L.I., N.Y.
1903	*Willie Anderson (82)	307	David Brown (84)	Baltusrol G.C. Short Hills, N.J.

Year	Winner	Score	Runner-Up	Played at
1904	Willie Anderson	303	Gil Nicholls	Glen View Club Golf, Ill.
1905	Willie Anderson	314	Alex Smith	Myopia Hunt Club Hamilton, Mass.
1906	Alex Smith	295	Willie Smith	Onwentsia Club Lake Forest, Ill.
1907	Alex Ross	302	Gil Nicholls	Philadelphia Cricket Club Chestnut Hill, Pa.
1908	*F. McLeod (77)	322	Willie Smith (83)	Myopia Hunt Club Hamilton, Mass.
1909	George Sargent	290	Tom McNamara	Englewood G.C. Englewood, N.J.
1910	*Alex Smith (71)	298	J. McDermott (75) M. Smith (77)	Philadelphia Cricket Club Chestnut Hill, Pa.
1911	*J. McDermott (80)	307	Mike Brady (82) G. O. Simpson (85)	Chicago G.C. Wheaton, Ill.
1912	J. McDermott	294	Tom McNamara	C.C. of Buffalo Buffalo, N.Y.
1913	*F. Ouimet (72)	304	Harry Vardon (77) Edward Ray (78)	The Country Club Brookline, Mass.
1914	Walter Hagen	290	Charles Evans, Jr.	Midlothian C.C. Blue Island, Ill.
1915	J. D. Travers	297	Tom McNamara	Baltusrol G.C. Short Hills, N.J.
1916	Charles Evans, Jr.	286	Jock Hutchison	Minikahda Club Minneapolis, Minn.
1917-1918	*No championships played—World War I*			
1919	*W. Hagen (77)	301	Mike Brady (78)	Brae Burn C.C. West Newton, Mass.
1920	Edward Ray	295	Harry Vardon Jack Burke Leo Diegel Jock Hutchison	Inverness C.C. Toledo, Ohio
1921	James M. Barnes	289	Walter Hagen Fred McLeod	Columbia C.C. Chevy Chase, Md.
1922	Gene Sarazen	288	John L. Black R. T. Jones, Jr.	Skokie C.C. Glencoe, Ill.
1923	*R. T. Jones, Jr. (76)	296	B. Cruickshank (78)	Inwood C.C. Inwood, L.I., N.Y.
1924	Cyril Walker	297	R. T. Jones, Jr.	Oakland Hill C.C. Birmingham, Mich.
1925	*W. MacFarlane (147)	291	R. T. Jones, Jr. (148)	Worcester C.C. Worcester, Mass.
1926	R. T. Jones, Jr.	293	Joe Turnesa	Scioto C.C. Columbus, Ohio
1927	*T. Armour (76)	301	Harry Cooper (79)	Oakmont C.C. Oakmont, Pa.
1928	*J. Farrell (143)	294	R. T. Jones, Jr. (144)	Olympia Fields C.C. Matteson, Ill.
1929	*R. T. Jones, Jr. (141)	294	Al Espinosa (164)	Winged Foot G.C. Mamaroneck, N.Y.
1930	R. T. Jones, Jr.	287	Macdonald Smith	Interlachen C.C. Hopkins, Minn.

Year	Winner	Score	Runner-Up	Played at
1931	*B. Burke (149-148)	292	George Von Elm (149-149)	Inverness Club Toledo, Ohio
1932	Gene Sarazen	286	Phil Perkins Bobby Cruickshank	Fresh Meadows C.C. Flushing, N.Y.
1933	Johnny Goodman	287	Ralph Guldahl	North Shore C.C. Glenview, Ill.
1934	Olin Dutra	293	Gene Sarazen	Merion Cricket Club Haverford, Pa.
1935	Sam Parks, Jr.	299	Jimmy Thompson	Oakmont C.C. Oakmont, Pa.
1936	Tony Manero	282	Harry Cooper	Baltusrol C.C. Springfield, N.J.
1937	Ralph Guldahl	281	Sam Snead	Oakland Hills C.C. Birmingham, Mich.
1938	Ralph Guldahl	284	Dick Metz	Cherry Hills C.C. Denver, Colo.
1939	*B. Nelson (68–70)	284	Craig Wood (68-73) Denny Shute (76-elim.)	Philadelphia C.C. Philadelphia, Pa.
1940	*L. Little (70)	287	Gene Sarazen (73)	Canterbury G.C. Cleveland, Ohio
1941	Craig Wood	284	Denny Shute	Colonial Club Fort Worth, Texas
1942-1945	*No championships played—World War II*			
1946	*Lloyd Mangrum (72-72)	284	Vic Ghezzi (72-73) B. Nelson (72-73)	Canterbury G.C. Cleveland, Ohio
1947	*Lew Worsham (69)	282	Sam Snead (70)	St. Louis C.C. Clayton, Mo.
1948	Ben Hogan	276	Jimmy Demaret	Riviera C.C. Los Angeles, Calif.
1949	Cary Middlecoff	286	Sam Snead Clayton Heafner	Medinah C.C. Medinah, Ill.
1950	*Ben Hogan (69)	287	Lloyd Mangrum (73) George Fazio (75)	Merion Cricket Club Haverford, Pa.
1951	Ben Hogan	287	Clayton Heafner	Oakland Hills C.C. Birmingham, Mich.
1952	Julius Boros	281	Ed Oliver	Northwood C.C. Dallas, Texas
1953	Ben Hogan	283	Sam Snead	Oakmont C.C. Oakmont, Pa.
1954	Ed Furgol	284	Gene Littler	Baltusrol C.C. Springfield, N.J.
1955	*Jack Fleck (69)	287	Ben Hogan (72)	Olympic C.C. San Francisco, Calif.
1956	Cary Middlecoff	281	Ben Hogan	Oak Hill C.C. Rochester, N.Y.
1957	*Dick Mayer (72)	282	Cary Middlecoff (79)	Inverness Club Toledo, Ohio
1958	Tommy Bolt	283	Gary Player	Southern Hills C.C. Tulsa, Okla.
1959	Billy Casper	282	Bob Rosburg	Winged Foot G.C. Mamaroneck, N.Y.
1960	Arnold Palmer	280	Jack Nicklaus	Cherry Hills C.C. Denver, Colo.

Year	Winner	Score	Runner-Up	Played at
1961	Gene Littler	281	Bob Goalby	Oakland Hills C.C.
			Doug Sanders	Birmingham, Mich.
1962	*Jack Nicklaus (71)	283	Arnold Palmer (74)	Oakmont C.C.
				Oakmont, Pa.
1963	*Julius Boros (70)	293	Jacky Cupit (73)	The Country Club
			Arnold Palmer (76)	Brookline, Mass.
1964	Ken Venturi	278	Tommy Jacobs	Congressional C.C.
				Washington, D.C.
1965	*Gary Player (71)	282	Kel Nagle (74)	Bellerive C.C.
				St. Louis, Mo.
1966	*Billy Casper (69)	278	Arnold Palmer (73)	Olympic Club
				San Francisco, Calif.
1967	Jack Nicklaus	275	Arnold Palmer	Baltusrol C.C.
				Springfield, N.J.
1968	Lee Trevino	275	Jack Nicklaus	Oak Hill C.C.
				Rochester, N.Y.
1969	Orville Moody	281	Deane Beman	Champions G.C.
			Al Geiberger	Houston, Texas
			Bob Rosburg	
1970	Tony Jacklin	281	Dave Hill	Hazeltine G.C.
				Chaska, Minn.
1971	Lee Trevino (68)	280	Jack Nicklaus (71)	Merion Cricket Club
				Haverford, Pa.
1972	Jack Nicklaus	290	Bruce Crampton	Pebble Beach G.L.
				Pebble Beach, Calif.
1973	Johnny Miller	279	John Schlee	Oakmont C.C.
				Oakmont, Pa.
1974	Hale Irwin	287	Forrest Fezler	Winged Foot G.C.
				Mamaroneck, N.Y.
1975	*Lou Graham (71)	287	John Mahaffey	Chicago, Ill.

* Winner in play-off. Figures in parentheses indicates play-off scores.

C. The British Open Championship

Year	Winner	Score	Runner-Up	Played at
1860	Willie Park	174	Tom Morris	Prestwick, Scotland
	(The first event was open only to professional golfers)			
1861	Tom Morris	163	Willie Park	Prestwick, Scotland
	(The second annual open was open to amateurs also)			
1862	Tom Morris	163	Willie Park	Prestwick, Scotland
1863	Willie Park	168	Tom Morris	Prestwick, Scotland
1864	Tom Morris	160	Andrew Strath	Prestwick, Scotland
1865	Andrew Strath	162	Willie Park	Prestwick, Scotland
1866	Willie Park	169	David Park	Prestwick, Scotland
1867	Tom Morris	170	Willie Park	Prestwick, Scotland
1868	Tom Morris, Jr.	154	Tom Morris (Sr.)	Prestwick, Scotland
1869	Tom Morris, Jr.	157	Tom Morris (Sr.)	Prestwick, Scotland
1870	Tom Morris, Jr.	149	David Strath	Prestwick, Scotland
			Bob Kirk	
1871	No championship			
1872	Tom Morris, Jr.	166	David Strath	Prestwick, Scotland
1873	Tom Kipp	179	—	St. Andrews, Scotland
1874	Mungo Park	159	—	Musselburgh, Scotland
1875	Willie Park	166	Robert Martin	Prestwick, Scotland

Year	Winner	Score	Runner-Up	Played at
1876	Robert Martin	176	David Strath (tied, but refused play-off)	St. Andrews, Scotland
1877	Jamie Anderson	160	R. Pringle	Musselburgh, Scotland
1878	Jamie Anderson	157	Robert Kirk	Prestwick, Scotland
1879	Jamie Anderson	169	Andrew Kirkaldy J. Allan	St. Andrews, Scotland
1880	Robert Ferguson	162	—	Musselburgh, Scotland
1881	Robert Ferguson	170	Jamie Anderson	Prestwick, Scotland
1882	Robert Ferguson	171	Willie Fernie	St. Andrews, Scotland
1883	*Willie Fernie	159	Robert Ferguson	Musselburgh, Scotland
1884	Jack Simpson	160	D. Rolland Willie Fernie	Prestwick, Scotland
1885	Bob Martin	171	Archie Simpson	St. Andrews, Scotland
1886	David Brown	157	Willie Campbell	Musselburgh, Scotland
1887	Willie Park, Jr.	161	Bob Martin	Prestwick, Scotland
1888	Jack Burns	171	B. Sayers D. Anderson	St. Andrews, Scotland
1889	*Willie Park, Jr.	155 (158)	Andrew Kirkaldy (163)	Musselburgh, Scotland
1890	John Ball	164	Willie Fernie	Prestwick, Scotland
1891	Hugh Kirkaldy	166	Andrew Kirkaldy Willie Fernie	St. Andrews, Scotland
1892	Harold H. Hilton	305	J. Ball Hugh Kirkaldy	Muirfield, Scotland
	(Championship extended from 36 to 72 holes)			
1893	William Auchterlonie	322	John E. Laidlay	Prestwick, Scotland
1894	John H. Taylor	326	Douglas Rolland	Royal St. George, England
1895	John H. Taylor	322	Alexander Herd	St. Andrews, Scotland
1896	*Harry Vardon (157)	316	John H. Taylor (161)	Muirfield, Scotland
1897	Harold H. Hilton	314	James Braid	Royal Liverpool, England
1898	Harry Vardon	307	Willie Park, Jr.	Prestwick, Scotland
1899	Harry Vardon	310	Jack White	Royal St. George, England
1900	John H. Taylor	309	Harry Vardon	St. Andrews, Scotland
1901	James Braid	309	Harry Vardon	Muirfield, Scotland
1902	Alexander Herd	307	Harry Vardon	Royal Liverpool, England
1903	Harry Vardon	300	Tom Vardon	Prestwick, Scotland
1904	Jack White	296	John H. Taylor	Royal St. George, England
1905	James Braid	318	John H. Taylor Rolland Jones	St. Andrews, Scotland
1906	James Braid	300	John H. Taylor	Muirfield, Scotland
1907	Arnaud Massy	312	John H. Taylor	Royal Liverpool, England
1908	James Braid	291	Tom Ball	Prestwick, Scotland
1909	John H. Taylor	295	James Braid Tom Ball	Deal, England
1910	James Braid	299	Alexander Herd	St. Andrews, Scotland
1911	Harry Vardon	303	Arnaud Massy	Royal St. George, England
1912	Edward Ray	295	Harry Vardon	Muirfield, Scotland
1913	John H. Taylor	304	Edward Ray	Royal Liverpool, England
1914	Harry Vardon	306	John H. Taylor	Prestwick, Scotland
1915-1919	*No championships*			
1920	George Duncan	303	Alexander Herd	Deal, England
1921	*Jock Hutchison	296 (150)	Roger Wethered (159)	St. Andrews, Scotland
1922	Walter Hagen	300	George Duncan James M. Barnes	Royal St. George, England

Year	Winner	Score	Runner-Up	Played at
1923	Arthur G. Havers	295	Walter Hagen	Troon, Scotland
1924	Walter Hagen	301	Ernest Whitcombe	Royal Liverpool, England
1925	James M. Barnes	300	Archie Compston	Prestwick, Scotland
			Ted Ray	
1926	Robert T. Jones, Jr.	291	Al Watrous	Royal Lytham, England
1927	Robert T. Jones, Jr.	285	Aubrey Boomer	St. Andrews, Scotland
1928	Walter Hagen	292	Gene Sarazen	Royal St. George, England
1929	Walter Hagen	292	Johnny Farrell	Muirfield, Scotland
1930	Robert T. Jones, Jr.	291	Macdonald Smith	Hoylake, England
			Leo Diegel	
1931	Tommy D. Armour	296	J. Jurado	Carnoustie, Scotland
1932	Gene Sarazen	283	Macdonald Smith	Princes, England
1933	*Denny Shute (149)	292	Craig Wood (154)	St. Andrews, Scotland
1934	Henry Cotton	283	S. F. Brews	Royal St. George, England
1935	Alfred Perry	283	Alfred Padgham	Muirfield, Scotland
1936	Alfred Padgham	287	J. Adams	Hoylake, England
1937	Henry Cotton	290	R. A. Whitcombe	Carnoustie, Scotland
1938	R. A. Whitcombe	295	James Adams	Royal St. George, England
1939	Richard Burton	290	Johnny Bulla	St. Andrews, Scotland
1940-1945	*No championships*			
1946	Sam Snead	290	Bobby Locke	St. Andrews, Scotland
			Johnny Bulla	
1947	Fred Daly	293	R. W. Horne	Hoylake, England
			Frank Stranahan	
1948	Henry Cotton	294	Fred Daly	Muirfield, Scotland
1949	*Bobby Locke (135)	283	Harry Bradshaw (147)	Sandwich, England
1950	Bobby Locke	279	Roberto DeVicenzo	Troon, Scotland
1951	Max Faulkner	285	A. Cerda	Portrush, Ireland
1952	Bobby Locke	287	Peter Thomson	St. Anne's on-the-Sea, England
1953	Ben Hogan	282	Frank Stranahan	Carnoustie, England
			D. J. Rees	
			Peter Thomson	
			A. Cerda	
1954	Peter Thomson	283	S. S. Scott	Royal Birkdale, England
			Dai Reese	
			Bobby Locke	
1955	Peter Thomson	281	John Fallon	St. Andrews, Scotland
1956	Peter Thomson	286	Flory van Donck	Hoylake, England
1957	Bobby Locke	279	Peter Thomson	St. Andrews, Scotland
1958	Peter Thomson (139)	278	Dave Thomas (143)	St. Anne's on-the-Sea, England
1959	Gary Player	284	Fred Bullock	Muirfield, Scotland
			Flory van Donck	
1960	Kel Nagle	278	Arnold Palmer	St. Andrews, Scotland
1961	Arnold Palmer	284	Dai Reese	Royal Birkdale, England
1962	Arnold Palmer	276	Kel Nagle	Troon, Scotland
1963	*Bob Charles	277	Phil Rodgers	Royal Lytham, England
1964	Tony Lema	279	Jack Nicklaus	St. Andrews, Scotland
1965	Peter Thomson	285	Brian Hugget	Southport, England
			Chris O'Connor	
1966	Jack Nicklaus	282	Doug Sanders	Muirfield, Scotland
			Dave Thomas	
1967	Robert DeVicenzo	278	Jack Nicklaus	Hoylake, England

Year	Winner	Score	Runner-Up	Played at
1968	Gary Player	289	Jack Nicklaus	Carnoustie, Scotland
			Bob Charles	
1969	Tony Jacklin	280	Bob Charles	Royal Lytham, England
1970	*Jack Nicklaus	283 (72)	Doug Sanders (73)	St. Andrews, Scotland
1971	Lee Trevino	278	Liang Huan Lu	Royal Birkdale, England
1972	Lee Trevino	278	Jack Nicklaus	Muirfield, Scotland

* Winner in play-off. Figures in parentheses indicates play-off scores.

D. The Western Open Championship

Year	Winner	Score	Runner-Up	Played at
1899	*Willie Smith	156	Laurie Auchterlonie	Golf, Ill.
1901	Laurie Auchterlonie	160	David Bell	Blue Island, Ill.
1902	Willie Anderson	299	Willie Smith	Cleveland, Ohio
			W. H. Way	
1903	Alex Smith	318	Laurie Auchterlonie	Milwaukee, Wis.
			David Brown	
1904	Willie Anderson	304	Alex Smith	Grand Rapids, Mich.
1905	Arthur Smith	278	James Maiden	Cincinnati, Ohio
1906	Alex Smith	306	John Hobens	Flossmoor, Ill.
1907	Robert Simpson	307	Willie Anderson	Hinsdale, Mich.
			Fred McLeod	
1908	Willie Anderson	299	Fred McLeod	St. Louis, Mo.
1909	Willie Anderson	288	Stewart Gardner	Glencoe, Ill.
1910	Chick Evans (am)	6 & 5	George Simpson	Chicago, Ill.
1911	Robert Simpson	2 & 1	Tom McNamara	Grand Rapids, Mich.
1912	Macdonald Smith	299	Alex Robertson	Flossmoor, Ill.
1913	John McDermott	295	Mike Brady	Memphis, Tenn.
1914	Jim Barnes	293	Willie Kidd	Minneapolis, Minn.
1915	Tom McNamara	304	Alex Cunningham	Glen Ellyn, Ill.
1916	Walter Hagen	286	Jock Hutchison	Milwaukee, Wis.
			George Sargent	
1917	Jim Barnes	283	Walter Hagen	Wilmette, Ill.
1919	Jim Barnes	283	Leo Diegel	Cleveland, Ohio
1920	Jock Hutchison	296	Jim Barnes	Olympia Fields, Ill.
			C. W. Hackney	
			Harry Hampton	
1921	Walter Hagen	287	Jock Hutchison	Cleveland, Ohio
1922	Mike Brady	291	Laurie Ayton	Birmingham, Mich.
1923	Jock Hutchison	281	Bobby Cruickshank	Memphis, Tenn.
			Leo Diegel	
			Walter Hagen	
1924	Bill Mehlhorn	293	Al Watrous	Chicago, Ill.
1925	Macdonald Smith	281	Leo Diegel	Youngstown, Ohio
			Johnny Farrell	
			Emmett French	
			Walter Hagen	
			Bill Mehlhorn	
			Harry Cooper	
1926	Walter Hagen	279	Gene Sarazen	Indianapolis, Ind.
			Al Espinosa	
1927	Walter Hagen	281	Bill Mehlhorn	Olympia Fields, Ill.
			Johnny Farrell	

Year	Winner	Score	Runner-Up	Played at
1928	Abe Espinosa	291	Horton Smith	Chicago, Ill.
1929	Tommy Armour	273	Al Espinosa	Milwaukee, Wis.
1930	Gene Sarazen	278	Walter Hagen	Detroit, Mich.
1931	Ed Dudley	280	Olin Dutra	Dayton, Ohio
1932	Walter Hagen	287	Tommy Armour	Cleveland, Ohio
1933	Macdonald Smith	282	Ky Laffoon	Olympia Fields, Ill.
1934	*Harry Cooper	274	Willie Goggin	Peoria, Ill.
1935	John Revolta	290	Ray Mangrum	South Bend, Ind.
1936	Ralph Guldahl	274	Horton Smith	Davenport, Iowa
1937	*Ralph Guldahl	288	Sam Snead	Cleveland, Ohio
1938	Ralph Guldahl	279	Lloyd Mangrum	St. Louis, Mo.
1939	Byron Nelson	281	Toney Penna	Medinah, Ill.
1940	*Jimmy Demaret	293	Ben Hogan	Houston, Texas
1941	Ed Oliver	275	Byron Nelson	Phoenix, Ariz.
			Henry Picard	
1942	Herman Barron	276	Lloyd Mangrum	Phoenix, Ariz.
1946	Ben Hogan	271	Bobby Locke	Sappington, Mo.
1947	Johnny Palmer	270	Ed Oliver	Salt Lake City, Utah
1948	*Ben Hogan	281	Cary Middlecoff	Buffalo, N.Y.
1949	Sam Snead	282	Jim Ferrier	St. Paul, Minn.
1950	Sam Snead	282	Cary Middlecoff	Los Angeles, Calif.
1951	Marty Furgol	270	Bobby Locke	Davenport, Iowa
1952	Lloyd Mangrum	274	Ed Furgol	St. Louis, Mo.
1953	Dutch Harrison	278	Fred Haas	St. Louis, Mo.
			Lloyd Mangrum	
			Ted Kroll	
1954	*Lloyd Mangrum	277	Mike Souchak	Cincinnati, Ohio
1955	Cary Middlecoff	272	Doug Ford	Portland, Oregon
1956	*Mike Fetchik	284	Jay Hebert	San Francisco, Calif.
			Don January	
			George Bayer	
1957	*Doug Ford	279	Gene Littler	Detroit, Mich.
			Billy Maxwell	
			Dow Finsterwald	
1958	Doug Sanders	275	Arnold Palmer	Detroit, Mich.
1959	Mike Souchak	272	Art Wall	Pittsburgh, Pa.
1960	*Stan Leonard	278	Sam Snead	Detroit, Mich.
1961	Arnold Palmer	271	Billy Casper	Belmont, Mich.
1962	Jacky Cupit	281	Jack Nicklaus	Medinah, Ill.
1963	*Arnold Palmer	280	Julius Boros	Chicago, Ill.
1964	Juan Rodriguez	268	Arnold Palmer	Niles, Mich.
1965	Billy Casper	270	Jack McGowan	Niles, Mich.
			Gay Brewer	
1966	Billy Casper	283	Doug Sanders	Medinah, Ill.
1967	Jack Nicklaus	274	Miller Barber	Chicago, Ill.
1968	Jack Nicklaus	273	Rocky Thompson	Olympia Fields, Ill.
1969	Billy Casper	276	Dale Douglass	Midlothian, Ill.
1970	Hugh Royer	273	Bobby Nichols	Chicago, Ill.
1971	Bruce Crampton	279	Labron Harris, Jr.	Olympia Fields, Ill.
1972	Jim Jamieson	271	Hale Irwin	Northbrook, Ill.
1973	Billy Casper	272	Larry Hinson	Midlothian, Ill.

* Winner in play-off.

E. The Ryder Cup Matches

The Ryder Cup matches developed from a match played between representatives of the American and British Professional Golfers' Association in England in 1926. That unofficial match, incidentally, was won by the British 13½ to 1½.

Following this highly successful exhibition, Samuel A. Ryder, a wealthy British seed merchant, offered to donate a solid gold trophy bearing his name to be competed for in a series of matches between professionals of these two nations.

In placing the Ryder Cup in competition, the donor set forth certain terms which were to be observed by the parties concerned so long as the matches are conducted. Included among these stipulations are the following:

(1) The matches will be played every other year on a home-and-home basis;

(2) While both parties must mutually agree on the specific dates for each match, the host team may select the site and will be responsible for such arrangements and details as are normally the function of a sponsoring group;

(3) The matches shall consist of two days of play with the first being devoted to foursomes and the second to singles matches;

(4) Each member of the competing teams must be a member of his country's PGA, and furthermore, must be a native born citizen of that country.

The matches for the Ryder Cup were first officially played in 1927 in the United States. They have been held continuously every other year since except for the period from 1937 through 1946 when the exigencies of World War II forced their suspension.

From 1927 to date, the United States has won every Ryder Cup match played in this country. It also won on British soil in 1937, 1949, 1953, 1961, and 1965, to run its list of victories to 14 in 17 matches. The British won at home in 1929, 1933, and 1957, and tied in 1969.

From the start of the series through the 1959 Ryder Cup matches, the competition was comprised of four foursomes matches one day and eight singles matches the other day, each at 36 holes.

In 1961, the format was changed to provide for four 18-hole foursomes the morning of the first day and four more that afternoon, then for eight 18-hole singles the morning of the second day and eight more that afternoon. As in the past, one point was at stake in each match, so the total number of points was doubled.

In 1963, for the first time, a day of fourball matches augmented the program to add new interest to the overall competition. This brought the total number of points to 32. The same format has been used since.

Year	Date	Played at	Total points	
1927	June 3, 4	Worcester Country Club Worchester, Massachusetts	United States Great Britain	9½ 2½
1929	April 27, 28	Moortown, England	United States Great Britain	5 7
1931	June 26, 27	Scioto Country Club Columbus, Ohio	United States Great Britain	9 3
1933	June 26, 27	Southport, England	United States Great Britain	5½ 6½
1935	September 28, 29	Ridgewood Country Club Ridgewood, New Jersey	United States Great Britain	9 3
1937	June 29, 30	Southport, England	United States Great Britain	8 4

Year	Date	Played at	Total points	

(Ryder Cup matches not held 1938-1946)

Year	Date	Played at	Total points	
1947	November 1, 2	Portland, Golf Club Portland, Oregon	United States Great Britain	11 1
1949	September 16, 17	Ganton Golf Course Scarborough, England	United States Great Britain	7 5
1951	November 2, 4	Pinehurst Country Club Pinehurst, North Carolina	United States Great Britain	$9\frac{1}{2}$ $2\frac{1}{2}$
1953	October 2, 3	Wentworth, England	United States Great Britain	$6\frac{1}{2}$ $5\frac{1}{2}$
1955	November 5, 6	Thunderbird Ranch and Country Club Palm Springs, California	United States Great Britain	8 4
1957	October 4, 5	Lindrick Golf Club Yorkshire, England	United States Great Britain	$4\frac{1}{2}$ $7\frac{1}{2}$
1959	November 6, 7	Eldorado Country Club Palm Desert, California	United States Great Britain	$8\frac{1}{2}$ $3\frac{1}{2}$
1961	October 13, 14	Royal Lytham and St. Anne's Golf Club St. Anne's-on-the-Sea, England	United States Great Britain	$14\frac{1}{2}$ $9\frac{1}{2}$
1963	October 11, 13	East Lake Country Club Atlanta, Georgia	United States Great Britain	23 9
1965	October 7, 9	Royal Birkdale Golf Club Southport, England	United States Great Britain	$19\frac{1}{2}$ $12\frac{1}{2}$
1967	October 20-22	Champions Golf Club Houston, Texas	United States Great Britain	$23\frac{1}{2}$ $8\frac{1}{2}$
1969	October 7, 9	Royal Birkdale Golf Club Southport, England	United States Great Britain	16 16
1971	September 16-18	Old Warson Country Club St. Louis, Missouri	United States Great Britain	$18\frac{1}{2}$ $13\frac{1}{2}$
1973	September 20-22	Muirfield, Scotland	United States Britain/Ireland	19 13
1975		Ryder Cup matches: Laurel Valley Country Club Ligonier, Pennsylvania		

F. The PGA Championship

Year	Winner	Score	Runner-Up	Played at
1916	James M. Barnes	1 up	Jock Hutchison	Siwanoy C.C. Bronxville, N.Y.
1917- 1918	*No championship played—* *World War I*			
1919	James M. Barnes	6 & 5	Fred McLeod	Engineers C.C. Roslyn, L.I., N.Y.
1920	Jock Hutchison	1 up	J. Douglas Edgar	Flossmoor C.C. Flossmoor, Ill.
1921	Walter Hagen	3 & 2	James M. Barnes	Inwood C.C. Far Rockaway, N.Y.

Year	Winner	Score	Runner-Up	Played at
1922	Gene Sarazen	4 & 3	Emmet French	Oakmont C.C. Oakmont, Pa.
1923	Gene Sarazen	1 up (38)	Walter Hagen	Pelham C.C. Pelham, N.Y.
1924	Walter Hagen	2 up	James M. Barnes	French Lick C.C. French Lick, Ind.
1925	Walter Hagen	6 & 5	William Mehlhorn	Olympia Fields C.C. Olympia Fields, Ill.
1926	Walter Hagen	5 & 3	Leo Diegel	Salisbury G.C. Westbury, L.I., N.Y.
1927	Walter Hagen	1 up	Joe Turnesa	Cedar Crest C.C. Dallas, Texas
1928	Leo Diegel	6 & 5	Al Espinosa	Five Farms C.C. Baltimore, Md.
1929	Leo Diegel	6 & 4	Johnny Farrell	Hillcrest C.C. Los Angeles, Cal.
1930	Tommy Armour	1 up	Gene Sarazen	Fresh Meadows C.C. Flushing, N.Y.
1931	Tom Creavy	2 & 1	Denny Shute	Wannamoisett C.C. Rumford, R.I.
1932	Olin Dutra	4 & 3	Frank Walsh	Keller G.C. St. Paul, Minn.
1933	Gene Sarazen	5 & 4	Willie Goggin	Blue Mount C.C. Milwaukee, Wis.
1934	Paul Runyan	1 up (38)	Craig Wood	Park C.C. Williamsville, N.Y.
1935	Johnny Revolta	5 & 4	Tommy Armour	Twin Hills C.C. Oklahoma City, Okla.
1936	Denny Shute	3 & 2	Jimmy Thomson	Pinehurst C.C. Pinehurst, N.C.
1937	Denny Shute	1 up (37)	Harold McSpaden	Pittsburgh F.C. Aspinwall, Pa.
1938	Paul Runyan	8 & 7	Sam Snead	Shawnee C.C. Shawnee-on-Delaware, Pa.
1939	Henry Picard	1 up (37)	Byron Nelson	Pomonok C.C. Flushing, L.I., N.Y.
1940	Byron Nelson	1 up	Sam Snead	Hershey C.C. Hershey, Pa.
1941	Vic Ghezzi	1 up (38)	Byron Nelson	Cherry Hills C.C. Denver, Colo.
1942	Sam Snead	2 & 1	Jim Turnesa	Seaview C.C. Atlantic City, N.J.
1943	*No championship played— World War II*			
1944	Bob Hamilton	1 up	Byron Nelson	Manito G. &. C.C. Spokane, Wash.
1945	Byron Nelson	4 & 3	Sam Byrd	Morraine C.C. Dayton, Ohio
1946	Ben Hogan	6 & 4	Ed Oliver	Portland G. C. Portland, Ore.
1947	Jim Ferrier	2 & 1	Chick Harbert	Plum Hollow C.C. Detroit, Mich.
1948	Ben Hogan	7 & 6	Mike Turnesa	Oakmont C.C. Oakmont, Pa.

Year	Winner	Score	Runner-Up	Played at
1949	Sam Snead	3 & 2	Johnny Palmer	Hermitage C.C. Richmond, Va.
1950	Chandler Harper	4 & 3	Henry Williams, Jr.	Scioto C.C. Columbus, Ohio
1951	Sam Snead	7 & 6	Walter Burkemo	Norwood Hills C.C. St. Louis, Mo.
1952	Jim Turnesa	1 up	Chick Harbert	Big Spring C.C. Louisville, Ky.
1953	Walter Burkemo	2 & 1	Felice Torza	Birmingham C.C. Birmingham, Mich.
1954	Chick Harbert	4 & 3	Walter Burkemo	Keller G.C. St. Paul, Minn.
1955	Doug Ford	4 & 3	Cary Middlecoff	Meadowbrook C.C. Detroit, Mich.
1956	Jack Burke	3 & 2	Ted Kroll	Blue Hill C.C. Boston, Mass.
1957	Lionel Hebert	2 & 1	Dow Finsterwald	Miami Valley G.C. Dayton, Ohio
1958	Dow Finsterwald	276	Billy Casper	Llanerch C.C. Havertown, Pa.
1959	Bob Rosburg	277	Jerry Barber Doug Sanders	Minneapolis G.C. St. Louis Park, Minn.
1960	Jay Hebert	281	Jim Ferrier	Firestone C.C. Akron, Ohio
1961	Jerry Barber (67)	277	Don January (68)	Olympia Fields C.C. Olympia Fields, Ill.
1962	Gary Player	278	Bob Goalby	Aronimink G.C. Newtown Square, Pa.
1963	Jack Nicklaus	279	Dave Ragan, Jr.	Dallas Athletic Club C.C. Dallas, Texas
1964	Bob Nichols	271	Jack Nicklaus Arnold Palmer	Columbus C.C. Columbus, Ohio
1965	Dave Marr	280	Billy Casper Jack Nicklaus	Laurel Valley G.C. Ligonier, Pa.
1966	Al Geiberger	280	Dudley Wysong	Firestone G. & C.C. Akron, Ohio
1967	Don January (69)	281	Don Massengale (71)	Columbine C.C. Littleton, Colo.
1968	Julius Boros	281	Bob Charles Arnold Palmer	Pecan Valley C.C. San Antonio, Texas
1969	Ray Floyd	276	Gary Player Arnold Palmer	NCR C.C. Dayton, Ohio
1970	Dave Stockton	279	Arnold Palmer Bob Murphy	Southern Hills C.C. Tulsa, Okla.
1971	Jack Nicklaus	281	Bill Casper	PGA National G.C. Palm Beach Gardens, Fla.
1972	Gary Player	281	Tommy Aaron Jim Jamieson	Oakland Hills C.C. Birmingham, Mich.
1973	Jack Nicklaus	277	Bruce Crampton	Canterbury C.C. Cleveland, Ohio
1974	Lee Trevino	276	Jack Nicklaus	Tanglewood G.C. Clemmons, N.C.

Figures in parentheses indicate play-off scores.

G. The PGA Seniors' Championship

Year	Winner	Score	Runner-Up	Played at
1937	Jock Hutchison	76-75-72—223	George Gordon	Augusta (Ga.) Natl. G.C.
1938	*Freddie McLeod	80-74—154	Otto Hackbarth	Augusta (Ga.) Natl. G.C.
1940	*Otto Hackbarth	76-70—146	Jock Hutchison	North Shore C.C. Sarasota, Fla.
1941	Jack Burke, Sr.	73-69—142	Eddie Williams	Sarasota Bay C.C. Sarasota, Fla.
1942	Eddie Williams	68-70—138	George Morris	Ft. Myers (Fla.) G. & C.C.
1945	Eddie Williams	74-74—148	Jock Hutchison	PGA Natl. G.C. Dunedin, Fla.
1946	*Eddie Williams	75-71—146	Jock Hutchison	PGA Natl. G.C. Dunedin, Fla.
1947	Jock Hutchison	74-71—145	Ben Richter	PGA Natl. G.C. Dunedin, Fla.
1948	Charles McKenna	69-72—141	Ben Richter	PGA Natl. G.C. Dunedin, Fla.
1949	Marshall Crichton	73-72—145	Lou Chiapetta George Smith Jock Hutchison	PGA Natl. G.C. Dunedin, Fla.
1950	Al Watrous	70-72—142	Bill Jellife	PGA Natl. G.C. Dunedin, Fla.
1951	*Al Watrous	69-73—142	Jock Hutchison	PGA Natl. G.C. Dunedin, Fla.
1952	Ernie Newnham	75-71—146	Al Watrous	PGA Natl. G.C. Dunedin, Fla.
1953	Harry Schwab	66-76—142	Gene Sarazen Charles McKenna	PGA Natl. G.C. Dunedin, Fla.
1954	Gene Sarazen	67-72-75—214	Al Watrous Perry Del Vecchio	PGA Natl. G.C. Dunedin, Fla.
1955	Mortie Dutra	70-71-72—213	Mike Murra Gene Sarazen Denny Shute	PGA Natl. G.C. Dunedin, Fla.
1956	Pete Burke	70-70-75—215	Ock Willoweit	PGA Natl. G.C. Dunedin, Fla.
1957	*Al Watrous	69-71-70—210	Bob Stupple	PGA Natl. G.C. Dunedin, Fla.
1958	Gene Sarazen	73-71-74-70—288	Charles Sheppard	PGA Natl. G.C. Dunedin, Fla.
1959	Willie Goggin	71-71-70-72—284	Duke Gibson Paul Runyan	PGA Natl. G.C. Dunedin, Fla.
1960	Dick Metz	71-70-73-70—284	Tony Longo Paul Runyan	PGA Natl. G.C. Dunedin, Fla.
1961	Paul Runyan	69-70-72-69—278	Jimmy Demaret	PGA Natl. G.C. Dunedin, Fla.
1962	Paul Runyan	71-69-68-70—278	Ernie Ball Joe Brown Dutch Harrison	PGA Natl. G.C. Dunedin, Fla.
1963	Herman Barron	67-67-69-69—272	John Barnum	Port St. Lucie (Fla.) C.C.
1964	Sam Snead	67-68-73-71—279	John Barnum	PGA Natl. G.C. Palm Beach Gardens, Fla.
1965	Sam Snead	71-68-68-71—278	Joe Lopez, Sr.	Fort Lauderdale (Fla.) C.C.

Year	Winner	Score	Runner-Up	Played at
1966	Fred Haas, Jr.	72-71-71-72—286	Dutch Harrison / John Barnum	PGA Natl. G.C. / Palm Beach Gardens, Fla.
1967	Sam Snead	71-69-73-66—279	Bob Hamilton	PGA Natl. G.C. / Palm Beach Gardens, Fla.
1968	Chandler Harper	70-73-64-72—279	Sam Snead	PGA Natl. G.C. / Palm Beach Gardens, Fla.
1969	Tommy Bolt	70-70-71-67—278	Peter Fleming	PGA Natl. G.C. / Palm Beach Gardens, Fla.
1970	Sam Snead	71-71-72-76—290	Fred Haas, Jr.	PGA Natl. G.C. / Palm Beach Gardens, Fla.
1971	Julius Boros	73-69-71-72—285	Tommy Bolt	PGA Natl. G.C. / Palm Beach Gardens, Fla.
1972	Sam Snead	69-73-73-71—286	Julius Boros / Tommy Bolt	PGA Natl. G.C. / Palm Beach Gardens, Fla.
1973	Sam Snead	66-66-67-69—268	Julius Boros / Joe Taylor	PGA Natl. G.C. / Palm Beach Gardens, Fla.
1974	Roberto De Vicenzo	68-68-71-66—273		Port St. Lucie (Fla.) C.C.
1975	Charley Sifford	68-71-72-69—280	F. Wampler	Disney World, Fla.

* Winner in play-off.

H. The PGA Seniors'-Juniors' Championship Winners

1959 Ivan Gantz and Joe Curtin
1960 Billy Burke and Sam Drake
1961 Walter Hall and Bob Nolus
1962 Henry Bontempo and Sam Bernardi
1963 Leland Gibson and Steve Isakov
1964 Walter Romans and Todd Hauck
1965 Lorin Shook and Bob Gajda
1966 Phil Greenwald and Frank Harned
1967 Bill Black and Ron Howell
1968 Herb Vogt and Pat Schwab
1969 Joe Lopez, Sr. and Jack Doser
1970 Rod Munday and J. C. Goosie
1971 Chuck Klein and Jim Logue
1972 Steve Doctor and Steve Bull
1973 Joe Lopez, Sr. and Tom Hanlon
1974 Monte Norcross and Denny Lyons
1975 Bob Gajda and Steve Bull

I. The PGA Club Professional Championship

Year	Winner and Runner-Up	Score	Played at
1968	Howell Fraser / Chuck Malchaski, Bob Rosburg	72-66-65-69: 272	Century C.C. & Roadrunner Resort, Scottsdale, Ariz.
1969	Bob Rosburg / Jimmy Wright	71-66-66-72: 275	Roadrunner Golf Resort & San Marcos C.C. Chandler, Ariz.
1970	Rex Baxter / Ernie George, Bob Duden	71-68-75-71: 285	Sunol Valley C.C. Sunol, Calif.
1971	Sam Snead / Jerry Steelsmith, Ron Letellier	67-65-74-69: 275	Pinehurst (N.C.) C.C.

Year	Winner and Runner-Up	Score	Played at
1972	Don Massengale	72-66-74-68:	Pinehurst (N.C.) C.C.
	Bob Bruno	280	
1973	Rives McBee	73-67-71-71:	Pinehurst (N.C.) C.C.
	Stan Brion	282	
1974	Roger Watson	71-73-71-69:	Pinehurst (N.C.) C.C.
	Sam Snead	284	

(One-hole sudden death play-off)

J. The PGA Match Play Champions

1964	Bob Frainey	1968	Steve Bull	1972	John Cook
1965	Chuck Malchaski	1969	Herb Hooper	1973	Bill Collins
1966	Jerry Cooper	1970	Dick Hart	1974	Joe Data
1967	Stan Brion	1971	Chick Evans	1975	Bobby Brue

K. The PGA Stroke Play Champions

1954	Ock Willoweit	1962	Jim Stamps	1969	Herb Hooper
1955	Gunnard Johnson	1963	John Barnum	1970	Gene Borek
1956	Al Huske	1964	John Barnum	1971	Dick Hart
1957	Matt Bartosek	1965	Sam Harvey	1972	Denny Lyons
1958	Henry Castillo	1966	Walker Inman, Jr.	1973	Gene Borek
1959	Skip Alexander	1967	Claude King	1974	Chick Evans
1960	Toby Lyons	1968	John Barnum	1975	Ron Letellier
1961	Sam Bernardi				

L. The 1974 PGA Section Champions

Carolinas	Terry Wilcox	New England	Charles Volpone
Central New York	Ed Kroll	New Jersey	Charles Huckaby
Colorado	Fred Wampler	Northeastern New York	Rudy Goff
Connecticut	Ed Rubis	Northern California	Harold Firstman
Dixie	Howell Fraser	Northern Ohio	Gene Ferrell
Eastern Missouri	Al Chandler	Northern Texas	Clayton Cole
Florida	Bill Robinson	Pacific Northwest	Jerry Mowlds
Georgia	DeWitt Weaver	Philadelphia	Dick Smith
Gulf States	David Smith	Rocky Mountain	Terry Malan
Illinois	Bill Ventresca	South Central	Dick Goetz
Indiana	Bob Placido	Southern California	Paul McGuire
Iowa	Bob Fry	Southern Ohio	Dick Plummer
Kentucky	Larry Gilbert	Southern Texas	Tommy Aycock
Metropolitan	Jimmy Wright	Southwest	Joe Porter
Michigan	Ron Aleks	Sun Country	Gene Torres
Middle Atlantic	Mac Main	Tennessee	Jim Riggins
Mid-West	James Davis	Tri-State	Norman Rack
Minnesota	Frank Freer	Western New York	Denny Lyons
Nebraska	John Frillman	Wisconsin	Bob Brue

INDEX